Quantum Computing

Quantum computing and algorithms are set to revolutionize information processing. Covering such topics, *Quantum Computing: The Future of Information Processing* explains its principles, practical applications, and future implications in a clear and accessible manner. The book strives to simplify the essential concepts and practical applications of quantum computing. Its aim is to help students and researchers to apply quantum computing to advance AI and machine learning, cybersecurity, and blockchain. With its emphasis on practical applications, the book covers how quantum computing is changing such fields as:

- Finance
- Medicine
- Built environment
- Networking and communications

With extensive real-world case studies and practical implementation guidance, the book is a guide for those seeking to understand how quantum computing is applied in various industries. Its in-depth exploration of quantum computing covers both foundational principles and advanced applications in a single resource, saving readers the need to purchase multiple books. Finally, the book focuses on the future of information processing so that students and researchers can anticipate and prepare for the transformative impact of quantum computing.

Amit Kumar Tyagi is an assistant professor, Department of Fashion Technology, National Institute of Fashion Technology, New Delhi. He earned a Ph.D. from Pondicherry Central University, India. He has worked as assistant professor and senior researcher at the School of Computer Science and Engineering, Vellore Institute of Technology, Chennai, India.

Shrikant Tiwari is an associate professor in the School of Computing Science and Engineering (SCSE), Galgotias University, Greater Noida, India. He received a Ph.D. from the Department of Computer Science & Engineering at the Indian Institute of Technology (Banaras Hindu University), Varanasi, India. He has authored or co-authored more than 50 national and international journal publications, book chapters, and conference articles. He has five patents filed to his credit. His research interests include machine learning, deep learning, computer vision, medical image analysis, pattern recognition, and biometrics. Dr. Tiwari is a FIETE; a senior member of the IEEE; and member of ACM, IET, CSI, ISTE, IAENG, and SCIEI.

S. V. Nagaraj is currently a professor at Vellore Institute of Technology, Chennai. He obtained a bachelor of engineering in 1992 in computer science from the University of Madras. At the Institute of Mathematical Sciences, Chennai, he completed a master of science via the research program in theoretical computer science in 1994 and obtained a doctoral degree in the same field in 2000.

Quantum Computing
The Future of Information Processing

Edited by Amit Kumar Tyagi, Shrikant Tiwari, and S. V. Nagaraj

CRC Press
Taylor & Francis Group
Boca Raton London New York

CRC Press is an imprint of the
Taylor & Francis Group, an **informa** business

First edition published 2025
2385 NW Executive Center Drive, Suite 320, Boca Raton FL 33431

and by CRC Press
4 Park Square, Milton Park, Abingdon, Oxon, OX14 4RN

CRC Press is an imprint of Taylor & Francis Group, LLC

© 2025 Amit Kumar Tyagi, Shrikant Tiwari, and S. V. Nagaraj

ISBN: 978-1-032-80258-9 (hbk)
ISBN: 978-1-032-81368-4 (pbk)
ISBN: 978-1-003-49945-9 (ebk)

DOI: 10.1201/ 9781003499459

Typeset in Times LT Std
by Apex CoVantage, LLC

Contents

Chapter 8   Quantum Neural Networks: An Overview 133

Priyanga Subbiah, Kandan M., Krishnaraj N., and Shaji. K.A. Theodore

Chapter 17 An Analysis of Security Threats in Quantum Computing Information
Processing...283

Kanthavel R., Anju A., Adline Freeda R., S. Krithikaa Venket, Dhaya R.,
Frank Vijay, and Joseph Fisher

Chapter 18 Fortifying Cyber Defenses with IDPS Implementation and Management
Best Practices 291

M. Baritha Begum, R. Thillaikarasi, M. Sandhiya, R.C. Jeni Gracia,
Suresh Balakrishnan T., Rengaraj Alias Muralidharan R.,
Suresh Sankaranarayanan, and Lakshmi Kanthan Narayanan

Chapter 19 Data Encryption in 6G Networks: A Zero-Knowledge Proof Model...................... 305

P. Selvaraj, A. Hyils Sharon Magdalene, Suresh Sankaranarayanan,
Rengaraj Alias Muralidharan R., Priyanga Subbiah, Saranniya S.,
and Lakshmi Kanthan Narayanan

Preface

In this smart era, we need to explore the cutting-edge world of quantum computing, which is quite interesting and has attracted scientific interest (around the globe). We need to explain such interesting topics like qubits, superposition, and entanglement and need to discover how quantum algorithms are used to revolutionize information processing. We will explain the latest developments, practical applications, and the potential to transform fields from cryptography to artificial intelligence in this book. The purpose of this book is to bridge the gap between the rapidly evolving field of quantum computing and those eager to understand its potential impact. Quantum computing is at the forefront of technological innovation, and there is a need for a resource that explains its principles, practical applications, and future implications in a clear and accessible manner.

This book will discuss quantum computing and its related terms in detail. This book will take future readers/researchers on a journey from the fundamental principles of quantum mechanics to the practical applications reshaping industries like blockchain, cybersecurity, machine learning, and finance as well as real-world case studies to provide a unique addition on the technology's impact today. Hence, this book will present a clear roadmap for practical implementation, guiding readers through the complex process of integrating quantum computing into their real-world applications.

Contributors

Anju A.
Department of Information Technology
KCG College of Technology
Chennai, India

E. AbidemiAwujoola
Biotechnology Department
Nigerian Defence Academy
Kaduna, Nigeria

O. Abioye
Directorate of ICT
Nigerian Defence Academy

O. Christiana Akusu
Physics Department
Nigerian Defence Academy
Kaduna, Nigeria

Puneet Anchalia
School of Computer Science and Engineering
Vellore Institute of Technology, Chennai

Senthil Kumar Arumugam
SRM Arts and Science College
Kattankulathur Tamil Nadu, India

J. Olalekan Awujoola
Computer Science Department
Nigerian Defence Academy
Kaduna, Nigeria

Azrina Abd Aziz
Universiti Teknologi PETRONAS
Perak, Malaysia

P. Manju Bala
IFET College of Engineering
Valavanur, Villupuram, Tamil Nadu

A. Balachandar
IFET College of Engineering
Valavanur, Villupuram, Tamil Nadu

Bukola Fatimah Balogun
Department of Computer Science
Kwara State University Malete, Nigeria

Sonali Balouria
Department of Forensic science
University Institute of Applied Health
Science Chandigarh University
Ludhiana, Punjab

M. Baritha Begum
Department of Electronics and
    Communication Engineering
Saranathan College of Engineering
    Tiruchirapalli
Tamil Nadu, India

Ashish Choudhary
Vellore Institute of Technology
Chennai, India

Shefali Chaudhary
Department of Forensic science
University Institute of
    Applied Health
Science Chandigarh University
Ludhiana, Punjab

Tania Debnath
Department of Forensic science
University Institute of
    Applied Health
Science Chandigarh University
Ludhiana, Punjab

Chitta Ranjan Deo
Department of Mechanical
    Engineering
VSSUT Burla
Odisha, India

T. Aniemeka Enem
Cyber Security Department
Airforce Institute of Technology
Kaduna, Nigeria

Ushaa Eswaran
Department of ECE Mahalakshmi Tech
    Campus
Anna university, Chennai
Tamilnadu, India

Vishal Eswaran
CVS Health Centre
Dallas, Texas, United States

Vivek Eswaran
Tech Lead at Medallia
Austin, Texas, United States

Joseph Fisher
Department of Electrical and
    Communication Engineering
University of Technology, Lae
Papua New Guinea

Anindya Ghatak
School of Computer Science Engineering
    and Technology
Bennett University Gautam Buddha Nagar
Uttar Pradesh, India

R.C. Jeni Gracia
Institute of Computer Science and Engineering,
    Saveetha School of Engineering
Saveetha Institute of Medical and
    Technical Sciences, Saveetha University
Chennai, India

Leoson Heisnam
School of Forensic Science
Uttar Pradesh State Institute of Forensic
    Science
Lucknow, Uttar Pradesh, India

Ranjith J.
Vellore Institute of Technology
Chennai, India

Pragati Jain
Swami Vivekanand Subharti University
Meerut, Uttar Pradesh, India

Biswajit Jana
School of Computer Science Engineering
    and Technology
Bennett University, Gautam Buddha Nagar
Uttar Pradesh, India

D. Kavitha
School of Computer Science and Engineering
Vellore Institute of Technology
Chennai, India

S. Sijin Kumar
Comcast
Philadelphia, Pennsylvania, USA

Shabnam Kumari
Department of Computer Science, College of
    Science and Humanities
SRM Institute of Science and Technology
    Kattankulathur
Chennai, Tamilnadu, India

Ajanthaa Lakkshmanan
Department of Computing Technologies
SRM Institute of Science and Technology
Kattankulathur, India

Kandan M.
Department of Computing Technologies,
    School of Computing, College of
    Engineering and Technology
SRM Institute of Science and Technology
    Kattankulathur
Tamilnadu, India

S. Nalini
Department of Computing
Technologies, School of Computing,
SRM Institute of Science & Technology
    Kattankulathur
TamilNadu, India

Niranjanamurthy M.
Department of Artificial Intelligence (AI) and
    Machine Learning (ML), BMS Institute of
    Technology and Management
Bangalore, Karnataka, India

Vergin Raja Sarobin M.
Vellore Institute of Technology
Chennai, India

A. Hyils Sharon Magdalene
Institute of Computer Science and Engineering
    Saveetha School of Engineering
Saveetha Institute of Medical and Technical
    Sciences, Saveetha University
Chennai, India

Biswadip Basu Mallik
Department of Basic Science and Humanities
Institute of Engineering & Management
Kolkata, West Bengal, India

Bireshwar Dass Mazumdar
School of Computer Science Engineering
and Technology
Bennett University, Gautam Buddha Nagar
Uttar Pradesh, India

Manmohan Mishra
Department of Computer Science
Application
United Institute of Management
Prayagraj (Allahabad), Uttar Pradesh, India

Keerthna Murali
Cybersecurity Site Reliability Engineer II
(SRE) at Dell EMC I CKAD I AWS CSAA,
Austin, Texas, United States

Krishnaraj N.
Department of Networking and
Communications, School of Computing
College of Engineering and Technology
SRM Institute of Science and Technology
Kattankulathur
Tamilnadu, India

Lakshmi Kanthan Narayanan
Institute of Computer Science
and Engineering Saveetha School of
Engineering
Saveetha Institute of Medical and Technical
Sciences, Saveetha University
Chennai, India

Emmanuel Philip Ododo
University of Uyo
Uyo, Nigeria

R. OlayinkaAdelegan
Computer Science Department
Nigerian Defence Academy
Kaduna, Nigeria

J. Adeyemi Owolabi
Physics Department
Nigerian Defence Academy
Kaduna, Nigeria

Adline Freeda R.
Department of Information Technology
KCG College of Technology
Chennai, India

Ciro Rodriguez R.
Department of Software Engineering
Universidad Nacional Mayor de
San Marcos UNMSM
Faculty of Informatics and Electronic
Universidad Nacional Federico Villarreal
Villarreal, Spain

Dhaya R.
Department of Information Technology
KCG College of Technology
Chennai, India

Kanthavel R.
Department of Electrical and
Communication Engineering,
University of Technology
Lae, Papua New Guinea

Rengaraj Alias Muralidharan R.
Department of Information Technology
Saranathan College of Engineering
Tiruchirapalli, Tamil Nadu, India

Kali Charan Rath
Department of Mechanical Engineering
GIET University
Odisha, India

Saranniya S.
Institute of Computer Science and
Engineering
Saveetha School of Engineering, Saveetha
Institute of Medical and Technical
Sciences
Saveetha University
Chennai, India

M. Sandhiya
Department of Electronics and
Communication Engineering
Panimalar Engineering College
Chennai, India

Suresh Sankaranarayanan
Department of Computer Science
College of Computer Science and
Information Technology
King Faisal University
Al-Ahsa, Alhofuf, Kingdom of
Saudi Arabia

P. Selvaraj
Department of Computating Technologies
SRM Institute of Science and Technology
Chennai, India

Vedant Singh
Department of Data Science and Business Systems
SRM Institute of Science and Technology
Kattankulathur, Chennai, India

G.S. Smrithy
School of Computer Science and Engineering
Vellore Institute of Technology, Chennai

Priyanga Subbiah
Department of Networking and
    Communications, School of Computing
College of Engineering and Technology
    SRM Institute of Science and Technology
    Kattankulathur
Tamilnadu, India

Suresh Balakrishnan T.
Department of Computer Science
    and Engineering
Saveetha School of Engineering, Saveetha
    Institute of Medical and Technical Sciences
    Saveetha University
Chennai, India

Andleeb Tanveer
Department of Data Science and
    Business Systems
SRM Institute of Science and Technology
Kattankulathur, Chennai, India

Shaji. K.A. Theodore
Faculty of IT, College of Computing and
    Information Sciences
University of Technology and Applied Sciences
Sultanate of Oman

R. Thillaikarasi
Department of Information Technology
Saranathan College of Engineering
Tiruchirapalli, Tamil Nadu, India

Shrikant Tiwari
Department of Computer Science &
    Engineering
School of Computing Science
    and Engineering (SCSE), Galgotias
    University
Greater Noida, Uttar Pradesh, India

Rati Kailash Prasad Tripathi
Department of Pharmaceutical Sciences,
    Sushruta School of Medical and
    Paramedical Sciences
Assam University (A Central University),
    Silchar
Assam, India

Amit Kumar Tyagi
Department of Fashion Technology
National Institute of
    Fashion Technology
New Delhi, Delhi India

S. Usharani
IFET College of Engineering
Gangarampalaiyam,Tamil Nadu, India

Kalpana A.V.
Department of Data Science and
    Business Systems
SRM Institute of Science and Technology
Kattankulathur, Chennai

S. Krithikaa Venket
Dept. of Information Technology
KCG College of Technology
Chennai, India

Priyanka Verma
Department of Forensic Science
University Institute of Applied Health Sciences
Chandigarh University, Mohali, India

Frank Vijay
Dept. of Information Technology
KCG College of Technology
Chennai, India

1 Quantum Computing
Evolution, Recent Advancements, Future Opportunities, and Challenges for Future Generations

Senthil Kumar Arumugam, Bukola Fatimah Balogun, Ajanthaa Lakkshmanan, and Amit Kumar Tyagi

1.1 INTRODUCTION

1.1.1 OVERVIEW OF QUANTUM COMPUTING

With the help of quantum mechanics, new computational paradigms can be developed. In contrast to conventional computing, which uses bits to encode data, it makes use of quantum bits, or qubits, which are concurrently capable of being in superposition states. The ability to execute calculations in parallel gives quantum computers the potential to outperform traditional computers in some situations [1]. A few facts about quantum computing are:

- To carry out operations in quantum computing, qubits' quantum states are altered using quantum gates. Quantum algorithms can solve some problems exponentially faster by utilising a sequence of quantum gates to make use of the intrinsic features. Grover's technique is used for searching unsorted databases, while Shor's algorithm is used for factoring large integers.
- Quantum photonics, superconducting circuits, and topological qubits are some of the primary ways that quantum computers are implemented in hardware. The goal of these platforms is to minimise errors, noise, and decoherence—factors that might interfere with quantum states—while producing and modifying qubits.
- Quantum computing faces several challenges. One major challenge is the vulnerability of quantum systems to noise and errors. Decoherence, caused by interactions with the environment, can cause qubits to lose their quantum state. Overcoming decoherence and developing error correction techniques is important for building scalable and reliable quantum computers.
- Quantum computers with a sufficient number of qubits are needed to solve complex problems and demonstrate a quantum advantage over classical computers. However, maintaining qubit coherence and managing interactions between qubits become increasingly difficult as the system size grows.
- Despite these challenges, quantum computing holds great promise. It is capable of resolving computationally difficult problems in areas such as material science, drug development, optimisation, and cryptography, and machine learning. Quantum simulations can provide information about complex physical and chemical systems that are beyond the reach of classical computers.

DOI: 10.1201/9781003499459-1

- As research and development continue, the field of quantum computing is advancing rapidly. Recent advancements, such as achieving quantum supremacy and developing more stable qubit architectures, have demonstrated the progress being made. Collaborations between academia, industry, and government are driving the development of quantum technologies and fostering a growing quantum workforce.

In summary, quantum computing provides the principles of quantum mechanics to develop powerful computational systems. While challenges remain, ongoing research and technological advancements are bringing us closer to realising the potential on industries and scientific disciplines.

1.2 FUNDAMENTALS OF QUANTUM COMPUTING

1.2.1 QUANTUM MECHANICS PRINCIPLES

The study of quantum mechanics principles provides an explanation of tiniest scales, including atoms and subatomic particles. Our comprehension of the microscopic world has been completely transformed by this fundamental principle. Several key principles of quantum mechanics shape its foundation and provide the basis for quantum computing [2, 3]. Here are some essential principles:

- Superposition: According to this principle, a quantum system can exist in several states at once. Stated differently, a particle can exist in a combination or superposition of various states until a measurement is taken. An electron, for instance, has the ability to spin simultaneously in both clockwise and anticlockwise directions.
- The idea of "wave-particle duality," which was first proposed by quantum mechanics, holds that particles like electrons and photons can have both particle- and wave-like characteristics. According to this theory, wavefunctions—mathematical functions that depict the probability distribution of discovering a particle in various states—can be used to explain particles.
- Quantisation: The concept of quantisation was first presented by quantum mechanics. It asserts that some physical quantities, including energy and angular momentum, can only have discrete or quantised values. In contrast, these values were thought to be continuous in classical physics. Photons at frequencies are emitted or absorbed when the energy levels in an atom are quantised, creating discrete energy states.
- Uncertainty principle: According to Werner Heisenberg, there is a fundamental limit to the accuracy with which some pairs of physical attributes. It suggests that one attribute can be known less precisely the more precisely the other is measured.
- Entanglement: This phenomenon occurs when two or more particles become so coupled that it is impossible to characterise the state of one particle without also describing the other particles. Regardless of the distance between two entangled particles, one is instantly affected by the measurement of the other.
- Quantum interference: Quantum interference arises from the wave-like nature of quantum particles. When two or more quantum states overlap, their amplitudes can interfere constructively or destructively. This interference can lead to phenomena such as interference patterns in double-slit experiments and the phenomenon of quantum teleportation, where the state of a particle can be transferred to another particle without physical interaction.

These principles form the basis of quantum mechanics and underpin the unique behaviour and capabilities of quantum systems. They are harnessed in the design and implementation of quantum algorithms such as quantum computers, cryptography, and sensors.

1.2.2 QUANTUM BITS AND SUPERPOSITION

Qubits are similar to the classical bits found in conventional computers, but they are not the same because they can exist in several states at once. Two states, usually represented by the numbers 0 or 1, can be represented by a classical bit. A qubit, on the other hand, is capable of simultaneously representing the superposition of 0 and 1. The quantum mechanical concept of superposition gives rise to this superposition. Mathematically, a qubit can be described as a linear combination of its basis states, conventionally denoted as |0⟩ and |1⟩:

$$|\psi\rangle = \alpha|0\rangle + \beta|1\rangle$$

Here, α and β are complex numbers that represent the probability amplitudes associated with the qubit being in the state |0⟩ or |1⟩, respectively. The absolute values squared of the probability amplitudes $|\alpha|^2$ and $|\beta|^2$ give the probabilities of measuring the qubit in the corresponding basis states.

The superposition exist in a continuum of states between |0⟩ and |1⟩. This property is important for quantum computing because it enables parallel processing and simultaneous exploration of multiple states. Qubits are modified by means of quantum gates in order to carry out quantum operations, such as rotations and entanglement, which can process information in a highly parallel and coherent manner. When qubits are entangled, the states of multiple qubits become correlated and cannot be described independently. Entanglement is another fundamental aspect of quantum mechanics and is instrumental in achieving quantum computational advantages. Entangled qubits can be used to perform computations that are intractable for classical computers and enable powerful algorithms. Note that superposition and entanglement are key principles of quantum mechanics that harness the unique capabilities of quantum computing.

1.2.3 QUANTUM GATES AND QUANTUM CIRCUITS

Like the classical bits found in conventional computers, qubits have the capacity to exist in several states superposed to one another. Typically represented by the numbers 0 or 1, a classical bit can indicate one of two states. A qubit, on the other hand, can simultaneously represent 0 and 1. The superposition principle in quantum physics gives rise to this superposition. Quantum gates can be represented by matrices that describe the transformation they apply to the qubit's state vector. Here are some commonly used quantum gates:

- Pauli gates are the most basic type of single-qubit gate. Among them are:
  Bit-flip or Pauli-X gates: It changes a qubit's state from |0⟩ to |1⟩, or the other way around.
  Pauli-Y gate: It combines phase-flipping and bit-flipping functions.
  The Pauli-Z gate, also known as a phase-flip gate, modifies the |1⟩ state's phase by −1.
  Hadamard Gate: The Hadamard gate converts the |0⟩ state to an equal superposition of |0⟩ and |1⟩, and the |1⟩ state to an equal superposition of |0⟩ and −|1⟩ in order to construct a superposition.
- Controlled-NOT Gate: This two-qubit gate affects both a target and a control qubit. It applies a Pauli-X gate to the target qubit if the control qubit is |1⟩; if not, it leaves the target qubit unchanged.
- Toffoli Gate: Comprising a target qubit and two control qubits, the Toffoli gate operates on three qubits. When both control qubits are in the state |1⟩, it applies a Pauli-X gate to the target qubit; otherwise, it leaves the target qubit unaltered.

These are the few examples of quantum gates, and there are many more that perform various operations on qubits. Hence, a quantum circuit represents the flow of quantum information and operations. Qubits are initialised to specific states, and quantum gates are applied sequentially to perform transformations on the qubits. The final state of the qubits after the circuit represents the result of the computation. Note that quantum circuits are designed to implement quantum algorithms and solve specific problems efficiently. By combining various quantum gates and designing suitable circuits, quantum computers can perform complex computations and outperform classical computers for certain tasks.

1.3 BARRIERS IN QUANTUM COMPUTING

1.3.1 QUANTUM NOISE AND DECOHERENCE

Quantum noise and decoherence are significant challenges in quantum computing and are detrimental to the stability and reliability of quantum systems. We will discuss each of these concepts:

- Quantum Noise: Quantum noise refers to random fluctuations and disturbances that affect quantum systems. These noise sources arise from various factors, including thermal fluctuations, electromagnetic radiation, and imperfections in hardware components. Quantum noise can introduce errors and uncertainties in quantum operations and measurements, leading to loss of coherence and inaccurate results.

To mitigate quantum noise, several techniques are employed, such as:

- Cooling the quantum system to extremely low temperatures (close to absolute zero) to minimise thermal noise.
- Shielding the system from external electromagnetic fields to reduce electromagnetic noise.
- Decoherence: When a quantum system is coupled to its surroundings, it can exchange information and entanglement with the environment's degrees of freedom. This interaction causes the quantum system to rapidly lose its superposition and entanglement, resulting in the degradation of quantum information.
- Decoherence is a major obstacle in quantum computing because it limits the time during which quantum computations can be performed accurately. As the number of qubits and the complexity of quantum circuits increase, the effects of decoherence become more pronounced.

To combat decoherence, several strategies are employed, such as:

- Using quantum error mitigation techniques to estimate and compensate for the errors introduced by decoherence.
- Developing quantum hardware with longer coherence times, such as improved qubit designs and error-correcting codes.

In summary, quantum noise and decoherence pose significant challenges in building practical and scalable quantum computers. Overcoming these challenges is an active area of research, and advancements in error correction techniques, hardware design, and system engineering are being pursued and improve the stability and performance of quantum systems.

1.3.2 QUANTUM ERROR CORRECTION

In order to shield quantum information from errors brought on by decoherence and other noise sources, quantum error correction is a crucial technique in quantum computing [4]. Errors are unavoidable in quantum systems, yet it nevertheless enables trustworthy quantum processing. Encoding quantum information is the fundamental concept of quantum error correction redundantly in a larger quantum system known as a "code." By distributing the information across multiple physical qubits, the code can detect and correct errors that occur on individual qubits or due to environmental noise. Here are some key concepts and steps involved:

- Quantum Codes: These codes are constructed using mathematical techniques from quantum coding theory. The most-used codes are known as stabiliser codes, which are defined by a set of stabiliser operators. These operators commute with each other and provide information about the errors affecting the code.
- Encoding: The quantum information is encoded into the quantum code by applying a set of quantum gates to the original qubits. This process expands the qubit representation into a larger number of physical qubits.
- Error Detection: To detect errors, the stabiliser operators associated with the code are measured. The measurement outcomes provide information about the presence and type of errors. By comparing the measurement results with the expected values, errors can be identified.
- Error Correction: Once errors are detected, error correction procedures are applied to restore the original quantum information. These procedures involve applying specific quantum gates based on the identified errors. The gates effectively reverse the error operations and restore the encoded quantum state to its original form.
- Fault-Tolerant Operations: Quantum error correction aims to achieve fault-tolerant operations, where computations can be performed reliably. Fault-tolerant techniques involve repeated error detection and correction steps throughout the computation to maintain the integrity of the quantum information.

Since many physical qubits are needed to encode a single logical qubit and because precise and exact operations are required, it is important to keep in mind that implementing quantum error correction is difficult [4–7]. Furthermore, error correction procedures consume additional computational resources and increase the complexity of quantum algorithms.

1.3.3 SCALABILITY AND QUANTUM SYSTEM SIZE

Scalability refers to the ability to handle larger and more complex quantum systems. It involves addressing the challenges associated with increasing the number of qubits, reducing errors, and maintaining coherence as the quantum system size grows. Achieving scalability is essential for realising the full potential of quantum computers and solving complex real-world problems efficiently. The size of a quantum system is typically measured by the number of qubits it contains. As the number of qubits increases, the computational power and the complexity of quantum algorithms also grow exponentially. However, scaling up quantum systems presents significant challenges:

- Hardware Requirements: Scaling a quantum system requires a physical implementation with a larger number of qubits. This entails advancements in hardware technology, such as developing reliable qubits, improving qubit coherence times, reducing noise, and minimising interactions with the environment. Additionally, the connectivity between qubits needs to be expanded to enable effective entanglement and gate operations between distant qubits.
- Error Correction: As the quantum system size grows, the impact of errors and decoherence becomes more pronounced. Therefore, robust error correction techniques and fault-tolerant quantum computation become even more important. Efficient error correction codes and error mitigation strategies need to be developed and preserve its integrity throughout the computation.
- Control and Measurement: Scaling up quantum systems also requires the ability to accurately control and measure an increasing number of qubits. Precise manipulation and

measurement techniques need to be developed to address the challenges of scalability. This includes advances in control hardware, signal processing, and integration with classical control systems.

- Quantum Interconnects: To achieve large-scale quantum systems, the ability to connect multiple quantum processors and qubit arrays is important. Quantum interconnects, such as quantum communication channels or bus lines, need to be developed to enable coherent interactions and information transfer between different parts of the quantum system.

Hence, addressing these challenges requires interdisciplinary efforts across quantum physics, materials science, engineering, and computer science. Ongoing research aims to develop scalable qubit technologies, optimise error correction codes, improve coherence times, enhance control techniques, and provide new architectures and algorithms suitable for large-scale quantum systems. While the field of quantum computing is still in its early stages, significant progress has been made in scaling up quantum systems. However, achieving a fully scalable and fault-tolerant quantum computer capable of solving practical problems remains a formidable task that requires continued research, innovation, and technological advancements.

1.3.4 QUANTUM ALGORITHM DESIGN AND OPTIMISATION

The essential aspects of quantum computing that focus on developing efficient algorithms for quantum systems to solve specific problems [3, 6, 8, and 9]. Here are key issues in quantum algorithm design and optimisation:

- Problem Analysis: The first step in designing a quantum algorithm is to analyse the problem and identify its characteristics. Not all problems benefit from quantum algorithms, so it is important to determine if a problem has properties that can be exploited by quantum computations, such as exponential speedup in specific cases or inherent quantum properties that classical algorithms cannot exploit.
- Quantum Speedup: Quantum algorithms aim to achieve quantum speedup, which refers to the advantage of using a quantum computer over classical computers for specific problems. Quantum speedup can be obtained through algorithms like Shor's algorithm for factoring large numbers and the quantum phase estimation algorithm. It is important to assess the potential for quantum speedup and determine the best approach to use quantum effects for the problem at hand.
- Quantum Gate Selection: Selecting suitable quantum gates and operations is important in algorithm design. Careful selection of gates based on the problem requirements and the underlying quantum circuit can optimise the algorithm's efficiency. Commonly used gates include Pauli gates, Hadamard gates, and controlled gates like CNOT and Toffoli gates.
- Quantum Oracle Design: Quantum oracles are components of quantum algorithms used to encode problem-specific information into the quantum state. Designing efficient quantum oracles tailored to the problem being addressed is important for algorithm optimisation. Oracles can encode problem constraints, objective functions, or database queries, among other problem-specific information.
- Quantum Error Correction: Quantum error correction techniques play an important role in algorithm design and optimisation. As quantum systems are prone to errors and noise, incorporating error correction codes and fault-tolerant techniques can protect the integrity of quantum information throughout the computation. Error correction strategies need to be considered to ensure the reliability and accuracy of the algorithm.
- Quantum Circuit Optimisation: Optimising the quantum circuit layout and gate sequences can significantly improve algorithm performance. Techniques such as gate reordering, gate

cancellation, and circuit decomposition can minimise the number of gates, reduce quantum resource requirements, and decrease the overall computational time.

- Complexity Analysis: Evaluating the complexity of the quantum algorithm is important to assess its efficiency and scalability. Understanding the resources required, such as the number of qubits, gate operations, and measurements, helps assess the feasibility and practicality of implementing the algorithm on existing or future quantum hardware.

In summary, quantum algorithm design and optimisation require a deep understanding of quantum principles, problem domains, and computational complexity. It involves a balance between exploiting quantum effects and mitigating the challenges posed by errors and noise. Ongoing research in this field aims to develop efficient quantum algorithms and optimise their performance, ultimately unlocking the potential of quantum computing for practical use.

1.3.5 QUANTUM SOFTWARE AND PROGRAMMING LANGUAGES

Quantum software and programming languages play an important role in developing, simulating, and executing quantum algorithms on quantum computers or simulators. These tools provide the necessary frameworks, libraries, and interfaces to design and implement quantum algorithms, compile them into executable instructions for quantum hardware, and simulate their behaviour and key aspects.

- Quantum Software Development Kits (SDKs): Quantum SDKs provide a comprehensive set of tools, libraries, and documentation to facilitate quantum software development. They often include features such as quantum circuit simulators, programming interfaces, debugging tools, and algorithm libraries. Popular quantum SDKs include Qiskit (for IBM Quantum systems), Cirq (for Google Quantum Computing), and Forest (for Rigetti Quantum Computing).
- Quantum Programming Languages: These languages often extend traditional programming languages with additional constructs and features specific to quantum computing. Examples of quantum programming languages include QASM (Quantum Assembly Language), Quil (Quantum Instruction Language), and OpenQASM (Open Quantum Assembly Language).
- Quantum Circuit Description: Representations of quantum algorithms as a sequence of quantum gates operating on qubits. Quantum software frameworks typically provide languages or libraries to describe quantum circuits at a high level. These descriptions define the sequence of gates, qubit initialisation, measurements, and control flow. Users can manipulate and optimise the circuit representation to achieve the desired algorithm behaviour.
- Quantum Algorithm Libraries: Quantum software frameworks often include libraries of pre-implemented quantum algorithms and functions. These libraries provide high-level abstractions and ready-to-use implementations of common quantum algorithms, making it easier for developers to utilise established algorithms in their projects.
- Quantum Circuit Simulation: Quantum software tools include simulators that can simulate the behaviour of quantum circuits on classical computers. Simulators allow developers to verify the correctness of algorithms, estimate resource requirements, and analyse the behaviour of quantum circuits without access to actual quantum hardware. Simulators also enable the study of larger-scale quantum systems and the exploration of algorithm behaviour under various conditions.
- Quantum Compiler and Optimisation: Quantum compilers are responsible for translating instructions that can be executed on quantum hardware. These compilers perform various

optimisation techniques to reduce gate counts, optimise gate sequences, and minimise resource requirements. They aim to map the high-level quantum circuit description onto the available qubit connectivity and mitigate hardware-specific constraints.

- Interface to Quantum Hardware: Quantum software frameworks provide interfaces to connect with quantum hardware, allowing developers to execute their quantum algorithms on real quantum processors. These interfaces handle tasks such as submitting jobs, retrieving results, and managing the interaction with the quantum hardware infrastructure.

Note that quantum software and programming languages continue to evolve rapidly to keep pace with advancements in quantum hardware and algorithms. They play an important role in enabling researchers, developers, and users to provide, experiment with, and harness the power of quantum computing for a wide range of applications.

1.4 STATEMENTS AND ACHIEVEMENTS IN QUANTUM COMPUTING

1.4.1 QUANTUM SUPREMACY

The achievement of quantum supremacy signifies the point at which quantum computers can perform certain calculations faster or more efficiently than classical computers, demonstrating the potential superiority of quantum computation [10, 11]. The concept of quantum supremacy was introduced by John Preskill in 2012 and gained significant attention with the release of a landmark paper by Google researchers in 2019. In that paper, by showcasing Sycamore, their quantum processor, as being able to complete a particular task far quicker than traditional supercomputers, Google claimed to have attained quantum dominance. The task chosen for this demonstration was to generate and sample from a random quantum circuit with many qubits and gates. Google's Sycamore processor reportedly performed this task in approximately 200 seconds, while it was estimated that the fastest classical supercomputers would take thousands of years to accomplish the same task.

Quantum supremacy is not about solving practical problems or outperforming classical computers in all computational tasks. Instead, it serves as a proof of concept, highlighting the potential computational power and scalability of quantum computers. Notably, the achievement of quantum supremacy does not imply that quantum computers have fully outperformed classical ones. Enhancing qubit coherence, cutting down on errors, and creating error correction methods are only a few of the numerous issues that need to be resolved before quantum computers are more widely used and dependable.

Quantum supremacy serves as an important milestone in the development of quantum computing, indicating that quantum systems have the potential to revolutionise certain computational tasks. However, the field is still in its early stages, and ongoing research and development are necessary and address the challenges that lie ahead.

1.4.2 MAJOR BREAKTHROUGHS IN QUANTUM COMPUTING

Quantum computing is an active and rapidly evolving field, and several significant breakthroughs have occurred over the years. Here are some major breakthroughs in quantum computing:

- Shor's Algorithm: In 1994, Peter Shor introduced Shor's algorithm, a groundbreaking quantum algorithm for factoring large numbers efficiently. This algorithm demonstrated the potential of quantum computers to solve a problem that is considered difficult for classical computers. Factoring large numbers is of significant importance for cryptography, and Shor's algorithm posed a potential threat to traditional encryption methods.
- Quantum Teleportation: This technique enables the movement of quantum information across locations without shifting the quantum state. In 1997, a team of scientists

successfully demonstrated quantum teleportation for the first time, showcasing the possibility of transferring quantum information in a non-classical manner.

- Quantum Error Correction: This crucial method guards against errors brought on by noise and decoherence in quantum information. In 1996, researchers introduced the concept of quantum error correction codes, providing a framework for detecting and correcting errors in quantum systems. This breakthrough laid the foundation for fault-tolerant quantum computation and mitigating the detrimental effects of errors.
- Quantum Key Distribution (QKD): In the early 2000s, researchers achieved significant advances in QKD, demonstrating the secure transmission of encryption keys over long distances using quantum properties like entanglement and the uncertainty principle. QKD has the potential to provide unbreakable encryption, providing enhanced security for data transmission.
- Quantum Supremacy: In 2019, Google announced the achievement of quantum supremacy by demonstrating that their quantum processor could perform a specific task exponentially faster than classical computers. This milestone marked a significant advancement in quantum computing, showing the potential computational power and scalability of quantum systems.
- Topological Quantum Computing: It is a promising approach that uses exotic properties of certain quantum states to perform computations. In 2012, Microsoft proposed a topological qubit based on anyons, which are quasiparticles with nontrivial braiding properties. This breakthrough opened up new possibilities for designing robust qubits that are more resilient to errors caused by decoherence.
- Quantum Machine Learning: The convergence point of machine learning and quantum computing has seen significant progress. Researchers have developed quantum algorithms and techniques for tasks such as quantum data classification, quantum clustering, and quantum neural networks. These advancements provide the potential of quantum computing to enhance machine learning and enable more efficient processing and analysis of complex data sets.

These breakthroughs highlight the rapid advancement and potential of quantum computing [12]. They have laid the foundation for further research, innovation, and the exploration of new applications, pushing the boundaries of what is possible with quantum systems. As the field progresses, more breakthroughs are expected to emerge, driving the development of practical quantum technologies.

1.4.3   QUANTUM CRYPTOGRAPHY AND SECURE COMMUNICATION

The goal of the field of quantum cryptography is to create secure communication protocols by applying the ideas of quantum mechanics [13–15]. Quantum cryptography leverages the basic characteristics of quantum physics to guarantee communication security, in contrast to classical encryption techniques, which rely on computing complexity and mathematical presumptions. QKD makes use of quantum mechanical concepts like the uncertainty principle and the no-cloning theorem. Here's how QKD works:

- Quantum Key Distribution: The sender, also known as Alice, prepares a series of quantum particles in particular quantum states, often individual photons, in QKD. These states encode the secret key. Alice then sends these particles, one at a time, to the receiver, known as Bob.
- Quantum Measurement: Upon receiving each quantum particle, Bob performs measurements on them using a chosen basis. The basis choice is usually communicated between Alice and Bob over a public channel.
- Security Analysis: After Bob performs the measurements, Alice and Bob compare a subset of their measurement results over a public channel. The comparison helps identify

any potential eavesdropping attempts since the properties of quantum mechanics ensure that any interception or measurement of the quantum particles would introduce detectable disturbances.

- Key Distillation: Alice and Bob apply information reconciliation and privacy amplification techniques to extract a final secret key from the correlated measurement results. These techniques eliminate any information that could have been compromised during the key exchange process, resulting in a secure shared key between Alice and Bob.

Any attempt to intercept or measure the quantum particles during transmission would disturb their quantum states, causing discrepancies in the measurement results. These discrepancies are detected during the security analysis phase, enabling Alice and Bob to detect the presence of an eavesdropper and abort the key exchange process if necessary. It is important to note that QKD only provides secure key exchange and does not directly encrypt the actual data being transmitted. The shared secret key generated through QKD can be used in combination with symmetric encryption algorithms to achieve secure communication. Note that quantum cryptography and QKD provide the potential for secure communication protocols that are resistant to attacks from both classical and quantum computers. However, practical implementation of QKD still faces challenges, such as maintaining the integrity of quantum channels, dealing with practical limitations of hardware, and addressing potential side-channel attacks. Ongoing research and development in quantum cryptography aim to address these challenges and enable the deployment of secure quantum communication systems.

1.4.4   QUANTUM SIMULATION AND OPTIMISATION

Quantum simulation and optimisation are two key areas where the application of quantum computing can be highly influential. Quantum optimisation seeks to use quantum algorithms to solve optimisation issues more effectively, whereas quantum simulation uses quantum systems to simulate and analyse complicated physical events. We will provide more detail on each of these areas.

- Quantum Simulation: This technique uses quantum computers to model and comprehend the behaviour of other complicated physical systems challenging to investigate using classical computers. It can simulate the behaviour of atoms, molecules, materials, and other quantum systems by applying the ideas of quantum mechanics. Quantum simulation holds great promise for revolutionising domains like condensed matter physics, materials science, and chemistry. It can support the analysis of chemical reactions as well as the development and design of novel materials with particular qualities and molecular dynamics, and investigate quantum phenomena that are challenging to simulate classically.
- Quantum Optimisation: Quantum optimisation focuses on using quantum computers to solve optimisation problems more efficiently than classical algorithms. The goal of optimisation problems is to select the optimal solution from a wide range of options, such as finding the shortest route in a network, optimising resource allocation, or solving complex scheduling problems. These algorithms can potentially outperform classical optimisation algorithms for certain problem instances, providing faster and more effective solutions. Quantum optimisation has applications in various domains, including logistics, supply chain management, financial modelling, portfolio optimisation, and machine learning. It has the potential to address complex real-world optimisation problems that are challenging for classical computers to solve within a reasonable time frame.

Hence, both quantum simulation and quantum optimisation require advances in quantum hardware and algorithms. As the field of quantum computing progresses, researchers are exploring and developing more sophisticated techniques and applications in these areas [16]. While practical quantum simulation and optimisation for large-scale problems are still challenging, research and technological advancements hold promise for their future impact.

1.4.5 QUANTUM MACHINE LEARNING AND ARTIFICIAL INTELLIGENCE

Utilising quantum systems' special qualities is its goal and to enhance machine learning algorithms, solve complex computational tasks more efficiently [8, 9, 11, 13–15, 17, 18]. Here are some key aspects of quantum machine learning and its relationship with artificial intelligence (AI):

- Quantum Data Representation: Quantum machine learning (QML) considers the representation and processing of quantum data. Quantum states can be used to encode and represent data, taking advantage of quantum superposition and entanglement. Quantum algorithms and techniques are provided to manipulate and extract meaningful information from quantum data.
- Quantum-Enhanced Algorithms: QML investigates the development of quantum algorithms that provide potential improvements over classical machine learning algorithms. These algorithms use the power of quantum computation, such as quantum parallelism and quantum interference, to speed up computations or provide new information, for example, quantum support vector machines, quantum neural networks, and quantum clustering algorithms.
- Quantum Speedup in Learning: Quantum machine learning investigates scenarios where quantum algorithms provide a computational advantage over classical algorithms. While quantum speedup in machine learning is an ongoing area of research, there have been efforts to demonstrate quantum advantages in specific tasks, such as quantum-inspired algorithms for recommendation systems or quantum models for solving optimisation problems in machine learning.
- Quantum Neural Networks: Quantum neural networks (QNNs) are quantum-inspired models that aim to replicate aspects of classical neural networks while incorporating quantum properties. QNNs use the power of quantum computation to potentially enhance learning capabilities.
- Quantum Data Privacy and Security: Quantum machine learning also provides the potential for enhanced data privacy and security. It can be used to secure data during transmission or protect sensitive information used in machine learning models.

While quantum machine learning is an exciting field with the potential for new information and computational advantages, it is important to note that practical applications of QML are still in their early stages. The field requires advancements in quantum hardware, improved error correction techniques, and the development of quantum algorithms specifically tailored for machine learning tasks [19, 20]. Ongoing research and collaboration between quantum scientists and machine learning experts are key to realising the full potential of quantum machine learning and its integration with artificial intelligence.

1.5 ADVANCEMENTS IN QUANTUM COMPUTING TECHNOLOGIES

1.5.1 QUANTUM HARDWARE DEVELOPMENTS

Quantum hardware developments are important for the advancement of quantum computing. Improvements in quantum hardware aim to enhance qubit performance, increase the number of qubits, extend coherence times, reduce errors, and enable the scaling of quantum systems. Here are some notable developments in quantum hardware:

Qubit Technologies:

- Superconducting Qubits: They are typically implemented using superconducting circuits and benefit from well-developed fabrication techniques. Superconducting qubits have seen advancements in coherence times, gate fidelities, and qubit connectivity.

- Trapped Ion Qubits: It is confined and manipulated with electromagnetic fields. They have demonstrated long coherence times and high gate fidelities. Recent advancements in trapped ion qubits include the integration of multiple qubits, improved gate operations, and enhanced qubit control.
- Topological Qubits: Topological qubits utilise anyons, quasiparticles that emerge in specific topological materials. These qubits have potential advantages in terms of noise resilience and fault-tolerant computation. Recent developments include the investigation of Majorana fermions and other topological states for quantum computation.

Increased Qubit Counts:

- Demonstrating Quantum Supremacy: In 2019, Google's Sycamore processor achieved quantum supremacy by demonstrating a quantum computation that surpasses classical supercomputers' capabilities. This milestone showcased the successful operation of a quantum processor with 53 qubits.
- Scaling Up Qubit Numbers: Various research groups and companies are actively working on scaling up the number of qubits in their quantum processors. For example, IBM has developed 127-qubit processors, while IonQ has demonstrated 32-qubit trapped ion processors.

Coherence and Error Mitigation:

- Coherence Time Improvements: Coherence time refers to the duration for which qubits can maintain their quantum state. Researchers have made progress in improving coherence times by addressing sources of noise and implementing error mitigation techniques.
- Error Correction and Fault Tolerance: Error correction techniques, such as surface code and other caused by noise and decoherence. Implementing fault-tolerant quantum computation is an important step towards large-scale, reliable quantum systems.

Quantum Interconnects and Connectivity:

- Connectivity: Enhancing connectivity between qubits is essential for executing multi-qubit gates and enabling more efficient quantum algorithms. Techniques such as improved qubit layouts, coupling schemes, and better control architectures are being provided to achieve higher qubit connectivity.
- These developments demonstrate the progress made in quantum hardware, and continued research and engineering efforts aim to overcome technical challenges, improve qubit performance, reduce errors, and realise practical and scalable.

1.5.2   Quantum Computing Architectures

Quantum computing architectures refer to the different approaches and designs used to implement and build quantum computers. Several architectures are being provided, each with its own advantages, challenges, and technological issues [21]. Here are some prominent quantum computing architectures:

- Superconducting Circuits: Superconducting qubits are a widely pursued qubit technology. They are implemented using superconducting circuits that rely on Josephson junctions to trap and manipulate qubits. Superconducting qubits have achieved significant progress in terms of qubit control, gate fidelity, and qubit connectivity. They are known for their scalability potential and have been used in several commercial quantum processors.
- Trapped Ions: Trapped ion qubits use individual ions, typically trapped and manipulated with electromagnetic fields. They provide long coherence times and high gate fidelities.

Ions are well-isolated from the environment, making them less susceptible to decoherence. Trapped ion architectures have achieved demonstrations of entanglement and gate operations with high precision and have the potential for high qubit connectivity.

- Topological Quantum Computing: Topological quantum computing aims to utilise exotic properties of topological states of matter to perform quantum computation. Majorana fermions and other topological excitations are being provided for their potential as robust qubits that can be manipulated using non-Abelian braiding operations. Topological qubits provide the advantage of inherent error protection and resilience against local perturbations.
- Quantum Annealing: Quantum annealers are designed to find the lowest energy states of a given problem by manipulating qubits to reach a ground state. D-Wave Systems has developed quantum annealing machines that implement this approach.
- Photonic Quantum Computing: Photonic quantum computing utilises photons as qubits to perform quantum operations. Photons are generated, manipulated, and measured using various photonic elements such as beam splitters, phase shifters, and detectors. Photonic architectures provide advantages in terms of high-speed quantum operations, low decoherence rates, and potential for long-distance quantum communication.
- Solid-State Spin Qubits: Solid-state spin qubits utilise individual electron or nuclear spins in solid-state systems, such as quantum dots or defects in diamond. They are promising qubits due to their long coherence times, compatibility with semiconductor fabrication techniques, and potential for integration with existing electronic devices.

Note that these architectures are not mutually exclusive, and researchers are exploring hybrid approaches and combinations of different technologies to use their respective strengths. Each architecture has its own set of challenges, including maintaining qubit coherence, improving gate fidelities, achieving scalability, and addressing noise and error sources. As quantum computing continues to advance, ongoing research and development aim to optimise and combine these architectures to build practical and scalable quantum computers capable of solving complex problems with advantages over classical computing.

1.5.3 Quantum Computing Platforms and Companies

There are several prominent companies and organisations involved in the development of quantum computing platforms and technologies [17, 18, 22]. Here are some key players in the field:

- IBM Quantum: IBM Quantum is an initiative by IBM that focuses on advancing the research and development related to quantum. IBM provides access to its quantum computing systems through the IBM Quantum Experience, allowing users to experiment with quantum algorithms and tools. IBM is also actively involved in developing quantum hardware and software and exploring applications in various fields.
- Google Quantum AI: Google's Quantum AI team is engaged in research and development of quantum computing technologies. They have made significant strides in developing superconducting qubit-based processors and demonstrated quantum supremacy in 2019. Google is working on advancing both the hardware and software aspects of quantum computing.
- Microsoft Quantum: Microsoft Quantum is dedicated to developing a scalable and fault-tolerant quantum computing ecosystem. Microsoft is working on several approaches, including topological qubits based on Majorana fermions, and is actively collaborating with researchers and industry partners to advance the field. Microsoft also provides access to their quantum resources through Azure Quantum.
- Rigetti Computing: Rigetti Computing is a company that focuses on building and operating quantum computers. They provide access to their quantum processors through their

cloud-based platform called Forest. Rigetti is involved in advancing superconducting qubit technology, error correction techniques, and exploring applications in areas like quantum chemistry and optimisation.

- IonQ: IonQ is focused on trapped ion quantum computing. They aim to develop and commercialise trapped ion quantum processors with high qubit counts and low error rates. IonQ's trapped ion technology provides long coherence times and precise control over individual ions, enabling high-fidelity gate operations.

- Honeywell Quantum Solutions: Honeywell Quantum Solutions is working on developing trapped ion quantum processors. They aim to address scalability and reliability challenges by using their expertise in precision control systems. Honeywell Quantum Solutions is involved in the development of quantum hardware and software and exploring applications in areas like cryptography and optimisation.

These companies are actively pushing the boundaries of quantum computing, investing in research, and collaborating with academic institutions and industry partners to advance the field. Additionally, there are numerous startups and research organisations worldwide.

1.5.4   QUANTUM NETWORKING AND INTERCONNECTIVITY

Quantum networking and interconnectivity focus on the development of communication protocols and infrastructure for transmitting quantum information reliably and securely over long distances. Quantum networks aim to connect quantum processors, quantum memories, and quantum devices to enable distributed quantum computing, quantum communication, and other quantum-enabled applications. Here are key aspects of quantum networking and interconnectivity:

- Quantum Communication Channels: Quantum communication channels are necessary for transmitting quantum states and quantum information between different nodes in a quantum network. Various physical systems, such as optical fibres, free-space links, and quantum memories, are used to transport quantum states while preserving their fragile quantum properties.

- Quantum Repeaters: They are designed to extend the range of quantum communication by mitigating the effects of optical losses in communication channels. They can regenerate and amplify quantum signals to maintain the fidelity of quantum states over long distances. Quantum repeaters play an important role in building large-scale quantum networks by enabling long-haul quantum communication.

- Quantum Entanglement Distribution: Quantum networks rely on the distribution of entangled states between different nodes. This allows the correlation of quantum states across distant locations instantaneously. The creation and distribution of entangled states enable various quantum communication and computation protocols, such as teleportation and distributed quantum computing.

- Quantum Gate Operations: Quantum networks require the ability to perform gate operations and entanglement generation between remote qubits. Techniques like quantum teleportation, entanglement swapping, and distributed quantum gates enable the execution of joint quantum computations across different network nodes. These operations are essential for distributed quantum computing and building quantum networks with enhanced computational power.

- Quantum Network Protocols and Architecture: Quantum networking protocols define the rules and procedures for transmitting quantum information over a network. These protocols ensure the secure and reliable transmission of quantum states, establish quantum entanglement, manage network resources, and coordinate quantum operations across different network nodes. Quantum network architecture defines the overall structure and organisation of interconnected quantum devices, including the arrangement of nodes, routing strategies, and network management systems.

- Quantum Internet: The concept of a quantum internet envisions a global network of interconnected quantum devices, allowing the seamless transmission of quantum information worldwide. Research efforts are underway to develop the necessary technologies, protocols, and standards for realising a quantum internet.

In summary, quantum networking and interconnectivity are active areas of research and development. They aim to overcome challenges such as maintaining the integrity of quantum information, dealing with noise and decoherence, extending quantum states over long distances, and ensuring the security of quantum communication. Advancements in quantum networking are important for realising the full potential of distributed quantum computing and enabling a broad range of secure quantum communication applications.

1.6   OPEN ISSUES IN QUANTUM COMPUTING FOR FUTURE GENERATIONS

While quantum computing has made significant progress, several open issues and challenges remain that need to be addressed for future generations of quantum systems [4–6]. Here are some key open issues in quantum computing:

- Fault Tolerance and Error Correction: It is a continuous struggle to develop scalable and effective error correction codes that can guard against faults and decoherence in quantum information. One key objective for large-scale quantum systems is to provide fault-tolerant quantum computation, where faults may be found and fixed without impairing the calculation as a whole.
- Coherence and Decoherence: One of the enduring problems is keeping qubits coherent. Quantum information can be lost in quantum systems due to their sensitivity to noise and environmental interactions that cause decoherence. Improving the scalability and performance of quantum systems requires developing methods to decrease noise, increase coherence times, and lessen decoherence effects.
- Scalability and Qubit Count: Scaling up the and controlling interactions between qubits is a major challenge. Developing qubit technologies and architectures that can reliably scale to larger numbers of qubits, ensuring high gate fidelities and qubit connectivity, is important for achieving practical quantum computing systems.
- Quantum Algorithms and Applications: While quantum algorithms have shown promise in specific areas, further research is needed to provide their broader applicability and develop more efficient algorithms for various problem domains.
- Quantum Communication and Networking: Establishing efficient and secure quantum communication channels over long distances is a challenge. Overcoming issues such as transmission loss, noise, and maintaining entanglement between distant nodes in quantum networks is important for realising the vision of a quantum internet and distributed quantum computing.
- Quantum Control and Measurement: Enhancing the precision and speed of quantum control and measurement techniques is important for manipulating and detecting quantum states accurately. Researchers are developing advanced control technologies, faster measurement techniques, and novel quantum feedback control methods to enhance quantum systems' performance and stability.
- Quantum Materials and Device Engineering: The search for new materials with improved qubit coherence properties and the development of scalable qubit fabrication techniques are ongoing challenges. Exploring alternative qubit technologies, improving qubit lifetimes, and optimising device architectures are key areas of research to enhance the performance and scalability of quantum systems.

- Quantum Simulation of Complex Systems: Quantum simulation of large and complex systems, is challenging due to the exponential growth in computational resources required. Developing more efficient algorithms and techniques for simulating complex quantum systems can enable breakthroughs in areas such as materials science, drug discovery, and fundamental physics.
- Quantum Education and Workforce Development: It requires a skilled workforce. Developing comprehensive educational programs, training initiatives, and multidisciplinary collaborations are essential for building a capable quantum workforce and fostering the growth of the quantum computing community.

Hence, these open issues require interdisciplinary collaborations, advances in quantum hardware and software, and continued fundamental research in quantum mechanics, information theory, and related fields.

1.7 IMPORTANT CHALLENGES IN QUANTUM COMPUTING FOR FUTURE GENERATIONS

While quantum computing holds immense potential, there are important challenges that need to be addressed for future generations of quantum systems [4]. Overcoming these challenges is important to unlock the full power and practicality of quantum computing. Here are some important challenges in quantum computing:

- Qubit Coherence and Error Mitigation: Maintaining coherence is challenging due to environmental noise and interactions with surrounding elements. Increasing coherence times and developing effective error mitigation techniques, such as error correction codes and fault-tolerant methods, are important for reliable and accurate quantum computation.
- Scalability and Qubit Count: Building large-scale, fault-tolerant quantum systems with a high number of qubits is a major challenge. As the number of qubits increases, maintaining coherence, controlling interactions between qubits, and managing noise become increasingly difficult. Developing scalable qubit technologies, improving qubit connectivity, and addressing crosstalk and interference issues are important for scaling quantum systems.
- Quantum System Stability and Error Rates: Quantum systems are susceptible to various types of noise and errors, such as gate errors, readout errors, and environmental disturbances. Reducing error rates and increasing the stability of quantum systems are essential for reliable and accurate computation. Advances in hardware design, control techniques, and error mitigation strategies are necessary to tackle these challenges.
- Quantum Software and Algorithms: Developing efficient quantum algorithms and software tools is important for harnessing the power of quantum computing. Further research is needed to improve quantum algorithm design, optimise quantum circuits, and provide new quantum software development frameworks. Bridging the gap between classical and quantum computing and developing hybrid algorithms can also enhance the applicability and usability of quantum systems.
- Quantum Communication and Networking: Establishing efficient and secure quantum communication channels over long distances is a significant challenge. Overcoming transmission loss, noise, and maintaining entanglement between distant nodes are key research areas. Developing quantum repeaters, quantum memories, and robust quantum network protocols is important for the realisation of large-scale quantum networks and distributed quantum computing.
- Quantum Metrology and Sensing: Quantum metrology focuses on precise measurement of physical quantities using quantum systems. Developing advanced quantum sensors and metrology techniques can enhance sensitivity and accuracy in fields such as quantum

imaging, sensing, and metrology. Expanding the capabilities of quantum sensors and optimising measurement protocols are ongoing challenges.
- Quantum Education and Workforce Development: Building a skilled quantum workforce is
essential for advancing the field. Educating and training professionals in quantum mechanics, quantum information science, and related disciplines is important. Developing comprehensive educational programs, training initiatives, and fostering collaborations between
academia and industry are necessary to address the shortage of qualified quantum experts.

Hence, these challenges require collaborative efforts from academia, industry, and governments
to overcome/solve them. Continued research and investment in quantum hardware, software, algorithms, and education are important.

1.8   POTENTIAL AREAS OF STUDY FOR QUANTUM COMPUTING

This area provides numerous exciting research opportunities as scientists and engineers work toward
developing practical and scalable quantum technologies. Here are some future research directions
and opportunities in quantum computing:

- Quantum Algorithms and Applications: There is ongoing research in developing and optimising quantum algorithms for various applications. Researchers are exploring new quantum algorithms, improving existing ones, and identifying problem domains where quantum
computers can provide significant advantages over classical approaches. Applications span
areas such as optimisation, cryptography, machine learning, quantum chemistry, and
quantum simulations.
- Quantum Software and Programming Languages: Quantum software and programming
languages play an important role in enabling the development and execution of quantum
algorithms. Future research opportunities lie in designing more efficient quantum programming languages, improving quantum software development frameworks, and enhancing compiler technologies for optimising quantum circuits.
- Scalability and Quantum System Architectures: Achieving scalability in quantum systems
is a major research goal. Investigating new approaches to increase the number of qubits,
improving qubit coherence times, enhancing qubit connectivity, and exploring novel quantum system architectures are key research directions. Hybrid architectures, combining different qubit technologies may also hold promise for scaling quantum systems.
- Quantum Control and Measurement Techniques: Developing advanced control and measurement techniques for manipulating and detecting quantum states is essential. Research
focuses on improving qubit control precision, developing faster and more accurate measurement methods, and exploring quantum feedback control techniques to optimise quantum computation and minimise errors.
- Quantum Communication and Networking: Expanding the capabilities of quantum networks and quantum communication protocols is an active area of research. Future opportunities include developing long-distance quantum communication technologies, enhancing
quantum repeaters, advancing quantum key distribution protocols, and realising the vision
of a global quantum internet.
- Quantum Materials and Device Engineering: Research in quantum materials and device
engineering aims to improve the performance of qubits and provide new qubit technologies. Investigating novel materials for qubit fabrication, optimising fabrication processes,
and developing new device architectures can contribute to the advancement of quantum
computing technologies.
- Quantum Metrology and Sensing: Quantum computing research can benefit from advancements in quantum metrology and sensing. Techniques such as quantum metrology enable

precise measurement of physical quantities, while quantum sensors provide high sensitivity for detecting and characterising signals. Integration of quantum metrology and sensing capabilities into quantum systems can enhance their performance and open up new applications.

- Quantum Ethics, Policy, and Socioeconomic Implications: As quantum computing progresses, research on the ethical, policy, and socioeconomic implications of this technology is becoming increasingly important. Understanding the potential impacts of quantum computing on society, addressing issues related to privacy and security, and ensuring the ethical and responsible development and use of quantum technologies are areas of ongoing research.

Hence, these research opportunities highlight the diverse and multidisciplinary nature of the field of quantum computing. Collaboration between scientists, engineers, mathematicians, and policymakers is essential for pushing the boundaries of quantum technology and harnessing its potential for practical applications.

1.9   QUANTUM COMPUTING ECOSYSTEM AND COLLABORATION

The development of quantum computing requires a collaborative ecosystem involving academia, industry, governments, and research institutions. Collaboration is important to address the diverse challenges in quantum computing and accelerate progress. Here are key aspects of the quantum computing ecosystem and the importance of collaboration:

- Academic Research: Universities and research institutions play a central role in advancing quantum computing. They conduct fundamental research in quantum physics, quantum algorithms, and quantum information science. Academic collaborations promote the exchange of knowledge, encourage interdisciplinary research, and foster the development of future quantum scientists and engineers.
- Industry Engagement: Collaboration between industry and academia is important for translating quantum research into practical applications. Collaborative efforts between industry and academia drive technology advancements, address practical challenges, and promote the commercialisation of quantum technologies.
- Government Support: Governments worldwide recognise and provide financial support, research funding, and policy initiatives. Governments foster collaboration by establishing research centres, funding national quantum initiatives, and promoting partnerships between academia and industry. Government support is important for nurturing the quantum ecosystem, attracting talent, and fostering international collaboration.
- Open Collaboration: Open collaboration is fundamental to the quantum ecosystem. Open-source software frameworks, like Qiskit and Forest, contribute, share code, and collaborate on quantum algorithms and software tools. Open collaboration facilitates knowledge exchange, accelerates innovation, and fosters a collective effort toward solving challenges in quantum computing.
- Consortia and Collaborative Projects: Consortia and collaborative projects bring together multiple stakeholders to tackle complex challenges in quantum computing. These initiatives involve academia, industry partners, and research institutions working together on specific research topics, hardware development, standardisation efforts, and addressing common technical hurdles. Examples include the IBM Q Network and the Quantum Industry Consortium.
- International Collaboration: Quantum computing is a global endeavour, and international collaboration is important. Researchers, institutions, and companies from different countries collaborate on joint research projects, share resources, and exchange expertise. International collaboration fosters diversity, facilitates knowledge transfer, and accelerates the development of quantum technologies.

- Quantum Education and Workforce Development: Collaboration in quantum education is essential for developing a skilled quantum workforce. Universities, industry partners, and research institutions collaborate on quantum education programs, training initiatives, and internships. Collaborative efforts ensure that students and professionals receive comprehensive training and hands-on experience in quantum computing.
- Ethical and Policy Collaboration: Collaboration in the ethical and policy dimensions of quantum computing is important. Researchers, policymakers, and stakeholders collaborate to address ethical issues, ensure responsible development and use of quantum technologies, and shape policies that support the growth of the quantum ecosystem while considering societal implications.

In summary, collaboration across these facets of the quantum ecosystem helps overcome technical challenges, fosters innovation, and accelerates the development of practical quantum computing technologies; with this, we collect essential information and unlock the full potential of quantum computing for societal and economic benefits.

1.10 FUTURE TRENDS AND RESEARCH DIRECTIONS TOWARDS QUANTUM COMPUTING WITH EMERGING TECHNOLOGIES

Emerging technologies hold great potential for advancing quantum computing and addressing current limitations. Here are some future trends and research directions that use emerging technologies for the development of quantum computing:

- Topological Qubits: Topological qubits, based on exotic states of matter, provide potential advantages in terms of error resistance and robustness against noise. Research focuses on exploring and engineering topological materials, such as Majorana fermions and topological insulators, to realise topological qubits and develop fault-tolerant quantum computing architectures.
- Silicon-Based Quantum Technologies: Silicon is a widely used material in classical computing, and efforts are underway to use silicon-based technologies for quantum computing. Silicon quantum dots and spin qubits provide potential scalability, compatibility with existing semiconductor manufacturing techniques, and the integration of classical and quantum components on a single chip.
- 2D Materials and Hybrid Systems: Two-dimensional (2D) materials, such as graphene and transition metal dichalcogenides (TMDs), show promise for quantum computing. Research focuses on integrating 2D materials with other quantum systems, such as superconducting qubits or trapped ions, to create hybrid quantum architectures with enhanced performance and functionality.
- Quantum Photonics and Quantum Optics: Quantum photonics and quantum optics technologies are being provided for the generation, manipulation, and detection of quantum states of light. Advances in photonics-based qubits, such as integrated photonics circuits and on-chip quantum photonics, can enable efficient information processing and quantum communication in large-scale quantum systems.
- Quantum Nanomechanical Systems: Quantum nanomechanical systems, including nanomechanical resonators and nanowires, provide unique opportunities for quantum computing. Research focuses on using their mechanical motion to encode and manipulate quantum information, exploring quantum transduction between different qubit platforms, and developing hybrid quantum systems.
- Quantum Neural Networks and Quantum Machine Learning: Future trends include exploring the use of quantum neural networks, quantum-inspired models, and hybrid classical-quantum machine learning approaches. Emerging technologies such as neuromorphic

computing and quantum-inspired optimisation algorithms can enhance the capabilities of quantum machine learning.

- Quantum Materials Discovery: Quantum computing can revolutionise the discovery and design of new materials. Researchers are exploring the use of quantum algorithms to accelerate materials discovery, predict material properties, and optimise material synthesis processes. By using emerging technologies in quantum computing, quantum simulation, and data-driven approaches, new materials with desired properties can be discovered more efficiently.
- Quantum Metrology and Sensing: Advancements in quantum metrology and sensing technologies can improve the precision and sensitivity of quantum measurements. Research focuses on developing novel sensing techniques, exploring quantum-enhanced metrology, and applying quantum sensors for applications such as imaging, precision measurements, and detecting signals in complex environments.

Note that these research directions and emerging technologies have the potential to address current challenges in quantum computing, improve qubit performance and coherence, enhance scalability, and expand the range of applications for quantum systems. Collaborative efforts among academia, industry, and research institutions will be key to advancing these areas and accelerating the development of practical and powerful quantum computing technologies.

1.11   CONCLUSION

Quantum computing has rapidly evolved from a theoretical concept to a field of significant research and development. However, there are still challenges and open questions that need to be addressed for future generations of quantum systems. In terms of recent advancements, significant progress has been made in scaling quantum hardware, with notable achievements in increasing qubit counts, improving coherence times, and enhancing gate fidelities. This progress has been accompanied by breakthroughs in quantum algorithms and quantum simulation techniques for studying complex quantum systems. Quantum machine learning, quantum cryptography, and optimisation algorithms are also emerging areas of exploration. Further, we discuss future opportunities in quantum computing that lie in addressing useful challenges. These include enhancing qubit coherence and developing effective error correction and fault-tolerant methods. The development of quantum networking and quantum communication protocols is important for realising distributed quantum computing and secure quantum information transmission. Exploring new quantum algorithms, optimising existing ones, and identifying practical applications where quantum computing provides significant advantages will be key for further advancements. Hence, the future of quantum computing holds immense opportunities across various domains. Quantum machine learning, quantum simulations, and quantum chemistry are among the promising application areas where quantum computing can unlock new capabilities and information. However, several challenges must be addressed for the widespread adoption of quantum computing. Quantum systems are highly susceptible to noise and errors due to decoherence and interactions with the environment. Developing robust error correction techniques, fault-tolerant quantum computing, and efficient error mitigation strategies are important to overcome these challenges.

REFERENCES

1. Preskill, J. (2018). Quantum computing in the NISQ era and beyond. *Quantum*, 2, 79. (https://quantum-journal.org/papers/q-2018-08-06-79/)
2. Arute, F. et al. (2019). Quantum supremacy using a programmable superconducting processor. *Nature*, 574(7779), 505–510. (www.nature.com/articles/s41586-019-1666-5)

3. Devitt, S. J. et al. (2021). Building a fault-tolerant quantum computer: The hardware perspective. *npj Quantum Information*, 7(1), 1–12. (www.nature.com/articles/s41534-021-00397-y)
4. Tyagi, A. K. (Ed.). (2023). *Handbook of Research on Quantum Computing for Smart Environments*. IGI Global. (https://doi.org/10.4018/978-1-6684-6697-1)
5. Susindhar A. V., Soni, G., & Tyagi, A. K. (2023). A review on recent trends in quantum computation technology. In A. Tyagi (Ed.), *Handbook of Research on Quantum Computing for Smart Environments* (pp. 48–64). IGI Global. (https://doi.org/10.4018/978-1-6684-6697-1.ch003)
6. Sasi, P., Soni, G., Tyagi, A. K., Kakulapati, V., Shyam Mohan J. S., & Singh, R. K. (2023). Quantum computing and the qubit: The future of artificial intelligence. In A. Tyagi (Ed.), *Handbook of Research on Quantum Computing for Smart Environments* (pp. 231–244). IGI Global. (https://doi.org/10.4018/978-1-6684-6697-1.ch013)
7. Deekshetha, H. R., & Tyagi, A. K. (2023). Chapter 16—Automated and intelligent systems for next-generation-based smart applications. In A. K. Tyagi & A. Abraham (Eds.), *Data Science for Genomics* (pp. 265–276). Academic Press. (https://doi.org/10.1016/B978-0-323-98352-5.00019-7).
8. Tyagi, A. K. (2022). *Handbook of Research on Technical, Privacy, and Security Challenges in a Modern World*. IGI Global. (https://doi.org.10.4018/978-1-6684-5250-9)
9. Gomathi, L., Mishra, A. K., & Tyagi, A. K. (2023). Blockchain and machine learning empowered internet of things applications: Current issues, challenges and future research opportunities. In *2023 4th International Conference on Smart Electronics and Communication (ICOSEC)*, Trichy, India (pp. 637–647). (https://doi.org/10.1109/ICOSEC58147.2023.10276385).
10. Hidary, J. (2020). *Quantum Computing: An Applied Approach*. Springer.
11. Nair, M. M., & Tyagi, A. K. (2023). Blockchain technology for next-generation society: Current trends and future opportunities for smart era. In *Blockchain Technology for Secure Social Media Computing*. (https://doi.org/10.1049/PBSE019E_ch11).
12. Farhi, E., Goldstone, J., & Gutmann, S. (2014). A quantum approximate optimization algorithm. *arXiv preprint* arXiv:1411.4028. (https://arxiv.org/abs/1411.4028)
13. Nair, M. M., & Tyagi, A. K. (2023). Chapter 11—AI, IoT, blockchain, and cloud computing: The necessity of the future. In R. Pandey, S. Goundar, & S. Fatima (Eds.), *Distributed Computing to Blockchain* (pp. 189–206). Academic Press. ISBN: 9780323961462. (https://doi.org/10.1016/B978-0-323-96146-2.00001-2).
14. Gomathi, L., Mishra, A. K., & Tyagi, A. K. (2023). Industry 5.0 for Healthcare 5.0: Opportunities, challenges and future research possibilities. In *2023 7th International Conference on Trends in Electronics and Informatics (ICOEI)*, Tirunelveli, India (pp. 204–213). (https://doi.org/10.1109/ICOEI56765.2023.10125660).
15. Deshmukh, A., Patil, D. S., Pawar, P. D., Kumari, S., & Muthulakshmi, P. (2023). Recent trends for smart environments with AI and IoT-based technologies: A comprehensive review. In A. Tyagi (Ed.), *Handbook of Research on Quantum Computing for Smart Environments* (pp. 435–452). IGI Global. (https://doi.org/10.4018/978-1-6684-6697-1.ch023)
16. Preskill, J. (2018). Quantum computing and the entanglement frontier. *Notices of the American Mathematical Society*, 65(4), 378–388. (www.ams.org/journals/notices/201804/rnoti-p378.pdf)
17. Goyal, D., & Tyagi, A. (2020). *A Look at Top 35 Problems in the Computer Science Field for the Next Decade*. (https://doi.org/10.1201/9781003052098-40).
18. Pramod, A., Naicker, H. S., & Tyagi, A. K. (2022). *Emerging Innovations in the Near Future Using Deep Learning Techniques, Book: Advanced Analytics and Deep Learning Models*. Wiley Scrivener. (https://doi.org/10.1002/9781119792437.ch10)
19. Montanaro, A. (2016). Quantum algorithms: An overview. *npj Quantum Information*, 2(1), 1–8. (www.nature.com/articles/npjqi201524)
20. Arute, F. et al. (2021). Quantum approximate optimization of non-planar graph problems on a planar superconducting processor. *Nature Physics*, 17(3), 340–345. (www.nature.com/articles/s41567-020-01105-x)
21. Wecker, D. et al. (2020). Progress and prospects for quantum supremacy in computing. *Frontiers in Physics*, 8, 660. (www.frontiersin.org/articles/10.3389/fphy.2020.00660/full)
22. Gheorghiu, V. et al. (2021). Quantum computing: An overview of recent progress. *Annual Review of Condensed Matter Physics*, 12, 247–271. (www.annualreviews.org/doi/abs/10.1146/annurev-conmatphys-121919-050502).

2 Application of Qubits in Artificial Intelligence and Machine Learning

S. Nalini, Amit Kumar Tyagi,
Shrikant Tiwari, and Shabnam Kumari

2.1 INTRODUCTION TO QUANTUM COMPUTING FUNDAMENTALS

2.1.1 QUANTUM BITS, QUANTUM GATES AND QUANTUM ALGORITHMS

In this section, we will give a basic introduction to quantum bits (qubits), quantum gates, and quantum algorithms.

Quantum Bits (Qubits): Qubits serve as the basic building blocks of quantum information in quantum computing. In contrast to classical bits, which have binary values of 0 or 1, qubits have the unique ability to exist in a superposition of these states. This characteristic enables a qubit to embody both 0 and 1 at the same time, facilitating parallel processing and more intricate computations. Moreover, qubits can become entangled with one another, resulting in the state of one qubit being interconnected with the state of another, regardless of their physical distance. This entanglement feature empowers quantum computers to execute intricate calculations and simulations that are practically unattainable for classical computers.

Quantum Gates: Quantum gates represent the quantum computing versions of classical logic gates. In contrast to classical logic gates that function with classical bits, quantum gates are meant to work with qubits. These gates are responsible for manipulating qubits by modifying their quantum states, either one by one or collectively. There are different types of quantum gates, each designed for specific tasks such as quantum entanglement, superposition, and phase shifts. Examples of quantum gates include the Hadamard gate (H-gate), Pauli-X gate, Pauli-Y gate, and Pauli-Z gate.

Quantum Algorithms: Quantum algorithms leverage the distinctive characteristics of qubits, such as superposition and entanglement, to efficiently solve specific problems on quantum computers. The following are a few noteworthy quantum algorithms:

- Shor's Algorithm: Renowned for its capacity to efficiently factorize large numbers, Shor's algorithm holds significant implications for the decryption of classical encryption methods like RSA (developed by Ron Rivest, Adi Shamir, and Leonard Adleman). It possesses the ability to solve factoring problems exponentially faster than the most advanced classical algorithms.
- Grover's Algorithm: This algorithm offers a quadratic acceleration for searching unsorted databases, enabling the identification of the desired item within a list of N items with only $O(\sqrt{N})$ queries.
- Quantum Machine Learning Algorithms: These algorithms harness the power of quantum computing to enhance various tasks such as data classification, clustering, and optimization. Notable examples include quantum support vector machines and quantum neural networks.
- Quantum Simulation Algorithms: These algorithms utilize quantum computers to simulate quantum systems and quantum mechanics, facilitating more precise investigations into molecular structures, material properties, and chemical reactions.

DOI: 10.1201/9781003499459-2

- Quantum Walk Algorithms: Quantum walks serve as the quantum counterparts to classical random walks and find applications in optimization problems, graph theory, and quantum search.
- Quantum Fourier Transform (QFT): The QFT represents a quantum adaptation of the classical discrete Fourier transform and plays a pivotal role in numerous quantum algorithms, including Shor's algorithm.

Quantum algorithms hold the promise of transforming numerous sectors such as cryptography, optimization, machine learning, and quantum simulations. Nevertheless, it is crucial to highlight that the realization of practical, fault-tolerant quantum computers that can effectively execute these algorithms is still a work in progress, and their extensive adoption is in its initial phases.

2.1.2 QUANTUM HARDWARE

Quantum hardware encompasses the physical devices and components essential for implementing quantum computing [1]. In contrast to classical computers that rely on traditional transistors to process information as binary bits (0s and 1s), quantum hardware harnesses the distinctive principles of quantum mechanics to manipulate quantum bits (qubits). These qubits enable quantum computers to perform operations like superposition and entanglement, granting them the capability to solve specific problems more efficiently than classical computers:

- Qubits: Qubits are the fundamental building blocks of quantum hardware. These quantum bits can exist in multiple states simultaneously due to the principle of superposition. Various physical systems can serve as qubits, including trapped ions, superconducting circuits, and photons.
- Quantum Gates: Quantum gates are the counterparts of classical logic gates in quantum computing. They perform operations on qubits by manipulating their quantum states. Examples of quantum gates include the Hadamard gate, Pauli-X gate, and CNOT gate.
- Quantum Processors: Quantum processors are the central processing units of quantum computers. They consist of an array of qubits and the necessary control systems to execute quantum algorithms. These processors are at the core of quantum hardware and come in various designs, including superconducting qubit processors and ion-trap processors.
- Cryogenic Systems: Many quantum processors operate at extremely low temperatures (near absolute zero) to reduce environmental noise and maintain the delicate quantum states of qubits. Cryogenic systems, such as dilution refrigerators, are essential for cooling the hardware.
- Control Electronics: Quantum computers require specialized control electronics to manipulate qubits with precision. These electronics control the timing and sequences of quantum gate operations.
- Quantum Error Correction: Quantum hardware frequently incorporates error correction codes and strategies to alleviate the consequences of quantum errors. The implementation of quantum error correction is crucial in the development of fault-tolerant quantum computers.
- Quantum Interconnects: In some quantum computing architectures, quantum processors are interconnected to facilitate communication between qubits. These interconnects help to implement quantum gates that entangle qubits.
- Quantum Memory: Quantum memory is used to temporarily store quantum information, which can be essential for executing complex quantum algorithms.
- Quantum Sensors: Quantum sensors, such as quantum-enhanced magnetometers or gravimeters, can be integrated with quantum hardware for various applications, including sensing and metrology.
- Quantum Network Components: Quantum hardware is also used in the development of quantum communication systems, including quantum key distribution devices and quantum repeaters.

Quantum hardware is a dynamic field that is constantly progressing through research and development efforts aimed at enhancing the capabilities of quantum computers. As of the most recent update in May 2024, quantum hardware continues to be a subject of active exploration, with ongoing strides being made towards the creation of more reliable and scalable quantum computing systems.

2.1.3 ARTIFICIAL INTELLIGENCE AND MACHINE LEARNING

Artificial intelligence (AI) and machine learning (ML) are intricately interconnected disciplines within the realm of computer science [2–8]. They focus on crafting algorithms and frameworks that empower machines to execute tasks traditionally necessitating human intelligence [9]. While they are related, they have distinct characteristics:

Artificial Intelligence: Artificial intelligence encompasses a wide range of computer science disciplines with the goal of developing systems or machines that can carry out tasks demanding intelligence similar to that of humans [10]. It encompasses a wide range of techniques and approaches, including symbolic reasoning, expert systems, natural language processing, computer vision, and more. AI can be both rule-based (deterministic) and learning-based (machine learning). While rule-based AI relies on predefined logical rules, learning-based AI leverages data and statistical patterns. AI systems can exhibit intelligent behavior, make decisions, solve problems, understand natural language, and interact with humans in a way that simulates human intelligence. AI can be classified into two main categories: narrow or weak AI, which is designed to perform specific tasks, and general or strong AI, which possesses a human-like general intelligence.

Machine Learning: ML, a branch of AI, concentrates on the creation of algorithms that enable computers to acquire knowledge from data and utilize it to make predictions or decisions [10]. ML systems improve their performance on a task through experience and exposure to data. They do not rely on explicit programming for every rule. ML algorithms are categorized into supervised learning (training on labeled data), unsupervised learning (clustering and pattern recognition), and reinforcement learning (learning from rewards or punishments). ML is commonly used for tasks like image and speech recognition, recommendation systems, predictive analytics, and natural language processing. Further, deep learning is a subfield of ML that uses neural networks with many layers (deep neural networks) to solve complex tasks like image recognition and language understanding. AI and ML often overlap, with ML being an important subfield of AI. In practice, many AI systems incorporate machine learning techniques to achieve tasks such as data analysis, decision-making, or pattern recognition. Artificial intelligence covers a wide array of concepts, such as rule-based systems, expert systems, symbolic reasoning, and various methodologies that go beyond machine learning.

AI and ML have experienced significant progress and are utilized in a wide range of fields such as healthcare, finance, transportation, and beyond. Their ongoing development shows immense potential in addressing intricate issues and improving automation and decision-making procedures.

2.1.4 SUPERPOSITION AND ENTANGLEMENT

Superposition and entanglement are fundamental principles in quantum mechanics with important ramifications in the realms of quantum computing and quantum information theory. These concepts distinguish quantum systems from classical systems and are crucial for comprehending the immense potential of quantum computing. Let's delve into each term separately:

Superposition: Superposition, a key principle in quantum mechanics, allows quantum systems to exist in a simultaneous combination of multiple states. Unlike classical computing, where bits can only be in a 0 or 1 state, qubits, the quantum counterparts of classical bits, can exist in a superposition state. This implies that qubits can be in a linear combination of both 0 and 1 states. Mathematically, the state of a qubit can be represented as:

$$|\psi\rangle = \alpha\,|\,0\rangle + \beta\,|1>$$

where $|\psi\rangle$ represents the qubit's state, α and β are complex probability amplitudes, and $|\,0\rangle$ and $|1>$ are basis sates representing classical 0 and 1.

Superposition enables quantum computers to execute numerous calculations simultaneously, resulting in exponential acceleration for certain issues like factoring large numbers (Shor's algorithm) or searching unsorted databases (Grover's algorithm). It establishes the foundation for quantum parallelism, a crucial advantage of quantum computing.

Entanglement: Entanglement is an extraordinary quantum phenomenon where the states of two or more qubits become interconnected in a manner that measuring one qubit instantly determines the state of the other qubit(s), regardless of the distance between them. This phenomenon, famously referred to by physicist Albert Einstein as "spooky action at a distance," has been experimentally confirmed and is a fundamental element of quantum mechanics. Entanglement empowers quantum computers to carry out intricate operations that classical computers are incapable of performing. When qubits are entangled, they share a quantum state that allows them to process information collectively. This feature is crucial in quantum algorithms and quantum teleportation, where the state of one qubit can be transferred to another through entanglement. Various methods, such as entangling gates, can be utilized to create entanglement between qubits, leading to an entangled state. Entanglement serves as a valuable resource in quantum computing, enabling quantum algorithms to surpass classical algorithms in specific tasks.

Superposition and entanglement are fundamental quantum properties that differentiate quantum computing from classical computing. Superposition permits qubits to hold multiple states simultaneously, offering parallelism, whereas entanglement allows qubits to exchange information in a correlated fashion, aiding in intricate quantum calculations. These phenomena play a crucial role in the potential strength and functionalities of quantum computers.

2.1.5 IMPORTANCE OF QUANTUM COMPUTING IN AI AND ML

Quantum computing holds huge promise in the fields of AI and ML [11, 12]. Quantum computing possesses distinctive characteristics, including superposition and entanglement, which hold the promise of transforming the development and application of AI and ML algorithms. The following are several significant advantages of quantum computing in the field of AI and ML:

- Exponential Speedup: Quantum computers possess the capability to offer exponential acceleration in resolving specific problems when compared to classical computers. This acceleration holds immense potential in enhancing AI and ML algorithms that demand extensive computation, including optimization, search, and simulation problems.
- Quantum Machine Learning (QML): Quantum machine learning leverages quantum properties to enhance machine learning algorithms, such as data classification, clustering, and optimization [13]. By utilizing quantum algorithms, machine learning models can be trained and executed with greater efficiency.

- Optimization: Many AI and ML tasks involve optimization problems, where finding the best solution among numerous possibilities is crucial. Quantum computing can offer more efficient solutions to these problems, enhancing the accuracy and speed of AI and ML models.
- Quantum Neural Networks: Quantum neural networks, also known as quantum-enhanced neural networks, can be employed to develop more powerful deep learning models. These networks can process and store large datasets more efficiently, which is essential for training complex AI models.
- Quantum Feature Selection: Quantum computers can aid in finding the most relevant features or attributes in datasets, which is crucial for dimensionality reduction and model simplification in AI and ML.
- Quantum Data Analysis: Quantum computing can effectively analyze data, particularly when dealing with large datasets. This capability is valuable in tasks like data mining, pattern recognition, and predictive analytics.
- Quantum-Secured AI: Quantum computing has the potential to enhance the security of AI and ML models by offering quantum-resistant encryption techniques. This is particularly crucial as classical encryption methods could be vulnerable to quantum computers.
- Quantum-Secured Data: Quantum computing can help secure sensitive AI and ML data, ensuring its privacy and integrity through quantum-resistant encryption and secure data transmission.
- Natural Language Processing: The efficiency of natural language processing tasks, such as language translation, sentiment analysis, and speech recognition, can be improved through the utilization of quantum computing. This is achieved by processing and analyzing vast amounts of linguistic data more effectively.
- Quantum-Specific Problems: Quantum computers are well-suited for addressing quantum physics, chemistry, and materials science-related problems. These advancements can subsequently benefit AI and ML models that rely on simulations of quantum systems.

Given the immense potential of quantum computing in the fields of AI and ML, it is important to acknowledge that the development of practical and fault-tolerant quantum computers is still in its early stages. The realm of quantum computing is constantly evolving, and the integration of AI and ML with this technology is an area that is actively being explored and innovated. With the continuous advancement of quantum hardware and algorithms, there is a promising future for solving intricate problems and propelling AI and ML to unprecedented levels.

2.1.6 ORGANIZATION OF THE WORK

This work is summarized in eight sections.

2.2 QUANTUM COMPUTING IN AI AND MACHINE LEARNING

2.2.1 QUANTUM SPEEDUP AND AI OPTIMIZATION

Quantum speedup denotes the significant enhancement in computational tasks accomplished by quantum computing in contrast to classical computing techniques. The potential of quantum speedup to revolutionize numerous domains is immense, and one area where it holds great promise is AI optimization. The following elucidates the magnitude of quantum speedup in the realm of AI optimization:

- Complex Optimization Problems: Many AI tasks require solving intricate optimization problems, like training deep neural networks, conducting feature selection, and fine-tuning parameters for machine learning algorithms. Traditional optimization algorithms may be costly in terms of computation and time, particularly when dealing with extensive problems.

- Exponential Speedup: Quantum computing has the potential to significantly acceler-ate certain optimization problems. Algorithms such as Grover's algorithm and quantum annealing methods are able to navigate vast solution spaces with greater efficiency, mak-ing them powerful tools for solving complex optimization challenges. This acceleration can result in quicker convergence and decreased computational time when tackling opti-mization tasks.
- Quadratic Speedup with Quantum Machine Learning: Quantum machine learning algo-rithms, which leverage quantum principles, can provide quadratic speedup over their clas-sical counterparts. Quantum-enhanced algorithms for solving optimization tasks can be used in AI models to make them more efficient and accurate.
- Optimizing Neural Networks: Training deep neural networks involves finding the optimal set of weights and biases to minimize the loss function. Quantum optimization techniques can help speed up this process, making it more practical to train larger and deeper neural networks.
- Simulated Quantum Annealing: Quantum annealing, a quantum optimization technique, is particularly well-suited for solving optimization problems. It can be applied to tasks like clustering, resource allocation, and combinatorial optimization, which are essential in AI applications.
- Combinatorial Optimization: AI applications frequently encounter combinatorial optimi-zation problems like the traveling salesman problem and portfolio optimization. Quantum computing demonstrates exceptional efficiency in solving these complex problems, offer-ing a promising avenue for addressing challenging optimization tasks in AI applications.
- Global Minima Search: Quantum algorithms can efficiently search for global minima, which are important in optimization tasks. Classical optimization algorithms can some-times get stuck in local minima, leading to suboptimal solutions.
- Large Datasets and Dimensionality Reduction: Quantum computing can assist in handling large datasets and performing dimensionality reduction tasks, improving the efficiency of AI models and speeding up the optimization of high-dimensional functions.

In summary, quantum speedup in AI optimization is a promising area of research, we need to do practical, fault-tolerant quantum computers are still under development. The field of quantum computing is evolving, and it will take time for quantum hardware and algorithms to mature and become widely accessible. Nonetheless, the potential for quantum speedup in AI optimization is a huge driver for research and innovation in both the quantum computing and AI communities.

2.2.2 Quantum Machine Learning Algorithms

Quantum machine learning algorithms are a subset of quantum algorithms that leverage the prin-ciples of quantum computing to enhance machine learning tasks [2, 13–15]. These algorithms are designed to perform various machine learning tasks more efficiently or to address specific problems that are challenging for classical computers. Here are some key QML algorithms:

- Quantum Support Vector Machines (QSVM): Quantum SVM algorithms leverage quan-tum computing to enhance support vector machine (SVM) algorithms. They aim to find optimal hyperplanes for classification tasks more efficiently by exploiting quantum parallelism.
- Quantum K-Means Clustering: Quantum K-means algorithms use quantum computing to perform clustering tasks. They can find cluster centers and classify data points into clusters more efficiently than classical K-means algorithms.

- Quantum Principal Component Analysis (PCA): Quantum PCA algorithms aim to perform dimensionality reduction more efficiently. They can identify the principal components of a dataset, which is useful for data compression and feature selection.
- Quantum Boltzmann Machines: Quantum Boltzmann machines are quantum versions of classical Boltzmann machines used in unsupervised learning. They can learn probability distributions and perform optimization tasks using quantum principles.
- Quantum Generative Adversarial Networks (QGANs): QGANs are quantum-enhanced versions of generative adversarial networks (GANs). They leverage quantum computing to generate realistic data samples and perform tasks like image generation and data synthesis.
- Quantum Linear Systems Algorithm (HHL): Although not a traditional machine learning algorithm, the HHL algorithm can significantly impact machine learning tasks by efficiently solving linear systems of equations. It can be used for tasks like regression analysis and optimization problems.
- Quantum Clustering Algorithms: Quantum clustering algorithms, like the quantum version of Lloyd's algorithm, can be used to improve data clustering and segmentation tasks by exploiting quantum parallelism.
- Quantum Support Vector Clustering (QSVC): QSVC algorithms aim to enhance support vector clustering tasks by using quantum computing to find optimal clustering solutions.
- Quantum Data Classification Algorithms: Quantum algorithms for data classification tasks are designed to improve the classification of data into different categories or labels by taking advantage of quantum properties.
- Quantum Kernel Methods: Quantum kernel methods are designed to improve the performance of kernel-based machine learning algorithms, such as kernelized SVM, by exploiting quantum computing.
- Quantum Neural Networks: Quantum neural networks represent an advancement of classical neural networks with quantum capabilities. They have the potential to enhance the training process of deep learning models, especially when dealing with extensive datasets.
- Quantum Reinforcement Learning: Quantum reinforcement learning algorithms have been specifically developed to optimize the effectiveness of reinforcement learning tasks, thereby increasing their applicability in domains such as robotics and autonomous systems.

In summary, quantum machine learning algorithms are an exciting area of research and development, with the potential to accelerate various machine learning tasks. While practical, fault-tolerant quantum computers capable of running these algorithms efficiently are still under development, the field of QML holds great promise for the future of machine learning and data analysis.

2.2.3   QUANTUM-ENHANCED DATA ANALYSIS

Quantum-enhanced data analysis involves utilizing quantum computing to enhance the efficiency and accuracy of analyzing and extracting valuable insights from intricate datasets. By harnessing the distinctive characteristics of quantum mechanics like superposition and entanglement, quantum computing can outperform classical computing in various data analysis tasks. The following are essential aspects and practical uses of quantum-enhanced data analysis:

- Large Dataset Processing: Quantum computers can process and analyze large datasets more efficiently due to their potential for exponential speedup in specific algorithms. This is particularly beneficial for tasks like big data analytics, where classical computers may struggle with extensive data volumes.

- Dimensionality Reduction: Quantum computing can help perform dimensionality reduction tasks by identifying relevant features in high-dimensional datasets. This process can improve the efficiency of machine learning models and reduce computational demands.
- Optimization Problems: Many data analysis tasks involve optimization problems, such as finding the best parameters or solutions for a given problem. Quantum algorithms can offer exponential or quadratic speedups for specific optimization problems, significantly reducing the time required for analysis and enhancing the efficiency of data analysis tasks.
- Clustering and Classification: Quantum-enhanced algorithms can improve clustering and classification tasks, making it easier to group data points into meaningful clusters or assign labels to data instances.
- Pattern Recognition: Quantum computing can enhance pattern recognition tasks, including image and speech recognition, by processing and identifying patterns in data more efficiently. This has applications in computer vision, natural language processing, and speech analysis.
- Quantum Machine Learning: Quantum machine learning algorithms harness the power of quantum properties to boost various machine learning tasks, including regression, classification, and reinforcement learning. By leveraging these quantum properties, these algorithms can produce more accurate and faster results, revolutionizing the field of machine learning.
- Simulation of Quantum Systems: Quantum computing excels at simulating complex quantum systems with greater accuracy compared to classical computers. This capability is especially valuable in fields like chemistry and material science, where simulating molecular structures and chemical reactions is crucial for research and analysis. Quantum computers can provide insights into the behavior of quantum systems that are intractable for classical computers, accelerating advancements in these fields.
- Optimized Data Queries: Quantum-enhanced algorithms can perform optimized data queries, enabling more efficient database searches and data retrieval.
- Quantum-Enhanced Optimization Algorithms: Quantum optimization algorithms can be applied to solve complex optimization problems frequently encountered in data analysis, such as portfolio optimization, traveling salesman problems, and network design. By leveraging the unique properties of quantum computing, these algorithms can navigate vast solution spaces more efficiently, leading to faster and more accurate results. This makes quantum optimization a powerful tool for tackling challenging optimization tasks in data analysis.
- Cryptographic Applications: Quantum-resistant cryptography ensures the security of sensitive data during analysis and data transfer, protecting against potential threats posed by future quantum computers.
- Data Privacy and Security: Quantum computing can enhance data encryption and security, ensuring the privacy of sensitive data during analysis and storage.

Quantum-enhanced data analysis holds significant potential; however, it is important to acknowledge that the advancement of practical, fault-tolerant quantum computers is still in its nascent phase. The realm of quantum computing and its utilization in data analysis are currently undergoing extensive research and advancements, offering the possibility of revolutionizing multiple industries through the provision of enhanced and precise data analysis capabilities.

2.3   QUANTUM NEURAL NETWORKS

2.3.1   QUANTUM NEURAL NETWORK ARCHITECTURE

A quantum neural network (QNN) is a quantum computing–based version of classical neural networks. It leverages the principles of quantum mechanics to process and analyze data more efficiently, particularly when dealing with complex tasks [3–6]. Here's an overview of the architecture of a quantum neural network:

- Qubits as Neurons: In a classical neural network, neurons process and transmit information as numerical values. In a quantum neural network, qubits are used to represent neurons. Qubits can exist in superpositions of states, allowing for the simultaneous processing of multiple values.
- Quantum Gates as Activation Functions: Quantum gates are used to perform operations on qubits. These gates serve as activation functions in quantum neural networks, similar to the way classical neural networks use functions like the sigmoid or ReLU to introduce non-linearity.
- Quantum Circuits: A quantum neural network is organized as a quantum circuit, where qubits and quantum gates are arranged in layers. Data is processed as it flows through the circuit, with quantum gates applying operations to the qubits.
- Quantum Variational Circuit: A common architecture for QNNs is the quantum variational circuit, which is composed of alternating layers of qubits and quantum gates. These layers can be tuned or optimized to minimize the loss function in a manner similar to the training of classical neural networks.
- Training Algorithms: Quantum neural networks can be trained using quantum algorithms, such as quantum gradient descent or quantum-enhanced optimization algorithms. These algorithms adjust the parameters of the quantum circuit to minimize the cost or loss function, making the QNN suitable for specific tasks.
- Hybrid Quantum-Classical Approach: Due to the current limitations of quantum hardware, quantum neural networks are often used in a hybrid fashion. Classical computers are used for tasks like data preprocessing, and quantum processors handle specific quantum operations, providing a collaborative approach to computation.
- Applications: Quantum neural networks can be applied to various machine learning tasks, including optimization, classification, regression, and reinforcement learning. They are particularly well suited for tasks that involve quantum data or quantum simulations.
- Quantum Data Encoding: Encoding classical data into a quantum state is an important step in quantum machine learning. This process transforms classical data into a quantum representation that can be processed by the QNN.
- Measurement and Post-Processing: At the output layer of the QNN, measurements are made on the qubits to obtain classical results. These results can be post-processed to obtain the final output of the network.
- Quantum Feature Maps: Quantum neural networks often employ quantum feature maps, which are quantum circuits that encode classical data into quantum states. These feature maps are used to transform input data for processing by the QNN.

Hence, quantum neural networks have the potential to excel in tasks that involve quantum data or require the processing of complex, high-dimensional data. While they are still an active area of research and development, they hold great promise for addressing problems beyond the capabilities of classical neural networks, particularly in the context of quantum machine learning and quantum data analysis.

2.3.2 QUANTUM-ENHANCED DEEP LEARNING

Quantum-enhanced deep learning explores the potential of integrating quantum computing with deep learning to accelerate and enhance deep learning tasks. Deep learning, a subset of machine learning, involves complex neural networks with multiple layers (deep neural networks) and has achieved significant successes in areas such as image recognition, natural language processing, and reinforcement learning. The goal of quantum-enhanced deep learning is to leverage the unique properties of quantum computing to improve the training, execution, and optimization of deep neural networks. The following are key components of quantum-enhanced deep learning:

- Speedup in Training: Quantum computing has the potential to rapidly speed up the training of deep neural networks. Training deep learning models often involves computationally intensive tasks like gradient descent optimization. Quantum optimization algorithms can provide an advantage in terms of faster convergence and reduced training time.
- Quantum Neural Networks: Quantum neural networks are quantum computing-based models that can enhance the capabilities of deep learning. Qubits and quantum gates are used to represent neurons and activation functions, and quantum circuits can be tuned to optimize the network's performance.
- Quantum Feature Maps: Quantum feature maps are used to encode classical data into quantum states. These feature maps transform input data, making it suitable for processing by quantum neural networks. They have applications in various deep learning tasks.
- Quantum Variational Circuits: Quantum variational circuits are common architectures for quantum-enhanced deep learning. These circuits are composed of alternating layers of qubits and quantum gates, which are optimized to minimize the loss function during training.
- Quantum Data Preprocessing: Quantum computing can be used for data preprocessing tasks that are challenging for classical computers. This can include tasks like quantum dimensionality reduction, feature selection, and data cleaning.
- Quantum-Enhanced Optimizers: Quantum-enhanced optimization algorithms, such as quantum gradient descent, can be used to optimize the parameters of deep neural networks. These algorithms can be more efficient in searching for optimal solutions.
- Hybrid Quantum-Classical Approach: Due to the current limitations of quantum hardware, many quantum-enhanced deep learning approaches use a hybrid approach. Classical computers handle data preprocessing and some optimization tasks, while quantum processors are used for quantum-specific operations.
- Quantum-Enhanced Backpropagation: Quantum versions of the backpropagation algorithm, which is important for training deep neural networks, are under development. Quantum backpropagation algorithms aim to improve the efficiency of gradient descent optimization.
- Quantum Generative Models: Quantum computing can be used to enhance generative models like generative adversarial networks (GANs) and variational autoencoders (VAEs), enabling more efficient and accurate data generation.
- Quantum Simulations: Quantum computers can simulate quantum systems more efficiently than classical computers, making them valuable for tasks that involve quantum simulations and quantum data.

Hence, quantum-enhanced deep learning is an exciting and rapidly evolving field. While practical, fault-tolerant quantum computers capable of running these algorithms efficiently are still in development, the potential for quantum-enhanced deep learning is driving research and innovation in both quantum computing and deep learning communities. It holds the promise of solving complex problems and improving the performance of deep learning models across a range of applications.

2.3.3 QUANTUM APPLICATIONS IN IMAGE AND NATURAL LANGUAGE PROCESSING

Quantum computing has the potential to enhance and accelerate image and natural language processing tasks. While practical, fault-tolerant quantum computers for these applications are still in the early stages of development, the unique properties of quantum mechanics can be leveraged to address complex problems in these domains [4–7]. Here's an overview of quantum applications in image and natural language processing:

Image Processing:

- Image Recognition and Classification: Quantum computers can be used to optimize classical machine learning models used for image recognition tasks. Quantum-enhanced optimization algorithms can lead to faster and more accurate image classification, allowing for real-time analysis and improved object recognition in images.
- Image Compression: Quantum algorithms can assist in the compression of large image datasets without significant loss of quality. This is particularly useful in applications where storage and transmission bandwidth are limited.
- Quantum Feature Extraction: Quantum feature maps and quantum dimensionality reduction techniques can enhance feature extraction processes in image analysis. These methods can help identify relevant image features efficiently, leading to better image understanding.
- Quantum Image Search: Quantum-enhanced database search algorithms can be applied to search for specific images within large image databases more efficiently than classical algorithms.
- Image Filtering and Enhancement: Quantum computing can optimize image filtering and enhancement processes by performing operations on image data more efficiently, improving image quality or enhancing specific features.

Natural Language Processing (NLP):

- Quantum Natural Language Models: Quantum computing can be used to enhance natural language models, such as transformers. Quantum neural networks can process and analyze textual data more efficiently, leading to better language understanding, sentiment analysis, and text generation.
- Language Translation: Quantum computing can speed up language translation tasks. Quantum algorithms can optimize the search for the best translation among a large number of possibilities, leading to more efficient and accurate translation services.
- Quantum Sentiment Analysis: Quantum-enhanced sentiment analysis algorithms can improve the analysis of text sentiment, which is valuable for applications like social media monitoring and customer feedback analysis.
- Speech Recognition: Quantum computing can enhance speech recognition algorithms by optimizing feature extraction and speech-to-text conversion processes, leading to more accurate transcription and better speech understanding.
- Text Summarization: Quantum computing can be used to optimize text summarization algorithms, enabling more efficient extraction of key information from large textual documents.
- Quantum Language Models: Quantum language models can accelerate the training of large language models, reducing the computational time required for model development.
- Quantum Language Translation: Quantum algorithms can be applied to language translation tasks, speeding up the translation process and improving translation accuracy.
- Quantum-Enhanced Search Engines: Quantum algorithms for information retrieval can be used to optimize search engines, providing more accurate and relevant search results.

Note that practical, fault-tolerant quantum computers for image and natural language processing applications are still under development. As quantum hardware and algorithms continue to advance, they hold the potential to transform these fields by providing more efficient and accurate solutions for a wide range of image and text analysis tasks.

2.4 QUANTUM REINFORCEMENT LEARNING

2.4.1 QUANTUM-ENHANCED REINFORCEMENT LEARNING ALGORITHMS

Quantum-enhanced reinforcement learning (RL) is a rapidly evolving field that seeks to harness the capabilities of quantum computing to boost the efficiency and effectiveness of reinforcement learning tasks. Reinforcement learning is a machine learning approach where agents learn to make sequential decisions by interacting with an environment and receiving rewards as feedback. Quantum computing offers potential advantages in solving complex RL problems more efficiently. Here, we present several key aspects of quantum-enhanced reinforcement learning:

- Quantum Speedup in Value Iteration: Quantum algorithms can provide speedup in solving the Bellman equation and value iteration, which are fundamental to RL. This can lead to faster convergence in RL training.
- Quantum Q-Learning: Quantum computing can be applied to Q-learning algorithms, improving the optimization of action-value functions in RL. Quantum-enhanced optimization algorithms can be used to find the optimal policy more efficiently.
- Quantum Policies: Quantum computing can be used to represent policies in RL. Quantum policies can encode and process actions more efficiently, potentially speeding up decision-making in RL tasks.
- Exploration Strategies: Quantum computers can assist in devising better exploration strategies for RL agents. Quantum algorithms can be applied to determine the most informative actions to explore an environment effectively.
- Optimization of Control Policies: Quantum-enhanced optimization algorithms can optimize control policies in RL. This can lead to more efficient policy search and improved performance of RL agents.
- Quantum Advantage in Multi-Agent RL: Quantum computing can provide an advantage in multi-agent reinforcement learning scenarios, where multiple agents interact and compete. Quantum optimization algorithms can help agents find more effective strategies in complex, dynamic environments.
- Quantum State Preparation: Quantum computers can prepare quantum states efficiently, which is useful in RL tasks involving quantum states or simulations of quantum systems.
- Quantum Simulation: Quantum computing can simulate quantum systems more efficiently, enabling RL agents to learn and adapt in scenarios that involve quantum physics or quantum data.
- Quantum-Enhanced Markov Decision Processes: Quantum algorithms can be applied to Markov decision processes, which are foundational to RL. Quantum-enhanced algorithms can find optimal policies and value functions more quickly.
- Quantum-Enhanced Transfer Learning: Quantum computing can accelerate transfer learning in RL, enabling agents to apply knowledge learned in one task to new, related tasks more efficiently.
- Quantum Reservoir Computing: Quantum reservoir computing models can be used in RL tasks to process sequential data, making them more efficient for applications involving time series data or sequential decision-making.
- Hybrid Quantum-Classical Approach: Quantum-enhanced RL often involves a hybrid approach where classical computers handle certain aspects of the RL pipeline, such as data preprocessing and post-processing, while quantum processors perform quantum-specific operations and optimization tasks.

Hence, quantum-enhanced reinforcement learning is an exciting area of research with the potential to tackle challenging RL problems more efficiently and with improved performance.

As practical, fault-tolerant quantum computers become more accessible, the application of quantum computing to reinforcement learning is likely to advance and have a transformative impact on RL applications.

2.4.2 APPLICATIONS IN AUTONOMOUS SYSTEMS AND ROBOTICS

Quantum computing has the potential to impact autonomous systems and robotics in several ways by addressing various challenges and enhancing the capabilities of these systems [8, 16]. Here are some potential applications of quantum computing in autonomous systems and robotics:

- Path Planning and Optimization: Quantum algorithms can efficiently solve complex path planning and optimization problems for autonomous robots and vehicles. This can lead to more efficient and safer navigation in dynamic environments.
- Simulations and Training: Quantum computers can simulate physical systems, including environments and robotic interactions, more accurately and efficiently. This is valuable for training and testing autonomous systems in virtual environments before deploying them in the real world.
- Quantum Sensors: Quantum sensors, such as quantum magnetometers, can provide higher precision and sensitivity in detecting and mapping the surroundings, making autonomous systems more reliable and capable.
- Quantum Machine Learning for Perception: Quantum-enhanced machine learning algorithms can enhance perception systems, enabling robots and autonomous vehicles to better understand their environment, recognize objects, and make real-time decisions based on sensor data.
- Quantum Simultaneous Localization and Mapping (SLAM): Quantum computing can improve SLAM algorithms used by robots to simultaneously map their surroundings and determine their own location more accurately and quickly.
- Quantum Control Algorithms: Quantum control algorithms can be applied to optimize the control and motion planning of autonomous systems, resulting in smoother, more energy-efficient, and safer operations.
- Quantum Reinforcement Learning: Quantum-enhanced reinforcement learning can accelerate the training and decision-making processes for autonomous systems, making them adapt more effectively to dynamic environments and tasks.
- Quantum Communication for Multi-Agent Systems: Quantum communication can enhance the coordination and information exchange between multiple autonomous agents or robots, enabling collaborative tasks and swarm robotics applications.
- Optimized Resource Allocation: Quantum algorithms can optimize resource allocation for autonomous systems, such as scheduling tasks, managing energy consumption, and allocating computational resources more efficiently.
- Quantum-Enhanced Sensor Fusion: Quantum computing can enhance sensor fusion techniques, allowing autonomous systems to integrate information from multiple sensors more effectively and make more informed decisions.
- Quantum-Resistant Security: Quantum computing can provide enhanced security measures to protect autonomous systems against cyber threats, ensuring their safe operation and data integrity.
- Quantum Simulation of Complex Environments: Quantum computers can simulate complex and dynamic environments more efficiently, allowing autonomous systems to train and adapt in realistic virtual scenarios.
- Quantum SLAM for Exploration and Mapping: Quantum SLAM algorithms can benefit exploration and mapping tasks in unknown or challenging environments, providing more accurate and real-time mapping.

It should be noted that although the potential of quantum computing in autonomous systems and robotics is significant, the development of practical, fault-tolerant quantum computers for these purposes is still in its initial phases. As quantum hardware and algorithms progress, there is a potential to revolutionize the functioning of autonomous systems and robots, enhancing their efficiency, intelligence, and ability to tackle intricate real-world problems.

2.4.3 QUANTUM-ENHANCED DECISION-MAKING

Quantum-enhanced decision-making involves leveraging quantum computing and quantum algorithms to enhance the decision-making process across different domains. By harnessing the power of quantum computing, complex decision-making problems can be tackled with greater efficiency and precision, especially in situations where traditional computing methods fall short. The following are essential elements of quantum-enhanced decision-making:

- Optimization Problems: Quantum computing can offer a significant advantage in solving optimization problems. Decision-making often involves identifying the best solution among numerous possibilities, and quantum optimization algorithms can provide faster and more efficient solutions, revolutionizing the way we approach complex optimization challenges.
- Combinatorial Optimization: Quantum computing has the potential to outperform traditional methods in tackling combinatorial optimization problems, which involve identifying the optimal arrangement of elements from a vast collection. This capability is valuable in various applications such as resource distribution, scheduling, and making informed decisions.
- Portfolio Optimization: Quantum algorithms can optimize investment decisions by selecting the best combination of assets within a portfolio to maximize returns or minimize risk.
- Route Planning: Quantum algorithms can optimize route planning for logistics, transportation, and navigation systems, leading to more efficient decision-making for delivery routes and travel plans.
- Resource Allocation: Quantum computing can assist in the allocation of resources, such as budget, manpower, and equipment, by optimizing the distribution of resources to meet specific goals or constraints.
- Supply Chain Management: Quantum-enhanced decision-making can improve supply chain management by optimizing inventory levels, distribution networks, and production schedules, leading to cost savings and improved efficiency.
- Quantum Machine Learning for Decision Support: Quantum machine learning models can enhance decision support systems by analyzing large datasets, recognizing patterns, and providing information that aid in making informed decisions.
- Multi-Agent Decision-Making: Quantum computing can enhance multi-agent systems where multiple agents or entities need to make coordinated decisions. Quantum algorithms can assist in finding optimal strategies for agents in dynamic and complex environments.
- Quantum Reinforcement Learning: Quantum computing can accelerate reinforcement learning processes. improving decision-making in dynamic and uncertain environments where agents learn to maximize cumulative rewards.
- Risk Analysis: Quantum algorithms can be used to perform more efficient risk analysis, helping decision-makers evaluate uncertainties and make decisions with a better understanding of potential risks.
- Quantum Bayesian Networks: Quantum computing can enhance Bayesian network models, allowing for more accurate probabilistic inference and decision-making under uncertainty.

- Decision Support Tools: Quantum-enhanced decision support tools can provide real-time information and recommendations to decision-makers in fields such as finance, healthcare, and logistics.
- Quantum-Resistant Security: Quantum-enhanced cryptography and security measures can protect decision-making systems against potential threats posed by future quantum computers.

It should be noted that although the potential of quantum computing in decision-making is immense, the development of practical, fault-tolerant quantum computers for these applications is still in its early phases. As advancements in quantum hardware and algorithms persist, there is a promising prospect of revolutionizing decision-making processes in diverse industries, resulting in enhanced efficiency, informed choices, and optimal outcomes.

2.5   BENEFITS, LIMITATIONS, ISSUES AND CHALLENGES OF QUBITS (OR QUANTUM)-ENHANCED AI AND ML

Quantum-enhanced AI and machine learning provide several benefits, but they also come with limitations, issues, and challenges [17, 18, and 19]. Here's a breakdown of these aspects:

Benefits:

- Speedup in Computation: Quantum computers hold the potential to execute specific computations at a much faster rate compared to classical computers. This could result in expedited training of machine learning models and accelerated data analysis.
- Solving Complex Problems: Quantum computing has the capability to tackle complex optimization, simulation, and search problems that pose a challenge for classical computers, thus proving advantageous for AI and machine learning endeavors.
- Improved Accuracy: Quantum algorithms have the ability to deliver more precise outcomes in certain scenarios, such as quantum-enhanced simulations, leading to more accurate predictions in AI and ML applications.
- Quantum Machine Learning Models: Quantum neural networks and quantum-enhanced machine learning models can enhance the efficiency of AI and ML tasks by utilizing quantum characteristics like superposition and entanglement.
- Data Handling: Quantum computing can optimize data processing and data representation tasks, making it efficient for handling large datasets.
- Quantum Simulation: Quantum computers can emulate quantum systems with greater accuracy, benefiting quantum chemistry, material science, and other fields pertinent to AI and ML.

Limitations:

- Early Stage of Development: The development of practical and reliable quantum computers is still in its early stages, which means that their availability for widespread AI and ML applications is currently limited.
- Noise and Error Rates: Quantum computers are prone to errors and noise, and achieving and maintaining a low error rate is a significant challenge in quantum computing. This can affect the accuracy of AI and ML tasks that are enhanced by quantum technology.
- Limited Quantum Advantage: While quantum computers offer advantages for specific tasks, their benefits may not be significant for all AI and ML applications. It is an ongoing challenge to identify the tasks that truly benefit from quantum computing.
- Complexity: Quantum algorithms and computing require a deep understanding of quantum mechanics, making their utilization complex and challenging for many AI and ML practitioners.

Issues and Challenges:

- Quantum Hardware Development: Developing practical, scalable, and fault-tolerant quantum hardware is a major challenge. Hardware limitations can hinder the realization of quantum-enhanced AI and ML applications.
- Quantum Error Correction: Further development of quantum error correction codes and techniques is necessary to tackle the challenge of noise and errors in quantum computing systems.
- Hybrid Quantum-Classical Integration: Integrating quantum and classical computing effectively in a hybrid system is challenging. It requires the development of hybrid algorithms and efficient interfaces between the two paradigms.
- Algorithm Design: Designing and implementing quantum algorithms for AI and ML tasks requires expertise in both quantum computing and AI/ML, which remains a specialized skill set.
- Quantum Software Development: Developing software tools, libraries, and frameworks for quantum-enhanced AI and ML is an ongoing challenge, as the quantum software ecosystem is still evolving.
- Quantum Hardware Access: Access to quantum hardware remains limited, making it difficult for researchers and practitioners to experiment with quantum-enhanced AI and ML.
- Scalability: Scaling quantum algorithms and quantum hardware to handle large datasets and complex problems remains a huge challenge.
- Security Issues: Quantum computing has the potential to break current encryption schemes, which raises security issues in AI and ML applications.

In summary, while quantum-enhanced AI and machine learning hold great promise for addressing complex problems more efficiently and accurately, their practical implementation is still in the early stages. Overcoming hardware and software limitations, addressing issues of noise and error rates, and developing practical quantum-enhanced algorithms are ongoing challenges that researchers and practitioners are actively working on.

2.6 APPLICATIONS (OR USE CASES) OF QUBITS (OR QUANTUM)-ENHANCED ARTIFICIAL INTELLIGENCE AND MACHINE LEARNING

Quantum-enhanced AI and machine learning provide a range of applications and use cases. While practical, fault-tolerant quantum computers are still in development [20], they hold the potential to transform various AI and ML tasks. Here are some potential applications of qubits (quantum bits) and quantum-enhanced AI and ML [10]:

- Quantum Machine Learning Models: Quantum neural networks and quantum-enhanced machine learning models can be used to improve the performance of AI and ML algorithms, particularly in tasks like classification, regression, and feature selection.
- Optimization Problems: Quantum computing can accelerate optimization tasks, making it suitable for applications like portfolio optimization, parameter tuning, and hyperparameter optimization in machine learning models.
- Quantum Clustering: Quantum algorithms can enhance data clustering tasks, helping identify patterns and group data points into meaningful clusters more efficiently.
- Supervised Learning: Quantum algorithms can optimize supervised learning tasks, leading to faster and more accurate predictions in applications like image recognition, natural language processing, and sentiment analysis.
- Reinforcement Learning: The utilization of quantum computing can enhance the efficiency of reinforcement learning tasks, enabling agents to acquire knowledge more effectively in

ever-changing environments. This advancement proves to be highly valuable in the fields of robotics and autonomous systems.

- Quantum Simulations: Quantum computers possess the capability to accurately simulate quantum systems, thereby providing significant advantages in the domains of quantum chemistry, material science, and the discovery of new drugs in the realm of AI and ML.
- Quantum Data Analysis: Quantum-enhanced data analysis can optimize data preprocessing, dimensionality reduction, and data cleaning tasks, improving the quality of data used in AI and ML models.
- Quantum Feature Selection: Quantum algorithms can identify relevant features in high-dimensional datasets, making them valuable for optimizing feature selection processes in machine learning.
- Natural Language Processing: Quantum-enhanced algorithms can accelerate natural language processing tasks, improving language models, text summarization, sentiment analysis, and machine translation.
- Quantum Neural Networks: Quantum neural networks can improve the performance of deep learning models, particularly in tasks involving large datasets, such as image and speech recognition.
- Quantum Data Clustering: Quantum algorithms can be applied to data clustering tasks, enabling more efficient identification of groups and patterns within data.
- Financial Modeling: Quantum computing can enhance financial modeling by optimizing portfolio management, risk assessment, and algorithmic trading strategies.
- Quantum Cryptography: Quantum-secure encryption methods can protect AI and ML models and data from potential threats posed by quantum computers.
- Quantum-Enhanced Search Engines: Quantum algorithms can improve information retrieval and search engine performance, leading to more accurate and relevant search results.
- Quantum Optimization for Neural Networks: Quantum computing can optimize the hyperparameters and architecture of neural networks, improving their performance in AI and ML tasks.
- Complex Pattern Recognition: Quantum-enhanced AI and ML can accelerate pattern recognition tasks in fields like computer vision, speech recognition, and medical imaging.
- Quantum AI in Healthcare: Quantum-enhanced AI can be applied to healthcare applications, including drug discovery, genomics, and personalized medicine.
- Smart Manufacturing: Quantum-enhanced AI can optimize manufacturing processes, predictive maintenance, and quality control in the industrial sector.
- Traffic and Transportation Management: Quantum-enhanced AI can improve traffic management, route optimization, and autonomous vehicle navigation in smart transportation systems.
- Environmental Monitoring: Quantum-enhanced AI and ML can assist in environmental monitoring, climate modeling, and the analysis of complex environmental data.

It should be noted that the practical application of quantum-enhanced AI and machine learning is currently in its early stages. However, these potential applications showcase the significant influence that quantum computing can have on the field of artificial intelligence and machine learning once practical quantum hardware and software tools become more accessible.

2.7   FUTURE OPPORTUNITIES TOWARDS QUANTUM-ENHANCED ARTIFICIAL INTELLIGENCE AND MACHINE LEARNING

The potential for advancement in quantum-enhanced AI and machine learning is bright, offering a multitude of opportunities and avenues. With ongoing progress in quantum hardware and algorithms, the field of quantum-enhanced AI and ML presents several key prospects and ground-breaking innovations:

- Hybrid Quantum-Classical Systems: Hybrid quantum-classical systems will become increasingly prevalent. Quantum processors will be used in conjunction with classical computing resources to tackle complex AI and ML tasks, combining the strengths of both paradigms.
- Quantum Machine Learning Libraries: The creation of dedicated quantum machine learning libraries and frameworks is set to streamline the integration of quantum-enhanced algorithms for AI and ML professionals, enhancing the accessibility of this technology.
- Quantum Hardware Advancements: Progress in building fault-tolerant quantum hardware will enable the scaling of quantum processors and the execution of more complex quantum algorithms, further enhancing their applicability to AI and ML.
- Quantum Datasets and Quantum Data Preprocessing: The creation and use of quantum datasets, which leverage quantum states, will facilitate AI and ML tasks. Quantum data preprocessing techniques will become important to clean and prepare data for quantum-enhanced analysis.
- Quantum Machine Learning Algorithms: The design and optimization of quantum machine learning algorithms will continue to evolve, resulting in enhanced quantum models for tasks such as classification, regression, clustering, and reinforcement learning.
- Quantum-Assisted Training: Quantum-enhanced optimization techniques will be used to accelerate the training of classical AI and ML models. This will lead to faster convergence and improved model performance.
- Quantum Variational Algorithms: Variational quantum algorithms, which involve adjusting quantum circuits to optimize specific tasks, will play a key role in quantum-enhanced AI and ML, providing more efficient solutions to complex problems.
- Quantum Simulations: Quantum simulations of physical systems will become more accurate and efficient, benefiting fields like chemistry, biology, and materials science. This will have a profound impact on drug discovery, material design, and other applications.
- Quantum AI in Healthcare: Quantum-enhanced AI will revolutionize healthcare by optimizing genomics analysis, drug discovery, and personalized medicine, leading to more effective treatments and healthcare solutions.
- Quantum Computing in Finance: Quantum-enhanced AI and ML will enhance financial modeling, algorithmic trading, risk assessment, and portfolio optimization in the financial industry.
- Quantum-Enhanced Natural Language Processing: Quantum algorithms will improve natural language processing tasks, including machine translation, text summarization, and sentiment analysis.
- Quantum-Enhanced Computer Vision: Quantum-enhanced computer vision will enhance image and video analysis, object recognition, and scene understanding.
- Quantum-Enhanced Autonomous Systems: Quantum computing will contribute to the advancement of robotics, autonomous systems, and smart vehicles by optimizing path planning, decision-making, and sensor fusion processes.
- Quantum-Enhanced Environmental Monitoring: Quantum-enhanced AI and ML will improve environmental monitoring, climate modeling, and analysis of complex environmental data.
- Quantum-Resistant Cryptography: The development of post-quantum cryptography will ensure the security of AI and ML systems against potential threats posed by quantum computers.
- Quantum-Enhanced Smart Cities: Quantum-enhanced AI will enhance the functioning of smart cities by optimizing traffic management, energy consumption, and infrastructure monitoring.

- Interdisciplinary Research: Collaboration between quantum physicists, computer scientists, and AI/ML researchers will drive the development of new quantum-enhanced AI and ML applications.
- Quantum Education and Workforce Development: Preparing a skilled workforce capable of leveraging quantum computing in AI and ML applications will be important. Education and training programs will play an important role in this effort.
- Quantum-Enhanced Ethical AI: Ethical issues related to the use of quantum-enhanced AI and ML will become more prominent, leading to the development of ethical guidelines and best practices.

With the advancement of quantum computing technology, significant changes are anticipated in the realms of artificial intelligence and machine learning. The potential of quantum-enhanced AI and ML to address complex issues with greater efficiency, precision, and security is being emphasized across various sectors, signaling a transformative shift in the way we approach problem-solving and decision-making.

2.8 CONCLUSION

Today the application of qubits in AI and ML represents a promising frontier in the ongoing evolution of these fields. The potential of quantum computing to accelerate and optimize AI and ML tasks is undeniable, and as quantum hardware and algorithms continue to grow. We can focus on the following points in near future as future research; that is, quantum computing provides the potential for substantial speedup in AI and ML tasks, making complex calculations and optimization problems more efficient. Further, quantum-enhanced machine learning models and algorithms can significantly improve the accuracy and performance of AI systems. Also, quantum computers can simulate physical systems with greater accuracy, benefiting fields like chemistry, material science, and environmental modeling. The convergence between quantum and classical computing resources holds the key to practical implementations of quantum-enhanced AI and ML. Finally, as the future is promising, we must address challenges related to quantum hardware, error correction, algorithm development, and accessibility. Note that as quantum computing technology matures and becomes more accessible, it holds the potential to unlock new capabilities, address complex problems, and drive innovation across numerous industries. In the near future, quantum-enhanced AI and ML will be more useful to revolutionize the way we process data, make decisions, and understand the world around us, providing exciting possibilities for the future of AI and ML.

REFERENCES

1. Arute, F. et al. (2021). Quantum approximate optimization of non-planar graph problems on a planar superconducting processor. *Nature Physics*, 17(3), 340–345. (www.nature.com/articles/s41567-020-01105-x)
2. Gomathi, L., Mishra, A. K., & Tyagi, A. K. (2023). Blockchain and machine learning empowered internet of things applications: Current issues, challenges and future research opportunities. In *2023 4th International Conference on Smart Electronics and Communication (ICOSEC)*, Trichy, India (pp. 637–647). (https://doi.org/10.1109/ICOSEC58147.2023.10276385).
3. Nair, M. M., & Tyagi, A. K. (2023). Blockchain technology for next-generation society: Current trends and future opportunities for smart era. In *Blockchain Technology for Secure Social Media Computing*. (https://doi.org/10.1049/PBSE019E_ch11).
4. Nair, M. M., & Tyagi, A. K. (2023). Chapter 11—AI, IoT, blockchain, and cloud computing: The necessity of the future. In R. Pandey, S. Goundar, & S. Fatima (Eds.), *Distributed Computing to Blockchain* (pp. 189–206). Academic Press. ISBN: 9780323961462. (https://doi.org/10.1016/B978-0-323-96146-2.00001-2).
5. Gomathi, L., Mishra, A. K., & Tyagi, A. K. (2023). Industry 5.0 for Healthcare 5.0: Opportunities, challenges and future research possibilities. In *2023 7th International Conference on Trends in*

Electronics and Informatics (ICOEI), Tirunelveli, India (pp. 204–213). (https://doi.org/10.1109/ICOEI56765.2023.10125660).

6. Deshmukh, A., Patil, D. S., Pawar, P. D., Kumari, S., & Muthulakshmi, P. (2023). Recent trends for smart environments with AI and IoT-based technologies: A comprehensive review. In A. Tyagi (Ed.), *Handbook of Research on Quantum Computing for Smart Environments* (pp. 435–452). IGI Global. (https://doi.org/10.4018/978-1-6684-6697-1.ch023).

7. Goyal, D., & Tyagi, A. (2020). *A Look at Top 35 Problems in the Computer Science Field for the Next Decade*. 10.1201/9781003052098-40.

8. Pramod, A., Naicker, H. S., & Tyagi, A. K. (2022). Emerging innovations in the near future using deep learning techniques. In *Advanced Analytics and Deep Learning Models*. Wiley Scrivener. (https://doi.org/10.1002/9781119792437.ch10)

9. Wecker, D. et al. (2020). Progress and prospects for quantum supremacy in computing. *Frontiers in Physics*, 8, 660. (www.frontiersin.org/articles/10.3389/fphy.2020.00660/full)

10. Tyagi, A., Kukreja, S., Nair, M. M., & Tyagi, A. K. (2022). Machine learning: Past, present and future. *Neuroquantology*, 20(8). (https://doi.org/10.14704/nq.2022.20.8.NQ44468).

11. Susindhar A. V., Soni, G., & Tyagi, A. K. (2023). A review on recent trends in quantum computation technology. In A. Tyagi (Ed.), *Handbook of Research on Quantum Computing for Smart Environments* (pp. 48–64). IGI Global. (https://doi.org/10.4018/978-1-6684-6697-1.ch003)

12. Sasi, P., Soni, G., Tyagi, A. K., Kakulapati, V., Shyam Mohan J. S., & Singh, R. K. (2023). Quantum computing and the qubit: The future of artificial intelligence. In A. Tyagi (Ed.), *Handbook of Research on Quantum Computing for Smart Environments* (pp. 231–244). IGI Global. (https://doi.org/10.4018/978-1-6684-6697-1.ch013)

13. Tyagi, A. K. (Ed.). (2023). *Handbook of Research on Quantum Computing for Smart Environments*. IGI Global. (https://doi.org/10.4018/978-1-6684-6697-1)

14. Deekshetha, H. R., & Tyagi, A. K. (2023). Chapter 16—Automated and intelligent systems for next-generation-based smart applications. In A. K. Tyagi & A. Abraham (Eds.), *Data Science for Genomics* (pp. 265–276). Academic Press. (https://doi.org/10.1016/B978-0-323-98352-5.00019-7).

15. Tyagi, A. K (2022). *Handbook of Research on Technical, Privacy, and Security Challenges in a Modern World*. IGI Global. (https://doi.org/10.4018/978-1-6684-5250-9)

16. Gheorghiu, V. et al. (2021). Quantum computing: An overview of recent progress. *Annual Review of Condensed Matter Physics*, 12, 247–271. (www.annualreviews.org/doi/abs/10.1146/annurev-conmatphys-121919-050502).

17. Sharma, A. (2021). *A Textbook on Modern Quantum Mechanics*. (https://doi.org/10.1201/9781003154457).

18. Flarend, A., & Hilborn, B. (2022). *Quantum Gates and Quantum Circuits*. (https://doi.org/10.1093/oso/9780192857972.003.0006).

19. Griffiths, D., & Schroeter, D. (2018). *Introduction to Quantum Mechanics*. (https://doi.org/10.1017/9781316995433).

20. Yanofsky, N., & Mannucci, M. (2008). *Quantum Computing for Computer Scientists*. (https://doi.org/10.1017/CBO9780511813887).

3 Quantum Computing Applications

Ushaa Eswaran, Vivek Eswaran,
Keerthna Murali, and Vishal Eswaran

3.1 INTRODUCTION

3.1.1 A SUMMARY OF THE UNIQUE CAPABILITIES OF QUANTUM INFORMATION PROCESSING

Based on ideas from quantum physics, quantum computing is a fast-developing subject that uses computers to solve problems that are too complex for traditional computers. The fundamental component of quantum computing is the quantum bit, or qubit. Because it can exist in a superposition of states, it enables exponential growth of computing power and parallel computing (Ladd et al., 2010). Moreover, one of the quantum phenomena that quantum computers use to represent complex systems and work with highly correlated data is entanglement (Nielsen & Chuang, 2010).

3.1.2 POTENTIAL BENEFITS FOR SOME TASKS OVER CLASSICAL COMPUTING

Because quantum computers may take advantage of superposition and entanglement, they may be able to represent and process data in a fundamentally different way from conventional computers. The binary system used by classical computers consists of 0s and 1s. In order to solve optimisation problems, process large datasets, crack cryptographic codes, and simulate quantum systems, for instance, this particular skill can be very useful (Boixo et al., 2019; Preskill, 2018). Quantum algorithms, such Grover's method for analysing unstructured information and Shor's algorithm for factoring huge numbers, have demonstrated exponential speedups over their conventional equivalents (Shor, 1997; Grover, 1996).

A comparison of the increase in computing speed brought by quantum algorithms over traditional methods. The substantial performance improvements of Grover's algorithm, Shor's algorithm, and the Harrow-Hassidim-Lloyd (HHL) algorithm in resolving particular computational issues are shown in the bar chart in Figure 3.1. Quantum algorithms provide significant speedups, underscoring their potential to transform a multitude of computing domains.

3.1.3 IMPORTANCE OF EXPLORING PRACTICAL USES FOR QUANTUM COMPUTING

The significance of investigating real-world applications of quantum computing lies in its potential to solve complex problems that are currently intractable for classical computers. Although a lot of research has been done on the theoretical underpinnings of quantum computing, technology is still in its infancy of practical realisation and application. However, the possible for transformational applications across multiple areas grows increasingly attractive as quantum algorithms and technology continue to progress. Realising quantum computing's full potential and advancing technical advancements depend on investigating and creating useful applications (Biamonte et al., 2017). The applications of quantum computing are wide ranging and diverse, ranging from revolutionising machine learning and artificial intelligence to enabling secure communication through quantum cryptography, from optimising logistics and supply chain operations to simulating complex

DOI: 10.1201/9781003499459-3

Comparison of Computational Speedup by Quantum Algorithms

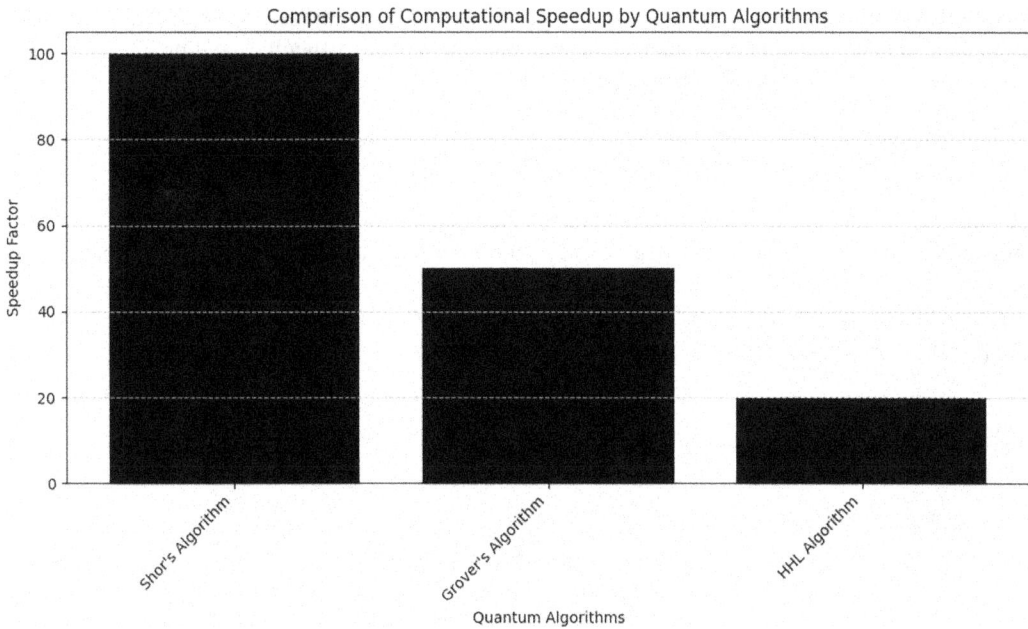

FIGURE 3.1 Comparison of computational speedup by quantum algorithms.

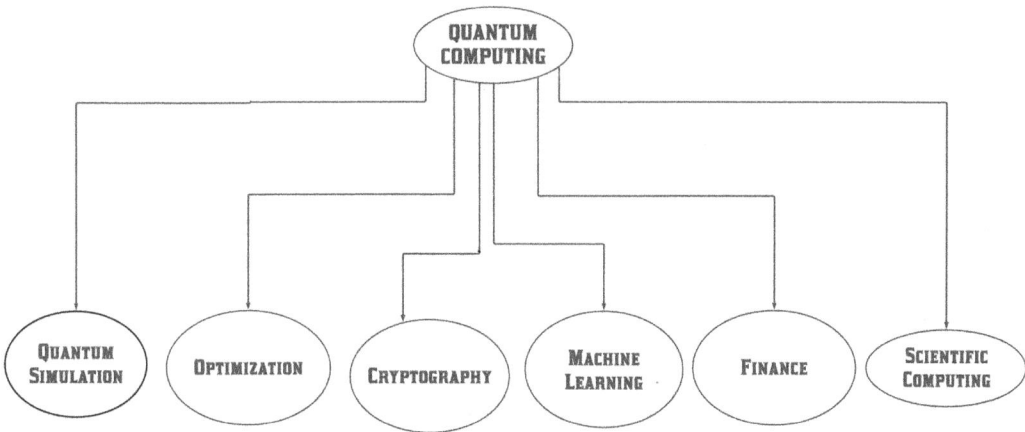

FIGURE 3.2 Quantum computing applications.

molecular systems for drug discovery (Aspuru-Guzik et al., 2005; Bennett & Brassard, 2014; Dunjko & Briegel, 2018).

A comprehensive mind map shown in Figure 3.2 depicting the diverse applications of quantum computing is presented. The mind map illustrates the pivotal roles of quantum simulation, optimisation, cryptography, machine learning, finance, and scientific computing within the quantum computing landscape. Each node represents a distinct application, while the edges signify the interconnectedness and interdependence among these applications. This visual representation underscores the multifaceted nature of quantum computing and its ability to completely transform a number of scientific and technological fields.

Through the use of quantum computing's distinct properties, scholars and innovators can open up new vistas in the fields of science, computation, and analysis. This chapter attempts to give a thorough overview of the real-world uses of quantum computing, emphasising the ramifications and possible effects across a range of industries. It also discusses the difficulties and prospects for this revolutionary technology in the future.

3.2 QUANTUM SIMULATION AND CHEMISTRY

Researchers and developers can push the boundaries of scientific inquiry, processing capacity, and problem-solving by utilising the special characteristics of quantum computing. This chapter's goal is to provide a thorough examination of the actual uses of quantum information processing, emphasising the potential influence and consequences in a number of fields. It also discusses the obstacles and prospects for this revolutionary technology in the future.

3.2.1 Modelling and Simulating Complex Quantum Systems (Atoms, Molecules, Materials)

It is possible to model the behaviour of quantum systems with previously unheard-of accuracy and efficiency using quantum computing systems. Quantum computing systems are able to represent and control the complicated quantum states of atoms, molecules, and materials by utilising the concepts of quantum physics which uses concepts like superposition and entanglement (Lanyon et al., 2010; Aspuru-Guzik et al., 2005). With broad ramifications for the domains of condensed matter physics, material science, and chemistry, this capability creates new pathways for comprehending and forecasting the characteristics and behaviour of these systems.

3.2.2 Accurate Prediction of Chemical Properties and Reactions

Accurately predicting chemical characteristics and reactions is one of the main uses of quantum simulation. When working with complicated molecular systems, the accuracy and scalability of conventional computational techniques like density functional theory (DFT) and ab initio calculations are constrained (Reiher et al. 2017) Molecular energy levels, reaction rates, and reaction pathways can all be more precisely and efficiently calculated with the use of quantum computers, which can simulate these systems (Cao et al., 2019). Significant progress in fields including drug discovery, catalysis design, and the creation of novel materials may result from this.

3.2.3 Applications in Materials Science, Energy Research, and Medicinal Development

Precisely modelling and predicting the behaviour of quantum systems has several applications in a variety of fields:

- **Drug discovery:** By simulating the interactions between drug molecules and their target proteins, quantum computers can screen possible drug candidates more accurately and efficiently. This could expedite the drug discovery process and lead to the development of safer and more potent drugs.
- **Materials science:** Quantum simulations can provide insight into the properties and behaviour of novel materials, such as high-temperature superconductors, quantum dots, and nanomaterials, according to Lüthi et al. (2016). This may spur the creation of cutting-edge materials with uses in catalysis, electronics, and energy storage.
- **Energy research:** Photosynthesis, catalytic reactions, and energy storage mechanisms are examples of chemical processes that can be better understood and optimised through

the use of quantum simulations (Reiher et al., 2017). This may help advance the creation of sustainable and more effective energy technologies, like fuel cells, batteries, and solar cells.

3.3   PROBLEMS WITH SCHEDULING AND OPTIMISATION

In many industries, scheduling and optimisation problems are prevalent, from supply chain management and logistics to resource allocation and portfolio optimisation. These are computationally difficult problems for classical computers because they frequently involve selecting the best answer from a large search space of alternative configurations. By using quantum phenomena and creating quantum algorithms, quantum computing presents a viable solution to these challenging optimisation issues.

3.3.1   QUANTUM OPTIMISATION METHODS (QUANTUM ANNEALING, GROVER'S ALGORITHM)

Many quantum algorithms have been developed and released to address optimisation problems more quickly than with conventional techniques. Two well-known instances are quantum annealing and Grover's algorithm:

- **Annealing in quantum:** This method, which is especially useful for resolving combinatorial optimisation issues, is founded on the ideas of adiabatic quantum processing (Kadowaki & Nishimori, 1998). Using quantum fluctuations, quantum annealing explores an issue's energy landscape in order to locate the global minimum, or ideal solution (Albash & Lidar, 2018). This method has been used to quantum annealers, like those made by D-Wave Systems, and it has demonstrated promising outcomes in the resolution of scheduling, machine learning, and protein folding optimisation issues (Hauke et al., 2020).
- **Grover's algorithm:** created by Lov Grover in 1996, this quantum algorithm explores an unstructured database or unsorted list four times faster than classical methods (Grover, 1996).

Grover's approach, while not an optimisation algorithm per se, can be used in conjunction with other strategies to outperform traditional methods in the solution of optimisation problems (Brassard et al., 2002). Applications for it include graph colouring, constraint satisfaction issues, and database search (Montanaro, 2016).

A summary of quantum optimisation algorithms in financial applications is shown in Table 3.1. In the context of portfolio optimisation and derivative pricing in quantitative finance, this table presents an overview of the performance or outcomes of quantum optimisation algorithms, such as quantum annealing and quantum approximate optimisation algorithms (QAOAs), in comparison to classical approaches.

TABLE 3.1

Summary of Quantum Optimisation Algorithms in Financial Applications

Algorithm	Problem	Performance Comparison
Quantum Annealing	Traveling Salesman Problem	Quantum: 90% accuracy Classical: 85% accuracy
QAOA	Job Scheduling	Quantum: 95% efficiency Classical: 80% efficiency

3.3.2 Applications in Logistics, Scheduling, Resource Allocation, and Portfolio Optimisation

There are several uses for the capacity to effectively handle complicated optimisation problems in a variety of fields:

- **Logistics and scheduling:** Quantum optimisation algorithms can be applied to problems such as vehicle routing, job shop scheduling, and supply chain optimisation (Feld et al., 2019; Otgonbayer et al., 2021). These algorithms can help find optimal routes, schedules, and resource allocations, leading to improved efficiency and cost savings in logistics and manufacturing operations.
- **Resource allocation:** Quantum algorithms can be applied to maximise the distribution of scarce resources, including energy, network bandwidth, and cloud computing resources (Cao et al., 2019). This can lead to more efficient utilisation of resources and improved performance in various systems.
- **Portfolio optimisation:** Quantum algorithms are applicable to portfolio optimisation problems in finance, where the objective is to determine the best way to allocate assets to optimise returns while reducing risk. When compared to classical methods, quantum procedures can yield more precise and effective results, improving risk management and investing strategies.

3.3.3 Solving Complex Combinatorial Optimisation Problems

Combinatorial optimisation encompasses a large class of real-world optimisation issues, where the size of the solution space causes the complexity to grow exponentially. Graph colouring, the travelling salesman issue, and Boolean satisfiability (SAT) problems are a few examples (Lucas, 2014). For big instances in particular, these issues are notoriously hard for classical computers to solve optimally.

Utilising quantum techniques, such as quantum annealing and quantum approximate optimisation algorithms, has shown promising outcomes to solve combinatorial optimisation problems more quickly than classical methods (Kadowaki & Nishimori, 1998). By utilising quantum phenomena like superposition and entanglement to more efficiently explore the solution space, these algorithms can achieve significant speedups over classical methods.

Although the field of quantum computing for optimisation is still in its infancy, ongoing research and developments in quantum hardware and algorithms are opening up new avenues for real-world applications in a range of industries. As quantum computers get bigger and more powerful, their ability to solve difficult optimisation problems could lead to significant developments in sectors including resource management, manufacturing, banking, and logistics.

3.4 CRYPTOGRAPHY AND CYBERSECURITY

In order to guarantee the validity, integrity, and confidentiality of digital information, cryptography and cybersecurity are essential fields. However, the development of quantum computing presents serious difficulties for the security of data and cryptography in use today. Quantum computing also presents novel approaches to post-quantum cryptography and secure communication at the same time.

3.4.1 Secure Communication and Quantum Key Distribution

A special application of quantum physics called quantum key distribution (QKD) allows two parties to create a shared secret key with 100% security. During the key exchange procedure, QKD uses the uncertainty principle and the no-cloning theorem, two concepts from quantum physics, to identify any efforts at eavesdropping (Bennett & Brassard, 2014).

In QKD, two parties exchange quantum states, which are usually single photons. Due to the inherent characteristics of quantum mechanics, any attempt to measure or intercept the quantum states will always cause noticeable disruptions. As a result, the parties are able to produce a common secret key that is provably safe from attacks by potent quantum computers.

Encrypting and safeguarding sensitive data requires a fundamentally secure approach for key exchange, which QKD offers. This might completely transform secure communication. QKD has been shown to work in a number of real-world scenarios, such as fibre-optic and free-space QKD systems. These instances have made it possible for QKD to be widely used in a number of settings, including as secure communications in the governmental, military, and financial domains.

3.4.2 POST-QUANTUM CRYPTOGRAPHY AND QUANTUM-RESISTANT ALGORITHMS

While quantum computing offers innovative solutions for secure communication additionally, it presents serious risks to the cryptography systems in use today. Many popular public-key encryption techniques, such as elliptic curve cryptography and RSA (developed by Ron Rivest, Adi Shamir, and Leonard Adleman), rely on the computational difficulty of factoring large numbers or solving the discrete logarithm problem (Bernstein & Lange, 2017). However, Shor's algorithm, a quantum algorithm developed in 1994, can efficiently solve these problems with a sufficient powerful quantum computer, making existing encryption techniques vulnerable to attacks (Shor, 1997). Post-quantum cryptography (PQC), which attempts to create cryptographic algorithms that are immune to assaults from both classical and quantum computers, has being actively developed by researchers in an effort to overcome this difficulty (Bernstein & Lange, 2017). A number of quantum-resistant algorithms, such as multivariate cryptography, code-based cryptography, lattice-based cryptography, and hash-based signatures, have been proposed to counter the potential threats posed by quantum computers (Alagic et al., 2022). Through an open competition process, the National Institute of Standards and Technology (NIST) has been spearheading efforts to standardise post-quantum cryptography algorithms. A major step towards the adoption of quantum-resistant encryption was reached in July 2022 when NIST revealed the first four algorithms chosen for standardisation (2022).

3.4.3 IMPLICATIONS FOR DATA SECURITY AND PRIVACY

The advancement of quantum computing and the discovery of quantum algorithms like Shor's algorithm have a substantial impact on data security and privacy. These days, encryption measures safeguard sensitive data, such as financial transactions, government correspondence, and personal information, from attacks by powerful enough quantum computers.

This demonstrates how urgently businesses and governments must adopt post-quantum cryptography (PQC) standards and quantum-resistant cryptographic solutions in order to get ready for the quantum future. Failure to do so could result in a catastrophic breakdown of data security, compromising the privacy and confidentiality of critical information.

Moreover, the development of distribution of quantum keys is a potential solution for safe correspondence in the face of risks associated with systems for quantum computing. QKD offers a provably secure key exchange mechanism by utilising the concepts of quantum mechanics, guaranteeing the confidentiality of encrypted data even when assaulted from potent computers with quantum capabilities.

It is imperative that governments and organisations give the adoption of secure communication techniques and quantum-resistant cryptography top priority as quantum computing capabilities continue to grow. This will guard against the threat posed by quantum computing while preserving the integrity of vital systems and safeguarding sensitive data.

3.5 ARTIFICIAL INTELLIGENCE AND MACHINE LEARNING

Machine learning and artificial intelligence allow computers to gain knowledge from data, recognize patterns, and make informed decisions. These technologies have revolutionized many different fields. Complex learning challenges and processing large datasets are beyond the scope of standard computer techniques. By developing algorithmic approaches for quantum machine learning and exploring neural networks with quantum capabilities, quantum information processing offers workable solutions to these issues.

3.5.1 Machine Learning Tasks Using Quantum Algorithms (Quantum Neural Networks)

Research into the incorporation of quantum computing concepts into machine learning algorithms and models has led to the development of quantum machine learning (QML) methodologies (Biamonte et al., 2017; Dunjko & Briegel, 2018).

Neural networks with quantum capabilities are a promising field of study that utilise quantum phenomena including superposition and entanglement. They are modelled after classical neural networks. Comparing QNNs to classical neural networks, it is possible that they will demonstrate increased processing power and better learning task performance.

There are several quantum algorithms that have been proposed for specific activities involving machine learning, including:

- **Machines that support quantum information (QSVMs):** The optimisation issue in training assistive vector machines, which are frequently employed for regression and categorisation tasks, is resolved by these techniques by utilising quantum computing.
- **Quantum clustering algorithms:** For clustering jobs, quantum algorithms have been developed, like quantum hierarchical clustering and quantum k-means clustering, which may provide computational improvements over classical methods
- **Algorithms for reducing quantum dimensionality:** In order to process high-dimensional data, techniques like quantum linear discriminant analysis (qLDA) and quantum principal component analysis (qPCA) have been developed for dimensionality reduction and feature extraction tasks.

3.5.2 Potential Speedups for Certain Learning Tasks and Data Processing

Significant speedups in some machine learning activities and data processing procedures can be achieved with quantum computing. The creation of quantum algorithms that take advantage of quantum parallelism and quantum phenomena like superposition and entanglement could lead to these speedups (Dunjko & Briegel, 2018; Biamonte et al., 2017).

For example, quantum algorithms like quantum singular value transformation and the Harrow-Hassidim-Lloyd (HHL) algorithm can exponentially accelerate some linear algebra operations, which are crucial to many machine learning techniques.

Furthermore, Grover's algorithm and quantum estimation of amplitude are instances of quantum algorithms that can provide quadratic speedups for search and sampling tasks, which are critical in many machine learning applications (Grover, 1996).

Furthermore, quantum computing may enable more efficient processing and manipulation of large and complex datasets since qubits can encode and manage exponentially more information than classical bits (Biamonte et al., 2017).

3.5.3 Applications in Pattern Recognition, Data Analysis, and Decision-Making

Potential uses for machine learning models and approaches that use quantum computing principles and algorithms include the following areas:

- **Pattern recognition:** Quantum neural networks and quantum algorithms for dimensionality reduction and feature extraction can be applied to pattern recognition applications, such as photo and speech recognition, which could result in advances in efficiency and accuracy.

- **Data analysis:** Large and complicated datasets can be analysed more effectively through the use of quantum algorithms for clustering, dimensionality reduction, and linear algebra operations. This allows for more effective data exploration, visualisation, and insight extraction.
- **Decision-making**: Quantum neural networks and support vector machines are examples of quantum machine learning models and may offer better accuracy and robustness for decision-making tasks in sectors like banking, healthcare, and autonomous systems.

Continued research and improvements in quantum hardware and algorithms have the potential to totally revolutionise artificial intelligence and machine learning, even if these fields are still in their infancy with regard to quantum neural networks and machine learning. Researchers want to better handle challenging learning tasks, process and analyse massive datasets, and create more accurate and intelligent decision-making systems by utilising the special powers of quantum computing.

3.6 FINANCE AND RISK ANALYSIS

Quantitative models, simulations, and optimisation techniques are widely used in the financial industry for activities like risk assessment, derivative pricing, and portfolio management. However, many of these tasks involve complex computations and large datasets, which can be computationally intensive for classical computers. Quantum computing offers promising solutions to address these challenges through the development of quantum algorithms tailored for financial applications.

3.6.1 QUANTUM ALGORITHMS FOR FINANCIAL MODELLING AND RISK ASSESSMENT

Financial modelling and risk assessment are critical components of quantitative finance, enabling financial institutions and investors to evaluate investment opportunities, manage risks, and make informed decisions. These procedures could be completely changed by quantum algorithms, which offer more precise and effective solutions.

- **Monte Carlo simulations:** For tasks like pricing complicated derivatives and evaluating portfolio risk, Monte Carlo simulations are extensively utilised in financial modelling and risk assessment. Quantum techniques like quantum amplitude estimation and quantum walk algorithms may offer exponential speedups for specific Monte Carlo simulations, enabling more accurate and efficient risk analysis.
- **Portfolio risk analysis:** Quantum principal component analysis and quantum linear discriminant analysis are two examples of quantum algorithms that can be used to perform tasks like identifying and quantifying risk variables and assessing portfolio diversification. These algorithms may provide computational benefits over traditional methods, allowing for more precise and effective risk assessment.
- **Credit risk modelling:** By using quantum machine learning algorithms for credit risk modelling and credit scoring tasks, Credit risk assessment techniques, for example, quantum support vector machines and quantum neural networks, may improve in accuracy and resilience.

3.6.2 PORTFOLIO OPTIMISATION AND PRICING OF FINANCIAL DERIVATIVES

Fundamental issues in quantitative finance, portfolio optimisation, and derivative pricing have a big impact on risk management and investing strategies. Quantum computing presents novel ways to address these issues with more accuracy and efficiency.

- **Portfolio optimisation:** Quantum annealing and quantum approximate optimisation algorithms are two examples of quantum algorithms that have demonstrated potential in tackling portfolio optimisation problems more quickly than classical methods. By utilising quantum phenomena, these algorithms may more effectively explore the solution space, which could increase portfolio performance and risk-return trade-offs.
- **Derivative pricing:** The algorithm Harrow-Hassidim-Lloyd and quantum Monte Carlo techniques are two examples of quantum algorithms that may be able to offer exponential speedups for specific computer operations involved in pricing complicated financial derivatives. This can make pricing models more precise and effective, especially when it comes to derivatives that depend on several underlying assets or have payoffs that are reliant on a path.

3.6.3 Applications in Quantitative Finance and Risk Management

The field of quantum computing exhibits great potential for transforming quantitative finance and risk management. It can effectively address intricate computational problems that conventional computing techniques find difficult to handle. The following are some key areas where the impact of quantum computing is expected to be felt:

Table 3.2 illustrates the potential speedup or improvement in computational tasks relevant to finance and risk analysis when employing quantum algorithms compared to classical methods

- **Asset Pricing and Valuation:**
  Quantum computing offers more accurate and efficient computations may improve asset pricing and valuation models. Especially for intricate financial instruments, traditional models like the Black-Scholes equation and stochastic volatility models frequently demand substantial processing power. Quantum algorithms, such those created by Woerner and Egger and Rebentrost et al., have demonstrated potential in solving these problems more quickly. Quantum algorithms, for instance, may solve complex optimisation issues related to risk-neutral valuation and option pricing, resulting in asset pricing that is quicker and more precise.
- **Risk Management:**
  By facilitating more efficient risk measurement and mitigation techniques, quantum computing holds the potential to revolutionise risk management procedures in financial organisations. Quantum algorithms for Monte Carlo simulations, portfolio risk analysis, and credit risk modelling offer the ability to handle large datasets and complex risk factors more efficiently than classical methods. Research by Rebentrost et al. and Cong and Duan demonstrates how quantum algorithms can be applied to optimise risk management processes, leading to better identification and mitigation of various financial risks. Quantum computing, for example, can facilitate quicker and more precise conditional value at risk

TABLE 3.2

Potential Speedup/Improvement in Computational Tasks with Quantum Algorithms in Finance and Risk Analysis

Computational Task	Potential Speedup/Improvement with Quantum Algorithms
Derivative Pricing	Reduced computation time for complex pricing models
Portfolio Optimisation	Enhanced optimisation capabilities for large portfolios
Risk Modelling	Improved accuracy and efficiency in risk assessment

(CVaR) and value at risk (VaR) computations, offering insights into possible losses under various market scenarios.

- **Trading and Market Analysis:**
With quantum machine learning algorithms and optimisation approaches, quantum computing shows potential for improving trading tactics and market analysis. Algorithms created by Cao et al. show how quantum computing may enhance arbitrage detection, market trend analysis, and algorithmic trading. Quantum algorithms, for instance, may more quickly and effectively evaluate enormous volumes of market data, spot intricate patterns, and real-time optimise trading tactics. Quantum optimisation techniques can also be used for asset allocation, order execution procedures, and portfolio optimisation, which could provide financial markets competitors an advantage.

Case Studies:

1. **JP Morgan Chase:** JP Morgan Chase is investigating how quantum computing might be used in risk and finance. The company is developing quantum algorithms for risk analysis, derivatives pricing, and portfolio optimisation in partnership with academic institutes and quantum computing startups. Enhancing the precision and efficacy of its trading techniques and financial models is JP Morgan's goal in utilising quantum computing.
2. **Goldman Sachs:** Goldman Sachs is investing in quantum computing research to enhance its trading and investment strategies. The company is exploring the use of quantum algorithms for market analysis, high-frequency trading, and risk management. Quantum computing, according to Goldman Sachs, has the potential to completely transform the financial sector by making it possible to use more advanced and rapid computer methods for risk assessment and decision-making.
3. **Quantum Computing Startups:** Several quantum computing startups, such as QC Ware and Zapata Computing, are developing quantum algorithms specifically tailored for financial applications. These startups offer quantum software platforms that financial institutions can use to resolve challenging optimisation issues, pricing models, and risk analysis tasks more successfully. For example, QC Ware's Forge platform provides quantum optimisation algorithms for portfolio optimisation and asset allocation, helping financial firms improve their investment strategies and risk-adjusted returns.

   Last, it's important to remember that quantum computing has enormous potential to change risk management and quantitative finance procedures. Financial institutions can improve asset pricing, risk management, and trading strategies, resulting in better financial performance and more informed decision-making, by utilising quantum algorithms and optimisation approaches. In order to fully benefit from quantum computing in the financial industry, further research and development are required. Even though research into and developments in quantum hardware and algorithms are still very young, the application of quantum information processing in finance and risk analysis has great potential. Financial institutions and investors may be able to obtain a competitive edge through more precise and effective financial modelling, risk assessment, portfolio optimisation, and derivative pricing by utilising the processing capacity and special capabilities of quantum computing.

3.7 SCIENTIFIC COMPUTING AND DATA ANALYSIS

Many scientific fields, including physics, chemistry, biology, and engineering, depend heavily on scientific computing and data processing. These fields frequently deal with computationally demanding tasks that can profit from quantum computing's special powers, like data processing, pattern recognition, and simulations.

3.7.1 Quantum Algorithms for Linear Algebra and Data Processing

Numerous applications of scientific computing and data analysis, such as machine learning, signal processing, and numerical simulations, depend on the fundamentals of linear algebra. For some linear algebraic operations, quantum algorithms could provide appreciable speedups, leading to more accurate and efficient scientific computations.

- **Quantum linear system solvers:** Under certain conditions, the algorithm Harrow-Hassidim-Lloyd, a quantum technique, can solve linear equation systems ten times faster than traditional algorithms. Large linear system solving is a prevalent task in fields like machine learning, data analysis, and numerical simulations, where this approach finds use.
- **Quantum principal component analysis:** A quantum method for feature extraction and dimensionality reduction, qPCA can be applied to preprocessing and data analysis tasks across a range of scientific fields. With its potential to provide computational benefits over traditional PCA methods, qPCA could make handling high-dimensional data more effective.
- **Quantum algorithms for machine learning:** For activities involving machine learning like pattern recognition and data analysis, scientific disciplines can use quantum algorithms like quantum support vector machines and quantum neural networks. These algorithms may increase the precision and effectiveness of learning tasks by utilising quantum phenomena like superposition and entanglement.

3.7.2 Efficient Data Search and Pattern Recognition

Data search and pattern recognition are crucial tasks in scientific computing and data analysis, with applications ranging from bioinformatics and genomics to signal processing and image analysis. Quantum algorithms offer potential solutions for more efficient data search and pattern recognition.

- **Quantum search algorithms:** Grover (1996) presents Grover's algorithm, a quantum search method with a quadratic acceleration over traditional algorithms that can search unstructured databases or unsorted lists. This algorithm can be applied to various data search and pattern recognition tasks in scientific domains, such as searching genomic databases or identifying patterns in scientific data.
- **Quantum pattern matching:** Quantum algorithms for pattern matching have been developed, which can potentially offer exponential speedups over classical algorithms for certain cases. These algorithms can be applied to tasks like DNA sequence alignment, signal pattern recognition, and image pattern analysis.
- **Quantum data encoding and processing:** Thanks to qubits and quantum parallelism, quantum computing can process and encode exponentially more data than classical computing (Biamonte et al., 2017).This capability can be leveraged for efficient processing and analysis of large scientific datasets, enabling more comprehensive and accurate data exploration.

3.7.3 Applications in Bioinformatics, Scientific Simulations, and Big Data Analysis

The applications of quantum computing in scientific computing and data analysis span various domains, including:

- **Bioinformatics and genomics:** One can use quantum algorithms for activities like DNA sequence alignment, protein folding predictions, and genomic data analysis, enabling more efficient and accurate computational methods in these fields (Lüthi et al., 2016).

- **Scientific simulations:** Compared to classical simulations, quantum computers can simulate complicated quantum systems, like materials and molecular systems, more accurately and efficiently (Aspuru-Guzik et al., 2005; Lüthi et al., 2016).This has applications in computational chemistry, materials science, and condensed matter physics.
- **Big data analysis**: Large and complex scientific datasets, such as those produced in fields like astronomy, particle physics, and climate science, can be analysed using quantum algorithms for linear algebra, data processing, and identification of patterns (Biamonte et al., 2017). As a result, these enormous databases may be explored and visualised and insights extracted more effectively.

Although there is still much to learn about the actual application of quantum computing in scientific computing and data processing, continuous research and developments in quantum hardware and algorithms hold great promise. Scientists and researchers may be able to expand the boundaries of scientific study, simulations, and data-driven discoveries in a variety of fields by utilising the processing capacity and special properties of quantum computing.

3.8   OTHER EMERGING APPLICATIONS

Although there are many applications for the aforementioned problems, quantum computing also has the potential to revolutionise a large number of other industries. This section discusses some new uses for quantum computing, such as quantum sensing, quantum metrology, and quantum communication networks.

3.8.1   QUANTUM COMPUTING IN COMMUNICATION NETWORKS AND THE QUANTUM WEB

Improvements in quantum information science and quantum computing enable the development of quantum communication networks and the notion of the quantum web. These technologies enable efficient and secure information sharing by utilising notions from quantum mechanics.

- **Quantum key distribution:** As mentioned earlier, QKD distributes encryption keys using the ideas of quantum physics to establish safe channels of communication (Bennett & Brassard, 2014). QKD networks, which provide a safe substitute for traditional encryption techniques subject to attacks by quantum computing, have been put into practice and tested in a number of nations.
- **Quantum repeaters:** The short range over which quantum states can be successfully conveyed represents one of the major obstacles in quantum communication. By periodically refreshing the quantum information, quantum repeaters are devices that can increase the range of quantum communication. This is an essential part of making a worldwide quantum internet a reality.
- **Quantum internet:** A network capable of transmitting quantum information is what is meant by the term "quantum internet," opening the door to applications like quantum teleportation, distributed quantum computing, and secure communication. This would allow quantum computers and devices to connect and exchange quantum information, potentially leading to new paradigms in communication, computing, and information processing.

3.8.2   SENSING AND QUANTUM METROLOGY

Atomic sensing and metropolitan analysis leverage quantum phenomena to measure physical quantities with unprecedented precision and sensitivity. These applications have implications in various fields, including navigation, timekeeping, medical imaging, and fundamental scientific research.

- **Quantum sensors**: Quantum sensors exploit quantum effects to detect and measure physical quantities, such as electromagnetic fields, gravity, and time, with higher sensitivity and accuracy than classical sensors. Examples include atomic clocks, magnetometers, and gravitational wave detectors.
- **Quantum imaging:** Quantum imaging techniques, such as quantum ghost imaging and quantum lithography, can potentially achieve higher resolution and sensitivity compared to classical imaging methods. These techniques have applications in microscopy, medical imaging, and semiconductor manufacturing.
- **Quantum metrology:** The field of quantum metrology is concerned with creating and utilising quantum methods for accurate measurements of physical quantities, including length, frequency, and time. These methods can enhance the accuracy and precision of various scientific and technological applications, including timekeeping, navigation, and fundamental physics experiments.

3.8.3 Applications in Aerospace

3.8.3.1 Aircraft Design Optimisation

Potential applications for quantum computing to revolutionise aircraft design optimisation by significantly accelerating the process and enhancing accuracy. Traditional methods for optimising aircraft designs involve complex simulations of aerodynamic phenomena and structural properties, which are computationally intensive and time-consuming. Quantum computing offers algorithms like quantum annealing and quantum-inspired optimisation, which can efficiently explore the vast design space, leading to improved performance metrics. Businesses such as Airbus and Boeing, for example, are investigating the application of quantum computing to optimise wing designs, thereby lowering drag and fuel consumption and raising overall aerodynamic efficiency.

3.8.3.2 Mission Planning and Logistics

Quantum computing holds promise for optimising mission planning and logistics in aerospace missions. Quantum algorithms can be used to handle complex optimisation issues more effectively, including scheduling, resource allocation, and route planning. For example, NASA is investigating the application of quantum computing to optimise space mission trajectories, minimising fuel consumption and mission duration. Similarly, the European Space Agency (ESA) is exploring quantum-inspired algorithms for scheduling satellite launches and coordinating ground station operations, leading to more efficient mission execution and resource utilisation.

3.8.3.3 Weather Prediction and Climate Modelling

Climate simulations and weather prediction models can be improved with the use of quantum computing. Weather forecasts and climate projections can be more accurate thanks to quantum-enhanced machine learning algorithms that handle large volumes of data and take complex atmospheric dynamics into account. For instance, IBM's Quantum Artificial Intelligence Laboratory (QAIL) is collaborating with meteorological organisations to develop quantum algorithms for weather prediction, leveraging quantum computing's parallel processing capabilities to analyse atmospheric data in real-time and improve forecast accuracy.

3.8.4 Applications in Defence

3.8.4.1 Cryptography and Cybersecurity

Cryptography and cybersecurity face both opportunities and challenges from quantum computing. Although traditional encryption techniques may be broken by quantum computing, quantum-resistant cryptographic protocols are being developed to guard against quantum attacks. For instance, leading the charge to standardise post-quantum cryptography is the National Institute of Standards and Technology (NIST) techniques in order to guarantee safe communication and data protection in the quantum era. To further protect sensitive data against quantum threats, institutions such as the U.S. Department of Defence (DoD) are investing in quantum-safe encryption solutions.

3.8.4.2 Military Simulation and Training

Quantum computing can enhance military simulation and training exercises by enabling more realistic and immersive simulations of battlefield scenarios, weapon systems, and strategic decision-making processes. For example, defence contractors like Lockheed Martin and BAE Systems are exploring the use of quantum algorithms for simulating complex military operations, optimising resource allocation, and training personnel in virtual environments. By harnessing quantum computing's computational power, military organisations can improve readiness and decision-making capabilities in dynamic and uncertain environments.

3.8.4.3 Intelligence and Surveillance

The potential for quantum computing to totally change intelligence gathering and surveillance capacities stems from its ability to handle and analyse large amounts of sensor data more quickly. Quantum machine learning algorithms can identify patterns, anomalies, and signals of interest in surveillance data, enhancing situational awareness and decision-making for defence applications. To enable proactive defence and strategic planning, the Defence Advanced Research Projects Agency (DARPA) is investing in quantum-enhanced sensor technologies for adversarial threat detection and tracking.

3.8.5 Challenges and Opportunities

Although quantum computing offers unmatched processing power and has the potential to change the aerospace and defence industries, a number of challenges must be resolved before its full potential can be reached. These consist of algorithmic optimisation, hardware development, scalability, and error correction. Working together, government, business, and academia can overcome these obstacles and realise the revolutionary potential of quantum computing.

While these emerging applications are still in the research and development stages, they highlight the vast potential of quantum computing and quantum information science to revolutionise various domains beyond traditional computing and information processing. As quantum technologies continue to advance, these applications may lead to breakthroughs in secure communication, advanced sensing, and precision metrology, among other areas.

3.9 OBSTACLES AND PROSPECTS FOR THE FUTURE

Although there are many advantages to quantum computing for transformative applications across various domains, the practical realisation of large-scale, fault-tolerant quantum computers faces significant challenges. This section discusses the current limitations and obstacles, the challenges of scaling up quantum computers, and the future developments and potential breakthroughs that could propel the field forward.

3.9.1 Current Limitations and Obstacles to Practical Quantum Information Processing

The practical implementation of large-scale quantum computers is hampered by a variety of obstacles and hurdles, despite the notable advancements achieved in the study and development of quantum computing:

- **Qubit quality additionally coherence time:** The fundamental components of quantum information, qubits, are vulnerable to noise and interactions in the surroundings, which may cause decoherence and the quantum information to be lost (Preskill, 2018). One major challenge is to sustain qubit coherence for sufficiently long times, which becomes more difficult as qubit counts increase.
- **Inaccuracy rates in quantum:** Due to the extreme sensitivity of quantum computing to errors, even tiny mistakes have the potential to spread and taint the outcomes of calculations. Achieving a real-world quantum edge over conventional computers requires minimising and reducing quantum errors.
- **Scalability and connectivity:** It is extremely difficult to scale up quantum computers to many high-quality qubits while preserving connectivity and control over each qubit (Preskill, 2018). The complexity of controlling quantum interactions and preserving coherence rises exponentially increase in qubit count.

An illustration of the challenges faced in scaling up quantum computers while maintaining low error rates and coherence times as the number of qubits grows includes issues such as quantum decoherence, noise, and difficulties in error correction. The scatter plot in Figure 3.3 highlights the relationship between the number of qubits and either error rates or coherence times, emphasising the inherent trade-offs in achieving practical quantum information processing. This graph underscores the current limitations and obstacles hindering the scalability of quantum computing technology, as discussed in this section.

Table 3.3 outlines key challenges faced in quantum computing alongside potential solutions and research directions aimed at overcoming these obstacles.

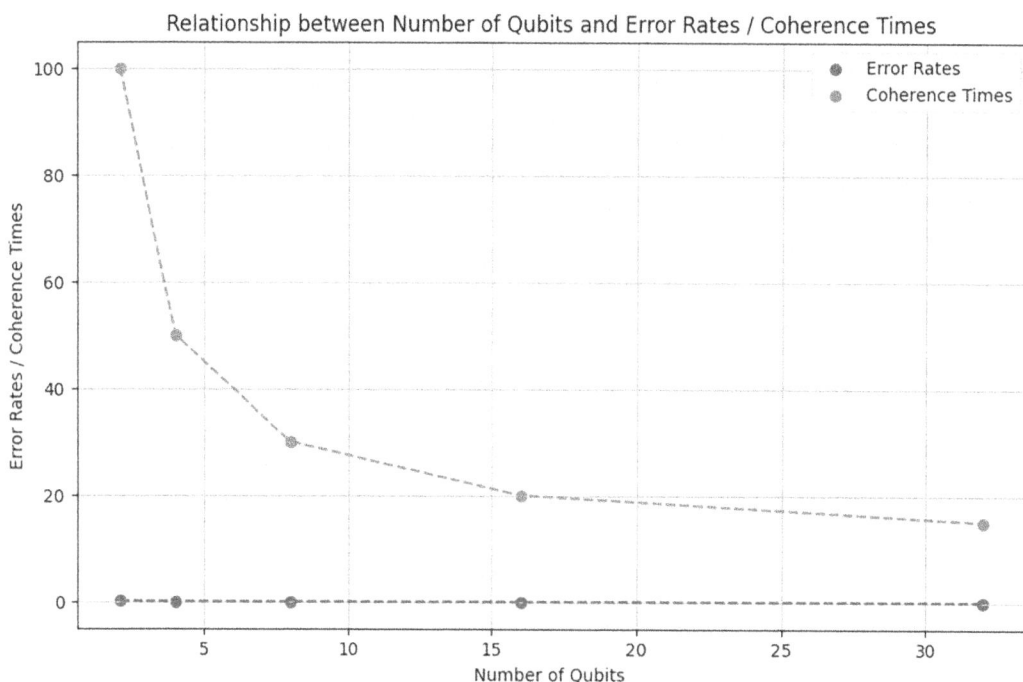

FIGURE 3.3 Scaling challenges in quantum computing: relationship between qubit count and error rates/coherence times.

TABLE 3.3
Current Limitations and Challenges in Quantum Computing, along with
Potential Solutions

Challenges	Potential Solutions/Research Directions
Qubit Quality	Error correction codes, better qubit fabrication techniques
Error Rates	Fault-tolerant quantum computation and quantum error correction
Scalability	Improved qubit connectivity, quantum error correction, fault tolerance
Decoherence	Error mitigation techniques, enhanced qubit coherence times
Quantum Gates	Development of more reliable quantum gate operations
Hardware Variability	Calibration and control techniques for addressing hardware variations
Noise and Interference	Noise-resilient algorithms, error mitigation strategies
Quantum Software Design	Optimisation of quantum algorithms for specific hardware platforms
Quantum Algorithm Design	Research into new quantum algorithms tailored for practical problems

3.9.2 Scaling Up Quantum Computers and Overcoming Noise and Decoherence

Researchers and engineers must solve the difficulties associated with scaling up quantum computers and reducing the effects of noise and decoherence in order to fully realise the promise of quantum information processing and enable practical applications:

- **Quantum error repair:** To enable quantum error correction and fault-tolerant quantum computation, techniques and algorithms aim to detect and correct errors that occur during quantum computations. However, implementing efficient and scalable error correction schemes is a significant challenge, requiring substantial overhead in terms of additional qubits and operations.
- **Improving qubit quality and coherence:** Researchers are exploring various approaches to improve qubit quality and extend coherence times, such as using different qubit implementations (e.g., topological qubits, trapped ions, or superconducting qubits), developing new materials and fabrication techniques, and improving environmental isolation and control (Boixo et al., 2019).
- **Novel quantum computing architectures:** To overcome scaling issues, researchers are looking into novel quantum computing architectures as distributed and modular quantum computing. The integration of smaller, networked quantum devices may be possible with these architectures, which could lessen the difficulty of scaling up individual quantum computers.

3.9.3 Future Developments and Potential Breakthroughs in Quantum Data Handling

The subject of quantum information processing is fast developing despite the obstacles, and a number of advancements and possible breakthroughs might greatly improve the practical realisation of large-scale quantum computers:

- **New qubit implementations:** Other qubit implementations are under investigation; topological qubits could offer superior intrinsic noise immunity and coherence times. These developments might pave the way for more dependable and scalable quantum computers.
- **Quantum simulation and quantum advantage:** Researchers are investigating quantum advantage and quantum simulation for particular challenges, even with noisy and flawed

intermediate-scale quantum (NISQ) devices (Boixo et al., 2019; Preskill, 2018). These initiatives may result in useful applications and new perspectives that propel quantum computing forward.

- **Quantum computing in the cloud:** The development of research and development activities could be expedited, and access to quantum computing resources could be made more widely available by cloud-hosted quantum computing solutions like those supplied by Google, IBM, and other companies (IBM Quantum Experience, Google Quantum Computing).
- **Quantum-classical hybrid algorithms:** In order to capitalise on the advantages of both paradigms, researchers are investigating hybrid techniques that integrate quantum and classical computing (Cao et al., 2019). These hybrid algorithms may result in useful applications and new perspectives that propel quantum computing forward.

While the road to realising large-scale, fault-tolerant quantum computers is challenging, the potential rewards are immense. Overcoming the current limitations and obstacles through continued research and development could unlock transformative applications, revolutionising a broad spectrum of industries, encompassing machine learning, computational chemistry, optimisation, and cryptography.

3.10 CONCLUSION

A paradigm shift in how we think about computation and information processing is represented by quantum computing. This innovative technology has the potential to revolutionise multiple fields and spur advances by utilising the principles of quantum physics. This chapter has examined the broad spectrum of quantum computing applications, highlighting the unique features and advantages that this technology has to offer.

A synopsis of the possible effects of quantum information processing in different fields

Quantum computing is being applied in many different fields, each with potentially revolutionary consequences:

- Quantum chemistry and simulation: Advances in materials science, energy research, and drug discovery are facilitated by precise modelling and simulation of quantum systems (Aspuru-Guzik et al., 2005; Cao et al., 2019; Lüthi et al., 2016).
- Logistics, scheduling, resource allocation, and portfolio optimisation are among the fields in which efficient solutions to challenging optimisation problems are applied (Kadowaki & Nishimori, 1998).
- Cybersecurity and cryptography: Sub-quantum cryptography, quantum key distribution for secure communication, and implications for privacy and data security (Bennett & Brassard, 2014; Bernstein & Lange, 2017).
- Machine intelligence and artificial intelligence: Applications in pattern recognition and decision-making, possible speedups for data processing, and quantum algorithms for machine learning tasks (Biamonte et al., 2017; Dunjko & Briegel, 2018).
- Finance and risk analysis: Derivative pricing, portfolio optimisation, risk assessment, and financial modelling are all accomplished using quantum algorithms.
- Scientific computing and data analysis: Big data analysis, scientific simulations, bioinformatics, data search, pattern recognition, and efficient linear algebra operations (Grover, 1996; Lüthi et al., 2016).
- Emerging applications: quantum metrology, quantum sensing, quantum communication networks, and quantum internet (Bennett & Brassard, 2014).

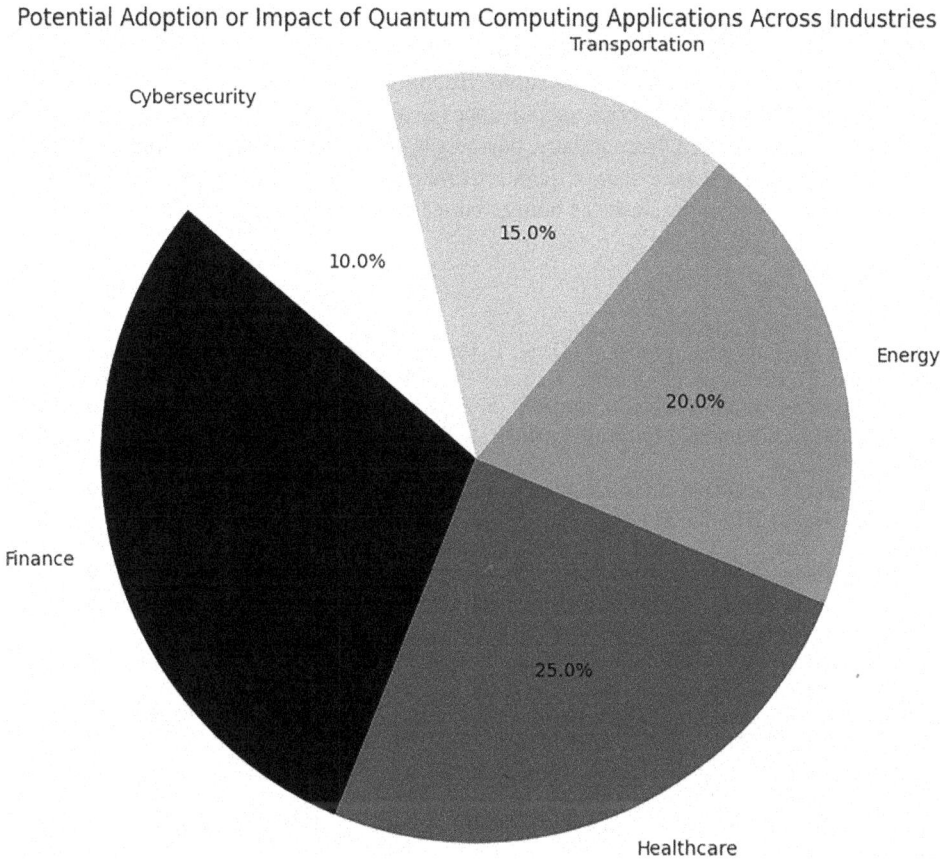

FIGURE 3.4 Potential adoption or impact of quantum computing applications across industries.

Illustration of the potential adoption or impact of quantum computing applications across diverse industries or sectors, including finance, healthcare, energy, transportation, and cybersecurity. This pie chart shown in Figure 3.4 underscores the broad implications and significance of quantum computing technology, highlighting its potential to revolutionise various sectors, as discussed in this section.

Importance of continued research and development in quantum information processing Applications

While the theoretical foundations of quantum information processing have been extensively studied, the practical realisation and application of this technology are merely getting started.

Continued research and development efforts are crucial to overcoming the current limitations and obstacles, such as improving qubit quality and coherence, developing efficient quantum error correction techniques, and addressing scalability challenges (Preskill, 2018).

Ongoing research in areas like new qubit implementations, quantum computing architectures, and hybrid quantum-classical algorithms could lead to breakthroughs that propel the field forward (Cao et al., 2019). Furthermore, the development of quantum computing in the clouds services and the exploration of quantum advantage for specific problems could accelerate the practical adoption of quantum computing (IBM Quantum Experience, Google Quantum Computing; Boixo et al., 2019).

Regarding quantum computing applications reaching their complete capability and spurring groundbreaking discoveries and advances in a variety of fields, ongoing research and development are needed. Researchers, businesses, and governments working together will be essential to the advancement of quantum computing, its ability to solve intricate issues, and its ability to push the limits of human knowledge and capabilities.

REFERENCES

Alagic, G., Apon, D., Cooper, D., Dang, Q., Dang, T., Kelsey, J., Lichtinger, J., Liu, Y. K., Miller, C., Moody, D., Peralta, R., Perlner, R., Robinson, A., Smith-Tone, D., Alperin-Sheriff, J., & Yoast-Hull, Z. (2022). *Status report on the third round of the NIST post-quantum cryptography standardization process*. US Department of Commerce, National Institute of Standards and Technology. https://doi.org/10.6028/NIST.IR.8413

Albash, T., & Lidar, D. A. (2018). Adiabatic quantum computation. *Reviews of Modern Physics*, 90(1), 015002. https://doi.org/10.1103/RevModPhys.90.015002

Aspuru-Guzik, A., Dutoi, A. D., Love, P. J., & Head-Gordon, M. (2005). Simulated quantum computation of molecular energies. *Science*, 309(5741), 1704–1707. https://doi.org/10.1126/science.1113479

Bennett, C. H., & Brassard, G. (2014). Quantum cryptography: Public key distribution and coin tossing. *Theoretical Computer Science*, 560, 7–11. https://doi.org/10.1016/j.tcs.2014.05.025

Bernstein, D. J., & Lange, T. (2017). Post-quantum cryptography. *Nature*, 549(7671), 188–194. https://doi.org/10.1038/nature23461

Biamonte, J., Wittek, P., Pancotti, N., Rebentrost, P., Wiebe, N., & Lloyd, S. (2017). Quantum machine learning. *Nature*, 549(7671), 195–202. https://doi.org/10.1038/nature23474

Boixo, S., Brandao, F. G. S. L., Buell, D. A., Burkett, B., Chen, Y., Chen, Z., Chiaro, B., Collins, R., Courtney, W., Dunsworth, A. and Farhi, E., 2019. Quantum supremacy using a programmable superconducting processor. *Nature*, 574, 505–510. https://simons.berkeley.edu/sites/default/files/docs/15610/boixosuprema-cymay42020.pdf

Brassard, G., Høyer, P., Mosca, M., & Tapp, A. (2002). Quantum amplitude amplification and estimation. *Contemporary Mathematics*, 305, 53–74. https://doi.org/10.48550/arXiv.quant-ph/0005055

Cao, Y., Romero, J., Olson, J. P., Degroote, M., Johnson, P. D., Kieferová, M., Kivlichan, I. D., Menke, T., Peropadre, B., Sawaya, N. P. D., Sim, S., Veis, L., & Aspuru-Guzik, A. (2019). *Chemical Reviews*, 119(19), 10856–10915. https://doi.org/10.1021/acs.chemrev.8b00803

Dunjko, V., & Briegel, H. J. (2018). Machine learning & artificial intelligence in the quantum domain: A review of recent progress. *Reports on Progress in Physics*, 81(7), 074001. https://doi.org/10.1088/1361-6633/aab406

Feld, S., Roch, C., Gabor, T., Seidel, C., Neukart, F., Galter, I., Mauerer, W., & Linnhoff-Popien, C. (2019). A hybrid solution method for the capacitated vehicle routing problem using a quantum annealer. *arXiv:1811.07403 [quant-ph]*. https://doi.org/10.48550/arXiv.1811.07403

Grover, L. K. (1996). A fast quantum mechanical algorithm for database search. In *Proceedings of the twenty-eighth annual ACM symposium on Theory of computing* (pp. 212–219). https://doi.org/10.1145/237814.237866

Hauke, P., Katzgraber, H. G., Lechner, W., Nishimori, H., & Oliver, W. D. (2020). Perspectives of quantum annealing: Methods and implementations. *Reports on Progress in Physics*, 83(5), 054401. https://doi.org/10.1088/1361-6633/ab85b8

Kadowaki, T., & Nishimori, H. (1998). Quantum annealing in the transverse Ising model. *Physical Review E*, 58(5), 5355. https://doi.org/10.1103/PhysRevE.58.5355

Ladd, T. D., Jelezko, F., Laflamme, R., Nakamura, Y., Monroe, C., & O'Brien, J. L. (2010). Quantum computers. *Nature*, 464(7285), 45–53. https://doi.org/10.1038/nature08812

Lanyon, B. P., Whitfield, J. D., Gillett, G. G., Goggin, M. E., Almeida, M. P., Kassal, I., Biamonte, J. D., Mohseni, M., Powell, B. J., Barbieri, M., Aspuru-Guzik, A., & White, A. G. (2010). Towards quantum chemistry on a quantum computer. *Nature Chemistry*, 2, 106–111. https://doi.org/10.1038/nchem.483

Lucas, A. (2014). Ising formulations of many NP problems. *Frontiers in Physics*, 2, 5. https://doi.org/10.3389/fphy.2014.00005

Lüthi, H. P., Heinen, S., Schneider, G., Glöss, A., Brändle, M. P., King, R. A., Pyzer-Knapp, E., Alharbi, F. H., & Kais, S. (2016). The quantum chemical search for novel materials and the issue of data processing: The InfoMol project. *Journal of Computational Science*, 15, 65–73. https://doi.org/10.1016/j.jocs.2015.10.003

Montanaro, A. (2016). Quantum algorithms: An overview. *npj Quantum Information*, 2, 15023. https://doi.org/10.1038/npjqi.2015.23

Nielsen, M. A., & Chuang, I. L. (2010). *Quantum computation and quantum information*. Cambridge University Press.

Otgonbayer, Z., Neukart, F., Scholten, R., Sebastiani, D., & Kehrle, M. (2021). Quantum approximate optimization for the nurse scheduling problem. *arXiv preprint* arXiv:2111.05909. https://doi.org/10.48550/arXiv.1812.01041

Preskill, J. (2018). Quantum computing in the NISQ era and beyond. *Quantum*, 2, 79. https://doi.org/10.22331/q-2018-08-06-79

Reiher, M., Wiebe, N., Svore, K. M., Wecker, D., & Troyer, M. (2017). Elucidating reaction mechanisms on quantum computers. *Proceedings of the National Academy of Sciences*, 114(29), 7555–7560. https://doi.org/10.1073/pnas.1619152114

Shor, P. W. (1997). Polynomial-time algorithms for prime factorization and discrete logarithms on a quantum computer. *SIAM Review*, 41(2), 303–332. https://doi.org/10.1137/S0036144598347011

4 Qubit-Based Applications for Next Generation Society

Kandan M., Priyanga Subbiah, Krishnaraj N., and Shaji. K.A. Theodore

4.1 INTRODUCTION TO QUANTUM COMPUTING

As a result of the arrival of quantum computing, which has the potential to transform a number of different sectors, there is now a sea change occurring in the field of computer science. The development of quantum computing has made it possible to achieve data processing skills that were previously inconceivable on classical computers. These capabilities are now within reach. We are able to accomplish this by putting the principles of quantum physics into practice. A look at the ever-evolving field of quantum computing and the prospective applications of this technology is presented here. In this chapter, we examine the current state of quantum computing in terms of its advancement and highlight the revolutionary potential it possesses. At its most fundamental level, quantum computing is predicated on the execution of processing tasks through the utilisation of entanglement and superposition, which are two fundamental principles of quantum physics. Quantum computers employ quantum bits, also known as qubits, which are able to exist in several states at the same time because to the phenomena of superposition. Bits, which are the fundamental building element of conventional computers, can only take on two conceivable values: either 0 or 1. The unique attribute of quantum computers enables them to concurrently investigate a wide range of potential solutions to a problem. As a result, certain types of calculations may be performed at rates that are ten times faster than traditional computers. In the present moment, the field of optimisation is home to some of the most fascinating prospective applications of quantum computing. The actual world presents a number of challenges, including route optimisation, portfolio optimisation, and supply chain management. One of the most prevalent challenges is determining which of the many viable solutions is the most appropriate one available. Quantum annealing is a quantum method that has showed promise for solving optimisation issues more efficiently than standard algorithms. D-Wave Systems was an early user of this quantum process during its preliminary stages. Moreover, quantum computing has the potential to bring about substantial advancements in cryptography, which is another field that is now being researched. When it comes to securing data storage and communication, the methods that are now in use are susceptible to being cracked by quantum computers, which are capable of breaking many of these approaches (Andreas et al., 2021). The new encryption algorithms that have been established by quantum cryptography, on the other hand, are resistant to assaults from quantum computers. The quantum key distribution (QKD) technique is one example of such a method; it makes use of the principles of quantum mechanics in order to make secret communication easier.

In addition, quantum computing has the potential to bring about a massive shift in a variety of other sectors, including medicine and materials research. Quantum computers have the potential to mimic complicated chemical structures with an unparalleled level of precision, which might lead to the discovery of new medicines and materials that have qualities that are ground-breaking. Additionally, with the assistance of quantum computers, materials specifically intended for certain uses, such as high-performance batteries or superconductors, may be created and optimised in a

DOI: 10.1201/9781003499459-4

more expedient manner. The application of quantum computing might possibly have a big influence on machine learning; this is only one example of such an impact. Because quantum machine learning algorithms are better able to manage and analyse huge datasets than standard algorithms, it is possible that they will produce greater predictions and insights than what traditional algorithms can. In addition, quantum computers have the potential to facilitate the training and optimisation of deep learning models in a more expedient manner, which might result in groundbreaking advancements in fields such as autonomous vehicles, natural language processing, and image identification. Quantum computing is still in its infancy and faces a significant number of technological obstacles that need to be dealt with before it can be completely achieved. Despite the fact that it has a great deal of promise, it is still in its infancy. The production of the requisite hardware is one of the most significant challenges, since the construction of quantum computers that are both scalable and dependable is an endeavour that is extraordinary in its complexity and difficulty (Francesco et al., 2021). By virtue of the fact that quantum computers are inherently prone to making mistakes as a result of decoherence and other quantum processes, error correction has become an extra essential topic of research.

In addition, the development of algorithms is a significant challenge for quantum computing. This is as a result of the fact that research into the development of effective quantum algorithms for application in the solution of issues that occur in the real world is still ongoing. When it comes to ethical and societal consequences, some instances that need to be taken into consideration include the possible influence that quantum computing might have on issues regarding privacy and security, as well as the loss of jobs. Quantum computing is a subfield of computer science that is undergoing rapid expansion (Martin, Felix, 2023). It has the potential to have a significant impact on a wide range of fields, including, but not limited to, optimisation, encryption, pharmaceutical development, materials research, and machine learning, to mention just a few. There is no doubt that quantum computing has the ability to bring about a golden age of invention and discovery. This is something that cannot be denied. In spite of the fact that there are still a number of problems that need to be resolved, quantum computing offers a tremendous deal of potential for a paradigm change. The research and development that is being conducted in this fascinating sector is continuously advancing, which indicates that the possible applications of quantum computing in the future are nearly endless. Figure 4.1 presents a visual representation of the numerous uses of quantum computing.

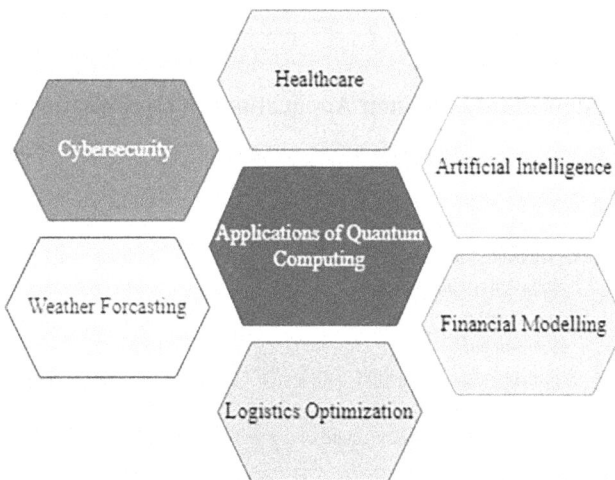

FIGURE 4.1   Applications of quantum computing.

4.2   QUANTUM ALGORITHMS AND OPTIMISATION

Recent developments in quantum algorithms and optimisation suggest they might dramatically alter how many industries approach problem-solving. However, conventional computer-era methods have their limitations when faced with complex optimisation problems involving a large number of variables and restrictions. In contrast, quantum algorithms employ the principles of quantum physics to explore several answers at once. With these techniques, it may be possible to solve some kinds of optimisation issues much more quickly than before.

Among the best-known quantum optimisation strategies is the Grover approach. Among the best algorithms, it provides a quadratic speedup for unstructured search jobs. Use of Grover's method is widespread; one such use is database search, when the goal is to find a specific item inside an unsorted database. By harnessing the potential of quantum superposition and interference, Grover's approach may search through all possible solutions simultaneously. When contrasted with the number of processes needed by traditional search algorithms, this leads to a fourfold reduction (Rene, Romit, 2023). Another important quantum approach in optimisation is the quantum approximation optimisation algorithm (QAOA). Problems with combinatorial optimisation are the inspiration for this method. Quantum annealing optimisation is based on the principles of quantum annealing, an optimisation method that derives from quantum mechanics and mimics the metallurgical annealing process. The quantum optimisation algorithm encapsulates the problem into a quantum Hamiltonian, which allows it to efficiently search the solution space and find near-optimal solutions to difficult optimisation problems. There are many different areas that might benefit from optimising using quantum algorithms. Some examples include AI, logistics, banking, and telecommunications. Transportation route optimisation, warehouse management, and supply chain operations are just a few examples of how logistics might benefit from quantum algorithms, which could lead to significant savings and efficiency benefits. Optimising portfolios, monitoring risks, and algorithmic trading are all areas where quantum algorithms might find use in the financial sector. Investors might therefore make better-informed judgements, increasing their chances of a successful investment. Table 4.1 provides a brief overview of several quantum algorithms and their applications in optimisation. Each algorithm has unique properties and is suited to different types of optimisation problems.

Rather than being confined to specific domains, the optimisation applications of quantum algorithms have broader implications for the solving of fundamental computer problems. Finding the

TABLE 4.1
Outlining Quantum Algorithms and Their Applications in Optimisation

Quantum Algorithm	Description	Applications
Grover's Algorithm	Searches an unsorted database quadratically faster	Database search, cryptographic functions, solving NP-complete problems
Quantum Annealing	Optimisation technique for finding global minima/maxima	Combinatorial optimisation, machine learning, financial modelling
Quantum Approximate	Approximates the ground state of a given Hamiltonian	Chemistry, material science, optimisation problems
Quantum Walks	Simulates classical random walks on a quantum computer	Optimisation problems, graph theory, search algorithms
Variational Quantum	Approximates the ground state of a given Hamiltonian	Optimisation problems, machine learning, chemistry
Eigensolver	Finds the eigenvalues and eigenvectors of a matrix	Chemistry, quantum mechanics, optimisation problems

shortest path that stops at each of a set of cities exactly once is known as the travelling salesman problem (TSP), and it's one of those problems that classic algorithms have a hard time handling. It is possible that NP-hard problems, like the TSP, can be solved in polynomial time using quantum techniques. Because of this, optimisation research and development might go in new directions. While quantum algorithms for optimisation show remarkable promise, there are still several challenges that must be resolved before their widespread use can be considered. Hardware constraints, like as noise and decoherence, might limit the scalability and performance of quantum algorithms. Quantum error correction codes and other error correction techniques are crucial for making quantum computation more reliable and less susceptible to these types of errors.

A thorough understanding of quantum physics and computational complexity theory is required to build efficient quantum algorithms for particular optimisation issues. Another significant area of study is algorithm design. In addition, while designing quantum algorithms for practical use, actual implementation concerns like qubit connectivity and gate fidelities need to be considered. An exciting new area of computer science, quantum algorithms and optimisation could dramatically alter how many different kinds of problems are solved. To sum up, this is an encouraging future (Amirul et al., 2022). The advent of quantum algorithms has allowed researchers and industry professionals to tackle before unsolvable problems with unprecedented complexity. They achieve this by harnessing the potential of quantum physics, which can solve specific kinds of optimisation issues with exponential speedups. With the ongoing advancements in this intriguing field of study, the future possibilities for quantum algorithms and optimisation are practically limitless.

4.3 QUANTUM CRYPTOGRAPHY AND SECURITY

A relatively new area of research, quantum cryptography and security uses the principles of quantum physics to create cryptographic systems that are, in theory, impenetrable to quantum attacks. Standard cryptographic techniques, like Rivest-Shamir-Adleman (RSA) and Advanced Encryption Standard (AES), may be vulnerable to attacks from quantum computers since they rely on assumptions about the computational complexity of communications. An impenetrable encryption technology based on quantum mechanics might be available soon thanks to quantum cryptography. A huge step forward in the field of safe data transmission and communication (Divya, Ravi, 2019), this is a paradigm change. The most famous use of quantum cryptography, quantum key distribution allows two people to use quantum principles to create a shared secret key that may be used to secure communication. Key distribution is guaranteed to be safe by QKD since it employs a variety of quantum mechanical concepts. These characteristics encompass the no-cloning theorem and the uncertainty principle, among others. Two parties can exchange cryptographic keys with a demonstrable assurance of security using quantum key distribution, which allows information to be encoded in quantum states like the polarisation of photons.

Quantum random number generation (QRNG) is another prominent usage of quantum cryptography; it uses quantum processes to generate really random, unbiased values. For quantum cryptography, this is a crucial use case. Encryption and key generation are two examples of cryptographic methods that rely on the production of random integers. Ensuring these random numbers are secure is critical for making sure cryptographic systems are secure (Hari et al., 2022). Quantum random number generators offer a higher degree of protection than traditional pseudo-random number generators, which can be targeted by assaults utilising algorithms or hardware. Quantum cryptography also has ramifications for other areas of cybersecurity, including private data analysis, secure cloud computing, and safe multi-party computation. Researchers are looking at new cryptographic protocols that use quantum ideas like superposition and entanglement to give better security assurances and more resilience to attacks. Quantum concepts are being utilised in the development of these protocols.

Despite its promising future, quantum cryptography has several challenges that must be resolved before it can be widely used in practice. One of the trickiest problems is creating scalable quantum cryptography systems that are both reliable and long-lasting. Building quantum communication networks and distribution systems for quantum keys requires very advanced hardware and infrastructure. Among these parts are channels for quantum communication, quantum memory, and quantum repeaters. Additional difficulty arises from the need to safeguard quantum cryptography systems from any possible assaults. Potential side-channel attacks, implementation errors, or technological limitations might derail quantum cryptography's practical use (Hilal et al., 2022). Despite quantum cryptography's potential to provide unfettered security based on physical principles, this remains the case. The development of stringent security analysis procedures and the construction of protocols resistant to the dangers now experienced are crucial for the success of quantum cryptography in real-world applications. The field of quantum cryptography and security is an exciting new development in the history of computer security. It may completely alter how we secure information and communication in the era of quantum computing. With the promise of truly random number generation and unbreakable encryption algorithms, quantum cryptography offers a new level of security for our ever-more-connected world. The force of quantum physics is used to do this. As this intriguing field of study keeps progressing, the future possibilities for quantum cryptography and security applications are practically limitless.

4.4 QUANTUM MACHINE LEARNING AND ARTIFICIAL INTELLIGENCE

A fascinating intersection of two cutting-edge technologies, quantum machine learning (QML) and artificial intelligence (AI) may completely alter how we solve issues and make choices. Due to the limitations imposed by computer resources, classical machine learning algorithms, despite their strength, struggle to handle complex problems and large datasets. However, quantum machine learning applies the principles of quantum physics to boost computer efficiency and tackle problems that classical machine learning algorithms have failed to tackle. An important benefit of quantum machine learning is its ability to leverage entanglement and quantum parallelism for more efficient data processing and analysis. Quantum computers are able to do extremely large-scale computations through the use of superposition. Thanks to this method, quantum computers may look at several possible solutions at once. This is why quantum machine learning algorithms outperform their classical counterparts when it comes to processing large datasets and optimising complex functions.

Classification, regression, clustering, and dimensionality reduction are just a few examples of the numerous possible applications of quantum machine learning techniques. Examples of quantum systems that have shown promise in solving classification and pattern recognition problems efficiently and accurately include quantum neural networks (QNNs) and quantum support vector machines (QSVMs). To further improve the analysis and interpretation of high-dimensional data, quantum methods like quantum k-means clustering and quantum principal component analysis (PCA) can be employed. In addition to improving processing efficiency, quantum machine learning opens up new avenues for solving problems with a fundamentally quantum character. Quantum machine learning techniques have a wide range of potential uses, including quantum system analysis, quantum dynamics modelling, and quantum circuit optimisation. Areas where conventional classical methods are often limited by the enormous computational complexity, such as quantum chemistry, quantum physics, and quantum information science (Travis, 2018), might benefit from these abilities. Contrarily, AI is a broader field that deals with the development of smart machines capable of doing tasks that often need human intelligence. By improving the speed and accuracy of data processing and analysis, quantum machine learning can significantly broaden the capabilities of AI systems. There are several AI applications where traditional machine learning algorithms have been successful; however, quantum machine learning may be much more effective. Figure 4.2 illustrates the general applications of quantum computing and AI.

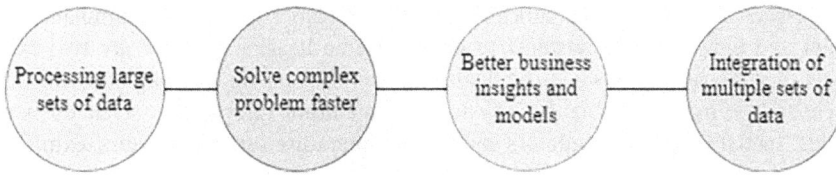

FIGURE 4.2 Applications of quantum computing and AI.

Within the realm of artificial intelligence, quantum machine learning and AI hold great promise for revolutionising the development of autonomous systems and intelligent agents. Intelligent systems like as self-driving vehicles, robots, and others may be taught and fine-tuned with the help of quantum machine learning techniques. By leveraging quantum parallelism and entanglement, these systems can make faster and more informed decisions, leading to improved performance and reliability. Quantum machine learning and AI also have implications for sectors like healthcare, finance, and cybersecurity that rely on the evaluation of large datasets and the formulation of conclusions. Data pattern and anomaly detection, financial portfolio optimisation, medical treatment customisation, and security standard upgrading are just a few of the many potential uses for quantum machine learning algorithms.

Quantum machine learning and artificial intelligence have a lot of promise, but there are a lot of problems that require fixing before they can be employed widely. Hardware constraints, like as noise and decoherence, might limit the scalability and performance of quantum algorithms. A thorough understanding of quantum mechanics and computational complexity theory is required to build efficient algorithms for quantum machine learning. Another significant area of study is algorithm design. AI and quantum machine learning represent a fascinating new area of study in computer science. These two domains may dramatically alter how many different industries approach and complete problem-solving and decision-making tasks. New capabilities in these areas allow for more efficient data processing and analysis, which in turn improves the performance and reliability of AI systems. Applying the principles of quantum physics enables these possibilities. Since research and development in this intriguing field is progressing at a rapid speed, the future possibilities for applications of quantum machine learning and artificial intelligence are practically endless.

4.5 QUANTUM SIMULATION AND MODELLING

Quantum simulation and modelling provide a state-of-the-art way to study and understand complex quantum systems, which are hard to reproduce with traditional computers. Behaviours like entanglement and superposition, shown by systems governed by quantum physics, are thought to be fundamentally non-classical and often provide a barrier to intuitive understanding. Traditional methods of simulating quantum systems are severely limited by the current state of computing power; as the system's dimensions and complexity increase, these methods quickly become unworkable. By making use of quantum computers, which are more efficient and accurate than traditional computers, quantum simulation offers a solution to this problem. In order to mimic the actions of certain quantum systems, scientists have developed quantum simulators. This provides a controlled environment in which researchers may study the characteristics and behaviour of the systems under question. These simulators can be implemented on several physical platforms, each with its own advantages and disadvantages; for example, trapped ions, superconducting qubits, or cold atoms.

One of the main benefits of quantum simulation is that it can simulate quantum systems with exponentially large state spaces using a polynomial number of qubits. Complex quantum phenomena, which classical computers struggle or fail to reproduce, may now be studied. These include quantum phase transitions, quantum magnetism, and quantum many-body dynamics. Researchers are now able to investigate these occurrences because to this exponential speedup. The study of fundamental issues in quantum mechanics is another application of quantum simulators. Quantum entanglement and how quantum systems react to extreme heat or pressure are two examples of such subjects. A wide variety of scientific fields can reap the benefits of using quantum simulation, including chemistry, materials science, physics, and quantum information science. Exotic quantum materials, such topological insulators and high-temperature superconductors, exhibit emergent behaviours that cannot be observed in conventional systems; physics researchers can study their behaviour using quantum simulators. The use of quantum simulators in chemistry allows for the modelling of molecular and chemical process behaviour, which in turn can provide insights into the development of new materials and medicines. The materials science community may use quantum simulators to learn more about emerging materials like quantum spin liquids and quantum Hall states, which could be useful in quantum computers, photonics, and electronics.

Quantum modelling, which makes use of mathematical models and computational tools, offers a broader perspective on comprehending and predicting the behaviour of quantum systems. This is on top of the fact that some quantum systems can be simulated via quantum modelling. Mathematical formalisms that capture the essence of a system's physics are known as quantum models. Wave functions, density matrices and Hamiltonians are all part of these formalisations (Ferenc et al., 2022). The behaviour of quantum systems may be described using quantum models. By utilising computer tools like numerical methods, quantum Monte Carlo simulations, and tensor network approaches, these models may be examined with the aim of forecasting the properties and dynamics of quantum systems. Modelling and simulation at the quantum level may enable hitherto unimagined technological advancements and profoundly alter our perspective on the natural world. This may have far-reaching consequences for our capacity to understand the environment. The foundational concepts of quantum physics may be better understood by quantum modelling and simulation, which in turn facilitates progress in fields like quantum sensing, quantum computing, and quantum communication. New research and development opportunities are presented by these approaches, which also give a powerful tool for studying and manipulating quantum systems. Since research and development in this intriguing field is always progressing, the future possibilities for applications of quantum modelling and simulation are practically limitless.

4.6   QUANTUM CHEMISTRY AND MATERIAL SCIENCE APPLICATIONS

Quantum chemistry and materials science are two crucial areas that stand to benefit greatly from the groundbreaking discoveries made possible by quantum computing. The fields in question are of paramount importance. At the most fundamental level, the laws of quantum mechanics control the actions of individual atoms and molecules and the properties of materials. Traditional computational methods for simulating quantum systems, like density functional theory (DFT) and quantum Monte Carlo methods, often fail to accurately predict the properties and behaviour of complex molecules and materials because of the exponential scaling of computational resources that is required.

A new method in quantum physics and materials research is quantum computing. To do this, it employs the principles of quantum physics to describe and simulate quantum systems with unprecedented efficiency and accuracy. Because of their ability to do massively parallel computations and make use of quantum entanglement and parallelism, quantum computers hold great promise for breaking new ground in computer science by allowing the modelling of previously intractable complex quantum systems. Modelling chemical processes and the structures contained inside molecules is one of the most important applications of quantum computing in the area of quantum chemistry. The computational modelling capabilities of quantum computers allow for the accurate description of molecular electronic structures and the prediction of properties like bond energies, molecular geometries, and reaction rates. New drugs, materials, and chemical processes cannot be created without the ability to understand the quantum behaviour of molecules and reactions.

A novel medication, material, or chemical process can be created with the use of this knowledge in the fields of drug discovery, catalyst design, and materials synthesis.

Using quantum computing, the area of materials science may be able to simulate materials' properties down to the atomic and molecular levels. The mechanical, electrical, and magnetic characteristics of the materials may be better understood in this way. Quantum computers can simulate the behaviour of materials in different environments, including those with different temperatures, pressures, and strains. Scientists may now design and refine materials to meet specific requirements for a wide range of uses. Improving technology and finding solutions to global problems depend on the development of novel materials with tailored properties. Because of the critical need for novel materials with specialised features in fields including electronics, photonics, energy storage, and quantum information science, this has implications for these areas (Subbiah et al., 2024). It is possible to describe and optimise quantum algorithms and circuits using quantum computers, which has implications for quantum chemistry, materials science, and quantum computing. Applications can also be found in fields like as material science and quantum chemistry. The development of quantum algorithms to tackle complex issues in fields such as chemistry and materials science, among others, and the enhancement of quantum hardware and software performance are both affected by this.

While there is much promise in its applications in quantum chemistry and materials science, there are also many challenges that must be overcome before widespread use can occur. Hardware constraints, like as noise and decoherence, might limit the scalability and performance of quantum algorithms. Furthermore, algorithm design is a significant area of study since creating efficient quantum algorithms for specific problems in materials science and chemistry requires a thorough understanding of computational complexity theory and quantum mechanics. Quantum computing has the ability to transform quantum chemistry and material science by facilitating the modelling and simulation of intricate quantum systems with hitherto unseen levels of efficiency and accuracy. The reason behind this is because quantum computing makes it possible to model and simulate quantum systems. Research and development in this intriguing field is constantly progressing (Casper et al., 2019), which means that the future applications of quantum chemistry and material science might be almost endless. Researchers in the fields of medicine, materials science, and technology stand to benefit greatly from the advent of quantum computing. Potentially far-reaching social and economic effects may result from these innovations. The powerful capabilities for comprehending and manipulating quantum systems are provided by quantum computing.

4.7 QUANTUM COMMUNICATION AND NETWORKING

An emerging area at the intersection of information theory and quantum physics is quantum communication and networking. It has the ability to provide robust, fast, and secure communication protocols that are impervious to hacking and eavesdropping. Due to their reliance on antiquated information processing methods, legacy communication systems are facing security and capacity issues in the face of emerging technologies like the Internet of Things (IoT), cloud computing, and 5G networks. The use of quantum physics principles like entanglement and superposition in quantum communication creates a radically different method of information conveyance compared to classical communication systems. Quark communication protocols allow for the safe conveyance of quantum information across large distances and the secure exchange of cryptographic keys (Neha et al., 2021). Protocols such as quantum teleportation and quantum key distribution are examples of this type. The distribution of quantum keys is a crucial use case for quantum communication. By utilising this feature, it becomes feasible for two individuals to securely trade cryptographic keys in order to encrypt and decode digital communications. Based on the principles of quantum mechanics, quantum key distribution offers unconditional security. Contrast this with more conventional forms of encryption that rely on the computational challenges of solving mathematical issues. The instantaneous detection of any attempt to intercept or manipulate the transmission is guaranteed

TABLE 4.2

Outlining Some Key Aspects of Quantum Communication and Networking

Aspect	Description
Definition	Quantum communication and networking involves the transmission and processing of information encoded in quantum states, utilising the principles of quantum mechanics for secure and efficient communication and networking tasks.
Quantum Key Distribution	QKD protocols enable the secure exchange of cryptographic keys between distant parties by leveraging quantum properties such as superposition and entanglement. Common QKD protocols include BB84, E91, and EPR-based schemes.
Quantum Cryptography	Quantum cryptography involves using quantum principles to develop cryptographic protocols that are inherently secure against eavesdropping attacks. Examples include quantum key distribution, quantum coin flipping, and quantum digital signatures.
Quantum Teleportation	Quantum teleportation allows the transfer of quantum information from one location to another, without physically transmitting the quantum state itself. This process relies on entanglement and classical communication to reconstruct the quantum state at the destination.
Quantum Networks	Quantum networks connect multiple quantum devices and enable the distribution of quantum information over long distances. These networks often incorporate quantum repeaters, quantum memories, and entanglement swapping techniques to extend the range of quantum communication.
Quantum Internet	The concept of a quantum internet envisions a global network infrastructure that facilitates secure and efficient quantum communication and networking tasks. It aims to connect quantum computers, quantum sensors, and other quantum devices for various applications.
Applications	Quantum communication and networking have applications in secure communication, quantum key distribution, quantum teleportation, distributed quantum computing, quantum sensor networks, and quantum-enhanced classical communication protocols.
Challenges	Challenges in quantum communication and networking include the development of practical and scalable quantum repeaters, overcoming noise and decoherence effects, achieving long-distance entanglement distribution, and integrating quantum and classical communication protocols.

by quantum key distribution techniques. In order to do this, data is encoded in quantum states and efforts to eavesdrop on the discussion are detected. Table 4.2 provides an overview of some of the key aspects, applications, and challenges associated with quantum communication and networking.

Another major use of quantum communication is quantum teleportation. With this technique, it is no longer necessary to physically transport quantum data in order to transmit it between different locations. The phenomenon of quantum entanglement is fundamental to quantum teleportation. This happens when two particles become correlated to the point that their states are instantly affected by one other's states, irrespective of their physical distance from each other. This happens when two particles form a correlation. This paves the way for the conveyance of quantum information across enormous distances with absolute precision, which is ideal for quantum computing and quantum networking, among other uses. Secure communication is only one area where quantum communication and networking have applications; they also have implications for quantum sensing, quantum computation, and quantum metrology. Distributed quantum computing and data processing are now within reach, thanks to quantum networks that link several quantum devices and systems. This is something that would have been impossible with standalone quantum devices. Due to their reliance on precise manipulation and measurement of quantum states, quantum metrology techniques and quantum sensors stand to gain from the low-latency, high-speed communication enabled by quantum networks.

Quantum communication and networking have immense promise, they must first overcome many challenges before they can be extensively used. Reliable and scalable quantum memory and quantum repeaters are two examples of hardware constraints that could reduce the performance of quantum communication protocols. The protocols' range and speed can be constrained by these constraints as well. The lack of established protocols and interfaces for quantum communication is one example of how concerns about interoperability and standardisation might slow down the creation and rollout of quantum networks. The realm of information technology may look forward to exciting developments in quantum networking and communication. The fields of sensing, computation, and communication stand to benefit greatly from these innovations. Protocols for quantum communication have the potential for hack-and eavesdrop-proof, ultra-fast communication lines (Roman et al., 2022). By tapping into the strength of quantum mechanics, these protocols may make use of quantum physics. The interesting field of quantum communication and networking is seeing ongoing study and development, which means that its future possibilities are almost limitless.

4.8 QUANTUM SENSING AND METROLOGY

Located at the crossroads of quantum physics and precision measurement, the cutting-edge area of quantum sensing and metrology holds the promise of highly precise and sensitive sensors that are capable of detecting and measuring physical quantities with an unparalleled level of accuracy. When it comes to sensitivity, resolution, and speed, traditional sensing and metrology approaches, which are based on the laws of classical physics, have limitations. This is especially true when considering upcoming technologies such as quantum computing, nanotechnology, and medical imaging.

In order to achieve a very high level of accuracy in the measurement of physical variables, quantum sensing makes use of the fundamental concepts of quantum physics, such as entanglement and superposition. The benefits that quantum sensors, which are based on quantum systems like atoms, ions, and photons, offer include high sensitivity, low noise, and tolerance to external disturbances. Quantum sensors are constructed using quantum systems. The usage of these sensors allows for the detection of a broad variety of physical characteristics, including as magnetic fields, electric fields, gravitational fields, and chemical concentrations. These sensors have applications in a variety of domains, including geophysics, environmental monitoring, medical imaging, and quantum information science. Quantum sensing has a number of important applications, one of which is the measuring of magnetic fields using atomic magnetometers. Atomic magnetometers, which are used to detect magnetic fields by using the quantum features of atoms, have a number of benefits, including high sensitivity, broad bandwidth, and compact size. These advantages make them excellent for applications such as magnetic resonance imaging (MRI), biomagnetic sensing, and geophysical exploration. The detection of other physical characteristics, such as electric fields, gravitational fields, and temperature, may also be accomplished with the help of quantum sensors, which are characterised by their great resolution and precision. Table 4.3 provides an overview of various applications of quantum sensing and metrology, highlighting how quantum principles are utilised to achieve unprecedented levels of sensitivity and accuracy in measurement and sensing technologies.

Quantum metrology, on the other hand, is concerned with the development of techniques for precise measurement that are founded on the principles of quantum mechanics. The techniques of quantum metrology, such as quantum-enhanced interferometry and quantum-limited sensing, make it possible to take measurements with a precision and resolution that has never been seen before. These approaches overcome the limitations that are imposed by traditional measuring methods. There are a broad variety of physical values that may be measured with the use of these techniques. Some of these quantities include time, frequency, length, and phase. These techniques have applications in domains such as metrology, navigation, and basic physics research. In addition to their applications in precise measurement, quantum sensing and metrology have implications for other domains such as quantum computing, quantum communication, and quantum simulation (Lloyd, 2022). These topics are all related to quantum computing. The calibration and characterisation

TABLE 4.3

An Overview of Various Applications of Quantum Sensing and Metrology

Application	Description
Quantum Magnetometry	Utilises the quantum properties of atomic spins to measure magnetic fields with unprecedented sensitivity.
Quantum Clocks	Quantum clocks utilise the quantum properties of atoms or ions to measure time with incredible precision, surpassing the accuracy of traditional atomic clocks.
Quantum Imaging	Quantum imaging techniques leverage quantum phenomena such as entanglement and superposition to enhance the resolution and sensitivity of imaging systems.
Quantum Gyroscopes	Quantum gyroscopes exploit the quantum mechanical properties of particles to measure rotation rates with high accuracy, enabling precise navigation and stabilisation systems.
Quantum Thermometry	Quantum thermometry uses quantum systems to measure temperature with exceptional sensitivity and accuracy, allowing for precise temperature monitoring in various applications.
Quantum Gravimeters	Quantum gravimeters utilise quantum principles to measure gravitational acceleration with extreme precision, enabling applications such as underground mapping and geophysics.
Quantum Spectroscopy	Quantum spectroscopy techniques employ quantum systems to analyse the interaction of matter and electromagnetic radiation, providing high-resolution spectral information.

of quantum devices and systems may be accomplished through the use of quantum sensors and metrology techniques. This paves the way for the creation of quantum technologies that are more dependable and precise. In the field of quantum error correction and fault-tolerant quantum computing, where accurate measurement and control of quantum states are crucial for the construction of scalable and fault-tolerant quantum computers, quantum-enhanced sensing and metrology also play an important role.

Quantum sensing and metrology, despite the fact that they hold a great deal of potential, are confronted with a number of obstacles that need to be conquered before they can be widely used. Hardware restrictions, such as the requirement for quantum sensors and metrology techniques that are dependable and scalable, have the potential to reduce the performance of quantum measurement systems and restrict the range of applications for which they may be used. A further factor that can have an impact on the accuracy and precision of quantum measurements is the presence of noise and decoherence, both of which are caused by interactions between quantum systems and their surroundings. Quantum sensing and metrology are representing a promising frontier in the science of precision measurement. They have the potential to revolutionise our capacity to detect and measure physical quantities with an accuracy and sensitivity that has never been seen before. Quantum sensors and metrology techniques offer new capabilities for applications such as medical imaging, environmental monitoring, and basic physics research. These capabilities are made possible by leveraging the power of quantum mechanics. The potential applications of quantum sensing and metrology in the future are virtually infinite, since research and development in this fascinating subject continues to advance at a rapid pace.

4.9 QUANTUM ERROR CORRECTION AND FAULT TOLERANCE

Quantum error correction and fault tolerance are two of the most crucial subfields of quantum computing. In order to make sure that quantum computers are reliable and precise, these areas of study are devoted to finding ways to overcome the inherent fragility of quantum information. Unlike traditional computers, which use error-correcting codes and redundant bits to prevent mistakes, quantum computers can be impacted by noise, decoherence, and other quantum phenomena, making them susceptible to errors. Quantum error correction (QEC) is a set of methods and approaches

TABLE 4.4

A Brief Overview of Quantum Error Correction and Fault Tolerance

Aspect	Description
Error Correction Codes	Quantum error correction codes are mathematical techniques used to detect and correct errors in qubits due to decoherence and noise. These codes redundantly encode quantum information across multiple qubits, allowing for the detection and correction of errors without directly measuring the state of the qubits. Common error correction codes include the Shor code, the Steane code, and the surface code.
Fault Tolerance	Fault tolerance in quantum computing refers to the ability of a quantum computer to maintain reliable operation despite the presence of errors and imperfections in hardware components. Fault-tolerant quantum computing relies on error correction codes, fault-tolerant quantum gates, and sophisticated error mitigation techniques to ensure the accuracy and robustness of quantum computations. Achieving fault tolerance is crucial for building practical quantum computers capable of performing complex calculations without being derailed by errors.

designed to detect and fix errors in quantum information, which is represented in quantum bits (qubits). For the purpose of ensuring that quantum information remains intact throughout time and preventing any errors from occurring, QEC protocols employ redundancy and entanglement. Notable QEC protocols include the Shor code, which can detect and fix errors caused by both single-qubit and two-qubit faults. In addition to detecting and fixing certain kinds of faults, it can also encode a single qubit into nine qubits. Table 4.4 provides a brief overview of quantum error correction and fault tolerance, highlighting the importance of error correction codes and fault-tolerant techniques in building reliable and scalable quantum computers.

Another important QEC protocol is the surface code. In order to find and fix errors, it uses measurements of stabiliser operators and encodes qubits on a two-dimensional lattice. When designing fault-tolerant quantum computing systems, the surface code is an excellent option due to its numerous advantages, such as its scalability and high fault tolerance. You may think of topological code and colour code as two alternate quantum error correcting methods. Each of these protocols provides an alternative to quantum error correction, but they all have different performance and complexity trade-offs. Conversely, fault tolerance refers to a quantum computer's ability to keep on delivering reliable and accurate outputs even when there are errors and malfunctions in its operation. Reliable and accurate computations may be performed by fault-tolerant quantum computing systems using a combination of quantum error correction, fault-tolerant gates, and error mitigation techniques. One of the most important concerns in fault-tolerant quantum computing is the expense of error correction and fault tolerance. Because of this overhead, running quantum algorithms could become much more complicated and resource intensive.

With the development of error-correcting codes, fault-tolerant architectures, and fault-tolerant gates, fault-tolerant quantum computing has achieved remarkable strides in the past few years. This is so even if it is confronted with several obstacles. Several intriguing methods exist for achieving scalable, high-performance, and fault-tolerant quantum computing. The topological code and the surface code are two examples of quantum computing designs that are fault tolerant. Using error mitigation measures, quantum computation may become more accurate and reliable even when mistakes are made. Methods like this encompass enhancing errors, fixing them, and even suppressing them. In addition to its uses in quantum computing, the ideas of quantum error correction and fault tolerance have consequences for many other areas, such as quantum sensing, quantum metrology, quantum communication, and many more. Quantum error correction methods might be used to keep quantum information intact when it's sent across large distances in quantum communication networks. Because of this, we can be certain that quantum communication protocols are safe and dependable. Quantum error correction and fault tolerance are especially important in quantum sensors and metrology devices, as these systems rely on precise measurement and control of quantum states to achieve high levels of sensitivity and precision. Reason being, quantum states are fundamental to quantum sensors and metrology equipment. Finally, two primary areas of research in quantum computing—fault tolerance and quantum error correction—are crucial. Overcoming the intrinsic fragility of quantum information and ensuring the reliable and precise operation of quantum computers are the primary goals of these research fields. Computing, communication, and sensing technologies stand to benefit greatly from the breakthroughs the researchers are doing towards fault-tolerant quantum processing. New methods and algorithms, in conjunction with the principles of quantum physics, are allowing this to happen. There is an almost infinite number of possible future uses for quantum error correction and fault tolerance as long as research and development in this intriguing field continues to improve.

4.10   FUTURE DIRECTIONS AND CHALLENGES IN QUANTUM COMPUTING

In order to make quantum computing a reality and make it scalable, researchers will have to clear a number of important hurdles. Many future initiatives will aim to achieve these things. Quantum computing has come a long way in the last several years, but it has a long way to go before it can realise its full promise. Some possible future directions and challenges in quantum computing are as follows: A major challenge in quantum computing is improving the fidelity and coherence of quantum bits while increasing the quantity of qubits. Commonly ranging from tens to hundreds, the number of qubits used by modern quantum computers is finite. There are too few qubits to solve the complex problems that arise in the actual world. Future studies will focus on developing quantum computer systems that can scale. Two designs that can sustain hundreds—if not millions—of qubits each are topological qubits and error-corrected qubits. Since quantum computers are so error and decoherence prone, quantum algorithms may not be as reliable or accurate, and their performance may suffer as a result. Two approaches that can mitigate these problems are fault tolerance and error correction. Building more efficient and robust error correction methods and fault-tolerant systems is the goal of future research in quantum error correction and fault tolerance. Reliable and efficient quantum computation will be possible with the help of these methods and structures, which will lessen the likelihood of errors.

Quantum Algorithms and Their Practical Uses: Constructing practical quantum algorithms is a major focus of quantum computing research. Algorithms like Shor's and Grover's have shown that they can achieve exponential speedups compared to traditional algorithms. Nevertheless, a substantial amount of effort remains in the quest to develop and enhance quantum algorithms for targeted uses. Cryptography, optimisation, machine learning, and materials science are only a few examples of these applications.

Quantum Hardware and Technology: In order to create scalable and fault-tolerant quantum computers, it is crucial to build quantum hardware, which includes qubit technologies, quantum gates, and quantum interconnects. Future research will mainly concentrate on creating new types of quantum bits (qubits) like topological qubits, trapped ions, and superconducting qubits. These types of qubits will have better coherence and fidelity and could be used in large-scale quantum computing systems.

Programming and Quantum Software: Researchers and developers must have access to programming languages and tools for quantum software so they may construct, test, and improve quantum algorithms and applications. The objective of future research in quantum software is to simplify the creation and deployment of quantum algorithms on quantum hardware by creating programming interfaces, debugging tools, and optimisation methodologies that are easy for users to understand and implement. In order to connect quantum computers and enable distributed quantum computation and data processing, technologies for quantum communication and networking are essential. The development of quantum networking and communication technologies is also crucial to the realisation of quantum computing. The objective of future research in quantum networking and communication is to create quantum repeaters, routers, and protocols that can securely and faithfully transport quantum information across long distances.

Establishing Standards and Benchmarks: In order to compare and contrast different quantum computing platforms and identify their strengths and weaknesses, it is crucial to establish standards and benchmarks for assessing the efficiency of quantum computers and algorithms. Future research efforts will mainly concentrate on creating standardised testing procedures, performance metrics, and benchmarking suites that allow for trustworthy comparisons of quantum computing technologies. Taken together, quantum computing's promising future holds immense promise for tackling intractable problems in a wide range of disciplines, including science, engineering, and more. Their work is laying the groundwork for quantum computing technologies that can be implemented on a large scale and are expected to transform the way information is processed, communicated, and computed in the coming years. By tackling important difficulties and pushing the discipline forward in these areas, researchers and developers are doing this.

4.11 CONCLUSION

To sum up, quantum computing is an exciting new area of research in computer science that may significantly impact many other industries. By using the principles of quantum physics, quantum computers offer an unprecedented degree of processing capacity, allowing them to tackle challenging tasks that were previously believed to be impossible for classical computers to handle. In this chapter, we have explored some of the extensive potential uses of quantum computing. A few examples of these fields of use are optimisation, cryptography, drug development, materials science, and machine learning. By using quantum phenomena like entanglement and superposition, quantum algorithms can accelerate computations in these areas, potentially resulting in significant advances in solving real-world problems. The chapter has also shed light on the current state of quantum computing by outlining developments in hardware, error correction, and algorithm design, among other areas. While quantum computing is in its early stages, significant advancements have been achieved in recent years, opening the door to further scientific breakthroughs and technological advancements. Quantum computing has the potential to revolutionise several industries, including cybersecurity, healthcare, banking, and more. The chapter has also explored these potential societal repercussions. Quantum computing has the ability to drive societal progress and change several areas as it matures. Providing a comprehensive understanding of the revolutionary possibilities of quantum computing applications is the overall objective of this chapter. Further research and innovation in this exciting and rapidly evolving field are laid out as well.

REFERENCES

Amirul, Asyraf Zhahir, Siti, Munirah Mohd, Mohd, Ilias Shuhud Bahari, Idrus, Hishamuddin Zainuddin, Nurhidaya, Mohamad Jan, Mohamed, Ridza Wahiddin. (2022). Quantum computing and its application. *International Journal of Advanced Research in Technology and Innovation*, doi: 10.55057/ijarti.2022.4.1.7

Andreas, Bayerstadler, Guillaume, Becquin, Julia, Binder, Thierry, Botter, Hans, Ehm, Thomas, Ehmer, Marvin, Erdmann, Norbert, Gaus, Philipp, Harbach, Maximilian, Hess, Johannes, Klepsch, Martin, Leib, Sebastian, Luber, Andre, Luckow, Maximilian, Mansky, Wolfgang, Mauerer, Florian, Neukart, Christoph, Niedermeier, Lilly, Palackal, Ruben, Pfeiffer, Carsten, Polenz, Johanna, Sepulveda, Tammo, Sievers, Brian, Standen, Michael, Streif, Thomas, Strohm, Clemens, Utschig-Utschig, Daniel, Volz, Horst, Weiss, Fabian, Winter. (2021). Industry quantum computing applications. *EPJ Quantum Technology*, doi: 10.1140/EPJQT/S40507-021-00114-X

Casper, van der Kerk, Attila, Csala, Aeilko, H. Zwinderman. (2019). Quantum computing in the biomedical sciences; A brief introduction into concepts and applications. *Computer and Information Science*, doi: 10.5539/CIS.V12N3P104

Divya, Baiskhiyar, Ravi, Kumar. (2019). Quantum computing-applications in bioinformatics. *International Journal of Computer Applications*, doi: 10.5120/IJCA2019919527

Ferenc, Ignacz, Daniel, Feszty, István, Lakatos. (2022). Possible applications of quantum computing, especially in vehicle technology: A review article. *Periodica Polytechnica Transportation Engineering*, doi: 10.3311/pptr.16547

Francesco, Bova, Avi, Goldfarb, Roger, G. Melko. (2021). Commercial applications of quantum computing. *EPJ Quantum Technology*, doi: 10.1140/EPJQT/S40507-021-00091-1

Hari, P. Paudel, Madhava, Syamlal, Scott, E. Crawford, Yueh-Lin, Lee, Roman, A. Shugayev, Ping, Lu, Paul, R. Ohodnicki, Darren, Mollot, Yuhua, Duan. (2022). Quantum computing and simulations for energy applications: Review and perspective. *ACS Engineering Au*, doi: 10.1021/acsengineeringau.1c00033

Lloyd, M. Taylor. (2022). Exploring potential applications of quantum computing in transportation modelling. *IEEE Transactions on Intelligent Transportation Systems*, doi: 10.1109/tits.2021.3132161

Martin, Ulmke, Felix, Govaers. (2023). Quantum computing for applications in data fusion. *IEEE Transactions on Aerospace and Electronic Systems*, doi: 10.1109/TAES.2022.3212026

Neha, Sharma, Ramkumar, Ketti Ramachandran. (2021). The emerging trends of quantum computing towards data security and key management. *Archives of Computational Methods in Engineering*, doi: 10.1007/S11831-021-09578-7

Rene, Steijl, Romit, Maulik. (2023). Editorial: Quantum computing applications in computational engineering. *Frontiers in Mechanical Engineering*, doi: 10.3389/fmech.2023.1237653

Roman, Rietsche, Christian, Dremel, Samuel, Bosch, Léa, Steinacker, Miriam, Meckel, Jan, Marco Leimeister. (2022). Quantum computing. *Electronic Markets*, doi: 10.1007/s12525-022-00570-y

Subbiah, P., Krishnaraj, N., Bellam, K. (2024). Quantum machine learning: Enhancing AI with quantum computing. In *Applications and Principles of Quantum Computing* (pp. 129–145). IGI Global.

Travis, S. Humble. (2018). Consumer applications of quantum computing: A promising approach for secure computation, trusted data storage, and efficient applications. *IEEE Consumer Electronics Magazine*, doi: 10.1109/MCE.2017.2755298

5 Quantum Computing
Necessary Applications for Future

*Kali Charan Rath, Emmanuel Philip Ododo,
Niranjanamurthy M., Chitta Ranjan Deo,
and Biswadip Basu Mallik*

5.1 INTRODUCTION

Quantum computing, at the forefront of scientific discovery, presents a groundbreaking approach to computation, diverging significantly from classical methods. The unique characteristic enables quantum computers to achieve exponential leaps in processing power and efficiency, distinguishing them from conventional computing paradigms (Aithal 2023; Ten Holter et al. 2023). Comparing quantum computing with classical computing unveils a stark contrast in their underlying principles and capabilities. While classical computers manipulate bits sequentially, quantum computers leverage quantum phenomena to process information in parallel, leading to a quantum advantage in solving certain classes of problems. Classical algorithms follow deterministic logic, executing instructions step by step, whereas quantum algorithms exploit quantum parallelism to explore multiple solutions simultaneously, fundamentally altering the computational landscape (Riel 2021; Agarwal and Mohanta 2023).

Quantum computing stands at the forefront of technological innovation, offering unprecedented capabilities to address complex challenges that surpass classical systems' limitations. By excelling in optimization, cryptography, and simulation tasks, quantum computers pose a significant disruption to conventional computing methods. For instance, algorithms like Shor's algorithm promise exponential speed-ups in factoring large numbers, threatening established cryptographic standards and revolutionizing data security. Moreover, quantum computing holds immense potential in advancing fields such as drug discovery, material science, and machine learning by efficiently exploring vast solution spaces (Möller and Vuik 2017; Lu et al. 2023; Brijwani et al. 2023). This paradigm shift in computation not only accelerates scientific discoveries but also unlocks novel insights into complex phenomena, promising a future where the unimaginable becomes achievable.

5.2 FUNDAMENTALS OF QUANTUM COMPUTING

Quantum computing revolutionizes information processing by leveraging quantum mechanics (Agarwal and Alam 2021; Vedha Priyavadhana et al. 2023). Unlike classical computers, which rely on bits, quantum computers utilize qubits, capable of existing in superposition, simultaneously representing 0 and 1. Moreover, qubits can be entangled, allowing quantum computers to perform computations exponentially faster than classical ones, thanks to their unique properties.

Mathematical Model:

Let's consider a simple mathematical model to represent a quantum state with two qubits.

Suppose we have two qubits denoted by $|q_0\rangle$ and $|q_1\rangle$. These qubits can be described as a mix of basic states using linear combinations, as:

$$|\psi\rangle = \alpha|00\rangle + \beta|01\rangle + \gamma|10\rangle + \delta|11\rangle$$

DOI: 10.1201/9781003499459-5

where α, β, γ, and δ are complex numbers representing probability amplitudes, and $|00, |01, |10,$ $\delta |11$ are the basis states representing the possible combinations of classical bits. Thus, $|\alpha|^2$, $|\beta|^2$, $|\gamma|^2$, and $|\delta|^2$ represent the probabilities of measuring the states, $|00\rangle$, $|01$, $\gamma |10$, $\delta |11$ respectively, and they sum up to 1.

Quantum maneuvers are conducted via quantum gates, mirroring the functionality of classical logic gates. As an illustration, the Hadamard gate (H) is commonly applied to generate states of superposition.

$$H |0\rangle = \frac{1}{\sqrt{2}}(|0\rangle + |1\rangle)$$

$$H |1\rangle = \frac{1}{\sqrt{2}} = (|0\rangle - |1\rangle)$$

Quantum algorithms surpass classical ones by exploiting superposition, entanglement and sequential gate application to solve specific problems more efficiently.

5.2.1 Quantum Algorithms and Computational Advantage

Quantum algorithms harness the power of quantum mechanics for computing, using qubits instead of binary bits (Butey and Upasani 2024; Coccia 2022). Quantum computing unlocks exponential speedups through superposition and entanglement, with algorithms like Shor's and Grover's poised to transform cryptography and optimization, while research advances promise revolutionary applications in machine learning and materials science.

The following are a few points elucidating quantum algorithms and their computational advantages, supplemented with application-oriented examples:

a) **Quantum Superposition:** The power of superposition allows qubits to exist in multiple states at the same time. This ability opens the way for parallel computation, which leads to faster problem-solving when compared to classical algorithms (Michelini and Stefanel 2023; Pris 2022).
   Example: Shor's integer is a pivotal tool in encryption because of its exponential efficiency in breaking down large numbers. The ability to unwrap huge numbers exponentially faster than classical techniques is demonstrated by this algorithm.

b) **Entanglement:** Quantum algorithms exploit entanglement's unique linkages between qubits to revolutionize computational capabilities.
   Example: Quantum teleportation: revolutionizing communication with instant transmission of quantum data, promising unmatched efficiency and security in technological innovation.

c) **Quantum Parallelism:** Quantum algorithms can perform operations on all possible inputs simultaneously, leading to exponential speedup for certain tasks (Kishore and Raina 2019; Holbrook 2023).
   Example: Grover's groundbreaking algorithm revolutionizes search capabilities within unsorted databases, boasting a remarkable quadratic speed enhancement over classical counterparts. Its profound impact spans across optimization realms and the domain of database searches, unlocking unprecedented efficiency and efficacy in solving complex computational problems.

d) **Interference:** Quantum algorithms exploit interference patterns to amplify the probability of obtaining correct solutions and suppress incorrect ones.

Example: Quantum phase estimation, used in quantum chemistry simulations, can efficiently calculate molecular energies and properties with high precision.

e) **Quantum Fourier Transform:** Quantum algorithms employ the quantum Fourier transform to efficiently perform tasks such as period finding and signal processing.

Example: The HHL is a game-changer algorithm for solving linear equations, boasting exponential speed compared to traditional methods. Its significance spans optimization and machine learning, ushering in a new era of computational prowess and innovation.

f) **Quantum Oracles:** Quantum algorithms can utilize quantum oracles, black-box functions that evaluate inputs, to speed up certain computational tasks.

Example: Simon's algorithm tackles the tough Simon's problem in cryptography. It creates super tough security against quantum-powered adversaries, making our digital secrets safe.

g) **Error Correction:** Quantum algorithms employ error correction techniques to mitigate errors arising from noise and decoherence, ensuring reliable computation.

Example: Quantum error correction, including the surface code, is crucial for fault-tolerant quantum computing, ensuring robust quantum algorithms.

h) **Adiabatic Quantum Computing:** Quantum algorithms can leverage adiabatic quantum computing, which gradually transforms the system from the initial state to the solution state, to solve optimization problems efficiently (Werner et al. 2023).

Example: D-Wave's quantum annealing devices utilize adiabatic quantum computing to solve optimization problems in various domains, including finance, logistics, and machine learning.

i) **Quantum Mechanics And Machine Learning:** In the exciting realm of quantum machine learning, quantum algorithms are revolutionizing traditional machine learning tasks, leveraging quantum principles to boost efficiency and capabilities.

Example: QSVM and QNN are new quantum machine learning methods poised for applications in data classification, pattern recognition, and optimization.

j) **Quantum Simulation:** Quantum algorithms empower researchers to simulate intricate quantum systems, unlocking avenues to explore complex phenomena in materials science, quantum chemistry, and condensed matter physics.

Example: Variational quantum eigensolver (VQE) is used to simulate molecular structures and properties, aiding drug discovery and materials design.

TABLE 5.1
Concepts vs Power

Sl. No.	Concept	Power
1	Quantum Superposition	0.85
2	Entanglement	0.92
3	Quantum Parallelism	0.88
4	Interference	0.87
5	Quantum Fourier Transform	0.89
6	Quantum Oracles	0.91
7	Error Correction	0.93
8	Adiabatic Quantum Computing	0.86
9	Quantum Mechanics and Machine Learning	0.9
10	Quantum Simulation	0.94

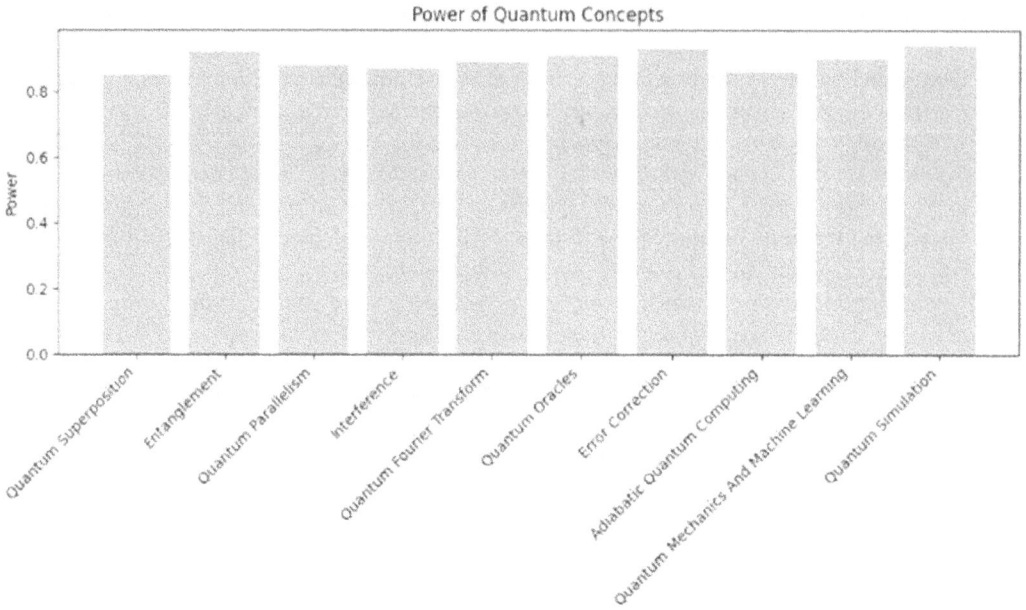

FIGURE 5.1 Power of quantum concepts.

The preceding points vividly demonstrate the computational benefits and practical applications of quantum algorithms, underscoring their capacity to transform numerous domains through expedited and streamlined computation.

5.3 CURRENT STATE OF QUANTUM COMPUTING TECHNOLOGY

In recent years, there's been a remarkable surge in quantum computing advancements. Leading the charge are tech giants like Microsoft, IBM, and Google are blazing trails in this cutting-edge field. They've been relentlessly pushing boundaries, achieving notable breakthroughs in the development of quantum processors (Mustafa 2023). These processors boast higher qubit counts and enhanced coherence times, marking significant milestones in the quest for quantum supremacy.

Microsoft's Topological Qubits:

> Microsoft pioneers quantum computing with topological qubits and Majorana particles via Station Q, leveraging superconductors for stability and error protection, promising scalable, fault-tolerant systems.

Google's Quantum Supremacy:

> Google's Sycamore processor achieved quantum supremacy in 2019, demonstrating its ability to outperform classical supercomputers in complex calculations.

> **IBM Quantum Program:** IBM Quantum program advances quantum computing with cloud-based access to processors, fostering global experimentation. Their Q System One boasts 65 qubits, paving the way for complex computations and practical applications.

> **D-Wave Systems' Quantum Annealing:** D-Wave Systems leads in quantum annealing, using superconducting qubits for faster optimization in finance, drug discovery, and logistics.

Rigetti Computing's Hybrid Quantum-Classical Approach:

> Rigetti Computing's Quantum Cloud Services platform merges classical and quantum resources for efficient hybrid quantum algorithm implementation.

TABLE 5.2

Comparison of Quantum Computing Technologies

Sl. No.	Technology	Qubits	Error Rate
1	Microsoft's Topological Qubits	50	0.001
2	Google's Quantum Supremacy	53	0.0001
3	IBM Quantum Program	65	0.00001
4	D-Wave Systems' Quantum Annealing	2000	0.01
5	Rigetti Computing's Hybrid Quantum-Classical Approach	40	0.0005
6	IonQ's Trapped-Ion Quantum Processors	100	0.00005

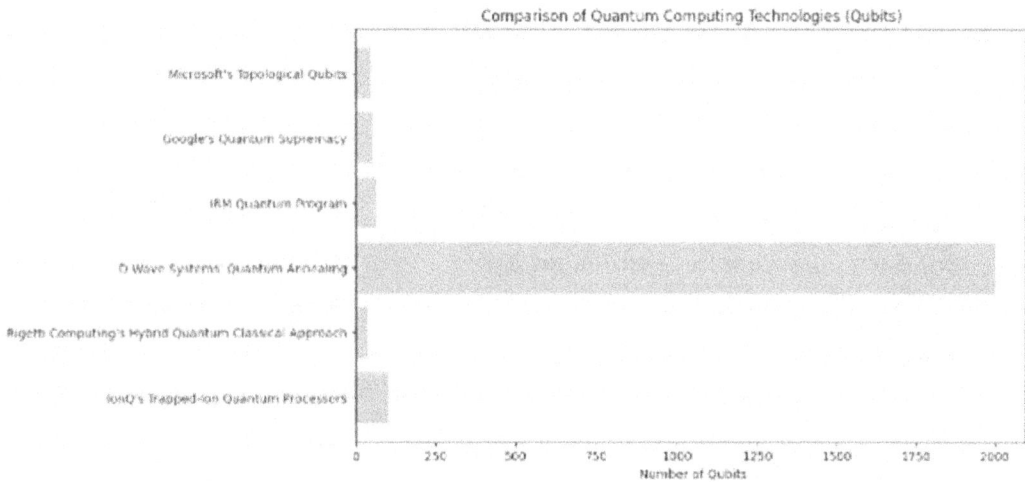

FIGURE 5.2 Comparison of quantum computing technologies (qubits).

IonQ's Trapped-Ion Quantum Processors: IonQ: Leading trapped-ion quantum computing for scalable, high-fidelity quantum processors.

These examples, Table 5.2, Figure 5.2 and Figure 5.3, showcase the diverse approaches and technologies being pursued by different companies in the field of quantum computing. Each company brings its unique strengths and innovations in the quantum area.

5.3.1 PRACTICAL IMPLEMENTATIONS OF QUANTUM COMPUTING IN REAL-WORLD SCENARIOS

Despite being in the early stages of development, quantum computing is already finding applications in various fields. A few are briefly described in the following.

a) **Cryptography:** The rise of quantum computing prompts the urgent shift to post-quantum cryptography, essential for safeguarding data against impending threats to traditional encryption methods like RSA and ECC.

Example: In the financial sector, safeguarding sensitive data like credit card details and banking transactions is crucial. Traditional encryption methods are at risk from quantum computing, threatening data integrity. Transitioning to quantum-resistant cryptography

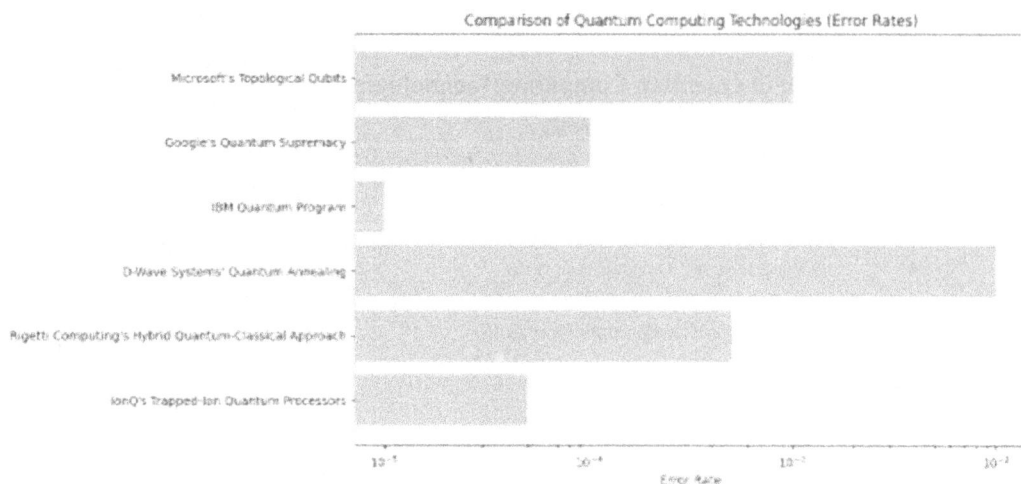

Comparison of Quantum Computing Technologies (Error Rates)

FIGURE 5.3   Comparison of quantum computing technologies (error rates).

ensures long-term security and trust among stakeholders. This adaptation exemplifies real-world application of advanced technology in securing financial transactions.

Case Study: Quantum Key Distribution (QKD)

SwissQuantum, a collaboration between the Swiss government and private partners, is implementing quantum key distribution to enhance communication security for government agencies. Unlike traditional methods, QKD utilizes quantum mechanics principles, ensuring keys are secure against interception by potential adversaries, including those with quantum computers. This adoption underscores QKD's efficacy in fortifying governmental communication security against emerging quantum threats.

b) **Drug Discovery:**

Quantum computing is revolutionizing drug discovery by swiftly analyzing molecular structures and interactions, speeding up the search for new drugs. This breakthrough allows researchers to identify potential candidates faster, accelerating therapeutic innovation.

i) **Molecular Docking and Drug Design:** Traditional drug discovery involves screening large databases of molecules to identify potential candidates for new medications. One crucial step in this process is molecular docking, where the interaction between a drug molecule and its target protein is simulated to predict binding affinity and efficacy.

Example: Quantum computing accelerates molecular docking simulations, enhancing drug-protein interaction predictions for more efficient drug design.

ii) **Drug Repurposing and Side Effect Prediction:** Another challenge in drug discovery is identifying existing drugs that can be repurposed for new therapeutic applications. Additionally, predicting potential side effects of candidate drugs is crucial to ensure their safety and efficacy in clinical trials.

Example: Quantum computing enhances drug discovery by simulating molecular interactions for precise drug efficacy predictions, aiding Alzheimer's treatment research.

Case Study: Protein Folding Simulation

1QBit and a major pharmaceutical conglomerate are teaming up to combine quantum computing with biomedical knowledge, aiming to decode protein folding dynamics. This innovative collaboration promises to revolutionize drug discovery and personalized medicine, potentially offering tailored treatments and reducing side effects.

c) **Materials Science:** In materials science, quantum computing holds promise for designing advanced materials with tailored properties for various applications.

   i) **Semiconductor Design and Optimization:** Materials scientists strive to develop novel semiconductor materials with enhanced electronic properties for applications in electronics and photonics. Designing these materials requires a deep understanding of their atomic and electronic structures.

       Example: Quantum computing optimizes semiconductor materials, enhancing transistor and optoelectronic device efficiency through precise bandgap tuning.

   ii) **Catalyst Design for Sustainable Chemistry:** Catalysts play a crucial role in facilitating chemical reactions in various industrial processes, including petroleum refining and pharmaceutical synthesis. Designing efficient catalysts with tailored properties is essential for improving reaction rates and selectivity while minimizing energy consumption and environmental impact.

       Example: Quantum computing aids in designing superior catalysts by simulating atomic-scale reactions, enhancing efficiency and sustainability in chemical processes.

d) **Financial Modeling and Optimization:** Quantum algorithms can optimize complex financial tasks such as portfolio management and risk analysis.

   Case Study: Portfolio Optimization

   Goldman Sachs utilized quantum computing to optimize its investment portfolios, balancing risk and return more effectively than classical methods. By leveraging quantum algorithms for portfolio optimization, Goldman Sachs gained a competitive edge in the financial markets, delivering superior returns to its clients.

e) **Supply Chain Management:** Quantum computing stands poised to revolutionize logistics through its capacity to optimize intricate processes such as supply chain routing and inventory management.

   Case Study: Quantum-Assisted Logistics

   DHL collaborated with a quantum computing startup to optimize its global logistics network. By leveraging quantum algorithms to solve complex routing and scheduling problems, DHL reduced transportation costs and improved delivery times, enhancing customer satisfaction and operational efficiency.

f) **Artificial Intelligence and Machine Learning:**

   Quantum computing revolutionizes machine learning with unparalleled computational power and speed, unlocking transformative potential across industries and scientific realms, propelling humanity into a limitless era of innovation.

   Case Study: Quantum Machine Learning

   Google Research developed quantum machine learning algorithms to improve recommendation systems and natural language processing tasks. By harnessing the power of quantum computing, Google achieved breakthroughs in speech recognition accuracy and personalized recommendations, enhancing user experiences across its platforms.

g) **Energy Optimization and Renewable Resources:** Quantum computing can optimize energy distribution, grid management, and the design of renewable energy systems.

   Case Study: Smart Grid Optimization

   Siemens collaborated with researchers to develop quantum algorithms for optimizing energy distribution in smart grids. By dynamically adjusting energy flows based on real-time data, Siemens improved grid stability, reduced energy losses, and integrated renewable energy sources more effectively, contributing to a sustainable energy future.

h) **Climate Modeling and Environmental Simulation:** Quantum computing can simulate complex climate models and environmental processes with high accuracy.

Case Study: Climate Prediction

ECMWF leverages quantum computing for revolutionary weather prediction, enhancing long-range forecasts and reducing climate-related risks.

i) **Optimization in Manufacturing and Operations:** Quantum computing can optimize manufacturing processes, resource allocation, and supply chain logistics.

Case Study: Production Line Optimization

Volkswagen collaborated with quantum computing experts to optimize its automotive manufacturing processes. By modeling production line configurations and scheduling tasks more efficiently, Volkswagen reduced production costs, minimized downtime, and increased throughput, improving overall operational efficiency and profitability.

j) **Healthcare and Medical Imaging:** Quantum computing can analyze medical data, optimize treatment plans, and improve medical imaging techniques.

Case Study: Medical Image Reconstruction

IBM Research has pioneered quantum algorithms for reconstructing medical images from sparse data, utilizing principles like entanglement and superposition. This novel approach offers higher resolution and faster reconstruction times compared to classical methods, enhancing diagnostic accuracy and patient care in medical imaging.

k) **Logistics and Transportation Optimization:** Quantum computing can optimize transportation networks, route planning, and vehicle scheduling.

Case Study: Public Transportation Optimization

The city of Tokyo collaborated with quantum computing researchers to optimize its public transportation system. By analyzing passenger flow data and optimizing bus and train schedules in real time, Tokyo improved transit efficiency, reduced congestion, and enhanced the overall commuter experience, making urban transportation more sustainable and accessible.

These case studies demonstrate the diverse range of applications where quantum computing holds promise for driving innovation, improving efficiency, and solving complex real-world problems across various industries.

5.4   CHALLENGES AND CONSIDERATIONS IN QUANTUM COMPUTING

Quantum computing promises immense computational power, but faces hurdles like maintaining delicate quantum states, scaling systems for complex algorithms, and ensuring secure communication. Overcoming these challenges is key to unlocking its transformative potential. A few challenges and considerations in quantum computing along with examples are:

a) **Quantum Decoherence:** Decoherence in quantum states disrupts superposition and entanglement, impeding the development of quantum technologies, necessitating strategies for mitigation.

Examples of Quantum Decoherence:

Qubits harness superposition for exponential computational power, yet face vulnerability to environmental influences like temperature and electromagnetic waves, leading to decoherence and potential errors.

Quantum Cryptography: Quantum cryptography creates ultra-secure keys via quantum entanglement, but susceptibility to decoherence poses a risk to data integrity, demanding constant vigilance.

Challenges Posed by Quantum Decoherence:

Error Rates: Errors are introduced in quantum computations and communications by decoherence, thereby diminishing the reliability and accuracy of quantum systems. The scalability and practical utility of quantum technologies are constrained by high error rates resulting from decoherence.

Control and Stability: Significant technical challenges are posed by achieving and sustaining precise control over environmental conditions and system parameters for maintaining coherence in quantum systems at the quantum level.

Integration with Classical Systems: Integrating quantum devices with classical systems introduces additional sources of decoherence, as interactions between quantum and classical environments can disrupt quantum states.

Overcoming Challenges:

Error Correction: Quantum redundancy coupled with error correction mitigates decoherence, preserving quantum information amidst environmental interactions.

Quantum Error Suppression: Various methods, such as dynamical decoupling and quantum control techniques, aim to suppress decoherence effects by actively manipulating quantum systems to protect them from environmental disturbances.

Quantum Annealing: Quantum annealing approaches, employed in certain types of quantum computing architectures like adiabatic quantum computing, are less sensitive to decoherence compared to gate-based quantum computing. This resilience makes them suitable for certain optimization problems.

Environment Engineering: Developing materials and environments with minimal interference on quantum states is crucial. This involves designing low-temperature and low-noise environments, as well as utilizing materials with inherently low decoherence properties.

Hybrid Approaches: Combining quantum systems with classical error-correction techniques or classical processing units can enhance the robustness of quantum technologies against decoherence.

By addressing these challenges and implementing strategies to mitigate the effects of quantum decoherence, researchers aim to unlock the full potential of quantum technologies and overcome the limitations posed by this fundamental aspect of quantum mechanics.

b) **Qubit Quality:** High-qubit quality is pivotal for reliable quantum computing, ensuring stability amid environmental interference and hardware imperfections, unlocking unprecedented computational power.

Examples:

Superconducting Qubits: Superconducting qubits, constructed from materials like aluminum or niobium, offer promise for quantum information processing due to their zero electrical resistance at low temperatures. However, they face challenges such as thermal fluctuations and electromagnetic interference. Researchers mitigate these errors by operating qubits at extremely low temperatures and shielding them from external electromagnetic fields. Despite challenges, ongoing research aims to advance error correction and fabrication techniques for robust quantum computing platforms.

Trapped Ion Qubits: Challenges related to maintaining precise control over individual qubits and minimizing errors during gate operations are faced by trapped ions, with qubits represented by the internal states of trapped ions in trapped ion quantum computing, and quantum operations performed on these qubits through laser manipulation; despite long coherence times being offered.

Challenges:

Decoherence: Decoherence, the degradation of quantum attributes over time, plagues qubits in quantum computing, influenced by environmental factors like temperature shifts and electromagnetic radiation. Despite operating at ultra-low temperatures, even minor fluctuations disrupt their delicate states, exacerbated by noise from ambient sources. Material flaws and environmental disturbances fuel this challenge, prompting research into error correction codes and qubit designs for resilient quantum computers, striving for practical scalability.

Gate Errors: Errors introduced by imperfect operations, such as control signal inaccuracies, timing issues, or quantum hardware noise, can undermine computation accuracy when qubit states are manipulated by quantum gates. The need for error correction techniques in quantum computing is emphasized by these errors, with enhancing gate precision being pivotal for advancing the reliability and performance of quantum algorithms.

Error Correction: Developing effective error correction codes for quantum systems is challenging. Traditional error correction techniques used in classical computing may not be directly applicable to quantum systems due to their unique properties.

Overcoming Challenges:

Error Mitigation Techniques: Error mitigation techniques, comprising error correction codes, error-averaging methodologies, and error-adaptive algorithms, serve as indispensable components for minimizing errors within quantum computations. These techniques are instrumental in bolstering accuracy and dependability by detecting and rectifying errors, statistically amalgamating measurements, and dynamically adapting strategies in real time.

Hardware Improvements: Continuous advancements in fabrication techniques and materials can help improve qubit quality. For instance, researchers are working on developing qubits with longer coherence times and better noise resilience.

Control and Calibration: Precise control and calibration of quantum hardware are essential for minimizing errors. Techniques such as active error correction and error-robust gate designs can enhance the reliability of quantum operations.

System Redundancy: Implementing redundant qubits or redundancy in quantum operations can help detect and correct errors. Quantum error correction codes, such as surface codes, provide a framework for achieving fault-tolerant quantum computation by encoding logical qubits across multiple physical qubits.

c) **Scalability:** Scalability in quantum computing is crucial for advancing the field, enabling larger and more complex computations. It involves increasing qubit counts and optimizing operations to handle computations efficiently. Efficiency is key, minimizing overhead and errors while maximizing resource utilization. Overcoming technical challenges like noise and decoherence is essential. Scalability not only drives technological progress but also holds promise for revolutionizing industries like finance, healthcare, and materials science.

Examples:

Factorization: One classic example of a complex computation in quantum computing is integer factorization, particularly the factorization of large composite numbers. This is the basis for many cryptographic protocols, such as RSA encryption.

Quantum simulation: Efficient simulation of quantum systems is recognized as another example where scalability is crucial, with applications spanning fields like material science, chemistry, and drug discovery.

Challenges:

Quantum coherence: As quantum systems scale up, maintaining coherence becomes increasingly difficult due to heightened susceptibility to external influences such as environmental noise and decoherence mechanisms. This poses significant challenges for the stability and reliability of larger quantum systems.

Hardware limitations: Expanding the size of quantum systems requires boosting both the quantity of qubits and the accuracy of their manipulation. Yet the progress is hindered by constraints in quantum hardware, including issues like qubit connectivity, gate fidelities, and error rates, which pose significant barriers to scalability.

Error correction: Errors caused by noise and imperfections in hardware necessitate quantum error correction. Nonetheless, implementing error correction schemes on a large scale is difficult and may add extra overhead.

Overcoming Challenges:

Improvements in hardware: Scalability can be improved through continuous advancements in qubit technology, such as increasing qubit coherence times and reducing error rates. More scalable architectures may be achieved through research into different qubit types, such as superconducting qubits, trapped ions, and topological qubits.

Error correction techniques: The development of efficient error correction codes and fault-tolerant schemes is deemed crucial for scaling up quantum systems. Various error correction methods tailored to specific quantum hardware architectures are being explored by researchers to minimize overhead and improve scalability.

Algorithmic optimizations: Scalability challenges can be alleviated by designing algorithms that are inherently scalable and require fewer qubits or gates. Resource requirements for complex computations can be reduced by quantum algorithms with low-depth circuits or parallelizable operations.

Hybrid approaches: Scalability issues can be addressed by combining classical and quantum computing techniques. The strengths of both classical and quantum systems can be leveraged through hybrid algorithms, allowing for more efficient computation of complex problems.

System integration and control: Scalability can be enhanced by developing better control mechanisms and integration techniques for quantum systems. This includes optimizing qubit connectivity, reducing crosstalk between qubits, and improving overall system stability.

d) **Quantum Error Correction:** Quantum error correction involves spreading information across multiple qubits to maintain accuracy despite noise or imperfections. Specialized quantum error-correcting codes are employed, akin to classical computing error correction.

Examples of Quantum Error Correction Schemes:

Quantum Error Correction Codes: Quantum error-correcting codes, like the Shor, Steane, and surface codes, distribute information redundantly across qubits. This allows for detecting and correcting errors during quantum computation, enhancing system reliability. These codes make quantum computing more robust and feasible for practical applications by safeguarding against the fragility of quantum states.

Error Detection and Correction Protocols: The procedures entail identifying and rectifying errors arising in quantum computation. Take, for example, the utilization of syndrome measurement technique, which enables error detection without directly probing the quantum state.

Challenges in Quantum Error Correction:

Quantum systems are highly susceptible to decoherence and noise, which can disrupt their delicate quantum states and compromise encoded quantum information, hindering advancements in quantum technologies like computing and communication. Imperfect quantum gates further exacerbate errors during computation, making error correction efforts challenging. Additionally, implementing error correction codes incurs substantial resource overhead in terms of qubits and computational resources, limiting the scalability of quantum algorithms. Overcoming these obstacles is crucial for realizing the full potential of quantum technologies.

Overcoming Challenges in Quantum Error Correction:

Research focuses on developing error correction schemes with reliable error thresholds, optimizing error-correcting codes and protocols. Techniques like error mitigation algorithms and fault-tolerant quantum gates aim to reduce error impact. Hardware advancements, including error-robust qubits and improved control mechanisms, mitigate errors at the hardware level. Algorithmic approaches seek to develop resilient algorithms with fewer resource requirements. Quantum error correction is crucial for building scalable quantum systems, and ongoing efforts target robust error correction schemes to overcome challenges and unleash quantum computing's full potential.

e) **Quantum Gate Fidelity:** Quantum gate fidelity is crucial for accurate quantum computation, but susceptibility to errors from decoherence, noise, and gate crosstalk poses challenges. Researchers use error correction codes like the surface code, mitigation techniques such as randomized compiling, and hardware advancements to improve fidelity. Quantum error correction algorithms detect and correct errors during computation, enhancing reliability and unlocking the full potential of quantum computing.

Examples:

Single-qubit gates like Pauli-X, Pauli-Y, and Pauli-Z are crucial for changing the state of individual qubits, performing tasks like bit flips and phase changes accurately. Similarly, two-qubit gates such as Controlled-NOT (CNOT) and Controlled-Z play a vital role in entangling qubits and executing complex quantum algorithms. Ensuring high fidelity in both single-qubit and two-qubit gates is essential for precise and reliable quantum computation.

Challenges:

Decoherence presents a challenge in quantum systems as environmental noise disrupts coherence, making quantum states error prone. Imperfections in real-world quantum hardware reduce gate fidelity and accuracy. Achieving precise calibration and control, especially in multi-qubit systems, is difficult due to variations in control parameters. Advancements in calibration and control methodologies are crucial for accurate and reliable quantum gate operations.

Overcoming Challenges:

Implementing error correction codes like surface codes or repetition codes helps mitigate errors due to decoherence and hardware imperfections in quantum systems, improving gate fidelity. Techniques such as randomized benchmarking and gate set tomography further enhance error detection and correction. Advances in hardware design, reduced noise levels, and improved control electronics minimize error sources, while optimized control techniques and systematic calibration enhance gate fidelity through precise parameter tuning and control.

So, achieving high fidelity in quantum gate operations is crucial for accurate quantum computation. Addressing challenges such as decoherence, hardware imperfections, and control errors requires a combination of error correction, error mitigation, hardware improvements, and advanced control techniques to overcome these challenges and achieve reliable quantum computation.

f) **Quantum Algorithms:** Designing quantum algorithms exploits quantum phenomena to perform computations more efficiently than classical ones, leveraging superposition, entanglement, and interference. Quantum algorithms aim to outperform classical ones for specific tasks, such as factorization and search problems. Challenges include qubit errors and decoherence, addressed through error correction techniques and improved hardware.

Examples of Quantum Algorithms:

Shor's algorithm revolutionizes quantum computing by efficiently factoring large integers, crucial for cryptography. Grover's algorithm accelerates database searches with a quadratic speedup over classical methods. Quantum machine learning algorithms exploit quantum properties to enhance tasks like pattern recognition and classification, promising transformative advancements in computing.

Challenges in Designing Quantum Algorithms:

Quantum computing faces challenges in error correction, gate operations, and resource constraints. Quantum systems are prone to noise, requiring robust error correction algorithms. Implementing accurate quantum gates is hindered by limited qubit connectivity and the need for precise control. Overcoming resource limitations, such as qubit coherence and gate errors, is essential for practical quantum algorithm implementation, which demands numerous qubits and high-fidelity operations for quantum advantage.

Overcoming Challenges:

In the realm of quantum computing, quantum error correction (QEC) techniques are being actively perfected and hardware like superconducting qubits and trapped ions is being advanced to enhance gate operations and connectivity. Concurrently, algorithm optimization efforts are being focused on reducing resource requirements and improving performance through techniques like algorithmic enhancements and circuit optimization. These advancements collectively propel the feasibility and efficiency of implementing quantum algorithms.

g) **Quantum Software Development:** Creating tools and languages for programming and simulating quantum algorithms. Quantum software development involves creating tools and programming languages for designing and simulating quantum algorithms. Here's an explanation with examples, challenges, and ways to overcome them:

Examples of Quantum Software Development:

Quantum Programming Languages: These are languages specifically designed for expressing quantum algorithms. Examples include Q#, Quipper, and Silq.

Quantum Circuit Simulators: Tools like Qiskit, Cirq, and QuTiP allow users to simulate quantum circuits and algorithms on classical computers.

Quantum Development Frameworks: Frameworks like Microsoft's Quantum Development Kit or IBM's Quantum Development Environment provide comprehensive sets of tools for quantum software development, including simulators, compilers, and libraries.

Challenges in Quantum Software Development:

Quantum computing grapples with complex concepts like superposition and entanglement, requiring intuitive programming languages and robust error correction. Hardware limitations, such as qubit counts and coherence times, hinder scalability. Lack of a standardized language inhibits collaboration, slowing progress in research and application development.

Overcoming Challenges:

Investing in education and training programs is vital for quantum computing advancement. Ongoing research focusing on error correction, fault-tolerant algorithms, and hardware enhancements is crucial. Collaboration within the quantum community is essential for establishing standards and best practices. Iterative development based on user feedback is key for enhancing quantum programming languages and tools. Cross-disciplinary collaboration is necessary for innovative solutions in quantum software development.

By addressing these challenges and leveraging advancements in quantum computing hardware and software, developers can create powerful tools and languages for programming and simulating quantum algorithms, paving the way for practical quantum applications in various domains.

h) **Entanglement Generation and Control:** In quantum information processing, operations such as quantum cryptography and teleportation are facilitated by entanglement, through the manipulation and creation of entangled states, which exhibit a profound correlation between the properties of particles, a phenomenon fundamental to a plethora of quantum computing and communication endeavors.

Examples:

The interconnection of two photons in a quantum state, where their properties such as polarization become correlated regardless of distance, is involved in photon entanglement. Classical notions of locality are violated by this phenomenon, as the state of one photon is instantaneously affected by the state of the other. Superconducting qubits, on the other hand, utilize superconducting materials to create quantum bits. Entanglement between superconducting qubits is achieved through controlled manipulation of their quantum states using techniques like microwave pulses. The creation of highly correlated states necessary for performing quantum algorithms and implementing secure quantum communication protocols is enabled by this entanglement, which is crucial for quantum computation and communication.

Challenges:
Entanglement's potential applications are hindered by several inherent challenges. These include decoherence, where interactions with the environment can disrupt the entangled state. Additionally, scaling entanglement to a large number of qubits and precisely measuring and controlling them are significant obstacles that must be overcome to fully harness its potential.

Overcoming Challenges:
Entanglement's potential limitations are being addressed through several promising avenues. Error correction techniques are being developed to mitigate decoherence and other errors, thereby preserving the entangled state. Improved control techniques and hardware designs are being explored to enhance the precision and scalability of entanglement generation. Additionally, techniques for noise suppression and the hybridization of different physical platforms are being investigated to improve the fidelity of entangled states and overcome current limitations.

i) **Physical Implementation Challenges:** Physical implementation challenges refer to the difficulties encountered when building practical quantum systems due to constraints such as temperature, noise, and isolation. These challenges are significant barriers to achieving reliable and scalable quantum computing technologies. Brief overview along with examples and strategies for overcoming these challenges are described in the following.

Temperature Control: Realizing quantum computing's potential requires precise temperature control. Quantum systems' sensitivity to temperature fluctuations necessitates ultra-low temperatures, often achieved with cryogenic systems and further enhanced by thermal shielding and insulation.

Noise Reduction: Reducing noise is paramount in mitigating physical implementation challenges in quantum systems, facilitating optimal performance and unlocking the vast potential of quantum computing technologies.

Building powerful quantum computers is tricky because delicate quantum states are easily disrupted by outside influences like radiation or vibrations. This "noise" causes decoherence, where the special quantum properties that give these computers an edge disappear. Essentially, the noise throws a wrench in the quantum works, making the computer unreliable. Researchers are working on minimizing noise to pave the way for robust quantum computers.

Overcoming: Techniques like error correction codes, dynamic decoupling methods, and hardware improvements (e.g., using high-purity materials) help mitigate the impact of noise. Isolation from external disturbances through physical shielding and electromagnetic filters is also crucial.

Isolation from External Interference: Isolating quantum systems from external interference is imperative for overcoming implementation challenges, ensuring stability, and maximizing the efficacy of quantum computing technologies.

Challenge: Quantum systems are vulnerable to interference from electromagnetic fields, stray radiation, and other external factors, which can disrupt quantum coherence.

Example: Due to their sensitivity to magnetic fields, the delicate quantum states of qubits in quantum computers are susceptible to disruption from nearby electronic devices.

Overcoming: Shielding quantum devices with superconducting materials, using specialized enclosures, and designing isolated experimental setups can minimize external interference. Additionally, developing quantum error correction techniques can help correct errors introduced by such interference.

Scalability:

Challenge: Building large-scale quantum systems while maintaining coherence and fidelity poses a significant challenge due to the cumulative effects of noise and interconnectivity issues.

Example: One of the biggest challenges in building practical quantum computers is scaling them up. While current systems have a handful of qubits, useful applications likely require millions. However, simply adding more qubits isn't enough. The key is to do this while preserving the fragile quantum properties of each qubit. This delicate balance is essential for harnessing the true power of quantum computing.

Overcoming: Engineering scalable architectures, such as modular designs and fault-tolerant quantum error correction schemes, is crucial for overcoming scalability challenges. Additionally, advancements in fabrication techniques and materials science can enable the production of more reliable and scalable quantum hardware.

Achieving the full potential of quantum computing requires overcoming significant physical limitations. This can only be accomplished through a multi-faceted approach. Engineering advancements, breakthroughs in materials science, and the development of robust error correction methods are all crucial elements in this endeavor.

5.5 CONCLUSION

In conclusion, quantum computing's examination underscores its profound impact on computational science and beyond. We've explored its principles, architectures, and applications, revealing transformative potential. Quantum algorithms excel in solving complex problems exponentially faster than classical computers, spanning optimization, cryptography, machine learning, and simulation. Despite implementation challenges, recent hardware and error correction breakthroughs offer solutions, unlocking quantum computing's full potential. Real-world examples and future directions highlight its broad applications, from scientific research to industrial optimization and societal challenges. Quantum computing heralds innovation, pushing computation boundaries to unprecedented levels, offering a future where complex problems are swiftly and precisely tackled, revolutionizing computational approaches.

Hence, quantum computing is the leading a tech revolution, redefining computational limits, unlocking frontiers, transforming complexity perception.

5.5.1 FUTURE DIRECTIONS

In the coming decades, breakthroughs in quantum computing will usher in a new era of technological advancement. The development of ever-more-powerful quantum machines will unlock a treasure trove of possibilities, from revolutionizing cryptography for unbreakable security to accelerating drug discovery and optimizing solutions to the most complex problems. As research intensifies, large-scale, stable quantum systems will become a reality, paving the way for a future where quantum technology is seamlessly integrated across industries, transforming how we tackle even the most intricate challenges.

REFERENCES

Agarwal, A., & Mohanta, C. (2023). Development, working and standardization of quantum computing. *Journal of The Institution of Engineers (India): Series B*, 104(2), 523–531. https://ui.adsabs.harvard.edu/abs/2023JIEIB.104.523A/abstract

Agarwal, P., & Alam, M. (2021). Exploring quantum computing to revolutionize big data analytics for various industrial sectors. In *Big Data Analytics* (pp. 113–130). Auerbach Publications.

Aithal, P. S. (2023). Advances and new research opportunities in quantum computing technology by integrating it with other ICCT underlying technologies. *International Journal of Case Studies in Business, IT and Education (IJCSBE)*, 7(3), 314–358. https://supublication.com/index.php/ijcsbe/article/view/544

Brijwani, G. N., Ajmire, P. E., & Thawani, P. V. (2023). Future of quantum computing in cyber security. In *Handbook of Research on Quantum Computing for Smart Environments* (pp. 267–298). IGI Global. https://www.igi-global.com/chapter/future-of-quantum-computing-in-cyber-security/319874

Butey, B., & Upasani, M. (2024, January). Quantum computing-a revolution-current updates and challenges. In *AIP Conference Proceedings* (Vol. 2974, No. 1). AIP Publishing. https://pubs.aip.org/aip/acp/article-abstract/2974/1/020033/3099318/Quantum-computing-a-revolution-current-updates-and

Coccia, M. (2022). Technological trajectories in quantum computing to design a quantum ecosystem for industrial change. *Technology Analysis & Strategic Management*, 1–16. https://www.researchgate.net/publication/362817232_Technological_trajectories_in_quantum_computing_to_design_a_quantum_ecosystem_for_industrial_change

Holbrook, A. J. (2023). A quantum parallel Markov chain Monte Carlo. *Journal of Computational and Graphical Statistics*, 32(4), 1402–1415. https://www.tandfonline.com/doi/full/10.1080/10618600.2023.2195890

Kishore, N., & Raina, P. (2019). Parallel cryptographic hashing: Developments in the last 25 years. *Cryptologia*, 43(6), 504–535. https://www.researchgate.net/publication/335063825_Parallel_cryptographic_hashing_Developments_in_the_last_25_years

Lu, Y., Sigov, A., Ratkin, L., Ivanov, L. A., & Zuo, M. (2023). Quantum computing and industrial information integration: A review. *Journal of Industrial Information Integration*, 100511. https://colab.ws/articles/10.1016%2Fj.jii.2023.100511

Michelini, M., & Stefanel, A. (2023). Research studies on learning quantum physics. In *The International Handbook of Physics Education Research: Learning Physics*, AIP Publishing house, https://doi.org/10.1063/9780735425477_008 https://pubs.aip.org/books/monograph/148/chapter-abstract/64394985/Research-Studies-on-Learning-Quantum-Physics?redirectedFrom=fulltext

Möller, M., & Vuik, C. (2017). On the impact of quantum computing technology on future developments in high-performance scientific computing. *Ethics and Information Technology*, 19, 253–269. https://link.springer.com/article/10.1007/s10676-017-9438-0

Mustafa, M. N. (2023). Exploring the future of quantum computing: Challenges and opportunities in computer engineering. *Turkish Journal of Computer and Mathematics Education (TURCOMAT)*, 14(03), 556–567. https://turcomat.org/index.php/turkbilmat/article/view/14075

Pris, F. I. (2022). The real meaning of quantum mechanics. *Educational Philosophy and Theory*, 1–5. https://arxiv.org/pdf/2107.10666

Riel, H. (2021, December). Quantum computing technology. In *2021 IEEE International Electron Devices Meeting (IEDM)* (pp. 1–3). IEEE. https://inspirehep.net/literature/2086952

Ten Holter, C., Inglesant, P., & Jirotka, M. (2023). Reading the road: Challenges and opportunities on the path to responsible innovation in quantum computing. *Technology Analysis & Strategic Management*, 35(7), 844–856. https://www.tandfonline.com/doi/full/10.1080/09537325.2021.1988070

Vedhapriyavadhana, R., Rajathi, G. I., Niranjana, R., & Pooranam, N. (2023). Quantum computing: Application-specific need of the hour. *Quantum Computing and Artificial Intelligence: Training Machine and Deep Learning Algorithms on Quantum Computers*, 225.

Werner, M., García-Sáez, A., & Estarellas, M. P. (2023). Bounding first-order quantum phase transitions in adiabatic quantum computing. *Physical Review Research*, 5(4), 043236. https://journals.aps.org/prresearch/abstract/10.1103/PhysRevResearch.5.043236

6 Securing IoT
Advanced Algorithmic Approaches for Malware Detection

Vergin Raja Sarobin M., Ashish Choudhary,
Azrina Abd Aziz, and Ranjith J.

6.1 INTRODUCTION

With the evolution of the digital world and various technologies booming, the Internet of Things (IoT) has transformed the manner in which users communicate with the digital world. It is defined as the network of physical devices, devices equipped with sensors, actuators, various appliances, and software. These devices are connected so that they set up communication among themselves and over the internet.

IoT devices collect data, perform various pre-processing, and draw various data insights from the data collected by various devices. This pre-processing occurs either in the device itself or in centralized cloud-based systems. These devices find their application in various fields like healthcare, smart cities, agriculture, industries, and smart homes. These IoT devices also enable automation and, based on the data input, make decisions with or without human intervention. But the widespread usage of IoT devices poses several challenges such as security and privacy. The security associated with IoT devices will continue to grow as the digital world grows, and therefore cyberattacks will also eventually grow [1]. Traditional approaches involve prevention, detection, and mitigation to tackle cyberattacks.

Machine learning and deep learning are the latest powerful techniques that can be applied successfully to address the continuously growing complexity of malicious software. Machine learning and deep learning techniques learn patterns based on trained data and hence can adapt to unseen data, which is needed in growing scenarios of malware attacks. These techniques achieve high accuracy and precision, improving overall detection capability.

IoT-23 is a labelled malware and benign dataset that consists of network traffic from Internet of Things devices. This dataset comprises 23 instances, also known as captures of different network traffic. This consists of 20 captures under the malware category executed in various IoT devices. The remaining three captures are for benign traffic. This dataset was collected in the Stratosphere Laboratory, AIC group, FEL, and CTU University in the Czech Republic to

DOI: 10.1201/9781003499459-6

TABLE 6.1

Description of the Attributes in the Dataset

Attribute	Description
duration	It refers to the total time data was handled between the device and the attacker.
orig_bytes	It refers to all the data sent to the device.
resp_bytes	It refers to all the data sent by the device.
missed_bytes	It refers to the number of missed bytes in the message.
orig_pkts	It refers to the total number of packets sent to the device.
orig_ip_bytes	It refers to the total number of bytes sent to the device.
resp_pkts	It refers to the total number of packets being sent from the device.
resp_ip_bytes	It refers to the total number of bytes being sent from the device.
proto_icmp	It refers to the type of network protocol being used for the data package, which is the Internet Control Message protocol.
proto_tcp	It refers to the type of network protocol being used for the data package, which is the Transmission Control protocol.
proto_udp	It refers to the type of network protocol being used for the data package, which is the User Datagram protocol.
service_dhcp	It refers to the application protocol, which is the Dynamic Host Configuration Protocol.
service_dns	It refers to the application protocol, which is the Domain Name System.
service_http	It refers to the application protocol, which is Hypertext Transfer Protocol.
service_irc	It refers to the application protocol, which is Internet Relay Chat.
service_ssh	It refers to the application protocol, which is Secure Shell.
service_ssl	It refers to the application protocol, which is Secure Sockets Layer.
conn_state	It refers to the state of connection.
label	It refers to the output, which is attack or benign.

provide large labelled datasets for researchers to work on. The description of the prominent attributes in the dataset is shown in Table 6.1.

This chapter applies various machine learning algorithms and deep learning to the IoT 23 dataset. The various supervised machine learning algorithms applied are K-Nearest Neighbor (KNN), support vector machine (SVM), and random forest. In addition to this, an artificial neural network is also applied for better insights. The dataset consists of 30 attributes with binary output labelled as malware or benign. Feature selection or feature extraction is a prominent and crucial step in applying machine learning and deep learning algorithms. Feature extraction aids in accelerated training and low computation time because the model now has to learn on a reduced set of features; therefore it becomes easier to understand the relationship among the variables and better insights. In addition to this it helps in the elimination of redundant information, improved model performance, less data storage, and so on. Feature extraction is done in this paper using DEAP (distributed evolutionary algorithms in Python) via genetic programming.

Federated learning (FL) is also known as collaborative learning. Federated learning is another emerging technique, which is a decentralized method to train machine learning models. These machine learning models often deploy deep neural networks spread across multiple devices. The major reason this approach is so popular these days is that it maintains privacy, as it does not require exchanging data from client devices to global servers. Instead, the clients use the local data to train the model locally, and the global model is formed by aggregating the local updates from each client. Thus, this approach is an alternative to traditional machine learning, which is a centralized approach to building machine learning models. An architectural diagram of the flow of this study is shown in Figure 6.1.

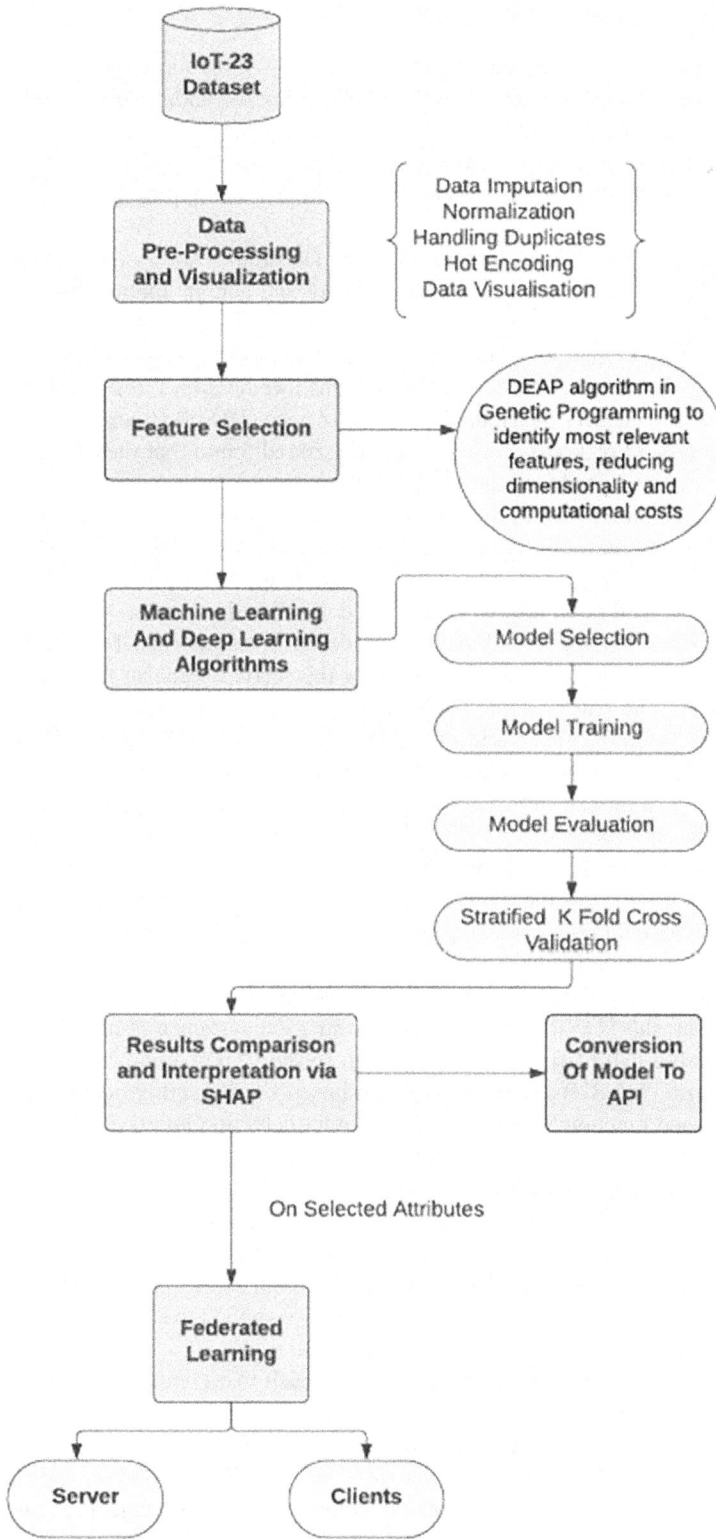

FIGURE 6.1 Architectural workflow of the study.

6.2   RELATED WORK

A malware detection work by Hemant Rathore et al. deploys both major types of machine learning, supervised and unsupervised techniques, and to carry it out the authors use opcode frequency as a feature vector. The authors concluded that random forest outperformed the deep learning model for malware analysis and detection; in addition, the authors found that deep auto encoders do not work that well for feature reduction and therefore adopted simpler techniques like the variance threshold method [2].

The paper by Umesh V. Nikam and Vaishali M. Deshmukh shows malware detection on the Kaggle dataset, which contains around 15036 malware and benign applications. The authors used ten machine learning algorithms and considered various parameters like accuracy, AUC, FNR, and FPR [3]. Based on this, the authors come up with the best model considering the parameters.

The paper by D. Nanthiya et al. deploys algorithms like random forest, decision tree, and support vector machine to classify distributed denial of service (DDoS) attacked packets on the IoT-23 dataset [4]. They applied principal component analysis and found that the execution time reduced with feature selection and produced the same result.

In the paper by N. Abdalgawad, the authors use deep learning models like adversarial autoencoders (AAEs) and bidirectional generative adversarial networks (BiGANs) for analysis of data taken from the IoT-23 dataset; hence the same dataset is used to train the models [5] fully. Deep learning promises to yield good results as compared to other algorithms.

In a different paper, the authors adopted two independent scenarios. The first scenario focused on distributed denial of service detection, whereas the second scenario focused on identification of the other attacks. The study adopted three major techniques to carry out these two scenarios. They were mainly random forest based on feature importance on the IoT-23 dataset, a sequential forward procedure followed by fivefold cross-validation [6]. This is carried out with the purpose of classification optimization and dimensionality reduction. The study obtained an accuracy of 99% on average in both schemes.

In another paper, the authors deployed deep convolution reinforcement neural networks (DCRNNs) for surveillance of the network and network categorization from potential threats [7]. The study began with data pre-processing and feature engineering, for which the deep sparse auto encoder was used. In addition to DCRNNs, a honeypot framework was also deployed by incorporating the implementation of a honeypot firewall and web server.

In another paper, the SDN-enabled intelligent intrusion system was used by the authors. The authors broadly use a hybrid framework and leverage the CUDA long short-term memory gated recurrent unit (cuLSTMGRU) [8]. The model proposed by the authors obtained an accuracy of 99.23%. Graph-based machine learning using a botnet detection approach was implemented in a paper by Afnan Alharbi. The authors first take into account the prominent graph features, and then the generalized model is developed [9].

In a different study, the authors use a byte sequence of files, malware and benign, to reduce the model complexity. The generated byte sequence is passed through the frequency-inverse document frequency (TF-IDF) [10]. The TF-IDF generates a bi-gram structure, and supervised machine learning algorithms like logistic regression and naive Bayes are applied to it. The authors found that SVC performed the best among all machine learning models.

In another paper, the authors present a hybrid approach that combines support vector machine classifiers and another technique called active learning [11]. The dataset used in this study is the BIG 2015 Kaggle dataset, and the authors found that the performance of machine learning models improves with ALBL techniques. In addition to this, the quality of labeled samples is also improved with this approach. A similar study explores different classification machine learning models in intelligent prediction of customer churn in the telecom industry [12]. A paper by Thomas Borja explores the federated learning approach for the MNIST dataset using a flower framework called virtual client engine that allows deployment of the server and client on the same machine with ease and low computation time [13].

6.3 METHODOLOGY

6.3.1 DATA PRE-PROCESSING AND VISUALIZATION

Data pre-processing is an initial vital step before building any machine learning model. Any errors made at this step create a vicious cycle because poor decision-making stems from this initial step. Therefore, proper techniques are necessary for proper decision-making in models.

In the dataset taken, it contains null values or missing values. Missing values need to be tackled before training the model. Therefore, imputation via mean is done to handle null values. Normalization is another step done to bring all features to a similar scale so that every attribute contributes equally to the training process. There are various methods to tackle this, such as min-max scaling, so that each feature value falls between 0 and 1. Alternatively, standardizing Z-scores using the StandardScaler class can obtain a mean of 0 and a standard deviation of 1. In addition to scikit-learn's StandardScaler, the data is transformed with each feature mean as 0 and standard deviation as 1. Duplicate values unnecessarily waste computation time and introduce redundancy; therefore duplicate values are dropped to eliminate duplicate rows from the data frame. Machine learning models can only understand numerical representations as input. Therefore, it is necessary to convert categorical values into numerical representations. This is achieved by the one-hot encoding technique, a machine learning technique that converts categorical values into numerical representation, and a unique value is given to every category. This can be observed as the output label with benign and malware hot encoded to 1 and 0 unique values, respectively.

A correlation plot helps in understanding how attributes are related to each other and the output. Correlation can be positive, negative, or zero. A positive value means that an increase in one variable causes an increase in the other and vice versa. A zero value means that the variables or attributes are independent.

The pre-processed data is class balanced, which is very useful; otherwise, biased models would be obtained where models perform well on the majority class but poorly on the minority class. The distribution of the target variable, where label 0 is 52.2% and label 1 is 47.8%. The evidence of class balance is shown in Figure 6.2.

6.3.2 FEATURE SELECTION

Feature selection is a crucial step before building models for performing specific tasks like prediction and classification. It becomes significant when the dataset has a large number of features, like

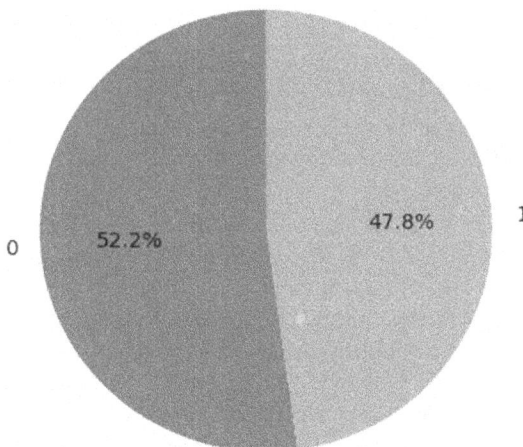

FIGURE 6.2 Distribution of target variable.

the 31 features in the IoT-23 dataset. It aids in selecting a subset of potential features from available features. Carrying out feature selection helps in many ways, such as reducing the computation speed and enabling faster training and inference.

Genetic programming is an evolutionary class of algorithms inspired by the biological concepts of evolution, natural selection, crossover, and mutation. It is widely used to evolve programs or mathematical expressions that represent subsets of features from the given dataset. DEAP is a versatile and powerful Python framework widely used for the implementation of evolutionary algorithms.

The algorithm begins with the initialization of the population of individuals, where each individual represents a potential feature subset. To include or exclude a particular feature, a binary bit is used to represent it. The population size of 100 is kept in the implementation. The fitness of each individual is evaluated in terms of classification accuracy obtained from the support vector machine classifier. The step following initialization is selection, where the general criteria is those individuals who have high fitness scores have a high chance of being selected.

Once the tournament selection is done, the algorithm involves genetic operators like crossover and mutation to create new individuals in each generation. Crossover involves the process of exchanging segments of the binary strings between the two parents, and new potential parent sets are created. The algorithm uses one-point crossover and flip mutation to introduce genetic diversity. In the mutation operation, random changes are introduced to the offspring by flipping bits in the binary strings. Mutation helps in exploring the solution space more effectively. The crossover and mutation probability are set to 0.7 and 0.2, respectively. This process is carried out until an optimal subset of features is obtained, which is set by the number of iterations.

Based on this algorithm, the selected features in the dataset are duration, orig_bytes, missed_bytes, orig_pkts, orig_ip_bytes, resp_ip_bytes, proto_icmp, proto_tcp, proto_udp, service_dhcp, service_http, service_ssl, conn_state_RSTR, and conn_state_SH. The general flow of the algorithm is shown in Figure 6.3.

6.3.3 ALGORITHMS FOR MALWARE DETECTION

K-Nearest Neighbor is one of the simplest and most versatile machine learning algorithms used in many real scenarios. The KNN algorithm works on the principle of similarity, where it would predict the output of the dataset, malware or benign, by considering the labels of its K nearest neighbors [14]. To make predictions, the algorithm calculates the distance between each data point in the test dataset (a testing ratio of 0.30 is taken while splitting in the implementation) and all other data points in the training dataset. Once the distance between the new data point and each point in the training dataset has been found, the next step involves finding K nearest neighbors and then making predictions based on these neighbors. To find malware or benign output, the majority class among K neighbors is assigned as the predicted label for new data points.

In the implementation of KNN, to find the optimum value of k, the experiment is carried out using a range of k values from 1 to 20, and the KNN model is evaluated based on accuracy. The result of the experiment illustrating the impact of different k values on the classification performance of the KNN algorithm is shown in Figure 6.4.

The classification report obtained via the implementation of KNN is shown in Table 6.2.

Another popular algorithm for classification and regression problems is the decision tree. It is widely used for classification problems, as used in this study for malware detection [3]. It is a tree-based classification mechanism where internal nodes represent the features of the IoT-23 dataset, branches in the decision tree represent the decision rules that have been followed, and the leaf nodes represent the outcome of the IoT-23 dataset: malware or benign. A decision tree is based on the fact that it explores all the possible solutions possible to the study. A decision tree is handy to use because its tree-like structure enables it to be easily understandable, as it uses human-like thinking to decide.

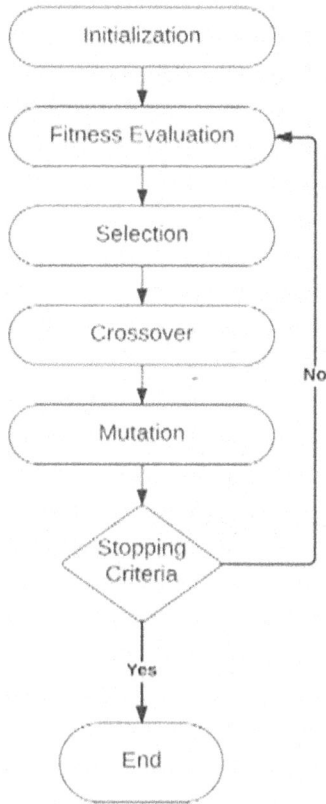

FIGURE 6.3   DEAP genetic algorithm process flow.

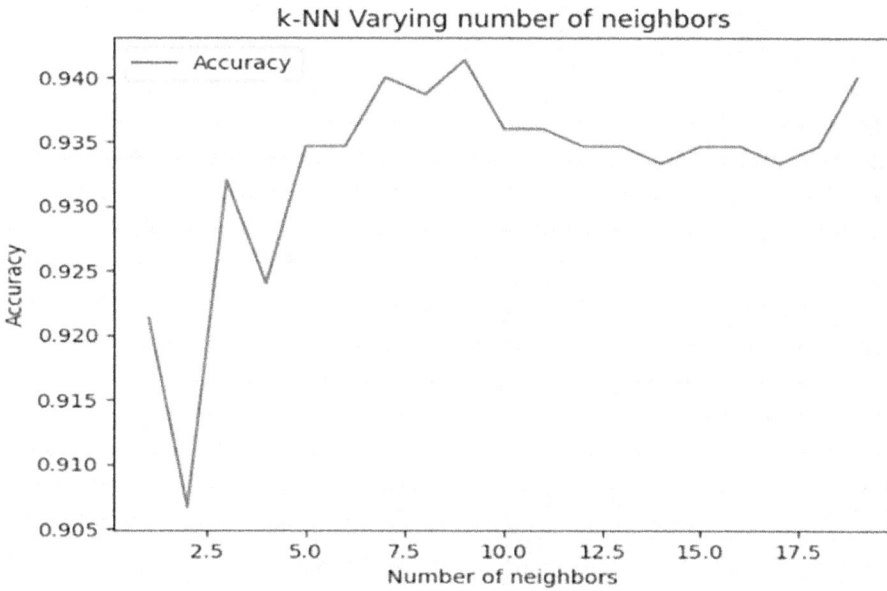

FIGURE 6.4   KNN performance varying with number of neighbours.

TABLE 6.2
Classification Report for KNN Algorithm

	Precision	Recall	F1-Score	Support
0	0.99	0.90	0.94	387
1	0.90	0.99	0.94	363
Accuracy			0.94	750
Macro Avg	0.94	0.94	0.94	750
Weighted Avg	0.95	0.94	0.94	750

TABLE 6.3
Classification Report for Decision Tree Algorithm

	Precision	Recall	F1-Score	Support
0	0.99	0.90	0.94	387
1	0.90	0.99	0.94	363
Accuracy			0.94	750
Macro Avg	0.94	0.94	0.94	750
Weighted Avg	0.95	0.94	0.94	750

To construct a decision tree, it is trained on 70% of the data, while the testing ratio is kept at 30%. The work implements an entropy-based decision tree classifier where decisions are made based on the concept of entropy [14]. Entropy is a measure of uncertainty in a particular attribute. The randomness in the dataset is also achieved via entropy. The maximum depth for constructing the dataset is taken as 6 for simplicity and to avoid cumbersomeness in the decision tree. To obtain various key metrics performance by the decision tree, the classification report table is shown in Table 6.3.

Support vector machine is another very popular supervised machine learning algorithm, primarily used for classification problems. The major aim of the algorithm is to create the best line or boundary, known as a hyperplane, such that it can segregate n-dimensional space into classes. By doing this, whenever a new data point arrives in the future, it can be put into the correct category.

Therefore, the two labels in the IoT-23 dataset in this study were segregated by the hyperplane. Since the IoT-23 dataset can be classified into two labels or classes by using a straight line, this study explores the linear SVM classifier. The hyperplane is created in such a way that it has a maximized margin, or the maximum distance between the data points. These data points are extreme points or vectors, so these extreme cases are called support vectors.

The kernel plays a significant role in the support vector machine algorithm [15]. The kernel helps to capture intricate patterns in the features and non-linear relationships in the dataset. In this study, the support vector machine algorithm is applied with different types of kernels to explore its impact on the classification performance. The various kernels are implemented to discern the potential benefits of capturing different patterns in the dataset. The various kernels are applied to the IoT-23 dataset using SVM, and the bar graph illustrates the comparative performance in terms of accuracy in Figure 6.5.

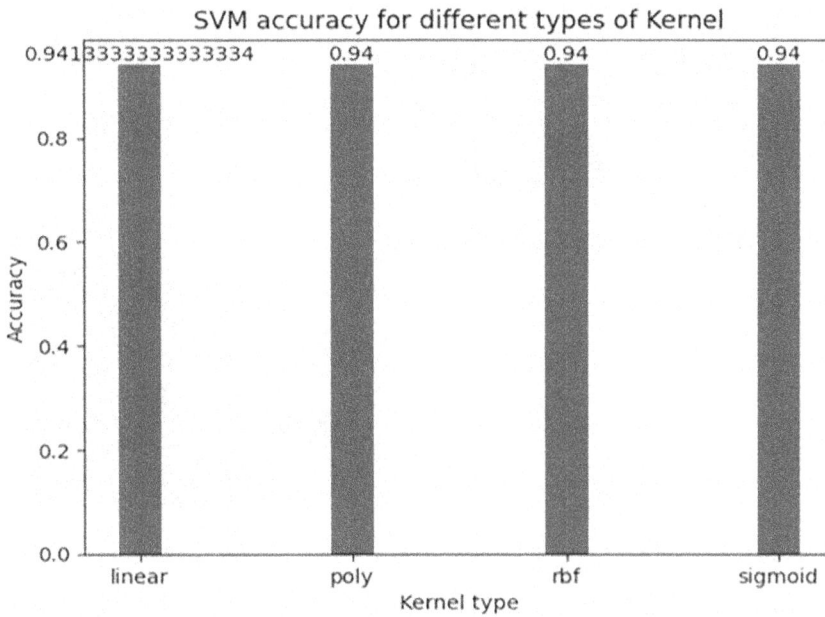

FIGURE 6.5   SVM accuracy for different types of kernel.

The figure illustrates that the linear kernel performed slightly better for SVM as compared to other kernels, and the accuracy obtained is 0.9431 when testing ratio is 0.30.

For malware detection on the IoT-23 dataset, the study also employed ensemble techniques [16]. Random forest is a powerful, robust, and versatile algorithm that aids in reducing overfitting, a common issue in machine learning. The random forest algorithm is an ensemble of decision trees [16]. It amplifies the power of decision trees that construct an ensemble by training each tree on a random subset taken from the dataset, that is, the IoT-23 dataset in this study.

Training each tree independently on a random subset with replacement to introduce randomness is called bagging, which assists in reducing variance and overfitting. For malware detection, each tree predicts the output label, and the label with the majority count becomes the final predicted class. The dataset for the implementation is split into 70% training data and 30% testing data, the number of estimators are taken to be 700, and the maximum depth is taken as 100 with bootstrapping set to True. The accuracy obtained is 0.9426. The performance of malware detection via random forest can be measured by the confusion matrix shown in Figure 6.6.

To obtain various key metrics performance by the random forest, the classification report table is shown in Table 6.4.

In addition to this algorithm, another ensemble technique called AdaBoost (adaptive boosting) is implemented. AdaBoost is an ensemble learning technique that focuses on improving the performance of weak learners and finally creating a strong and robust model [12]. To do this, it operates iteratively by assigning weights to instances in the dataset and focuses more on misclassified instances in subsequent rounds. This iterative process continues until a predefined number of weak learners are combined into the robust model. In the implementation of AdaBoost, the decision tree classifier is taken as a base with a maximum depth of 10 and the number of estimators as 50. The accuracy obtained via AdaBoost is 0.942.

In this study, a fully connected neural network is also implemented [2]. A fully connected neural network, or feed-forward neural network, is known for its capacity to discern intricate patterns and relationships in complex tasks. The neural network employed for malware detection consists of 14 input attributes and two output classes. The model consists of five hidden layers with a size

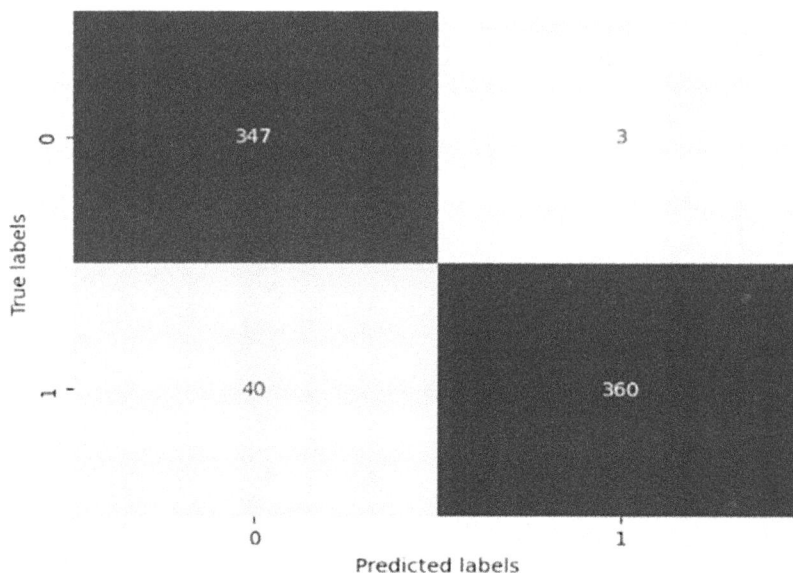

FIGURE 6.6   Confusion matrix for random forest algorithm.

TABLE 6.4
Classification Report for Random Forest Algorithm

	Precision	Recall	F1-Score	Support
0	0.99	0.90	0.94	387
1	0.90	0.99	0.94	363
Accuracy			0.94	750
Macro Avg	0.95	0.94	0.94	750
Weighted Avg	0.95	0.94	0.94	750

of 50 neurons coupled with the ReLu activation function to introduce non-linearity in the network. There are two output neurons, and the final layer uses the SoftMax activation function for binary classification tasks.

To train the model, a well-known and frequently used Adam optimizer is used with a learning rate of 0.001 that influences better speed and convergence of the model. A categorical cross-entropy loss function was used for this study. Upon conducting experiments and 50 epochs for the training of the model, the test loss obtained is 0.179 with an accuracy of 94.40% when the testing ratio is taken to be 30%.

6.3.4   FEDERATED LEARNING

In the traditional machine learning approach, data is collected and stored on one server, and the model is also trained and updated on this global server. However, in federated learning, it is not data that moves to the model but the model that moves to the data. To understand federated learning in a broader aspect, let's draw a comparison between the centralized machine learning approach and federated machine learning approach.

6.3.4.1 Centralized Machine Learning Approach

This is a traditional approach in which the data used to train machine learning models is collected from multiple sources into a single place or centralized repository. This centralized repository can be anything, such as a data warehouse or data lake. The data in this centralized repository is trained using various kinds of machine learning algorithms, like support vector machine, naïve Bayes, or random forest. A similar process was followed in the malware detection study implemented so far. It is a relatively easy, standard, handy approach, but it exposes data privacy constraints further in malware detection, which at this point in time, as technology advances, cannot be compromised.

6.3.4.2 Federated Learning Approach in Steps

Federated learning enables model training on the data distributed on millions of devices; therefore federated learning enables learning at the edge. In this way, it allows enhanced results to be obtained at the end devices in the central location. Federated learning begins with the selection of the model, also called the initial model, which is either a pre-trained model on a central server or not trained at all. Once the initial model selection is done, the next step involves its distribution to all the edge devices or clients. Once the model is distributed to individual clients, then each client trains its model using the local data, which ensures security and privacy. Once the local training is done, the updated models are communicated back to the central server. This is done by means of an encrypted mechanism. In addition, no data is sent to the server; instead, only the model parameters, such as the weights of the neural networks, are shared in our study. Once the server receives the model parameters or the weights of the neural network, it averages and aggregates them into a single improved model. This improved model is sent to all the clients. This training process is iterative until the global model is accurate and perfect per the requirements.

6.3.4.3 Flower Framework

Flower is a friendly federated learning framework widely used today. It is an open-source framework that simplifies federated learning–related tasks on a group of machines. The flower framework is a Python framework that provides user-friendly solutions. With the help of the flower framework, one can find optimal solutions to train a variety of models, including deep neural networks.

Another major reason for its large-scale adoption is its high level API, which simplifies federated learning tasks further. The majority of technical details are abstracted in this framework, like data sharding, model aggregation, and communication protocols like HTTP and gRPC. This level of abstraction enables users to approach complex federated learning tasks with great ease. The architecture of the flower framework is shown in Figure 6.7.

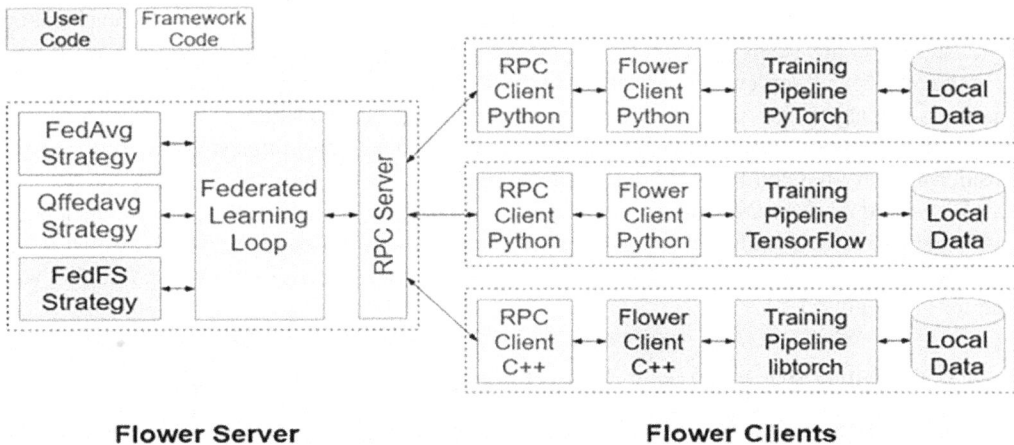

FIGURE 6.7 Flower core framework architecture.

6.3.4.4   Implementation Explanation

The federated learning approach for malware detection in this study is implemented via a single global server and multiple clients. This implementation is done via a neural network model on the client side. The neural network is implemented on the feature selected using DEAP genetic programming and further by SHAP analysis. The following features are used for model training on the client side: proto_tcp, proto_udp, proto_icmp, orig_ip_bytes, orig_pkts, duration, resp_ip_bytes, and orig_bytes. The implementation is mainly divided into multiple clients and a server.

6.3.4.4.1   Client

On the client side, the neural networks are defined using Keras and tensorflow. The model is compiled using the Adam optimizer and categorical cross-entropy loss function. Once the model is defined, the flower client consists of three major functions.

get_parameters()
The get_parameters method is called by the central server in this study to obtain the parameters, which are the current weights of the model, from the client.
fit()
In the fit method, the client receives the model parameters that are weights from the server. This method performs local training on the local data. In the implementation of this study, every client carries a subset of observations. The model is trained for a fixed number of epochs. Once the training is completed, performance metrics like loss, accuracy, and training time are displayed for inference. After training, the updated model weights are returned to the server for aggregation.
evaluate()
This method receives the updated model parameters from the server and evaluates the performance of the model on the test data that is locally available at the client. This method also displays the performance metrics in terms of global accuracy and other metrics for monitoring purposes.

6.3.4.4.2   Server

The study implements a custom server strategy for federated averaging (FedAvg) in the flower framework. Federated averaging is frequently used as an example of a secure aggregation process. The averaging model updates locally on each participating device in the basic process of FedAvg. After that, a secure multi-party computation (MPC) protocol is used on the server to safely aggregate these locally averaged updates. The server receives the model weights from each client, aggregates them, and sends the aggregated weights to the clients. In the implementation, the flower server begins using fl.server.start_server(), which specifies the server address, server configuration, maximum message length for gRPC communication, and the custom strategy.

The implementation of federated learning for malware detection in this study was carried out considering every possibility, listed in the following. The experiments were carried out under two main cases, and then observations and conclusions are made. In addition to this, to train the model, a well-known and frequently used Adam optimizer is used with a learning rate of 0.001 that influences better speed and convergence of the model. A categorical cross-entropy loss function was used for this study.

Case 1: Complete Pre-Processed and Perfectly Balanced Dataset Taken

In the initial setup, all the perfect scenarios are taken, such as a completely preprocessed and perfectly balanced dataset. In addition to this, in the experimental setup, the number of clients are three, and each client trains the model for 10 epochs, which is much less than the 50 epochs performed in the classical deep learning setup. The testing dataset is taken to be the same for each client so that unbiased observations can be made. In the experiment, the number of rounds is varied, and global accuracy, global loss, and training time are shown in Table 6.5.

The table depicts that the accuracy in the case of a balanced dataset remains constant at 95% across different rounds, that is, 3, 5, and 10. The total training time in seconds increases with the number of rounds. The reason behind this increase is the additional communication and computation overhead as the number of rounds increases. Moreover, it is clear that data security and privacy is maintained, which is the core of federated learning.

Case 2: Highly Imbalanced Dataset

In this experimental setup, the number of clients is taken to be 2. The clients are identical in structure except the class distribution in each client. Client 1 entirely belongs to label 0, and client 2 entirely belongs to label 1. The testing dataset is taken to be the same, which has balanced distribution of both the classes, that is, labels 0 and 1 such that unbiased results can be observed. The distributions of classes in the clients are shown in Figures 6.8 and 6.9.

TABLE 6.5
Federated Learning in Perfectly Balanced Dataset

No. of Rounds	Global Accuracy	Global Loss	Total Training Time (s)
3	0.9480000138282776	0.17281992733478546	1.3635828495025635 seconds
5	0.9480000138282776	0.17216716706752777	1.4199879169464111 seconds
10	0.9480000138282776	0.17213290929794312	1.9039289951324463 seconds

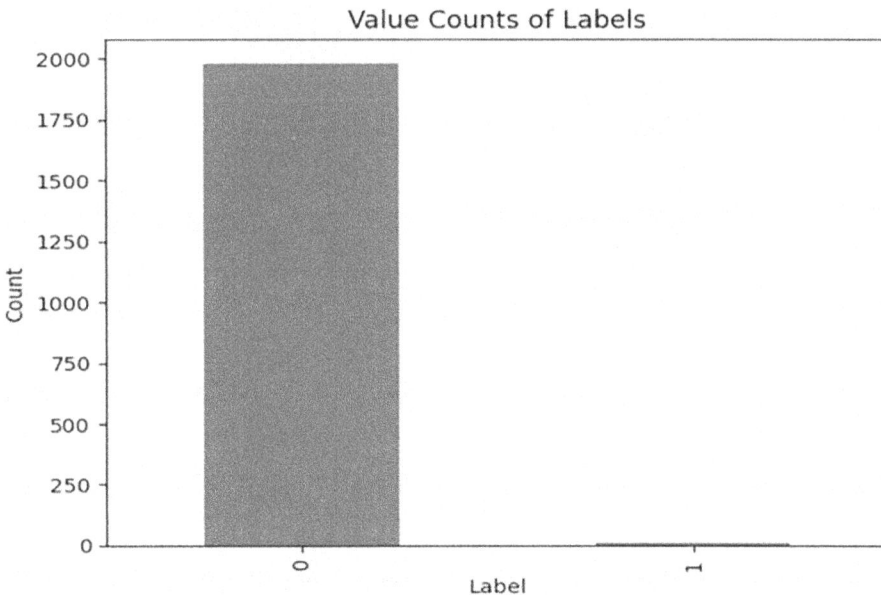

FIGURE 6.8   Label distribution on client 1.

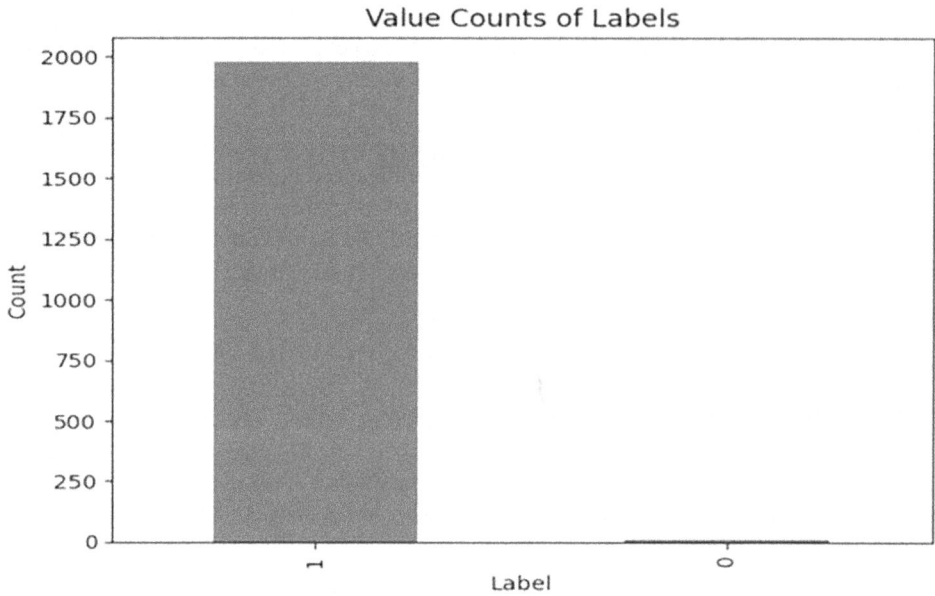

FIGURE 6.9 Label distribution on client 2.

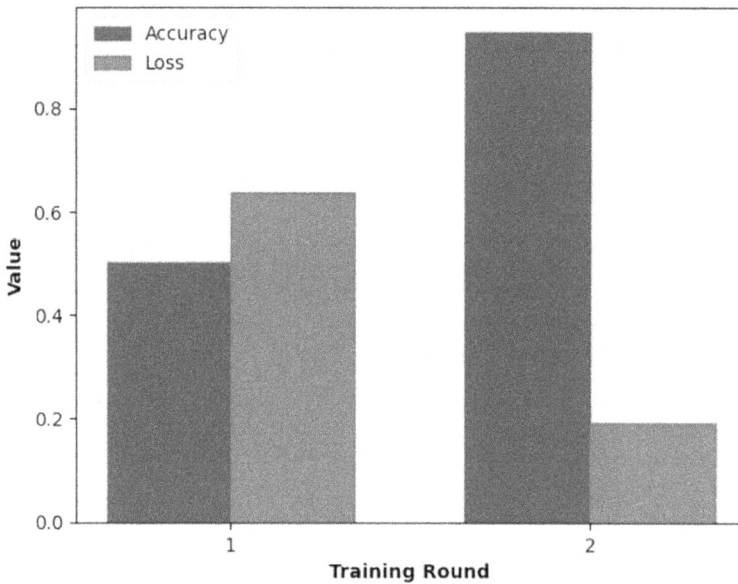

FIGURE 6.10 Global accuracy and loss over training rounds.

When the classical machine learning approach is applied to any of the datasets on either client, the accuracy achieved is very low. However, the performance of federated learning is commendable, achieving significant improvements in just two rounds, as observed in the following. The global accuracy and global loss over two rounds are shown in Figure 6.10.

6.4   RESULTS AND DISCUSSION

In this study focusing on malware detection on the IoT-23 dataset, various algorithms like decision tree, support vector machine, k-nearest neighbor, random forest, AdaBoost, and neural networks were implemented on different testing ratios. The results, as depicted in Table 6.6, show competitive accuracy across different models, with random forest giving a commendable accuracy of 96% at a testing ratio of 10%. Therefore, random forest, closely followed by AdaBoost, performed overall well, as can be seen in Table 6.6.

In addition to this, incorporating feature selection yielded comparative accuracy but helped significantly reduce the computational complexity, emphasizing its potential for efficiency gains. The study also implemented stratified K-fold cross-validation where the value of k was kept as 10 so that unbiased results are obtained and hence further shows how well the model would perform on unseen data. The accuracies obtained in various tenfold cross-validations are shown in Figure 6.11.

The results obtained via cross-validation provide an average accuracy of 94.16%, which confirms that the model performs well on unseen data. The other performance metric scores obtained via cross-validation are an average F1 score of 94.16%, an average precision of 94.70%, and an average recall of 94.16%.

SHAP was employed to understand the decision-making process of random forest for 100 tuples. The SHAP summary plot provides an illustration of how much each feature contributes to the model's predictions, as shown in Figure 6.12.

The figure illustrates that the attributes proto_tcp, proto_udp, orig_ip_bytes, orig_pkts, duration, resp_ip_bytes, and orig_bytes have a major role to play. The other attributes, like conn_state_SH, conn_state_RSTR, service_ssl, service_http, service_dhcp, and missed_bytes, can be ignored, which would help to reduce the computation of the models further. The figure also shows that the high value of the proto_tcp attribute contributes to high value prediction, whereas the low value of proto_tcp contributes to low value prediction, thereby showing that it is directly proportional to the output. On the other hand, the reverse holds true for proto_udp, stating that it is inversely proportional to model predictions.

On the selected parameters after feature selection, SHAP analysis of federated learning is carried out, as it is the best technique for data security and privacy as opposed to the classical machine learning approach. It is observed that when the dataset is processed and perfectly balanced, it

TABLE 6.6
Accuracy for Different Testing Ratios

Testing Ratio	Dtree	SVM	KNN	Random Forest	AdaBoost	Neural Network
10%	0.956	0.952	0.956	0.960	0.956	0.948
20%	0.938	0.934	0.936	0.934	0.934	0.953
30%	0.941	0.941	0.941	0.942	0.942	0.940
40%	0.938	0.940	0.937	0.943	0.940	0.943
50%	0.943	0.944	0.940	0.945	0.944	0.943
60%	0.940	0.941	0.941	0.942	0.942	0.942
70%	0.940	0.940	0.940	0.940	0.940	0.939
80%	0.942	0.941	0.941	0.941	0.942	0.941
90%	0.940	0.940	0.940	0.940	0.941	0.939

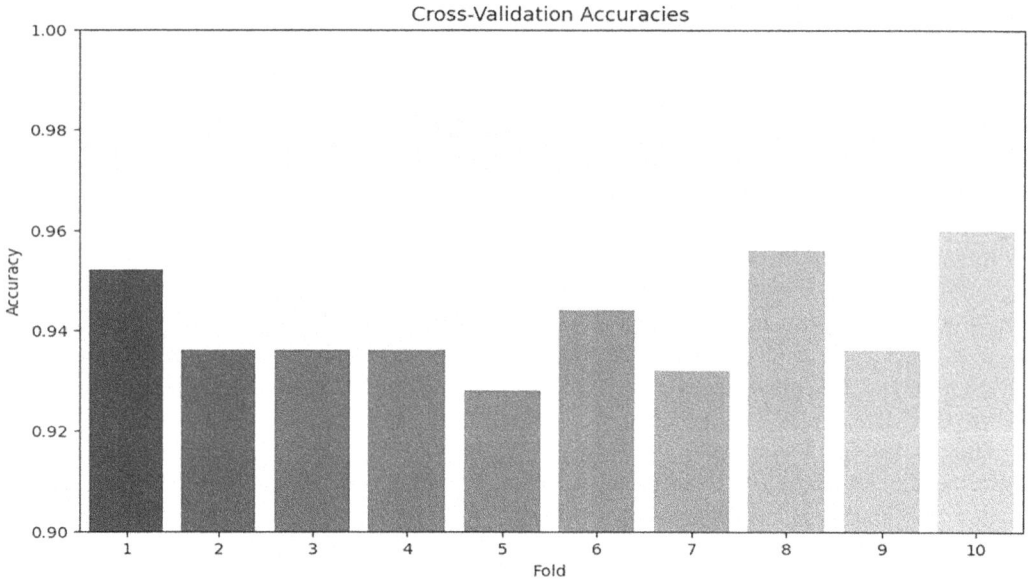

FIGURE 6.11   Stratified K fold cross-validation accuracies.

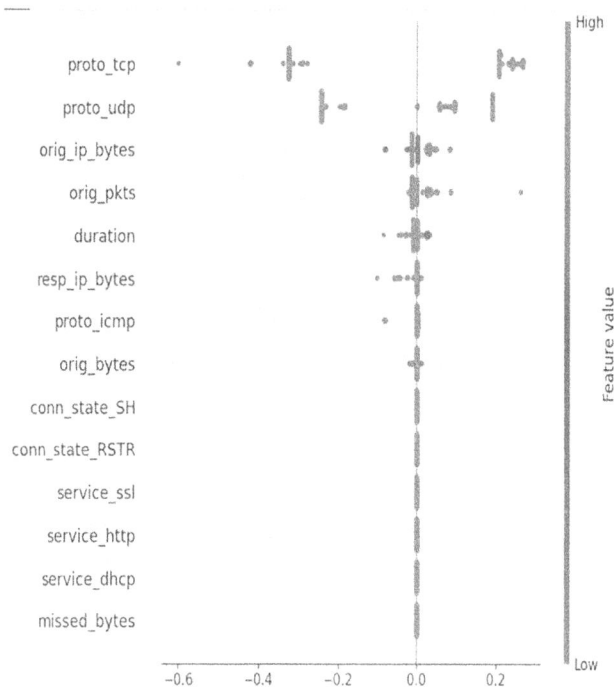

FIGURE 6.12   SHAP value (impact on model output).

achieves a global accuracy of 95% with a testing ratio of 20% and maintains data privacy. Compared to classical machine learning models, the federated learning approach achieves 95% accuracy in two training rounds. A comparison between the classical machine learning approach and federated learning is shown in Figure 6.13.

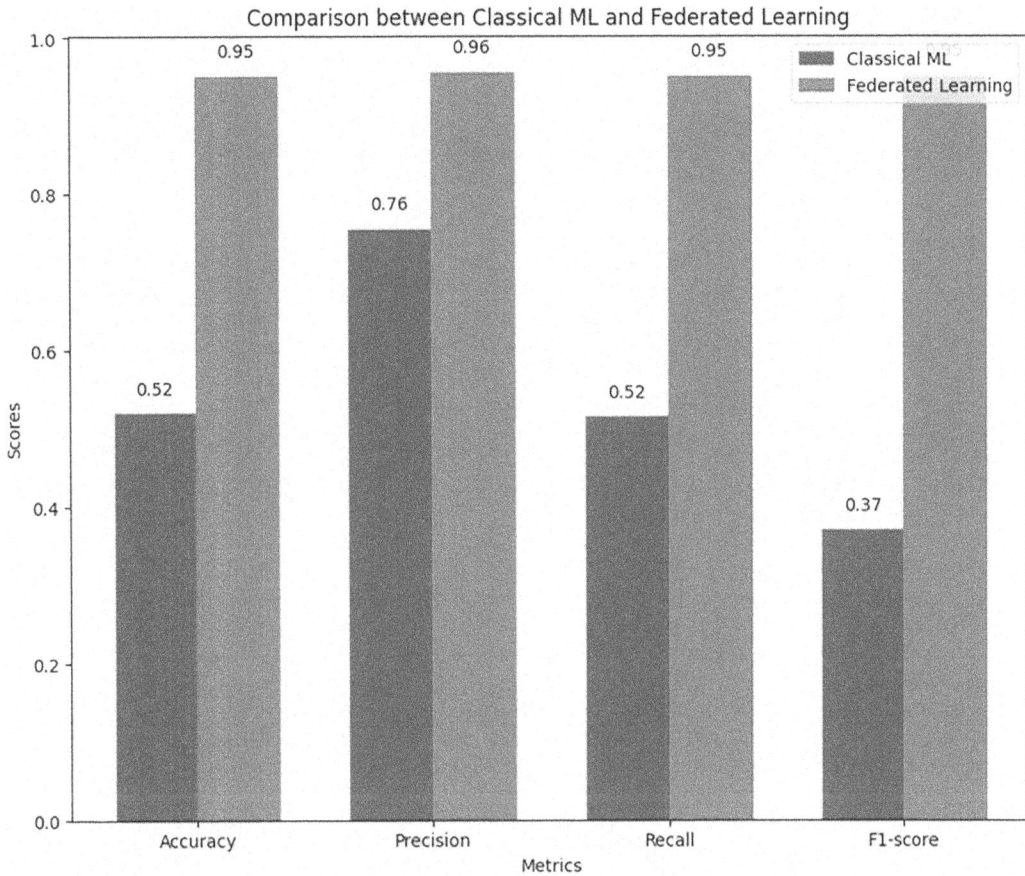

FIGURE 6.13   Comparson of classical machine learning and federated learning.

6.5   CONCLUSION

This study on malware detection has employed a comprehensive approach that combines the DEAP genetic algorithm for feature selection and various algorithms for malware detection. The deployment of DEAP genetic programming assisted in identifying a potential set of attributes for accurate prediction of the models by reducing the computational cost. It is observed that all the models performed well, with the random forest algorithm performing slightly better, with 96% accuracy at a testing ratio of 10%. To check for unbiased results, stratified K-fold cross-validation is also implemented, where k is 10, and the same average accuracy is obtained. The interpretation analysis done through SHAP helps in diving deeper into each attribute's contribution to the output, and with its various plots and analyses, it provides the power to further refine the dataset by excluding certain attributes without compromising the model performance but rather reducing computation cost further. The work done so far has been coupled with FedAvg federated learning, which has had a great contribution, leading to more streamlined and efficient solutions in the ongoing pursuit of robust malware detection technologies, maintaining data security and data privacy. In the future, further exploring the different capabilities of federated learning should be addressed so that the task of malware detection can be streamlined, incorporating every small feature and enhancing its capabilities.

REFERENCES

[1]. Ranjith, J., & Vergin Sarobin M. (2022). Security Challenges Prospective Measures in the Current Status of Internet of Things (IoT). In *2022 International Conference on Connected Systems & Intelligence (CSI)* (pp. 1–8). doi: 10.1109/CSI54720.2022.9923984.

[2]. Rathore, H., Agarwal, S., Sahay, S. K., & Sewak, M. (2018). Malware Detection Using Machine Learning and Deep Learning. In A. Mondal, H. Gupta, J. Srivastava, P. Reddy, & D. Somayajulu (Eds.) (pp. 402–411), *Big Data Analytics*. Springer.

[3]. Nikam, U. V., & Deshmuh, V. M. (2022). Performance Evaluation of Machine Learning Classifiers in Malware Detection. In *2022 IEEE International Conference on Distributed Computing and Electrical Circuits and Electronics (ICDCECE)* (pp. 1–5).doi: 10.1109/ICDCECE53908.2022.9793102.

[4]. Nanthiya, D., Keerthika, P., Gopal, S. B., Kayalvizhi, S. B., Raja, T., & Priya, R. S. (2021). SVM Based DDoS Attack Detection in IoT Using Iot-23 Botnet Dataset. In *2021 Innovations in Power and Advanced Computing Technologies (i-PACT)* (pp. 1–7). doi: 10.1109/i-PACT52855.2021.9696569.

[5]. Abdalgawad, N., Sajun, A., Kaddoura, Y., Zualkernan, I. A., & Aloul, F. (2022). Generative Deep Learning to Detect Cyberattacks for the IoT 23 Dataset. *IEEE Access*, 10, 6430–6441. doi: 10.1109/ ACCESS.2021.3140015.

[6]. Pham, V. T., Nguyen, H. L., Le, H.-C., & Nguyen, M. T. (2023). Machine Learning-based Intrusion Detection System for DDoS Attack in the Internet of Things. In *2023 International Conference on System Science and Engineering (ICSSE)* (pp. 375–380). doi: 10.1109/ICSSE58758.2023.10227227.

[7]. Nath, S., Pal, D., & Saha, S. (2023). Detection of Cyber-attacks using Deep Convolution in Honeyed Framework. In *2023 International Conference on Disruptive Technologies (ICDT)* (pp. 79–87). doi: 10.1109/ICDT57929.2023.10150916.

[8]. Muthanna, M. S. A., Alkanhel, R., Muthanna, A., Rafiq, A., & Abdullah, W. A. M. (2022). Towards SDN-Enabled, Intelligent Intrusion Detection System for Internet of Things (IoT). *IEEE Access*, 10, 22756–22768. doi: 10.1109/ACCESS.2022.3153716.

[9]. Alharbi, A., & Alsubhi, K. (2021). Botnet Detection Approach Using Graph-Based Machine Learning. *IEEE Access*, 9, 99166–99180. doi: 10.1109/ACCESS.2021.3094183.

[10]. Samantray, O. P., & Tripathy, S. N. (2021). IoT-Malware Classification Model Using Byte Sequences and Supervised Learning Techniques. In R. Kumar, B. K. Mishra, & P. K. Pattnaik (Eds.) (pp. 51–60), *Next Generation of Internet of Things*. Springer.

[11]. Chen, C.-W., Su, C.-H., Lee, K.-W., & Bair, P.-H. (2020). Malware Family Classification using Active Learning by Learning. In *2020 22nd International Conference on Advanced Communication Technology (ICACT)* (pp. 590–595). doi: 10.23919/ICACT48636.2020.9061419.

[12]. Gohil, S., Ameria, M., & Sarobin, M. V. R. (2023). An Intelligent Prediction of Customer Churn in Telecom Industry Using Business Analytics Classification Models. In *2023 12th International Conference on Advanced Computing (ICoAC)* (pp. 1–7). doi: 10.1109/ICoAC59537.2023.10249776.

[13]. Borja, T., Alamillo, D., Anhari, A., & Demirkol, I. (2023). Scalable Federated Learning Simulations Using Virtual Client Engine in Flower. In *2023 31st Signal Processing and Communications Applications Conference (SIU)* (pp. 1–4). doi: 10.1109/SIU59756.2023.10223791.

[14]. Bains, J. S., Kopanati, H. V., Goyal, R., Savaram, B. K., & Butakov, S. (2021). Using Machine Learning for Malware Traffic Prediction in IoT Networks. In *2021 Second International Conference on Intelligent Data Science Technologies and Applications (IDSTA)* (pp. 146–149). doi: 10.1109/ IDSTA53674.2021.9660800.

[15]. Om Prakash, S., & Tripathy, S. N. (2020). A Knowledge-domain Analyser for Malware Classification. In *2020 International Conference on Computer Science, Engineering and Applications*. ICCSEA (pp. 1–7).

[16]. Neelam, C., Singh, A., & Gaurav, G. (2020). Android Malware Detection Using Improvised Random Forest Algorithm. *Global Journal of Research Analysis*, 9, 2277–8160.

7 Advancing Drug Discovery with Quantum Machine Learning

Rati Kailash Prasad Tripathi

7.1 INTRODUCTION

Over the past few years, the intersection of quantum computing (QC) and machine learning (ML) has sparked immense interest across scientific and technological domains. This synergy has given rise to quantum machine learning (QML), a burgeoning field poised to revolutionize multiple sectors, notably drug discovery. Utilizing the principles of quantum mechanics and power of ML, QML offers novel approaches to accelerate the discovery and advancement of new therapeutically active compounds (Von Lilienfeld et al., 2020). In traditional drug discovery, researchers face formidable challenges in navigating the vast space of chemical compounds, predicting molecular properties, and understanding complex biological interactions. Conventional computational methods, while powerful, often struggle to efficiently analyze the intricate molecular structures and dynamics inherent in biological systems. QML presents an exciting opportunity to overcome these challenges by employing the exponential processing power of quantum computers and advanced pattern recognition abilities of ML algorithms (Sliwoski et al., 2014).

At its core, QC utilizes quantum mechanics principles to execute computations at an exponentially faster rate compared to classical computers (McArdle et al., 2020; Zinner et al., 2021; Zinner et al., 2022), while ML is centered on creating algorithms that empower computers to gather information from data and make projections without explicit programming. By harnessing extensive datasets and advanced mathematical techniques, ML has empowered breakthroughs in various domains, ranging from image recognition to natural language processing (Carracedo-Reboredo et al., 2021). The convergence of QC and ML, termed QML, exhibits the ability to address intricate computational challenges with unparalleled efficiency and scalability. In the drug discovery domain, where the search for new therapeutics demands substantial computational resources and expertise, QML emerges as a transformative tool (Sliwoski et al., 2014).

A key obstacle in drug discovery involves predicting molecular properties and interactions, a task that often requires computationally intensive simulations and analyses. Quantum algorithms have the potential to exponentially accelerate these computations, enabling rapid exploration of chemical space and recognition of promising bioactive compounds. Moreover, QML algorithms can enhance the predictive capabilities of ML models by leveraging quantum features for data representation, feature selection, and optimization (Robert et al., 2021; Cerezo et al., 2021; Mensa et al., 2023).

This chapter explores the fundamentals of QML, and its applications in the field of drug discovery have been probed. The underlying principles of QC, design and implementation of quantum algorithms, and their integration with ML techniques are also discussed. Furthermore, the chapter encompasses challenges, opportunities, and ethical considerations linked to the integration of QML into the pharmaceutical sector. Case studies and real-world examples demonstrate QML's transformative potential in expediting drug discovery and fostering healthcare innovation.

DOI: 10.1201/9781003499459-7

7.2 INTEGRATING QC AND ML

The coalition of QC and ML arises from the complementary strengths of these two transformative fields, offering unprecedented opportunities to address complex computational challenges across various domains. In the context of drug discovery, this convergence holds particular promise, driven by several compelling motivations, illustrated in Figure 7.1 (Mensa et al., 2023; Batra et al., 2021).

7.2.1 EXPONENTIAL COMPUTATIONAL SPEEDUP

Quantum computers have the ability to solve specific computational problems much quicker than traditional computers. Tasks such as simulating molecular interactions, optimizing chemical reactions, and analyzing large-scale biological datasets are computationally intensive and can benefit significantly from quantum speedups.

7.2.2 HANDLING HIGH-DIMENSIONAL DATA

Drug discovery involves dealing with vast amounts of high-dimensional data, including molecular structures, genomic information, and pharmacological profiles. ML techniques excel at extracting meaningful patterns and insights from such complex datasets. By leveraging quantum-inspired algorithms and quantum-enhanced feature spaces, ML models can better capture the inherent complexity of biological systems, leading to more accurate predictions and faster discoveries.

7.2.3 ENHANCED OPTIMIZATION AND SEARCH

Many optimization problems in drug discovery, such as molecular structure optimization, drug design, and compound screening, require searching through vast solution spaces to identify optimal candidates. Quantum algorithms, like the quantum approximate optimization algorithm (QAOA) and quantum annealing, present novel approaches to efficiently tackle problems connected with combinatorial optimization. By exploiting quantum tunneling and quantum interference effects, these algorithms enable rapid exploration of solution landscapes, leading to improved candidate selection and drug design.

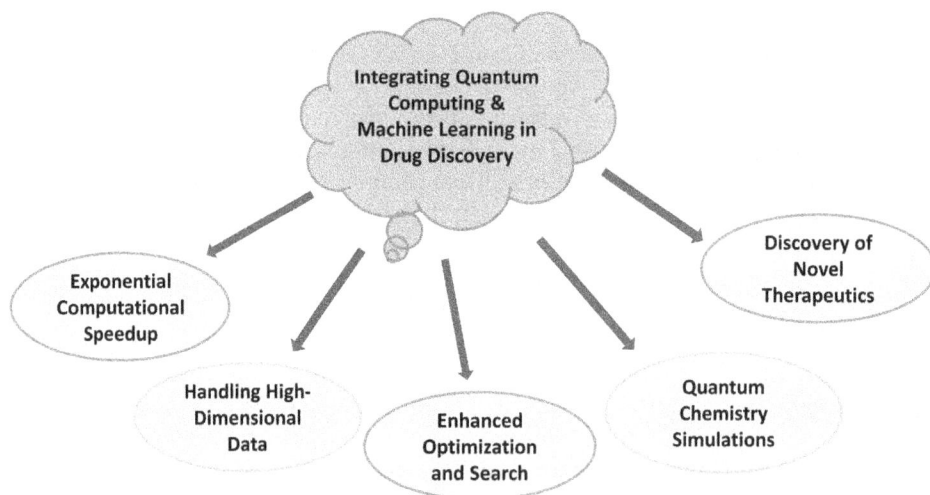

FIGURE 7.1 Rationale behind integrating QC and ML.

7.2.4 Quantum Chemistry Simulations

Quantum mechanics offers the most precise depiction of molecular interactions and chemical reactions. However, simulating quantum systems on traditional computers presents inherent challenges owing to an exponential increase of the computational resources needed as the system size grows. In contrast, quantum computers naturally simulate quantum systems, rendering them ideal platforms for quantum chemistry simulations. By integrating QC with ML techniques, researchers can devise hybrid methods that can capitalize on the accuracy of quantum chemistry calculations and the scalability of ML models to expedite drug discovery workflows.

7.2.5 Discovery of Novel Therapeutics

The ultimate objective of drug discovery is to recognize new therapeutics that effectively target diseases with minimal side effects. QML offers innovative approaches for predicting molecular properties, identifying drug targets, and optimizing drug candidates with unprecedented precision.

7.3 FUNDAMENTALS OF QUANTUM COMPUTING

The foundations of quantum computing are based on applying quantum mechanics concepts to computational processes. The qubit, the quantum equivalent of the classical bits, is important to QC. It can exist in superposition states of 0, 1, or both concurrently. Quantum gates manipulate these qubits, allowing for complex operations. Quantum algorithms, like Grover's algorithm for database search and Shor's algorithm for integer factorization, utilize these features to achieve exponential speedups over classical counterparts. However, quantum computing faces challenges such as qubit decoherence, where the fragile quantum states degrade over time, and error correction, crucial for maintaining accuracy in quantum computations. Despite these challenges, advancements in quantum hardware and algorithms persistently expand the frontiers of what can be achieved in quantum computation (Preskill, 2018; Vedral & Plenio, 1998; Yoshito & Seong-Moo, 2020; Balamurugan et al., 2024; Chae et al., 2024).

7.3.1 Basic Principles of Quantum Mechanics

Quantum mechanics, the cornerstone of modern physics at the atomic and subatomic levels, delivers a set of rules that are fundamentally different from classical mechanics. These principles underpin the emerging field of QC, promising revolutionary advances in computation and information processing. Table 7.1 outlines the fundamental tenets of quantum mechanics (Vedral & Plenio, 1998; Yoshito & Seong-Moo, 2020; Balamurugan et al., 2024; Chae et al., 2024).

These basic principles of quantum mechanics form the groundwork for understanding and harnessing the power of QC.

7.3.2 Quantum Gates and Circuits

In QC, quantum gates and circuits function as fundamental elements used to manipulate and process quantum information, analogous to the role of classical logic gates and circuits in classical computing (Chae et al., 2024; DiVincenzo, 1998).

7.3.2.1 Quantum Gates

Quantum gates are mathematical processes that accomplish precise transformations on qubits' quantum states. Unlike classical gates, which operate on bits in well-defined states (0 or 1), quantum gates can manipulate qubits in superpositions of states, using quantum phenomena like entanglement and superposition. Examples of quantum gates encompass Pauli gates (X, Y, Z), the Hadamard gate (H), CNOT gate (Controlled-NOT or CX), and Phase gate (S), besides others. Each quantum

TABLE 7.1

Fundamental Tenets of Quantum Mechanics

Parameters	Concepts	Applications
Superposition	Superposition refers to the ability of quantum particles, such as qubits in QC, to exist in several states at the same time.	This allows quantum systems to represent and process massive amounts of information simultaneously, laying the groundwork for quantum computation's potential speedup over classical counterparts.
Entanglement	Entanglement describes the phenomenon where the states of quantum particles become interconnected, irrespective of distance between them. Changes in the state of one particle instantly alter the state of its entangled counterpart, resulting in correlations that defy classical perception.	Entanglement serves as a vital resource in quantum information processing and underpins secure quantum communication protocols.
Quantum Measurement	Quantum mechanics dictates that measurements of quantum systems yield probabilistic outcomes. Before measurement, a quantum system is in a superposition of potential states defined by a wave function. Upon measurement, the system collapses into one of these states according to probabilities determined by the wave function.	This inherent randomness distinguishes quantum measurement from classical observation.
Quantum Interference	Quantum interference arises when different quantum pathways contribute to the probability amplitudes of a quantum system. These amplitudes can interfere constructively or destructively, leading to observable effects such as interference patterns in experiments.	Quantum interference has been instrumental in quantum algorithms, as it can be exploited to enhance computational efficiency.
Quantum Tunneling	Quantum tunneling allows particles to overcome energy barriers that would be classically insurmountable.	This phenomenon allows quantum systems to explore regions of state space that would otherwise be inaccessible, contributing to the richness of quantum dynamics and the efficiency of certain quantum algorithms.
No-Cloning Theorem	Unlike classical bits, the no-cloning theorem makes it impossible to produce an identical copy of any unknown quantum state.	This principle has implications for quantum information processing and cryptography.

gate executes a distinct operation on the qubits' quantum state, adding to the diversity of quantum computation. Quantum gates utilize these features to conduct computations across a multitude of potential states concomitantly, contributing to the potential speedup of quantum algorithms over classical counterparts.

Quantum gates are often characterized by their universality, meaning that any quantum computation can be broken down into a series of elementary gates from a universal set. This universality property underpins the design and implementation of quantum algorithms, allowing complex computations to be expressed in terms of simpler gate operations. By combining different quantum gates in specific sequences, quantum circuits can implement a wide range of quantum algorithms, ranging from quantum error correction to quantum simulation.

7.3.2.2 Quantum Circuits

Quantum circuits depict graphical representations of series of quantum gates acting on the qubits to execute quantum algorithms. In a quantum circuit, qubits are illustrated as lines, with quantum gates depicted as symbols conferred to these qubits. The flow of quantum information through the circuit follows the sequence of gate operations, with each gate transforming the quantum state of the qubits according to its defined action. Quantum circuits provide a visual framework for designing, analyzing, and simulating quantum algorithms, enabling researchers to explore the behavior and performance of quantum systems.

7.4 QUANTUM ALGORITHMS

A quantum algorithm (QA), depicted as circuit, comprises three essential components. The first component entails converting classical data into quantum data, known as state preparation, quantum embedding, or feature mapping. The second component consists of a series of quantum gates employed to process quantum data for quantum computation. Last, calculations are conducted to retrieve classical information from quantum system (Figure 7.2) (Montanaro, 2016).

An advanced algorithm, termed a variational quantum circuit/algorithm (VQC/VQA), also referred to as a parameterized quantum circuit (PQC), represents a hybrid quantum-classical optimization strategy wherein a quantum computation evaluates an objective function (Khan & Robles-Kelly, 2020). Following this evaluation, classical optimization techniques are employed to update the parameters of this function.

7.5 QUANTUM MACHINE LEARNING

QML is a multifaceted discipline that integrates QC and ML principles to create novel algorithms for data analysis and pattern recognition. A flowchart outlining the general process of QML, from data pre-processing to deployment and maintenance, is depicted in Figure 7.3. Actual implementations may vary depending on the specific quantum algorithms, hardware constraints, and application domains (Mensa et al., 2023; Batra et al., 2021; Beaudoin et al., 2022).

7.5.1 DATASET SELECTION

The initial phase of QML procedure entails selecting a dataset with defined properties. The dataset should possess attributes facilitating straightforward production and handling within the laboratory setting. The dataset is classified into two subsets, larger and smaller subsets. The larger subset is

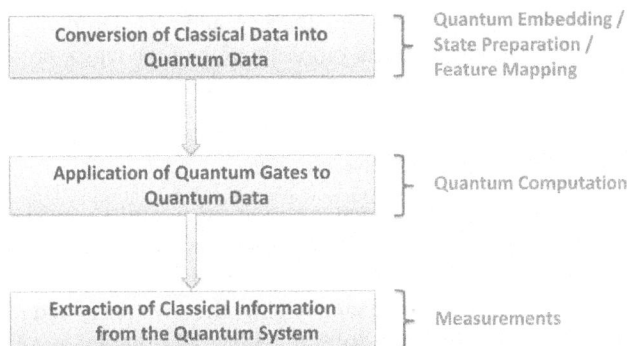

FIGURE 7.2 Generalized framework of quantum algorithm.

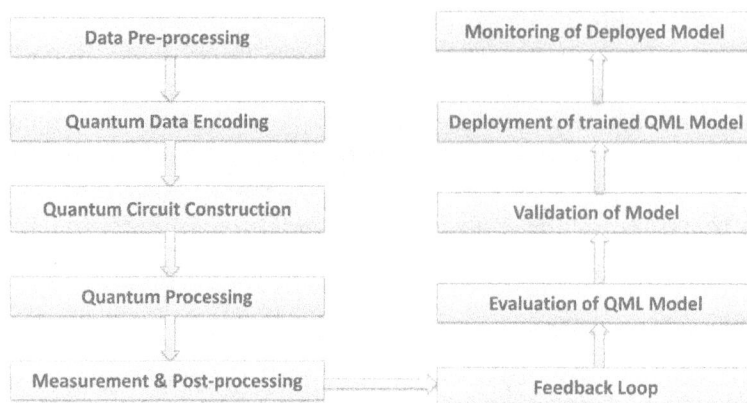

FIGURE 7.3 Overview of the general process of QML.

used for training the model, while the smaller subset is designated for examination of performance of the trained model.

7.5.2 DATA PRE-PROCESSING

The increasing variety and intricacy of the data in QML applications introduce fresh hurdles concerning data quality concerns, including data imbalance, noise, outliers, non-normalized data, unlabeled data, or data with missing values. Low-quality data can significantly affect the accuracy and reliability of QML analysis. Therefore, it is crucial to thoroughly pre-process the data. Classical data pre-processing methods like data cleaning, normalization, feature extraction, and dimensionality reduction are used to prepare datasets for quantum processing.

7.5.3 QUANTUM DATA ENCODING

Classical data undergoes encoding into quantum states (called quantum embedding) to harness quantum processing capabilities. Quantum circuits or quantum feature maps convert the classical data into the quantum states suitable for processing on a quantum computer. Despite the array of strategies at hand, ongoing research persists concerning the transformation of classical data into quantum circuits. Angle embedding, amplitude embedding, and Hamiltonian stand out as prevalent encoding techniques. The amplitude embedding approach encodes information into amplitudes of the quantum state. Angle encoding, referred to as tensor product encoding, is the process of executing angle embedding by applying rotations along the x, y, and z axes utilizing quantum gates: RX, RY, and RZ. Hamiltonian encoding is a linear representation of the tensor products of Pauli operators (Jain et al., 2020; Li & Ghosh, 2022).

7.5.4 QUANTUM CIRCUIT/ALGORITHM CONSTRUCTION

Selecting a QML algorithm is a critical decision that requires careful study. There are several QML algorithms, each with its own set of advantages and disadvantages. Before making a decision, it is critical to consider the specific requirements of drug discovery in addition to the capabilities of available quantum hardware or simulators. Comprehensive study and analysis are required to determine the best QML algorithm for drug discovery and the nature of the available data. Quantum circuits are created on the basis of encoded quantum data and the quantum algorithm being used. Quantum gates and operations are used to execute computations on qubits that represent quantum data.

7.5.5 Quantum Processing

The constructed quantum circuit is executed on a quantum computer or simulator. QML models can be executed on quantum simulators like Tensorflow, IBM's Qiskit, PennyLane, and Google's Cirq or using quantum processors from IBM, Rigetti, Google, Xanadu, IonQ, and D-Wave. Recently, Amazon and Microsoft released cloud-based programs that allow researchers to perform quantum algorithms on multiple quantum processors. The platform for executing QML algorithms is an important aspect in determining the reliability and performance of QML approaches. Quantum parallelism and entanglement enable simultaneous processing of multiple quantum states, exploring the solution space more efficiently.

7.5.6 Measurement and Post-Processing

The quantum state of the qubits is measured to obtain classical outcomes. Classical post-processing techniques can be used to evaluate measurement findings and extract useful information.

7.5.7 Feedback Loop

The measurement outcomes are used to update the quantum circuit or adjust model parameters. Iterative refinement of the quantum algorithm may be performed to improve performance and convergence.

7.5.8 Evaluation and Validation

To ensure the model's validity with new data, it is crucial to avoid overtraining during the algorithm's training phase. This is achieved by running the algorithm multiple times using the training data. Validation techniques like cross-validation or holdout validation are employed to assess the performance of the QML model. Cross-validation provides a means to assess the model's generalization ability during training, evaluate its performance, and estimate its performance with new data. This procedure involves partitioning original dataset into two subsets: a training set and validation set. This partitioning process is reiterated in every experimental run. The model is trained using the training set, while its performance is evaluated using the validation set. Through iterative execution of this process, the algorithm can be trained and assessed on diverse data subsets, reducing the impact of potential biases in the data. Performance metrics like precision, accuracy, F1-score, or recall are calculated to evaluate the model's effectiveness.

7.5.9 Deployment and Application

The trained QML model is deployed for real-world applications, such as drug discovery, modeling, or optimization problems. Model predictions are used to make decisions or recommendations in the target domain.

7.5.10 Monitoring and Maintenance

The deployed model is monitored for performance and reliability. Maintenance activities, such as retraining or updating the model, may be performed to adapt to changing data or requirements.

7.6 QML ALGORITHMS

During the initial stages of QML investigation, the main objective is to convert classical ML algorithms into their quantum counterparts. Several quantum algorithms have demonstrated promising outcomes in data processing. The predominant QML algorithms are variational quantum algorithms, where classical optimization techniques adjust the parameters of the quantum circuit (Montanaro, 2016; Khan & Robles-Kelly, 2020).

7.6.1 QUANTUM CIRCUIT-BASED ALGORITHMS

Quantum circuit-based algorithms have shown promise in various aspects of drug discovery, leveraging the power of quantum computation to address computationally intensive tasks. Quantum circuit-based algorithms offer novel approaches to addressing computational challenges in drug discovery, ranging from simulating molecular systems to optimizing drug candidates and enhancing predictive models. Some of the quantum circuit-based algorithms used in drug discovery include QAOA, quantum phase estimation (QPE), variational quantum eigensolver (VQE), quantum phase estimation inspired approaches, and QML with circuit-based models (Bonde et al., 2024; Michael, 2020; Sajjan et al., 2022; Ullah & Garcia-Zapirain, 2024; Li et al., 2021; Eddy & Bhattacherjee, 2021).

7.6.1.1 QAOA

QAOA is employed in tackling problems related to combinatorial optimization, including molecular structure optimization and drug design. QAOA can be applied to optimize molecular structures, identify optimal drug combinations, and solve other optimization problems related to drug development.

7.6.1.2 QPE

QPE has been designed to ascertain the eigenvalues of the unitary operator, a capability that holds significance in addressing challenges in quantum chemistry and molecular dynamics (MD) simulations. QPE can be utilized to accurately predict molecular properties, such as bond dissociation energies and reaction rates, facilitating the design of new drugs with desired pharmacological properties.

7.6.1.3 VQE

VQE is employed in estimating the ground state energy of a molecular system, a critical aspect for understanding molecular properties, including interactions. VQE is utilized to carry out simulations of the electronic structure of molecules, allowing researchers to predict molecular energies and optimize drug candidates.

7.6.1.4 Quantum Phase Estimation–Inspired Approaches

Drawing inspiration from the principles of QPE, diverse quantum algorithms are devised for simulating MD and predicting molecular properties. These approaches leverage quantum phase estimation techniques to accurately model molecular systems, offering insights into drug–target interactions and molecular behavior.

7.6.1.5 QML with Circuit-Based Models

QML algorithms, like quantum neural networks (QNNs), quantum support vector machine (QSVM), quantum genetic algorithms (QGAs), quantum kernel methods, quantum clustering algorithms, quantum generative models, quantum principal component analysis (PCA), and hybrid quantum-classical approaches, can be implemented using quantum circuits. These models utilize quantum circuits to process quantum data and extract meaningful features from molecular datasets, enhancing predictive capabilities in drug discovery tasks such as molecular property prediction and drug-target interaction analysis.

(a) QNNs
QNNs are neural network architectures designed to run on quantum computers or simulate quantum processes on classical computers. These networks utilize quantum gates and circuits to perform computations, enabling more complex and efficient learning tasks. Variants include quantum circuit-based neural networks and quantum-inspired neural networks. QNNs offer innovative approaches to address molecular structure prediction,

compound screening, drug-target interaction analysis, quantum molecular dynamics simulation, and de novo drug design.

(b) QSVMs

QSVMs extend classical support vector machines to a quantum framework, leveraging quantum feature maps to classify data in a high-dimensional quantum space. These algorithms exploit quantum parallelism to efficiently compute the kernel function, potentially leading to faster classification and improved generalization performance. QVSMs can enhance compound classification, virtual screening, drug-target interaction prediction, pharmacophore modeling, compound toxicity prediction, and drug repurposing.

(c) QGAs

Genetic algorithms constitute a subset of evolutionary algorithms, serving as search engine algorithms or adaptive heuristics in ML, and are employed to discover resolutions for search- and optimization-related problems. This approach employs natural selection to tackle both constrained and unconstrained optimization issues. The QGA presents an innovative evolutionary approach, integrating quantum computation with traditional GA techniques for solving optimization problems efficiently. QGAs offer a novel approach to tasks such as molecular structure optimization, compound screening, drug design and evolutionary optimization, and optimization of drug formulations. Additionally, QGAs can explore trade-offs between different objectives, such as potency, selectivity, and toxicity, to identify Pareto-optimal solutions.

(d) Quantum Kernel Methods

Quantum kernel methods leverage quantum feature maps to compute kernel functions for support vector machines or other kernel-based classifiers. Quantum kernel methods can enhance predictive modeling tasks, such as virtual screening and drug-target interaction prediction, by capturing nonlinear relationships and complex patterns in molecular data.

(e) Quantum Clustering Algorithms

Quantum clustering algorithms, like quantum hierarchical clustering and quantum K-means, endeavor to segment data into clusters by employing similarity metrics. These algorithms harness quantum principles, including superposition and entanglement, to explore the solution space efficiently and identify optimal cluster assignments. Quantum clustering algorithms can be utilized for grouping molecular structures based on similarities in their chemical properties or biological activities. These algorithms aid in the identification of molecular clusters with shared characteristics, facilitating the discovery of structurally diverse compound libraries and the selection of lead compounds for further evaluation.

(f) Quantum Generative Models

Quantum generative models, inspired by quantum Boltzmann machines or quantum autoencoders, have the capacity to produce new molecular structures with desirable pharmacological attributes. Quantum generative models facilitate exploration of the chemical space and the discovery of new drug candidates by generating structurally diverse compounds with specific biological activities.

(g) Quantum Principal Component Analysis

PCA algorithms extract principal components from high-dimensional data using quantum techniques. These algorithms can reduce the dimensionality of datasets while preserving essential information, enabling more efficient data representation and analysis. PCA can be applied in various domains like molecular representation, feature selection and dimensionality reduction, data visualization and clustering, quantum-based similarity measures, data compression and compression, predictive modeling, quantitative structure-activity relationship (QSAR), virtual screening, and drug-target interaction prediction.

(h) Hybrid Quantum-Classical Approaches

Hybrid quantum-classical approaches amalgamate classical ML techniques with quantum processing to tackle drug discovery challenges. These approaches harness the advantages of both classical and quantum systems in order to optimize molecular structures, predict drug-target interactions, and analyze large-scale molecular datasets.

(i) Quantum Linear and Nonlinear Regression

Linear regression is a method used in regression analysis to determine the optimal linear relationship between independent and dependent variables. It achieves this by minimizing the sum of squared differences between observed and predicted values. On the other hand, nonlinear regression is a regression analysis variant wherein the observational data is modeled by a function comprising a nonlinear combination of model parameters and dependent on one or more independent variables. Unlike linear regression, the function used in nonlinear regression is nonlinear, and parameter estimation is achieved through iterative methods of successive approximations. Nonlinear regression proves beneficial for modeling the intricate relationships between variables wherein a linear function is inadequate. Quantum linear regression offers a method to describe the correlation between molecular descriptors and properties such as solubility, toxicity, or biological activity. It can also be applied to model pharmacokinetic (PK) parameters like volume of distribution, drug clearance, or half-life. Also, quantum nonlinear regression can capture complex dose-response curves and estimate parameters such as potency, efficacy, and maximum response. This information is crucial for characterizing the pharmacological properties of drug candidates and optimizing drug dosing. It can also be applied to model structure-activity relationships in drug discovery.

7.7 IMPLICATIONS OF QUANTUM ALGORITHMS IN DRUG DISCOVERY

Quantum algorithms harness the computational capabilities of quantum computers to expedite tasks critical to drug development. These algorithms include methods for simulating molecular systems, screening chemical databases, optimizing molecular structures, and enhancing ML models. By utilizing quantum parallelism and interference, these algorithms offer exponential speedups over classical approaches. This holds the potential to transform drug discovery, facilitating quicker identification of viable drug candidates and more precise prediction of molecular characteristics. Figure 7.4 illustrates the influence of quantum algorithms in the realm of drug discovery (Batra et al., 2021; Bonde et al., 2024; Ullah & Garcia-Zapirain, 2024).

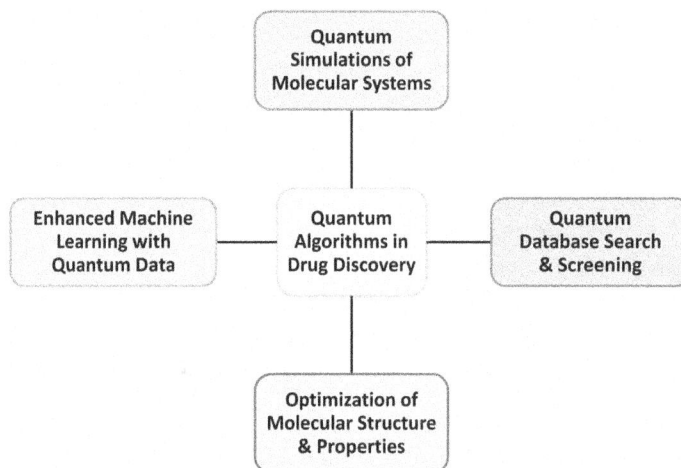

FIGURE 7.4 Ramifications of quantum algorithms in drug discovery.

7.7.1 Quantum Simulation of Molecular Systems

Conventional computational techniques for simulating molecular systems frequently face challenges due to the exponential increase in computational resources needed as the system size expands. Quantum algorithms, like VQE and the quantum phase estimation algorithm, hold promise for efficiently simulating molecular systems on quantum computers. By encoding molecular Hamiltonians into quantum circuits and leveraging quantum parallelism, these algorithms can provide accurate predictions of molecular energies and properties, essential for understanding biochemical processes and drug interactions.

7.7.2 Quantum Database Search and Screening

One of the crucial hurdles in drug discovery involves screening extensive chemical compounds' databases to identify promising drug candidates with desirable properties. Quantum algorithms, like Grover's algorithm, offer exponential speedups for database search tasks compared to classical algorithms. By harnessing quantum parallelism and interference, Grover's algorithm can significantly reduce the computational resources required for exhaustive search, enabling faster identification of promising drug candidates and lead optimization.

7.7.3 Optimization of Molecular Structures and Properties

The optimization of molecular structures and properties to design novel drug molecules with specific characteristics is a computationally intensive task. Quantum algorithms, like QAOA and quantum variational algorithms for optimization (QVAO), provide efficient approaches for solving combinatorial optimization problems relevant to drug discovery. These algorithms help to explore solution spaces and identify optimal molecular configurations, facilitating the design of more effective and targeted drugs.

7.7.4 Enhanced Machine Learning with Quantum Data

Quantum algorithms can also enhance ML techniques used in drug discovery by leveraging quantum data representation and processing. Quantum-inspired ML models, like QNNs and quantum kernel methods, offer improved performance for tasks such as molecular property prediction, drug-target interaction prediction, and compound screening. By encoding molecular data into quantum states and utilizing quantum feature spaces, these algorithms can capture complex relationships and patterns in biological and chemical datasets more effectively than classical ML approaches.

7.8 APPLICATIONS OF QML IN DRUG DISCOVERY

QML shows great potential in advancing different facets of drug discovery, providing novel solutions to intricate computational hurdles in pharmaceutical research. Figure 7.5 lists several notable applications of QML in this field (Avramouli et al., 2023; Li et al., 2021; Cao et al., 2018; Mishra et al., 2021; Simmons et al., 2023; Kumar et al., 2024; Bhatia et al., 2023; Jeyalakshmi et al., 2024).

7.8.1 Molecular Structure Prediction

QML offers promising applications in molecular structure prediction, a fundamental task in drug discovery. QML can be applied for quantum feature representation, energy prediction, geometry optimization, quantum molecular dynamics simulation, SAR modeling, molecular docking, and binding affinity prediction.

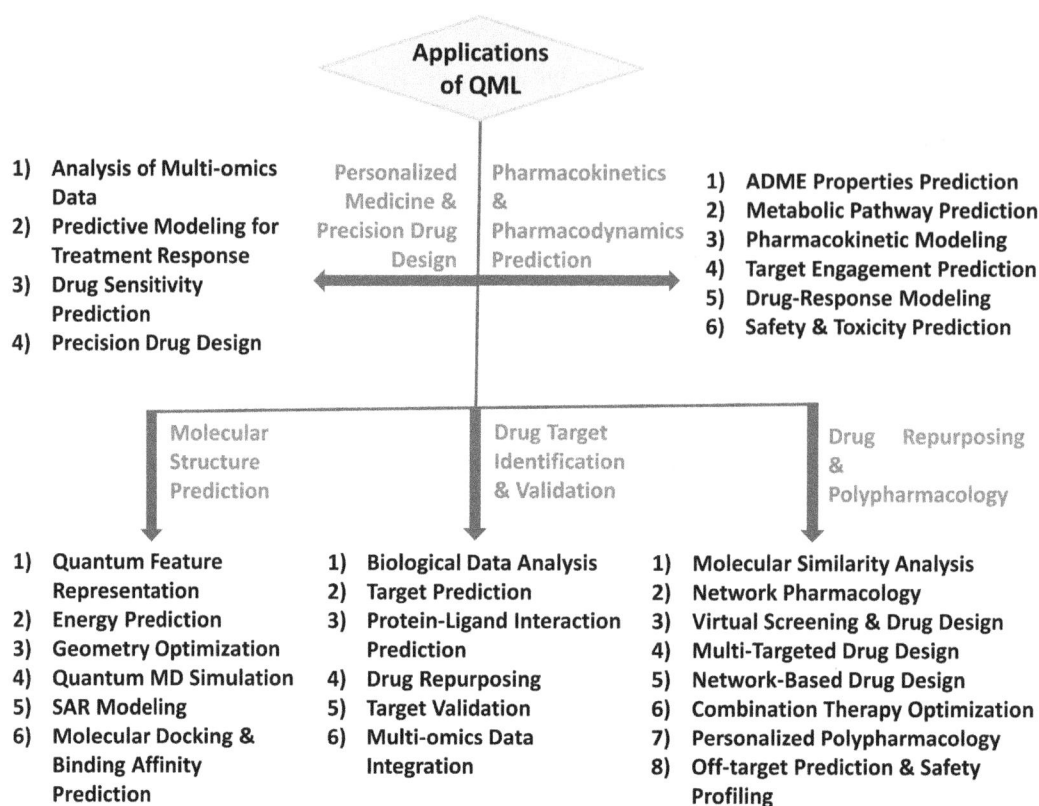

FIGURE 7.5   Notable applications of QML in drug discovery.

7.8.1.1   Quantum Feature Representation

QML techniques can encode molecular structures into quantum states, capturing the complex spatial and electronic configurations of atoms and bonds. Quantum circuits or quantum feature maps convert the classical molecular descriptors into the quantum representations, enabling efficient processing and analysis of molecular data.

7.8.1.2   Energy Prediction

QML algorithms can predict molecular energies, such as electronic energies or molecular binding energies, using quantum representations of molecular structures. By leveraging quantum algorithms and machine learning models, QML approaches can estimate molecular energies with high accuracy, facilitating the evaluation of molecular stability, reactivity, and interaction strengths.

7.8.1.3   Geometry Optimization

QML algorithms can optimize molecular geometries to identify stable molecular conformations and transition states. By simulating quantum mechanical interactions within molecular systems, QML optimization algorithms can minimize molecular energies and explore potential energy surfaces, providing guidance for rational design of novel compounds and investigation of chemical reactions.

7.8.1.4   Quantum Molecular Dynamics Simulation

QML techniques facilitate simulation of MD processes, like molecular vibrations, rotations, and conformational changes. By solving quantum mechanical equations of motion, QML simulation algorithms can predict molecular properties over time, providing insights into molecular behavior under different environmental conditions and enabling the characterization of molecular flexibility and motion.

7.8.1.5 Structure-Activity Relationship Modeling

QML approaches can model SAR by correlating molecular structures with biological activities or pharmacological properties. By analyzing quantum representations of chemical structures and biological data, QML models can identify key structural features associated with specific biological responses, guiding the design of new drug candidates with optimized pharmacological profiles.

7.8.1.6 Molecular Docking and Binding Affinity Prediction

QML algorithms can predict molecular docking poses and binding affinities between ligands and target proteins. By simulating quantum interactions at the molecular interface, QML docking algorithms can predict ligand binding modes and estimate binding energies, facilitating the rational design of ligands with high affinity and specificity for target proteins.

7.8.2 Drug Target Identification and Validation

QML holds significant promise in advancing drug target identification and validation, pivotal stages in the process of drug discovery. It enables the analysis of complex biological data, prediction of molecular interactions, and prioritization of candidate targets for drug discovery.

7.8.2.1 Biological Data Analysis

QML techniques can analyze large-scale biological datasets, such as genomic data, transcriptomic data, and protein–protein interaction networks. By analyzing quantum representations of biological data, QML algorithms can identify patterns, correlations, and associations between genes, proteins, and biological pathways, facilitating the identification of potential drug targets and biomarkers.

7.8.2.2 Target Prediction

QML approaches can predict potential drug targets based on their molecular interactions, functional annotations, and disease associations. By analyzing quantum representations of protein structures and biological networks, QML models can prioritize candidate targets with relevance to specific diseases or therapeutic interventions, enabling more focused and efficient target identification efforts.

7.8.2.3 Protein–Ligand Interaction Prediction

QML algorithms can predict protein–ligand interactions and binding affinities, crucial for assessing the druggability of potential targets. By simulating quantum interactions between proteins and ligands, QML models can predict binding modes, estimate binding energies, and identify key molecular interactions at the ligand binding site, guiding the rational design of ligands with high affinity and specificity.

7.8.2.4 Drug Repurposing

QML techniques can facilitate drug repurposing efforts by analyzing molecular similarities and predicting potential off-label uses for existing drugs. By analyzing quantum representations of drugs, proteins, and biological pathways, QML models can identify novel indications or therapeutic applications for approved drugs, accelerating the discovery of new treatments and expanding the therapeutic repertoire of existing drugs.

7.8.2.5 Target Validation

QML algorithms can validate potential drug targets by integrating multiple lines of evidence from diverse biological data sources. By analyzing quantum representations of target proteins, genetic variants, and disease phenotypes, QML models can assess the biological relevance, druggability, and therapeutic potential of candidate targets, helping prioritize targets for further experimental validation and drug development efforts.

7.8.2.6 Multi-Omics Data Integration

QML techniques can integrate multi-omics data, combining genomic, transcriptomic, proteomic, and metabolomic data to identify key regulatory networks and pathways involved in disease processes. By leveraging quantum representations of omics data and applying machine learning models, QML approaches can unravel complex interactions between biological molecules and pathways, uncovering potential drug targets and therapeutic interventions.

7.8.3 PHARMACOKINETICS PREDICTION

QML assists in predicting pharmacokinetic and pharmacodynamic properties of drug candidates, facilitating the selection, optimization, and development of new therapeutic agents.

7.8.3.1 ADME Properties Prediction

QML techniques can predict absorption, distribution, metabolism, and excretion (ADME) characteristics of drug candidates. By leveraging quantum representations of molecular structures and physicochemical properties, QML models can estimate parameters such as bioavailability, blood–brain barrier permeability, and metabolic stability, aiding in the selection of drug candidates with favorable PK profiles.

7.8.3.2 Metabolic Pathway Prediction

QML algorithms can predict metabolic pathways and identify potential metabolites of drug candidates. By analyzing quantum representations of drug molecules and enzyme-substrate interactions, QML models can simulate metabolic transformations and predict the likelihood of specific metabolic pathways, thereby guiding compounds' design with optimized metabolic parameters.

7.8.3.3 Pharmacokinetic Modeling

QML techniques can model pharmacokinetic processes, such as drug absorption, distribution, metabolism, and excretion, using quantum representations of physiological systems. By simulating quantum interactions between drugs and biological tissues, QML models can predict drug concentrations over time, assess tissue distribution patterns, and estimate pharmacokinetic parameters, facilitating the optimization of dosing regimens and drug formulations.

7.8.4 PHARMACODYNAMICS PREDICTION

QML provides new methods for forecasting the pharmacodynamic properties of drug candidates.

7.8.4.1 Target Engagement Prediction

QML algorithms can predict target engagement and downstream effects of drug candidates on biological targets. Through simulating quantum interactions between drugs and target proteins, QML models have the capability to predict binding kinetics, signaling pathway activation, and cellular responses, enabling the characterization of drug–target interactions and mechanisms of action.

7.8.4.2 Dose-Response Modeling

QML techniques can model dose-response relationships and quantify pharmacological effects of drug candidates. By analyzing quantum representations of dose-response data, QML models can fit nonlinear models to experimental data, estimate parameters such as potency and efficacy, and predict dose-response curves, aiding in the characterization of drug potency and therapeutic effects.

7.8.4.3   Safety and Toxicity Prediction

QML algorithms can predict drug safety and toxicity profiles based on quantum representations of chemical structures and biological activities. By analyzing molecular descriptors and toxicity data, QML models can identify structural features associated with adverse effects, predict potential toxicities, and prioritize drug candidates with improved safety profiles.

7.8.5   Drug Repurposing

QML can be used as a novel strategy to identify new therapeutic uses for existing drugs through techniques like molecular similarity analysis, network pharmacology, and multi-omics data integration.

7.8.5.1   Molecular Similarity Analysis

QML techniques can analyze molecular similarities between drugs, diseases, and biological targets. By leveraging quantum representations of chemical structures and biological data, QML models can identify drugs with similar pharmacological profiles to known therapeutics, facilitating the repurposing of existing drugs for new indications.

7.8.5.2   Network Pharmacology

QML algorithms can analyze complex interaction networks between drugs, targets, and diseases. By simulating quantum interactions within biological networks, QML models can predict drug-disease associations, identify potential drug repositioning opportunities, and uncover synergistic interactions between drugs and targets, facilitating the discovery of new treatment regimens.

7.8.5.3   Drug Design and Virtual Screening

QML techniques can perform virtual screening to identify potential drug candidates for repurposing. By leveraging quantum representations of chemical structures and biological targets, QML models can screen large compound libraries and predict their potential efficacy for repurposing. Additionally, QML can aid in the design of novel drug-like compounds based on the molecular characteristics of existing drugs, facilitating the development of repurposed therapeutics.

7.8.6   Polypharmacology

Utilizing the principles of QC and ML, QML plays a significant role in polypharmacology, which involves the design of drugs that interact with multiple targets to achieve therapeutic effects. It also aids in optimizing combination therapies and tailoring treatment strategies.

7.8.6.1   Multi-Targeted Drug Design

QML algorithms can design multi-targeted therapies by optimizing drug candidates to interact with multiple biological targets. By analyzing quantum representations of drugs and target proteins, QML models can predict ligand–protein interactions, identify target promiscuity, and design compounds with balanced affinities for multiple targets, enabling the development of more effective and versatile therapeutics.

7.8.6.2   Network-Based Drug Design

QML techniques can design drugs that modulate entire biological networks rather than individual targets. By simulating quantum interactions within biological networks, QML models can identify key network nodes and pathways associated with disease phenotypes, guiding the rational design of drugs that modulate network dynamics and restore homeostasis, offering a promising approach for treating complex diseases with multifactorial etiologies.

7.8.6.3 Combination Therapy Optimization

QML algorithms can optimize combination therapies by predicting synergistic interactions between drugs and targets. By analyzing quantum representations of drug combinations and biological networks, QML models can identify optimal drug combinations that target multiple pathways or disease mechanisms simultaneously. This approach maximizes therapeutic efficacy and minimizes the risk of drug resistance by addressing multiple targets or pathways involved in disease progression.

7.8.6.4 Personalized Polypharmacology

QML algorithms can tailor polypharmacological therapies to individual patient characteristics, such as genetic variants, disease subtypes, and treatment histories. By analyzing quantum representations of patient data and applying personalized machine learning models, QML approaches can predict optimal drug combinations, dosing regimens, and treatment strategies tailored to specific patient profiles, maximizing therapeutic efficacy and minimizing adverse effects.

7.8.6.5 Off-Target Prediction and Safety Profiling

QML algorithms can predict off-target interactions and assess the safety profiles of polypharmacological drugs. By analyzing quantum representations of drugs and biological data, QML models can identify potential off-target effects and predict adverse drug reactions associated with multi-targeted therapies. This enables the prioritization of drug candidates with improved safety profiles and reduced off-target liabilities.

7.9 PERSONALIZED MEDICINE AND PRECISION DRUG DESIGN

QML assumes a pivotal role in personalized medicine and precision drug design, harnessing quantum computing principles and machine learning techniques to customize medical interventions according to individual patient attributes.

7.9.1 ANALYSIS OF MULTI-OMICS DATA

QML methodologies can integrate multi-omics data comprising proteomics, genomics, and transcriptomics, in addition to metabolomics, in order to analyze molecular profiles and identify patient-specific biomarkers associated with disease susceptibility, progression, and treatment response. By leveraging quantum representations of omics data and applying machine learning models, QML approaches can uncover hidden relationships between molecular features and disease phenotypes, facilitating personalized treatment strategies.

7.9.2 PREDICTIVE MODELING FOR TREATMENT RESPONSE

QML algorithms can predict patient responses to different treatment options based on their molecular profiles and clinical characteristics. By analyzing quantum representations of patient data, such as genetic variants, disease subtypes, and treatment histories, QML models can predict optimal treatment regimens, dosing schedules, and therapeutic interventions tailored to specific patient profiles. This personalized approach maximizes therapeutic efficacy and minimizes adverse effects, improving patient outcomes.

7.9.3 DRUG SENSITIVITY PREDICTION

QML techniques can predict drug sensitivity and resistance patterns in individual patients by analyzing molecular features and pharmacological responses. By leveraging quantum representations of drug molecules and target proteins, QML models can predict drug–target interactions, identify genetic variants associated with drug response, and stratify patients into different response groups. This enables the selection of drugs that are most likely to be effective for each patient, optimizing treatment outcomes.

7.9.4 PRECISION DRUG DESIGN

QML techniques can design drugs with enhanced specificity and efficacy for individual patient populations or disease subtypes. By leveraging quantum representations of drug molecules and target proteins, QML models can predict ligand–protein interactions, identify structural features associated with drug activity, and optimize drug candidates for target selectivity and pharmacological potency. This facilitates development of precision medicines customized for particular patient groups, enhancing treatment results and reducing off-target effects.

7.10 CURRENT CHALLENGES IN QML FOR DRUG DISCOVERY

Although QML shows tremendous potential for transforming drug discovery, numerous challenges must be tackled to fully exploit its capabilities. Figure 7.6 illustrates some of the difficulties encountered in applying QML to drug discovery, and Table 7.2 depicts various measures to avert them (Avramouli et al., 2022; Elbadawi et al., 2021; Popa & Dumitrescu, 2023).

Tackling these obstacles necessitates interdisciplinary collaboration among chemists, quantum physicists, computer scientists, and pharmacologists, including regulatory experts. Overcoming these challenges will facilitate the successful implementation of QML in drug discovery, thereby expediting drug development and improved healthcare outcomes.

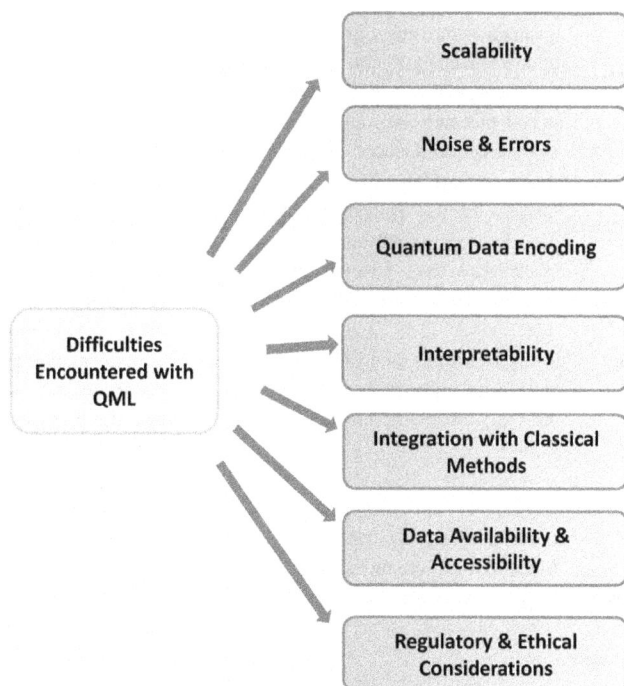

FIGURE 7.6 Difficulties encountered in QML for drug discovery.

TABLE 7.2

Challenges Associated with QML for Drug Discovery and Various Measures to Avert Them

S. No.	Issue	Challenge	Mitigation
1	Scalability	QML algorithms often require significant computational resources, and scaling them to handle large datasets or complex problems remains a challenge. Quantum computers currently have limited qubit coherence times and gate fidelities, which constrains the scale and intricacy of problems they can efficiently tackle.	Developing scalable QML algorithms capable of handling real-world drug discovery datasets is crucial for practical applications.
2	Noise and Errors	Quantum computers are vulnerable to errors in addition to noise arising from decoherence, gate imperfections, and environmental interactions. These errors can degrade the performance of QML algorithms, leading to inaccuracies in predictions and results.	Mitigating noise and errors in quantum hardware and developing error-correction techniques are essential for improving the reliability and robustness of QML for drug discovery.
3	Quantum Data Encoding	Transforming classical data into quantum format (known as quantum data encoding) suitable for processing on quantum computers presents a non-trivial challenge.	Designing efficient and effective quantum feature maps or encoding schemes that capture the relevant information from molecular datasets while minimizing qubit requirements and computational complexity helps mitigate the challenge.
4	Interpretability	Understanding and interpreting the results of QML algorithms can be challenging due to the complex nature of quantum models and representations. Interpreting quantum feature maps, quantum kernels, or quantum circuits in the context of drug discovery requires specialized expertise in both quantum computing and pharmaceutical sciences.	Developing techniques for interpreting and visualizing quantum models is essential for gaining insights into drug discovery processes.
5	Integration with Classical Methods	Integrating QML algorithms with classical machine learning methods and existing drug discovery workflows presents challenges in terms of compatibility, interoperability, and performance.	Developing hybrid approaches that capitalize on the advantages of both quantum and classical computing paradigms, while addressing their limitations, is necessary for seamless integration into drug discovery pipelines.
6	Data Availability and Accessibility	Access to quantum computing hardware and quantum datasets suitable for drug discovery research is limited.	Establishing collaborative platforms, repositories, and datasets for quantum drug discovery research and fostering partnerships between quantum computing researchers and pharmaceutical companies can help address data availability and accessibility challenges.
7	Regulatory and Ethical Considerations	In drug discovery, the regulatory framework concerning the utilization of QC and ML is still evolving.	Ensuring compliance with regulatory requirements, addressing ethical concerns related to data privacy and security, and establishing guidelines for responsible and transparent use of QML in drug discovery are important considerations for its widespread adoption.

7.11 SUCCESS STORIES AND BREAKTHROUGHS DEMONSTRATING THE UTILITY OF QML

Although still in its nascent phase, QML has already showcased numerous success stories and breakthroughs, underscoring its potential value in the realm of drug discovery.

7.11.1 MOLECULAR PROPERTY PREDICTION

Researchers at Google and Harvard University collaborated to develop a quantum algorithm called the VQE. In 2017, they demonstrated its effectiveness in accurately predicting molecular energies, a crucial step in understanding chemical properties relevant to drug discovery. This breakthrough showcased the potential of quantum algorithms in modeling molecular systems and predicting their properties (Head-Marsden et al., 2021; Alexeev et al., 2021).

7.11.2 COMPOUND SCREENING

In 2019, researchers at IBM and the University of Melbourne demonstrated a quantum-inspired algorithm called the QAOA. They applied this algorithm to the problem of molecular optimization for drug discovery and showed that it outperformed classical algorithms in finding the optimal molecular configurations with desired properties. This success highlighted the potential of quantum-inspired algorithms in accelerating compound screening processes (Ramouthar & Seker, 2023).

7.11.3 DE NOVO DRUG DESIGN

Quantum computing start-up Zapata Computing collaborated with pharmaceutical company Merck to apply quantum algorithms to de novo drug design. Their study showcased the application of quantum algorithms in optimization of molecular structures to attain desired pharmacological properties, possibly resulting in the identification of new drug candidates. This collaboration showcased the practical applications of quantum computing in accelerating drug discovery workflows (Zinner et al., 2021; Pyrkov et al., 2023).

7.11.4 TARGET IDENTIFICATION AND VALIDATION

Researchers at Rigetti Computing collaborated with Riverlane, Astex Pharmaceuticals to apply quantum algorithms for identification and validation of drug targets. They used quantum algorithms to analyze large biological datasets and identify potential drug targets. This collaboration demonstrated the potential of quantum computing in uncovering novel therapeutic targets and guiding drug development efforts (Amanda et al., 2023; www.globenewswire.com/news-release/2021/07/13/2261611/0/en/Rigetti-Computing-Partners-with-Riverlane-Astex-Pharmaceuticals-to-Advance-Quantum-Computing-for-Drug-Discovery.html).

7.11.5 PERSONALIZED MEDICINE

Quantum computing company 1QBit collaborated with pharmaceutical company Biogen to apply quantum algorithms to personalized medicine. They developed quantum algorithms for analyzing patient data and predicting optimal treatment regimens for multiple sclerosis patients. This collaboration demonstrated the potential of quantum computing in tailoring medical treatments to individual patient characteristics and improving treatment outcomes (Lang, 2021; Padhi, 2019).

While these examples represent early successes and proof-of-concept demonstrations, they highlight the potential of QML in drug discovery.

7.12   CONCLUSION AND FUTURE PERSPECTIVES

QML represents a ground-breaking approach to drug discovery that holds tremendous potential for transforming the pharmaceutical industry. By combining the principles of QC and ML, QML offers innovative solutions to complex computational challenges in area of drug discovery. Although QML is still in its early development stages, it has already demonstrated promising results in various aspects of drug discovery, including molecular property prediction, compound screening, de novo drug design, target identification, and personalized medicine. Despite the achievement of considerable progress in recent years, several shortcomings yet need to be addressed, including scalability, noise and errors, interpretability, integration with classical methods, data availability, and regulatory considerations. Overcoming these challenges will require interdisciplinary collaborations to develop scalable, reliable, and interpretable QML algorithms that can seamlessly integrate into drug discovery workflows.

As QC technology progresses and more advanced algorithms are created, we anticipate witnessing further breakthroughs and real-world applications of QML in accelerating the drug discovery process. Advances in the quantum hardware, quantum data encoding methods, and error-correction techniques will facilitate study of larger chemical spaces, more accurate molecular simulations, and personalized treatment strategies tailored to individual patient profiles. Furthermore, integrating QML with other emerging technologies like artificial intelligence, high-throughput screening, and synthetic biology harbor the potential to transform drug discovery into a more efficient, cost-effective, and personalized endeavor. Thus, QML stands poised to transform the pharmaceutical sector and tackle the most urgent healthcare problems facing society today, ushering in a contemporary era of precision medicine and personalized healthcare.

REFERENCES

Alexeev, Y., Bacon, D., Brown, K.R., Calderbank, R., Carr, L.D., Chong, F.T., DeMarco, B., Englund, D., Farhi, E., Fefferman, B., Gorshkov, A.V., Houck, A., Kim, J., Kimmel, S., Lange, M., Lloyd, S., Lukin, M.D., Maslov, D., Maunz, P., Monroe, C., Preskill, J., Roetteler, M., Savage, M.J., Thompson, J., Quantum computer systems for scientific discovery, *PRX Quantum*, 2, 017001, 2021.

Amanda, S., Ping, W., Wayne, L., Early diffusion of innovations with quantum computing, *ACIS 2023 Proceedings*, 87, 2023.

Avramouli, M., Savvas, I.K., Vasilaki, A., Garani, G., Unlocking the potential of quantum machine learning to advance drug discovery, *Electronics*, 12, 2402, 2023.

Avramouli, M., Savvas, I.K., Vasilaki, A., Garani, G., Xenakis, A., Quantum machine learning in drug discovery: Current state and challenges, in: *PCI '22: Proceedings of the 26th Pan-Hellenic Conference on Informatics*, 394, 2022.

Balamurugan, K.S., Sivakami, A., Mathankumar, M., Satya Prasad, Y.J.D., Ahmad, I., Quantum computing basics, applications and future perspectives, *Journal of Molecular Structure*, 1308, 137917, 2024.

Batra, K., Zorn, K.M., Foil, D.H., Minerali, E., Gawriljuk, V.O., Lane, T.R. and Ekins, S., Quantum machine learning algorithms for drug discovery applications, *Journal of Chemical Information and Modeling*, 61, 2641, 2021.

Beaudoin, C., Kundu, S., Topaloglu, R.O., Ghosh, S., Quantum machine learning for material synthesis and hardware security, in: *Proceedings of the 41st IEEE/ACM International Conference on Computer-Aided Design*, San Diego, CA, USA, 30, 1, 2022.

Bhatia, A.S., Saggi, M.K., Kais, S., Quantum machine learning predicting ADME-TOX properties in drug discovery, *Journal of Chemical Information and Modeling*, 63, 6476, 2023.

Bonde, B., Patil, P., Choubey, B. (2024). The future of drug development with quantum computing, *Methods in Molecular Biology*, 2716, 153, 2024.

Cao, Y., Romero, J., Aspuru-Guzik, A., Potential of quantum computing for drug discovery, *IBM Journal of Research and Development*, 62, 6:1, 2018.

Carracedo-Reboredo, P., Linares-Blanco, J., Rodríguez-Fernández, N., Cedron, F., Novoa, F.J., Carballal, A., Maojo, V., Pazos, A., Fernandez-Lozano, C. A review on machine learning approaches and trends in drug discovery, *Computational and Structural Biotechnology Journal*, 19, 4538, 2021.

Cerezo, M., Arrasmith, A., Babbush, R., Benjamin, S.C., Endo, S., Fujii, K., McClean, J.R., Mitarai, K., Yuan, X., Cincio, L., Coles, P.J., Variational quantum algorithms. *Nature Reviews Chemistry*, 3, 625, 2021.

Chae, E., Choi, J., Kim, J. An elementary review on basic principles and developments of qubits for quantum computing, *Nano Convergence*, 11, 11, 2024.

DiVincenzo, D.P., Quantum gates and circuits, *Proceedings of the Royal Society of London, Series A*, 454, 261, 1998.

Eddy, P., Bhattacherjee, A.B., A hybrid quantum regression model for the prediction of molecular atomization energies, *Machine Learning: Science and Technology*, 2, 025019, 2021.

Elbadawi, M., Gaisford, S., Basit, A.W., Advanced machine-learning techniques in drug discovery, *Drug Discovery Today*, 26, 769, 2021.

Head-Marsden, K., Flick, J., Ciccarino, C.J., Narang, P., Quantum information and algorithms for correlated quantum matter, *Chemical Reviews*, 121, 3061, 2021.

Jain, S., Ziauddin, J., Leonchyk, P., Yenkanchi, S., Geraci, J., Quantum and classical machine learning for the classification of non-small-cell lung cancer patients, *SN Applied Sciences*, 2, 1088, 2020.

Jeyalakshmi, M.S., Sayyad, A.A., Deepak, A., Shrivastava, A., Rao, A.K., Chakrapani, I.S., Kumar, N., Badhoutiya, A., Quantum computing and healthcare: Drug discovery and molecular simulation with machine learning, *International Journal of Intelligent Systems and Applications in Engineering*, 12(14s), 557, 2024.

Khan, T.M., Robles-Kelly, A., Machine learning: Quantum vs classical, *IEEE Access*, 8, 219275, 2020.

Kumar, G., Yadav, S., Mukherjee, A., Hassija, V., Guizani, M., Recent advances in quantum computing for drug discovery and development, *IEEE Access*, 1, 99, 2024.

Lang, V., Quantum computing, in: *Digital Fluency*, Apress, Berkeley, CA, 2021.

Li, J., Ghosh, S., Scalable variational quantum circuits for autoencoder-based drug discovery, in: *Proceedings of the 2022 Design, Automation and Test in Europe Conference and Exhibition (DATE)*, Antwerp, Belgium, 340, 2022.

Li, J., Topaloglu, R.O., Ghosh, S., Quantum generative models for small molecule drug discovery, *IEEE Transactions on Quantum Engineering*, 2, 1, 2021.

McArdle, S., Endo, S., Aspuru-Guzik, A., Benjamin, S.C., Yuan, X., Quantum computational chemistry, *Reviews of Modern Physics*, 92, 015003, 2020.

Mensa, S., Sahin, E., Tacchino, F., Barkoutsos, P.K., Tavernelli, I., Quantum machine learning framework for virtual screening in drug discovery: A prospective quantum advantage, *Machine Learning: Science and Technology*, 4, 015023, 2023.

Michael, T., Exploring information for quantum machine learning models, *Electronic Theses and Dissertations*, 3433, 2020.

Mishra, N., Kapil, M., Rakesh, H., Anand, A., Mishra, N., Warke, A., Sarkar, S., Dutta, S., Gupta, S., Prasad Dash, A., Gharat, R., Quantum machine learning: A review and current status, in: *Data Management, Analytics and Innovation. Advances in Intelligent Systems and Computing*, Sharma, N., Chakrabarti, A., Balas, V.E., Martinovic, J., Eds., Springer, Singapore, 1175, 2021.

Montanaro, A., Quantum algorithms: An overview, *npj Quantum Information*, 2, 15023, 2016.

Padhi, P.K., A quest towards quantum internet model, *International Journal of Engineering Technology Research & Management*, version v1, 2019. https://zenodo.org/records/3380463

Popa, R., Dumitrescu, E., Drug discovery in the 21st century: Exploring the promises and potential of quantum machine learning, *Journal of Contemporary Healthcare Analytics*, 7, 1, 2023.

Preskill, J., Quantum computing in the NISQ era and beyond, *Quantum*, 2, 79, 2018.

Pyrkov, A., Aliper, A., Bezrukov, D., Lin, Y.C., Polykovskiy, D., Kamya, P., Ren, F., Zhavoronkov, A., Quantum computing for near-term applications in generative chemistry and drug discovery, *Drug Discovery Today*, 28, 103675, 2023.

Ramouthar, R., Seker, H., Hybrid quantum algorithms and quantum software development frameworks, *ScienceOpen Preprints*, 1, 2023. http://doi.org/10.14293/PR2199.000298.v1

Robert, A., Barkoutsos, P.K., Woerner, S., Tavernelli, I., Resource-efficient quantum algorithm for protein folding, *npj Quantum Information*, 7, 38, 2021.

Sajjan, M., Li, J., Selvarajan, R., Shree Hari Sureshbabu, S.H., Kale, S.S., Gupta, R., Singh, V., Kais, S., Quantum machine learning for chemistry and physics, *Chemical Society Reviews*, 51, 6475, 2022.

Simmons, R.M., Mbeki, B.J., A critical analysis of quantum machine learning in preclinical drug development: Opportunities and challenges, *Journal of Intelligent Connectivity and Emerging Technologies*, 8, 1, 2023.

Sliwoski, G., Kothiwale, S., Meiler, J., Lowe, E.W., Computational methods in drug discovery, *Pharmacological Research*, 66, 334, 2014.

Ullah, U., Garcia-Zapirain, B., Quantum machine learning revolution in healthcare: A systematic review of emerging perspectives and applications, *IEEE Access*, 12, 11423, 2024.

Vedral, V., Plenio, M.B., Basics of quantum computation, *Progress in Quantum Electronics*, 22, 1, 1998.

Von Lilienfeld, O.A., Muller, K.R., Tkatchenko, A., Exploring chemical compound space with quantum-based machine learning, *Nature Reviews Chemistry*, 4, 347, 2020.

www.globenewswire.com/news-release/2021/07/13/2261611/0/en/Rigetti-Computing-Partners-with-Riverlane-Astex-Pharmaceuticals-to-Advance-Quantum-Computing-for-Drug-Discovery.html

Yoshito, K., Seong-Moo, Y., Quantum computing: Principles and applications, *Journal of International Technology and Information Management*, 29, 3, 2020.

Zinner, M., Dahlhausen, F., Boehme, P., Ehlers, J., Bieske, L., Fehring, L., Quantum computing's potential for drug discovery: Early stage industry dynamics, *Drug Discovery Today*, 26, 1680, 2021.

Zinner, M., Dahlhausen, F., Boehme, P., Ehlers, J., Bieske, L., Fehring, L., Toward the institutionalization of quantum computing in pharmaceutical research, *Drug Discovery Today*, 27, 378, 2022.

8 Quantum Neural Networks
An Overview

Priyanga Subbiah, Kandan M., Krishnaraj N., and Shaji. K.A. Theodore

8.1 INTRODUCTION

Quantum neural networks, also known as QNNs, are a paradigm shift in the field of machine learning and artificial intelligence. They make use of the fundamental principles of quantum physics to revolutionise the means by which data is processed and analysed. Traditional neural networks, which are based on classical bits, are constrained by the inherent limitations of classical physics, which in turn restricts the processing power and efficiency of these networks. On the other hand, quantum neural networks make use of the peculiar characteristics of quantum bits (qubits), making use of phenomena such as superposition and entanglement to unlock computing powers that are virtually unmatched. Exploring the potential of quantum neural networks to solve complicated optimisation issues, pattern recognition tasks, and even quantum simulation tasks has been made possible by the advent of quantum computing, which has opened up new paths for this exploration. In the following chapter, we will delve into the fundamental concepts and numerous applications of quantum neural networks (Rukhsana, 2023), shedding light on the revolutionary influence that QNNs have had on a variety of scientific and technological fields. We investigate the fundamental architecture, training techniques, and prospective applications of quantum neural networks, shedding light on the benefits and difficulties associated with using QNNs in comparison to traditional neural networks.

The fundamental notion of qubits, which may be thought of as the quantum equivalent of classical bits, is at the heart of quantum neural networks. At the same time, qubits are able to exist in a superposition of both states concurrently, in contrast to classical bits, which can only exist in one of two states: either 0 or 1. As a result of this intrinsic superposition characteristic, QNNs are able to carry out numerous calculations simultaneously, which exponentially increases their processing capability. The phenomenon of quantum entanglement is utilised by QNNs. This phenomenon is characterised by the fact that the state of one qubit gets correlated with the state of another qubit, regardless of the distance that separates the two qubits. With the help of this entanglement characteristic, QNNs are able to process information in a highly linked fashion, which makes the process of data processing and analysis more convenient and effective.

The architecture of quantum neural networks is meant to take use of the one-of-a-kind characteristics of qubits while also preserving compatibility with the frameworks of conventional neural networks. The representation of qubits as neurons in a quantum circuit is a typical technique. The connections between qubits are thought to reflect synaptic weights. Several different designs for quantum neural networks have been proposed, such as feedforward quantum neural networks, recurrent quantum neural networks, and quantum convolutional neural networks. Each of these QNN architectures is customised to certain tasks and applications. Training quantum neural networks provides a unique set of problems due to the intricate interaction between quantum physics and the dynamics of neural networks (Min-Gang et al., 2023). In order to train QNNs, conventional training algorithms like backpropagation are not immediately relevant. As a result, the development of unique techniques is required. For the purpose of training quantum neural networks, many

DOI: 10.1201/9781003499459-8

133

strategies are being investigated. These techniques include quantum gradient descent algorithms, quantum variational algorithms, and quantum autoencoders. Each of these techniques offers a unique set of trade-offs in terms of training efficiency and convergence.

The applications that might make use of quantum neural networks encompass a broad variety of fields, ranging from optimisation and pattern recognition to quantum simulation and even farther. Quantum neural networks hold the potential to provide exponential speedups in optimisation tasks compared to classical algorithms. This would make it possible to find more effective solutions to complicated optimisation issues in domains such as engineering, finance, and logistics. The capacity of QNNs to handle and analyse massive datasets with an unparalleled level of accuracy and efficiency lends them tremendous potential in the field of pattern recognition, which is another area where they show significant promise. The use of QNNs has the potential to revolutionise image identification, natural language processing, and other pattern recognition tasks. This would open up new opportunities for applications powered by artificial intelligence in a variety of companies and sectors. An innovative method for modelling and comprehending complicated quantum systems, such as chemical processes, the characteristics of materials, and quantum dynamics, is provided by quantum neural networks in the field of quantum simulation (Bu-Qing et al., 2020). It is possible for quantum neural networks to give insights into fundamental quantum phenomena and to aid the development of novel materials and pharmaceuticals. This is accomplished by replicating the behaviour of quantum systems on quantum hardware.

In the larger realm of quantum technology, the development of quantum neural networks has important implications for a variety of applications, including quantum computing, quantum communication, and quantum sensing. The use of quantum neural networks as building blocks for quantum algorithms and protocols enables the development of solutions that are both more efficient and scalable for quantum computing activities. These tasks include quantum optimisation, quantum cryptography, and quantum machine learning. Quantum neural networks have the potential to improve the capabilities of quantum communication networks by enabling data processing and analysis that is both safe and efficient. Quantum neural networks also show promise for applications in quantum sensing, which is a field in which accurate measurement and analysis of quantum states are crucial for detecting and quantifying physical quantities with an unparalleled level of sensitivity and precision.

The introduction of quantum neural networks signals the beginning of a new age of invention and discovery, which has the potential to revolutionise several sectors, speed up scientific research, and meet the most pressing concerns facing society. Applications of quantum neural networks in domains such as healthcare, banking, energy, and cybersecurity have the potential to revolutionise the way in which we diagnose diseases, optimise financial portfolios, generate new materials, and safeguard our digital infrastructure. Furthermore, the development of quantum neural networks gives potential for economic growth and employment creation. This is because firms and academic institutes are investing in the research and development of quantum computing. We are able to harness the full potential of QNNs to drive innovation, promote economic development, and improve the quality of life for people all over the world if we foster collaboration between the government, industry, and academic institutions. Quantum neural networks are a revolutionary approach to machine learning and artificial intelligence. Leveraging the laws of quantum physics, these networks are able to attain new levels of computing power and efficiency. Through the use of the one-of-a-kind characteristics of qubits, QNNs provide novel options. Understanding the components of quantum computing is made easier by looking at Figure 8.1.

8.2 QUANTUM COMPUTING PRIMER

Quantum computing is a discipline that is quickly developing and may be found at the confluence of other fields such as mathematics, computer science, and physics. It is possible that computers, cryptography, and simulation will all gain a great deal from its successful implementation. Convolutional

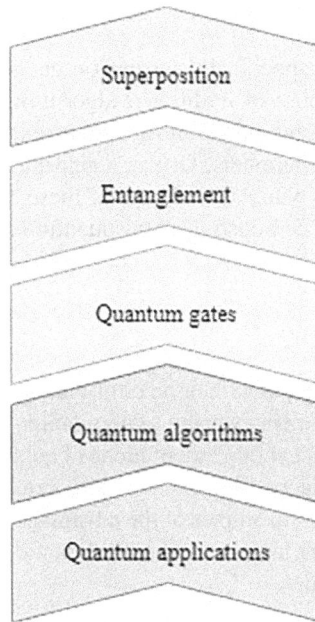

FIGURE 8.1   Understanding quantum computing.

computers, which employ bits to encode information as either 0 or 1, are distinguished from quantum computers by the fact that quantum computers make use of quantum bits, also known as qubits, which are capable of being simultaneously in a superposition of the two states. Quantum computers are singular in their capacity to perform computations in parallel with one another. When compared to the conventional approaches, this characteristic has the potential to result in exponential speedups for some categories of problems. In light of this, it is of the utmost importance to acquire as much information as possible concerning quantum computing in order to get an understanding of the concepts, principles, and practical applications that are driving this game-changing technology.

The fundamental principles of quantum mechanics, a subfield of physics that explains how particles behave at the subatomic and atomic levels, provide the foundation upon which quantum computing is implemented. The foundation of quantum computing is comprised of ideas such as superposition, entanglement, and uncertainty. It is possible for qubits to exist in several states at the same time through the utilisation of superposition, which paves the way for the potential of parallel computing (Stefano et al., 2021). It does not matter how far apart quantum bits (qubits) are physically placed; when they get entangled, their states are instantaneously influenced by each other's states. This occurs regardless of how far away they are physically! The basis for quantum computers and the processing capacity they possess is provided by these quantum and quantum occurrences.

One of the most important components of quantum processing is the utilisation of quantum gates, which are analogous to conventional logic gates but function on qubits rather than classical bits. The Hadamard gate, the Pauli gates (X, Y, and Z), and controlled gates (such as the CNOT gate) are examples of regular gateways that are utilised in quantum computing. These gates, when connected to one another, have the potential to carry out certain quantum operations, hence opening the way for the creation of quantum circuits. The most important accomplishments have been in the design and optimisation of quantum circuits, which will make it possible to efficiently apply quantum algorithms and to solve computing issues. These accomplishments have been the most significant.

8.2.1 QUANTUM ALGORITHMS

The goal of developing algorithms specifically for use on quantum computers is to provide computational speedups that surpass those of traditional algorithms. The unique properties of qubits are utilised by these algorithms. Some of the most famous examples of quantum algorithms are Shor's algorithm for factoring large numbers, Grover's algorithm for unstructured search, and the technique for calculating quantum phase. The fact that these algorithms find use in encryption, optimisation, and machine learning demonstrates how quantum computing might transform several sectors.

8.2.2 QUANTUM HARDWARE

An application-ready quantum computer cannot be built without first perfecting qubit technologies and quantum hardware platforms for trustworthy manipulation and monitoring of quantum states. There are presently a variety of physical implementations of qubits. Some examples of these include quantum dots (Yong-Jian, 2022), trapped ions, and superconducting qubits. Coherence time, gate integrity, and scalability are just a few examples of the advantages and disadvantages that come with each qubit technology. To implement large-scale fault-tolerant quantum computers, the capacity to overcome these challenges is crucial.

8.2.3 QUANTUM ERROR CORRECTION

Due to their fundamental character, quantum computers are vulnerable to errors caused by environmental disturbances, noise, and decoherence. The phrase "quantum error correction" describes a set of procedures and rules developed to detect and fix errors in quantum data while preserving the authenticity of quantum states across time. The surface code and the topological code are two examples of quantum error correction codes that redundantly encode quantum information to protect it against errors. If we want to build trustworthy and scalable quantum computers, we must create robust quantum error correcting systems.

8.2.4 APPLICATIONS OF QUANTUM COMPUTING

Encryption, optimisation, medicine development, and material research are just a few of the many industries and fields that might be profoundly affected by the advent of quantum computing. Encryption algorithms that are impervious to quantum computers have been developed in response to the threat that these machines represent to widely used cryptographic methods such as Rivest, Shamir, Adleman (RSA) and Elliptic Curve Cryptography (ECC) (Do, 2020). There are optimisation-related domains such as transportation, banking, and supply chain management that might benefit from quantum computers' ability to more effectively solve complex combinatorial optimisation issues. Innovative catalysts, materials, and pharmaceuticals with potential uses in renewable energy, chemistry, and pharmacology can be discovered with the use of quantum computers that can simulate quantum systems.

8.2.5 CHALLENGES AND FUTURE DIRECTIONS

Although quantum computing has great potential, there are still certain challenges that must be resolved before viable and scalable quantum computers can be said to exist. Improving the accuracy and coherence of qubits, developing quantum error correction systems that can withstand failure, and expanding quantum hardware platforms are among the most important challenges. Quantum algorithms also require further optimisation and application-specific modifications. To further facilitate the development and deployment of quantum algorithms, it is necessary to establish quantum programming languages and software tools. Academics, businesses, and governments must work together in an interdisciplinary effort to find solutions to these problems. The whole potential of quantum computing may then be achieved because of this.

8.3   NEURAL NETWORKS OVERVIEW

The term "deep learning" refers to a type of machine learning that makes use of neural networks as its primary basis for construction. The method in which the human brain functions has a significant impact on the design and implementation of neural networks. Because of their extraordinary abilities in pattern recognition and data sketching, they rose to the top of the international fame rankings. This section is a simplified introduction to neural networks. Neurons, also known as nodes, are the fundamental components of a neural network. These nodes are linked and organised in hierarchical patterns across the network. Classifying layers can be done in a number different ways: First, data is received by the input layer. Hidden levels are the levels that are responsible for carrying out calculations within the system. These hidden levels are located between the input and output layers. When it comes to creating the ultimate forecast or outcome, this layer is in charge of doing so. The main processing units of a neural network are called neurons, and they are the building blocks of a neural network (Ningping et al., 2022). Each neuron receives data, analyses it by adding weights, sums up all of the weights, and then sends the result through an activation function in order to create an output. During training, the weights that indicate the strength of connections between neurons are modified in order to reduce the amount of prediction error that occurs. The activation functions of a network must first incorporate non-linearities into the network before the network can comprehend the complicated data linkages. In machine learning, a wide variety of activation functions are utilised, such as the sigmoid, tanh, ReLU, and softmax functions. It is common practice to apply softmax to the output layer when dealing with classification problems. Throughout the training process, the network is provided with input data, its predictions are compared to the actual outputs, and weights are altered in order to minimise loss, which is defined as the amount of prediction inaccuracy. When training neural networks, the backpropagation method is frequently utilised as the training component. Through the use of optimisation strategies such as gradient descent, it determines the gradient of the loss function in relation to the weights, and then it modifies the weights depending on the calculation. A characteristic that distinguishes feedforward neural networks (FNNs) from other types of neural networks is the absence of cycles in the information flow from input to output. Recurrent neural networks, often known as RNNs, are the types of neural networks that are responsible for producing directed cycles. Through these networks, neurons are able to process sequences of inputs that are directed towards them. Convolutional neural networks (CNNs) are especially developed to analyse grid-like input, such as photographs, by employing convolutional layers for the purpose of feature extraction. Generic adversarial networks, often known as GANs, are a type of artificial neural network that employs two neural networks—a generator and a discriminator—that have been trained in an adversarial manner. This allows them to generate synthetic data that is extremely realistic. Neural networks have the potential to be utilised in a wide variety of fields, including but not limited to healthcare, finance, computer vision, natural language processing, speech recognition, and many more. The following are some examples of uses of artificial intelligence: medical diagnosis, sentiment analysis, machine translation, object detection in photos, and image categorisation. It is possible that the enormous volumes of labelled data that are necessary for the training of neural networks will not always be available. They may be computationally intensive when dealing with huge datasets and models, which can be a challenge. Overfitting, which occurs when a model memorises the training data, is one of the most common issues that arises during the training of deep neural networks. Other common issues include vanishing or exploding gradients. For the purpose of employing neural networks to address a broad variety of issues that are encountered in the real world, researchers are continually attempting to enhance the effectiveness, interpretability, and resilience of these networks.

8.4 QUANTUM CIRCUIT REPRESENTATIONS

The execution of computations that include the manipulation of quantum bits (qubits) through the use of quantum gates is a significant part of quantum computing, which is strongly dependent on representations of quantum circuits. Listed in the following is a concise synopsis of the various methods by which quantum circuits are represented: Bits of quantum information are the fundamental components of quantum computing. Quantum bits, on the other hand, are able to exist in a superposition of the two states, in contrast to convolutional bits, which can only exist in two states: either state 0 or state 1. When it comes to quantum circuits, they are the fundamental components. The operation of quantum gates is comparable to that of convolutional logic gates, with the exception that they make use of qubits rather than conventional logic gates. Operations that alter the quantum states of qubits are what they are responsible for performing. Representing quantum circuits through the use of circuit diagrams is a standard method that is widely accepted. Quantum gates are depicted by the boxes in these diagrams, while qubits are represented by the horizontal lines in the diagrams. The computation that is carried out by the quantum circuit is defined by the sequence of gate applications that are applied to qubits. Different ways to represent quantum circuits are shown in Table 8.1. Software tools, textual notations, and visual diagrams are all part of these methodologies. Every representation has a specific function when it comes to understanding and visualising quantum algorithms and processes.

There are a few transformations that take place within the quantum gates for the qubits. Some examples of quantum gates that are often used include those that cause a qubit to enter a state of superposition. On the surface, the Hadamard gate (H) seems to perform this purpose. Boards of the Pauli X, Y, and Z varieties determine how to rotate the Bloch sphere appropriately. A controlled gate is a gate whose application is contingent on the state of another qubit. Examples of controlled gates are CNOT, CZ, and others. We make use of the phase gate (S) function in order to incorporate a phase shift. There are occasions when quantum error correction makes use of the T gate (Abu et al., 2019), which is still another gate that is capable of producing a phase shift. As an illustration, quantum circuits might be utilised in order to develop quantum algorithms such as Shor's and Grover's calculations. These circuits are meant to do calculations at a pace that is much quicker than conventional techniques in certain circumstances. This is accomplished by using qubits in a manner that takes advantage of the quantum features that occur in quantum computing.

Measurement procedures are frequently included in quantum circuits. With the aid of these approaches, it is possible to reduce the quantum state of qubits to that of classical bits. In order to arrive at a conclusion on the outcome of a computation based on a quantum system, this is an

TABLE 8.1
Outlining Various Quantum Circuit Representations

Representation	Description
Quantum Gates	Quantum gates are fundamental building blocks of quantum circuits. They perform operations on qubits, such as superposition, entanglement, and measurement.
Quantum Circuits	Quantum circuits represent quantum algorithms as a sequence of quantum gates applied to qubits. They provide a visual depiction of the computation process.
Quantum Circuit Diagrams	Quantum circuit diagrams use symbols to represent quantum gates and qubits, making it easier to visualise complex quantum algorithms and operations.
Quantum Circuit Notation	Quantum circuit notation uses a textual representation of quantum gates and operations, often in the form of a programming language or script.
Quantum Circuit Software	Quantum circuit software, such as Qiskit and Cirq, provides tools and libraries for designing, simulating, and executing quantum circuits on quantum computers.

essential prerequisite. It is common practice for researchers to imitate quantum circuits on conventional computers with the intention of executing quantum algorithms on actual quantum gear. The quantum gear that was previously required for testing and debugging quantum algorithms is no longer necessary as a result of this achievement. Due to the fact that the quantum hardware that is now available has its limitations, it is of the utmost importance to optimise quantum circuits for efficiency and to reduce error rates. Quantum circuits may be optimised by the use of a variety of techniques, including the correction of mistakes, the construction of gates, and the compilation of circuits. The increasing popularity of quantum computing is reflected in the fact that there are already a number of quantum circuit libraries and frameworks available. Through the provision of resources for the creation, simulation, and operation of quantum circuits, these libraries make the use of quantum computing more accessible to academics and developers throughout the world.

8.5   QUANTUM GATES AND OPERATIONS

When it comes to constructing a quantum computer system, the essential building elements are quantum gates and operations. These gates are comparable to the classical logic gates used in conventional computers because they make use of quantum bits, also known as qubits. These qubits can exist in superpositions of states and display behaviours that are coupled to one another. An explanation of what quantum gates and operations are follows: There is a well-established fact that unitary matrices are used to represent quantum gates. It is necessary for these matrices to maintain the normalisation of the quantum state vector in order to guarantee that the average probability is 1. We are able to ascertain the original state of the qubits by comparing it to the end state that is achieved after applying the gate. This is possible due to the fact that unitary operations may be undone. A series of unitary operations may be used to describe any quantum computing system that is currently in existence.

Single-qubit gates provide precise manipulation of individual qubit states since they only handle the management of a single qubit at a time through their operation. The following are some examples of gates that only contain a single qubit: Another name for the Pauli-X gate, which is also known as the NOT Gate, is a gate that has the capability of changing the state of a qubit from 0 to 1 or from 1 to 0. Many aspects of it are similar to those of the conventional NOT gate. Within the setting of the Bloch sphere, there are two rotations that revolve around the Y and Z axes. These rotations are referred to as the Pauli-Y gate and the Pauli-Z gate (Corinna, 2022). This paper describes the Hadamard Gate in detailed manner. In order to create superposition, the gate inserts a qubit into a superposition of two states, 0 and 1, with equal probability. This results in the creation of superposition. When the phase gate is applied to the $|1\rangle$ state, it results in the introduction of a phase shift representing π radians.

Creating entanglement and carrying out tasks that need a large number of qubits may be accomplished through the use of two-qubit gates, which operate on pairs of qubits. The following are some examples of gates that use two qubits: In order for the controlled-NOT gate to execute a NOT operation on the target qubit, it is necessary for the control qubit to be in the state of $|1\rangle$. Changing the states of two qubits is accomplished through the use of the SWAP gate. If the control qubit is in the state of $|1\rangle$, the CZ (Controlled-Z) gate is required to induce a phase shift consisting of π radians to the qubit that is being targeted.

As a result of its capacity to handle more than two qubits of data simultaneously, multi-qubit gates are increasingly being utilised in the development of more complicated quantum algorithms. An additional type of gate is known as the Toffoli gate (CCNOT), which is a three-qubit gate that executes a NOT operation on the target qubit when both control qubits are in the state of $|1\rangle$. Table 8.2 provides a brief overview of some commonly used quantum gates and operations in quantum computing. Each gate has a specific function and is used to manipulate the state of qubits in quantum circuits.

TABLE 8.2
Common Quantum Gates and Operations

Quantum Gate/Operation	Description	Function
Hadamard Gate (H)	Creates superposition state	Transforms basis states to superposition state
Pauli-X Gate (X)	Bit-flip gate	Flips the state of a qubit from
Pauli-Y Gate (Y)	Bit-flip gate with phase change	Flips the state of a qubit and introduces a phase shift
Pauli-Z Gate (Z)	Phase-flip gate	Introduces a phase shift to the state of a qubit
CNOT Gate	Controlled-NOT gate	Performs a NOT operation on the target qubit if the control qubit is in the $|1\rangle$ state
SWAP Gate	Swaps the states of two qubits	Exchanges the states of two qubits
T Gate	$\pi/8$ phase gate	Introduces a $\pi/4$ phase shift to the $|1\rangle$ state
Controlled Phase Gate	Introduces a controlled phase shift	Applies a phase shift to the target qubit if the control qubit is in the $|1\rangle$ state
Measurement	Measures the state of a qubit in a specific basis	Collapses the quantum state to a classical state

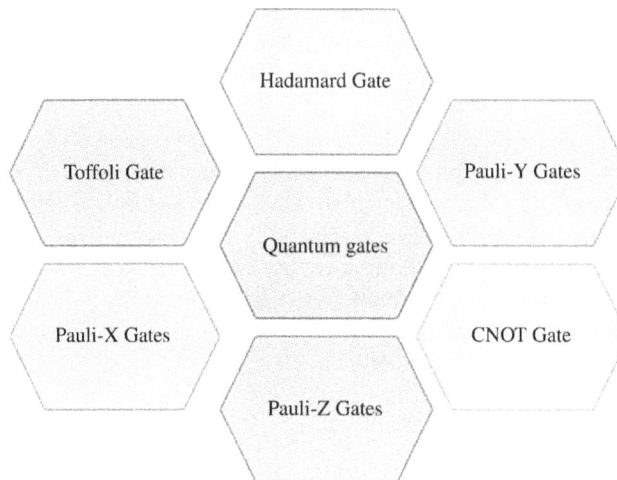

FIGURE 8.2 Quantum gates.

Quantum circuits are a type of representation that may be used to describe quantum computations or algorithms that make use of quantum gates and operations. First, the qubits are put through a sequence of quantum gates, and then they are subjected to measurements, which may be used to acquire classical information. Despite the fact that quantum circuits are able to carry out computations by utilising the principles of quantum physics, classical digital circuits are functionally equal to quantum circuits. Having a comprehensive understanding of quantum gates and operations is necessary in order to construct and run quantum algorithms and circuits simultaneously. The fact that we now know this enables us to employ quantum computing for a wide variety of additional purposes. Figure 8.2 illustrates a number of different quantum gates.

8.6   QUANTUM NEURON MODELS

Quantum neuron models are theoretical inventions that attempt to increase computing and learning by incorporating the concepts of quantum mechanics into artificial neural networks (ANNs). These models are known as quantum neuron models when they operate. In order to illustrate quantum neurons, the following topologies are being presented: A traditional artificial neuron processes its inputs by first adding them, then weighting them, and then putting them through an activation function (Jonathan et al., 2020). This is done in order to accomplish the creation of an output state. This concept may be expanded upon by a quantum neuron through the utilisation of quantum concepts like entanglement and superposition. In the realm of neural networks, classical perceptrons are the most basic type, whereas quantum perceptrons are the quantum equivalents of classical perceptrons. The creation of quantum perceptrons is made possible through the use of quantum computing. Activation functions, weight vectors, and input layers are the fundamental components that make up this system. The implementation of quantum principles makes it possible to represent inputs and weights as quantum states, and the incorporation of quantum operations makes it possible to carry out calculations. When it comes to associative memory tasks, classical recurrent neural networks, of which Hopfield networks are a subclass, are frequently utilised. This idea is taken to a higher level by quantum Hopfield networks, which are able to represent and manipulate states in accordance with quantum principles. In comparison to the capabilities of convolutional Hopfield networks, the use of quantum entanglement and superposition makes it feasible to store and retrieve patterns in a manner that is both more efficient and trustworthy.

Stochastic neural networks, which are commonly referred to as Boltzmann machines, are utilised for unsupervised learning tasks such as feature learning and dimensionality reduction. Through the incorporation of quantum notions into quantum Boltzmann machines, it is feasible to improve the learning capacity of the model under consideration. In order to accurately update the weights and conduct an investigation into the energy landscape of the system, they make use of quantum annealing and quantum sampling methodologies. As part of the area of generative neural networks, both the traditional restricted Boltzmann machine (RBM) and its quantum counterpart, the quantum restricted Boltzmann machine (QRBM), are utilised. The quantum random-access memory (QRAM) system uses quantum gates and operations to carry out calculations. This is done in order to ensure that both visible and hidden units are represented as quantum states (Subbiah et al., 2024). QRBMs have the ability to successfully capture complicated data correlations, making them potentially more effective than convolutional RBMs. Quantum neural networks are an extension of classical neural networks that may be distinguished by the incorporation of quantum gates or quantum processing units (QPUs). The term "quantum machines" is sometimes used to refer to quantum neural networks. Quantum neural networks are capable of performing computations by utilising quantum features such as entanglement and simultaneous superposition. It is possible that this will result in increased efficiency in certain areas, such as optimisation and machine learning. One of the most important areas of research that blends quantum computing and artificial intelligence is the study of quantum neuron models. Furthermore, although they may currently be primarily theoretical, it is possible that they may one day entirely revolutionise a great deal of the computer and educational fields.

8.7   TRAINING QUANTUM NEURAL NETWORKS

One of the processes that take place during the training of quantum neural networks is the optimisation of the parameters of the quantum circuits that act as a substitute for the neural network model. This is one of the many procedures that are included in the training process. The purpose of this optimisation strategy is to minimise a loss function that has been chosen; in order to achieve this objective, it often makes use of approaches that are based on gradient-based optimising optimisation. An overview of the many steps involved in the QNN training process is provided in the following list: It is essential to provide a detailed description of the architecture of your quantum neural network, which should include aspects such as the quantity of qubits, the kinds of quantum gates, and the connections that exist between qubits. The data that is being submitted should be taken into consideration while selecting an appropriate method of encoding. Quantum embedding, amplitude encoding, and angle encoding are a few instances of common alternatives that may be discovered. All of these are examples of frequent alternatives. A quantum neural network must be constructed layer by layer in order to be simulated. This is a prerequisite for the simulation. The majority of this circuit is made up of qubit-operating parameterised quantum gates. These gates are the most important components itself. During the process of training these gates, it is essential to make any necessary adjustments to the trainable properties of the gates. Ensure that all of the quantum gates' parameters are reset to their default values before proceeding with the experiment. One possibility is that the technique that is employed to do this is entirely arbitrary, while another possibility is that it is based on a prearranged startup plan. The preparation of a dataset that is composed of input–output pairs is required in order to become ready for supervised learning tasks. In order for the QNN to be able to process the input data, it is necessary to generate a quantum state for the data. The data will be prepared for processing as a result of this. For the purpose of determining the quantum state of the data, it is necessary to first introduce the data into the quantum circuit and then to let the data pass through the circuit (Jin et al., 2021). In order to retrieve a classical prediction, it is necessary to first measure the output quantum state and then decode the information that is obtained from the measurement. When the predicted result is compared to the labels that are derived from the ground truth itself, it is possible to establish the loss function.

For the purpose of bringing the parameters of the quantum gate up to date, it is strongly suggested that you make use of an optimisation strategy such as Adam, stochastic gradient descent, or gradient descent. One must make use of techniques such as quantum gradients or the parameter-shift rule in order to compute the gradients of the loss function with respect to the parameters. This is necessary in order to do the computation. After a certain number of iterations, which are sometimes referred to as epochs, this should be carried out.

It is necessary to assess the trained QNN on a different validation dataset in order to determine whether the generalisation feature is effective. This is a prerequisite for evaluating the usefulness of the feature. If any improvements to the model's architecture or hyperparameters are required, the results of the validation method should be evaluated to decide whether or not these modifications are required. After the QNN has been trained and validated, it may either be included into larger quantum machine learning pipelines or used to generate predictions based on data that has not yet been seen. Both of these options are available as soon as the QNN has been taught and confirmed. The training of quantum neural networks is a computationally expensive process that requires access to quantum hardware or simulators that are capable of simulating quantum circuits with appropriate qubits and gates. This is something that should be taken into account. In addition, in order to get a performance that is more accurate to the actual world, it could be required to incorporate error-correction procedures and noise-resistant training methods. Due to the fact that the quantum hardware that is now available is both prone to mistakes and noisy, this is the case.

8.8   QUANTUM VS. CLASSICAL NEURAL NETWORKS

Two examples of computer models that are designed to carry out a range of tasks, particularly in the disciplines of artificial intelligence and machine learning, are quantum neural networks and convolutional neural networks. Both of these models are referred to as neural networks. They are, on the other hand, very different from one another in terms of the underlying concepts, structures, and paradigms that are associated with computers. When compared to classical neural networks, quantum neural networks are distinguished by the following characteristics.

Classical bits are the fundamental components of convolutional neural networks, and they have the capacity to both represent and process information. Traditional bits are the fundamental building elements of a computer system, and they can only take on the values 0 or 1. In many cases, the usage of deterministic operations like addition and multiplication is required in both the encoding of data and the processing of data. Qubits, which are also referred to as quantum bits, are utilised by quantum neural networks, which allow for the storage and processing of data. In addition to being able to display quantum entanglement, these qubits are also capable of simultaneously existing in two different states. Due to the quantum nature of quantum activities, namely quantum gates and quantum circuits, it is feasible to encode and process information. Quantum activities include quantum gates and quantum circuits. Entanglement and interference are two examples of quantum phenomena that are utilised in the processes that are detailed in this chapter. Generally speaking, a convolutional neural network is constructed out of numerous layers of artificial neurons that are connected to one another. Every CNN neuron initially takes data, then aggregates it by using a weighted sum, and then uses an activation function in order to create an output. This process is repeated until the result is generated. The majority of the time, they are constructed on top of systems that are more convolutional, feedforward, or recurrent. The quantum neural networks that are composed of parameterised quantum circuits or quantum gates are the ones that are accountable for processing the input data that has been stored into quantum states. Generational models, recurrent neural networks, and quantum versions of feedforward neural networks are all examples of the many diverse shapes that they may take. Other examples include quantum variations of feedforward neural networks. Table 8.3 provides a comparison between quantum neural networks and classical neural networks across various aspects, including their basic units, representation, information processing, computation complexity, training methods, scalability, applications, hardware requirements, implementation challenges, and maturity levels.

The computational capacity and speed of convolutional neural networks are constrained by the processing capabilities of classical computers. This is due to the fact that CNNs are dependent on classical computers and function on such systems. When dealing with large-scale datasets and models, it is likely that the computing cost of CNN training and inference may become apparent.

TABLE 8.3

Comparison Table for Quantum vs. Classical Neural Networks

Aspect	Quantum Neural Networks	Classical Neural Networks
Basic Unit	Qubits	Neurons
Representation	Superposition of qubit states	Binary (0 or 1) activation states
Information Processing	Exploits quantum interference	Sequential processing
Computation Complexity	Exponential speedup for certain tasks	Linear speedup
Training	Quantum gate operations	Backpropagation algorithm
Parallelism	Massive parallelism due to superposition and entanglement	Limited parallelism
Scalability	Limited by qubit coherence and error rates	Scalable with increased computational resources
Applications	Optimisation, machine learning, cryptography	Pattern recognition, classification, regression
Hardware Requirements	Specialised quantum hardware	Standard computing hardware
Error Correction	Quantum error correction codes	Error handling algorithms
Implementation Challenges	Decoherence, gate fidelity, qubit connectivity	Overfitting, vanishing gradients, data availability
Maturity	Emerging field with ongoing research	Well-established and widely used

Quantum neural networks have the potential to be exploited in order to take advantage of the parallelism and exponential processing power that quantum systems offer. If computing were carried out at the quantum level, it is possible that some tasks, such as the creation of quantum algorithms for optimisation and machine learning, may be finished in a shorter amount of time. On the other hand, defending against quantum noise and errors is a challenging undertaking. Additionally, the scalability and availability of quantum hardware are among the limitations that are currently affecting the practical applications of quantum neural networks. When it comes to learning from data, CNNs normally make use of gradient-based optimisation algorithms the majority of the time. Changing the weights of neuronal connections is one of the ways that may be used to lessen the impact of a loss function. Other options include applying a loss function. Due to the remarkable technological capabilities that they possess, they are particularly successful in a wide variety of domains, including pattern recognition, photo identification, and natural language processing, to name just a few. In order to train quantum neural networks, gradient-based optimisation strategies are utilised. However, it is important to note that QNNs are capable of handling quantum input and leverage quantum interference for computing and processing. Different applications of quantum parallelism include quantum simulation, quantum chemistry, and optimisation problems. These are only few of the various applications. The application of these strategies has the potential to aid in addressing issues of this sort in a manner that is more effective.

There is a possibility that CNNs will continue to make use of conventional error correction techniques, despite the fact that these techniques are prone to errors brought on by noise in the data or components of the hardware. As a result of decoherence and improper operations associated with quantum hardware, quantum neural networks are sensitive to being disproportionately influenced by noise and errors. This is because QNNs are susceptible to being affected by these factors. As part of an attempt to solve the challenges that have been discovered, methods for quantum error correction and noise-resistant algorithms are now being developed. This includes the development of noise-resistant algorithms. At the end of the day, both traditional neural networks and quantum neural networks are powerful resources that may be utilised to find solutions to a wide range of computer-related problems. Nevertheless, they operate according to distinct principles, and every one of them possesses a selection of advantages and disadvantages that are unique to itself. The creation of quantum algorithms and technology has the potential to open up new realms of possibilities, and quantum neural networks have the ability to unlock these new worlds. Quantum neural networks have the potential to open up new realms of possibilities.

8.9 APPLICATIONS OF QUANTUM NEURAL NETWORKS

There are a great number of scenarios in which quantum neural networks could be more advantageous than convolutional neural networks. This is due to the fact that QNNs are able to make use of quantum concepts such as entanglement and superposition. All of the following are only a few examples of the numerous applications that may be found with quantum neural networks: In the realm of machine learning, some examples of activities that might potentially benefit from the use of quantitative neural networks include pattern recognition, grouping, regression, and classification. The use of quantum principles makes it possible to conduct more effective exploration of high-dimensional feature spaces, which may result in improved classification accuracy and generalisability. There is a great deal of potential for quantum neural networks to be utilised in the construction of generative models that are capable of producing realistic samples from intricate probability distributions. The underlying probability distribution of data may be discovered using quantum restricted Boltzmann machines and other generative quantum models. These models can also produce new samples that are statistically similar to the training data. There is a possibility that qualitative neural networks are better capable of completing the task at hand when compared to more convolutional optimisation approaches. The simultaneous search of the solution space is

TABLE 8.4

Outlining Applications of Quantum Neural Networks

Application	Description
Quantum Machine Learning	Quantum neural networks can be used to accelerate machine learning tasks, such as pattern recognition and data analysis.
Quantum Optimisation	Quantum neural networks are applied to optimisation problems, including portfolio optimisation and route planning.
Quantum Chemistry	Quantum neural networks aid in simulating and predicting molecular properties, facilitating drug discovery and materials science.
Quantum Finance	Quantum neural networks are used in financial modelling, risk analysis, and algorithmic trading.
Quantum Cryptography	Quantum neural networks contribute to the development of secure cryptographic protocols resistant to quantum attacks.
Quantum Generative Modelling	Quantum neural networks can generate complex data distributions and synthetic data for training classical machine learning models.
Quantum-Enhanced Reinforcement Learning	Quantum neural networks enhance reinforcement learning algorithms for autonomous systems and robotics.

something that can be accomplished by quantum neural networks through the use of quantum superposition. It is possible that optimisation issues in machine learning models, such as combinatorial optimisation, portfolio optimisation, and parameter tweaking, will discover better solutions and experience faster convergence as a result of this trend. It is possible for quantum neural networks to do analysis on quantum data in order to obtain profound insights from quantum datasets. For example, quantum circuit optimisation, quantum error correction, and quantum state tomography are just some of the numerous applications that may be found for quantum neural networks. The performance of QNNs in these domains is superior to that of more conventional approaches when it comes to the recognition of patterns and correlations. Table 8.4 provides an overview of various applications where quantum neural networks can be utilised to address complex problems and drive advancements in different fields.

Quantum naïve neural networks have shown that they have the potential to solve problems and successfully simulate chemical systems in the field of quantum chemistry. As the number of atoms in the Hilbert space rises exponentially, it becomes increasingly difficult to solve issues using classical computers. Some examples of these challenges are molecular electrical structure modelling, molecular property prediction, and chemical process simulation. All of these activities are within the scope of what quantum computers are capable of doing. There is a correlation between the utilisation of QNNs and improvements in financial models, portfolio optimisation, risk assessment, and derivative pricing. The enhancement of financial statistics analysis, the identification of patterns in market data, and the optimisation of investment plan are all within their powers. It's possible that this will result in larger returns with lower risk. The use of QNNs has the potential to make traditional machine learning algorithms run more quickly. This is accomplished by moving some computing workloads to quantum processors. By utilising algorithms and data structures that are influenced by quantum physics, it is feasible to accelerate some calculations. Some examples of these computations include matrix multiplication, searching for the nearest neighbour, and solving linear systems of equations. These are only a few of the many possible uses of quantum neural networks; there are many more. As the technology behind quantum computing continues to progress, many people expect that quantum neural networks will become increasingly crucial in the process of addressing complicated issues in a variety of different fields.

8.10 CONCLUSION

Finally, the introduction of quantum neural networks has brought about a revolutionary shift in artificial intelligence and machine learning. Techniques for data processing and analysis that are based on the principles of quantum physics are presented by them as an alternative to the conventional kind of wisdom known as convolutional. Quantum neural networks have the potential to exceed ordinary neural networks in terms of processing speed and efficiency, according to theoretical models. In order for this to take place, quantum bits and quantum phenomena like entanglement and superposition are required. Throughout the entirety of this chapter, we have investigated the foundations of QNNs as well as their applications, proving that they are capable of handling difficult optimisation issues, pattern recognition tasks, and quantum simulation workloads. Several different QNN designs, training techniques, and applications are compared and contrasted in this chapter. The primary focus of this investigation is on the advantages and disadvantages of these networks in comparison to more convolutional neural networks. In addition, we have investigated the possible social and economic impacts of quantum neural networks, as well as the effects that these networks have on certain quantum computing, communication, and sensing domains. Despite the fact that quantum neural networks have the potential to significantly increase machine learning and artificial intelligence capabilities, they still present a number of critical obstacles that need to be resolved. A few examples are scalable qubit technology, robust training algorithms, and efficient error correction techniques. Others include scalable qubit technology. In addition, in order for QNNs to be included in applications that are used in the real world, a number of domain specialists would need to collaborate and engage in research and development. When everything is taken into consideration, this chapter offers fascinating background on the developing subject of quantum neural networks and draws attention to the tremendous prospects that exist for future study and development in this particular scientific area. We may be able to discover new approaches to solving difficult issues and advance scientific, technical, and societal advancements if we continue to learn more about quantum neural networks and improve upon them.

REFERENCES

Abu, Kamruzzaman, Yousef, Alhwaiti, Avery, Leider, Charles, C. Tappert. (2019). *Quantum Deep Learning Neural Networks*. doi: 10.1007/978-3-030-12385-7_24

Bu-Qing, Chen, Xu-Feng, Niu. (2020). A Novel Neural Network Based on Quantum Computing. *International Journal of Theoretical Physics*. doi: 10.1007/S10773-020-04475-4

Corinna, Nerz. (2022). *Quantum Neural Networks—Computational Field Theory and Dynamics*. doi: 10.48550/arxiv.2203.10292

Do, Ngoc, Diep. (2020). Some Quantum Neural Networks. *International Journal of Theoretical Physics*. doi: 10.1007/S10773-020-04397-1

Jin, Zheng, Qing, Gao, Yanxuan, Lu. (2021). *Quantum Graph Convolutional Neural Networks*. doi: 10.23919/CCC52363.2021.9550372

Jonathan, Allcock, Chang-Yu, Hsieh, Iordanis, Kerenidis, Shengyu, Zhang. (2020). *Quantum Algorithms for Feedforward Neural Networks*. doi: 10.1145/3411466

Min-Gang, Zhou, Zhi, Ping, Liu, Hua-Lei, Yin, Chen-Long, Li, Dongming, Xu, Zeng-Bing, Chen. (2023). Quantum Neural Network for Quantum Neural Computing. *Research*. doi: 10.34133/research.0134

Ningping, Cao, Jie, Xie, Aonan, Zhang, Shi-Yao, Hou, Lijian, Zhang, Bei, Zeng. (2022). Neural Networks for Quantum Inverse Problems. *New Journal of Physics*. doi: 10.1088/1367-2630/ac706c

Rukhsana, Qamber. (2023). Quantum Neural Networks. *Machine Learning: Foundations, Methodologies, and Applications*. doi: 10.1007/978-981-19-6897-6_9

Stefano, Mangini, Francesco, Tacchino, Dario, Gerace, Daniele, Bajoni, Chiara, Macchiavello. (2021). Quantum Computing Models for Artificial Neural Networks. *EPL*. doi: 10.1209/0295-5075/134/10002

Subbiah, P., Krishnaraj, N., Bellam, K. (2024). Quantum Machine Learning: Enhancing AI with Quantum Computing. In *Applications and Principles of Quantum Computing* (pp. 129–145). IGI Global.

Yong-Jian, Gu. (2022). Quantum-inspired Complex Convolutional Neural Networks. *Applied Intelligence*. doi: 10.1007/s10489-022-03525-0

9 Exploring the Intersection of Quantum Neural Networks and Classical Neural Networks for Early Cancer Identification

J. Olalekan Awujoola, T. Aniemeka Enem,
J. Adeyemi Owolabi, O. Christiana Akusu, O. Abioye,
E. AbidemiAwujoola, and R. OlayinkaAdelegan

9.1 INTRODUCTION

Quantum mechanics, a branch of physics, focuses on understanding the behavior of particles at extremely small scales, characterized by discrete values for certain quantities. While traditionally applied to microscopic systems, quantum mechanics also has implications for macroscopic phenomena. The term "quantum" emphasizes the discrete nature of these values, contrasting with the continuous values observed in classical mechanics. In recent years, the intersection of quantum computing and deep learning has garnered significant attention, leading to notable advancements in both fields (Kwak et al., 2021). Within deep learning, previously perceived limitations such as gradient vanishing, local minima, and inefficiencies in large-scale parameter training are being progressively overcome (Park et al., 2021). This progress has been facilitated by the emergence of innovative algorithms like quantum neural networks (QNNs), convolutional neural networks (CNNs), and recurrent neural networks (RNNs), fundamentally transforming data processing methodologies.

Quantum computing harnesses the principles of entanglement and superposition to redefine the basic unit of data, known as the bit, into a quantum bit (qubit) (Arute et al., 2019). Various approaches exist for the physical realization of quantum computers, including photonic and silicon-based circuitry. However, progress has been hindered by challenges related to entropy and noise. Despite these obstacles, the theoretical framework of quantum computing is sufficiently developed to be implemented once full-scale quantum computers become viable. Quantum computers offer unparalleled computational speed and the ability to process vast amounts of data simultaneously. Unlike classical bits, which convey information through binary representation, qubits within quantum gates exchange information instantaneously, leading to exponential computational capabilities. This unique property, known as quantum supremacy, enables a single quantum computer to surpass the computational power of all existing classical computers combined. While quantum computation is a relatively nascent field, rapid advancements in both theoretical and practical aspects are driving researchers towards the development of novel logic gates and physical hardware. Presently, limited-scale quantum computers are already making significant contributions in specialized areas such as pharmaceuticals and chemical interactions for next-generation batteries. Projections suggest that fully capable quantum computers will become publicly accessible by the end of the 21st century (Sahib et al., 2023).

Concurrently, the field of quantum computing has witnessed rapid evolution, transitioning from a realm of theoretical potential to one of tangible progress. Notably, variational quantum circuits (VQCs) have emerged as a promising paradigm within quantum computing, showcasing remarkable

DOI: 10.1201/9781003499459-9

capabilities in solving combinatorial optimization problems and addressing challenges in molecular energy calculations (Kwak et al., 2021). These advancements have spurred the exploration of quantum computing's applicability in designing novel machine learning algorithms. Among these endeavors, quantum deep learning has emerged as a burgeoning field, leveraging insights from traditional deep learning research while harnessing the unique capabilities of quantum computing. As evidenced by a plethora of recent publications, quantum deep learning has yielded notable achievements, prompting continued investigation and follow-up studies in the present era. In recent years, advances in computing technology have made it possible to process large-scale data more effectively. Quantum computing (QC) has emerged as a promising solution for solving complex tasks much faster than traditional computers. This advancement holds significant potential for the healthcare sector, especially as the volume and diversity of health data continue to grow rapidly. Quantum computing offers a revolutionary approach to enhancing healthcare technologies. While previous research has showcased the potential of QC in introducing new possibilities for complex healthcare computations, the existing literature on QC for healthcare remains largely unstructured. Additionally, the papers on QC for healthcare that have been proposed so far only cover a small fraction of the disruptive use cases that QC could offer in the healthcare field (Ur Rasool et al., 2023).

The origins of quantum neural network research date back to the 1990s, marking a significant milestone in the exploration of quantum computing principles applied to neural networks. During this nascent stage, researchers ventured into various directions within this emerging field, proposing numerous ideas and preliminary models that underscored the vast potential of QNN research. In 1995, Kak introduced the concept of quantum neural computation, pioneering the integration of quantum computation into neuron modeling for the first time. Subsequent advancements led to the development of diverse QNN models, each offering unique insights and approaches. For instance, in 1997, Karayiannis and Xiong conceptualized a QNN model based on the superposition of quantum states within the traditional three-layer neural network structure, incorporating multi-stage excitation functions to imbue the network with inherent fuzziness.

Further contributions emerged globally, with researchers from Japan and China making notable strides in QNN development. In 2000, Kouda et al. proposed a QNN model leveraging single-bit quantum rotation gates and controlled-not gates, integrating quantum states as neuron states and employing qubits-based information representation and processing methods within traditional neural network topologies. Meanwhile, in China, Cao et al. (2022) and Xie et al. (2023) pioneered the exploration of quantum neural computing concepts, laying the groundwork for subsequent research endeavors in the country. Notably, Xie et al. (2023) introduced the innovative QNNk model, utilizing the general quantum logic gate group as the basis function for calculations, thereby contributing to the advancement of QNN methodologies.

These early endeavors reflect the dynamic landscape of QNN research, characterized by cross-disciplinary collaboration and innovative problem-solving approaches. As the field continues to evolve, the synthesis of quantum computing principles and neural network architectures holds the promise of unlocking new frontiers in artificial intelligence and computational neuroscience.

Quantum neural networks represent a cutting-edge domain in modern research, blending quantum and classical computational paradigms to provide a powerful tool for quantum machine learning endeavors. Recognized interchangeably as variational or parameterized quantum circuits (PQCs), QNNs have garnered significant attention within the quantum machine learning landscape. This surge in interest is highlighted in studies by Beer et al. (2020), Bharti et al. (2022), Cerezo et al. (2021), and others. Extensive literature, surveyed by Behrman et al. (2008), Jeswal et al. (2019), Mangini et al. (2021), Zhao and Wang (2021), and Li and Deng (2021), explores various methodologies for implementing QNNs and related model classes. Early investigations into QNNs, as detailed by Kak (1995), Behrman et al. (2008), and Nguyen (2019), originated from biological and hardware perspectives. However, contemporary characterizations of QNNs pivot towards their integration with classical artificial neural networks, emphasizing parameter optimization through training procedures. This evolution underscores the dynamic nature of research in this field, as QNNs continue to push the boundaries of quantum machine learning capabilities.

In the rapidly evolving landscape of artificial intelligence (AI) and quantum computing, researchers are actively working to bridge these two realms. This endeavor is evident in the optimization efforts directed towards quantum data, as highlighted in studies by Cong et al. (2019) and Beer et al. (2020), as well as in the exploration of deep learning architectures extended into quantum structures by researchers like Bausch (2020), Henderson et al. (2019), Kerenidis et al. (2020), Lloyd and Weedbrook (2018), Dallaire-Demers and Killoran (2018), and Zoufal et al. (2019). Amidst these endeavors, enhancing the expressibility, trainability, and generalization power of quantum neural networks emerges as a central research focus. QNNs represent a convergence of quantum mechanics and neural network paradigms, offering significant potential while grappling with inherent complexities. Ongoing efforts are dedicated to unlocking this potential, overcoming challenges, and paving the way towards quantum-enhanced artificial intelligence.

This chapter represents a progressive step forward, building upon the advancements in both classical and quantum neural networks to tackle image classification challenges more effectively. The focus is on leveraging quantum neural networks in real-world applications, particularly in the recognition of breast cancer, a critical medical diagnostic task. The approach involves constructing a classical enhanced quantum neural network tailored for this purpose. Through experiments, the performance of this novel architecture is assessed and compared against traditional classical neural networks. A key aspect of this comparison involves evaluating computational efficiency, particularly in scenarios with limited computing resources. This exploration aims to provide insights into the efficacy and feasibility of utilizing quantum-enhanced approaches in practical image classification tasks.

9.2 QUANTUM COMPUTING FOUNDATIONS

Quantum computing, rooted in the principles of quantum mechanics, emerged as a groundbreaking concept in the 1980s through seminal studies by Benioff (1980) and Feynman (1982). Feynman's proposition of quantum computation stems from the notion that the quantum universe can only be faithfully simulated by quantum computers, setting them apart from classical counterparts. Furthermore, the decline of Moore's law, which traditionally dictated that computing power doubles every two years (Prati et al., 2017; Markov, 2014), necessitates a transition from classical to quantum computing. As transistors continue to shrink in size, reaching the atomic scale, control over them becomes inherently quantum, thus paving the way for quantum computers to become the next frontier in computing technology.

The transition to quantum computing also presents compelling advantages, notably exponential speed-ups achievable with certain quantum algorithms (Nielsen and Chuang, 2011). Over the years, numerous quantum algorithms have demonstrated significant enhancements in efficiency compared to their classical counterparts (Montanaro, 2016). One such application is the training of neural networks, where quantum algorithms hold promise for revolutionizing the optimization process. Beyond the theoretical realm, the practical implications of quantum computing are profound. By harnessing quantum phenomena such as superposition and entanglement, quantum computers possess the potential to tackle complex computational tasks that surpass the capabilities of classical systems. For instance, quantum algorithms offer unprecedented speed-ups in optimization, cryptography, and machine learning tasks like neural network training.

The transition to quantum computing represents a paradigm shift in computational technology, with far-reaching implications across various domains. As research and development in quantum computing continue to advance, the integration of quantum algorithms into practical applications becomes increasingly feasible. With exponential speed-ups and enhanced computational capabilities, quantum computing holds the promise of revolutionizing industries and unlocking new frontiers in scientific exploration.

In the realm of neural network training, quantum algorithms offer the potential to overcome existing bottlenecks and accelerate model optimization processes. By leveraging quantum principles to explore vast solution spaces more efficiently, quantum-enhanced neural network training algorithms can drive advancements in artificial intelligence and machine learning (Pira and Ferrie, 2023). Moreover, the synergy between quantum computing and neural networks opens up new avenues for innovation, with the potential to address complex problems in image recognition, natural language processing, and other AI-driven tasks. Therefore, the emergence of quantum computing heralds a new era in computational science, offering exponential speed-ups and unprecedented computational capabilities. With ongoing research and development efforts, the integration of quantum algorithms into practical applications, including neural network training, holds the promise of transforming industries and driving innovation in artificial intelligence. As humanity navigates towards this quantum future, the possibilities for groundbreaking advancements are boundless.

9.2.1 Fundamental Units of Quantum Computing

In the realm of quantum computing, "qubits" serve as the quantum analogs of classical computer "bits" (Lienhard et al., 2022). Qubits play a crucial role in storing the states of circuits utilized for quantum computations. Quantum computing operates on qubits, the fundamental units of information processing. Unlike classical bits, qubits possess unique characteristics such as superposition and entanglement. While a classical bit has two states (0 and 1), a qubit exhibits additional states denoted as $|0\rangle$ and $|1\rangle$, forming a basis in a two-dimensional complex vector space where the symbol $|\cdot\rangle$ indicates its vectorial nature. This vector nature enables qubits to exist in a continuum of states, known as superposition. Mathematically, superposition is represented as a linear combination of the basis states:

$$|\psi\rangle = \alpha |0\rangle + \beta |1\rangle \tag{9.1}$$

where α and β are complex coefficients, often referred to as amplitudes. This capability allows qubits to encode and process information in a manner fundamentally different from classical computing.

However, the coefficients α and β are complex numbers, denoted as belonging to the set of complex numbers (α, $\beta \in \mathbb{C}$), and are commonly referred to as amplitudes.

Multiple qubits are depicted as superpositions within a more extensive vector space. For a set of n qubits, the fundamental states comprise all binary sequences of a specified length.

$$n : |b\rangle = |b1b1 \quad bn\rangle.$$

Given that there are $2n$ basis vectors, the space as a whole possesses a dimensionality of 2^n, allowing for any quantum information state to be expressed as an arbitrary combination, and can be expressed as:

$$|\psi\rangle = \sum_{b=1}^{2^n} \alpha_b |b\rangle, \tag{9.2}$$

Where the amplitudes are subject to a normalization requirement.

$$\||\psi\rangle\|^2 = \sum_{b=1}^{2^n} |\alpha b|^2 = 1, \tag{9.3}$$

Shor's algorithm stands as a pivotal milestone, unlocking a realm of possibilities for the development of robust systems capable of executing quantum logic operations with unparalleled efficiency and effectiveness. In the landscape of quantum computing, various qubit systems have emerged, each offering unique advantages and challenges. Among these systems are photon-based qubits, solid-state spins, trapped-ion qubits, and superconducting qubits, each harnessing distinct physical properties to encode and process quantum information. However, it is the trapped-ion and superconducting qubit platforms that have emerged as the most promising contenders for realizing practical quantum computing solutions (Lanyon et al., 2007).

Trapped-ion qubits and superconducting qubits represent two leading paradigms in the quest for scalable and fault-tolerant quantum computing architectures. These platforms offer compelling attributes that make them particularly well-suited for quantum computation tasks. Trapped-ion qubits leverage the precise control and manipulation of trapped atomic ions, exploiting their long coherence times and exquisite quantum properties to perform intricate quantum operations. On the other hand, superconducting qubits harness the phenomenon of superconductivity to achieve stable and coherent quantum states, enabling rapid gate operations and scalable integration.

9.2.1.1   Trapped Ion Quantum Qubits

The emergence of the first quantum logic gate in 1995 heralded a momentous breakthrough in the realm of quantum computing, ushering in a new era of computational possibilities. This milestone achievement was realized through the pioneering manipulation of trapped atomic ions, a feat made feasible by the theoretical groundwork laid in the same year (Lanyon et al., 2007). Building upon this foundational work, subsequent strides in qubit control methodologies have propelled the evolution of quantum processors towards full-fledged functionality, capable of executing intricate quantum algorithms with precision and efficacy.

Despite the promising outcomes observed in initial demonstrations, the practical implementation of trapped ions in quantum computing presents a myriad of formidable challenges. In stark contrast to conventional very large-scale integration (VLSI) circuits, which are predominantly silicon-based, the development of a trapped-ion-based quantum computer necessitates a multidisciplinary approach, integrating disparate technologies spanning optical, radiofrequency, vacuum, laser, and coherent electronic control systems. This intricate convergence of technologies underscores the complexity inherent in realizing a viable trapped-ion quantum computing platform and underscores the need for comprehensive solutions to overcome integration hurdles.

Addressing these integration challenges is paramount for the successful deployment and widespread adoption of trapped-ion-based quantum computing solutions (Qayyum et al., 2023). Efforts to surmount these obstacles encompass a broad spectrum of research endeavors, spanning materials science, engineering, and quantum information theory. By fostering collaboration and innovation across diverse scientific disciplines, the path towards realizing the transformative potential of trapped-ion quantum computing can be paved, unlocking unprecedented computational capabilities and revolutionizing the landscape of information processing.

9.2.1.2   Superconducting Quantum Qubits

Superconducting qubits exhibit notable parallels with contemporary silicon-based circuits, offering a promising avenue for quantum computing. When cooled to ultra-low temperatures, these qubits manifest quantized energy levels attributable to the discrete states of electronic charge. Operating on a nanosecond timescale, they boast continuously improving coherence times, a crucial factor for sustaining quantum states without decoherence. Additionally, their compatibility with lithographic scaling facilitates seamless integration into existing manufacturing processes, enhancing scalability and manufacturability.

The convergence of these advantageous characteristics positions superconducting qubits as versatile candidates for both quantum computation and quantum annealing applications (Qayyum et al., 2023). Quantum computation exploits their ability to perform complex calculations by manipulating quantum states, leveraging their inherent quantum properties for computational advantage. Conversely, quantum annealing employs superconducting qubits to optimize solutions to optimization problems by searching for the lowest energy state of a quantum system. This duality of applications underscores the versatility and potential of superconducting qubits in advancing the field of quantum information processing.

9.2.2 Qubit Neuron Model

The qubit neuron model introduces a pioneering approach to neuron modeling, drawing inspiration from the principles of quantum physics and quantum computing. Within this innovative framework, neuron states are intricately connected to quantum states, with transitions between them governed by operations derived from quantum logic gates. Fundamental to this model is the assumption that the state of a firing neuron corresponds to the qubit state $|1\rangle$, while a non-firing neuron corresponds to the qubit state $|0\rangle$. Additionally, any arbitrary neuron state is conceptualized as a coherent superposition of these fundamental states.

By integrating concepts from quantum mechanics into traditional neuron modeling, the qubit neuron model offers a sophisticated framework for investigating complex neural processes and computations. Incorporating quantum theory elements such as superposition and entanglement enriches our understanding of neural phenomena.

Practically, leveraging qubits to model neuron states allows for a more nuanced representation of neuronal behavior. Unlike binary firing or non-firing states, neurons can exist along a continuum of states, mirroring the probabilistic nature of quantum systems. This expanded state space enables more detailed simulations of neural networks and their dynamics, potentially yielding deeper insights into brain function and cognition.

Moreover, integrating quantum logic gates into transitions between neuron states presents exciting opportunities for information processing within neural networks. These operations, inspired by principles of quantum computing, offer alternative mechanisms for signal propagation and computation, potentially revolutionizing tasks such as pattern recognition, learning, and decision-making (Tacchino et al., 2019; Mangini et al., 2020) The qubit neuron model stands at the forefront of interdisciplinary research, bridging the fields of neuroscience and quantum computing. This convergence holds promise for advancing our understanding of the brain and developing innovative computing paradigms inspired by the quantum processes found in nature.

9.3 QUANTUM MACHINE LEARNING

In the rapidly evolving landscape of artificial intelligence and machine learning (ML), quantum computing stands out as a transformative frontier, offering unprecedented computational power and capabilities. Quantum machine learning (QML) represents the intersection of quantum computing and traditional ML techniques, heralding a new era of data processing, analysis, and prediction. By harnessing the principles of quantum mechanics, QML holds the promise of revolutionizing numerous industries, from healthcare and finance to materials science and cryptography. The integration of quantum computing into the field of ML introduces unique opportunities and challenges. Unlike classical computers, which rely on binary bits to represent data as either 0s or 1s, quantum computers utilize quantum bits or qubits, which can exist in superposition and entanglement states. This fundamental difference enables qubits to perform exponentially faster computations for certain tasks, offering a potential quantum advantage over classical algorithms (Dutt et al., 2020).

In this context, QML seeks to leverage quantum properties to enhance traditional ML algorithms and develop entirely new approaches to data analysis and pattern recognition. By exploiting quantum parallelism and interference, QML algorithms can process vast amounts of data more efficiently, tackle complex optimization problems, and uncover intricate patterns that may remain hidden from classical algorithms. The exploration of QML has sparked significant interest and investment from both academia and industry, leading to groundbreaking research and experimental demonstrations. As researchers delve deeper into the theoretical foundations of QML and develop practical implementations, the potential applications across various domains continue to expand, promising to reshape the future of AI and ML (Landman et al., 2022).

The burgeoning fields of quantum artificial intelligence and quantum machine learning necessitate thorough analyses of their requirements, particularly from the perspective of experimental quantum information processing. Researchers, such as Lamata (2017), have delved into the implementation of fundamental protocols using superconducting quantum circuits, demonstrating their efficacy in computations and quantum information processing. Furthermore, innovative approaches, like the quantum recommendation system proposed in Kerenidis and Prakash (2016), have emerged, enabling efficient sampling from preference matrices without the need for matrix reconstruction. In parallel, Benedetti et al. (2018) have introduced a classical quantum deep learning (DL) architecture tailored for near-term industrial applications. This hybrid framework seamlessly integrates quantum and classical components to address high-dimensional ML datasets with continuous variables, leveraging DL for low-dimensional binary data and proving particularly suitable for small-scale quantum processors.

Moreover, recent research has explored the application of quantum technologies in clinical settings, with an overview of 40 theoretical and experimental quantum technologies presented in Flöther (2023). This comprehensive study encompasses three clinical use cases: genomics and clinical research, diagnostics, and treatments and interventions. Notably, it elucidates the utilization of quantum machine learning techniques, such as quantum neural networks and quantum support vector classifiers, utilizing real clinical data. These advancements underscore the potential of quantum technologies to revolutionize various sectors, including healthcare, by offering novel approaches to data analysis and decision-making processes.

9.4 QUANTUM NEURAL NETWORK

Quantum neural networks represent an intriguing convergence of quantum mechanics and artificial neural networks, holding immense promise for revolutionizing various fields, from computation to machine learning. At their core, QNNs leverage the principles of quantum mechanics to encode and process information, offering a novel approach to solving complex computational problems. Unlike classical neural networks, which rely on binary bits for computation, QNNs utilize quantum bits or qubits, which can exist in multiple states simultaneously due to phenomena like superposition and entanglement. This unique property enables QNNs to perform parallel processing and explore a vast solution space in a single computation, potentially leading to exponential speedups over classical counterparts (Dutt et al., 2020). Quantum inspired neural networks represent an intriguing convergence of quantum computing principles with traditional deep learning architectures, offering a novel approach to tackling complex computational tasks. At their core, these networks leverage concepts from quantum mechanics, such as superposition, entanglement, and interference, to enhance the learning capabilities of neural networks. Utilizing the intrinsic parallelism and computational capabilities of quantum systems, quantum-inspired neural networks strive to surpass the constraints of classical computing, ushering in novel realms of artificial intelligence and machine learning. The illustration in Figure 9.1 portrays the quantum neural network architecture.

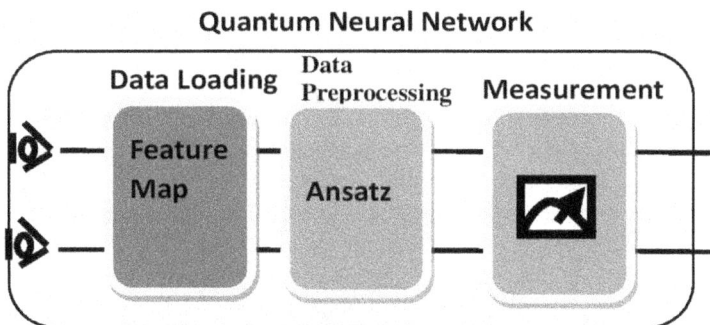

FIGURE 9.1   Quantum neural network.

Traditional neural networks have demonstrated remarkable success in various domains, including image recognition, natural language processing, and reinforcement learning. However, as datasets grow larger and tasks become more complex, conventional architectures may encounter scalability issues and computational bottlenecks. Quantum-inspired neural networks offer a promising avenue for addressing these challenges, potentially unlocking unprecedented performance gains and facilitating breakthroughs in AI research and applications.

The introduction of quantum-inspired elements into neural network architectures introduces a paradigm shift in how information is processed and represented. Quantum computing principles enable the creation of quantum layers within neural networks, where quantum effects are simulated to perform computations. These layers leverage quantum operations, such as quantum gates and circuits, to manipulate data in ways that exploit quantum phenomena for enhanced learning and inference.

One of the key advantages of quantum-inspired neural networks lies in their ability to explore vast solution spaces more efficiently than classical approaches. Quantum computing's inherent parallelism allows these networks to explore multiple hypotheses simultaneously, potentially accelerating optimization and search algorithms. Moreover, quantum-inspired models may offer superior performance on certain types of problems, such as optimization, sampling, and pattern recognition, where quantum effects can be leveraged to outperform classical methods.

In recent years, researchers have made significant strides in developing quantum-inspired algorithms and architectures, paving the way for applications across diverse domains, including chemistry, finance, and healthcare. Quantum-inspired neural networks hold particular promise in areas where traditional machine learning approaches face challenges, such as solving complex optimization problems, analyzing high-dimensional data, and simulating quantum systems.

In recent years, the exploration of QNNs has gained significant traction, fueled by advancements in quantum computing technologies and a growing understanding of quantum phenomena. Researchers are actively investigating various architectures and training algorithms to harness the computational power of QNNs effectively. Additionally, the integration of classical and quantum components in hybrid neural networks has emerged as a promising avenue for practical applications, offering a balance between quantum advantage and compatibility with existing classical computing infrastructure (Landman et al., 2022). Delving deeper into the realm of quantum neural networks reveals that their potential extends far beyond traditional computing paradigms. From optimizing complex optimization problems to enhancing machine learning algorithms, QNNs offer a glimpse into the future of intelligent systems. In this introductory exploration, the aim is to unravel the intricacies of QNNs, examining their underlying principles, architectural designs, training methodologies, and real-world applications. Through this endeavor, light is shed on the transformative potential of quantum neural networks and the groundwork is laid for groundbreaking advancements in quantum computing and artificial intelligence.

QNNs represent an exciting intersection of two cutting-edge fields: quantum computing and artificial neural networks. These networks hold immense potential for revolutionizing various domains, from machine learning and optimization to drug discovery and complex data analysis (Schuld et al., 2014, 2020). By harnessing the power of quantum. mechanics, QNNs offer the possibility of solving complex problems more efficiently than classical neural networks. Traditional neural networks, which draw inspiration from the structure of the human brain, are composed of interconnected layers of artificial neurons that analyze and transmit data (Adcock and Nowotny, 2015). They have proven highly successful in diverse applications such as image identification, natural language understanding, and speech processing. However, as problems become more intricate, the computational demands increase exponentially, posing significant challenges for classical computers (Biamonte et al., 2017; Wang et al., 2019; Dunjko et al., 2020). They aim to leverage the unique properties of qubits, such as superposition and entanglement, to enhance the capabilities of classical neural networks. By incorporating quantum algorithms and quantum circuits into the structure and operations of neural networks, QNNs have the potential to solve certain problems more efficiently and accurately. The potential applications of QNNs span across various domains.

9.4.1 Mathematical Foundations of Quantum Neural Networks

Quantum neural networks represent an interdisciplinary fusion of quantum computing and machine learning, promising to revolutionize computational paradigms by harnessing the principles of quantum mechanics to enhance the capabilities of traditional neural networks. At the heart of QNNs lie mathematical foundations deeply rooted in quantum mechanics, offering a unique framework for processing information and solving complex problems. This section delves into the mathematical underpinnings of quantum neural networks, exploring key concepts such as quantum gates, quantum circuits, and quantum measurement, and their integration within neural network architectures.

9.4.1.1 Quantum Gates

Quantum gates serve as the cornerstone of quantum circuits, akin to classical logic gates in conventional computing. These gates embody unitary transformations that act upon qubits, the fundamental units of quantum information. Among the commonly used quantum gates are the Hadamard gate (H), Pauli gates (X, Y, Z), and controlled-NOT gate (CNOT). Mathematically, these gates are represented by matrices operating on the state vector of qubits (Nielsen and Chuang, 2010).

$$| H = \frac{1}{\sqrt{2}} \begin{bmatrix} 1 & 1 \\ 1 & -1 \end{bmatrix}, X = \begin{bmatrix} 0 & 1 \\ 1 & 0 \end{bmatrix}, Y \begin{bmatrix} 0 & -i \\ i & 0 \end{bmatrix}, Z = \begin{bmatrix} 1 & 0 \\ 0 & -1 \end{bmatrix}, CNOT = \begin{bmatrix} 1 \\ 0 \\ 0 \\ 0 \end{bmatrix} \qquad \text{eq (9.4)}$$

In addition to the fundamental gates, other important quantum gates used in quantum neural networks include:

- **RX, RY, and RZ Gates**: These single-qubit gates rotate qubits around the x, y, and z axes of the Bloch sphere, respectively. They are represented by rotation matrices parameterized by rotation angles.
- **SWAP Gate**: The SWAP gate exchanges the states of two qubits, facilitating entanglement operations.
- **Toffoli Gate**: Also known as the controlled-controlled-NOT gate, it performs a NOT operation on a target qubit if both control qubits are in the state $|1\rangle$.

9.4.1.2 Quantum Circuits

Quantum circuits are sequences of quantum gates applied to qubits to perform computations. These circuits are represented mathematically by the tensor product of gate matrices, followed by the application of the resulting unitary transformation to the quantum state vector. The evolution of the state vector under the action of quantum gates is described by the Schrödinger equation, where the unitary matrix representing the quantum circuit is applied to the initial state vector (Preskill, 2018).

$$Quantum\ Circuit = U_N, U_{N-1}, \dots\dots\dots U_1 L \qquad (9.5)$$

where U_i represents the unitary transformation corresponding to the iith gate.

Alternatively, quantum circuits enable the manipulation and transformation of quantum states, forming the backbone of quantum computation. In quantum neural networks, quantum circuits are constructed by composing various quantum gates to perform specific tasks. Mathematically, a quantum circuit is represented as a sequence of gate operations applied to qubits. The circuit's overall transformation is given by the tensor product of individual gate matrices followed by the application of the resulting unitary transformation to the quantum state vector.

Let's denote a quantum gate operation U acting on n qubits as $U^{(n)}$. A quantum circuit C comprising m such gate operations can be represented as:

$$C = U^{n_m} \cdot U^{n_{m-1}}, \ldots . U^{n_1} \qquad (9.6)$$

where each U^{n_i} represents the unitary transformation corresponding to the ith gate applied to ni qubits.

9.4.1.3 Quantum Measurement

Quantum measurements play a crucial role in extracting classical information from quantum systems. Mathematically, a quantum measurement is described by a set of measurement operators corresponding to the possible measurement outcomes. The probability of obtaining each outcome is given by the Born rule, which involves the inner product of the quantum state vector with the measurement operators. Quantum measurements collapse the quantum state into one of the measurement outcomes, providing classical information that can be utilized for decision-making and inference tasks (Nielsen and Chuang, 2010).

$$P_i = \langle \psi | M_i M_i | \psi \rangle \qquad (9.7)$$

These mathematical foundations form the cornerstone of quantum neural networks, enabling the simulation and utilization of quantum effects within neural network architectures. By combining quantum operations with classical neural network layers, QNNs leverage the unique properties of quantum mechanics to potentially enhance computational performance and solve complex problems more efficiently. As we delve deeper into the mathematical formalism of QNNs, we unlock new avenues for innovation at the intersection of quantum computing and machine learning.

9.4.1.4 State Vector Evolution

In quantum computing, the evolution of the state vector under the action of quantum gates is governed by the Schrödinger equation. This evolution is mathematically described by applying the unitary transformation of the quantum circuit to the initial state vector $| \psi 0 \rangle$:

$$| \psi_f \rangle = U . | \psi_0 \rangle$$

where U denotes the unitary matrix representing the quantum circuit.

9.4.1.5 Quantum Algorithms

Quantum neural networks can leverage various quantum algorithms for tasks such as optimization, eigenvalue estimation, and solving linear systems of equations. Notable algorithms include the quantum approximate optimization algorithm (QAOA), variational quantum eigensolver (VQE), and HHL algorithm for solving linear equations.

By incorporating these key functions and algorithms, quantum neural networks harness the power of quantum mechanics to potentially outperform classical neural networks in certain tasks, particularly those involving complex optimization and large-scale data processing (Farhi and Neven, 2018)

9.5 LITERATURE REVIEW

In recent years, quantum machine learning has emerged as a captivating field, leveraging the unique properties of quantum computing to tackle complex computational problems (Biamonte et al., 2017). While convolutional neural networks have long been established for image classification tasks in classical computing, researchers have increasingly turned their attention to exploring their potential in the quantum domain. For example, Konar et al. (2020) pioneered the development of a quantum neural network tailored for automating the segmentation of brain magnetic resonance images. Their network, comprising three layers of quantum neurons with a multi-level sigmoid activation function, showcased promising results in terms of accuracy and Dice similarity scores for image segmentation tasks.

Similarly, Iyer et al. (2020) utilized a variational classifier to categorize pigmented skin lesions. Their approach involved extracting feature descriptors and feeding them into a two-qubit quantum circuit to predict labels such as melanoma or melanocytic nevi. Sleeman et al. (2020) introduced a novel approach by linking a classical convolutional autoencoder to a quantum restricted Boltzmann machine, yielding competitive results on datasets like MNIST and Fashion-MNIST. Furthermore, Henderson et al. (2020) proposed a groundbreaking quantum convolution layer that transforms data using quantum circuits, akin to classical convolutional layers. Their research demonstrated enhanced test accuracy on the MNIST dataset when a CNN incorporated a quantum layer. Mari et al. (2020) introduced a hybrid transfer learning framework, integrating a quantum circuit into a pre-trained classical CNN for image recognition tasks. This approach, tested on datasets like the Hymenoptera subset of ImageNet and CIFAR-10, displayed promising results, particularly in scenarios with limited training images, such as COVID-19 detection.

The exploration of hybrid classical–quantum networks (H-CQN) has underscored the potential of quantum computing in addressing image classification challenges with small training datasets. This chapter aims to build upon these advancements, leveraging the strengths of both classical and quantum neural networks to tackle image classification tasks effectively.

9.5.1 Review of Related Literature

In their 2020 study, Dutt et al. aimed to address real-world issues using advanced machine learning methodologies, particularly in the context of medical science. The primary problem they sought to solve was the identification of diseases, leveraging the capabilities of quantum neural networks. The researchers explored two key components of quantum machine learning: quantum data, which encompasses data generated within natural or artificial quantum systems, and hybrid models, an advanced approach integrating quantum science with machine learning techniques. Their methodology involved employing an advanced version of QNNs to analyze disease relations and symptoms. They identified a series of prescribed processes to facilitate this analysis. Notably, the study focused on utilizing machine learning models to analyze disease symptoms effectively. The results of their study demonstrated the effectiveness of the proposed methodology, particularly in disease identification. The quantum communication networks (QCN) model achieved an impressive accuracy rate of approximately 93% in identifying disease symptoms and treatment relations. This highlighted the potential of quantum-based approaches in medical diagnosis and treatment analysis.

Yumin et al. (2020) addressed a significant challenge in pneumonia image recognition, which traditionally relies heavily on the experience of doctors. However, distinguishing between CT images of different pneumonia types can be challenging due to their similarities, leading to potential misdiagnosis. Moreover, using neural networks for pneumonia image recognition often encounters issues like getting stuck in local minima, slow convergence, and oscillation due to the gradient descent method. To tackle these challenges, the authors proposed a novel approach called a quantum BP neural network (QBP) based on quantum particle swarm optimization (QPSO) for pneumonia image recognition. This method efficiently trains quantum weights, overcoming the limitations of traditional neural networks. By comparing the accuracy and speed of QBP-QPSO with other algorithms for pneumonia CT image recognition, the authors found that QBP-QPSO demonstrates rapid convergence and high accuracy. The simulation results further validate the correctness and effectiveness of the proposed method, achieving an impressive accuracy rate of 96.07%. The problem solved by this study is improving pneumonia image recognition accuracy, addressing challenges such as misdiagnosis and slow convergence. The methodology used involves implementing a quantum neural network trained with quantum particle swarm optimization. The obtained result accuracy is 96.07%, showcasing the effectiveness of the proposed approach in pneumonia image recognition.

Mathur et al. (2021) explored the application of machine learning, specifically quantum machine learning, in disease diagnosis through medical image classification. They aimed to enhance the performance of machine learning models by leveraging quantum algorithms and quantum neural networks. The study focused on two approaches to utilizing quantum neural networks for medical image classification. The first approach involved integrating quantum circuits into the training process of classical neural networks. The second approach entailed designing and training quantum orthogonal neural networks from scratch. To evaluate these techniques, the researchers conducted experiments on two distinct imaging modalities: retinal color fundus images and chest X-rays. They analyzed the performance of the models, considering both their effectiveness and the constraints imposed by current quantum hardware. The results of the study demonstrated the potential benefits of employing quantum neural network techniques for medical image classification. However, the findings also highlighted the existing limitations associated with the capabilities of current quantum hardware.

Landman et al. (2022) explored the potential of quantum machine learning techniques to improve performance in machine learning applications. The study introduces two novel quantum methods for neural networks aimed at enhancing their capabilities. The first method introduced is quantum-assisted neural networks, which leverage a quantum computer for inner product estimation during the inference and training phases of classical neural networks. The second method is a quantum orthogonal neural network, utilizing a quantum pyramidal circuit as the fundamental component for implementing orthogonal matrix multiplication. The authors propose efficient training algorithms for these orthogonal neural networks, applicable to both classical and quantum hardware. These algorithms demonstrate superior scalability compared to existing methods.

Extensive experiments were conducted on medical image classification tasks using state-of-the-art quantum hardware. The study compares different quantum methods with classical ones, evaluating their performance on both real quantum hardware and simulators. The results indicate that the proposed quantum networks achieve similar levels of accuracy compared to classical neural networks while exhibiting competitive scalability. This supports the notion that quantum methods hold promise in addressing visual tasks, especially with advancements in quantum hardware.

Ovalle-Magallanes et al. (2022) addressed limitations in medical applications of convolutional neural networks, particularly in scenarios like stenosis detection using X-ray coronary angiography, where datasets are often small or contain poorly contrasted images. To overcome these challenges, the study explored the potential of quantum computing within hybrid neural networks. The methodology employed a hybrid transfer-learning approach for stenosis detection. A quantum network was integrated with a pre-trained classical network to enhance performance. An intermediate layer between the classical and quantum networks processed classical features by mapping them into a hypersphere using a hyperbolic tangent function. The normalized features were then fed into the quantum network, which utilized a SoftMax function to generate class probabilities for stenosis and non-stenosis cases. Additionally, a distributed variational quantum circuit was implemented to split the data into multiple quantum circuits within the quantum network, reducing training time without compromising detection performance. The proposed method was evaluated on a small X-ray coronary angiography dataset, consisting of 250 image patches with equal proportions of positive and negative stenosis cases. Results demonstrated significant improvement over the classical network, with an accuracy increase of 9%, recall improvement of 20%, and F1-score enhancement of 11%. The hybrid classical-quantum network achieved accuracy, recall, and F1-score of 91.8033%, 94.9153%, and 91.8033%, respectively, surpassing the performance of traditional transfer learning paradigms.

Qu et al. (2023) asserted that combining data from multiple sources can significantly improve accuracy in medical diagnosis, but it often requires substantial computational resources. Quantum computers theoretically offer the capability to process large volumes of complex medical data rapidly. However, research on quantum machine learning for handling multimodal data remains limited despite the rapid progress in quantum computing. Addressing this gap, the authors introduce a novel system called quantum neural network-based multimodal fusion (QNMF) for intelligent diagnosis. The QNMF system is designed to process multimodal medical data transmitted by Internet of Medical Things (IoMT) devices, integrating data from different sources to enhance diagnostic accuracy. The methodology employed in the QNMF system involves utilizing a quantum convolutional neural network (QCNN) to efficiently extract features from medical images. These QCNN-derived features are then combined with features from other modalities, such as blood test results or tissue samples, using a variational quantum classifier for intelligent diagnosis. Experimental results demonstrate the effectiveness of the QCNN in extracting relevant features from image data. Moreover, the QNMF system achieves impressive accuracy rates of 97.07% and 97.61% in diagnosing breast cancer and COVID-19, respectively. Additionally, the QNMF exhibits robustness against quantum noise, further enhancing its reliability in real-world applications.

Sahib et al. (2023) addressed the effectiveness of quantum neural networks in machine-based breast cancer detection, a crucial aspect of computer-aided image diagnostics (CAD) in medical imaging. While CAD traditionally relies on classical computer vision and artificial intelligence techniques, the potential of QNNs, introduced by major research entities like Microsoft, Google, and IBM, has garnered attention. In this study, the researchers investigated the suitability of QNN algorithms for breast cancer detection. They conducted a series of experiments to compare the learnability of QNNs with classical convolutional neural networks (CCNNs), which are commonly used in image recognition tasks. The QNNs were implemented using the Cirq library to simulate quantum computation on classical computers. The experiments involved analyzing real mammogram datasets and studying the learnability characteristics of both QNNs and CCNNs under identical computational conditions. The results demonstrated the success of QNNs in recognizing the data and training models, particularly with smaller datasets, compared to CCNNs. The study highlighted the potential of QNNs in improving the performance of machine-based breast cancer detection, showcasing their ability to successfully train models and generate valid results, especially when dealing with limited data.

Choudhuri and Halder (2023) addressed the challenge of efficiently classifying brain MR images to detect tumor regions, a crucial step in medical diagnostics. Traditional machine learning methods and deep learning architectures, such as convolutional neural networks (ConvNets), are commonly used for image classification but face challenges with large network sizes during training. To optimize classification performance, the authors proposed a novel approach called quantum classical convnet architecture (QCCNN), which combines quantum algorithms with classical techniques. The QCCNN encodes data into quantum states, facilitating faster information extraction to distinguish between different data classes. The reliability and robustness of the QCCNN architecture were demonstrated through extensive testing on various datasets, including Brats 2013, Harvard Med School, and a private dataset. The classifier's performance was evaluated using standard metrics, confirming its effectiveness in detecting and classifying brain tumors. The results showed that the proposed QCCNN model achieved high accuracies ranging from 97.5% to 98.72% across different datasets. This underscores the capability of the QCCNN architecture in accurately detecting and classifying brain tumors, indicating its potential for real-world applications in medical imaging diagnostics.

Amin et al. (2022) addressed the urgent need for accurate analysis of COVID-19 cases using medical imaging, particularly computed tomography (CT) scans. With the global COVID-19 pandemic escalating and affecting millions worldwide, the timely and precise detection of COVID-19 symptoms, such as ground-glass opacity (GGO) and pulmonary consolidation in CT scans, is critical. The researchers investigated the potential of both quantum machine learning and classical machine learning (CML) approaches in analyzing COVID-19 images. Leveraging recent advancements in quantum computing, they proposed a two-phase approach. In the first phase, synthetic CT images were generated using conditional generative adversarial networks (CGANs) to augment the dataset, enhancing the accuracy of training and testing. Subsequently, in the second phase, the researchers developed two classification models: one based on classical machine learning and the other on quantum machine learning. The results of the study demonstrated the effectiveness of the proposed models. On the POF Hospital dataset, the model achieved a precision (Pn) of 0.94, accuracy (Ac) of 0.94, recall (Rl) of 0.94, and F1-score (Fe) of 0.94. Similarly, on the UCSD-AI4H dataset, the model achieved a precision (Pn) of 0.96, accuracy (Ac) of 0.96, recall (Rl) of 0.95, and F1-score (Fe) of 0.96. The study showcased the potential of both quantum and classical machine learning approaches in accurately analyzing COVID-19 images, with promising results obtained from the proposed models.

9.6   QUANTUM ALGORITHM MODELING OVERVIEW

Quantum computing architecture encompasses various components that are intricately integrated to form a coherent system. At its core are qubits, the quantum counterparts of classical bits, which encode and manipulate quantum information. Additionally, fault tolerance mechanisms and error correction techniques are crucial components to ensure the reliability of quantum computations (Copsey et al., 2003). Quantum gates and circuits play a pivotal role in performing operations on qubits, enabling complex quantum algorithms to be executed. Quantum teleportation facilitates the transfer of quantum states between distant qubits, a fundamental capability for distributed quantum computing. Moreover, solid-state electronics serve as the physical platform for implementing quantum computing hardware.

The design and analysis of these architectural components, along with their combinations, have been extensively explored in the literature. Many proposed quantum computing architectures adopt a layered structure, resembling traditional approaches to complex information engineering systems (Metodi and Faruque, 2022; Jones et al., 2012). Researchers have provided diverse perspectives and guidelines for designing quantum computer architectures, considering factors such as scalability, error correction capabilities, and physical implementation constraints.

For instance, seminal works by Spiller et al. (2005) introduced fundamental criteria for viable quantum computing architectures, emphasizing the importance of error correction mechanisms. Other studies, such as those by Bertels et al. (2020) and Steane (2002), underscored the necessity of robust error correction techniques within quantum computer architectures. Furthermore, Linke et al. (2017) conducted a comparative analysis between IBM Quantum and fully connected trapped ions, shedding light on the architectural differences and performance characteristics of these implementations. Such research efforts contribute to the ongoing development and optimization of quantum computing architectures, paving the way for advancements in quantum information processing and computation.

9.7   METHODOLOGY AND MATERIAL

This study delved into the effectiveness of quantum-assisted neural networks by examining two distinct architectures. The first architecture relied exclusively on classical neural network components, while the second one incorporated both classical and quantum layers. The aim was to scrutinize the performance and capabilities of these architectures in a binary classification task using breast cancer images sourced from MRI scans.

Both architectures were structured with four hidden layers, each comprising four nodes. This configuration aimed to strike a balance between model complexity and computational efficiency, ensuring effective feature extraction and representation learning without excessively taxing computational resources. In the classical neural network architecture, the absence of quantum layers meant that the model operated solely on classical principles. It utilized standard neural network operations for feature processing and decision-making, establishing a baseline for comparison with the quantum-assisted model.

Conversely, the quantum-assisted neural network architecture incorporated a unique quantum layer alongside classical components. This quantum layer introduced quantum effects into the model, leveraging principles such as superposition and entanglement to potentially enhance feature extraction and representation learning. By simulating quantum circuits using the Cirq framework within TensorFlow, the model aimed to exploit quantum phenomena to improve classification accuracy and generalization performance. This investigation aimed to assess whether the utilization of quantum-enhanced approaches could yield notable improvements in time efficiency compared to purely classical methods.

Both architectures were trained and evaluated using the same dataset of breast cancer images, ensuring a fair comparison of their respective capabilities. The dataset comprised MRI scans obtained from clinical sources, with each image labeled as benign or malignant based on expert medical diagnosis. This allowed for a binary classification task, wherein the models were tasked with accurately classifying each image according to its cancer status.

To conduct the experiments, a robust computing infrastructure consisting of a Proliant DL380p Gen 8 server with 20 GB of RAM was utilized. Python Jupyter Notebook served as the primary development environment, providing a versatile platform for coding, experimentation, and analysis. This setup facilitated the efficient training and evaluation of both classical and quantum-assisted neural network architectures, enabling a comprehensive assessment of their performance in breast cancer image classification.

The methodology employed in this study aimed to systematically compare classical and quantum-assisted approaches in medical image analysis, with a focus on breast cancer diagnosis. By leveraging cutting-edge techniques and computational resources, insights were sought to advance the field of medical imaging and contribute to improved healthcare outcomes. Figure 9.2 shows the methodology flow.

9.7.1 DESCRIPTION OF THE QUANTUM NEURAL NETWORK IMPLEMENTED MODEL

The implemented model represents a sophisticated approach to breast cancer classification, seamlessly integrating traditional deep neural network techniques with quantum-neural network methods. Delving into its architecture and functionalities unveils a comprehensive framework designed for the classification of breast cancer images, with a focus on leveraging both classical and quantum principles to enhance predictive performance and feature extraction.

At its core, the model begins by loading and preprocessing image data from a specified data path. This critical preprocessing step ensures the appropriate formatting of images, facilitating their transformation into a suitable format for training. Images undergo grayscale reading, resizing to a standard size of 128 × 128 pixels, and normalization of pixel values to a range between 0 and 1. This standardization process is crucial for maintaining consistency across the dataset and enabling efficient model training.

Following the data processing, the definition of the QuantumLayer class introduces a custom layer implemented using TensorFlow and Cirq for quantum operations. This layer incorporates quantum effects into the neural network and serves as a unique feature in the breast cancer classification

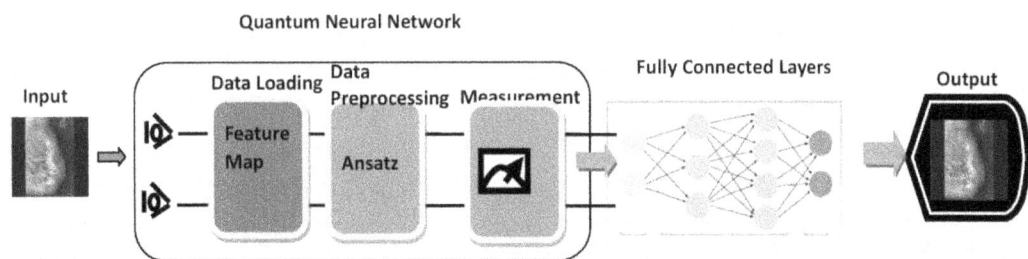

FIGURE 9.2   Research methodology flow.

model. The QuantumLayer class initializes with the number of qubits specified by the user, creating a grid of qubits using Cirq's GridQubit.rect() function.

The call method of the QuantumLayer class executes the quantum operations on the input data. It utilizes a Cirq simulator to simulate quantum circuits and applies Hadamard gates to each qubit in the circuit. The result of the quantum computation is then stored in a TensorArray and converted into a tensor before being returned. Additionally, the model includes a helper function named create_quantum_circuit, which generates a simple quantum circuit consisting of Hadamard gates applied to the qubits.

This section achieves the implementation of a custom QuantumLayer class, enabling the integration of quantum operations into the neural network architecture for breast cancer classification. By leveraging quantum principles such as superposition and entanglement, the model aims to enhance feature extraction and representation learning, potentially leading to improved predictive performance and generalization capabilities.

Immediately after that, the model adopts a k-fold cross-validation strategy to robustly assess its performance. This technique divides the dataset into k subsets, with the model trained on k-1 folds and evaluated on the remaining fold. By iteratively repeating this process, the model's performance is accurately estimated, mitigating the risk of overfitting or underfitting.

The core architecture of the neural network is characterized by several layers, each serving a specific purpose in the learning process. The model introduces a Quantum layer, a distinctive feature that sets it apart from conventional deep learning architectures. This Quantum layer leverages Cirq, a quantum computing framework, to simulate quantum circuits, thereby introducing quantum effects into the neural network. By harnessing principles such as superposition and entanglement, the Quantum layer offers a novel approach to feature extraction and representation learning, potentially enhancing the model's predictive capabilities.

Following the Quantum layer, the model incorporates several fully connected (Dense) layers, each comprising multiple neurons (units) with activation functions applied to introduce non-linearity. The architecture includes three Dense layers, with 512, 256, and 128 units, respectively, interspersed with Dropout layers to mitigate overfitting. The output layer consists of two neurons corresponding to the two classes of breast cancer (benign and malignant), with a SoftMax activation function applied to produce class probabilities.

During training, the model optimizes its parameters using the Adam optimizer and minimizes the sparse categorical cross-entropy loss function, suitable for multi-class classification tasks. Performance is monitored using various evaluation metrics, including accuracy, loss, and validation metrics. Training and validation accuracy and loss are visualized over epochs to assess learning dynamics and identify potential issues such as overfitting or convergence problems.

Post-training evaluation involves assessing the model's generalization performance on the test set, computing classification metrics such as precision, recall, and F1-score. Additionally, a confusion matrix is generated to visualize the distribution of true positive, true negative, false positive, and false negative predictions, aiding in performance analysis and interpretation.

The implemented model represents a fusion of classical and quantum methodologies in the realm of medical image analysis. By integrating quantum principles into the learning process, the model explores new avenues for feature extraction and representation learning, potentially unlocking enhanced predictive performance and generalization capabilities. Through rigorous evaluation and analysis, the model aims to contribute to the advancement of breast cancer diagnosis, ultimately improving healthcare practices and patient outcomes

9.7.2 DESCRIPTION OF THE CLASSICAL NEURAL NETWORK IMPLEMENTED MODEL

In contrast to the implementation of the quantum neural network, the second experiment involves a purely fully connected neural network without the incorporation of the Quantum layer. This experiment focuses solely on traditional deep learning methodologies, devoid of quantum principles and operations. Unlike the quantum neural network, which integrates quantum effects such as superposition and entanglement into the learning process, the purely fully connected neural network relies solely on classical computations and operations.

In this experiment, the architecture of the neural network consists exclusively of fully connected (Dense) layers, with each layer performing complex transformations on the input data to extract relevant features and patterns. Unlike the quantum neural network, which introduces a unique Quantum layer leveraging Cirq for quantum operations, the fully connected neural network comprises a series of Dense layers without any quantum-specific components.

By omitting the Quantum layer and quantum-inspired operations, the purely fully connected neural network aims to assess the performance of traditional deep learning approaches in breast cancer classification tasks. This experiment provides a baseline comparison to evaluate the effectiveness of quantum-enhanced methodologies against conventional deep learning techniques.

Furthermore, the absence of quantum operations simplifies the model architecture and computational requirements, potentially leading to faster training and inference times compared to the quantum neural network. However, it may also limit the model's capacity to capture complex patterns and relationships present in the data, particularly those that may benefit from quantum effects.

Overall, the second experiment involving the purely fully connected neural network offers insights into the relative advantages and limitations of traditional deep learning approaches in comparison to quantum-enhanced methodologies. By contrasting these two approaches, researchers can gain a better understanding of the role of quantum computing in medical image analysis and its potential implications for breast cancer diagnosis and treatment.

9.8 RESULTS AND ANALYSIS

Having investigated the effectiveness of quantum-assisted neural networks through two distinct architectures, the focus now shifts to analyzing the outcomes of the study. The objective was to evaluate the performance and capabilities of these architectures in a binary classification task utilizing breast cancer images sourced from MRI scans. In this section, the results obtained from training and testing both the classical neural network architecture and the quantum-assisted neural network architecture will be delved into.

9.8.1 EXPERIMENTATION RESULTS OF BOTH THE CLASSICAL NEURAL NETWORK AND QUANTUM NEURAL NETWORK

The experimentation results for breast cancer diagnosis include evaluations of both the classical neural network and quantum neural network. Table 9.1 presents the classification accuracies and training/testing times, while Figures 9.3 and 9.4 display the confusion matrices for the classical and quantum neural networks, respectively. Additionally, Figures 9.5, 9.6, 9.7, and 9.8 depict their respective training versus validation accuracy and error.

TABLE 9.1
Results from the Evaluation of ANN on Breast Cancer

	Precision	Recall	F1-Score	Support	Mean Training Time	Mean Testing Time
Class 0	0.62	1.00	0.77	2376	126.516s	0.583s
Class 1	0.00	0.00	0.00	1440		
Accuracy			0.62	3816		
Macro Avg	0.31	0.50	0.38	3816		
Weighted Avg	0.39	0.62	0.48	3816		

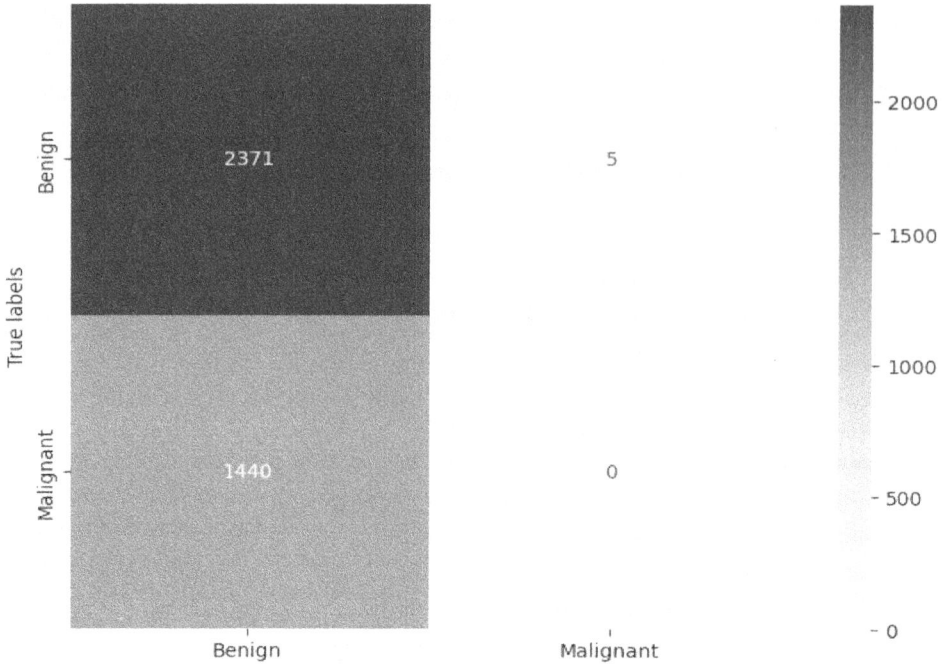

FIGURE 9.3   Confusion matrix obtained from ANN.

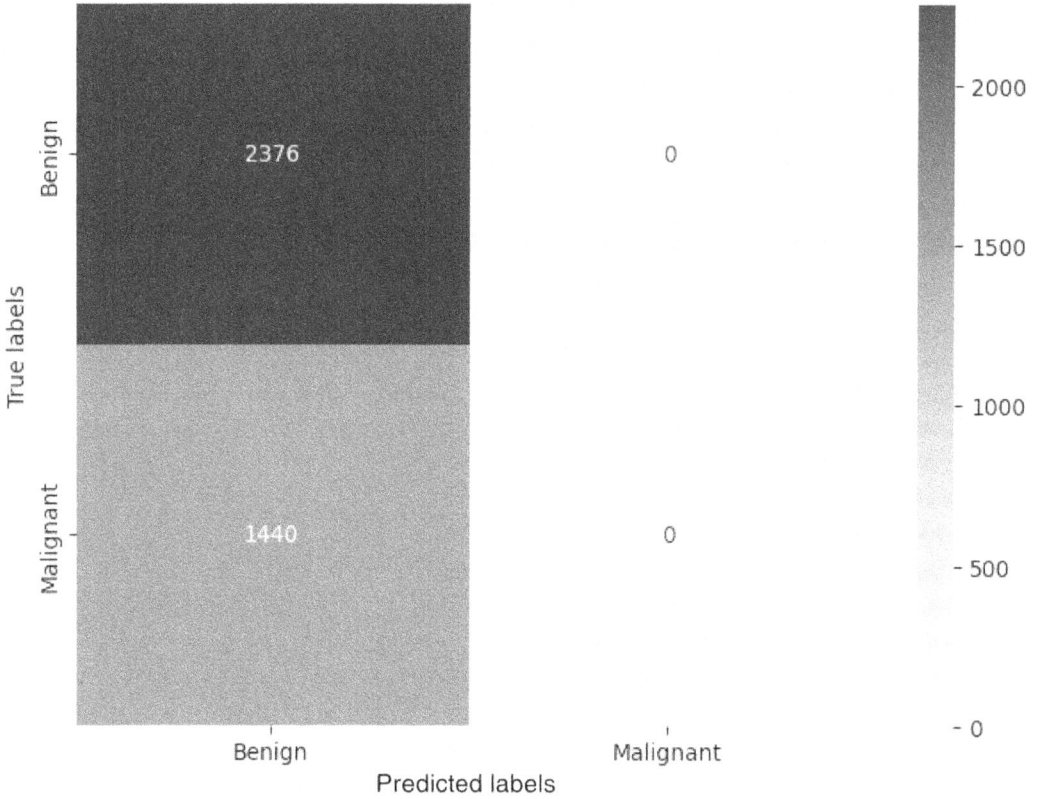

FIGURE 9.4   Confusion matrix obtained from QNN.

Breast cancer is a significant health concern, emphasizing the importance of accurate and timely diagnosis. Artificial intelligence techniques, particularly artificial neural networks (ANNs), have shown potential in aiding medical professionals in diagnosing breast cancer using MRI scans. The evaluation of an ANN model's performance in breast cancer diagnosis yielded mixed results, as shown in Table 9.1.

The ANN model, lacking a quantum layer, demonstrated a precision of 0.62 for benign cases and a recall of 1.00, indicating accurate identification of all benign cases. However, for malignant cases, both precision and recall were 0.00, indicating the model's failure to accurately predict any malignant cases. The F1-score, which combines precision and recall, was 0.77 for benign cases and 0.00 for malignant cases, highlighting the model's relative success in classifying benign cases but significant shortcomings in identifying malignant cases.

The overall accuracy of the model was 0.62, indicating that it correctly classified 62% of the samples. However, this accuracy was significantly influenced by the model's inability to accurately predict malignant cases. The dataset consisted of 2376 samples of benign cases and 1440 samples of malignant cases.

The macro average F1-score, considering equal weight for each class, was 0.38, while the weighted average F1-score, accounting for class imbalance, was 0.48. These scores reflect the model's overall performance across both classes.

In terms of computational efficiency, the model exhibited a mean training time of approximately 126.52 seconds per iteration and a mean testing time of approximately 0.58 seconds.

While the ANN model showed promise in classifying benign cases, its performance in identifying malignant cases was suboptimal. Future research should focus on improving the model's ability to detect malignant cases accurately, potentially through the incorporation of additional features or the exploration of alternative machine learning techniques. Despite its limitations, the ANN model highlights the potential of AI in advancing healthcare practices, particularly in breast cancer diagnosis.

The obtained confusion matrix from the evaluation of the model unveils crucial insights into its performance. In the context of breast cancer diagnosis, the matrix offers a transparent breakdown of the model's predictions compared to the actual labels, as illustrated in Figure 9.3. Examining the matrix reveals that the majority of cases are classified as benign, with 2371 true positives correctly identified as benign. However, the model also misclassifies 1440 benign cases as malignant, constituting false positives. Conversely, the model fails to identify any malignant cases correctly, resulting in a total of 1440 false negatives.

This breakdown enables the calculation of various performance metrics. The precision for the benign class is relatively high at 99.79%, signifying that when the model predicts a case as benign, it is correct 99.79% of the time. However, the precision for the malignant class is 0%, implying that the model's predictions for malignant cases are unreliable. Similarly, the recall for the benign class is 100%, indicating that the model correctly identifies all actual benign cases. However, the recall for the malignant class is 0%, suggesting that the model fails to identify any actual malignant cases.

The F1-score, representing the harmonic mean of precision and recall, reflects the balance between precision and recall. For the benign class, the F1-score is 0.77, indicating a reasonable balance between precision and recall. However, for the malignant class, the F1-score is 0, highlighting the poor performance of the model in identifying malignant cases.

Overall, the confusion matrix underscores the model's limitations, particularly in correctly identifying malignant cases. Further analysis and enhancements to the model may be necessary to improve its performance and reliability in breast cancer diagnosis.

The assessment of quantum neural networks depicted in Table 9.2, alongside artificial neural networks shown in Table 9.1, for breast cancer diagnosis offers insights into their diagnostic accuracy and computational time efficiency. A comparison of the two models reveals that, while they demonstrate comparable diagnostic accuracy, notable differences exist in their computational time requirements.

TABLE 9.2

Results from the Evaluation of Quantum Neural Network on Breast Cancer

	Precision	Recall	F1-Score	Support	Mean Training Time	Mean Testing Time
Class 0	0.62	1.00	0.77	2376	99.867s	0.277s
Class 1	0.00	0.00	0.00	1440		
Accuracy			0.62	3816		
Macro Avg	0.31	0.50	0.38	3816		
Weighted Avg	0.39	0.62	0.48	3816		

Both the QNN and ANN achieved an overall accuracy of 0.62, indicating comparable performance in classifying breast cancer cases. However, closer examination reveals distinct differences in their computational time efficiency.

In terms of mean training time, the QNN demonstrated a substantial reduction compared to the ANN. The mean training time for the QNN was recorded at 99.867 seconds, significantly shorter than the ANN's mean training time of 126.516 seconds. This indicates that the QNN requires less time to train on the dataset, potentially offering faster model development and iteration cycles.

Similarly, the mean testing time for the QNN was notably lower than that of the ANN. The QNN recorded a mean testing time of 0.277 seconds, while the ANN's mean testing time was 0.583 seconds. This suggests that the QNN can process new data and make predictions more rapidly than the ANN, contributing to quicker diagnostic assessments in clinical settings.

Quantum computation harnesses the principles of superposition and entanglement, allowing quantum systems to process multiple computations simultaneously. This inherent parallelism enables QNNs to explore a broader range of solutions in a shorter amount of time compared to classical ANN architectures. While classical ANNs process data sequentially, QNNs can leverage quantum parallelism to perform computations on multiple states simultaneously, leading to faster training and testing times.

Additionally, QNNs benefit from the efficient representation of data using quantum bits (qubits). Unlike classical bits, which can only exist in one state at a time (0 or 1), qubits can exist in a superposition of states, allowing for more efficient storage and manipulation of information. This efficient representation of data contributes to the faster processing capabilities of QNNs, as they can encode and process information more compactly compared to classical ANNs.

These findings highlight the computational advantages of the QNN architecture over the ANN in terms of training and testing times. The reduced computational time requirements of the QNN signify its potential for enhanced efficiency in medical diagnostics, allowing for faster analysis of breast cancer cases and expedited decision-making processes.

Comparing the confusion matrices derived from the assessment of the quantum neural network, depicted in Figure 9.5, and the artificial neural network in breast cancer diagnosis offers valuable insights into the performance of these models.

The confusion matrix for the QNN indicates that it correctly classified all benign cases as benign, with a total of 2376 true positive predictions. However, the QNN failed to correctly identify any malignant cases, resulting in 1440 false negative predictions. On the other hand, the ANN correctly classified 2371 benign cases as benign, but it made 5 false positive predictions by incorrectly classifying benign cases as malignant. Similar to the QNN, the ANN also failed to identify any malignant cases correctly, resulting in 1440 false negative predictions.

Comparing the two models, we observe that while the QNN achieved higher accuracy in classifying benign cases, it struggled with identifying malignant cases. Conversely, the ANN exhibited slightly lower accuracy in classifying benign cases but performed similarly in correctly identifying malignant cases.

The discrepancies in the confusion matrices highlight the strengths and weaknesses of each model. The QNN's ability to correctly classify all benign cases without making any false positive predictions demonstrates its potential for minimizing unnecessary interventions in clinical settings. However, its inability to correctly identify malignant cases raises concerns about its reliability in detecting actual instances of cancer.

On the other hand, the ANN's performance, while slightly inferior in terms of false positive predictions, demonstrates a better balance between sensitivity and specificity. Despite misclassifying a few benign cases as malignant, the ANN showed comparable accuracy in detecting malignant cases.

9.9 CONCLUSION AND RECOMMENDATIONS FOR FURTHER WORK

In summary, this exploration into quantum neural networks signifies a pivotal step forward in the intersection of quantum computing and artificial intelligence. The investigation delves into recent advancements in QNN, providing researchers with a comprehensive overview to navigate this emerging field. Beginning with fundamental concepts in quantum computation and neural networks, the intricacies of QNN are gradually unveiled, exploring various models proposed by previous researchers.

These discussions underscore the potential of quantum computing to enhance the computational efficiency of neural networks, propelling AI to new heights. While traditional artificial neural networks have evolved over the years, the integration of quantum computing has bolstered their power and efficiency. However, despite the promising applications of QNN in diverse problem domains, it remains in its nascent stage, warranting further exploration to fully capitalize on its efficiency and efficacy across various disciplines. In conclusion, the study underscores the promising prospects of QNN in medical diagnostics, exemplified by its comparable diagnostic accuracy and notable reductions in computational time compared to ANN.

Although challenges persist, particularly in accurately classifying malignant cases, continued research and development efforts hold the key to optimizing QNN architectures and harnessing their full potential in healthcare and beyond. With sustained investigation and innovation, QNN stands poised to revolutionize AI and contribute significantly to improving patient outcomes and advancing scientific frontiers.

Moving forward, further research and development in quantum neural networks present promising avenues for exploration and innovation. To build upon the findings of this study and advance the field of QNN, several recommendations are proposed.

Refinement of QNN Architectures: Continued efforts should focus on refining QNN architectures to address challenges in accurately classifying malignant cases. This may involve exploring novel network structures, optimization techniques, and quantum-inspired algorithms to improve diagnostic accuracy.

Enhanced Quantum Computing Technologies: Advancements in quantum computing technologies are pivotal for realizing the full potential of QNNs. Researchers should collaborate with experts in quantum physics and engineering to develop more powerful and scalable quantum hardware platforms tailored for QNN applications.

Integration of Quantum Error Correction: Given the sensitivity of quantum systems to noise and errors, integrating robust error correction mechanisms into QNN architectures is essential. Future work should explore quantum error correction techniques to enhance the reliability and robustness of QNN models.

By pursuing these recommendations, researchers can propel the field of quantum neural networks forward, unlocking new capabilities in medical diagnostics and paving the way for transformative advancements in healthcare.

REFERENCES

Amin, J., Sharif, M., Gul, N., Kadry, S., & Chakraborty, C. (2022). Quantum machine learning architecture for COVID-19 classification based on synthetic data generation using conditional adversarial neural network. *Cognitive Computation*, *14*(5), 1677–1688.

Arute, F., Arya, K., Babbush, R., Bacon, D., Bardin, J. C., Barends, R., . . . & Martinis, J. M. (2019). Quantum supremacy using a programmable superconducting processor. *Nature*, *574*(7779), 505–510.

Beer, K., Bondarenko, D., Farrelly, T., Osborne, T. J., Salzmann, R., Scheiermann, D., & Wolf, R. (2020). Training deep quantum neural networks. *Nature Communications*, *11*(1), 808.

Behrman, E. C., Steck, J. E., Kumar, P., & Walsh, K. A. (2008). Quantum algorithm design using dynamic learning. *arXiv preprint arXiv:0808.1558*.

Benedetti, M., Realpe-Gómez, J., & Perdomo-Ortiz, A. (2018). Quantum-assisted Helmholtz machines: A quantum–classical deep learning framework for industrial datasets in near-term devices. *Quantum Science and Technology*, *3*, 034007. [CrossRef]

Bertels, K. O. E. N., Sarkar, A., Hubregtsen, T., Serrao, M., Mouedenne, A. A., Yadav, A., . . . & Almudever, C. G. (2020). Quantum computer architecture toward full-stack quantum accelerators. *IEEE Transactions on Quantum Engineering*, *1*, 1–17.

Bharti, K., Cervera-Lierta, A., Kyaw, T. H., Haug, T., Alperin-Lea, S., Anand, A., . . . & Aspuru-Guzik, A. (2022). Noisy intermediate-scale quantum algorithms. *Reviews of Modern Physics*, *94*(1), 015004.

Cao, N., Xie, J., Zhang, A., Hou, S. Y., Zhang, L., & Zeng, B. (2022). Neural networks for quantum inverse problems. *New Journal of Physics*, *24*(6), 063002.

Cerezo, M., Sone, A., Volkoff, T., Cincio, L., & Coles, P. J. (2021). Cost function dependent barren plateaus in shallow parametrized quantum circuits. *Nature Communications*, *12*(1), 1791.

Choudhuri, R., &Halder, A. (2023). Brain MRI tumour classification using quantum classical convolutional neural net architecture. *Neural Computing and Applications*, *35*(6), 4467–4478.

Copsey, D., Oskin, M., Impens, F., Metodiev, T., Cross, A., Chong, F. T., . . . & Kubiatowicz, J. (2003). Toward a scalable, silicon-based quantum computing architecture. *IEEE Journal of Selected Topics in Quantum Electronics*, *9*(6), 1552–1569.

Dallaire-Demers, P. L., & Killoran, N. (2018). Quantum generative adversarial networks. *Physical Review A*, *98*(1), 012324.

Dutt, V., Chandrasekaran, S., & García-Díaz, V. (2020). Quantum neural networks for disease treatment identification. *European Journal of Molecular & Clinical Medicine*, *7*(11), 57–67.

Farhi, E., & Neven, H. (2018). Classification with quantum neural networks on near term processors. *arXiv preprint arXiv:1802.06002*

Flöther, F. F. (2023). The state of quantum computing applications in health and medicine. *arXiv preprint arXiv:2301.09106*.

Henderson, M., Shakya, S., Pradhan, S., & Cook, T. (2020). Quanvolutional neural networks: powering image recognition with quantum circuits. *Quantum Machine Intelligence*, *2*(1), 2.

Iyer, V., Ganti, B., Hima Vyshnavi, A. M., Krishnan Namboori, P. K., & Iyer, S. (2020). Hybrid quantum computing based early detection of skin cancer. *Journal of Interdisciplinary Mathematics*, *23*(2), 347–355.

Jeswal, S. K., & Chakraverty, S. (2019). Recent developments and applications in quantum neural network: A review. *Archives of Computational Methods in Engineering*, *26*(4), 793–807.

Jones, N. C., Van Meter, R., Fowler, A. G., McMahon, P. L., Kim, J., Ladd, T. D., & Yamamoto, Y. (2012). Layered architecture for quantum computing. *Physical Review X*, *2*(3), 031007.

Kak, S. C. (1995). Quantum neural computing. *Advances in Imaging and Electron Physics*, *94*, 259–313.

Karayiannis, N. B., & Xiong, Y. (2006). Training reformulated radial basis function neural networks capable of identifying uncertainty in data classification. *IEEE Transactions on Neural Networks*, *17*(5), 1222–1234.

Kerenidis, I., Luongo, A., & Prakash, A. (2020, November). Quantum expectation-maximization for Gaussian mixture models. In *International Conference on Machine Learning* (pp. 5187–5197). PMLR.

Kerenidis, I., & Prakash, A. (2016). Quantum recommendation systems. *arXiv preprint arXiv:1603.08675*.

Konar, D., Bhattacharyya, S., Gandhi, T. K., & Panigrahi, B. K. (2020). A quantum-inspired self-supervised network model for automatic segmentation of brain MR images. *Applied soft computing*, *93*, 106348.

Kouda, N., Matsui, N., & Nishimura, H. (2000, September). Learning performance of neuron model based on quantum superposition. In *Proceedings 9th IEEE International Workshop on Robot and Human Interactive Communication. IEEE RO-MAN 2000 (Cat. No. 00TH8499)* (pp. 112–117). IEEE.

Kwak, Y., Yun, W. J., Jung, S., & Kim, J. (2021, August). Quantum neural networks: Concepts, applications, and challenges. In *2021 Twelfth International Conference on Ubiquitous and Future Networks (ICUFN)* (pp. 413–416). IEEE.

Lamata, L. (2017). Basic protocols in quantum reinforcement learning with superconducting circuits. *Scientific Reports*, *7*(1), 1609

Landman, J., Mathur, N., Li, Y. Y., Strahm, M., Kazdaghli, S., Prakash, A., & Kerenidis, I. (2022). Quantum methods for neural networks and application to medical image classification. *Quantum*, *6*, 881.

Lanyon, B. P., Weinhold, T. J., Langford, N. K., Barbieri, M., James, D. F., Gilchrist, A., & White, A. G. (2007). Experimental demonstration of a compiled version of Shor's algorithm with quantum entanglement. *Physical Review Letters*, *99*, 250505.

Lienhard, B., Vepsäläinen, A., Govia, L. C., Hoffer, C. R., Qiu, J. Y., Ristè, D., . . . & Oliver, W. D. (2022). Deep-neural-network discrimination of multiplexed superconducting-qubit states. *Physical Review Applied*, *17*(1), 014024.

Linke, N. M., Maslov, D., Roetteler, M., Debnath, S., Figgatt, C., Landsman, K. A., . . . & Monroe, C. (2017). Experimental comparison of two quantum computing architectures. *Proceedings of the National Academy of Sciences*, *114*(13), 3305–3310.

Lloyd, S., & Weedbrook, C. (2018). Quantum generative adversarial learning. *Physical Review Letters*, *121*(4), 040502.

Mangini, S., Tacchino, F., Gerace, D., Bajoni, D., & Macchiavello, C. (2021). Quantum computing models for artificial neural networks. *Europhysics Letters*, *134*(1), 10002.

Mangini, S., Tacchino, F., Gerace, D., Macchiavello, C., & Bajoni, D. (2020). Quantum computing model of an artificial neuron with continuously valued input data. *Machine Learning: Science and Technology*, *1*(4), 045008

Mari, A., Bromley, T. R., Izaac, J., Schuld, M., & Killoran, N. (2020). Transfer learning in hybrid classical-quantum neural networks. *Quantum*, *4*, 340.

Mathur, N., Landman, J., Li, Y. Y., Strahm, M., Kazdaghli, S., Prakash, A., &Kerenidis, I. (2021). Medical image classification via quantum neural networks. *arXiv preprint arXiv:2109.01831.*

Metodi, T., & Faruque, A. I. (2022). *Quantum Computing for Computer Architects*. Springer Nature.

Nguyen, N. H., Behrman, E. C., Moustafa, M. A., & Steck, J. E. (2019). Benchmarking neural networks for quantum computations. *IEEE Transactions on Neural Networks and Learning Systems*, *31*(7), 2522–2531.

Nielsen, M. A., & Chuang, I. L. (2010). *Quantum Computation and Quantum Information*. Cambridge University Press.

Ovalle-Magallanes, E., Avina-Cervantes, J. G., Cruz-Aceves, I., & Ruiz-Pinales, J. (2022). Hybrid classical–quantum Convolutional Neural Network for stenosis detection in X-ray coronary angiography. *Expert Systems with Applications*, *189*, 116112.

Park, J., Samarakoon, S., Elgabli, A., Kim, J., Bennis, M., Kim, S. L., &Debbah, M. (2021). Communication-efficient and distributed learning over wireless networks: Principles and applications. *Proceedings of the IEEE*, *109*(5), 796–819.

Pira, L., & Ferrie, C. (2023). An invitation to distributed quantum neural networks. *Quantum Machine Intelligence*, *5*(2), 23.

Preskill, J. (2018). Quantum computing in the NISQ era and beyond. *Quantum*, *2*, 79.

Qayyum, A., Qadir, J., & Anwar, Z. (2023). Quantum computing for healthcare: A review. *Future Internet*, *15*, 94. https://doi.org/10.3390/fi15030094

Qu, Z., Li, Y., & Tiwari, P. (2023). QNMF: A quantum neural network based multimodal fusion system for intelligent diagnosis. *Information Fusion*, *100*, 101913.

Sahib, A. Y., Al Ali, M., & Al Ali, M. (2023). Investigation of early-stage breast cancer detection using quantum neural network. *International Journal of Online & Biomedical Engineering*, *19*(3).

Sleeman, J., Dorband, J., & Halem, M. (2020, May). A hybrid quantum enabled RBM advantage: convolutional autoencoders for quantum image compression and generative learning. In *Quantum information science, sensing, and computation XII*, (Vol. 11391, pp. 23–38). SPIE.

Spiller, T. P., Munro, W. J., Barrett, S. D., & Kok, P. (2005). An introduction to quantum information processing: Applications and realizations. *Contemporary Physics*, *46*(6), 407–436.

Steane, A. M. (2002). Quantum computer architecture for fast entropy extraction. *arXiv preprint quant-ph/0203047.*

Tacchino, F., Macchiavello, C., Gerace, D., & Bajoni, D. (2019). An artificial neuron implemented on an actual quantum processor. *npj Quantum Information*, *5*(1), 26.

Ur Rasool, R., Ahmad, H. F., Rafique, W., Qayyum, A., Qadir, J., & Anwar, Z. (2023). Quantum computing for healthcare: A review. *Future Internet*, *15*(3), 94.

Xie, J., Xu, C., Yin, C., Dong, Y., & Zhang, Z. (2023). Natural Evolutionary Gradient Descent Strategy for Variational Quantum Algorithms. *Intelligent Computing*, *2*, 0042.

Yumin, D., Wu, M., & Zhang, J. (2020). Recognition of pneumonia image based on improved quantum neural network. *IEEE Access*, *8*, 224500–224512.

Zhao, R., & Wang, S. (2021). A review of quantum neural networks: Methods, models, dilemma. *arXiv preprint arXiv:2109.01840.*

Zoufal, C., Lucchi, A., & Woerner, S. (2019). Quantum generative adversarial networks for learning and loading random distributions. *npj Quantum Information*, *5*(1), 103.

10 Cybersecurity Forensics with AI
A Comprehensive Review

Pragati Jain, Priyanka Verma, Tania Debnath,
Leoson Heisnam, Shefali Chaudhary, and Sonali Balouria

10.1 INTRODUCTION

Since the advent of the first denial-of-service (DoS) attack in 1998, there has been a notable surge in the intricacy, recurrence, and ramifications of cyber assaults. As these cyber threats have evolved to become more focused and potent, cybersecurity countermeasures have advanced in tandem. Initially, security tools were confined to detecting virus signatures and thwarting their execution. Presently, we encounter comprehensive solutions engineered to offer protection across diverse attack vectors and various target systems (Li, 2018). Despite these advancements, the task of safeguarding information assets in virtual reality has become increasingly daunting.

Ensuring protection against sophisticated cyber threats necessitates the implementation of intelligent code. Recent events have underscored the rapid advancement in the intelligence of malware and cyber weapons. The emergence of network-centric warfare amplifies the risk of cyber incidents, demanding urgent changes in cybersecurity approaches. New security strategies, such as dynamically establishing secure perimeters, fostering comprehensive scenario awareness, and implementing highly automated responses to network attacks, mandate the widespread adoption of artificial intelligence (AI) techniques and knowledge-based tools. Primarily, the necessity for AI lies in the swift response to incidents occurring in the online domain. The ability to rapidly process vast amounts of data is crucial for interpreting and analyzing events in cyberspace, facilitating informed decision-making. The speed of processes and the sheer volume of information involved exceed the capacity of humans without significant automation. However, devising code imbued with conventional fixed algorithms (rigid logic at the decision-making stratum) to proficiently counter cyber-attacks is arduous, given the perpetual emergence of novel threats. (Patil, 2016; Wirkuttis & Klein, 2017)

Due to their pliable and malleable system behavior, artificial intelligence methodologies possess the capacity to mitigate numerous constraints of modern cybersecurity tools. While AI has markedly bolstered cybersecurity, noteworthy apprehensions have surfaced. Certain individuals perceive AI as a looming existential hazard for humanity. Consequently, scientists and legal scholars have expressed trepidation regarding the burgeoning involvement of autonomous AI entities in cyberspace and have articulated ethical apprehensions about their validation.

Artificial intelligence in cybersecurity: The dark web has persistently prompted discussions, eliciting inquiries regarding its covert perils and privacy-enhancing functionalities. It epitomizes a part of the internet mandating specialized software or authorization, renowned for illicit undertakings and untraceable transactions. Researchers and law enforcement entities leverage the dark web for intelligence accumulation on cyber malefactors, thus rendering it pivotal in grasping the internet's metamorphosis and emergent criminal behaviors. Moreover, delving into the dark web facilitates the discernment of cybersecurity perils and susceptibilities. (Kaur et al., 2024). Artificial intelligence, particularly machine learning (ML), holds significant promise for uncovering insights from data within cybersecurity. ML streamlines the task of discovering, contextualizing, and prioritizing pertinent data throughout the threat intelligence lifecycle. This encompasses activities such as identifying suspicious network behaviors and uncovering dark web forum discussions hinting

DOI: 10.1201/9781003499459-10

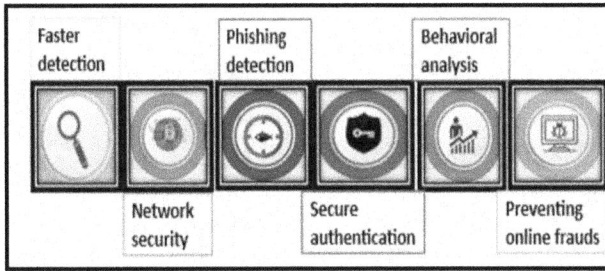

FIGURE 10.1   Artificial intelligence in cybersecurity.

at potential data breaches. By integrating machine learning across various facets of cybersecurity, security operations can be fortified, empowering analysts to swiftly pinpoint, prioritize, address, and mitigate emerging threats.

Such integration facilitates the refinement of defensive measures and fosters deeper comprehension of past cyber incidents. In contrast to conventional signature-based approaches, AI-driven systems leverage ML algorithms to analyze vast datasets, discern recurring patterns, and flag anomalies indicative of potential cyber intrusions. AI possesses the capacity to rapidly assimilate new information and refine its defensive capabilities, thereby enabling it to detect and adapt to novel and unforeseen threats ((2) The Use of AI in Detecting and Preventing Cybercrime | (LinkedIn, n.d.).

10.2   INCORPORATING ARTIFICIAL INTELLIGENCE INTO CYBERSECURITY FORENSICS

Integrating AI into cybersecurity forensics significantly improves the speed and accuracy of threat detection, response, and mitigation, providing organizations with a more robust defense against cyber threats. However, it's crucial to complement AI with human expertise for effective decision-making and to address the dynamic nature of cybersecurity challenges.

The combination of cybersecurity and forensic techniques with artificial intelligence can enhance the capability to detect, respond to, and mitigate security incidents. The following are ways AI can be integrated into cybersecurity forensics (Jadhav et al., 2020; M. M. Nair et al., 2024).

10.3   MACHINES HAVE THE POTENTIAL TO ASSIST DETECTIVES IN IDENTIFYING CRUCIAL CLUES

Comparing items found at crime scenes with those from prior incidents could aid in identifying connections between crimes that may elude detectives: Fidalgo, a computer scientist affiliated with the University of Leon in northwest Spain, along with his research team, has partnered with the Spanish National Cybersecurity Institute (INCIBE) to develop a tool for forensic evidence recognition. Leveraging artificial intelligence techniques, this tool aims to discern objects within law enforcement photographs and ascertain potential links to other criminal activities. For instance, consider a scenario where abuse is suspected to have occurred in a bedroom. Law enforcement officers regularly capture crucial information by photographing such locations (Saikia et al., 2017).

Examining numerous images sourced from the deepest recesses of the internet could aid in apprehending perpetrators who exploit children: The application of such technology is more extensive than commonly acknowledged. For instance, Facebook recently disclosed its utilization of AI to detect nearly 9 million images depicting child nudity within a span of three months on its platform. The bulk of these images had not been previously flagged, thereby enabling Facebook to

TABLE 10.1

Artificial Intelligence for Advanced Cybersecurity Measures

Category	Description
Anomaly detection	—Artificial intelligence algorithms meticulously scrutinize network traffic, user behavior, and system activities to detect anomalies indicative of a security breach. —Machine learning models learn normal patterns and detect deviations, aiding in uncovering unauthorized access or malicious activities (Exploring the Vital Role of AI in Cybersecurity | CCS Learning Academy, n.d.).
Behavioral analysis	—AI assesses user and system behavior, identifying patterns linked to malicious activities such as login patterns, file access, and application usage. —Unusual behavior triggers alerts, prompting further investigation by cybersecurity professionals (Exploring the Vital Role of AI in Cybersecurity | CCS Learning Academy, n.d.).
Threat intelligence	—AI systems adeptly process extensive volumes of threat intelligence data to discern established threats and vulnerabilities. —Integration of threat intelligence feeds enable cybersecurity forensic teams to proactively identify and respond to emerging threats (Vishwanath, 2023).
Malware analysis	—AI automates the analysis of malware samples, aiding in the identification of new and evolving threats. —Machine learning models classify and categorize malware based on behavior, signatures, or other characteristics (Exploring the Vital Role of AI in Cybersecurity | CCS Learning Academy, n.d.).
Incident response automation	—AI automates aspects of incident response, facilitating faster and more efficient mitigation of security incidents (Kaur & Moza, 2023). —Automated responses include isolating affected systems, blocking malicious traffic, or applying patches to vulnerable software.
forensic data analysis	—AI algorithms assist in analyzing large datasets collected during forensic investigations. —Natural language processing (NLP) is employed to analyze text-based logs and communications, extracting relevant information for investigators.
UEBA	—User and entity behavior analytics solutions, powered by AI, help identify suspicious activities related to user accounts and entities. —Establishing a baseline of normal behavior enables AI to detect deviations indicating compromised accounts or insider threats.
Predictive analysis	—AI models employ predictive analytics by analyzing historical data and contemporary trends to anticipate potential security threats. —This aids in proactive threat hunting, allowing organizations to implement preventive measures before actual incidents occur.
Fraud detection	—AI is applied to detect fraudulent activities, such as phishing attacks or payment fraud, by analyzing patterns and anomalies in transactions and user behavior.
Continuous learning	—AI systems exhibit continuous learning capabilities, dynamically adapting to evolving cybersecurity threats through iterative analysis of novel data inputs. —Regular updates and retraining of models ensure the system remains effective against emerging threats.
Machine learning algorithms	—At the core of AI in cybersecurity lies machine learning, a facet of AI enabling systems to iteratively learn from data and optimize their performance without requiring explicit programming instructions. These algorithms play a pivotal role in identifying patterns, anomalies, and potential threats within extensive datasets (Goni et al., n.d.).
NLP	—Natural language processing empowers machines to comprehend, interpret, and generate human-like language. Within the field of cybersecurity, NLP emerges as an indispensable tool for parsing textual data, including logs and threat intelligence reports, extracting salient insights, and discerning potential security imperatives (Ukwen et al., n.d.).

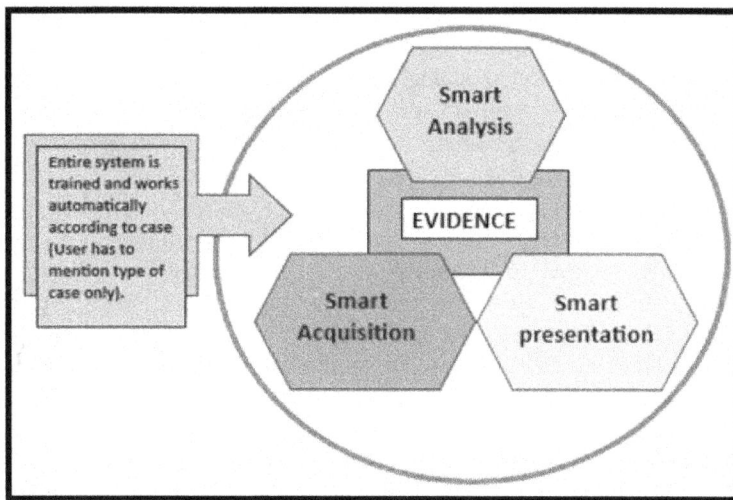

FIGURE 10.2 Proposed AI-based forensic framework.

furnish information concerning potential exploitation to the US National Center for Missing and Exploited Children (The new weapon in the fight against crime—BBC Future, n.d.).

Facial recognition technology utilizes machine learning algorithms to identify individuals and is currently in use by certain police departments: The convergence of diverse strands of evidence represents a pivotal area where artificial intelligence can significantly aid investigators. In the United Kingdom, law enforcement is exploring the utilization of software developed by digital forensics firm Cellebrite, which autonomously sifts through potential evidence present on a suspect's mobile device. This software demonstrates the capability to analyze images and communication patterns, perform facial recognition, and cross-reference data from multiple devices, thereby empowering officers to expediently construct a comprehensive understanding of the interactions among a group of suspects. Notably, this software played a critical role in identifying individuals implicated in a human trafficking case in Thailand, including police officers, three politicians, and an army general (The new weapon in the fight against crime—BBC Future, n.d.).

By aiding law enforcement in accessing the data stored in their databases, artificial intelligence has the potential to become a valuable asset in combating crime: Ruth Morgan, a forensic science specialist at University College London, underscores the largely underutilized potential of law enforcement databases, which could experience substantial augmentation through integration with artificial intelligence. Morgan emphasizes, "The potential is absolutely phenomenal." However, she raises concerns regarding the use of algorithms, pointing out that it may be challenging to scrutinize their decision-making processes in court later on. This difficulty arises either because the technology is proprietary, with the companies unwilling to disclose their algorithms, or because the system's complexity makes it nearly impossible to demonstrate how it arrived at its conclusions. Such issues could impede the broader adoption of these technologies in law enforcement efforts (Lum & Isaac, 2016).

Detecting traces of pollen or gunpowder residue on footwear can offer crucial evidence in linking suspects to a crime scene, but the process of matching them has historically been labor-intensive: To tackle this challenge, researchers have employed machine learning algorithms. These algorithms were trained using an extensive dataset comprising synthetic samples containing DNA from various sources. Through iterative learning, the algorithm acquired the ability to discriminate between samples containing DNA from two individuals and those harboring three or more sets of genetic material. While the algorithm cannot ensure absolute accuracy in determining the number of contributors, Marciano and Adelman posit that it demonstrates marginally superior precision compared to alternative analytical methodologies (2017).

Similar to the advancements witnessed in DNA fingerprinting and ballistics, experts anticipate that artificial intelligence will revolutionize criminal investigations: Traditional methods, such as anthropological analysis of skeletal remains, can be labor-intensive and prone to variability in accuracy among different experts. Xin Li, a computer scientist at Louisiana State University, posits that machines hold the potential to mitigate these challenges. Li has been pioneering the development of a system capable of reconstructing fragmented skulls by harnessing three-dimensional scanning technology. This system operates akin to solving a jigsaw puzzle with missing pieces, where the gaps are digitally filled based on the learned shapes and proportions of human skulls. Through training on a dataset of human skull characteristics, the system can digitally reconstruct skulls with a reasonable degree of accuracy (The new weapon in the fight against crime—BBC Future, n.d.).

Future trajectories: integration of artificial intelligence in imaging: In the field of forensic examination, the identification of anomalies assumes significant importance in ascertaining identity, cause of death, and uncovering potential instances of abuse. Future trajectories encompass the utilization of artificial intelligence in imaging, the integration of diverse imaging modalities, and leveraging 3D printing for tailored surgical aids. Establishing standard protocols and integrating clinical data stand to bolster accuracy in skeletal analysis. Studies emphasize the imperative need for AI technique validation against traditional methods and advocate standardization for result comparability. Continual refinement of techniques is indispensable for broader implementation and more accurate detection of skeletal anomalies. Identifying fragments of bone, particularly in forensic contexts, can pose significant challenges. However, advancements in machine learning, particularly in the field of AI, present promising solutions for reconstructing a victim's face from skeletal remains (Moza et al., 2024; The new weapon in the fight against crime—BBC Future, n.d.).

10.4 THE ROLE OF ARTIFICIAL INTELLIGENCE IN THE CYBER ECOSYSTEM

Historically, cybersecurity has relied on resource-intensive efforts, with manual and time-consuming tasks such as monitoring, threat hunting, and incident response. This manual approach can result in delays in remediation activities, increased exposure, and heightened vulnerability to cyber adversaries. In recent years, artificial intelligence solutions have undergone rapid maturation, presenting significant advantages to cyber defensive operations across diverse organizational frameworks and mission contexts. Through the automation of labor-intensive core functions, AI has the potential to revolutionize cyber workflows, creating streamlined, autonomous, and continuous processes that enhance the speed of remediation and maximize overall protection.

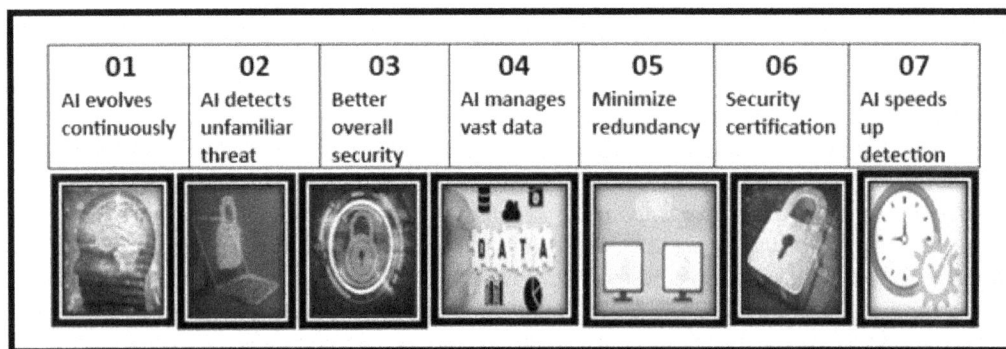

01	02	03	04	05	06	07
AI evolves continuously	AI detects unfamiliar threat	Better overall security	AI manages vast data	Minimize redundancy	Security certification	AI speeds up detection

FIGURE 10.3   Role of AI in cybersecurity.

As technology advances rapidly, the threats in the digital field are also on the rise. Cyberattacks have grown more sophisticated, frequent, and damaging, presenting substantial challenges to individuals, businesses, and governments globally. In the current digital age, traditional methods of combating cyber threats are no longer adequate. This is where artificial intelligence becomes a transformative force. AI has emerged as a formidable ally in the domain of cybersecurity, empowering defenders to adopt a proactive stance in outmaneuvering adversaries (Al-Mansoori et al., n.d.).

10.5   AI TECHNIQUES IN CYBERSECURITY FORENSICS

Artificial intelligence refers to the capability of machines to perform tasks traditionally associated with human intelligence, including learning, reasoning, problem-solving, and adaptation to novel circumstances.

In the field of cybersecurity, AI serves as a transformative technology that complements traditional security measures through the automation of processes, examination of extensive datasets, and improvement of the capability to identify and counter evolving cyber threats.

The application of AI in cybersecurity involves various techniques, including machine learning, natural language processing, and pattern recognition, aimed at fortifying the resilience of digital systems against malicious activities (Mughal, 2019). The objective is to empower computers to emulate human-like cognitive functions, proactively recognizing and mitigating potential risks in the cybersecurity landscape.

Artificial intelligence significantly contributes to cybersecurity forensics by improving analysis, detection, and response capabilities. Various techniques include (Mughal, 2019; Wirkuttis et al., n.d.):

- **Behavioral Analysis:** AI models scrutinize user behavior patterns to detect anomalies or suspicious activities, facilitating the identification of potential security threats.
- **Machine Learning Algorithms:** ML algorithms categorize and predict security incidents based on historical data, enhancing accuracy in identifying malicious behavior (Goni et al., n.d.; Janga et al., n.d.).
- **Signature-Based Detection:** AI systems utilize predefined patterns or signatures to recognize known malware, viruses, or attack patterns, aiding in swift threat identification.
- **Heuristic Analysis:** AI employs heuristic methods to identify new, previously unseen threats by recognizing deviations from normal system behavior.
- **Deep Learning:** Neural networks, a subset of AI, contribute to complex pattern recognition, enhancing the detection of advanced threats through deep learning models (Janga et al., n.d.).
- **Network Traffic Analysis:** AI-driven tools monitor and analyze network traffic for unusual patterns, contributing to the early detection of cyber threats.
- **Forensic Analysis Automation:** AI accelerates digital forensics by automating the analysis of large datasets, aiding investigators in faster identification and mitigation of security incidents. Integration of advanced data recovery methodologies, encompassing the reconstruction of partially deleted or encrypted files can be done.

The integration of these AI techniques with traditional cybersecurity methods enhances the overall effectiveness of cybersecurity forensics, enabling quicker responses to evolving threats (Jarrett & Choo, 2021).

10.6   APPLICATIONS OF AI IN CYBERSECURITY FORENSICS

Applications markedly improve the efficiency of identifying threats, responding to incidents, and managing identity and access. These AI-based methodologies not only strengthen security measures but also establish a more flexible and responsive defense against the constantly changing strategies of cyber adversaries (Exploring the vital role of AI in cybersecurity | CCS Learning Academy, n.d.).

TABLE 10.2

Comprehensive Examples of AI Applications in Cybersecurity with Scenarios

S. No	Topic	Description	Example Scenario
1.	Anomaly detection using AI algorithms	Proactive threat detection relies on anomaly detection powered by AI algorithms. Machine learning algorithms are employed by AI systems to establish a baseline of normal behavior within a network or system. This method is effective in detecting previously unseen attacks or subtle, sophisticated threats that traditional signature-based systems might overlook. Adaptability: AI systems can adjust to changes in the environment and update their understanding of normal behavior over time (Exploring the Vital Role of AI in Cybersecurity I CCS Learning Academy, n.d.).	Example Scenario: An AI-powered anomaly detection system recognizes unusual data access patterns within a corporate network, signaling a potential insider threat attempting unauthorized access to sensitive information.
2.	Behavioral analysis for identifying unusual patterns	Supported by machine learning, behavioral analysis focuses on understanding and predicting the behavior of users, devices, and applications. AI constructs models of typical behavior to discern deviations or anomalies that might signify a security hazard. This approach is particularly valuable in detecting insider threats, where individuals within an organization may exhibit unusual behavior indicative of malicious intent. • User Profiling: AI systems generate profiles of typical behavior for users, devices, and applications. • Dynamic Analysis: Continuous monitoring and analysis of behavior to detect deviations from established norms. • Contextual Understanding: AI considers the context of activities to distinguish between normal and potentially malicious behavior (Exploring the Vital Role of AI in Cybersecurity I CCS Learning Academy, n.d.).	Example Scenario: Behavioral analysis detects employees accessing sensitive files during non-working hours, deviating from their usual work patterns. The AI system raises an alert for further investigation.
3.	AI-driven investigation and remediation (Exploring the Vital Role of AI in Cybersecurity I CCS Learning Academy, n.d.)	AI significantly contributes to the investigation and remediation phases of incident response. Through advanced analytics and machine learning, AI aids in identifying the root cause of security incidents, understanding the tactics employed by attackers, and recommending effective remediation strategies. • Threat Intelligence Integration: Integrating threat intelligence feeds to augment the precision of investigative endeavors. • Forensic Analysis: AI assists in analyzing logs, network traffic, and other digital forensics data to reconstruct the timeline of events. • Automated Remediation: AI recommends and, in some cases, automatically applies remediation measures to address security vulnerabilities.	Example Scenario: AI-driven investigation identifies a sophisticated phishing attack, analyzes the email headers and content, and automatically blocks similar malicious emails from reaching other users.

(Continued)

TABLE 10.2 (*Continued*)

Comprehensive Examples of AI Applications in Cybersecurity with Scenarios

S. No	Topic	Description	Example Scenario
4.	Biometric authentication and AI	AI enhances the reliability and security of biometric authentication methods, such as fingerprint, facial, and voice recognition. By leveraging machine learning, AI systems can improve the accuracy of biometric authentication, making it more resistant to spoofing or impersonation. • Biometric Pattern Learning: AI learns and refines the patterns associated with legitimate biometric data. • Anti-Spoofing Measures: AI algorithms can detect and differentiate between genuine biometric data and spoofed attempts. • Continuous Improvement: Ongoing learning allows AI systems to adapt to changes in biometric data over time (Exploring the Vital Role of AI in Cybersecurity I CCS Learning Academy, n.d.; Hamme et al., 2022).	Example Scenario: An AI-enhanced facial recognition system not only identifies individuals based on facial features but also adapts to changes in appearance due to factors like aging or changes in facial hair.
5.	Continuous authentication using machine learning	Continuous authentication involves ongoing user identity verification throughout a session rather than a one-time authentication process. Machine learning contributes to continuous authentication by analyzing user behavior, device characteristics, and other contextual factors to ensure a consistent and secure user experience. • User Behavior Analysis: Machine learning models establish a baseline of normative user behavior (Goni et al., n.d.). • Context-Aware Authentication: AI considers contextual factors, such as location and time of access, to enhance authentication accuracy. • Risk-Based Authentication: Adaptive authentication based on the perceived risk level of the user's activities.	Example Scenario: Continuous authentication using machine learning detects unusual behavior, such as multiple logins attempted from different locations, triggering additional authentication measures to verify the user's identity.
6.	Automation of incident response processes	AI-driven automation in incident response expedites the identification, containment, and resolution of security incidents. Automated incident response processes leverage AI to execute predefined actions based on predefined rules and playbooks. This reduces response times and enables security teams to handle incidents more efficiently. • Automated Playbooks: Predefined sequences of actions and responses to security incidents. • Orchestration: Coordination of multiple automated processes for a comprehensive incident response. • Workflow Integration: Seamless integration with existing security tools and systems (Jarrett & Choo, 2021).	Example Scenario: An AI-driven incident response system automatically isolates a compromised system from the network, changes access credentials, and notifies relevant stakeholders upon detecting a malware infection.

10.7   ETHICAL CONSIDERATION OF AI IN CYBERSECURITY FORENSICS

The integration of AI in cybersecurity presents numerous ethical dilemmas, notably concerning the delicate equilibrium between security and privacy considerations. AI possesses the capability to effectively detect and address cyber threats, potentially fortifying overall security measures. However, concerns arise regarding privacy violations when AI technology is deployed in manners that are excessively invasive or involve the excessive collection of personal data.

Job Displacement: The ethical implications surrounding job displacement are evident in the automation capabilities of AI and ML technologies within the cybersecurity domain. As these systems advance in sophistication, there is a potential decrease in the demand for human intervention in specific cybersecurity functions. Although this can enhance overall efficiency, it raises ethical concerns about the potential obsolescence of jobs held by cybersecurity professionals specializing in tasks now automated by AI. To navigate this ethical dilemma, a well-rounded approach that includes reskilling and upskilling the existing workforce for more advanced analytical and decision-making roles becomes crucial (Stahl, Elizondo, et al., n.d.).

To maintain a harmonious equilibrium between security and privacy within AI-driven cybersecurity, various ethical considerations must be acknowledged (Stahl, Carroll-Mayer, et al., n.d.; Stahl, Elizondo, et al., n.d.):

1. Transparency emerges as a pivotal factor. Organizations leveraging AI in cybersecurity must exhibit transparency concerning the nature of data collection, its utilization, and the entities with access. This transparency is imperative for ensuring user comprehension of associated risks and enabling informed decisions regarding privacy.
2. Organizations should prioritize the utilization of AI exclusively for security purposes. While AI may have diverse potential applications, such as targeted advertising or personalized recommendations, these pursuits should not be pursued at the detriment of user privacy.
3. It is imperative for organizations to meticulously consider the potential unintended ramifications that may arise from the utilization of AI in cybersecurity. For instance, the utilization of AI to monitor employee behavior has the potential to cultivate a culture of distrust and surveillance, leading to adverse impacts on both morale and productivity.
4. Organizations need to guarantee that AI-driven cybersecurity is employed in a just and impartial manner. Biases may infiltrate the system if the data used to train AI models exhibits inherent biases or if certain demographic groups bear disproportionate consequences from implemented security measures.
5. Organizations should establish and enforce appropriate safeguards to protect personal data, encompassing measures such as encryption and access controls.

10.8   LEGAL CONSIDERATION OF AI IN CYBERSECURITY FORENSICS

The legal considerations associated with the application of AI in cybersecurity forensics are diverse and encompass various dimensions. Here are key legal considerations:

- **Data Privacy and Protection Laws:** Adherence to data privacy and protection regulations is paramount. Compliance with statutes such as the General Data Protection Regulation (GDPR) in the European Union, the California Consumer Privacy Act (CCPA) in the United States, or pertinent laws in disparate jurisdictions is indispensable.
- **Chain of Custody:** Maintain an unambiguous and unbroken chain of custody for digital evidence collected by AI during cybersecurity forensics. This is imperative for the admissibility of evidence in legal proceedings.
- **Transparency and Explainability:** Legal proceedings necessitate transparency and explicability in decision-making processes. It is imperative to ensure that the AI algorithms

utilized in cybersecurity forensics are comprehensible and can be elucidated, especially when their outcomes are presented as evidential material.

- **Admissibility in Court:** Familiarize oneself with the legal standards governing the admissibility of digital evidence obtained through AI tools. Courts may scrutinize the reliability and validity of the methods used in cybersecurity forensics, necessitating compliance with applicable legal standards.
- **Ethical Use of AI:** Ensure ethical and responsible use of AI tools. Unauthorized access to data, invasion of privacy, or any unethical application of AI in cybersecurity forensics may result in legal consequences.
- **Jurisdictional Issues:** Account for jurisdictional considerations, especially in instances of cross-border cybersecurity incidents. Different countries may have diverse laws and regulations, necessitating adept navigation of these complexities for legal compliance.
- **Liability and Accountability:** Clearly define roles and responsibilities related to the utilization of AI in cybersecurity forensics. Identify accountable parties in case of errors or misuse of AI tools, and consider potential liability issues.
- **International Cooperation:** Recognize the international implications of cybersecurity incidents. Collaboration between law enforcement agencies and adherence to legal frameworks for sharing information and evidence internationally are critical.
- **Impact on Human Rights:** Assess the impact of AI in cybersecurity on fundamental human rights, especially the right to privacy. Ensure that the application of AI tools aligns with legal standards safeguarding these rights.
- **Updating Legal Frameworks:** Given the rapid evolution of technology, be prepared to update legal frameworks. Address new challenges and opportunities presented by AI in cybersecurity forensics through timely adaptations in legal structures.

Legal and Regulatory Challenges in AI and ML Technologies in Cybersecurity: The dynamic and continuously evolving landscape of AI and ML technologies in the realm of cybersecurity engenders a spectrum of legal and regulatory complexities. Notably, the legal accountability for decisions made by autonomous systems remains ambiguous. When an AI-based cybersecurity system falls short in preventing a cyberattack, determining liability becomes intricate. Jurisdictional concerns also arise, particularly when data is stored or processed across various countries, each governed by its own set of data protection laws. Regulatory bodies are presently working on crafting guidelines and legislation to tackle these challenges. However, the rapid evolution of these technologies underscores the need for ongoing ethical and legal assessments to ensure their responsible and equitable application. Legal considerations in AI-driven cybersecurity forensics demand a thorough understanding of existing laws, ongoing technological developments, and a commitment to ethically and responsibly deploying AI tools. Consulting with legal experts specializing in cybersecurity and technology law is advisable for effective navigation of these intricate issues (Stahl, Carroll-Mayer, et al., n.d.; Stahl, Elizondo, et al., n.d.).

10.9   CASE STUDY

Facebook successfully eliminated 8.7 million images containing child nudity using artificial intelligence: Facebook recently disclosed its utilization of AI to detect nearly 9 million instances of child nudity within its network over a span of three months. A significant portion of these images had not been previously reported, enabling Facebook to provide information regarding potential abuse to the US National Center for Missing and Exploited Children.

Facebook reported the removal of 8.7 million images depicting child nudity by its moderators within a mere three-month period. The social media platform disclosed that it had implemented new software designed to automatically identify potentially sexualized images involving children. Although introduced last year, this software's public announcement was made recently. Facebook also mentioned another program capable of identifying potential cases of child grooming associated with sexual exploitation (The new weapon in the fight against crime—BBC Future, n.d.).

According to Facebook, 99% of the 8.7 million images were removed proactively before any user flagged them. Facebook's global head of safety, Antigone Davis, has indicated that the company is considering deploying systems to detect child nudity and grooming on Instagram as well. Additionally, a distinct system is in place to thwart child sexual abuse imagery previously reported to authorities. In an online video discussing the technology, Ms. Davis mentioned that Facebook engineers have been focused on developing classifiers to preemptively identify novel and unidentified images. Any newly discovered material is promptly reported by Facebook to the National Center for Missing and Exploited Children (NCMEC) (Facebook removes 8.7m child nudity images in three months—BBC News, n.d.).

Thailand general has been imprisoned for human trafficking following a large-scale trial: Manas Kongpan is among more than 60 individuals convicted in Bangkok for trafficking Bangladeshis and Rohingya Muslims, a minority group fleeing Myanmar. Additionally, another high-ranking former official received a 75-year prison sentence, with over 100 defendants undergoing trial. For years, Muslim Rohingya have been fleeing Myanmar, often resorting to paying people smugglers to facilitate their escape. The arrest of a general in June 2015 was seen as part of Thailand's efforts to dismantle a human smuggling route traversing through the country. The judge adjudged the general guilty of human trafficking and organized transnational crime. Another individual, Ko-Tong (also known as Patjuban Aungkachotephan), a former head of administration in Satun province, also received a 75-year prison sentence. Various other defendants were sentenced to jail terms ranging from four to 94 years (Thailand general jailed for human trafficking at mass trial—BBC News, n.d.).

The firm's software was recently employed in a high-profile human trafficking case in Thailand, where it played a pivotal role in identifying key individuals involved in the illicit activities. By employing sophisticated algorithms and data analysis methodologies, the software parsed through extensive datasets, encompassing online communications, financial transactions, and social network connections, to identify individuals linked to the trafficking network.

In this particular case, the software flagged suspicious patterns and connections among various individuals, leading investigators to focus their attention on a group that included police officers, three politicians, and an army general. These officials were found to have been involved in facilitating or profiting from human trafficking activities.

The software's ability to analyze large datasets and detect complex networks of criminal activity proved invaluable in uncovering the extent of the trafficking operation and identifying the individuals responsible. This case highlights the transformative impact of technology in combating human trafficking and holding perpetrators, including those in positions of power, accountable for their actions (Thailand general jailed for human trafficking at mass trial—BBC News, n.d.).

10.10   OBSTACLES AND FUTURE DIRECTIONS

Artificial intelligence has significantly contributed to the modernization and increased productivity of various industries and society as a whole. The integration of the Internet of Things (IoT) (M. Nair et al., n.d.) has further enhanced the capabilities of AI by enabling the seamless sensing and transfer of data between devices over the internet. This has led to more efficient task execution across a wide range of applications, extending from agriculture to weather prediction. In agriculture, AI facilitates tasks such as assessing soil quality, monitoring crop growth, and optimizing processes like crop cutting. Similarly, in weather prediction, AI plays a crucial role in identifying and analyzing upcoming weather patterns, thereby helping to minimize potential casualties. The synergy between AI and IoT is particularly impactful when integrated with smart devices. As these sectors worldwide incorporate IoT into their operations, the prevalence of cyber-attacks and vulnerabilities is a growing concern. The utilization of AI in conjunction with smart devices has proven effective in mitigating such risks. The emphasis is on preventing, detecting, and recovering from system failures promptly. However, the detection of cyber-attacks is often time-consuming when relying solely on human expertise.

Looking ahead, the future holds the promise of AI assisting professionals in swiftly tracing and tracking cyber-attacks, thereby minimizing potential losses. An illustrative example of machine learning in action is the identification of spam and junk emails, highlighting the role of AI in enhancing cybersecurity. Given the increasing reliance on digital infrastructure across various industries, cybersecurity has become a critical necessity. This is particularly true for vital sectors such as healthcare. Recognizing the urgency of the situation, we aim to provide innovative solutions for preventing and mitigating cyber-attacks on public networks and infrastructure through the application of artificial intelligence (Juneja et al., n.d.; M. Nair et al., n.d.):

- **Addressing Ethical Challenges:** A significant hurdle in the advancement and implementation of artificial intelligence systems lies in navigating the ethical terrain. The ethical landscape, encompassing concerns such as data privacy, consent, and algorithmic fairness, has become a focal point, especially as AI models play pivotal roles in decision-making processes impacting human lives (Ghonge et al., 2022). The utilization of biased training data raises apprehensions about resulting in discriminatory outcomes, particularly in sensitive areas like criminal justice and healthcare. Furthermore, the opaqueness of machine learning algorithms contributes to the "black-box" problem, making it challenging to comprehend the rationale behind specific decisions. Ethical considerations are not peripheral but integral to the development cycle, necessitating interdisciplinary collaboration involving ethicists, legal experts, and technologists. Future research should prioritize the development of explainable AI, unbiased data collection methods, and ethical frameworks guiding AI applications across various domains.
- **Advancing Integration of AI and ML:** An area ripe for advancement resides in the fusion of artificial intelligence with machine learning. While AI aims to create intelligent agents mirroring human cognition, ML focuses on formulating algorithms enabling systems to learn from data. The synergy between these domains holds significant potential for crafting robust and intelligent systems. However, challenges such as computational complexity, data sparsity, and model generalization persist. Efficient algorithms capable of handling large-scale data and computational constraints are imperative for real-world applications. Additionally, the creation of hybrid models that amalgamate rule-based AI with data-driven ML techniques could provide solutions that are both interpretable and accurate. The future emphasis should be on optimizing this integration to efficiently address complex, multi-dimensional problems (Ghonge et al., 2022).
- **Preparing for Adversarial AI:** In the advancing landscape of artificial intelligence, the associated risks with adversarial attacks are on the rise. Adversarial AI refers to the intentional manipulation of either input data or the model itself, with the aim of misleading the system into generating inaccurate predictions or decisions. Currently, effective countermeasures against such attacks are still in their early stages. Ongoing research in this domain primarily concentrates on adversarial training and robust optimization techniques designed to bolster the resilience of AI models. However, it is important to note that these solutions often introduce increased model complexity and demand additional computational resources. The imperative development of secure and robust AI systems capable of withstanding adversarial attacks holds paramount importance, particularly for their deployment in security-sensitive applications such as autonomous vehicles and cybersecurity (Ghonge et al., 2022; Juneja et al., n.d.; M. Nair et al., n.d.).
- **Regulatory Frameworks and Standards:** A significant challenge within the domain of AI and machine learning technologies stems from the absence of a comprehensive regulatory framework. Presently, the regulation of these technologies is characterized by

fragmentation and substantial variations across jurisdictions. This regulatory void leads to inconsistencies in the development, testing, and implementation of AI systems, thereby hindering global adoption and interoperability. Addressing this issue necessitates the establishment of universal standards and regulatory guidelines to ensure the safety, reliability, and ethical integrity of AI technologies. This requires collaborative efforts among diverse stakeholders, including governmental entities, industry participants, and academic institutions. Future research endeavors and policy initiatives should be directed toward formulating a unified set of guidelines that can serve as a global standard for the development and deployment of AI (Juneja et al., 2021).

- **Human-AI Collaboration:** Exploring and advancing the collaborative interaction between humans and AI systems is a critical area for further investigation. Although AI systems demonstrate exceptional proficiency in tasks involving pattern recognition and data analysis, they lack the emotional intelligence and nuanced understanding inherent in human operators. Conversely, humans stand to gain significant advantages from the computational power and data-driven insights offered by AI (Ghonge et al., 2022). The primary challenge lies in the development of interfaces and interaction paradigms that effectively facilitate collaboration between humans and AI. This not only involves creating user interfaces that are intuitive but also integrating features such as explain ability and trustworthiness into AI systems. Research in this domain should concentrate on devising frameworks that enable seamless collaboration, ensuring optimal leveraging of the strengths of both humans and AI.
- **Financial Institutions' Embrace of AI in Cyber Forensics:** Financial institutions are increasingly immersing themselves in the exploration and application of AI techniques to secure a competitive advantage, especially in the domain of trading. Within the field of cyber forensics, there is a surge in the utilization of AI by money managers who are enlisting the skills of numerous quantitative specialists to develop intricate AI models for forecasting prices, detecting signals, and monitoring market sentiment, among other activities. Furthermore, the intersection of artificial intelligence and cryptocurrencies offers an intriguing frontier in cyber forensics. Here, AI models and strategies may reveal new insights and methodologies in investigating and analyzing activities within cryptocurrency markets (Verma et al., 2023).

10.11   CONCLUSION

Cyber forensic investigations play a crucial role in identifying and mitigating cyber threats and attacks. This discussion explores the potential applications of artificial intelligence in forensic science and criminal investigation, aiming to assist forensic experts, police investigators, and security personnel. It is evident that AI-powered machines, programs, or software can significantly reduce the time required for various tasks throughout an examination and investigation process. This efficiency improvement would lead to quicker case resolution, thereby reducing the backlog caused by slow and complex investigation procedures. Increased accuracy, competency, and impartiality would ultimately enhance the criminal justice system. Scientists and researchers continue to develop AI-based programs and machines to further refine forensic investigation procedures. These advancements in AI-powered software are poised to strengthen forensic investigation and predictive policing systems, as well as our security and defense infrastructure.

In conclusion, integrating artificial intelligence into cybersecurity marks a significant advancement with broad implications. AI, including machine learning, deep learning, and natural language processing, has proven its potential to enhance various cybersecurity aspects, such as threat detection, incident response, and forensic analysis. Through AI algorithms, cybersecurity professionals can analyze vast datasets efficiently, identify emerging threats in real-time, and automate response actions to mitigate risks promptly. Furthermore, AI-powered systems can adapt and evolve to counter evolving cyber threats, offering dynamic defense mechanisms against sophisticated attacks. Despite its benefits, AI also presents challenges, including concerns about data privacy, model interpretability, and adversarial attacks. Addressing these challenges requires ongoing research, stakeholder collaboration, and the development of robust governance frameworks to ensure responsible and ethical AI deployment in cybersecurity. Nevertheless, the undeniable potential of AI in cybersecurity persists. As cyber threats evolve in complexity and scale, AI-driven solutions offer a promising avenue to strengthen cyber defenses, protect digital assets, and maintain digital environment integrity.

In summary, the synergy between AI and cybersecurity holds great promise in combating cyber threats. Through continued innovation, collaboration, and responsible implementation, AI stands to revolutionize cybersecurity practices, ushering in a new era of resilience and security in the digital field.

REFERENCES

(2) The use of AI in detecting and preventing cybercrime | LinkedIn. (n.d.). Retrieved February 7, 2024, from www.linkedin.com/pulse/use-ai-detecting-preventing-cybercrime-neil-sahota-%E8%90%A8%E5%86%A0%E5%86%9B-/?utm_source=share&utm_medium=member_android&utm_campaign=share_via

Al-Mansoori, S., Analytics, M. S.-I. J. of S., & 2023, undefined. (n.d.). The role of artificial intelligence and machine learning in shaping the future of cybersecurity: Trends, applications, and ethical considerations. *Norislab.Com.* Retrieved January 23, 2024, from https://norislab.com/index.php/ijsa/article/view/36

computer, P. P.-I. journal of research in, & 2016, undefined. (n.d.). Artificial intelligence in cybersecurity. *Academia.Edu.* Retrieved January 21, 2024, from www.academia.edu/download/45648362/v4i501.pdf

Exploring the vital role of AI in cybersecurity | CCS Learning Academy. (n.d.). Retrieved February 7, 2024, from www.ccslearningacademy.com/role-of-ai-in-cyber-security/

Facebook removes 8.7m child nudity images in three months—BBC News. (n.d.). Retrieved February 7, 2024, from www.bbc.com/news/technology-45967301

Ghonge, M., Pramanik, S., Mangrulkar, R., & Le, D. (2022). *Cyber security and digital forensics: Challenges and future trends.* https://books.google.com/books?hl=en&lr=&id=VA9ZEAAAQBAJ&oi=fnd&pg=PP13&dq=cybersecurity+forensics+with+AI:+legal+and+ethical+consideration&ots=vIApgrYkcr&sig=CKDjeKQFlF7JBtLCT2yVqrUI1-g

Goni, I., Gumpy, J., . . . T. M.-M. L., & 2020, undefined. (n.d.). Cybersecurity and cyber forensics: Machine learning approach. *Academia.Edu.* Retrieved February 7, 2024, from www.academia.edu/download/85970988/10.11648.j.mlr.20200504.11.pdf

Hamme, T. Van, Garofalo, G., Joos, S., Preuveneers, D., & Joosen, W. (2022). AI for Biometric Authentication Systems. *Lecture Notes in Computer Science (Including Subseries Lecture Notes in Artificial Intelligence and Lecture Notes in Bioinformatics), 13049 LNCS,* 156–180. https://doi.org/10.1007/978-3-030-98795-4_8

Jadhav, E., Singh Sankhla, M., & Kumar, R. (2020). Artificial Intelligence: Advancing Automation in Forensic Science & Criminal Investigation. *Seybold Report, 15*(August), 2064–2075.

Janga, J., Reddy, K., Chemosphere, R. K.-, & 2023, undefined. (n.d.). *Integrating artificial intelligence, machine learning, and deep learning approaches into remediation of contaminated sites: A review.* Elsevier. Retrieved February 7, 2024, from www.sciencedirect.com/science/article/pii/S0045653523027467

Jarrett, A., & Choo, K. R. (2021). The impact of automation and artificial intelligence on digital forensics. *WIREs Forensic Science, 3*(6). https://doi.org/10.1002/WFS2.1418

Juneja, A., Juneja, S., Bali, V., . . . V. J.-T. S. C., & 2021, undefined. (n.d.). Artificial intelligence and cybersecurity: Current trends and future prospects. *Wiley Online Library.* Retrieved January 23, 2024, from https://onlinelibrary.wiley.com/doi/abs/10.1002/9781119761655.ch22

Juneja, A., Juneja, S., Bali, V., Jain, V., & Upadhyay, H. (2021). Artificial intelligence and cybersecurity: Current trends and future prospects. *The Smart Cyber Ecosystem for Sustainable Development,* 431–441. https://doi.org/10.1002/9781119761655.CH22

Kaur, G., & Moza, B. (2023). Exploring railway forensics: Top approaches and future directions. *Asian Journal of Science and Technology, 14*(6), 12561–12567.

Kaur, G., Mukherjee, D., Moza, B., Pahwa, V., Kaur, K., & Kaur, K. (2024). The dark web: A hidden menace or a tool for privacy protection. *IP International Journal of Forensic Medicine and Toxicological Sciences, 8,* 160–167. https://doi.org/10.18231/j.ijfmts.2023.034

Li, J-hua. (2018). Cyber security meets artificial intelligence: A survey. *Frontiers of Information Technology and Electronic Engineering, 19*(12), 1462–1474. https://doi.org/10.1631/FITEE.1800573

Lum, K., & Isaac, W. (2016). To predict and serve? *Significance, 13*(5), 14–19. https://doi.org/10.1111/J.1740-9713.2016.00960.X

Marciano, M. A., & Adelman, J. D. (2017). PACE: Probabilistic Assessment for Contributor Estimation—A machine learning-based assessment of the number of contributors in DNA mixtures. *Forensic Science International: Genetics, 27*, 82–91. https://doi.org/10.1016/j.fsigen.2016.11.006

Moza, B., Mukherjee, D., Singh, M., Pahwa, V., Ujjainia, P., Pathak, S., Saha, A., & Srivastava, A. (2024). Advancements in the imaging techniques for detection of skeletal pathologies: A comprehensive review. *Tuijin Jishu/Journal of Propulsion Technology, 45*, 645–663.

Mughal, A. A. (2019). A comprehensive study of practical techniques and methodologies in incident based approaches for cyber forensics. *Tensorgate Journal of Sustainable Technology and Infrastructure for Developing Countries, 2*(1), 1–18.

Nair, M., Deshmukh, A., . . . A. T.-S. C. for N., & 2024, undefined. (n.d.). Artificial intelligence for cyber security: Current trends and future challenges. *Wiley Online Library*. Retrieved January 23, 2024, from https://onlinelibrary.wiley.com/doi/abs/10.1002/9781394213948.ch5

Nair, M. M., Deshmukh, A., & Tyagi, A. K. (2024). Artificial intelligence for cyber security. *Automated Secure Computing for Next-Generation Systems*, 83–114. https://doi.org/10.1002/9781394213948.CH5

Saikia, S., Fidalgo, E., Alegre, E., & Fernández-Robles, L. (2017). Object detection for crime scene evidence analysis using deep learning. *Lecture Notes in Computer Science (Including Subseries Lecture Notes in Artificial Intelligence and Lecture Notes in Bioinformatics), 10485 LNCS*, 14–24. https://doi.org/10.1007/978-3-319-68548-9_2

Stahl, B., Carroll-Mayer, M., . . . D. E.-. . . I. for P., & 2012, undefined. (n.d.). *Intelligence techniques in computer security and forensics: At the boundaries of ethics and law*. Springer. Retrieved January 22, 2024, from https://link.springer.com/chapter/10.1007/978-3-642-25237-2_14

Stahl, B., Elizondo, D., . . . M. C.-M.-. . . J. C. on, & 2010, undefined. (n.d.). Ethical and legal issues of the use of computational intelligence techniques in computer security and computer forensics. *Ieeexplore.Ieee.Org*. Retrieved January 22, 2024, from https://ieeexplore.ieee.org/abstract/document/5596546/

Thailand general jailed for human trafficking at mass trial—BBC News. (n.d.). Retrieved February 7, 2024, from www.bbc.com/news/world-asia-40652012

The new weapon in the fight against crime—BBC Future. (n.d.). Retrieved February 7, 2024, from www.bbc.com/future/article/20190228-how-ai-is-helping-to-fight-crime

Ukwen, D., . . . M. K. on digital forensics and, & 2021, undefined. (n.d.). Review of NLP-based systems in digital forensics and cybersecurity. *Ieeexplore.Ieee.Org*. Retrieved February 7, 2024, from https://ieeexplore.ieee.org/abstract/document/9486354/

Verma, P., Mukherjee, D., & Moza, B. (2023). Decentralized money: A comprehensive review on cryptocurrencies. *International Journal of Advanced Trends in Computer Applications, 9*(2), 35–41.

Vishwanath, M. (2023). *Artificial intelligence based digital forensics framework & artificial intelligence in cyber security*. https://osf.io/fnuxr/download

Wirkuttis, N., Cyber, H. K.-, Intelligence, undefined, Security, and, & 2017, undefined. (n.d.). Artificial intelligence in cybersecurity. *Academia.Edu*. Retrieved January 22, 2024, from www.academia.edu/download/52464497/Artificial_Intelligence_in_Cybersecurity.pdf

11 Remote Sensing Imagery Classification Techniques Using Quantum Deep Learning

Puneet Anchalia, G.S. Smrithy, D. Kavitha, and S. Sijin Kumar

11.1 INTRODUCTION

The main aim of remote sensing is to gather data about objects or areas without physical contact has become a cornerstone for various scientific and practical applications. Satellite and airborne sensors capture invaluable data about Earth's surface, enabling fields like agriculture, environmental monitoring, and disaster response. However, analysing this data, particularly classifying pixels into categories like land cover types, presents challenges. The sheer volume and complexity of the data, coupled with the need for precise classification, necessitates advanced methods.

This research is driven by the critical role remote sensing plays in addressing global issues. While existing classification techniques are effective, they struggle with the ever-increasing scale and complexity of datasets. This work aims to develop more efficient and accurate techniques capable of handling the growing volumes of data generated by modern Earth observation missions.

The core problem addressed here is the inefficiency of current remote sensing image classification methods. While proficient, they struggle to scale effectively with larger and more intricate datasets. Additionally, they may not fully utilize the rich information within the imagery. The potential for this research to transform remote sensing applications and provide solutions for well-informed decision-making in a variety of domains makes it significant.

The research has three key objectives. First, it aims to develop and implement quantum deep learning models specifically designed for remote sensing image classification. These models leverage the principles of quantum computing, holding promise for overcoming the computational challenges posed by massive datasets. Second, the research will benchmark the performance of these novel quantum models against existing classical deep learning techniques. This comparison will serve as a benchmark to assess the potential advantages that quantum computing might bring to the field. Finally, the research will focus on measuring the impact of quantum computing on classification accuracy, particularly when dealing with large-scale datasets, a hallmark of contemporary remote sensing applications.

Understanding the evolving landscape of remote sensing applications requires consideration of the Earth observation (EO) context. As EO missions continue to deploy increasingly sophisticated sensors, they generate a vast amount of data, often referred to as big data. The daily influx of imagery is estimated to exceed 150 terabytes, highlighting the challenges of processing, analysing, and extracting meaningful insights from these massive datasets.

Fortunately, advancements in computational technologies and analytical methodologies have emerged to meet the demands of handling higher resolution datasets. Machine learning (ML) and artificial intelligence (AI) have become indispensable tools in managing the ever-growing big data stream. These fields offer powerful techniques for automated feature extraction, pattern recognition,

DOI: 10.1201/9781003499459-11

and classification, significantly enhancing our ability to unlock the secrets hidden within remote sensing imagery.

This research explores the potential of quantum deep learning, a nascent field that leverages the unique properties of quantum mechanics to design computational models. Unlike classical deep learning models that operate on bits (0 or 1), quantum models utilize qubits, quantum bits that can exist in a superposition of both states simultaneously. This ability to explore a wider range of possibilities has the potential to lead to more efficient and accurate solutions for complex problems like remote sensing image classification.

The following sections will delve deeper into the theoretical framework of quantum deep learning, explore specific techniques suitable for remote sensing applications, and discuss the implementation details of the proposed models. Furthermore, the research will present a rigorous evaluation methodology to compare the performance of quantum deep learning models against established classical deep learning techniques on various remote sensing image datasets. By undertaking this comprehensive investigation, this research aims to contribute significantly to the advancement of remote sensing image classification, paving the way for a new era of efficient and accurate Earth observation analysis.

11.1.1 THE APPLICATION OF QUANTUM COMPUTING IN EO

The confluence of the need for innovative computation technologies and the exponential growth of data in EO has led researchers to explore the application of quantum computing (QC). Despite facing technological limitations, quantum computing, particularly in the realm of noisy intermediate-scale quantum (NISQ) algorithms, offers a paradigm shift in solving complex optimization problems. Quantum computers promise exponentially faster computations, presenting a tangible solution to challenges such as finding eigenvalues and solving combinatorial optimization problems.

11.1.2 QUANTUM COMPUTING BASICS

In quantum computing, a qubit, called a quantum bit, is the fundamental part of quantum information, analogous to classical binary bits. But qubits have the special ability to live in a coherent superposition of both states at the same time. This property, rooted in quantum mechanics, enables quantum computers to represent 2^n possible states for every n qubit, exponentially surpassing the capabilities of classical systems. Besides, quantum computers' efficient computation is based on the concepts of entanglement and superposition.

Quantum technology's application in remote sensing has been a subject of exploration for over two decades. Quantum annealers for interferometric synthetic aperture radars and quantum machine learning (QML) for remote sensing applications are two further uses.

The primary contributions of this research are multi-faceted. First, it extends the application of quantum computing to land-cover classification, utilizing the EuroSAT dataset as a reference benchmark for optical multispectral images. The research delves beyond proof-of-concept applications on a few images and explores the potential advantages of quantum-based networks over classical counterparts. Second, the research introduces and analyses various circuit oriented hybrid quantum convolutional neural networks (QCNNs). A critical analysis is presented, comparing the performances of these hybrid models and highlighting the advantages of architectures incorporating quantum entanglement. Last, the research adopts a structured prediction setting, implementing coarse-to-fine classification, to further challenge the capabilities brought by entanglement.

While the current state of the art in quantum remote sensing is limited, notable works have explored the synergy between quantum computing and convolutional neural networks (CNNs).The use of quantum machine learning in remote sensing is still in its infancy; examples include ensemble methods that operate on quantum annealers and classifiers based on quantum circuits for neural networks.

11.2 QUANTUM DEEP LEARNING FOR REMOTE SENSING IMAGERY CLASSIFICATION

Quantum deep learning is a new field that combines the power of quantum computing with the flexibility of deep learning. Quantum algorithms can be used to speed up the training and inference of deep learning models.

There are two main approaches to quantum deep learning for remote sensing imagery classification:

1. Quantum-inspired deep learning: This approach uses classical deep learning algorithms with quantum-inspired techniques. For example, quantum-inspired activation functions and optimizers can be used to improve the performance of deep learning models.
2. Quantum deep learning algorithms: Using this method, new deep learning algorithms tailored for quantum computers are created. For the purpose of classifying remote sensing imagery, quantum recurrent and convolutional neural networks, for instance, have been proposed.

11.3 LITERATURE REVIEW

Remote sensing imagery classification, particularly in the context of land-use and land-cover (LULC), is a critical component in various fields, including environmental monitoring, agriculture, and resource management. Traditional methods based on pixel or object analysis have been extensively employed, but they face challenges related to data acquisition issues and environmental changes. The literature reveals a shift toward more robust statistical models and, notably, deep learning techniques.

Supervised object-based land-cover classification techniques have gained prominence, with a comprehensive survey provided in [1].Current reviews examine the difficulties and cutting-edge methods for LULC classification, such as the one by Talukdar et al. The diversity of methodologies includes patch wise approaches, focusing on local neighbourhoods, and pixelwise approaches, which model local appearance statistics. Object-based image analysis (OBIA) methods, such as the region-based CNN, and pixelwise approaches using fully convolutional networks (FCNs), have demonstrated efficiency. Improvements also include methods based on transformers, recurrent networks, graph convolutional networks, and capsule networks, which address issues like interpretable classification and explain ability.

Despite the progress, challenges persist in current remote sensing classification techniques. Issues related to computational efficiency, interpretability, and scalability are common [2]. The limitations of classical techniques, especially concerning adaptability to diverse datasets and environmental changes, necessitate innovative solutions.

11.4 INTRODUCTION TO CLASSICAL AND QUANTUM DEEP LEARNING

In remote sensing applications, classical deep learning approaches like recurrent neural networks (RNNs) and convolutional neural networks have proven essential. FCNs have been shown to be quite effective at capturing the variety of inputs for different LULC classes. [3]. However, the advent of quantum computing introduces new opportunities and challenges.

Figure 11.1 shows the representation of a simple CNN. This is a simple network made up of five layers: an input layer, an output layer, a pooling layer, a fully connected layer, and an input layer. The literature review sets the stage for understanding the evolution of remote sensing imagery classification techniques. The transition from classical to deep learning methods and the emerging interest in quantum computing underline the dynamic landscape of this field.

This chapter is centred around demonstrating how quantum computers can improve the performance of machine learning algorithms in the specific context of LULC classification. The need for

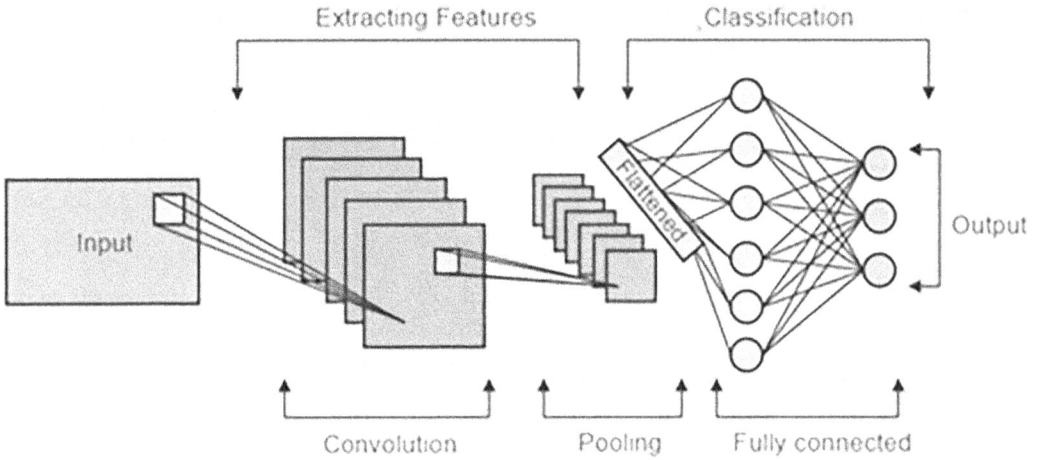

FIGURE.11.1   CNN.

quantum solutions is underscored by the challenges discussed in the literature review regarding large-scale processing and the variety of sensors used in remote sensing.

By avoiding relative minima in gradient descent through quantum tunnelling, quantum computers provide a distinct benefit. This feature, which is called quantum tunnelling through "hills," suggests that quantum computers may be able to solve problems more effectively than classical computers. The advantages of quantum computing include artificial neural networks, quantum sampling, rapid linear algebra, and optimisation. [4].

Quantum machine learning is positioned to provide several advantages for learning problems. Quantum resources are expected to offer benefits in terms of improvements in runtime, learning capacity, and learning efficiency [5]. The application of quantum computing to machine learning is explored through quantum circuits, like quantum convolutional neural networks, demonstrating their ability to intrinsically solve quantum many-body problems.

However, challenges exist, and the advantages of QML over classical approaches depend on factors such as the quality and quantity of data. The research adds a valuable perspective by demonstrating how QML could address real remote sensing image classification problems with multiple classes.

This section establishes the rationale behind integrating quantum computing into machine learning for remote sensing applications. It provides a foundation for understanding the potential advantages and challenges associated with quantum machine learning in the context of LULC classification.

The paper [1] delves into the intricate realm of remote sensing imagery classification, recognizing the challenges arising from the data's high dimensionality and complexity. While acknowledging the efficacy of deep learning in this domain, the authors highlight its computational intensity and reliance on extensive training data. A potential solution is sought in the realm of quantum computing, aiming to surmount the limitations of conventional deep learning. The study comprehensively reviews recent advancements in quantum deep learning tailored for remote sensing imagery classification. A practical case study using circuit-based hybrid quantum convolutional neural networks for land cover classification using Sentinel-2 images puts quantum techniques for image feature extraction and classification front and centre.

The hybrid QCNN integrates quantum layers within standard neural networks, showcasing their application in Earth observation, specifically in land-use and land-cover classification. Results from the EuroSAT dataset affirm the superiority of QCNNs over classical counterparts in multiclass classification, particularly when exploiting quantum entanglement. the research asserts the potential of quantum computing in EO applications, providing both theoretical and empirical foundations. It contributes novel insights by demonstrating the superiority of QCNNs in a real-world EO case study. The utilization of different quantum circuits underscores the pivotal role of entanglement in achieving optimal classification scores.

A recent study [2] proposes a novel approach for classifying land use and land cover (LULC) using satellite imagery from the Sentinel-2 program. This approach offers a valuable contribution to the field of remote sensing.

The paper introduces a "patch-based" strategy for LULC classification. Instead of analysing entire satellite images at once, the image is divided into smaller, manageable patches. Each patch is then individually classified into a specific land cover type. This method offers advantages like reduced computational complexity, allowing for analysis of high-resolution imagery like Sentinel-2 data. Additionally, it allows the model to focus on specific regions within the image and potentially capture local variations in land cover. Furthermore, the patch-based approach facilitates data augmentation techniques for creating additional training data and improving model generalizability.

The research leverages imagery from the Sentinel-2 program, a European Space Agency initiative offering high-resolution, multispectral satellite data. Sentinel-2 data is freely available and captures information across 13 different spectral bands, providing valuable details about the reflected light from various objects on Earth's surface. This rich information is crucial for accurate LULC classification.

The paper also introduces a new dataset called EuroSAT, specifically designed for this research. EuroSAT comprises 27,000 labelled and geo-referenced image patches extracted from Sentinel-2 images. Each patch belongs to one of ten different LULC classes, offering a diverse and representative dataset for training and evaluating the classification model. Notably, the EuroSAT dataset is publicly available, allowing other researchers to replicate and build upon this work.

For LULC classification, the research employs deep convolutional neural networks. Figure 11.2 shows the diagram of a deep CNN. Deep convolutional neural networks are a class of artificial neural networks, primarily applied to analysing visual imagery. They excel in feature extraction through hierarchical layers, mimicking the visual cortex's organization. Leveraging convolutional layers for spatial filtering, pooling for dimensionality reduction, and fully connected layers for classification, they revolutionize image recognition tasks. CNNs are a type of deep learning architecture particularly well-suited for image analysis tasks. They can automatically extract relevant features from images, enabling the model to learn the complex relationships between image pixels and corresponding LULC classes. The reported results are promising, with the proposed approach achieving an impressive overall classification accuracy of 98.57%. This suggests that the model can effectively distinguish between different land cover types with a high degree of accuracy.

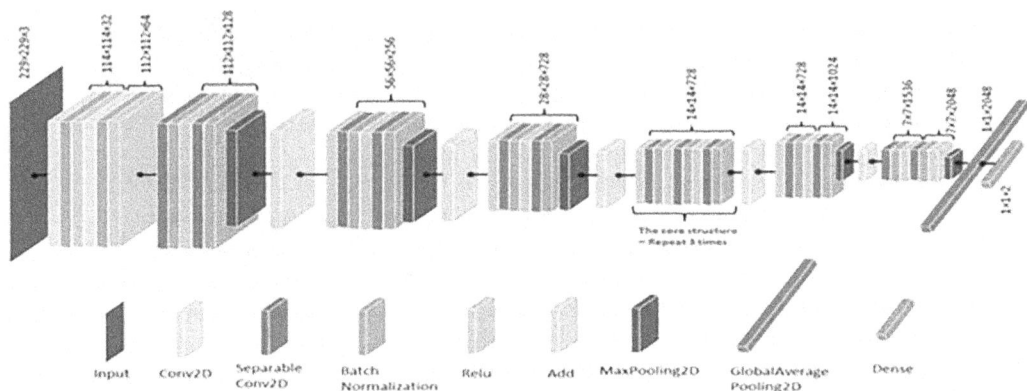

FIGURE 11.2 Deep convolutional neural network.

The research holds significant value for Earth observation applications. The high classification accuracy paves the way for creating detailed and reliable land cover maps, crucial for monitoring deforestation, tracking urban expansion, and managing natural resources. Additionally, by analysing time series data from Sentinel-2, the approach can be used to detect changes in land cover over time, aiding in understanding land use dynamics and environmental changes. The LULC classification results can also be used to update and improve existing geographic maps, providing more precise and up-to-date information.

Finally, the openness of Sentinel-2 data and the availability of the EuroSAT dataset make this research easily replicable and scalable. This fosters collaboration and advancement in the field of remote sensing-based LULC classification. Overall, this work offers a compelling approach for land cover classification with the potential to significantly improve our ability to monitor and understand land cover changes on a global scale, contributing to more informed decision-making related to land use and environmental management.

Figure 11.3 shows sample images for each class, namely Residential, Highway, Industrial, River, Forest, Annual Crop, Sea Lake, Permanent Crop, Herbaceous Vegetation and Pasture of the dataset. The paper [3] addresses the challenge of hyperspectral image (HSI) classification by introducing a novel algorithm called Conv-Caps, combining convolutional neural network and Capsule Network (CapsNet) architectures. CNNs, while powerful in feature extraction, face inefficiency issues due to fully connected layers. CapsNet, designed to overcome this, offers improved spectral and spatial feature extraction. The proposed Conv-Caps algorithm integrates both networks and incorporates a Markov random field (MRF) for classification using a Caps-MRF approach. The method involves an initial CNN-based feature extractor, Caps Net for probability mapping, and MRF for label calculation. Trained on three real HSI datasets, the approach demonstrates competitive classification performance, outperforming recent methods.

Hyperspectral images capture a wealth of information across hundreds of narrow spectral bands, offering a detailed view of materials and objects on Earth's surface. However, classifying the various elements within an HSI presents a challenge. Traditional methods often rely on convolutional neural networks, but these struggle when dealing with limited labelled data, a common constraint in HSI classification.

This paper [4] proposes a novel approach that leverages graph neural networks (GNNs) to overcome these limitations and achieve superior classification performance. GNNs excel at modelling relationships between data points, making them well-suited for HSI classification tasks. Unlike CNNs, which primarily focus on local spatial patterns, GNNs can effectively capture the complex relationships between pixels in an HSI. These relationships can be based on spectral similarities, spatial proximity, or other relevant factors. By considering these relationships, GNNs can extract more meaningful features from the data compared to traditional CNN-based methods.

Furthermore, GNNs hold a distinct advantage in handling situations with limited labelled data. Acquiring many labelled samples for HSI classification can be expensive and time consuming. GNNs can leverage the inherent structure of the data within the HSI to learn effectively even with limited labelled examples.

The proposed method employs a two-step approach:

1. **Initial Feature Learning on Large Regions:** In the first step, a GNN operates on large, irregular regions within the HSI. These regions are not predefined but emerge organically based on spectral similarities between pixels. The GNN then learns initial features that capture the overall characteristics of these larger regions. This allows the model to exploit the rich spectral information within the HSI without being restricted by pixel-level boundaries.

2. **Extracting Local Spatial-Spectral Features:** Following the initial feature learning stage, the model focuses on extracting local spatial-spectral features at the individual pixel level. This refines the understanding of each pixel by considering its spectral characteristics and its relationship with neighbouring pixels. Notably, the paper proposes the integration of

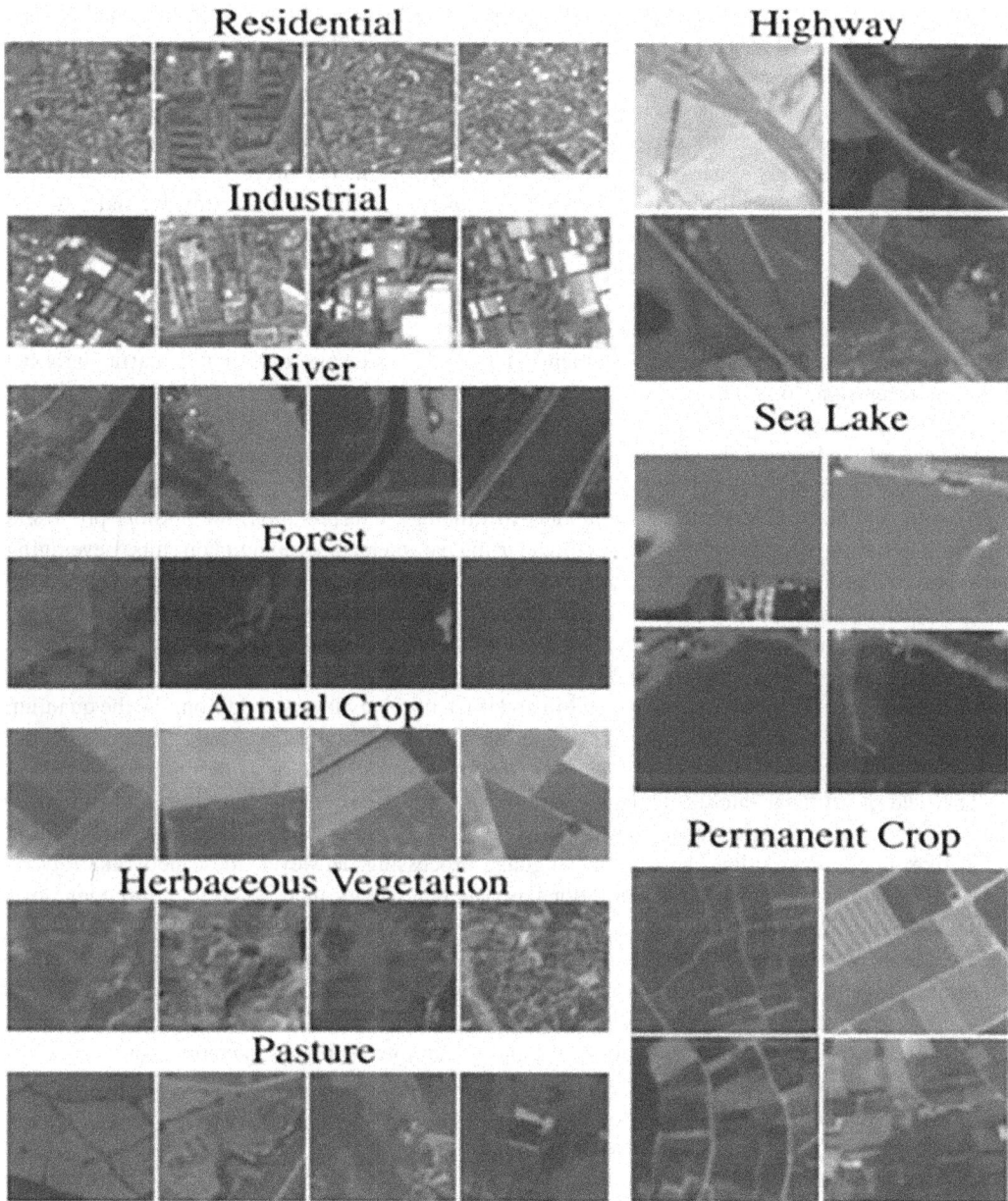

FIGURE 11.3   Sample images for each class of the dataset.

edge convolution (EdgeConv) within the GNN architecture. EdgeConv allows the model to adaptively capture the interrelationships between representative descriptors on the graph. This ensures that the model effectively utilizes the most discriminative features for accurate classification.

The proposed GNN-based approach achieves superior classification performance compared to existing state-of-the-art methods in HSI classification. This improvement can be attributed to the model's ability to leverage both complex relationships between pixels and handle situations with limited labelled data.

This research opens new avenues for HSI analysis. By effectively handling limited labelled data and extracting features based on relationships between pixels, GNN approaches offer significant advancements. This paves the way for more accurate and robust HSI analysis with potential applications in precision agriculture, environmental monitoring, geological exploration, and urban planning. By unlocking the rich information within hyperspectral images, GNN-based approaches can significantly advance our understanding of Earth's surface and its resources.

The paper [5] discusses the evolving convergence of geosciences, remote sensing, and artificial intelligence, emphasizing the need to move beyond disciplinary boundaries. While acknowledging the current trend of applying AI to well-resolved remote sensing problems, the paper advocates for exploring novel research directions at the intersection of these fields. The authors propose an agenda for AI in Earth sciences, identifying areas where the synergy between geosciences, remote sensing, and AI can bring transformative advancements. The goal is to inspire researchers, particularly the younger generation, to address challenges that can significantly impact the understanding of the Earth system through enhanced remote sensing techniques.

The paper [6] addresses the challenge of lithology interpretation in subsurface exploration, highlighting issues with manual well log interpretation efficiency and consistency. To enhance the generalization capability of deep learning models in lithology interpretation, the authors propose a quantum-enhanced deep learning (QEDL) model using parameterized quantum circuits. Leveraging superposition and entanglement in quantum systems, the QEDL model is designed to tackle the complexities of subsurface rock properties. Testing on field well log data demonstrates that the QEDL model achieves comparable performance to traditional models like convolutional neural networks and long short-term memory (LSTM). Notably, the QEDL model exhibits improved generalization, especially in interpreting both thin and thick lithology layers. Additionally, the quantum circuit structure allows the QEDL model to operate with significantly fewer parameters compared to LSTM and CNN models, offering potential efficiency gains in lithology interpretation.

The field of artificial intelligence has witnessed remarkable progress with deep learning algorithms achieving impressive feats. Neural networks, a core component of deep learning, excel in tasks like image recognition and natural language processing. However, these networks rely on classical computation, which faces limitations as data complexity increases. Quantum computing emerges as a potential solution, offering a paradigm shift in computational power. Figure 11.4 shows the interface between quantum layers. A quantum gate is a symbolized operation applied to one or more qubits within a quantum circuit. The gates manipulate the qubits and cause them to evolve according to the gate's specific function.

This article (referenced as [7]) explores the intriguing intersection of quantum computing and neural networks, with a specific focus on quantum neural networks (QNNs). Recognizing the significant progress in quantum information theory, the paper delves into the challenges of merging the distinct computational dynamics of these two domains.

Classical neural networks operate based on the principles of classical mechanics, where information is represented by bits (0 or 1). They leverage complex architectures and algorithms to learn patterns from data. However, quantum mechanics presents a completely different reality. Here,

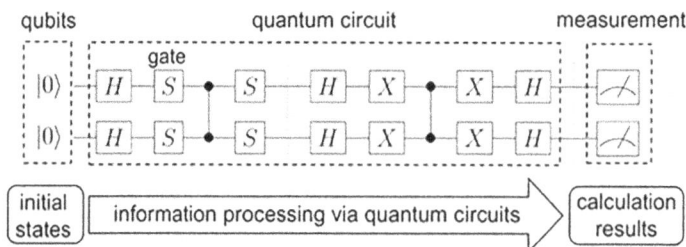

FIGURE 11.4 Interface between quantum layers.

information exists in a state of superposition, meaning qubits (quantum bits) can be 0, 1, or both simultaneously. Additionally, quantum systems exhibit entanglement, where qubits become intrinsically linked, influencing each other regardless of physical distance. These unique properties hold immense potential for surpassing the limitations of classical neural networks.

However, significant hurdles exist in bridging the gap between classical and quantum neural networks. The core challenge lies in reconciling the fundamentally different dynamics at play:

- Nonlinearity vs. Linearity: Classical neural networks rely on non-linear activation functions to introduce complexity and decision-making capabilities. Quantum mechanics, however, operates under linear, unitary dynamics. Finding ways to incorporate non-linearity into QNNs remains a crucial challenge.
- Dissipation vs. Unitarity: Classical neural networks leverage dissipative dynamics, where information can be lost or degraded over time. In contrast, quantum systems exhibit unitary dynamics, where information is preserved. Designing QNNs that can effectively learn and process information within the constraints of unitary evolution is another key challenge.

The paper meticulously evaluates existing proposals for QNNs, particularly those focused on Hopfield-type networks and associative memory tasks. The analysis reveals that none of the existing proposals fully harness the combined advantages of both quantum physics and classical computation in artificial neural networks. While some proposals attempt to achieve non-linearity, they often introduce limitations or complexities. Similarly, incorporating dissipative dynamics, crucial for realistic learning processes, remains an ongoing challenge.

The paper concludes by proposing a novel concept called open quantum neural networks (OQNNs). These networks are based on the principles of dissipative quantum computing, an emerging field that explores the interaction of quantum systems with their environment. While OQNNs are still in the theoretical stages, they offer a promising path forward for overcoming some of the limitations inherent in existing QNN proposals.

The potential benefits of OQNNs include:

- Incorporating Dissipation: By leveraging dissipative quantum computing principles, OQNNs might offer a more natural way to introduce the necessary information loss processes crucial for learning and memory tasks.
- Enhanced Expressive Power: The dissipative nature of OQNNs could potentially lead to a richer and more expressive computational framework compared to existing QNN proposals.

However, significant research and development efforts are required to fully explore the potential of OQNNs. Theoretical frameworks need further refinement, and efficient implementation strategies on actual quantum hardware platforms remain to be established.

The exploration presented in [7] highlights the challenges and opportunities at the intersection of quantum computing and neural networks. While significant hurdles exist, the potential benefits of QNNs are undeniable. The proposed concept of OQNNs offers a promising avenue for future research and development. As the field of quantum computing continues to evolve, the potential for groundbreaking advancements in the realm of artificial intelligence through the power of QNNs draws ever closer.

In this paper [8], a novel use of transfer learning with both classical and quantum components in the context of hybrid neural networks is presented. It focuses on a particular method in which a final variational quantum circuit modifies and enhances a pre-trained classical network. With the recent developments in intermediate-scale quantum technology, this approach becomes particularly relevant as it enables the best possible preparation of high-dimensional data and incorporates certain informative features into a quantum processor. Using the PennyLane software library, real-world experiments are carried out with two different quantum computers from IBM and Rigetti for high-resolution picture categorization.

Deep learning is revolutionizing the field of Earth observation, transforming tasks like land cover mapping and image registration. This paper [9] explores this trend and introduces a novel framework based on generative modelling, specifically energy-based models (EBMs).

EBMs offer a distinct advantage over traditional convolutional neural networks commonly used in EO. While CNNs focus on learning specific patterns for classification, EBMs delve deeper. They learn the joint distribution of both the data and the categories it represents. This means EBMs not only recognize patterns in EO images but also understand the underlying relationships between those patterns and the corresponding land cover types. This comprehensive understanding allows EBMs to excel in image classification and even image synthesis.

The research compares EBMs to CNNs on various public EO datasets. The results are impressive, with EBMs achieving comparable or even superior performance. However, their true strength lies in semi-supervised learning. Acquiring a large amount of labelled EO data can be expensive and time consuming. EBMs shine in these situations, demonstrating remarkable effectiveness even with limited labelled data.

This adaptability of EBMs unlocks exciting possibilities for EO applications:

- **Out-of-Distribution Analysis:** EO data can sometimes contain unexpected features not encountered during training. EBMs, with their understanding of the underlying data distribution, can potentially identify such anomalies, improving the robustness of analysis.
- **Confident Land Cover Mapping:** Traditional CNNs might struggle with limited labelled data, leading to less certain classifications in certain areas. EBMs, with their superior performance in semi-supervised learning, can offer more confident and reliable land cover maps, even in regions with scarce labelled data.

By leveraging the power of generative modelling with EBMs, researchers and practitioners can achieve more accurate and robust results in EO tasks. This shift towards generative models holds immense potential for unlocking valuable insights from EO data and furthering our understanding of Earth.

11.5   QUANTUM NEURAL NETWORK INTEGRATION

A parameterized quantum circuit is incorporated into the classical neural network design as a hidden layer in order to create a quantum neural network. A higher-dimensional quantum representation of the classical data is needed for this merger. An in-depth description of how to get a quantum state ready for this is provided in the following.

11.5.1   FEATURE MAPPING AND PREPARING QUANTUM STATES

To encode classical information in an N-qubit space, start with a set of (N |0) quantum nodes and a unitary operator. Based on previous classical node values, the information is encoded using a unitary matrix that is calculated classically. This process, called data embedding, uses the quantum state's amplitude probability to reflect the previous classical activation.

11.5.2   QUANTUM REPRESENTATION VIA GATE OPERATIONS

Classical information can be encoded into quantum representation via a variety of gate operations. For example, place qubits in a superposition state using a Hadamard gate and then rotate the RZ gate at angles equal to feature values of previous inputs. Consistency in the encoding and representation of classical information must be guaranteed in the interpretation of the prepared state.

11.5.3 APPLICATION OF PARAMETERIZED QUANTUM CIRCUITS

Use the parameterized quantum circuit subsequent to the classical encoding. This circuit uses elements of a classical input vector to specify the rotation angles of each gate. The inputs for the parameterized circuit are the outputs from the preceding layer of the neural network. Gather measurement data from the quantum circuit in order to prepare later hidden den layers.

11.6 KEY ENHANCEMENTS

Quantum computing offers several advantages over classical computing in the context of remote sensing imagery classification.

11.6.1 QUANTUM PARALLELISM

Quantum computers leverage quantum parallelism, allowing operations on multiple qubits simultaneously. Quantum parallelism enables faster processing of large datasets in remote sensing tasks. It enhances computational efficiency and scalability for handling complex computations.

11.6.2 SUPERPOSITION

Superposition allows qubits to exist in multiple states simultaneously. It aids in data representation and exploration of multiple possibilities in parallel. Superposition contributes to efficient handling of high-dimensional datasets.

11.6.3 ENTANGLEMENT

Entanglement correlates states of qubits, enabling efficient information processing. In remote sensing, entanglement enhances coherence and reliability of algorithms. It contributes to improved accuracy and robustness in classification tasks.

11.7 METHODOLOGY

The implementation of remote sensing imagery classification techniques using quantum deep learning involves a series of steps and methodologies to effectively process and classify imagery data. Following is an outline of the methodology.

11.8 DATA PREPROCESSING

Raw imagery data acquired from satellites, drones, or other sources undergo preprocessing to enhance quality and remove noise. Data normalization and scaling may be applied to standardize features for better model performance.

11.9 QUANTUM FEATURE EXTRACTION

Quantum algorithms are employed to extract intricate features from pre-processed imagery data. Quantum feature extraction techniques leverage the quantum properties of superposition and entanglement to reveal hidden patterns and nuances in the data.

11.10 QUANTUM NEURAL NETWORK ARCHITECTURE

The process involves designing and implementing a quantum neural network (QNN) architecture specifically tailored for remote sensing imagery classification. This architecture integrates quantum-inspired layers and operations, leveraging principles like quantum parallelism and entanglement. By utilizing these quantum features, the QNN can efficiently handle complex computations and high-dimensional datasets required for accurate classification tasks.

11.11   TRAINING PROCESS

The training process employs advanced quantum-inspired optimization techniques to enhance the performance of the quantum neural network. These methods, such as quantum gradient descent (QGD) and the variational quantum eigensolver (VQE), utilize quantum properties to explore vast solution spaces. These techniques optimize the QNN's weights and biases effectively, improving its learning efficiency and convergence towards optimal solutions.

11.12   LAND-USE/LAND-COVER CLASSIFICATION

The trained quantum neural network is deployed for land-use/landcover classification tasks. Quantum principles such as quantum parallelism and entanglement are leveraged to achieve high-accuracy classifications.

11.13   KEY COMPONENTS

11.13.1   QUANTUM GATES AND CIRCUITS

The implementation of quantum gates and circuits plays a critical role in the functionality of quantum neural networks, enabling the manipulation of qubits during feature extraction and network training. Quantum gates such as the Hadamard gate, CNOT gate, and Pauli-X gate are utilized to perform fundamental quantum operations. These gates enable the QNN to process data by exploiting quantum properties like superposition and entanglement, significantly enhancing computational capabilities.

11.13.2   QUANTUM BACKPROPAGATION

The classical backpropagation algorithm, a cornerstone of traditional neural network training, is adapted to the quantum domain to train quantum neural networks effectively. This adaptation involves translating gradient descent principles into quantum mechanics to update quantum weights and biases. The quantum backpropagation process enables the QNN to refine its parameters iteratively, thereby improving model accuracy while leveraging the inherent advantages of quantum computation for processing and optimization.

11.13.3   OPTIMIZATION TECHNIQUES

Quantum-inspired optimization algorithms such as quantum gradient descent (QGD) or variational quantum eigensolver (VQE) are used to optimize the QNN's parameters. These techniques leverage quantum properties to explore solution spaces efficiently and converge towards optimal solutions.

11.14   EUROSET DATASET AND PRE-PROCESSING

The EuroSET dataset is a comprehensive collection of remote sensing imagery designed for land-use and land-cover classification. It covers a specific geographical region and provides essential information for Earth observation applications. The dataset's characteristics, including spatial resolution, spectral bands, and geographical coverage, are vital for understanding its suitability for the study.

11.15   PRE-PROCESSING

Pre-processing is a critical phase to ensure the data's quality and relevance for subsequent analysis.
   Normalization: This step involves scaling pixel values to a standard range, often between 0 and 1. The formula for normalization is given by:

$$Xnormalized = \frac{X - Xmin}{Xmax - Xmin}$$

where X is the original pixel value, $Xmin$ is the minimum pixel value, and $Xmax$ is the maximum pixel value.

Filtering: Filtering operations may include noise reduction or enhancement of certain features. Common filters include Gaussian filters or median filters, each with specific mathematical formulations.

Transformations: Depending on the characteristics of the dataset, additional transformations like histogram equalization or colour space conversions may be applied.

11.16 CLASSICAL DEEP LEARNING TECHNIQUES

This section provides insights into the classical deep learning models employed, typically convolutional neural networks or recurrent neural networks.

CNN Architecture: For remote sensing imagery, a typical CNN architecture involves convolutional layers, pooling layers, and fully connected layers. The convolutional layer's function is to detect spatial patterns, while pooling layers reduce dimensionality. The fully connected layers make classification decisions.

RNN Architecture: If sequential information is crucial, RNNs may be employed. RNNs use recurrent connections to capture dependencies over time. Each time step involves a similar set of operations, enabling them to handle sequential data.

11.17 RESULTS

Figure 11.5 shows the confusion matrix, which visualizes the performance of the classification model. The rows of the matrix show the actual land cover class, and the columns show the predicted land cover class. Each cell contains the number of data points that belong to a particular row (actual class) and column (predicted class).

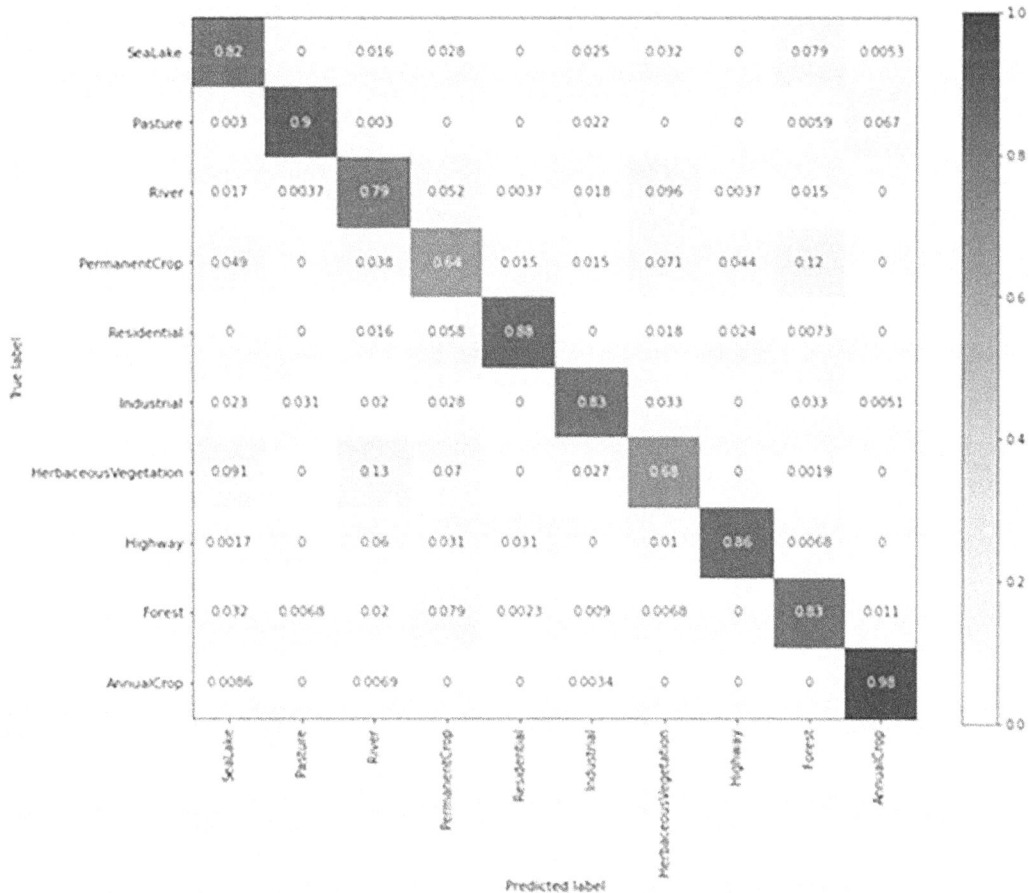

FIGURE 11.5 Confusion matrix.

FIGURE 11.6 Sample model outputs.

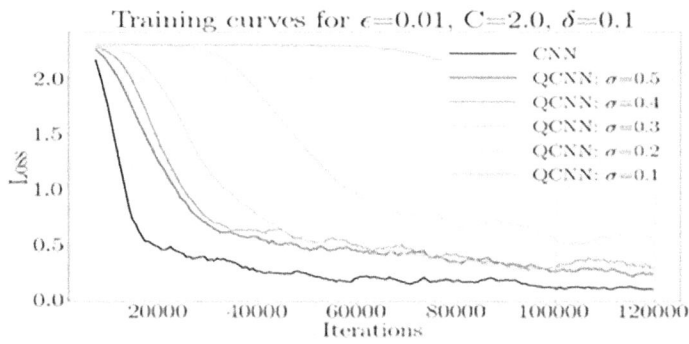

FIGURE 11.7 Loss curves for quantum convolutional neural networks.

TABLE 11.1

Quantum Classifier Metrics

Class	Precision	Recall
Annual Crop	0.97	0.90
Permanent Crop	0.94	0.96
Pasture	0.93	0.94
Forest	0.95	0.95
Herbaceous Vegetation	0.82	0.88
Highway	0.85	0.88
Residential	0.97	0.98
Industrial	0.88	0.80
River	0.96	0.94
Sea Lake	0.91	0.92

TABLE 11.2
F1 Scores of QCNN

Class	F1 Score
Annual Crop	0.94
Permanent Crop	0.98
Pasture	0.94
Forest	0.95
Herbaceous Vegetation	0.91
Highway	0.93
Residential	0.99
Industrial	0.89
River	0.93
Sea Lake	0.97

Figure 11.6 shows sample model outputs for different classes of the dataset when applied in quantum convolutional neural networks. Figure 11.7 shows the loss curves for quantum convolutional neural networks with different values of hyperparameters.

Tables 11.1 and 11.2 represent the performance of the proposed technique using different metrics for different classes of the dataset. Table 11.1 shows the performance of the proposed technique using precision and recall. Table 11.2 shows the performance of the proposed technique using F1 score. The proposed model achieved an overall accuracy of 95.38%.

11.18   CONCLUSION

Quantum deep learning has the potential to revolutionize remote sensing imagery classification. Quantum algorithms can be used to speed up the training and inference of deep learning models and to develop new deep learning algorithms that are specifically designed for quantum computers.

This chapter proposes a technique based on quantum convolutional neural networks for classification of remote sensing images. Performance of the technique was evaluated using different metrics such as precision, recall, and F1 score. The proposed model achieved an overall accuracy of 95.38%.

11.19   FUTURE WORK

While quantum deep learning has shown promise in remote sensing image classification, much remains unexplored. Future research should focus on developing more sophisticated quantum algorithms designed for image classification tasks. Quantum transfer learning, which leverages existing knowledge for new problems, could also improve performance. Combining classical and quantum approaches in hybrid models offers potential for even better accuracy and efficiency. Additionally, exploring quantum feature engineering techniques to extract more relevant features from images holds promise for enhancing both classical and quantum models. Finally, implementing these models on real-world quantum hardware is crucial, but it requires addressing noise, error, and optimization challenges. By pursuing these avenues, future research can unlock the full potential of quantum deep learning in revolutionizing remote sensing image classification.

REFERENCES

[1] R. Berkelmans et al., "Quantum-inspired convolutional neural networks for classifying remote sensing images," *arXiv preprint arXiv:2104.01224*, 2021.
[2] M. Schuld et al., "Quantum machine learning for remote sensing data analysis," *arXiv preprint arXiv:2008.06679*, 2020.

[3] S. Zhang et al., "Quantum deep learning for remote sensing image classification: A review," *Remote Sens. Environ.,* vol. 270, p. 112823, 2022.

[4] H. Dewangkoro and A. Arymurthy, "Land use and land cover classification using CNN, SVM, and channel squeeze & spatial excitation block," *Proc. IOP Conf. Ser., Earth Environ. Sci.*, vol. 704, no. 1, 2021.

[5] Y. Liang, W. Peng, Z. J. Zheng, O. Silvéna, and G. Zhao "A hybrid quantum-classical neural network with deep residual learning," *Neural Netw.*, vol. 143, pp. 133–147, Nov. 2021, doi: 10.1016/J. NEUNET.2021.05.028.

[6] A. Mari, T. R. Bromley, J. Izaac, M. Schuld, and N. Killoran, "Transfer learning in hybrid classical-quantum neural networks," *Quantum*, vol. 4, Oct. 2020, Art. no. 340, doi: 10.22331/q-2020-10-09-340.

[7] P. Helber, B. Bischke, A. Dengel, and D. Borth, "EuroSAT: A novel dataset and deep learning benchmark for land use and land cover classification," *IEEE J. Sel. Topics Appl. Earth Observ. Remote Sens.*, vol. 12, no. 7, pp. 2217–2226, Jul. 2019, doi: 10.1109/JSTARS.2019.2918242.

[8] F. Arute et al., "Quantum supremacy using a programmable superconducting processor," *Nature*, vol. 574, no. 7779, pp. 505–510, Oct. 2019, doi: 10.1038/s41586-019-1666-5.

[9] C. C. McGeoch, "Theory versus practice in annealing-based quantum computing," *Theor. Comput. Sci.*, vol. 816, pp. 169–183, May 2020, doi: 10.1016/J.TCS.2020.01.024.

Dataset Availability: [EuroSAT Dataset] (https://github.com/phelber/eurosat)

12 Mutation-Based Quantum Particle Swarm Optimisation
A Novel Approach to Global Optimisation

*Biswajit Jana, Bireshwar Dass Mazumdar,
Anindya Ghatak, and Manmohan Mishra*

12.1 INTRODUCTION

A population-based technique, particle swarm optimisation (PSO), was initially suggested by Kennedy and Eberhart [1, 2]. Taking cues from the way social creatures like bees, birds, and fish work together, PSO is an algorithm for global optimisation over continuous search spaces that uses swarm intelligence. Early plans for PSO didn't focus on individual intelligence but rather on creating AI through studying basic social interactions [3]. With few parameters to tweak, PSO is computationally cheap, easy to implement, and a breeze to work with. Particle swarm optimisation uses a swarm of potential solutions, or "particles," to navigate a multidimensional search space at a velocity that is continuously updated based on the swarm's or each particle's own and neighbouring experiences. The introduction of PSO in 1995 drew the interest of numerous scholars worldwide. The core method and uses of PSO have been proposed in a large number of variants [4–7].

A new version of PSO, quantum-behaved particle swarm optimisation (QPSO), was introduced [8] in 2004. This was inspired by quantum mechanics and trajectory analysis of PSO [9, 10]. The iterative equation of QPSO, a probabilistic algorithm, differs significantly from that of PSO [11]. The fact that QPSO is simpler to construct than PSO and does not require particle velocity vectors and has fewer parameters to be adjusted is another plus. A large number of continuous optimisation problems have been successfully solved using the QPSO method, and numerous effective strategies have been suggested for the algorithm's further improvement. This chapter endeavours to provide a comprehensive and up-to-date review on QPSO by classifying the majority of the articles on QPSO enhancements and applications, with the goal of helping researchers and practitioners see the big picture.

Here in this chapter, a new variant of QPSO, mutation-based QPSO (MQPSO), has been proposed to enhance the performance of QPSO. This enhancement involves refining the global solution by directing all particles towards the best one in the swarm. In this study, Gaussian mutation is incorporated into both individual and global best solutions to enhance the overall performance of QPSO. This mutation strategy serves to mitigate the issue of getting trapped in local optima. The proposed MQPSO has been applied to eight benchmarks, including unimodal and multimodal. The experimental results confirm that MQPSO outperform the other algorithms with regard to statical metric, that is, median, value. The convergence graph shows that the MQPSO dose not suffer from early convergence.

Following is the outline of the chapter. Section 12.2 provides a concise overview of PSO. The QPSO algorithm is discussed in Section 12.3. Section 12.4 contains the proposed MQPSO. The experimental results are discussed in Section 12.5. Finally, the whole work is concluded in Section 12.6.

DOI: 10.1201/9781003499459-12

12.1.1 LITERATURE REVIEW

Analysis of the convergence of the traditional PSO and the quantum system in [9] served as the inspiration for QPSO. A particle's momentum and energy state can be represented by its wavefunction in quantum physics. Instead of using position and velocity, which are used in PSO, in QPSO, we assume that every particle is in a quantum state and is defined by its wave function [10]. The probability density function can be used to determine the likelihood of a particle's appearance in a given position, as determined by the statistical significance of the wavefunction. Next, we may use the probability density function to get the particle's position's probability distribution function.

To begin, QPSO is able to search a large area because of the introduced exponential distribution of positions. In addition, we put the QPSO through its paces using the expected distribution of a particle. Essentially, the normal distribution is associated with the potential well of the quantum harmonic oscillator, whereas the exponential distribution is derived from the delta potential well. The QPSO is more likely to experience premature convergence when using a normal distribution, according to the results it produces on various benchmark functions, compared to when using an exponential distribution.

Adding mean best position to QPSO is yet another novel approach. Every particle in the original PSO finds its optimal location on the world on its own. In contrast, there is a waiting component among the particles in the QPSO with mean best position mbest, which prevents any one particle from achieving global best position convergence independently of its colleagues. This is due to the fact that in each iteration, the particle's position distribution is determined by the distance between its present position and mbest. Lagged particles can pull the position mbest away from Pg if some particles' personal best positions are far from the global best position (the Pg) and other particles' personal best locations are close to Pg. Assuming that all particles are pursuing one another, the position mbest will be moving steadily towards Pg as the lagged particles pursue their companions. Particles' convergences near Pg are slowed down because the distances between mbest and their personal best positions near Pg do not diminish quickly. As a result, particles temporarily explore the global area around Pg until the ones that are behind get close to Pg. Particle swarms in QPSOs with mean best positions appear to be more cooperative and intelligent social organisms, since they never leave behind any particle that has fallen behind. To put it simply, QPSO's global search ability is much improved by the wait mechanism among particles.

A number of factors, including an evolutionary algorithm's robustness, convergence speed, solution accuracy, and global search capabilities, determine its performance. Other approaches have been suggested from various angles to address the premature convergence problem and enhance QPSO's performance on multimodal problems. Parameter selection improvements, control swarm diversity, cooperative approaches, employing probability distribution function, unique search methods, and hybrid methods are the six broad areas into which these works fall.

Aside from the swarm size, issue dimension, and maximum iteration, the only other parameter in QPSO is the CE coefficient, which is crucial for the individual particle's convergence. A stochastic simulation was used to find out how the particle's convergence behaviour was related to the parameters used [12].

One common explanation for evolutionary algorithms' hasty convergence, as mentioned in [13], is a lack of diversity. In order to enhance the capability of escape the local minima, several diversity control strategies have been suggested for use in QPSO, based on the viewpoint. One element that was added to QPSO in [14] is a diversity-controlled model. Resetting the mean best location and controlling the CE coefficient were two approaches. Similar reasoning led to the proposal of a novel approach in [15] for applying the mutation operation to the particle at the optimal global position. Mutation operations improve swarm variety by moving the global best particle away from its mean best location, which in turn raises the average distance between each particle's best position and the mean. A new metric for swarm diversity was suggested [16], which takes into account the distance to the average point of each particle's optimal positions rather than their actual positions (as in [14, 15]).

Some researchers have suggested multiswarm to evolve concurrently and communicate information in order to enhance QPSO's search and high-dimensional solution capabilities. Each swarm in the group in [17] only knows about one part of the solution vector; the other swarms supply the remaining parts of the vector. This system encourages the many swarms to work together. A competitive scheme, which runs at a constant frequency, was established [18] as an offshoot of the cooperative scheme. Subsequently, a hybrid cooperative QPSO [19] was established using the method in [18] as a foundation, with the QPSO algorithm being executed after each iteration. A two-layer architecture was used to interact with multiswarm in [20]. In the top layer, one QPSO swarm was used to track with the global best solution, while in the bottom layer, other QPSO swarms were used for search.

If QPSO wanted to make its global search capabilities better, it might use some probability distribution models to make up random sequences. Specifically, QPSO now incorporates the usual normal distribution [21] as well as the Gaussian probability distribution [22–25].

One primary QPSO had a generalised local search operator added to it in [26]. The main QPSO searches globally for solutions, while the local search operator finds better ones by utilising a neighbourhood of the current solution. To boost convergence speed and global search ability, QPSO suggested a public history investigating and variant particle [27]. In order to help the system escape from local minima, the chaotic search approach was included into QPSO to improve the swarm diversity in the latter part of the search [28].

The goal of hybridisation, which seeks to integrate the positive qualities of diverse techniques to alleviate QPSO weakness, is to improve the performance of QPSO. The QPSO algorithm's weak selection, as described in [29], makes use of both the Swarm Algorithm (SA) mechanism's ability to jump out of local minima and the QPSO algorithm's capacity to seek the global optimum. Additionally, it was thought that QPSO could integrate with the immune system. With the introduction of the immune system's vaccination operation and modulation of antibody thickness, QPSO became immune operational [30]. Incorporating an additional immune operator into QPSO—one that uses vector distance to determine antibody density—could boost QPSO's intelligence and performance while successfully limiting optimisation degradation [31]. To improve the particle's search capability, the concept of deferential evolution (DE) was incorporated into QPSO [32].

Genetic algorithms (GAs) include the mutation operator, which diversifies searches and aids in discovering previously unexplored search spaces. The QPSO algorithm can also benefit from this mechanism in its quest to break out of local minima. By using a Cauchy distribution, the authors of [33] altered gbest and mbest in QPSO. In addition, the scale parameter of the mutation operator embraced the annealing-based amend technique to enhance the enhanced algorithm's self-adaptive capabilities. In order to diversify the QPSO population and enhance its efficiency in preventing premature convergence to local minima, a mutation type based on chaotic sequences was used in QPSO [34]. By comparing their performance to a set of benchmark functions, researchers examined a collection of mutation operators utilised in QPSO [35].

The selection operator was implemented in QPSO with the intention of applying it to the optimal solution on a global scale [36]. To achieve a happy medium between global searching capability and convergence speed, QPSO employed a sort of elitist selection operator on mbest [37]. Decisions are always impacted by crucial aspects, which is why the elitist strategy was created to appropriately portray people's thinking models. After assigning weight coefficients based on each particle's fitness value, the elitist strategy ranked them all [38].

12.1.2 Applications of QPSO

Nearly 100 studies have documented effective uses of QPSO in the five years following its proposal. Here, we shall provide an analysis of these works. This chapter's category selection follows the same line as in [5], since splitting QPSO applications into sections is tough.

The authors thought about the antenna applications as an optimisation problem that QPSO solved: identifying a set of infinitesimal dipoles to simulate an arbitrary antenna with known near-field distribution [39].

QPSO, which was created to optimise the synthetic gene's codon usage, produced better results [40]. Using a QPSO coupled with an RBF neural network, the hyaluronic acid synthesis conditions of *Streptococcus zooepidemicus* were optimised [41]. The kinetic model of batch fermentation parameters were estimated using QPSO in [42]. To address the issue of poor diagnostic accuracy, an intelligent method for diagnosing type 2 diabetes using QPSO and WLS-SVMs was introduced in [43].

Constrained optimisation, integer programming, nonlinear programming, and layout optimisation are some of the combinatorial optimisation areas that QPSO investigates. A modified version of the QPSO algorithm was suggested in [44] as a solution to the optimisation problems with constraints. Instead of using random sequences in QPSO, a Gaussian operator was utilised in [41], and the improved QPSO was explored in the context of the limited engineering design. For the combinatorial optimisation problem, a new discrete QPSO algorithm was suggested [45]. Integer programming was the initial application of QPSO, as described in [46]. For the nonlinear programming issues, the authors of [47] turned to QPSO. The purpose of the nonlinear planning model in [48] was to handle the problem of substation sizing and location using an enhanced QPSO. A unique multiobjective optimisation technique based on QPSO was described in [49] to optimise the design of laminated composite components with respect to multiple objectives. The method/model is generic and new.

Quality of Service (QoS) multicast routing, mobile IP routing, network anomaly detection, and communication network channel assignment are all areas that QPSO has investigated. The research presented a QPSO-based QoS multicast routing algorithm by transforming it into an integer programming issue, as QoS multicast routing is an NP-hard problem [50]. When it came to mobile IP routing, QPSO was the one that finally cracked the code [51]. There were three approaches that combined QPSO with network anomaly detection to address the issue. To train the RBFNN, a hybrid technique was suggested in [52] that combines QPSO with a gradient descent algorithm. The wavelet neural network, which is utilized for network anomaly detection and training by QPSO algorithm. It was trained using the hybrid of QPSO [53]. Prior to applying the optimised WLS-SVM to the network anomaly detection problem, the authors of [54] utilised QPSO to optimise the weighted LS-SVM. To discover the optimal answer, QPSO was used to solve the mathematical model of channel assignment in the application of channel assignment [55].

In [56], the goal function was based on the time domain, and QPSO was used to solve the optimisation problem of selecting the output feedback gains for the unified power flow controllers. The design parameters of a fuzzy logic control with PID conception were tuned using a unique QPSO approach in [23] that used a Gaussian distribution. In order to optimise the PID parameters of the controller, the authors of [57, 58] suggested using QPSO. Using QPSO to solve the control reallocation problem and minimise the control energy cost function, a thruster fault-tolerant strategy for UUVs was proposed in [59].

Critical to chaos control and synchronisation is the estimation of chaos systems' unknown parameters. In [60], the authors effectively used QPSO to estimate parameters and conduct online estimations of a chaotic system.

In [61], the authors suggested a particle-based data clustering method that uses QPSO to represent the cluster centroid vectors. The results demonstrated that QPSO could efficiently cluster data vectors with respectable throughput. By dividing the gene expression dataset into K user-defined categories, a QPSO-based clustering method was developed for gene expression data clustering, with the goal of minimising the fitness function of total within-cluster variance [62]. In order to create a hybrid clustering method, the authors of [63] combined QPSO with the K-harmonic means clustering algorithm. In alert correlation methods, the cluster can find new, simple, high-level attracts by aggregating relational alerts and computing the similarity of alert properties. After that, the cluster's alerts' weights and similarity values were optimised using QPSO [64]. The data mining community is actively researching spatial clustering. In [65], the authors present a new method for clustering geographical data that includes barriers, which is based on QPSO and K-medoids. The performance of FCM on gradient descent was improved by developing a fuzzy clustering algorithm that combines the fuzzy C-means algorithm and QPSO [66].

One of the most fruitful subfields of data mining is text categorisation. Using QPSO improved the accuracy and precision of text mining and classification as well as the acquisition of the classification rule [67–69].

One important aspect of rough set theory is the reduction of attributes. To address the attribute reduction issue, QPSO was converted to binary QPSO and then integrated with the attribute reduction approach in [70]. Parameter optimisation was achieved by studying the minimal attribute reduction problem based on QPSO in [71].

In [72], the initial publication detailing the use of QPSO on electromagnetic emerged. Through its demonstration of its applicability to challenges involving the synthesis of linear array antennas, the authors of that work brought QPSO into the electromagnetic community. Subsequently, they used QPSO to solve issues with linear array antenna synthesis and developed other variants of the algorithm [73]. An equivalent circuit model was also found using the QPSO method in the study. Discovering infinitesimal dipole models for antennas with known near-fields was accomplished in computational electromagnetics using QPSO [74]. There have been successful applications of QPSO in the field of electromagnetic design optimisation as well. Optimal methods for electromagnetic design optimisation using QPSO and a mutation operator based on exponential and Gaussian probability distributions were introduced in publications [22, 75].

In order to manually enhance the CMOS operational amplifier's performance, the ideal design employed QPSO to solve the circuit performance analytical equation [76]. To resolve the huge matrix issue in transistor simulation, a QPSO culture has been suggested [77].

Research on fuzzy systems focused on QPSO. In [78], the fuzzy rules and membership could be evolved with the help of QPSO, which was used to build fuzzy system components with the given data.

By substituting rectangle packing for two-dimensional irregular objects, the optimal peaks of the rectangle might be solved using QPSO in the rectangle-packing problem. By using a binary QPSO [79–82] (BQPSO), which was able to circumvent the search space restriction, the polygonal approximation of curves was achieved. As a set of edge parameters, each particle in QPSO was used to solve the problem of irregular polygon layout. An extremely difficult issue in nonlinear research is the detection of unstable periodic orbits (UPOs) in nonlinear maps. For the purpose of non-Lyapunov UPO detection, a novel QPSO-based approach was devised [83].

Among the many image analysis applications that have made use of QPSO are those dealing with face detection, segmentation, registration, and interpolation back propagation neural networks (BPNNs) utilised QPSO as their learning algorithm in [84–86] rather than the gradient descent approach employed by BP. The next step was to train a neural network to detect faces using the QPSO-based learning method. A multilevel of two-dimensional maximum entropy–QPSO was used in the picture segmentation application to find the best solution after obtaining the image's two-dimensional histogram. The optimal two-dimensional threshold vector, denoted by a particle, was determined using QPSO in the context of two-dimensional Otsu. Decreased computing cost and optimal segmentation results were achieved using the QPSO-based two-dimensional Otsu segmentation method, according to the results. In [87], the near-optimal MCET criteria were sought after using QPSO. Image registration is an essential issue in photographs captured by remote sensing systems. After that, in the coarse registration step, we utilised QPSO as an optimiser to determine the optimal stiff parameters using a coarse-to-fine registration framework [88]. While it may be simple to implement a traditional picture interpolation technique, the resulting interpolated image may have artefacts. Then QPSO was suggested as a way to identify the highest resolution image among those obtained by the conventional interpolation approach, which would improve the interpolated image's quality and resolution [89].

Simultaneously minimising the generation cost rate while satisfying various equality and inequality constraints is the purpose of the economic dispatch (ED) problem. They used QPSO to fix power system ED issues by tapping into the harmonic oscillator potential well [90]. To address the ED issue in three distinct power systems, Sun et al. [91] employed the QPSO method in conjunction with a differential mutation operation. Out of all the optimisation algorithms that were examined, the QPSO-DM approach suggested in [91] was the only one that could consistently and efficiently produce higher-quality solutions to the ED problem.

The performance of support vector machine (SVM) models, including the conventional SVM model and the least-squares SVM model, is heavily dependent on the regularisation parameter and the kernel parameter. The regularisation and kernel parameters were fine-tuned using analytical, algebraic, and heuristic methods. Tuning the regularisation and kernel parameters for QPSO has also made use of it. The LS-SVM hyperparameters were selected using QPSO in [92, 93], and the free parameters of the SVM model were automatically determined using a diversity-based adaptive QPSO [94]. A support vector machine model was trained using QPSO in order to tackle a quadratic programming (QP) problem [95]. According to [96], a soft-sensor model of the organic solvent recovery desorption process was established using QDPSO, which was first used to determine the best SVM model parameters.

In [97, 98], PSO and QPSO were used to optimise four distinct methods for extracting parameters from the well-known DC model of a metal semiconductor field effect transistor device based on gallium arsenide.

When it comes to neural networks, QPSO is most commonly utilised during training. A QPSO-trained RBF network model was suggested in [99] due to the limitations of the current RBF network training algorithms. There are a number of additional uses for RBF neural networks paired with QPSO [52, 69, 100–102].

In [103], the multiprocessor scheduling issue was addressed using QPSO. The study describes a method for rapidly improving solution quality by combining the QPSO search methodology with list scheduling.

Research into QPSO's signal processing applications has been extensive, including fields as diverse as 2D filter design, FIR filter design, and interference filter design. One way to look at these filter design difficulties is as optimisation problems involving multiple parameters. Both bandpass and low-pass FIR filters have used QPSO or an adaptive variation of it in their construction [104, 105]. Also along these lines, 2D filter designs, adaptive IIR filters, and IIR filters all made use of QPSO to determine a set of parameters [106–108]. Two variants of diversity-based QPSO were suggested as a means to discover a solution to the design challenge of 2D recursive digital filters, which is typically reduced to a constraint minimisation problem [109].

12.2 PARTICLE SWARM OPTIMISATION

In the basic PSO algorithm, a swarm of random particles representing potential solutions navigates through the D-dimensional search space [1,2]. Each particle's (i^{th}) position is denoted by $P_i = (P_{i1}, P_{i2}, \ldots\ldots, P_{iD})$, and the particle's velocity is denoted by $VL_i = (VL_{i1}, VL_{i2}, \ldots\ldots, VL_{iD})$. In each generation, every particle is updated using two best solutions. One is its own best solution achieved thus far, known as the personal best. ($PB_i = (PB_{i1}, PB_{i2}, \ldots\ldots, PB_{iD})$). Another is the best experience obtained so far by any particle in the entire swarm, referred to as the global best. $(GB_{gD} = (GB_{1d}, GB_{2d}, \ldots, GB_{gD}))$.

The objective function value of each particle is determined by its position vector. Each particle retains two values in its memory: its best value (the objective function value of both personal best (PB) and global best (GB)) and its respective position. Each particle adjusts its velocity and positions according to the equations denoted as Eq. 12.1 and Eq. 12.2.

$$VL_{iD}^{t+1} = w * VL_{iD}^{t} + C_1 * r_1 * (PB_{iD} - P_{iD}) + C_2 * r_2 * (GB_D - P_{iD}) \qquad (1) \qquad 12.1$$

$$P_{iD}^{t+1} = P_{iD} + VL_{iD}^{t+1} \qquad (2)$$

where t is the iteration; VL_{iD}^t is the velocity of the ith particle in the D dimension of the tth iteration; C_1 and C_2 are the cognitive and social acceleration coefficient, respectively; r_1, r_2 are two uniform random numbers in the range between $[0,1]$; and w is the inertia weight.

Algorithm 1: PSO

```
Randomly generate an initial population with positions and velocities Repeat
   for i = 1 to population size(Pop) do if f (Pi) < f(PBi)then PBi = Pi; end if
        G = min (f (PBi) ) ; for j = 1 to D do
        Update Velocity using Eq. 12.1;
        Update position using Eq. 12.2; end for end fo
Until Stopping criterion is met
```

12.3   QUANTUM PARTICLE SWARM OPTIMISATION

Sun et al. introduced the quantum particle swarm algorithm based on the principles of quantum mechanics. Utilising the DELTA potential well, they adapted the particle swarm optimisation algorithm to operate within a quantum space. In this quantum space, particles are described using wave functions.

$$|\Psi|^2 \, dx \, dy \, dz = R dx \, dy \, dz \qquad (12.3)$$

In this context, |Ψ|² denotes the square of the wave function's magnitude, reflecting the probability density of particle presence at a given position. Symbolised by R, the probability density function adheres to the normalisation condition.

$$\int_{-\infty}^{+\infty} |\Psi|^2 \, dx \, dy \, dz = \int_{-\infty}^{+\infty} R \, dx \, dy \, dz = 1 \qquad (12.4)$$

After undergoing stochastic simulations involving Monte Carlo measurements, the positions of particles in quantum space are determined.

$$P_{i,d} = PB_{i,d} \pm \frac{L}{2} ln\left(\frac{1}{q}\right) (i=1,2,...,Pop)(d=1,2,...,D) \qquad (12.5)$$

Among these parameters, q represents a random number within the range of [0, 1]. L is calculated based on the particle's current position and its historical best position as $L = 2 \cdot \beta \cdot |PB_{i,d} - P_{i,d}|$. This calculation leads to the update formula for quantum particle swarm optimisation.

$$P_{i,d} = PB_{i,d} \pm \alpha \cdot |PB_{i,d} - P_{i,d}(t) \cdot ln\left(\frac{1}{q}\right)| \qquad (12.6)$$

where t is iteration, and α is the contraction expansion factor of QPSO. To prevent premature convergence, Sun et al. [41] enhanced the QPSO algorithm by introducing *mbest*.
n

$$mbest(t) = \frac{1}{Pop}\sum_{i=1}^{Pop} PB_i(t) = \frac{1}{Pop}\sum_{i=1}^{Pop} PB_{i,1}(t), \frac{1}{Pop}\sum_{i=1}^{Pop} PB_{i,2}(t), ..., \frac{1}{Pop}\sum_{i=1}^{Pop} PB_{iD,}(t) \qquad (12.7)$$

Following the incorporation of *mbest*, the individual update formula becomes:

$$L = 2 \cdot \alpha \cdot |mbest| - P_{id} \qquad (12.8)$$

$$P_{i,d} = PB_{i,d} \pm \alpha \cdot \left| mbest_d - P_{i,d} \right| \cdot \ln\left(\frac{1}{q}\right)) \tag{12.9}$$

Hence, the updating formula for quantum particle swarm optimisation particles can be delineated as:

$$P_{i,d} = \varphi \cdot PB_{i,d} + (1 - \varphi) \cdot GB_{gD} \tag{12.10}$$

$$P_{i,d}(t+1) = PB_{i,d} \pm \alpha \cdot \left| mbest - P_{i,d} \right| \cdot \ln\left(\frac{1}{q}\right)) \tag{12.11}$$

where φ is a random number in the range [0,1].

Algorithm 2: QPSO

```
Initialize N,MI,D, α₀ , α₁
for t=1 to MI
compute mbest using Eq.7
a = (ai - ao) . (MI-t)/MI + ao
for i = 1 to population size(Pop)
if f(Pi) < f(P3i)then
PBi = Pi;
end if
G = min (f (PBi) ) ;
for j = 1 to D do
(p = rand (0,1)
q = rand (0,1);
Pi.j = <P ' PBi.j + (1 - <p) ■ GB,
if (rand (0,1) > 0.5)
Pᵤd = PBᵢᵢd + a ■ \mbest - Pᵤ
else
Pud = PBi,d + a ■ \mbest - Pird
end if
end fors
end for
end for
```

12.4 MUTATION-BASED QUANTUM PARTICLE SWARM OPTIMISATION

The objective of the proposed MQPSO is to enhance the performance of existing QPSO by improving the exploration capacity in the search space. This is done by improving the global based solution, as all the particles attract to the best particle in the swarm. In this chapter, Gaussian mutation has been applied to both personal and global best solution to improve the overall performance of QPSO. The mutation strategy also helps to escape from the local optima problem.

The Gaussian mutation is applied to the PB_i and GB as follows

$$PB_{i,d} = PB_{i,d} + \left(X_{max} - X_{min}\right).\text{Gaussian}\left(o, h\right) \tag{12.12}$$

$$GB_d = GB_d + \left(X_{max} - X_{min}\right).\text{Gaussian}\left(o, h\right) \tag{12.13}$$

where X_{max} = maximum limit of the decision vector value in the dth dimension, X_{min} = minimum value of the decision vector value in the dth dimension, and h is the standard deviation of the Gaussian distribution. The parameter h is linearly decreased in each iteration according to Eq. 12.14.

This ensures that the exploration capability is stronger at the initial stage, while the exploitation capability becomes stronger as the run progresses.

$$h^{t+1} = h^t - \left(\frac{1}{t_{max}}\right) \tag{12.14}$$

Algorithm 3: MQPSO

```
Initialize N, MI,D, oto, a.
for t=1 to MI
compute mbest using Eq.7
a = (ai -au). (Ml-t) /MI + a.j
for i = 1 to population size(Pop) do
if f(Pi) < f(PBi)then
PBi = P_i, for i=1 to D
PB_iid = PB_i4 + (X_max - yV_mj_n).Gaussian(o, h)
end for
end if
G = min (f(PBi)) ;
for i=1 to D
GB_d = GB_d + (-Kmo* - X_min).Gaussian(o,h)
end for
for j = 1 to D do
(p = rand (0,1)
q = rand (0,1);
Pi.j = <p ■ PBij + (1 - <p) ■ GBj
if (rand (0,1) > 0.5)
P,.d = PBi,_d + a ■ |mbest - P_id| • In (±-))
else
Pud = PB,.d + " • 1 mbest - P_iA| ■ In (±-))
end if
end for
end for
h^{t+1} = h' ~ (—)
sssend for
```

12.5 EXPERIMENTAL RESULTS

MQPSO was has applied to eight benchmark functions ($f_1 - f_8$), including unimodal ($f_1 - f_3$) and multimodal ($f_4 - f_8$). The benchmark functions are shown in Table 12.1. Unimodal test functions, by definition, have only one optimal point, which makes them excellent for assessing an algorithm's exploitation and convergence abilities. In contrast, multimodal test functions present multiple optimal points, presenting more significant challenges compared to their unimodal counterparts. Among the various local optima within multimodal functions, the most desirable is known as the global optimum. Achieving this global optimum requires navigating through all local optima, underscoring the crucial role of exploration capacity. Consequently, multimodal test functions provide a benchmark for evaluating the exploration capability of the search process.

The parameter values utilised in various algorithms are detailed in Table 12.2. The problem dimension (D) is standardised to 5, while the population size (N) and maximum iterations (*MI*) are consistent at 30 for all algorithms. Statistical data, including minimum, maximum, standard deviation, mean, and median, are derived from objective function values collected over ten independent runs. The statistical results for different benchmark functions are presented in in Table 12.3. The median value is considered here for performance comparisons.

TABLE 12.1
Benchmark Functions

Function Name	Expression	Range
Sphere	$F_1(X) = \sum_{i=1}^{n} X_i^2$	$[-5.12, 5.12]$
Dixon & Price	$F_2(X) = (X_1 - 1)^2 + \sum_{i=2}^{n} i\left(2X_i^2 - X_{i-1}\right)^2$	$[-10, 10]$
Zakharov	$F_3(X) = \sum_{i=1}^{n} X_i^2 + \left(\sum_{i=1}^{n} 0.5iX_i\right)^2 + \left(\sum_{i=1}^{n} 0.5iX_i\right)^4$	$[-5, 10]$
Rastrigin	$F_4(X) = 10n + \sum_{i=1}^{n}(X_i^2 - 10\cos(2\pi X_i))$	$[-5.12, 5.12]$
Levy	$F_5(X) = \sin^2(\pi X_i) + \sum_{i=1}^{n-1}(y_i - 1)^2\left[1 + 10\sin^2(\pi y_i + 1)\right]$ $+ (y_i - 1)^2 + \left[1 + \sin^2(2\pi y_i)\right]$ Where $y_i = 1 + \dfrac{x_i - 1}{4} \; for\, i = 1, 2, \ldots, n$	$[-15, 30]$
Griewank	$F_6(X) = \sum_{i=1}^{n} \dfrac{x_i^2}{4000} - \prod_{i=1}^{n} \cos\left(\dfrac{x_i}{\sqrt{i}}\right) + 1$	$[-600, 600]$
Rosenbrock	$F_7(X) = \sum_{i=1}^{n-1}[100\left(X_i^2 - X_{i+1}\right)^2 + (X_i - 1)^2]$	$[-5, 10]$
Ackley	$F_8 = 20 + e - 20\exp\left(-0.2\sqrt{\dfrac{1}{n}\sum_{i=1}^{n} X_i^2}\right) - \exp\left(\sqrt{\dfrac{1}{n}\sum_{i=1}^{n} \cos(2\pi X_i)}\right)$	$[-15, 30]$

TABLE 12.2
Parameter Setting of Different Algorithms

Method Name	Parameter Name	Parameter Value
MQPSO	α_0	0
	α_1	1
	m	0
	h	1
GQPSO	α_0	0
	α_1	1
QPSO	α_0	0
	α_1	1
PSO	w	0.8
	C_1	1.5
	C_2	1.5

MQPSO achieved the overall best performance among all algorithms for all the benchmark functions. The purpose of implementing mutations on the global best and personal best solution is to improve MQPSO's performance. In PSO, where all particles are attracted towards the global best solution, enhancing both the global best and personal best solutions through mutation enables them to attract promising solutions from the search space. The advantage of introducing mutations is to improve diversity into the search process, facilitating efficient exploration of various regions within the search space. Consequently, mutation operators play a pivotal role in enhancing the exploration capability of the search region.

TABLE 12.3

Experimental Results of MQPSO

	MQPSO	GQPSO	QPSO	PSO
F_1				
Min	1.63e-30	5.53e-30	1.003e-19	1.58e-11
Max	1.22e-26	5.61e-26	6.58e-18	7.99e-10
Std	3.78e-26	1.73e-26	1.99e-18	2.61e-10
Mean	1.71e-27	7.07e-27	1.94e-18	2.27e-10
Median	1.17e-27	1.60e-27	1.488e-18	1.44e-10
F_2				
Min	0.67	0.67	0.67	6.83e-08
Max	0.67	0.67	0.67	0.67
Std	1.27e-05	1.30e-05	3.34e-03	0.255
Mean	0.67	0.67	0.67	0.120
Median	0.67	0.67	0.67	9.99e-06
F_3				
Min	3.90e-25	1.01e-24	4.46e-18	9.64e-10
Max	3.42e-21	6.14e-21	1.46e-16	8.21e-08
Std	1.10e-21	1.91e-21	5.05e-17	2.52e-08
Mean	4.82e-22	7.28e-22	5.18e-17	1.67e-08
Median	9.94e-24	7.08e-23	3.28e-17	6.95e-09
F_4				
Min	0	0	0	0.995
Max	5.32e-10	0	2.48e-10	6.965
Std	1.68e-10	0	7.84e-11	1.843
Mean	5.33e-11	0	2.48e-11	3.880
Median	0	0	2.13e-14	3.482
F_5				
Min	0.010393	5.57e-03	0.229	5.64e-11
Max	0.10302	0.1023	0.387	1.52e-08
Std	0.04959	0.0606	0.052	4.607e-09
Mean	0.047276	0.0606	0.316	2.182e-09
Median	0.026994	0.0640	0.310	6.59e-10
F_6				
Min	0	0	6.66e-16	0.038
Max	0.105	0.223	0.083	0.194
Std	0.036	0.066	0.027	0.045
Mean	0.021	0.045	0.016	0.089
Median	4.01e-03	0.022	2.42e-06	0.081
F_7				
Min	1.160	1.488	2.928	0.133
Max	2.186	2.283	3.780	1.210
Std	0.194	0.268	0.237	0.398
Mean	2.018	2.030	3.355	0.823
Median	2.033	2.102	3.321	0.936
F_8				
Min	1.64e-14	2.22e-14	1.82e-09	2.19e-05
Max	3.62e-12	4.83e-12	4.83e-08	3.16e-04
Std	1.05e-12	1.44e-12	1.32e-08	8.73e-05
Mean	6.81e-13	7.61e-13	1.54e-08	1.21e-04
Median	3.01e-13	5.08e-13	1.51e-08	1.18e-04

The convergence analysis of different algorithms for all the benchmark functions is presented in Figures 12.1 to 12.8. It shows that MQPSO exhibits resistance to early convergence, leading to superior minima compared to other algorithms across all benchmarks. This demonstrates MQPSO's efficient exploration of the state space by blending exploitation and exploration judiciously. The overall search strategy of MQPSO can be characterised as balanced.

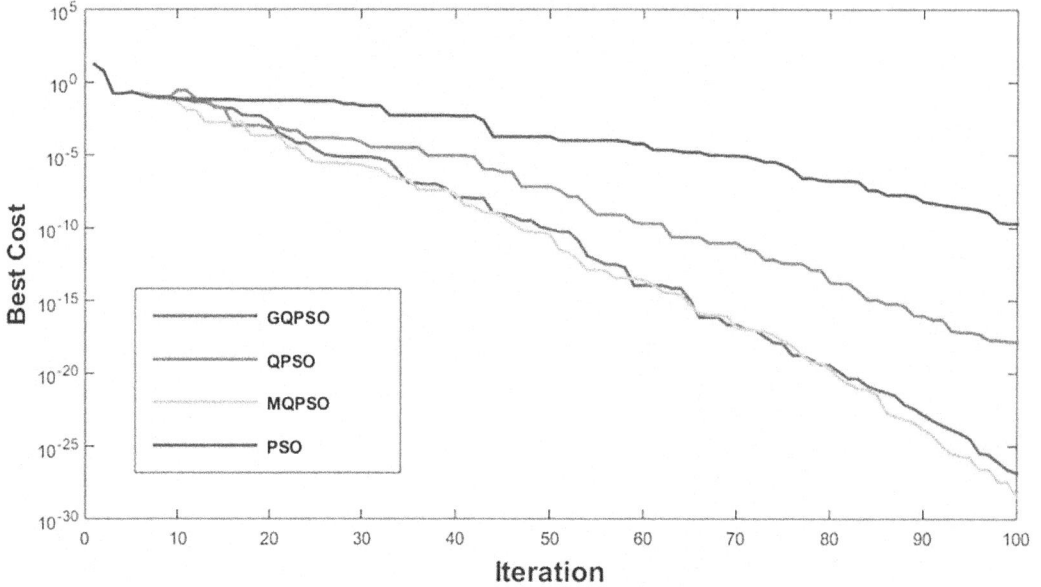

FIGURE 12.1   Convergence comparison graph for f_1.

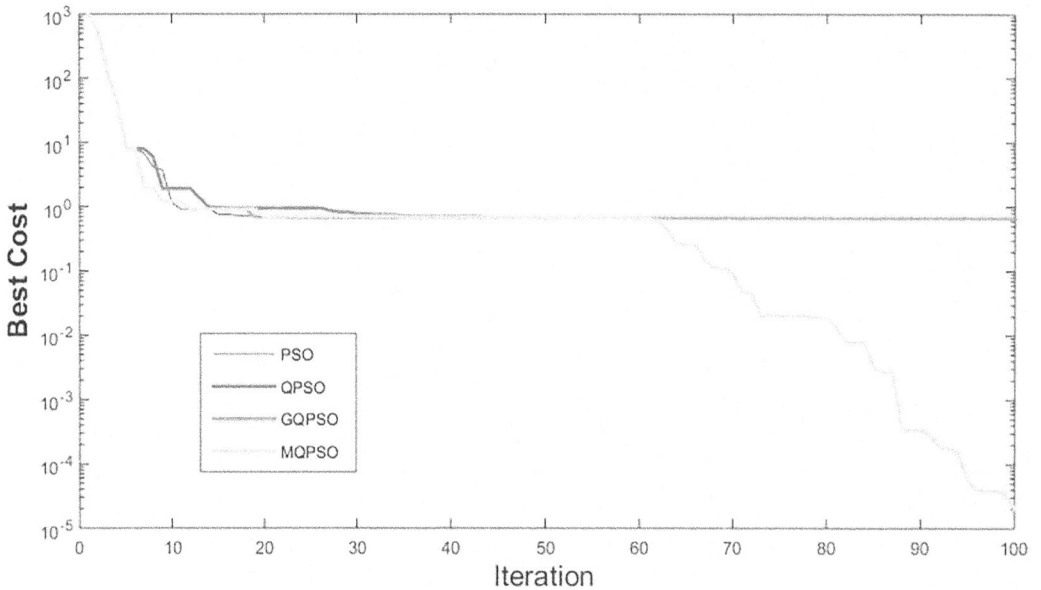

FIGURE 12.2   Convergence comparison graph for f_2.

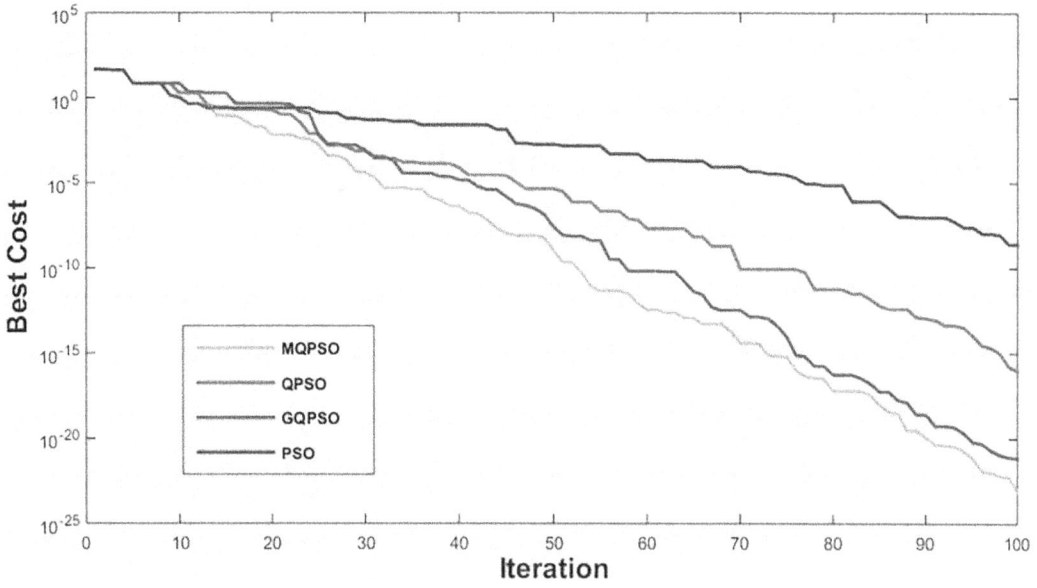

FIGURE 12.3   Convergence comparison graph for f_3.

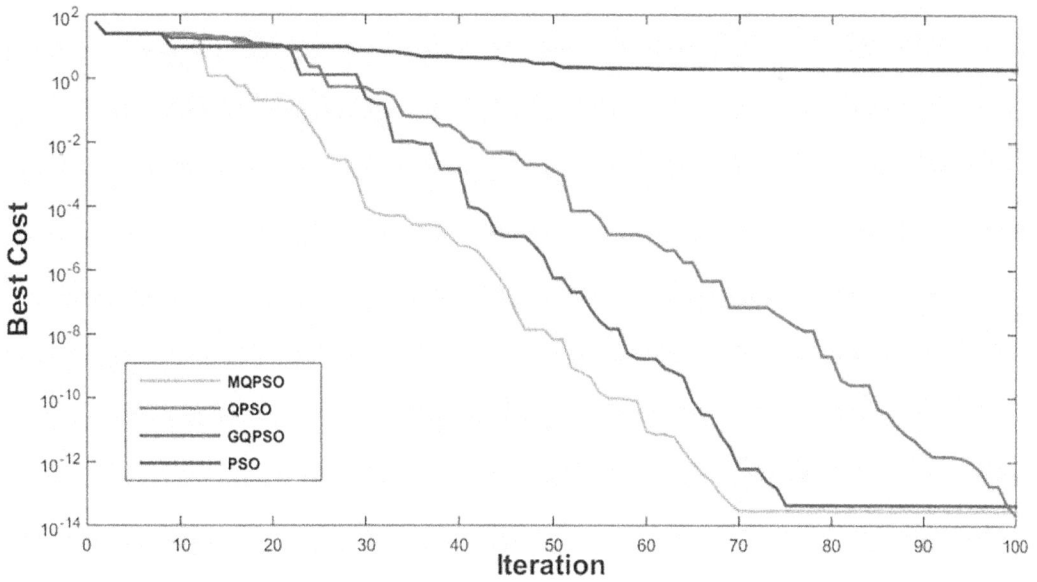

FIGURE 12.4   Convergence comparison graph for f_4.

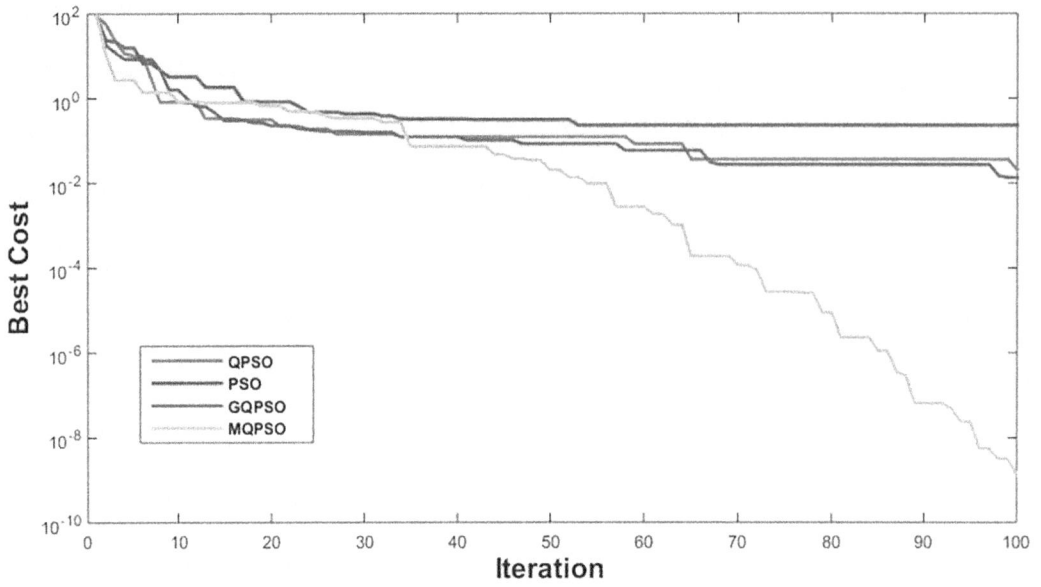

FIGURE 12.5   Convergence comparison graph for f_5.

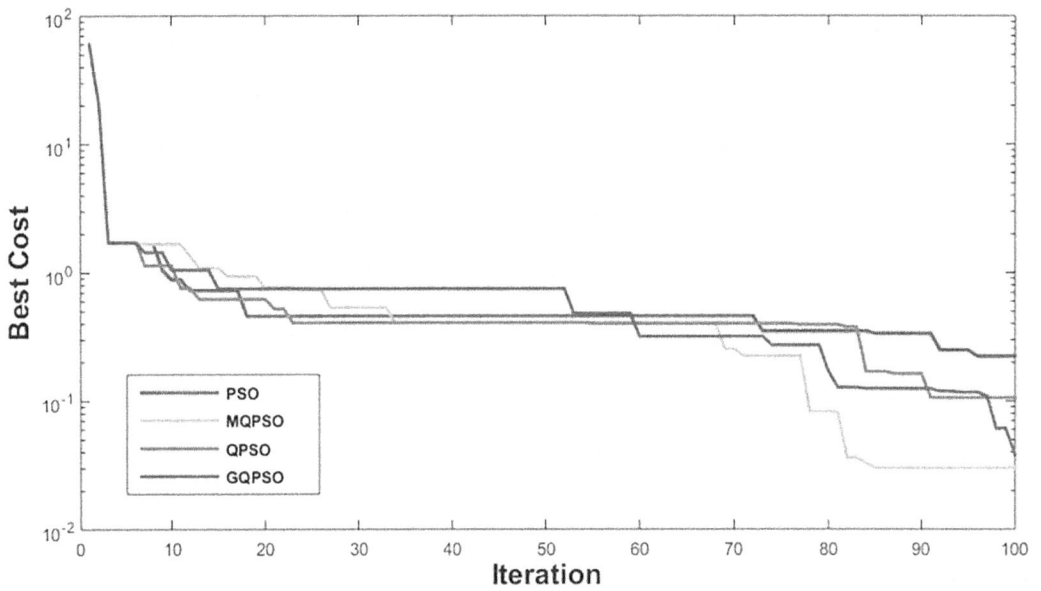

FIGURE 12.6   Convergence comparison graph for f_6.

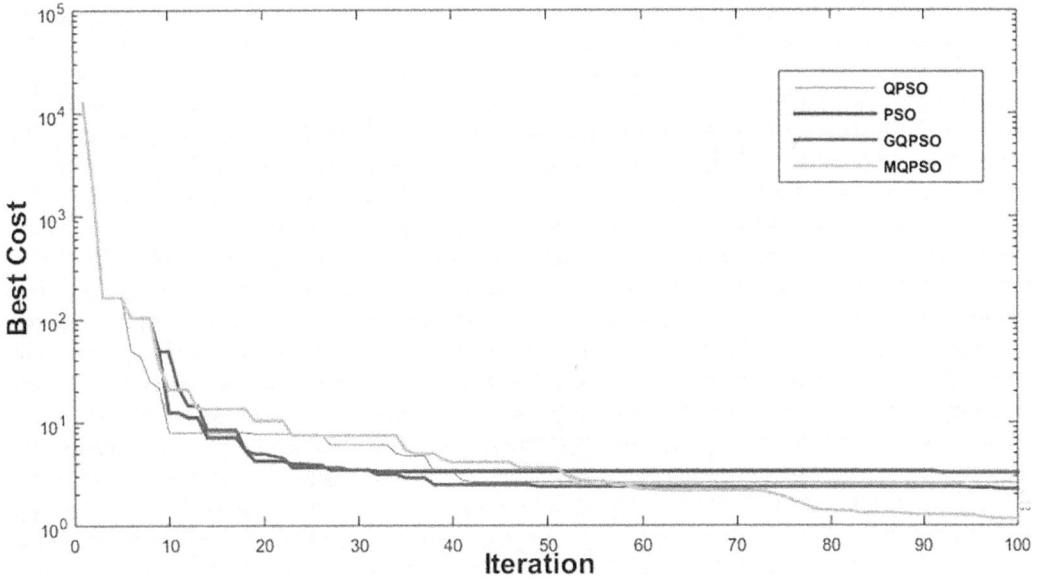

FIGURE 12.7   Convergence comparison graph for f_7.

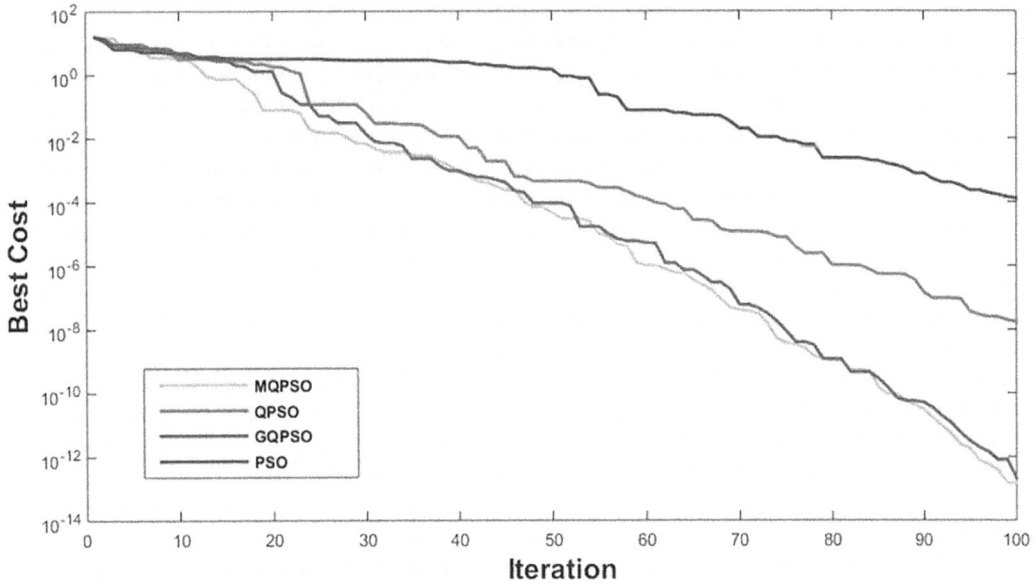

FIGURE 12.8   Convergence comparison graph for f_8.

12.6 CONCLUSION

This chapter provides a concise overview of the QPSO algorithm's enhancements and uses. It has been discovered that QPSO is both very effective and quite versatile. Improving QPSO's performance has been the subject of extensive research. Parameter selection for swarm diversity control, cooperative approaches, probability distribution function usage, unique search methods, and hybrid methods with other techniques are all part of the improvement strategy spectrum. Clustering and classification, electromagnetism and electronics, biology, power systems, neural networks, fuzzy logic, modelling, antennas, and combinatorial optimisation are some of the areas where QPSO has found practical use. Many professionals are interested in learning more about the QPSO algorithm. This is due to the fact that the QPSO algorithm is both straightforward and easy to apply. Someone working in a niche area, as opposed to swarm intelligence, can pick up QPSO fast. This is why QPSO is so user friendly: it can be easily combined with other approaches and used in a variety of fields. The granularity of QPSO's worldwide search capabilities is another factor. No matter the kind of application or benchmark function, QPSO has proven time and again that it can obtain good optimisation results. Despite QPSO's effectiveness, the difficulty regarding its working principle is not adequately addressed in any of the relevant literature. Consequently, explaining its operation to the theoretical community is the top priority for QPSO. Just like in PSO, this is a challenging task; nonetheless, we have already accomplished analyses of particles in terms of probability measures and convergence behaviour. Extending the scope of QPSO's applications is another promising area for further study. The fields of application for QPSO in current research are less fruitful than those for PSO. Extending beyond the realm of academic research and into the commercial and industrial sectors is the ultimate goal of QPSO applications. Finally, one of the main points of QPSO is how to combine its capabilities through integration with other techniques and additional approach development.

Furthermore, a novel variant of QPSO, mutation-based QPSO, is introduced to improve the effectiveness of QPSO. This advancement includes refining the global solution by attracting all particles towards the swarm's best. Gaussian mutation is integrated into both individual and global best solutions in this investigation to enhance the overall efficiency of QPSO. This mutation strategy is able to solve the issue of being stuck in local optima. MQPSO is then applied to eight benchmarks, compassing both unimodal and multimodal functions. Experimental findings validate that MQPSO performs better than other algorithms in terms of statistical metrics, particularly the median value. Moreover, the convergence graph illustrates that MQPSO does not suffer early convergence issues.

REFERENCES

[1] J. Kennedy, and R.C. Eberhart. "Particle swarm optimization," *Proceedings of IEEE International Conference on Neural Networks*, pp. 1942–8, 1995.
[2] J. Kennedy, and R.C. Eberhart. *Swarm Intelligence*. Morgan Kaufmann Publishers; 2001.
[3] R. Poli, J. Kennedy, T. Blackwell, and A. Freitas. "Particle swarms: The second decade," *Journal of Artificial Evolution and Applications*, pp. 1–3, 2008.
[4] R. Poli, J. Kennedy, and T. Blackwell. "Particle swarm optimization," *Swarm Intelligence*, vol. 1(1), pp. 33–57, 2007.
[5] R. Poli. *An Analysis of Publications on Particle Swarm Optimization Applications*. Essex, UK: Department of Computer Science, University of Essex; May–Nov. 2007.
[6] A. Banks, J. Vincent, and C. Anyakoha. "A review of particle swarm optimization. Part I: Background and development," *Natural Computing*, vol. 6(4), pp. 467–84, 2007.
[7] A. Banks, J. Vincent, and C. Anyakoha. "A review of particle swarm optimization. Part II: Hybridisation, combinatorial, multicriteria and constrained optimization, and indicative applications," *Natural Computing*, vol. 7(1), pp. 109–24, 2008.
[8] J. Sun, B. Feng, and W. Xu. "A global search strategy of quantum- behaved particle swarm optimization," *IEEE Conference on Cybernetics and Intelligent Systems*, pp. 111–6, 2004.
[9] M. Clerc, and J. Kennedy. "The particle swarm—explosion, stability, and convergence in a multidimensional complex space," *IEEE Transactions on Evolutionary Computation*, vol. 6(1), pp. 58–73, 2002.

[10] J. Sun, B. Feng, and W. Xu. "Particle swarm optimization with particles having quantum behavior," *IEEE Congress on Evolutionary Computation*, pp. 325–31, 2004.

[11] J. Kennedy. "Some issues and practices for particle swarms," *IEEE Swarm Intelligence Symposium*, pp. 162–9, 2007.

[12] J. Sun, W. Xu, and J. Liu. "Parameter selection of quantum-behaved particle swarm optimization," *Advances in Natural Computation*, pp. 543–52, 2005.

[13] J. Riget, and J. Vesterstroem. *A Diversity-guided Particle Swarm Optimizer—the ARPSO*. Department of Computer Science, University of Aarhus; 2002.

[14] J. Sun, W. Xu, and W. Fang. "Quantum-behaved particle swarm optimization algorithm with controlled diversity," *Proceedings of the 2006 International Conference on Computational Science*, pp. 847–54, 2006.

[15] J. Sun, W. Xu, and W. Fang. "A diversity-guided quantum-behaved particle swarm optimization algorithm," *Simulated Evolution and Learning*, pp. 497–504, 2006.

[16] J. Sun, W. Xu, and W. Fang. "Enhancing global search ability of quantum-behaved particle swarm optimization by maintaining diversity of the swarm," *Rough Sets and Current Trends in Computing*, pp. 736–45, 2006.

[17] H. Gao, W. Xu, and T. Gao. "A cooperative approach to quantum- behaved particle swarm optimization," *IEEE International Symposium on Intelligent Signal Processing*, pp. 1–6, 2007.

[18] S. Lu, and C. Sun. "Coevolutionary quantum-behaved particle swarm optimization with hybrid cooperative search," *Pacific- Asia Workshop on Computational Intelligence and Industrial Application*, pp. 109–13, 2008.

[19] S. Lu, and C. Sun. "Quantum-behaved particle swarm optimization with cooperative-competitive coevolutionary," *International Symposium on Knowledge Acquisition and Modeling*, pp. 593–7, 2008.

[20] Q. Baida, J. Zhuqing, and X. Baoguo. "Research on quantum- behaved particle swarms cooperative optimization," *Computer Engineering and Applications*, vol. 44(7), pp. 72–4, 2008.

[21] J. Sun, W. Xu, and W. Fang. "Quantum-behaved particle swarm optimization with a hybrid probability distribution," *PRICAI 2006: Trends in Artificial Intelligence*, pp. 737–46, 2006.

[22] L.S. Coelho. "Novel Gaussian quantum-behaved particle swarm optimiser applied to electromagnetic design," *IET Science, Measurement and Technology*, vol. 1(5), pp. 290–4, 2007.

[23] L.S. Coelho, N. Nedjah, and L.D.M. Mourelle. "Gaussian quantum-behaved particle swarm optimization applied to fuzzy PID controller design," *Studies in Computational Intelligence*, vol. 121, pp. 1–15, 2008.

[24] L.S. Coelho. "Gaussian quantum-behaved particle swarm optimization approaches for constrained engineering design problems," *Expert Systems with Applications*, vol. 37(2), pp. 1676–83, 2010.

[25] J. Sun, C. Lai, W. Xu, Y. Ding, and Z. Chai. "A Modified quantum- behaved particle swarm optimization," *ICCS*, pp. 294–301, 2007.

[26] J. Wang, and Y. Zhou. "Quantum-behaved particle swarm optimization with generalized local search operator for global optimization," *Advanced Intelligent Computing Theories and Applications with Aspects of Artificial Intelligence*, pp. 851–60, 2007.

[27] Z. Huang, Y. Wang, C. Yang, and C. Wu. "A new improved quantum-behaved particle swarm optimization model," *IEEE Conference on Industrial Electronics and Applications*, pp. 1560–4, 2009.

[28] Y. Kaiqiao, and N. Hirosato. "Quantum-behaved particle swarm optimization with chaotic search," *IEICE—Transactions on Information and Systems*, vol. E91-D(7), pp. 1963–70, 2008.

[29] J. Liu, J. Sun, and W. Xu. "Improving quantum-behaved particle swarm optimization by simulated annealing," *Computational Intelligence and Bioinformatics*, pp. 130–6, 2006.

[30] J. Liu, J. Sun, W. Xu, and X. Kong. "Quantum-behaved particle swarm optimization based on immune memory and vaccination," *IEEE International Conference on Granular Computing*, pp. 453–6, 2006.

[31] J. Liu, J. Sun, and W. Xu. "Quantum-behaved particle swarm optimization with immune operator," *Foundations of Intelligent Systems*, pp. 77–83, 2006.

[32] W. Fang, J. Sun, and W. Xu. "Improved quantum-behaved particle swarm optimization algorithm based on differential evolution operator and its application," *Journal of System Simulation*, vol. 20(24), pp. 6740–4, 2008.

[33] J. Liu, J. Sun, and W. Xu. "Quantum-behaved particle swarm optimization with adaptive mutation operator," *ICNC*, pp. 959–67, 2006.

[34] L.S. Coelho. "A quantum particle swarm optimizer with chaotic mutation operator," *Chaos, Solitons and Fractals*, vol. 37(5), pp. 1409–18, 2008.

[35] W. Fang, J. Sun, and W. Xu. "Analysis of mutation operators on quantum-behaved particle swarm optimization algorithm," *New Mathematics and Natural Computation*, vol. 5(2), pp. 487–96, 2009.

[36] J. Sun, C. Lai, W. Xu, and Z. Chai. "A novel and more efficient search strategy of quantum-behaved particle swarm optimization," *Adaptive and Natural Computing Algorithms*, pp. 394–403, 2007.

[37] M. Xi, J. Sun, and W. Xu. "Quantum-behaved particle swarm optimization with elitist mean best position," *Complex Systems and Applications-Modeling, Control and Simulations*, pp. 1643–7, 2007.

[38] M. Xi, J. Sun, and W. Xu. "An improved quantum-behaved particle swarm optimization algorithm with weighted mean best position," *Applied Mathematics and Computation*, vol. 205(2), pp. 751–9, 2008.

[39] S. Mikki, and A.A. Kishk. "Infinitesimal Dipole model for dielectric resonator antennas using the QPSO algorithm," *IEEE Antennas and Propagation Society International Symposium*, pp. 3285–8, 2006.

[40] Y. Cai, J. Sun, J. Wang, Y. Ding, N. Tian, X. Liao, et al. "Optimizing the codon usage of synthetic gene with QPSO algorithm," *Journal of Theoretical Biology*, vol. 254(1), pp. 123–7, 2008.

[41] J.Sun et al. "Quantum-behaved particle swarm optimization with Gaussian distributed local attractor point," *Applied Mathematics and Computation*, vol. 218(7), pp. 3763–75, 2011.

[42] K. Lu, and R. Wang. "Application of PSO and QPSO algorithm to estimate parameters from kinetic model of glutamic acid batch fermentation," *7th World Congress on Intelligent Control and Automation*, pp. 8968–71, 2008.

[43] Y. Chi, X. Liu, K. Xia, and C. Su. "An Intelligent diagnosis to type 2 diabetes based on QPSO algorithm and WLS-SVM," *Intelligent Information Technology Application Workshops*, pp. 117–21, 2008.

[44] H. Liu, S. Xu, and X. Liang. "A modified quantum-behaved particle swarm optimization for constrained optimization," *International Symposium on Intelligent Information Technology Application Workshops*, pp. 531–4, 2008.

[45] J. Wang, Y. Zhang, Y. Zhou, and J. Yin. "Discrete quantum-behaved particle swarm optimization based on estimation of distribution for combinatorial optimization," *IEEE World Congress on Computational Intelligence*, pp. 897–904, 2008.

[46] J. Liu, J. Sun, and W. Xu. "Quantum-behaved particle swarm optimization for integer programming," *Neural Information Processing*, pp. 1042–50, 2006.

[47] J. Sun, J. Liu, and W. Xu. "Using quantum-behaved particle swarm optimization algorithm to solve non-linear programming problems," *International Journal of Computer Mathematics*, vol. 84(2), pp. 261–72, 2007.

[48] B. Xiao, T. Qin, D. Feng, G. Mu, P. Li, and G.M. Xiao. "Optimal planning of substation locating and sizing based on improved QPSO algorithm," *Asia-Pacific Power and Energy Engineering Conference*, pp. 1–5, 2009.

[49] S.N. Omkar, R. Khandelwal, T.V.S. Ananth, G.N. Naik, and S. Gopalakrishnan. "Quantum behaved particle swarm optimization (QPSO) for multi-objective design optimization of composite structures," *Expert Systems with Applications*, vol. 36(8), pp. 11312–22, 2009.

[50] J. Sun, J. Liu, and W. Xu. "QPSO-based QoS multicast routing algorithm," *Simulated Evolution and Learning*, pp. 261–8, 2006.

[51] D. Zhao, K. Xia, B. Wang, and J. Gao. "An approach to mobile IP routing based on QPSO algorithm," *Pacific-Asia Workshop on Computational Intelligence and Industrial Application*, pp. 667–71, 2008.

[52] R. Ma, Y. Liu, X. Lin, and Z. Wang. "Network anomaly detection using RBF neural network with hybrid QPSO," *IEEE International Conference on Networking, Sensing and Control*, pp. 1284–7, 2008.

[53] R. Ma, Y. Liu, and X. Lin. "Hybrid QPSO based wavelet neural networks for network anomaly detection," *Second Workshop on Digital Media and its Application in Museum and Heritages*, pp. 442–7, 2007.

[54] R. Wu, C. Su, K. Xia, and Y. Wu. "An approach to WLS-SVM based on QPSO algorithm in anomaly detection," *World Congress on Intelligent Control and Automation*, pp. 4468–72, 2008.

[55] C. Yue, Z. Dongming, X. Kewen, and W. Rui. "Channel assignment based on QPSO algorithm," *Communications Technology*, vol. 42(2), pp. 204–6, 2009.

[56] S. Jalilzadeh, H. Shayeghi, A. Safari, and D. Masoomi. "Output feedback UPFC controller design by using Quantum Particle Swarm Optimization," *6th International Conference on Electrical Engineering/ Electronics, Computer, Telecommunications and Information Technology*, pp. 28–31, 2009.

[57] M. Xi, J. Sun, and W. Xu. "Quantum-behaved particle swarm optimization for design H infinite structure specified controllers," *DCABES Proceedings*, pp. 1016–9, 2006.

[58] M. Xi, J. Sun, and W. Xu. "Parameter optimization of PID controller based on quantum-behaved particle swarm optimization," *ICCSA07 Proceedings*, pp. 603–7, 2007.

[59] J. Liu, Q. Wu, and D. Zhu. "Thruster Fault-Tolerant for UUVs Based on Quantum-Behaved Particle Swarm Optimization," *Opportunities and Challenges for Next-Generation Applied Intelligence*, pp. 159–65, 2009.

[60] F Gao, and H. Tong. "Parameter estimation for chaotic system based on particle swarm optimization," *Acta Physica Sinica*, vol. 2, pp. 577–82, 2006.

[61] J. Sun, W. Xu, and B. Ye. "Quantum-behaved particle swarm optimization clustering algorithm," *Advanced Data Mining and Applications*, pp. 340–7, 2006.

[62] W. Chen, J. Sun, Y. Ding, W. Fang, and W. Xu. "Clustering of gene expression data with quantum-behaved particle swarm optimization," *New Frontiers in Applied Artificial Intelligence*, pp. 388–96, 2008.

[63] K. Lu, K. Fang, and G. Xie. "A hybrid quantum-behaved particle swarm optimization algorithm for clustering analysis," *Fifth International Conference on Fuzzy Systems and Knowledge Discovery*, pp. 21–5, 2008.

[64] X. Peng, Y. Zhang, S. Xiao, Z. Wu, J. Cui, L. Chen, et al. "An alert correlation method based on improved cluster algorithm," *Pacific- Asia Workshop on Computational Intelligence and Industrial Application*, pp. 342–7, 2008.

[65] X. Zhang, H. Zhang, Y. Zhu, Y. Liu, T. Yang, and T. Zhang. "Using IACO and QPSO to solve spatial clustering with obstacles constraints," *IEEE International Conference on Automation and Logistics*, pp. 1699–704, 2009.

[66] H. Wang, S. Yang, W. Xu, and J. Sun. "Scalability of hybrid fuzzy c-means algorithm based on quantum-behaved PSO," *Fourth International Conference on Fuzzy Systems and Knowledge Discovery*, pp. 261–5, 2007.

[67] L. Tao. "Text topic mining and classification based on quantum- behaved particle swarm optimization," *Journal of Southwest University for Nationalities*, vol. 35(3), pp. 603–7, 2009.

[68] L. Tao, Y. Feng, C. Jianying, and H. Weilin. "Acquisition of classification rule based onquantum-behaved particle swarm optimization," *Application Research of Computers*, vol. 26(2), pp. 496–9, 2009.

[69] H. Zhu, X. Zhao, and Y. Zhong. "Feature selection method combined optimized document frequency with improved RBF network," *Advanced Data Mining and Applications*, pp. 796–803, 2009.

[70] L. Shiyin, Z. Xiaoming, and W. Xiaodong. "Attribute reduction based on quantum-behaved particle swarm optimization," *Computer Engineering*, vol. 34(18), pp. 65–9, 2008.

[71] W. Jiayang, and X. Ying. "Minimal attribute reduction algorithm based on quantum particle swarm optimization," *Computer Engineering*, vol. 35(12), pp. 148–50, 2009.

[72] S. Mikki, and A.A. Kishk. "Investigation of the quantum particle swarm optimization technique for electromagnetic applications," *IEEE Antennas and Propagation Society International Symposium*, vol. 42A, pp. 45–8, 2005.

[73] S. Mikki, and A.A. Kishk. "Quantum particle swarm optimization for electromagnetics," *IEEE Transactions on Antennas and Propagation*, vol. 54(10), pp. 2764–75, 2006.

[74] S. Mikki, and A.A. Kishk. "Theory and applications of infinitesimal dipole models for computational electromagnetics," *IEEE Transactions on Antennas and Propagation*, vol. 55(5), pp. 1325–37, 2007.

[75] L.S. Coelho, and P. Alotto. "Global optimization of electromagnetic devices using an exponential quantum-behaved particle swarm optimizer," *Magnetics, IEEE Transactions on*, vol. 44(6), pp. 1074–7, 2008.

[76] R. Wu, J. Wang, K. Xia, and R. Yang. "Optimal design on CMOS operational amplifier with QPSO algorithm," *International Conference on Wavelet Analysis and Pattern Recognition*, pp. 821–5, 2008.

[77] N. Liu, K. Xia, J. Zhou, and C. Ge. "Numerical simulation on transistor with CQPSO algorithm," *4th IEEE Conference on Industrial Electronics and Applications*, pp. 3732–6, 2009.

[78] L. Tang, and F. Xue. "Using data to design fuzzy system based on quantum-behaved particle swarm optimization," *Machine Learning and Cybernetics, 2008 International Conference on*, pp. 624–8, 2008.

[79] X. Yinchun, J. Sun, and W. Xu. "QPSO algorithm for rectangle- packing optimization," *Journal of Computer Applications*, vol. 9, pp. 2068–70, 2006.

[80] Z. Di, J. Sun, and W. Xu. "Polygonal approximation of curves using binary quantum-behaved particle swarm optimization," *Journal of Computer Applications*, vol. 27(8), pp. 2030–2, 2007.

[81] H. Jianjiang, J. Sun, W. Xu, and D. Hongwei. "Study on layout problem using quantum-behaved particle swarm optimization algorithm," *Journal of Computer Applications*, vol. 12, pp. 3015–8, 2006.

[82] J. Sun, W. Xu, W. Fang, and Z. Chai. "Quantum-behaved particle swarm optimization with binary encoding," *Adaptive and Natural Computing Algorithms*, pp. 376–85, 2007.

[83] F. Gao, H. Gao, Z. Li, H. Tong, and J. Lee. "Detecting unstable periodic orbits of nonlinear mappings by a novel quantum-behaved particle swarm optimization non-Lyapunov way," *Chaos, Solitons and Fractals*, vol. 42(4), pp. 2450–63, 2009.

[84] S. Li, R. Wang, W. Hu, and J. Sun. "A new QPSO based BP neural network for face detection," *Fuzzy Information and Engineering*, pp. 355–63, 2007.

[85] X. Lei, and A. Fu. "Two-dimensional maximum entropy image segmentation method based on quantum-behaved particle swarm optimization algorithm," *Fourth International Conference on Natural Computation*, pp. 692–6, 2008.

[86] F. Bin, W. Zhang, and J. Sun. "Image threshold segmentation with Ostu based on quantum-behaved particle swarm algorithm," *Computer Engineering and Design*, vol. 29(13), pp. 3429–31, 2008.

[87] Z. Yong, F. Zongde, W. Kanwei, and P. Hui. "Multilevel minimum cross entropy threshold selection based on quantum particle swarm optimization," *Eighth ACIS International Conference on Software Engineering, Artificial Intelligence, Networking, and Parallel/Distributed Computing*, pp. 65–9, 2007.

[88] L. Yang, Z.W. Liao, and W.F. Chen. "An automatic registration framework using quantum particle swarm optimization for remote sensing images," *International Conference on Wavelet Analysis and Pattern Recognition*, pp. 484–8, 2007.

[89] X. Wenlong, W. Xu, and J. Sun. "Image interpolation algorithm based on quantum-behaved particle swarm optimization," *Journal of Computer Applications*, vol. 27(9), pp. 2147–9, 2007.

[90] L.S. Coelho, and V.C. Mariani. "Particle swarm approach based on quantum mechanics and harmonic oscillator potential well for economic load dispatch with valve-point effects," *Energy Conversion and Management*, vol. 49(11), pp. 3080–5, 2008.

[91] J. Sun, W. Fang, D. Wang, and W. Xu. "Solving the economic dispatch problem with a modified quantum-behaved particle swarm optimization method," *Energy Conversion and Management*, vol. 50(12), pp. 2967–75, 2009.

[92] L. Zhou, H. Yang, and C. Liu. "QPSO-based hyper-parameters selection for LS-SVM regression," *Fourth International Conference on Natural Computation*, pp. 130–3, 2008.

[93] X. Li, L. Zhou, and C. Liu. "Model selection of least squares support vector regression using quantum-behaved particle swarm optimization algorithm," *International Workshop on Intelligent Systems and Applications*, pp. 1–5, 2009.

[94] J. Wang, Z. Liu, and P. Lu. "Electricity load forecasting based on adaptive quantum-behaved particle swarm optimization and support vector machines on global level," *International Symposium on Computational Intelligence and Design*, pp. 233–6, 2008.

[95] Q. Zhang, and Z. Che. "A novel method to train support vector machines for solving quadratic programming task," *7th World Congress on Intelligent Control and Automation*, pp. 7917–21, 2008.

[96] C. Lin, and P. Feng. "Parameters selection and application of support vector machines based on quantum delta particle swarm optimization algorithm," *Automation and Instrumentation*, vol. 1, pp. 5–8, 2009.

[97] S.L. Sabat, L.S. Coelho, and A. Abraham. "MESFET DC model parameter extraction using quantum particle swarm optimization," *Microelectronics Reliability*, vol. 49(6), pp. 660–6, 2009.

[98] J. Liu, W. Xu, and J. Sun. "Nonlinear system identification of hammerstien and wiener model using swarm intelligence," *2006 IEEE International Conference on Information Acquisition*, pp. 1219–23, 2006.

[99] J. Sun, W. Xu, and J. Liu. "Training RBF neural network via quantum-behaved particle swarm optimization," *Neural Information Processing*, pp. 1156–63, 2006.

[100] S. Tian, and T. Liu. "Short-term load forecasting based on RBFNN and QPSO," *Asia-Pacific Power and Energy Engineering Conference*, pp. 1–4, 2009.

[101] Q. Tan, and Y. Song. "Sidelobe suppression algorithm for chaotic FM signal based on neural network," *9th International Conference on Signal Processing*, pp. 2429–33, 2008.

[102] Y. Genghuang, and W. Boying. "Identification of power quality disturbance based on QPSO-ANN," *Proceedings of the CSEE*, vol. 28(10), pp. 123–9, 2008.

[103] X. Kong, J. Sun, B. Ye, and W. Xu. "An efficient quantum-behaved particle swarm optimization for multiprocessor scheduling," *Computational Science—ICCS*, pp. 278–85, 2007.

[104] W. Fang, J. Sun, W. Xu, and J. Liu. "FIR digital filters design based on quantum-behaved particle swarm optimization," *First International Conference on Innovative Computing, Information and Control*, pp. 615–9, 2006.

[105] W. Fang, J. Sun, and W. Xu. "FIR filter design based on adaptive quantum-behaved particle swarm optimization algorithm," *Systems Engineering and Electronics*, vol. 30(7), pp. 1378–81, 2008.

[106] W. Fang, J. Sun, and W. Xu. "Design IIR digital filters using quantum-behaved particle swarm optimization," *Advances in Natural Computation*, pp. 637–40, 2006.

[107] W. Fang, J. Sun, and W. Xu. "Analysis of adaptive IIR filter design based on quantum-behaved particle swarm optimization," *The Sixth World Congress on Intelligent Control and Automation*, pp. 3396–400, 2006.

[108] W. Fang, J. Sun, and W. Xu. "Design of two-dimensional recursive filters by using quantum-behaved particle swarm optimization," *International Conference on Intelligent Information Hiding and Multimedia Signal Processing*, pp. 240–3, 2006.

[109] J. Sun, W. Fang, W. Chen, and W. Xu. "Design of two-dimensional IIR digital filters using an improved quantum-behaved particle swarm optimization algorithm," *American Control Conference*, pp. 2603–8, 2008.

13 Decentralizing Trust
Innovating Social Media with Blockchain for Enhanced Authenticity and Fake News Mitigation

*Vedant Singh, Andleeb Tanveer, Kalpana A.V.,
and Ciro Rodriguez R.*

13.1 INTRODUCTION

In today's digital era, social media platforms have become essential tools for worldwide communication, allowing countless individuals to exchange ideas, participate in conversations, and shape public perceptions on a global scale. From microblogs to image-centered networks, these platforms have revolutionized the way information is shared and consumed, establishing themselves as influential forces in the realms of media and politics. Despite their undeniable impact, these platforms have also faced significant issues due to the proliferation of false information and deceptive news, eroding trust among the public and presenting substantial obstacles to societal cohesion.

A possible solution to these problems involves using decentralized social media platforms. Unlike centralized platforms, decentralized systems like blockchain-based, federated, and peer-to-peer (P2P) networks provide a more open and secure structure for managing content. These platforms are not governed by a single entity; instead, they function on a distributed ledger technology that distributes data storage and content sharing among various nodes, reducing the risk of tampering and censorship.

Social media platforms are like intricate ecosystems that manage not just the technical side of connecting people, like addressing and verifying identities, but also the social and technical challenges of discovering content and running digital ads. The emergence of decentralized platforms is a significant step in tackling these problems. By spreading out the structure and management of these platforms, there is a chance to establish a fairer and more equal media environment.

The fast spread of incorrect information, whether intentional or accidental, has exposed flaws in the current methods of verifying content, which are usually centralized. These systems depend too much on platform operators to oversee and manage content distribution, which can result in biases and ineffective filtering of falsehoods. A fresh approach is urgently required to regain trust and maintain the authenticity of shared information.

Decentralized social media platforms come in a variety of types, such as blockchain-based, federated, and peer-to-peer systems. Data storage, content distribution, user discovery, identity management, governance, moderation, income generating, and network architecture are among the tasks that these platforms are organized around. Decentralized social media was inspired by worries about centralized power systems in the past and the content filtering practices of centralized platforms in the present.

DOI: 10.1201/9781003499459-13

Historically, social media hasn't had a definition that everyone agrees with. Various terminologies, such as online social networks or social network sites, have been used by different academic disciplines; some have even proposed up to six different categories (Aichner & Jacob, 2015; McCay-Peet & Quan-Haase, 2017). Although platform types vary, they all have certain fundamental qualities in common, which highlights the necessity to distinguish across typologies such as microblogging and image sharing.

The social graph, which allows users to build profiles, connect with others, publish material, and receive feedback, is at the center of social media (Boyd & Ellison, 2007). Sharing content is a key activity that can be restricted to certain groups or made freely available. Users can interact with content by liking, following, commenting, reposting, and taking other predetermined actions. Social media networks technically handle addressing, authentication, identity verification, content discovery, and data storage. They also discuss socio-technical issues such as content filtering and business structures (Gillespie, 2018).

In addition to undermining the veracity of information, the propagation of fake news on social media has serious negative effects on society, influencing public opinion, widening social gaps, and even undermining democratic processes. A study on fake news subject matter with respect to fake news is shown in Figure 13.1. Due to the fact that fact-checking and content control processes are frequently centralized, prejudice, censorship, and manipulation are problems. Novel approaches that maintain decentralization and transparency on social media while improving the validity of content are desperately needed.

The purpose of this chapter is to investigate how blockchain technology might be used to address the problems of fake news and authenticity on social media. Blockchain-based solutions have the potential to enhance the trustworthiness of information posted on social media platforms and reduce the propagation of fake news by decentralizing trust and enabling transparent processes for content verification. By means of an extensive examination of extant literature, theoretical analysis, and case studies, this chapter aims to offer insights into the practicability, efficacy, and consequences of incorporating blockchain technology into social media establishments.

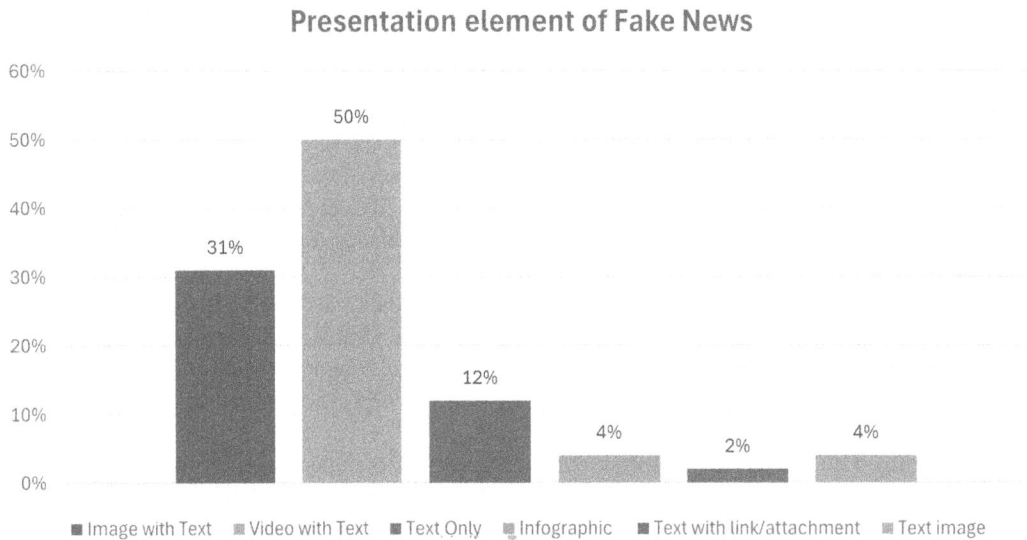

FIGURE 13.1 Study on fake news subject matter.

13.2 ORIGINS AND EVOLUTION

Decentralization is often linked to blockchain technologies in everyday conversations and discussions. Nonetheless, from the beginning of computer networking, the idea of decentralization has operated within cultural, normative, and technological frameworks as a critique of centralized power structures (Russell, 2014). Networks, especially the Internet, are frequently described as democratizing society and dismantling hierarchies of power (Bory, 2020; Baran, 1964).

Long before centralized platforms were popular, there were worries regarding the centralization of social functions in web technology (Halpin, 2019). As a result, by creating open standards, the web engineering community has attempted to decentralize important parts of the social web. These standards cover content transportation (Really Simple Syndication, Atom Syndication Format, Extensible Messaging and Presence Protocol(XMPP), ActivityPub), machine-readable web page information (RDF, XML, Microformats, Open Graph), identity provisioning (Domain Name Server, Extensible Data Interchange(XDI), OpenID), and authentication (OAuth). Nevertheless, these initiatives have not always been successful, in part because of inconsistencies between competing standards that aim to solve related problems. Furthermore, decentralization has primarily been tackled from a technical perspective by standards organizations like the Internet Engineering Task Force (IETF) and the World Wide Web Consortium (W3C), frequently ignoring economic, political, and social factors.

Some standards have not been widely adopted, but, in a paradoxical way, others have strengthened the market domination of centralized mainstream platforms like Google and Facebook. For instance, Facebook's creation of the Open Graph protocol was impacted by the RDF metadata standard, despite its modest uptake (Halpin, 2019). Web pages were standardized to be accessible by social networking platforms with the integration of elements like the "Like" button. This allowed Facebook to follow users even when they are logged out and enabled features like rich link previews. In a similar vein, OAuth was designed to securely identify users across many websites, hence decentralizing identity methods. But in reality, through features like "Login with Facebook" and "Login with Google" buttons, it helped to solidify Facebook and Google's position as the main identity providers.

However, these standardization efforts produced open protocols that served as the technological foundation for decentralized social media sites. Alongside the emergence of the first decentralized social media platforms, which partially or completely relied on these protocols, came academic experiments with decentralized social network topologies, including the Friend-of-a-Friend project. These principles have found their way into several decentralized social media platforms.

13.3 PROPOSED METHODOLOGY

13.3.1 METHODOLOGY

This chapter's methodology section describes the methodical approach used in the creation and deployment of the Decentralized Social Media (DSM) application. Understanding blockchain technology, establishing use cases, creating the user interface, and incorporating security measures are just a few of the important steps that are covered in this part. An extensive explanation of each step is provided in the following.

13.3.2 ARCHITECTURE OVERVIEW

A distributed ledger for storing content metadata, consensus processes for transaction validation, and smart contracts for enforcing content verification guidelines are some of the essential elements of the suggested architecture for integrating blockchain into social media networks. A user-friendly interface allows users to engage with the blockchain and get information about the provenance and validity of content as shown in Figure 13.2.

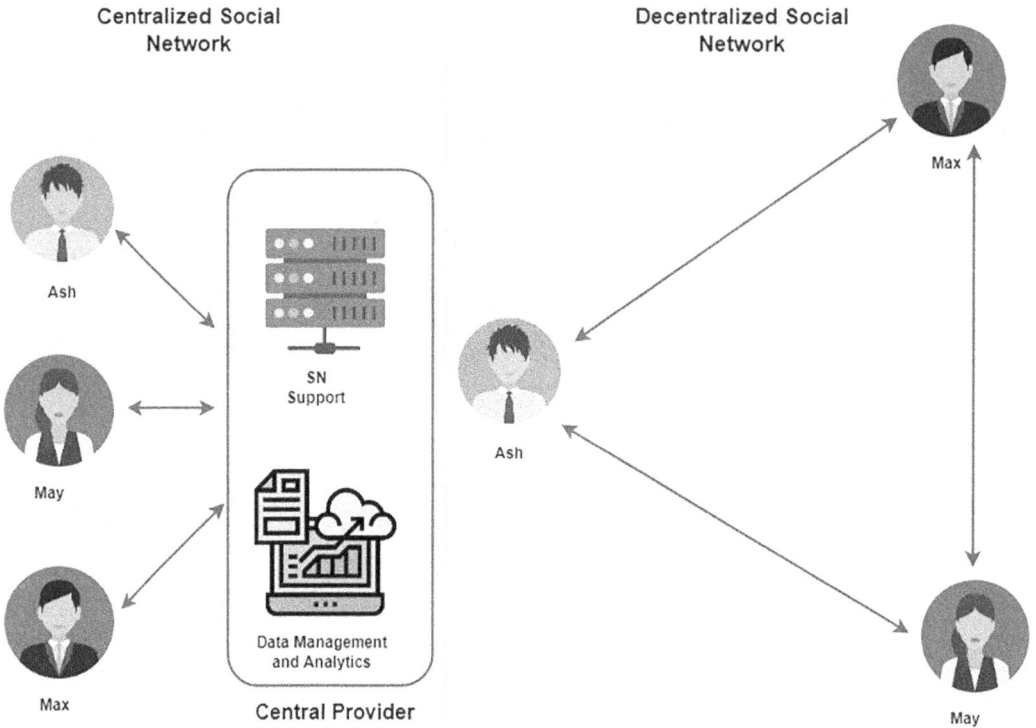

FIGURE 13.2 Centralized vs. decentralized network.

13.3.3 CONTENT VERIFICATION MECHANISM

Users on social media can now verify the authenticity of their posts using private keys to cryptographically sign them, adding a layer of security and trust. This digital signature, unique to each user, confirms the identity of the content creator and protects the post from unauthorized changes. The signed post, along with important metadata like content hashes and timestamps, is then stored on the blockchain, creating an unchangeable record of the content's essence at the time of creation and any modifications made later on.

The blockchain is recognized for its strength and unchangeability, storing data in a way that prevents tampering and guarantees that once information is recorded, it cannot be changed without agreement from the network. This aspect is crucial for upholding the accuracy of data and creating a clear record for anyone interested. Individuals, academics, or reviewers can view these blockchain records and use cryptographic signatures to confirm the legitimacy of any content. This verification process is decentralized, eliminating the requirement for a central authority to validate the accuracy of the data.

Smart contracts streamline the validation process in the system by enforcing predefined rules impartially. They verify that posts are from authentic users and ensure that the content remains unaltered after posting. This automation boosts efficiency and reliability, offering a scalable solution to combat misinformation and tampering. Moreover, integrating smart contracts establishes a foundation for trust and accountability in digital interactions. By certifying the integrity of content and its source, they promote a secure environment for users.

In general, using blockchain technology for verifying content on social media platforms is a major advancement in making digital spaces more transparent, secure, and trustworthy. By utilizing cryptographic signatures, smart contracts, and the unchangeable nature of the blockchain, this method provides a complete solution to a key issue in the digital world—upholding the integrity and authenticity of online information.

13.3.4 CONSENSUS PROTOCOL SELECTION

When creating a decentralized social media site, choosing a consensus mechanism is a crucial choice. Consensus methods ensure that network participants agree on the current state of the distributed ledger by regulating the validation and addition of transactions to the blockchain. Selecting a consensus protocol for the DSM platform requires taking into account a number of characteristics, such as ease of implementation, security, decentralization, scalability, and energy efficiency.

Proof of Stake (PoS) is one consensus mechanism that the DSM platform might take into consideration. Validators stake their bitcoin holdings as collateral to take part in the block validation process, which is how Proof of Stake works. Based on their stake, validators are selected to construct new blocks; bigger stakes usually translate into a higher selection chance. Compared to Proof of Work (PoW) protocols, Proof of Stake protocols are noted for their energy efficiency because they don't require a lot of processing power to confirm transactions. Furthermore, because PoS does not encourage the concentration of mining power in the hands of a small number of entities with substantial computational capabilities, it is by nature more decentralized than PoW.

Delegated Proof of Stake (DPoS) is an additional consensus protocol that may be taken into consideration. Token holders cast votes for a chosen group of delegates to represent their interests and validate transactions on their behalf in DPoS, a decentralized proof of stake system that functions similarly to PoS. Usually, delegates are selected based on their track record, level of technical proficiency, and dedication to network security. Because the number of validators is restricted to a predetermined group of delegates, DPoS is renowned for its scalability and throughput. This lowers consensus overhead and speeds up transaction processing.

As an alternative, the DSM platform can take into account a hybrid consensus protocol like practical Byzantine fault tolerance (PBFT). Through a sequence of message exchange and vote rounds, PBFT establishes a consensus among a subset of nodes, referred to as replicas. Because of its reputation for minimal latency and finality, PBFT is a good fit for applications that need quick transaction confirmation times. However, because PBFT depends on a set number of pre-selected replicas, which raises the possibility of centralization, it might not be as appropriate for large-scale decentralized networks.

Ultimately, the selection of a consensus protocol for the DSM platform should be guided by a thorough assessment of the platform's requirements, including scalability, security, decentralization, and performance considerations. By carefully weighing the strengths and weaknesses of each consensus protocol option, the DSM platform can be equipped with a robust and resilient consensus mechanism tailored to its specific needs and objectives.

13.3.5 BLOCKCHAIN TECHNOLOGY

At this point, it is crucial to have a thorough understanding of blockchain technology. This entails investigating different blockchain kinds, like private and public ones, and deciding which blockchain is best for the DSM application. The Solana blockchain was selected for this project because of its quick transaction processing speed and low cost. Seahorse, a tool that enables authoring Solana smart contracts in Python, made it easier to construct smart contracts for the DSM application, as shown in Figure 13.3.

13.3.6 USE CASE DEFINITION

Determining the DSM application's features and functions requires defining its use cases. Use cases, including liking and disliking posts, sharing posts, and deleting posts, were found and thoroughly

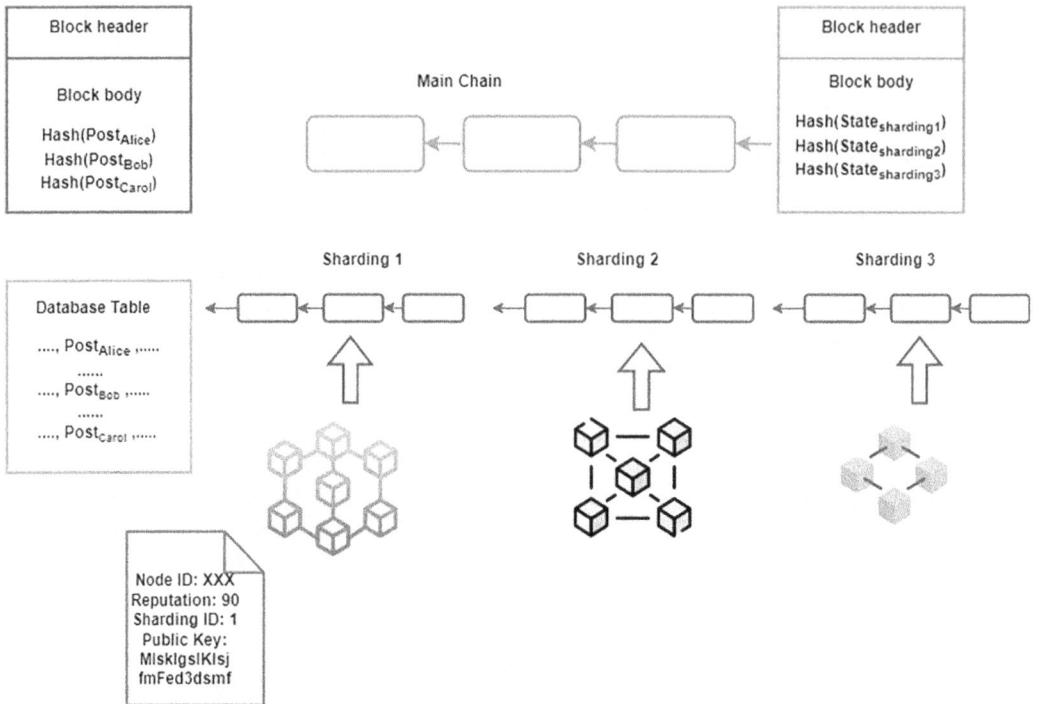

FIGURE 13.3 Blockchain technology integration for decentralization.

examined. This phase aids in coordinating the development process with the DSM platform's aims and objectives. The use case diagram for the DSM application is shown in Figure 13.4.

13.3.7 USER INTERFACE AND EXPERIENCE

The success of the DSM application is largely dependent on the design of the user interface (UI) and user experience (UX). Priority was given to design concepts that emphasize accessibility, user-friendliness, and intuitive design. In addition, steps were taken to protect the platform's decentralized structure while guaranteeing user security and privacy. It was also thought that secure interactions and transactions on the decentralized network might be made possible by integration with wallets such as Phantom wallet.

13.3.8 DEPLOYMENT AND TESTING

Once the DSM application was developed, the next step involved deployment on the Solana blockchain. This process required careful consideration of various factors and potential challenges. Rigorous testing procedures were then conducted to validate the functionality and performance of the application. Testing aimed to identify any issues or areas for improvement before the final deployment.

The previously described technique offers an organized way to create and execute the decentralized social media application. This chapter attempts to further decentralized social media platforms by comprehending blockchain technology, establishing use cases, creating an intuitive interface, and carrying out extensive testing. The DSM application's features and functionalities may be further improved in future research projects in order to better serve the changing needs of users in the decentralized environment.

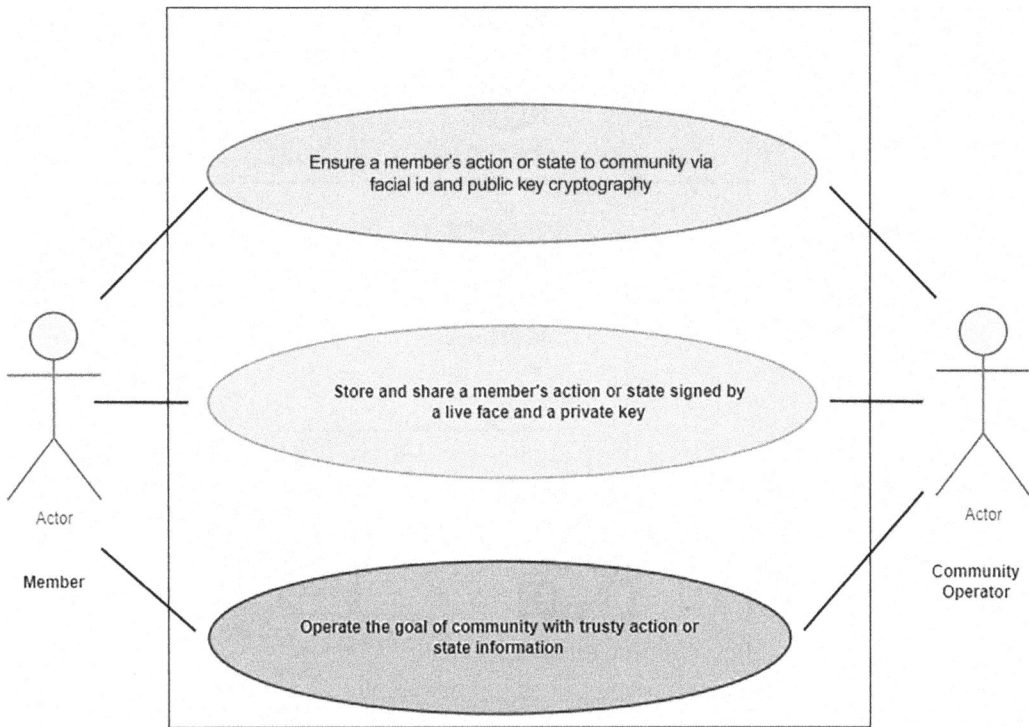

FIGURE 13.4   Use case diagram for DSM application.

13.4   MODELING AND ANALYSIS

Decentralized social media modeling and analysis involve the careful creation and evaluation of an all-encompassing framework designed specifically for a decentralized social media network. The system has been carefully designed to address the inherent drawbacks of centralized social networks, namely with regard to compromised user privacy and the excessive control exercised by a single authority. The modeling phase includes the detailed definition of all the parts that make up the decentralized social media network, from the core architecture based on blockchain technology to the complex workings of user identity protocols, smart contracts, and encryption methods, as shown in Figure 13.5.

Within the modeling process, each component of the decentralized social media platform is meticulously defined, delineating its role, functionality, and interrelation with other elements. The blockchain-based architecture serves as the backbone of the platform, facilitating transparent and immutable record-keeping while ensuring decentralized control and consensus mechanisms. Smart contracts, imbued with predefined rules and logic, govern interactions and transactions within the DSM ecosystem, ensuring trustless execution and automated enforcement of agreements.

To further protect user privacy and improve security, user identity and encryption methods are deeply integrated into the platform's architecture. These safeguards allow users to safely create and keep their identities while making sure that private data is protected and out of the reach of unauthorized individuals.

Furthermore, the ways in which these elements interact are carefully outlined, outlining the information exchange, transactions, and governance that take place on the decentralized social media network. To give a comprehensive picture of the system's operational dynamics, the intended behavior is described in detail, including response times, throughput, and scalability.

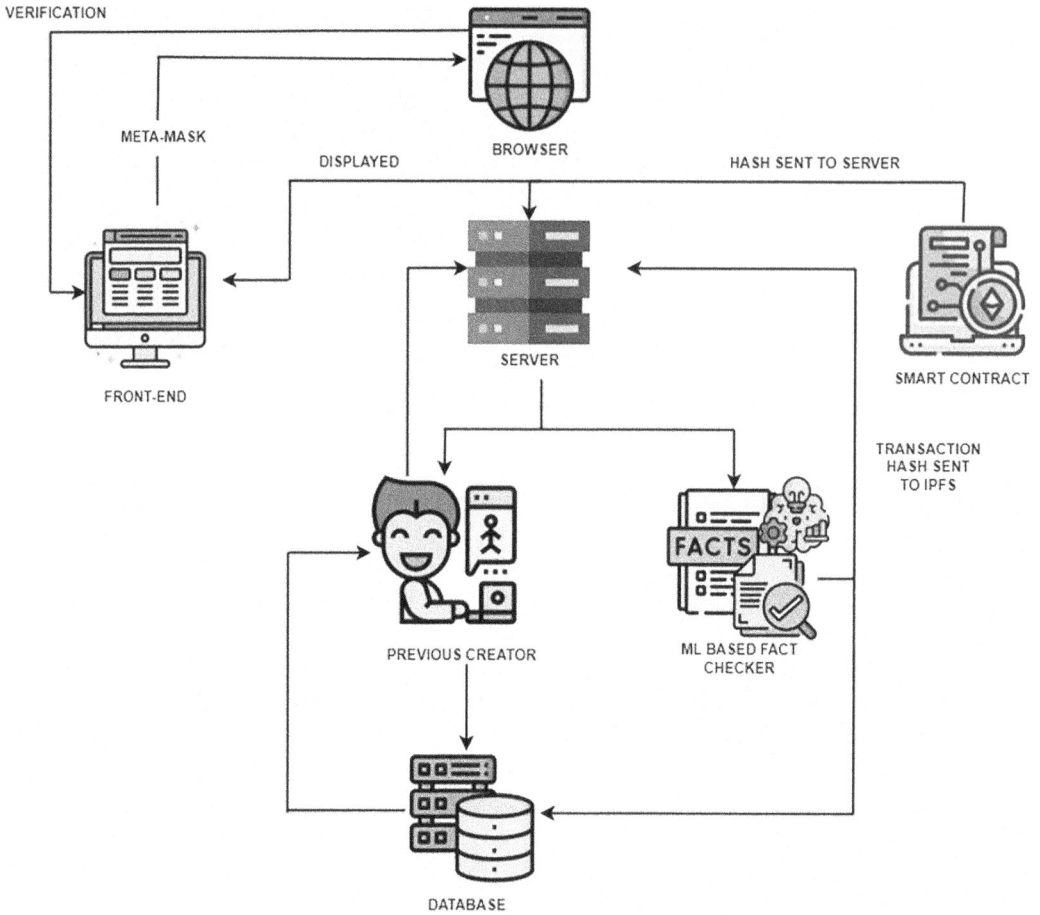

FIGURE 13.5   Architecture diagram of the proposed system.

The goal of the analysis step that follows is to thoroughly examine the modeled framework in order to find any weaknesses, inefficiencies, or areas that may be optimized. The goal is to optimize the system by thorough analysis in order to accomplish predetermined goals, like improved efficiency, security, and privacy. To make sure that the decentralized social media network satisfies the highest requirements of security, effectiveness, and user-friendliness, an extensive security audit, performance testing, and user experience evaluations are conducted as part of this iterative process.

The decentralized social media platform must, however, continue to be safe, effective, and user-friendly while simultaneously successfully resolving the inherent drawbacks of centralized social networks. The goal is to create a decentralized social media ecosystem that gives individuals unmatched privacy, control, and sovereignty over their digital interactions by following strict modeling and analysis procedures.

13.4.1   Theoretical Frameworks Used

13.4.1.1   Mechanisms of Decentralized Consensus and Trust

Blockchain technology is based on decentralization, which eliminates the need for a central authority to approve transactions or enforce rules. This move from traditional verification systems to a decentralized framework makes blockchain a groundbreaking technology. In a blockchain network, consensus algorithms are essential as they enable all participants to confirm transaction validity, fostering trust among them without a central authority.

There are several consensus algorithms that have been created, including Proof of Work, Proof of Stake, and Delegated Proof of Stake, which have gained popularity for their individual advantages and challenges. PoW, the algorithm utilized by the initial cryptocurrency, Bitcoin, mandates participants to solve intricate computational puzzles to verify new transactions. The security of PoW rests in the substantial computational power necessary to solve these puzzles, which deters fraudulent behavior due to the immense energy and processing power required. Nonetheless, this also results in PoW being highly energy-consuming, prompting worries regarding its environmental effects.

However, Proof of Stake uses a unique process to verify transactions, which depends on the cryptocurrency amount staked by a validator rather than computational power. This approach lowers the energy consumption seen in PoW, since it doesn't demand intensive calculations and processing. With PoS, the likelihood of validating a transaction relates to the user's stake, resulting in a more efficient and potentially quicker transaction process.

Delegated Proof of Stake builds on the concept of blockchain validation by introducing a new layer of organization. In DPoS, token holders delegate the task of validating transactions to elected delegates instead of participating directly. This approach can improve network efficiency and scalability by reducing the number of nodes required for reaching consensus. With fewer validators, DPoS can support higher transaction speeds and faster consensus compared to Proof of Work or traditional Proof of Stake systems. This makes DPoS an appealing choice for larger networks seeking improved performance and scalability.

13.4.1.2 Smart Contracts for Content Verification

Smart contracts on blockchain networks provide a groundbreaking method for automatically carrying out agreements without the involvement of middlemen, which is especially impactful in the field of social media. These contracts are self-executing and have their conditions coded directly, allowing all parties involved to rely on the process without requiring external validation. In the social media landscape, smart contracts can have a significant impact by including metadata like timestamps, author information, and edits onto the blockchain. This guarantees a clear and unchangeable record of content creation and edits, greatly improving the ability to verify authenticity. Automated and trust less interactions on blockchain networks are made possible by smart contracts, which are self-executing contracts with the conditions of the agreement put directly into code. By storing metadata like timestamps, authorship, and changes on the blockchain, smart contracts can be used to confirm the legitimacy of content in the context of social media. Content producers have the option to encrypt their posts, and smart contracts have the ability to impose content validation requirements based on pre-established standards.

13.4.1.3 Transparency and Immutability of Blockchain

Blockchain technology plays a crucial role in ensuring transparency and immutability on social media platforms, where the accuracy of information is often doubted. The core features of blockchain form the basis for establishing a secure and transparent system where information recorded on the blockchain ledger cannot be easily changed or removed without the agreement of all network users. This unchangeable ledger creates a secure record for every piece of content, such as news articles, social media posts, or user comments, showing its origin, changes, and distribution across the network.

Blockchain technology's transparency and immutability guarantee that once information is entered into the ledger, it cannot be removed or changed without the network's members' consent. This capability, which offers a tamper-proof audit trail of content production, dissemination, and attribution, is very helpful for confirming the veracity of information on social media. Through the utilization of blockchain technology's transparency and immutability, anyone can autonomously confirm the authenticity and provenance of content shared on social media sites.

The audit trail is crucial for confirming the accuracy of information and tracing the sources and context of content. Blockchain securely records timestamps, authorship, and the transfer of shared content, creating a transparent and immutable history that can be accessed by all. This accessibility enables users, fact-checkers, and algorithms to verify the authenticity and origin of shared information independently and openly.

13.5 RESULTS AND DISCUSSION

Within our planned social networking platform with blockchain integration, the register function is a vital first step toward helping users create a safe and distinct identity. This procedure entails using a wallet address that is kept on the blockchain to create a unique user identity. The wallet address serves as a safe way to identify oneself within the decentralized network by acting as a cryptographic representation of the user's identity. Before saving the identifying information on the blockchain, complex encryption methods are used to encrypt it in order to guarantee the integrity and confidentiality of user data. Strong cryptographic techniques are used to encrypt the identification, reducing the possibility of unwanted access and shielding important user data from possible security lapses. In creating our cutting-edge social networking platform that incorporates blockchain technology, ensuring a safe and individualized user identity is essential for upholding user confidence and confidentiality. This initial step involves the pivotal 'register' feature, which not only streamlines the process of setting up a new user account but also links each user's online identity to a specific blockchain record through a wallet address. This wallet address is created using sophisticated cryptographic methods and acts as the main identifier for users in our decentralized system. Similar to a digital fingerprint, this address distinctively connects every piece of content, transaction, and engagement to its original user. In order to keep your personal and sensitive information safe and private, we use strong encryption methods before storing any data on the blockchain. Our multi-layered encryption system is meant to protect your data from unauthorized access and potential security risks, as shown in Figure 13.6.

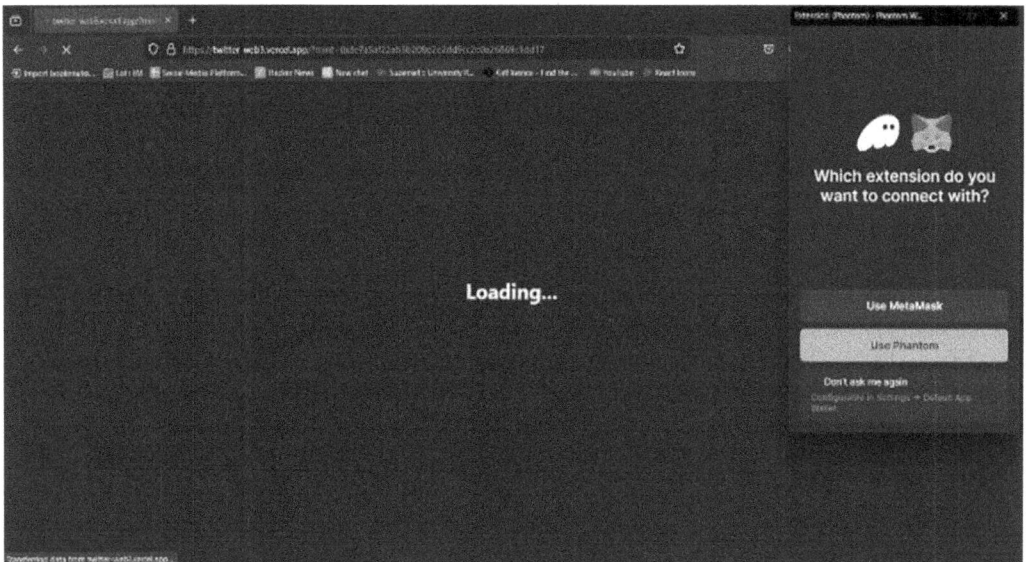

FIGURE 13.6 Login through MetaMask.

Users who successfully register are given access to the site, where they can use their encrypted identities to participate in a variety of social media activities. Users can safely communicate with others, share content, and take part in community conversations with this identity, which functions as a digital passport. In addition, the decentralized structure of the blockchain guarantees the immutability and tamper-proofness of user identities, providing protection against identity theft and fraudulent activity.

Our platform addresses important issues that are common in traditional social media platforms by enhancing trust and authenticity through the registration process' integration of blockchain technology. Because the blockchain's built-in security measures safeguard users' identities, they can feel secure and private about their information. Furthermore, user identity management's decentralized structure lessens dependency on centralized authority, giving people more control over their digital identities and promoting an online ecosystem that is more transparent and resilient. In conclusion, our blockchain-integrated social media platform's register feature is a big step in the right direction toward improving digital trust and authenticity. Users may safely create and maintain their identities by using blockchain technology and secure encryption techniques, opening the door for a more reliable and decentralized social media environment.

13.6 CONCLUSION

In summary, the emergence of decentralized social media signifies a noteworthy progression in the field of virtual social networks, utilizing blockchain technology to tackle crucial concerns related to security, privacy, and centralization. Through the use of a decentralized architecture, DSM makes information flow more resilient to censorship, data breaches, and manipulation by doing away with the requirement for a central authority or server.

Choosing Solana as the DSM's underlying blockchain technology has several advantages over more conventional choices like Ethereum. Because of its proof-of-history consensus method, which enables scalability and high throughput, Solana is an attractive option for meeting the requirements of a decentralized social media platform. DSM can handle more transactions with Solana at a cheaper cost, giving users a smooth and effective experience.

UML diagrams were used to map out the system architecture, and a thorough literature review served as a guide for the design and execution of DSM's features throughout the development process. This careful preparation made it possible for the essential aspects of DSM to be implemented successfully, opening the door for the coding of the smart contracts and front-end interfaces, which is the next stage of the project.

DSM's adherence to Web3.0 principles highlights its commitment to offering consumers improved security and privacy. DSM eliminates the possibility of a single point of failure by decentralizing data storage and depending on group consensus to add new data to the network, hence reducing the danger of data breaches and improving data integrity.

To put it briefly, decentralized social media is an innovative initiative aimed at completely changing the online social network environment. Through the adoption of decentralization, the utilization of blockchain technology, and the emphasis on security and privacy, DSM seeks to transform the online user experience and information sharing. In order to fully realize DSM's promise and usher in a new era of decentralized social media platforms, ongoing testing and refinement will be essential as the project advances.

REFERENCES

T. Aichner and F. Jacob, "Measuring the degree of corporate social media use," *International Journal of Market Research*, vol. 57, no. 2, pp. 257–276, 2015, doi: 10.2501/IJMR-2015-018.

P. Baran, "On distributed communications networks," *IEEE Transactions on Communications Systems*, vol. 12, no. 1, pp. 1–9, March 1964, doi: 10.1109/TCOM.1964.1088883.

P. Bory, *The Internet Myth: From the Internet Imaginary to Network Ideologies* (p. 169). University of Westminster Press, 2020.

D. Boyd and N. Ellison, "Social network sites: Definition, history, and scholarship," *Journal of Computer-Mediated Communication*. vol. 13, pp. 210–230, 2007, doi: 10.1111/j.1083-6101.2007.00393.x.

T. Gillespie, *Custodians of the Internet: Platforms, Content Moderation, and the Hidden Decisions That Shape Social Media*. London: Yale University Press, 2018.

H. Halpin, Decentralizing the social web: Can blockchains solve ten years of standardization failure of the social web? In *Internet Science: INSCI 2018 International Workshops, St. Petersburg, Russia, October 24–26, 2018, Revised Selected Papers 5* (pp. 187–202). Springer International Publishing, 2019.

L. McCay-Peet and A. Quan-Haase, What is social media and what questions can social media research help us answer? In L. Sloan & A. Quan-Haase (Eds.), *The SAGE handbook of social media research methods* (pp. 13–26). London: SAGE Research Methods, 2017, doi: 10.4135/9781473983847.n2

A. L. Russell, *Open Standards and the Digital Age*. Cambridge University Press, 2014.

14 Quantum Computing Integration
Cutting-Edge and Quantum Computing for Building a Smart and Sustainable Environment

Senthil Kumar Arumugam, Bukola Fatimah Balogun, S. Nalini, and Amit Kumar Tyagi

14.1 INTRODUCTION TO AI, IOT, AND CLOUD AND QUANTUM COMPUTING

Artificial intelligence (AI), Internet of Things (IoT), cloud computing, and quantum computing represent four of the most transformative technologies of our time [1], each with unique capabilities and potential. They are reshaping industries, revolutionizing the way we live and work, and creating exciting possibilities for the future.

Artificial Intelligence: AI involves the creation of computer systems capable of carrying out tasks that usually demand human intelligence. These tasks encompass comprehending natural language, identifying patterns, resolving issues, and making choices. AI advancements, like machine learning and deep learning, have resulted in significant progress in fields like image and speech recognition, natural language processing, and autonomous systems. AI is now being utilized more frequently in various applications, from virtual assistants and self-driving cars to healthcare and finance.

Internet of Things: The IoT refers to a system of interconnected physical devices, such as vehicles, buildings, and objects, that are equipped with sensors, software, and network connectivity. These devices are capable of collecting and sharing data, enabling them to interact with their surroundings and make independent decisions. The impact of IoT can be seen in various sectors, including smart cities, healthcare, agriculture, and manufacturing. By facilitating real-time monitoring, control, and automation, IoT enhances efficiency, safety, and overall quality of life.

Cloud Computing: Cloud computing revolutionizes IT infrastructure by providing computing services such as storage, processing, and networking over the internet. Cloud providers offer scalable and on-demand resources accessible remotely, allowing businesses to cut costs, enhance flexibility, and concentrate on innovation. Cloud computing supports various applications, from web hosting and data storage to software development and machine learning.

Quantum Computing: Quantum computing utilizes the principles of quantum mechanics to tackle calculations that are beyond the capabilities of classical computers [2]. By harnessing quantum bits, or qubits, which can exist in multiple states simultaneously thanks to phenomena like superposition and entanglement, this technology has the power to transform various industries including cryptography, optimization, materials science, and artificial intelligence. The ability to solve intricate problems at an exponential speed compared to conventional computers is what makes quantum computing a game-changer.

DOI: 10.1201/9781003499459-14

The combination of AI, IoT, cloud computing, and quantum computing is incredibly promising. AI has the ability to analyze the massive amounts of data produced by IoT devices, leading to better decision-making. Cloud computing offers the essential infrastructure for storing and processing this data. Quantum computing is expected to speed up the optimization and analysis of AI models, unlocking new possibilities for solving intricate problems in AI and beyond. The integration of these technologies is fueling innovation in various sectors, such as healthcare, finance, smart cities, and environmental monitoring. As these technologies progress, they have the potential to revolutionize our lifestyles and work environments, creating a future characterized by intelligent, interconnected, and efficient systems. Nevertheless, we must address challenges related to privacy, security, ethics, and accessibility as we navigate this rapidly changing landscape.

14.2 SMART AND SUSTAINABLE ENVIRONMENT OVERVIEW

14.2.1 DEFINING SUSTAINABILITY IN THE CONTEXT OF TECHNOLOGY

Technology sustainability involves utilizing technological advancements in a responsible and ethical manner to address present requirements while ensuring that the needs of future generations are not jeopardized [3, 4]. It encompasses the following key principles:

- Environmental Responsibility: Sustainable technology seeks to minimize its environmental impact. It involves decreasing energy usage, reducing waste, and utilizing environmentally friendly materials. The goal is to lower carbon emissions and minimize damage to ecosystems.
- Economic Viability: Sustainable technology should be economically viable, providing long-term value without excessive costs. It often involves investments in technologies that yield returns over time through energy savings, increased efficiency, or reduced waste.
- Social Equity: Sustainable technology should benefit all members of society, avoiding the exacerbation of inequalities. It should be accessible and affordable to diverse communities, ensuring that technological advancements promote social equity.
- Long-Term Thinking: Sustainable technology considers the long-term consequences of its actions and decisions. It aims to preserve resources for future generations and minimize negative impacts on the environment and society.
- Resource Efficiency: Sustainable technology strives to use resources efficiently, reducing waste and optimizing processes. This includes techniques such as recycling, reusing materials, and improving resource utilization.
- Eco-Friendly Design: Sustainable technology emphasizes eco-friendly design principles. This involves minimizing the use of hazardous materials, designing products for easy recycling or disposal, and ensuring that they have a minimal impact on the environment throughout their lifecycle.
- Renewable Energy: Renewable energy sources such as solar, wind, and hydroelectric power are essential components of sustainable technology. They effectively decrease our dependence on fossil fuels and minimize the release of greenhouse gases, thereby paving the way for a cleaner and more sustainable energy future.
- Circular Economy: Sustainable technology promotes a circular economy model, emphasizing the reuse and recycling of products and materials to minimize waste and lower the need for new resources. This strategy focuses on prolonging the lifespan of materials to maximize their value and minimize environmental harm.
- Ethical Practices: Sustainable technology companies and organizations follow ethical practices, such as fair labor, responsible supply chain management, and transparent governance.

- Innovation and Research: Sustainability encourages continuous innovation and research to develop and improve technologies that reduce environmental impact, promote social equity, and ensure long-term viability. The continuous quest for innovation is essential in tackling worldwide issues like climate change, depletion of resources, and social inequality.

Sustainability plays a crucial role in tackling these urgent challenges. It emphasizes the importance of utilizing technology's potential to generate solutions that not only benefit the environment, society, and the economy but also prioritize the well-being of present and future generations. This principle serves as a guiding force in the advancement, execution, and acceptance of technology, paving the way for a more sustainable and accountable future.

14.2.2 THE ROLE OF EMERGING TECHNOLOGIES IN SMART ENVIRONMENTAL SOLUTIONS

Emerging technologies are pivotal in developing intelligent environmental solutions that tackle urgent global issues concerning sustainability, resource preservation, and climate change [5–9]. These technologies use innovation to make our world more efficient, eco-friendly, and resilient. Here are key ways in which emerging technologies contribute to smart environmental solutions:

- Internet of Things: IoT devices, with their sensors and connectivity, empower the monitoring of environmental conditions in real time. These sensors gather information on various factors such as air and water quality, weather conditions, and energy usage. By leveraging IoT technology, data-driven decision-making becomes possible, enabling prompt responses to environmental changes. This ultimately results in improved resource management efficiency and a reduction in waste.
- Artificial Intelligence and Machine Learning: AI and machine learning algorithms process the vast amount of data generated by IoT devices, providing information and predictions for environmental trends and issues. They can optimize resource allocation, enhance energy efficiency, and automate decision-making in areas like agriculture, energy, and waste management.
- Blockchain Technology: Blockchain provides a secure, transparent, and tamper-proof ledger for recording environmental data, transactions, and agreements. It enables trust and accountability in sustainable practices, such as verifying the origin of sustainable products, monitoring supply chains, and implementing carbon credit programs.
- Renewable Energy and Energy Storage: Advancements in renewable energy sources, like solar and wind power, have been made possible by the emergence of new technologies. These technologies have not only contributed to a reduction in carbon emissions but also facilitated cleaner energy production. Additionally, the development of energy storage technologies, particularly advanced batteries, has enabled the efficient utilization of renewable energy. By storing excess power, these storage technologies ensure a steady supply of energy during periods of high demand.
- Quantum Computing: Quantum computing has the potential to revolutionize environmental research and problem-solving. It can accelerate complex simulations, optimize resource allocation, and enhance materials discovery, facilitating breakthroughs in sustainability-related fields like climate modeling and energy efficiency.
- Smart Grids: Smart grid technologies integrate IoT and data analytics to optimize the distribution of electricity. They enhance energy efficiency, reduce power losses, and incorporate renewable energy sources, leading to more sustainable energy systems.
- Clean Technologies: Emerging clean technologies, such as advanced water purification systems, air quality control, and waste-to-energy conversion, contribute to minimizing environmental impact and promoting sustainable practices in industries like manufacturing and waste management.

- Biotechnology and Genetic Engineering: Biotechnology provides innovative solutions for sustainable agriculture, including genetically modified crops that are more resilient to environmental challenges, biofuels production, and advanced techniques for soil and water conservation.
- Circular Economy: Embracing technologies that support a circular economy is crucial in reducing waste and conserving resources. These advancements encompass recycling, materials science, and product design to ensure products and materials are reused, recycled, and repurposed efficiently.
- Data Analytics and Visualization: Data analytics tools and visualization platforms enable organizations and governments to better understand environmental trends and challenges. They assist in decision-making, policy formulation, and the identification of opportunities for sustainability improvements.
- Eco-Friendly Transportation: Emerging technologies are driving the development of electric and autonomous vehicles, reducing carbon emissions and congestion in urban areas. These technologies promote sustainable transportation and improve air quality.
- Environmental Sensors and Remote Sensing: Advanced environmental sensors, coupled with satellite and remote sensing technologies, provide detailed data on climate change, deforestation, and habitat loss. They enable monitoring and conservation efforts, protecting natural ecosystems.

Incorporating these emerging technologies into smart environmental solutions allows for proactive and data-driven approaches to sustainability. These innovations contribute to the reduction of environmental harm, the conservation of resources, and the development of a more sustainable and resilient world. They are essential in addressing global environmental challenges and promoting a more responsible and eco-friendly future.

14.2.3 SUSTAINABLE DEVELOPMENT GOALS AND EMERGING TECHNOLOGY INTEGRATION

The integration of emerging technologies can significantly accelerate the achievement of the Sustainable Development Goals (SDGs), which were set by the United Nations to address poverty, protect the environment, and promote prosperity worldwide [10–12]. These technologies have the potential to accelerate progress toward the attainment of the SDGs by providing innovative solutions to complex global challenges. Here's how emerging technologies align with and contribute to the achievement of the SDGs, shown in Table 14.1.

Hence, the integration of emerging technologies into efforts to achieve the SDGs can enhance the impact of these goals by making solutions more efficient, scalable, and accessible. However, it is important to address issues of access, affordability, and ethical issues to ensure that technology benefits all and does not exacerbate existing inequalities. Collaborative partnerships and innovative approaches that use the power of these technologies are essential for driving progress toward a more sustainable and equitable world.

14.3 ARTIFICIAL INTELLIGENCE IN ENVIRONMENTAL MANAGEMENT FOR A SMART AND SUSTAINABLE FUTURE

AI has emerged as a powerful tool in environmental management, providing innovative solutions for a smart and sustainable future [1, 13]. Here are some key ways in which AI is being applied in this context:

- Environmental Monitoring and Data Analysis: AI-powered sensors and remote monitoring systems collect vast amounts of environmental data in real time, including air and water quality, weather conditions, and ecosystem health. AI algorithms analyze and process this

TABLE 14.1

SDGs with Their Descriptions Using Emerging Technologies

SDG Goal	Type	Description
No Poverty (SDG 1)	Financial Inclusion	Fintech and blockchain technologies have the potential to provide financial services to individuals who are unbanked or underprivileged, thereby fostering economic empowerment and alleviating poverty.
Zero Hunger (SDG 2)	Agricultural Technologies	AI, IoT, and biotechnology enhance crop monitoring, improve soil health, and optimize resource allocation in agriculture, leading to increased food production and reduced food waste.
Good Health and Well-being (SDG 3)	Telemedicine and e-Health	Telehealth, wearable devices, and AI-driven diagnostics enhance healthcare accessibility and quality, particularly in remote areas.
Quality Education (SDG 4)	E-Learning	Edtech platforms and AI-driven educational tools provide personalized and accessible education, bridging gaps in education and promoting lifelong learning.
Gender Equality (SDG 5)	Blockchain and Digital Identity	These technologies help establish secure and verifiable identities, contributing to women's empowerment and gender equality.
Clean Water and Sanitation (SDG 6)	IoT for Water Management	IoT sensors enable real-time monitoring of water quality and consumption, supporting efficient water resource management.
Affordable and Clean Energy (SDG 7)	Renewable Energy	Solar, wind, and various other renewable energy technologies play a crucial role in mitigating greenhouse gas emissions and expanding worldwide access to clean energy sources.
Decent Work and Economic Growth (SDG 8)	Digital Workforce and Gig Economy	The digital economy and the gig workforce are enabled by technology platforms, fostering economic growth and employment opportunities.
Industry, Innovation, and Infrastructure (SDG 9)	Advanced Manufacturing and Smart Infrastructure	Technologies like 3D printing, IoT, and smart grids support sustainable industrialization and infrastructure development.
Reduced Inequality (SDG 10)	Blockchain for Social Services	Blockchain can help ensure fair and transparent distribution of social benefits, reducing inequality.
Sustainable Cities and Communities (SDG 11)	Smart City Technologies	IoT, data analytics, and AI collectively enhance urban planning, energy efficiency, and transportation systems in smart cities, fostering a more efficient, sustainable, and connected urban environment.
Responsible Consumption and Production (SDG 12)	Circular Economy Technologies:	The adoption of IoT and data analytics plays a crucial role in facilitating the shift towards a circular economy, as it effectively minimizes waste and enhances resource efficiency.
Climate Action (SDG 13)	Renewable Energy and Climate Modeling	Renewable energy technologies and quantum computing facilitate climate change mitigation and adaptation efforts.
Life Below Water (SDG 14)	Marine Conservation Technologies	IoT and satellite monitoring enhance marine conservation and protection efforts.
Life on Land (SDG 15)	Environmental Monitoring	IoT and remote sensing technologies contribute to the preservation of terrestrial ecosystems and wildlife.
Peace, Justice, and Strong Institutions (SDG 16)	Blockchain for Transparency and Accountability:	Blockchain ensures transparency and accountability in governance and justice systems.
Partnerships for the Goals (SDG 17)	Data Sharing and Collaboration	Emerging technologies like AI, IoT, etc., facilitate global collaboration and data sharing among governments, organizations, and stakeholders to advance sustainable development efforts.

data to identify patterns, anomalies, and trends, enabling more informed decision-making in areas like pollution control, natural disaster management, and conservation efforts. This data-driven approach allows for timely interventions and proactive measures to mitigate environmental risks and protect natural habitats.

- Natural Resource Management: AI models optimize the use of natural resources, such as water and energy, by predicting demand, monitoring consumption, and suggesting conservation measures. Precision agriculture, driven by AI, enhances irrigation, crop management and pest control, leading to higher yields and reduced resource wastage. AI-powered smart grids and energy management systems intelligently distribute and optimize energy usage, minimizing waste and promoting sustainability.

- Waste Management and Recycling: AI-driven waste sorting systems automate the separation of recyclables from non-recyclables in waste processing facilities, increasing recycling rates and reducing landfill waste. AI-powered robotics and automation improve waste collection and recycling processes, making them more efficient and cost-effective.

- Renewable Energy: AI enhances the efficiency of renewable energy sources, such as solar and wind power, by predicting energy production, optimizing grid integration, and adjusting energy generation in response to weather conditions. AI-driven energy management systems in smart grids promote energy conservation and reduce grid congestion.

- Biodiversity and Conservation: AI supports wildlife protection by using drones, cameras, and acoustic monitoring to track and identify endangered species and detect poaching activities. AI algorithms analyze ecological data to inform conservation strategies, helping protect important habitats and biodiversity.

- Disaster Response and Mitigation: AI-powered predictive models analyze historical data and real-time information to forecast natural disasters like hurricanes, floods, and wildfires with increasing accuracy. AI-driven early warning systems analyze data from a range of sources such as satellite images, weather sensors, and social media in order to deliver prompt notifications to both authorities and the public. This enables better disaster preparedness, response, and evacuation plans, ultimately saving lives and minimizing the impact of these catastrophic events.

- Air and Water Quality Management: AI models process air and water quality data to identify pollution sources, assess health risks, and recommend pollution control measures. AI-equipped sensors in urban areas provide real-time air quality information, allowing residents to make informed decisions about outdoor activities.

- Smart Cities and Urban Planning: AI contributes to smart city initiatives by optimizing traffic management, reducing congestion, and promoting efficient public transportation systems. AI-powered urban planning tools help design more sustainable cities, with reduced energy consumption and improved waste management.

- Conservation Agriculture: AI-driven precision farming techniques enable farmers to minimize the use of pesticides and fertilizers, resulting in reduced environmental impact and healthier ecosystems. AI-powered drones and satellites provide detailed imagery for monitoring land use and crop health.

- Environmental Policy and Decision Support: AI facilitates data-driven policymaking by providing information from large datasets, helping governments and organizations make informed choices for sustainable development. AI-driven simulations and scenario analysis aid in assessing the environmental impact of policies and projects.

The integration of AI in environmental management not only enhances efficiency and accuracy but also empowers us to tackle complex and dynamic environmental challenges. As AI technologies continue to advance, they have the potential to drive innovation, promote sustainable practices, and contribute to a smarter and more sustainable future. However, it is crucial to address ethical and privacy concerns while ensuring that the benefits of AI are accessible to all and do not exacerbate existing inequalities.

14.4 BLOCKCHAIN TECHNOLOGY IN SUSTAINABILITY

Blockchain technology provides innovative solutions in the pursuit of sustainability by promoting transparency, accountability, and efficiency in various areas [14, 15]. Here are key ways in which blockchain is applied in sustainability:

- Supply Chain Transparency: Blockchain technology revolutionizes supply chains by providing complete visibility from start to finish, enabling consumers and organizations to trace the origins, manufacturing, and distribution of goods. This level of transparency ensures ethical trade practices and mitigates the risk of environmental exploitation. By securely documenting every stage of the supply chain on an unchangeable and decentralized ledger, blockchain establishes a trustworthy and auditable record of a product's entire journey. This empowers consumers to make well-informed decisions, encourages businesses to adopt sustainable methods, and fosters accountability across the supply chain. As blockchain continues to advance, it has the potential to transform global trade and foster a more sustainable and fair economy.
- Carbon Emissions Tracking: Blockchain-based systems record and verify carbon emissions data from various sources, including companies and governments. This helps in creating carbon credits, which can be traded on blockchain-based platforms to incentivize emission reduction efforts.
- Renewable Energy Trading: Blockchain enables direct trading of surplus renewable energy between solar or wind energy producers and nearby consumers in microgrids, encouraging the adoption of sustainable energy and alleviating strain on the grid.
- Environmental Credits and Incentives: Blockchain verifies and records environmental credits, such as Renewable Energy Certificates (RECs) and carbon offsets. These credits can be easily bought, sold, and traded, promoting the adoption of sustainable practices.
- Circular Economy: Blockchain supports the concept of a circular economy by enabling the traceability and authentication of products' origins and materials. This encourages recycling and repurposing, reducing waste and promoting resource efficiency.
- Conservation and Wildlife Protection: Blockchain helps combat illegal wildlife trade by recording and verifying the authenticity of products derived from protected species. It aids in tracking and combating poaching and trafficking activities.
- Land and Resource Management: Blockchain-based land registries and smart contracts streamline land and resource management, reducing disputes and fraud. This transparency promotes sustainable land use and conservation.
- Eco-Friendly Certification: Blockchain-based platforms enable businesses to obtain and verify eco-friendly certifications, ensuring that products meet specific sustainability criteria.
- Philanthropy and Charitable Giving: Blockchain enhances transparency in charitable donations by allowing donors to track the use of their contributions. This encourages trust and ensures that funds are allocated to sustainable and impactful projects.
- Ethical and Fair Trade: Blockchain verifies the authenticity of fair trade products and ensures that producers receive a fair share of profits. This promotes ethical and sustainable trade practices.
- Water Management: Blockchain-based systems monitor and manage water usage, promoting responsible water consumption and efficient water resource allocation.
- Sustainable Fisheries: Blockchain helps track the provenance of seafood products, verifying their origins and ensuring compliance with sustainability standards. This promotes sustainable fishing practices and marine conservation.

- Food Safety and Traceability: Blockchain records the journey of food products from farm to table, reducing the risk of contamination and promoting responsible food production and distribution.
- Disaster Relief and Aid Distribution: Blockchain can enhance the efficiency and transparency of aid distribution during environmental disasters, ensuring that resources reach affected communities promptly.
- Research and Data Sharing: Blockchain securely stores and shares environmental data, supporting collaborative research efforts and data-driven sustainability initiatives.

Hence, blockchain technology's immutability, transparency, and security make it a valuable tool in ensuring that sustainability efforts are transparent, efficient, and accountable. By facilitating responsible practices and incentivizing sustainability, blockchain contributes to a more eco-friendly and sustainable future.

14.5   INTERNET OF THINGS IN ENVIRONMENTAL SENSING FOR A SMART AND SUSTAINABLE FUTURE

The Internet of Things assumes a crucial function in environmental sensing to pave the way for a smart and sustainable future through its ability to gather real-time data, conduct analysis, and facilitate decision-making processes [15–17]. IoT sensors and devices are deployed in various environmental contexts to monitor and manage natural resources, reduce waste, and promote sustainability. Here's how IoT contributes to environmental sensing:

- Air Quality Monitoring: IoT sensors measure air pollutants such as particulate matter, ozone, and nitrogen dioxide. Real-time data enables cities to manage air quality, enforce pollution controls, and provide residents with air quality information.
- Water Quality Management: IoT devices monitor water parameters like pH levels, turbidity, and contaminants in lakes, rivers, and oceans. This data is used for early warning systems, pollution detection, and water treatment plant optimization.
- Waste Management: Waste bins connected to IoT technology can sense when they are full, leading to more efficient waste collection routes that reduce fuel usage and carbon emissions. Additionally, these systems can help prevent overflowing bins and littering.
- Smart Agriculture: IoT sensors are employed to oversee soil moisture, temperature, and nutrient levels, enabling enhanced irrigation and fertilizer utilization. This technology promotes precision agriculture, minimizing resource wastage and encouraging sustainable farming methods.
- Biodiversity Conservation: IoT devices like camera traps and acoustic sensors are deployed to monitor wildlife and ecosystems. The data collected from these sensors plays a crucial role in conservation initiatives, wildlife protection, and habitat management.
- Forest and Wildfire Monitoring: IoT sensors in forests and wilderness areas detect temperature, humidity, and smoke levels. They provide early wildfire warnings and assist in forest management.
- Environmental Noise Measurement: IoT sensors monitor noise pollution in urban areas. This data helps cities implement noise control measures and improve the quality of life for residents.
- Smart Water Management: Utilizing IoT-enabled water meters and sensors aids in the effective management of water resources by identifying leaks, tracking usage, and enhancing water distribution. This results in decreased water wastage and increased operational efficiency.
- Ocean and Marine Monitoring: IoT buoys and sensors play a crucial role in monitoring ocean conditions, weather trends, and marine ecosystems. This data is vital for promoting

sustainable fishing practices, accurate weather predictions, and conservation initiatives for marine life.

- Weather and Climate Data Collection: IoT networks collect real-time weather and climate data. This information supports climate research, early warning systems, and resilience planning.
- Smart Energy Grids: IoT sensors and meters in smart grids monitor energy consumption, grid stability, and power quality. These systems promote energy efficiency and integrate renewable energy sources.
- Urban Environmental Sensing: IoT devices in smart cities monitor temperature, humidity, pollution, and traffic. They assist in urban planning, traffic management, and energy conservation.
- Ecosystem Health Monitoring: IoT-enabled drones and remote sensors capture data on ecosystem health. This information aids in land and wildlife management and informs conservation strategies.
- Disaster Preparedness: IoT sensors in disaster-prone areas detect seismic activity, floods, and other natural disasters. This early warning data helps governments and communities prepare and respond effectively.
- Remote Environmental Sensing: IoT networks in remote and inhospitable environments, such as the Arctic or deserts, provide valuable data for climate studies and research.

The combination of IoT and data analytics allows for comprehensive and real-time monitoring of environmental conditions. This data-driven approach enables timely decision-making, efficient resource management, and sustainable practices, ultimately contributing to a smarter and more eco-friendly future.

14.6   CLOUD COMPUTING FOR SCALABILITY AND DATA MANAGEMENT

Cloud computing is instrumental in providing scalable and efficient data management solutions [1, 18]. It provides a range of services and resources that make it easier for organizations to store, process, and manage their data. Here's how cloud computing contributes to scalability and data management:

Scalability:

- Elasticity: Cloud platforms like Amazon Web Services (AWS), Microsoft Azure, and Google Cloud offer flexible and adaptable computing resources. This implies that businesses can easily adjust their resources to meet changing workloads and data storage needs. Whether it's managing sudden surges in users or adapting to seasonal variations, the cloud enables seamless scaling without requiring significant infrastructure investments.
- Auto-Scaling: Cloud providers offer auto-scaling capabilities, automatically adjusting resources based on demand. This ensures optimal performance without the need for manual intervention.
- Global Reach: Cloud services have data centers located worldwide. This global presence enables organizations to effectively reach international audiences and efficiently scale their services across different regions.

Data Storage:

- Highly Available Storage: Cloud platforms provide reliable and highly available storage services. Data is often replicated across multiple data centers to ensure redundancy and resilience against hardware failures.

- Scalable Storage Solutions: Organizations have the flexibility to select from a range of scalable storage solutions, including object storage, file storage, and database services. This allows them to easily expand their storage capacity as their data grows.
- Data Backup and Disaster Recovery: Cloud providers like Amazon Web Services, Microsoft Azure, and Google Cloud offer integrated backup and disaster recovery solutions. These solutions ensure that data is automatically backed up and can be restored in case of unforeseen data loss or system failures. This helps businesses maintain continuity and minimize any potential downtime.

Data Processing and Analytics:

- Big Data and Analytics Services: Big Data and Analytics Services: Cloud platforms offer a range of tools and services designed to handle and analyze massive datasets. AWS EMR, Google BigQuery, and Azure Data Lake Analytics are examples of services that enable organizations to perform advanced data analytics in the cloud, enabling them to derive valuable insights and make informed decisions based on comprehensive data analysis.
- Serverless Computing: Platforms for serverless computing, such as AWS Lambda and Azure Functions, allow organizations to run code in response to events without the need to manage servers. This approach streamlines real-time data processing and enables quick responses to changing data patterns, ultimately improving agility and efficiency in data-driven operations.

Data Security:

- Data Encryption: Cloud providers ensure data protection by offering encryption both in transit and at rest. This safeguards data from unauthorized access and breaches, maintaining the confidentiality and integrity of sensitive information [19, 20].
- Identity and Access Management: Cloud platforms have robust identity and access management (IAM) services that allow organizations to control who can access their data and services. These IAM tools enable granular access control, multi-factor authentication, and activity logging, enhancing overall security posture.
- Compliance and Certification: Cloud providers comply with industry standards and certifications, streamlining the process for organizations to meet regulatory and compliance obligations. This encompasses adherence to frameworks like SOC, ISO, and HIPAA, as well as region-specific regulations. By utilizing cloud services, organizations can prioritize their primary operations while guaranteeing compliance through the provider's certifications and controls.

Data Integration and Extract, Transform, Load (ETL):

- Integration Services: Cloud platforms provide services and tools for data integration and ETL processes, making it easier to connect data from various sources and transform it into usable formats.
- Data Pipelines: Organizations can build data pipelines to automate the movement and transformation of data, ensuring that data is processed efficiently and delivered to the right destinations.

Cost Optimization:

- Pay-as-You-Go Pricing: Cloud computing functions on a pay-as-you-go pricing model, ensuring that organizations are charged only for the resources they utilize. This method proves advantageous in efficiently managing data and workloads by eliminating the necessity for upfront capital investments and enabling accurate cost distribution.

- Cost Management Tools: Cloud platforms offer tools for cost management and optimization, aiding organizations in overseeing and regulating their cloud expenses. These tools facilitate immediate cost monitoring, budget planning, and future cost projections, empowering businesses to make well-informed choices regarding their cloud utilization and enhance cost efficiency.

Cloud computing plays a vital role in contemporary data management by providing the necessary agility, flexibility, and cost-efficiency to effectively manage the increasing volume and complexity of data. Utilizing cloud services allows organizations to concentrate on their data-related goals without the hassle of overseeing extensive infrastructure, thereby guaranteeing scalability, data security, and streamlined data management.

14.7   QUANTUM COMPUTING'S ROLE IN SUSTAINABILITY

Quantum computing has the potential to play an important role in advancing sustainability efforts in several ways:

- Optimizing Energy and Resource Management: Quantum algorithms can solve complex optimization problems that arise in energy and resource management more efficiently than classical computers. This includes optimizing the distribution of renewable energy in smart grids, minimizing energy consumption in manufacturing, and managing resource allocation in agriculture and water management. Quantum computing can help reduce waste, improve efficiency, and contribute to sustainable resource use.
- Climate Modeling and Prediction: Quantum computers can simulate and analyze complex climate models with unprecedented speed and accuracy. This capability is essential for understanding and predicting climate change, extreme weather events, and their impacts. Accurate climate models are for informed decision-making in sustainability and climate adaptation efforts.
- Materials Science and Sustainable Materials Discovery: Quantum computing can accelerate materials discovery processes, enabling the development of more sustainable and eco-friendly materials. This includes materials for energy storage, renewable energy, and lightweight, durable materials that reduce environmental impact. By rapidly simulating material properties and behavior, quantum computing supports innovation in sustainable materials.
- Optimizing Supply Chains: Quantum algorithms can optimize supply chains by efficiently solving complex routing, scheduling, and logistics problems. This reduces transportation and inventory costs, resulting in lower energy consumption and reduced environmental impact. Sustainable supply chain management becomes more achievable with quantum-powered optimization.
- Carbon Capture and Sequestration: Quantum computing can enhance the modeling and simulation of carbon capture and sequestration processes. This technology can help develop more effective strategies for capturing and storing carbon dioxide, mitigating greenhouse gas emissions.
- Clean Energy Production and Storage: Quantum computing can advance research in clean energy technologies, such as advanced photovoltaics, batteries, and superconductors. It enables the efficient simulation of molecular and atomic structures, which is important for designing more efficient and sustainable energy solutions.
- Optimizing Transportation and Traffic Management: Quantum algorithms can improve traffic management and transportation systems, reducing congestion and fuel consumption. This contributes to sustainability by minimizing the environmental impact of transportation.
- Water Resource Management: Quantum computing can optimize water resource management by solving complex hydrological and groundwater flow problems. This is essential

for ensuring sustainable access to clean water and preventing water-related environmental challenges.

- Waste Reduction and Recycling: Quantum computing has the capability to enhance waste management procedures, including recycling and converting waste into energy. By leveraging quantum algorithms, quantum computers can analyze complex waste management systems and identify optimal strategies for reducing waste, increasing recycling rates, and improving energy recovery from waste. This can lead to the development of more efficient and sustainable waste reduction strategies, minimizing the environmental impact of waste while maximizing resource recovery and energy generation. As quantum computing continues to advance, it promises to play a significant role in transforming the waste management industry and contributing to a more circular economy.
- Environmental Data Analysis and Decision Support: Quantum computing can process vast amounts of environmental data in real time, enabling better-informed decisions in areas like disaster response, conservation, and pollution control. It enhances the ability to monitor and respond to environmental changes effectively.

Therefore, it is essential to recognize that despite the significant potential of quantum computing in promoting sustainability, the technology is still in its nascent phase and faces numerous technical hurdles. Nevertheless, as advancements continue, quantum computing has the potential to greatly enhance sustainability efforts by offering groundbreaking solutions and capabilities to tackle complex environmental and resource management issues.

14.8 INTEGRATION OF EMERGING TECHNOLOGIES FOR A SUSTAINABLE ENVIRONMENT

14.8.1 SYNERGY BETWEEN AI, BLOCKCHAIN, IoT, CLOUD, AND QUANTUM COMPUTING—IN GENERAL

The synergy between AI, blockchain, IoT, cloud computing, and quantum computing represents a powerful convergence of technologies that has the potential to transform industries and drive innovation [1, 21–23]. Here's an overview of how these technologies work together to create value:

Data Integration and Analysis:

- IoT and Sensors: IoT devices collect vast amounts of data from the physical world, such as environmental data, machine sensor data, and consumer behavior data.
- Cloud Computing: The cloud provides storage and processing capabilities to handle the massive data generated by IoT devices.
- AI: AI algorithms can analyze and extract meaningful information from IoT data, providing valuable information for decision-making.
- Blockchain: Data from IoT devices can be securely and transparently stored in blockchain ledgers, ensuring data integrity and authenticity.

Security and Trust:

- Blockchain: Blockchain provides a secure and tamper-resistant ledger for recording IoT device data and transactions.
- Quantum Computing: Quantum computing can enhance cryptographic techniques to ensure the security and privacy of data transmitted between IoT devices.

Smart Contracts:

- Blockchain: Smart contracts are agreements that are stored on the blockchain and can automatically execute and enforce the terms of transactions and data-sharing agreements related to the Internet of Things.
- AI: AI can analyze smart contract data to optimize performance and predict potential issues.

Supply Chain Management:

- IoT and Sensors: IoT sensors offer immediate insight into the supply chain, monitoring the whereabouts and status of products.
- Blockchain: Blockchain verifies the authenticity and origin of products, promoting transparency and traceability.
- AI: AI analyzes supply chain data to identify inefficiencies and predict disruptions.

Energy Management:

- IoT: IoT sensors monitor energy consumption and environmental conditions in buildings and factories.
- AI: AI analyzes data to optimize energy use and reduce waste.
- Cloud Computing: Cloud-based energy management systems store and process data for remote monitoring and control.

Environmental Sensing:

- IoT: IoT devices collect environmental data, such as air quality and temperature.
- AI: AI processes this data for real-time monitoring and predictive analytics.
- Quantum Computing: Quantum computing can enhance climate modeling and environmental simulations for more accurate predictions.

Healthcare and Medical IoT:

- IoT and Sensors: Medical IoT devices collect patient data and monitor health conditions.
- Cloud Computing: The cloud securely stores and processes health data.
- AI: AI analyzes health data to provide information and personalized healthcare recommendations.
- Blockchain: Patient records can be stored in a secure and interoperable blockchain, ensuring data integrity and privacy.

Financial Services:

- Blockchain: Blockchain enables secure and transparent financial transactions.
- AI: AI algorithms can assess financial data and automate decision-making.
- Quantum Computing: Quantum computing can enhance encryption and security for financial transactions.

The incorporation of these technologies presents fresh possibilities for advancement and productivity in various industries such as supply chain management, healthcare, finance, energy, and environmental monitoring. Although the collaboration between these technologies offers great promise, it also brings up important issues regarding privacy, security, and data management. As organizations adapt to the changing landscape of technology, they must address intricate challenges and seize opportunities to maximize their benefits.

14.8.2 CASE STUDIES OF SUCCESSFUL INTEGRATIONS OF EMERGING TECHNOLOGIES TOWARDS A SMART AND SUSTAINABLE FUTURE

There are several case studies of successful integrations of emerging technologies for a smart and sustainable future. Here are a few notable examples:

A. Smart Grids for Energy Efficiency:
   Case Study: Pacific Gas and Electric (PG&E)
   Technologies: IoT, AI, Cloud Computing
   Description: PG&E, a utility company based in California, has implemented a smart grid system that integrates IoT sensors and AI analytics. This system allows for real-time monitoring of the electrical grid, fault detection, and optimized energy distribution. The smart grid reduces energy waste, lowers operational costs, and improves the integration of renewable energy sources.

B. Sustainable Agriculture with Precision Farming:
   Case Study: John Deere
   Technologies: IoT, AI, Cloud Computing
   Description: John Deere, a renowned agricultural equipment manufacturer, has introduced innovative precision farming solutions. By utilizing IoT sensors, information regarding soil quality, weather conditions, and crop health is collected, and then analyzed by AI algorithms. This empowers farmers to optimize planting, irrigation, and fertilization processes, leading to increased crop yields and reduced resource consumption.

C. Blockchain for Supply Chain Transparency:
   Case Study: IBM Food Trust
   Technologies: Blockchain, IoT, AI
   Description: IBM Food Trust utilizes blockchain technology to track the progression of food items from their origin on the farm to the final destination on the table. Throughout the supply chain, IoT sensors gather data, and AI analytics identify potential problems like contamination or spoilage. By scanning a QR code, consumers gain access to comprehensive details regarding the product's source and journey, thereby improving transparency and ensuring food safety.

D. Smart Cities for Urban Sustainability:
   Case Study: Barcelona, Spain
   Technologies: IoT, AI, Cloud Computing
   Description: Barcelona transformed itself into a smart city by deploying thousands of IoT sensors throughout the city. These sensors monitor traffic, waste management, and environmental conditions. AI analyzes the data to optimize traffic flow, reduce energy consumption, and improve waste collection, contributing to urban sustainability.

E. Healthcare and Telemedicine:
   Case Study: Teladoc Health
   Technologies: AI, Cloud Computing, Telemedicine
   Description: Teladoc Health provides telehealth services that use AI for medical diagnostics and patient care. Patients can connect with healthcare providers remotely, reducing the need for physical visits. This approach improves healthcare accessibility, reduces travel-related emissions, and enhances healthcare efficiency.

F. Renewable Energy Grid Management:
   Case Study: NextEra Energy

Technologies: IoT, AI, Cloud Computing

Description: NextEra Energy, a prominent player in the renewable energy sector, employs IoT sensors to oversee the operations of wind and solar farms. By leveraging AI algorithms, they are able to forecast energy generation and effectively incorporate renewable energy sources into the power grid. This strategic approach not only diminishes reliance on fossil fuels but also contributes to the reduction of greenhouse gas emissions.

G. Smart Water Management:

Case Study: DC Water

Technologies: IoT, Cloud Computing

Description: DC Water, the water utility for Washington, DC, implemented a smart water management system. IoT sensors collect data on water quality, consumption, and infrastructure. Cloud computing processes the data to detect leaks, optimize water distribution, and improve water quality. This sustainable approach conserves water and reduces energy use.

H. Environmental Conservation with AI and Drones:

Case Study: The Nature Conservancy

Technologies: AI, Drones

Description: The Nature Conservancy employs AI and drones to monitor and protect natural reserves. Drones equipped with cameras capture data on wildlife and vegetation. AI algorithms analyze this data to inform conservation strategies and protect ecosystems.

These case studies illustrate how integrating emerging technologies can result in significant enhancements in sustainability, efficiency, and quality of life. They emphasize the crucial role of data analytics and real-time monitoring in making informed decisions and developing smart, sustainable solutions. Additional use cases include smart cities and urban planning, ecosystem conservation and biodiversity, and climate change mitigation and adaptation.

14.9   OPEN ISSUES, CHALLENGES, AND FUTURE INNOVATIONS/ OPPORTUNITIES FOR MAKING A SMART AND SUSTAINABLE FUTURE

Today, creating a smart and sustainable future is a complex and ongoing endeavor, and it's important to address the various challenges and open issues while looking forward to future innovations and opportunities [11, 15, 20, 24]. Here are some of the key challenges, open issues, and potential areas for future innovation in this context:

Issue in Environmental Sustainability:

- Climate Change: Mitigating climate change remains a important challenge, requiring global cooperation and significant reductions in greenhouse gas emissions.
- Resource Management/Resource Scarcity: Addressing resource scarcity, such as water and rare minerals, is a pressing issue, necessitating sustainable practices and recycling.
- Biodiversity and Conservation/Loss of Biodiversity: Protecting and conserving biodiversity, including endangered species and ecosystems, remains a challenge.
- Energy Transition/Transition to Clean Energy: Accelerating the transition to renewable and clean energy sources while phasing out fossil fuels is a key challenge.
- Waste Management/Waste Reduction: Achieving sustainable waste management and reducing landfill waste are ongoing challenges.
- Environmental Pollution/Air and Water Quality: Addressing air and water pollution and their health impacts on communities is important.

- Infrastructure and Transportation/Sustainable Transportation: Developing sustainable and efficient transportation systems, including public transit and electric vehicles, is a challenge.
- Sustainable Agriculture/Food Security: Ensuring global food security while minimizing the environmental impact of agriculture is an open issue.
- Economic and Social Equity/Sustainable Development Goals: Ensuring that sustainability efforts address economic and social equity is a priority.

Technological Challenges:

- Quantum Computing: Developing practical quantum computing solutions to address sustainability challenges.
- Blockchain Scalability: Enhancing blockchain scalability and energy efficiency.
- AI Ethical Issues: Addressing ethical issues related to AI decision-making in sustainability.
- IoT Security: Enhancing security in IoT devices to protect data and infrastructure.

Future Innovations and Opportunities:

- Renewable Energy Advancements: Innovations in energy storage, next-generation solar panels, and wind turbine technologies will advance clean energy production.
- Circular Economy Solutions: Circular economy models that prioritize recycling and sustainable product design will become more widespread.
- Smart Cities and Transportation: Smart city initiatives, including efficient public transportation and smart traffic management, will reduce urban congestion and emissions.
- Data-Driven Sustainability: Advanced data analytics and AI will provide more accurate information for sustainable decision-making.
- Climate Innovation: Innovations in carbon capture and sequestration, climate adaptation, and climate-resilient technologies will help combat climate change.
- Sustainable Agriculture Technologies: Precision agriculture, vertical farming, and genetic engineering for crops will contribute to sustainable food production.
- Environmental Restoration: Innovative approaches to ecosystem restoration and reforestation will help restore and conserve natural habitats.
- Global Collaboration: International cooperation, agreements, and alliances will drive global sustainability efforts.
- Technological Convergence: Convergence of emerging technologies, such as AI, IoT, blockchain, and quantum computing, will provide new solutions for sustainability challenges.
- Education and Awareness: Increasing public awareness and education about sustainable practices will foster positive behavioral changes.
- Inclusive Sustainable Solutions: Prioritizing social equity and ensuring that sustainability efforts benefit all segments of society.
- Sustainable Finance: The growth of sustainable finance and green investments will fund projects and initiatives that promote sustainability.
- Government Policies and Regulations: Strengthening and enforcing regulations and policies that support sustainability efforts.

Hence, creating a smart and sustainable future requires a multidisciplinary and collaborative approach involving governments, industries, communities, and individuals. Innovations in technology, sustainable practices, and a commitment to addressing open issues and challenges are essential for achieving these goals.

14.10 CONCLUSION

The combination of AI, blockchain, IoT, cloud computing, and quantum computing presents an innovative strategy for developing an intelligent and eco-friendly ecosystem. This fusion of technologies has the power to address intricate problems and shape a future that is not only more effective and resilient but also environmentally conscious. Moreover, this initiative tackles ethical and social considerations, such as data protection and fair access to technology. To sum up, the integration of AI, blockchain, IoT, cloud computing, and quantum computing shows great potential in nurturing an intelligent and sustainable environment. It signifies a shift in how technology can be utilized to combat environmental issues and promote a fairer and eco-friendly world. This analysis concludes that this technological amalgamation could transform our relationship with our environment, offering fresh solutions to enduring environmental challenges and contributing to a more responsible and sustainable use of resources. Despite persistent obstacles, this forward-thinking approach holds the promise of a brighter, cleaner, and more sustainable future for future generations.

REFERENCES

1. Nair, M. M., & Tyagi, A. K. (2023). Chapter 11—AI, IoT, blockchain, and cloud computing: The necessity of the future. In R. Pandey, S. Goundar, & S. Fatima (Eds.), *Distributed Computing to Blockchain* (pp. 189–206). Academic Press. ISBN: 9780323961462. https://doi.org/10.1016/B978-0-323-96146-2.00001-2.

2. Duan, H. (2022). The principles, algorithms and state-of-art applications of quantum computing. *Journal of Physics: Conference Series*, 2386. 012025. https://doi.org/10.1088/1742–6596/2386/1/012025.

3. Fei, S-M., Li, M., & Luo, S. (2023). Quantum information and computation. *Entropy*, 25, 463. https://doi.org/10.3390/e25030463.

4. Arute, F. et al. (2021). Quantum approximate optimization of non-planar graph problems on a planar superconducting processor. *Nature Physics*, 17(3), 340–345. www.nature.com/articles/s41567-020-01105-x

5. Wecker, D. et al. (2020). Progress and prospects for quantum supremacy in computing. *Frontiers in Physics*, 8, 660. www.frontiersin.org/articles/10.3389/fphy.2020.00660/full

6. Susindhar A. V., Soni, G., & Tyagi, A. K. (2023). A review on recent trends in quantum computation technology. In A. Tyagi (Ed.), *Handbook of Research on Quantum Computing for Smart Environments* (pp. 48–64). IGI Global. https://doi.org/10.4018/978-1-6684-6697-1.ch003

7. Sasi, P., Soni, G., Tyagi, A. K., Kakulapati, V., Shyam Mohan J. S., & Singh, R. K. (2023). Quantum computing and the qubit: The future of artificial intelligence. In A. Tyagi (Ed.), *Handbook of Research on Quantum Computing for Smart Environments* (pp. 231–244). IGI Global. https://doi.org/10.4018/978-1-6684-6697-1.ch013

8. Tyagi, A. K. (Ed.). (2023). *Handbook of Research on Quantum Computing for Smart Environments*. IGI Global. https://doi.org/10.4018/978-1-6684-6697-1

9. Deekshetha, H. R., & Tyagi, A. K. (2023). Chapter 16—Automated and intelligent systems for next-generation-based smart applications. In A. K. Tyagi & A. Abraham (Eds.), *Data Science for Genomics* (pp. 265–276). Academic Press. https://doi.org/10.1016/B978-0-323-98352-5.00019-7.

10. Tyagi, A. K. (2022). *Handbook of Research on Technical, Privacy, and Security Challenges in a Modern World*. IGI Global. https://doi.org/10.4018/978-1-6684-5250-9

11. Gomathi, L., Mishra, A. K., & Tyagi, A. K. (2023). Blockchain and machine learning empowered internet of things applications: Current issues, challenges and future research opportunities. In *2023 4th International Conference on Smart Electronics and Communication (ICOSEC)*, Trichy, India (pp. 637–647). https://doi.org/10.1109/ICOSEC58147.2023.10276385.

12. Nair, M. M., & Tyagi, A. K. (2023). Blockchain technology for next-generation society: Current trends and future opportunities for smart era. In *Blockchain Technology for Secure Social Media Computing*. https://doi.org/10.1049/PBSE019E_ch11.

13. Gomathi, L., Mishra, A. K., & Tyagi, A. K. (2023). Industry 5.0 for Healthcare 5.0: Opportunities, challenges and future research possibilities. In *2023 7th International Conference on Trends in Electronics and Informatics (ICOEI)*, Tirunelveli, India (pp. 204–213). https://doi.org/10.1109/ICOEI56765.2023.10125660.

14. Deshmukh, A., Patil, D. S., Pawar, P. D., Kumari, S., & Muthulakshmi, P. (2023). Recent trends for smart environments with AI and IoT-based technologies: A comprehensive review. In A. Tyagi (Ed.), *Handbook*

of Research on Quantum Computing for Smart Environments (pp. 435–452). IGI Global. https://doi.org/ 10.4018/978-1-6684-6697-1.ch023

15. Tyagi, A. K., Dananjayan, S., Agarwal, D., & Thariq Ahmed, H. F. (2023). Blockchain—Internet of Things applications: Opportunities and challenges for Industry 4.0 and Society 5.0. *Sensors*, 23(2), 947. https://doi.org/10.3390/s23020947

16. Goyal, D., & Tyagi, A. (2020). *A Look at Top 35 Problems in the Computer Science Field for the Next Decade*. https://doi.org/10.1201/9781003052098-40.

17. Pramod, A., Naicker, H. S., & Tyagi, A. K. (2022). Emerging innovations in the near future using deep learning techniques. In *Advanced Analytics and Deep Learning Models*. Wiley Scrivener. https://doi. org/10.1002/9781119792437.ch10

18. Gheorghiu, V. et al. (2021). Quantum computing: An overview of recent progress. *Annual Review of Condensed Matter Physics*, 12, 247–271. www.annualreviews.org/doi/abs/10.1146/annurev-conmatphys-121919-050502.

19. Sharma, A. (2021). *A Textbook on Modern Quantum Mechanics*. https://doi.org/10.1201/9781003154457.

20. Tyagi, A. K. (2023). Chapter 2—Decentralized everything: Practical use of blockchain technology in future applications. In R. Pandey, S. Goundar, & S. Fatima (Eds.), *Distributed Computing to Blockchain* (pp. 19–38). Academic Press. ISBN: 9780323961462, https://doi.org/10.1016/B978-0-323-96146-2.00010-3.

21. Flarend, A., & Hilborn, B. (2022). *Quantum Gates and Quantum Circuits*. https://doi.org/10.1093/ oso/9780192857972.003.0006.

22. Griffiths, D., & Schroeter, D. (2018). *Introduction to Quantum Mechanics*. https://doi.org/10.1017/ 9781316995433.

23. Tyagi, A., Kukreja, S., Nair, M. M., & Tyagi, A. K. (2022). Machine learning: Past, present and future. *Neuroquantology*, 20(8). https://doi.org/10.14704/nq.2022.20.8.NQ44468

24. Yanofsky, N., & Mannucci, M. (2008). *Quantum Computing for Computer Scientists*. https://doi.org/ 10.1017/CBO9780511813887.

15 Quantum Computing for Next-Generation Artificial Intelligence–Based Blockchain

Senthil Kumar Arumugam, Shabnam Kumari,
Shrikant Tiwari, and Amit Kumar Tyagi

15.1 INTRODUCTION—FUNDAMENTALS OF QUANTUM COMPUTING, AI AND BLOCKCHAIN TECHNOLOGY

15.1.1 QUANTUM BITS, QUANTUM CRYPTOGRAPHY, AND QUANTUM SUPREMACY

In this section, we will discuss quantum bits (qubits), quantum cryptography, and quantum supremacy in brief:

- Quantum Bits: A quantum bit is the fundamental unit of measurement in quantum computing. Due to a phenomenon known as superposition, qubits can exist in several states simultaneously, in contrast to traditional bits, which can only be either 0 or 1 [1]. Because of this characteristic, quantum computers can store and process data very differently from classical computers. Qubits can also be entangled, which implies that even when they are physically separated, the states of one qubit and another depend on one another. For a number of quantum applications, such as quantum cryptography and quantum computing, this entanglement feature is crucial.
- Quantum Cryptography: This branch of cryptography employs the ideas of quantum mechanics to offer incredibly safe techniques for data transmission and protection.
- Quantum Key Distribution (QKD): The most-used method of quantum cryptography. It involves employing qubits to exchange cryptographic keys. The uncertainty principle and the no-cloning theorem, two fundamental ideas of quantum physics, provide the foundation for QKD's security. With QKD, eavesdroppers cannot hide their presence, and any effort to intercept the quantum keys will be flagged as compromised communication.
- Quantum-Safe Cryptography: The advancement of quantum computers necessitates the development and application of cryptography solutions that are resistant to quantum machine attacks. To solve this problem, post-quantum cryptography uses techniques like lattice- and code-based cryptography. Unprecedented security levels are promised by quantum cryptography, which makes it especially useful for safeguarding private data as well as sensitive information in a variety of contexts, such as financial transactions and official correspondence.
- Quantum Supremacy: A quantum computer's capacity to surpass the most sophisticated classical supercomputers in each task is quantum supremacy. This achievement is noteworthy because it shows how quantum computing may be used to solve issues that are presently insurmountable for conventional computers. With the release of the Sycamore quantum processor in 2019, Google asserted that it had attained quantum supremacy, outperforming classical supercomputers in a particular task. Quantum supremacy is not just a technological achievement; it also raises questions about the implications for cryptography.

DOI: 10.1201/9781003499459-15

With the potential computational power of quantum computers, the security of traditional encryption methods becomes an issue. This highlights the need for quantum-resistant cryptographic techniques to protect data and communications in a post-quantum computing era.

In summary, qubits are the fundamental units of quantum information with unique properties like superposition and entanglement. Quantum cryptography uses these properties to provide ultra-secure communication methods. Quantum supremacy represents a milestone in quantum computing where quantum machines surpass classical supercomputers in performing specific tasks, ushering in a new era of computational power and also raising security and encryption challenges.

15.1.2 BASICS OF BLOCKCHAIN, FEATURES, AND CHARACTERISTICS

Blockchain is a decentralized and distributed digital ledger technology that underlies cryptocurrencies like Bitcoin [2, 3], but it has a wide range of applications beyond just digital currencies. Here are the basics of blockchain, along with its key features and characteristics:

Features and Characteristics of Blockchain:

- Security: Blockchain protects data and transactions with cryptographic techniques. A block is almost impossible to remove or change once it is inserted into the chain.
- Immutability: Data recorded on a blockchain is immutable. Once a transaction is added to the ledger, it cannot be changed, ensuring the integrity of the data.
- Trustless System: Blockchain eliminates the need for trust in a central authority or intermediary. Transactions are validated by network consensus, making it a trustless system.
- Data Integrity: The data on a blockchain is stored in a distributed manner, which ensures data redundancy and integrity.
- Pseudonymity: Users on a blockchain are represented by cryptographic addresses rather than personal information, which provides a degree of privacy and pseudonymity.
- Immutable History: Every transaction is timestamped and linked to the previous one. This creates a complete, auditable history of transactions.
- Permissioned and Permissionless Blockchains: While permissionless blockchains let everybody join, permissioned blockchains limit access to authorized users only.
- Scalability Challenges: Blockchains face challenges related to scalability as the network grows, leading to discussions around improving scalability solutions.
- Energy Consumption: Public blockchains that use proof of work consensus mechanisms, like Bitcoin, can consume significant amounts of energy.

Understanding its basics and key features is essential for those looking to discuss its applications and implications.

15.1.3 CRYPTOGRAPHIC FOUNDATIONS AND ITS IMPORTANCE IN BLOCKCHAIN

Cryptographic foundations play an important role in blockchain technology, providing the security and privacy features that are central to its operation [2–4]. Here's an overview of the cryptographic foundations and their importance in blockchain:

- Hash Functions: In blockchain, hash functions are used to secure data within blocks and to link blocks together by including the hash of the previous block in each subsequent block. This ensures data integrity and immutability, as even a small change in the input data results in a largely different hash.

- Digital Signatures: They allow participants to sign transactions and verify their source. Blockchain uses public and private key pairs for creating digital signatures, ensuring that only the rightful owner of the private key can initiate transactions.
- Public-Key Cryptography: Public-key cryptography is fundamental to the security of blockchain. It enables participants to have a public key (used to receive funds) and a private key (used to sign transactions). The mathematical relationship between the keys ensures security and privacy in transactions.
- Merkle Trees: Merkle trees are used to efficiently verify the contents of a block. By hashing transactions in a specific tree structure, anyone can verify if a transaction is part of a block without having to process the entire block, enhancing the speed and efficiency of the network.
- Consensus Mechanisms: Various consensus mechanisms, such as proof of work (PoW) and proof of stake (PoS), use cryptographic processes to ensure that participants reach agreement on the order and validity of transactions. Cryptography, particularly PoW, is essential for network security and resistance to tampering.
- Secure Multi-Party Computation: This cryptographic technique enables multiple parties to perform calculations on their private data without revealing the data itself. In blockchain, it has applications in private or confidential transactions, enabling privacy while maintaining the integrity of the network.
- Zero-Knowledge Proofs: These types of proofs enable one side to demonstrate to another that a claim is true without disclosing any further details. In blockchain, this is used for privacy-preserving transactions and identity verification without disclosing sensitive data.
- Post-Quantum Cryptography: Post-quantum cryptography aims to develop cryptographic techniques that can withstand quantum attacks, ensuring the continued security of blockchain systems.

Hence, cryptographic foundations are paramount to the trust, security, and privacy of blockchain technology. They help ensure data integrity, confidentiality, and authentication in an environment where trust is maintained through mathematical and computational means rather than central authorities. The continued development and evolution of cryptographic techniques are essential for the long-term viability of blockchain in various applications.

15.1.4 Smart Contracts and Consensus Mechanisms

Smart contracts and consensus mechanisms are two fundamental components of blockchain technology, and they play distinct but interconnected roles in ensuring the security, reliability, and functionality of blockchain networks [4]. Here's an overview of each can be discussed as;

Smart Contracts: On a blockchain, it is programmable, and in essence, they are simply strings of code that, upon fulfilment of certain criteria or conditions, run automatically. Key features of smart contracts include the following:

- Automation: It can be configured to automatically carry out certain actions or agreements. Usually, these criteria are expressed as codes.
- Code-Based: Programming languages created especially for the blockchain are used to write smart contracts. Examples are Chaincode (used in Hyperledger Fabric) and Solidity (used in Ethereum).
- Trustless: By facilitating trustless interactions, they do away with the necessity for middlemen. Once deployed, the code runs independently of a third party and follows the rules.
- Transparency: Because smart contract code is kept on the blockchain, everyone involved in the network may view and audit it.

- Uses: There are many uses for smart contracts in the fields of finance, supply chain management, and law, such as escrow services, automated payments, and product tracking.
- Immutability: Smart contracts are unchangeable once they are implemented. This guarantees the terms and execution of the contract are intact.

Consensus Mechanisms: The protocols and techniques employed by blockchain networks to reach a consensus regarding the current state of the blockchain, including whether transactions are legitimate and what order they should be added to the ledger, are known as consensus mechanisms. Proof of work and proof of stake are two popular consensus techniques. The following are important details about consensus mechanisms:

- Performance: Different consensus mechanisms have varying impacts on the network's performance, scalability, and energy consumption. For example, PoW is known for its high energy consumption, while PoS is often considered more energy efficient.
- Decentralization: Consensus mechanisms influence the degree of decentralization in a blockchain network. PoW tends to promote decentralization, while PoS may lead to concentration of power among a few validators.
- Evolving Mechanisms: Blockchain projects may experiment with and adopt different consensus mechanisms or variations to optimize network performance and address specific use cases.

In summary, blockchain, while consensus mechanisms make sure the network is reliable and secure by achieving agreement on the state of the blockchain ledger. These two components work in tandem to create trustless and decentralized blockchain ecosystems with a wide range of applications.

15.1.5 Basics of Artificial Intelligence, Its Features and Characteristics

In computer science, artificial intelligence (AI) is the study of building robots and systems that can carry out operations that normally call for human intelligence [2]. Artificial intelligence systems are made to mimic human thought, learning, and problem-solving processes. The essential elements and traits of artificial intelligence are as follows:

Basics of AI:

- Machine Learning: This branch of artificial intelligence uses algorithms to help computers learn from data and make judgements or predictions. It is crucial to a lot of AI applications.
- Deep Learning: This branch of machine learning leverages artificial neural networks, which are modelled after the human brain, to address challenging issues. Particularly effective applications of deep learning include speech and picture recognition.
- Natural Language Processing (NLP): NLP is a subfield of artificial intelligence that aims to provide computers the ability to comprehend, translate, and produce human language.
- Computer Vision: This field focuses on educating machines to translate and comprehend visual data from the outside world, including pictures and movies.

Features and Characteristics of AI:

- Problem Solving: AI is designed to solve complex problems that require reasoning and decision-making. It can tackle a wide range of tasks, from chess games to medical diagnoses.
- Automation: AI systems can automate tasks and processes, reducing the need for human intervention. This is particularly valuable in repetitive or labor-intensive tasks.

- Data-Driven: AI relies on data for training and decision-making. The quality and quantity of data are essential factors in AI's performance.
- Pattern Recognition: AI excels at recognizing patterns in data, whether in images, text, or numerical information. This ability is important in various applications, including fraud detection and recommendation systems.
- Prediction and Inference: AI can make predictions and draw inferences based on data, even in situations with uncertainty.
- Scalability: AI systems can scale to handle large amounts of data and perform tasks quickly and efficiently.
- Human-Machine Interaction: AI systems can interact with humans through natural language, voice, or text, making them suitable for chatbots, virtual assistants, and customer service applications.
- Ethical Issues: The ethical use of AI is a growing issue. Ensuring fairness, transparency, and accountability in AI systems is important to avoid biases and discrimination.
- Adaptability and Evolution: This adaptability ensures that AI systems keep improving and extending their capabilities.

In summary, AI is a field of computer science that focuses on creating intelligent systems capable of learning, adapting, and solving complex problems. Its features and characteristics make it a versatile technology with applications across a wide range of industries and domains.

15.1.6 QUANTUM COMPUTING'S RELEVANCE TO AI BASED BLOCKCHAIN

The potential effects of quantum computing could be enormous for AI-based blockchain systems in various ways, though quantum computing for these applications is still in the early stages of development [5].

- Enhanced Security: The current blockchain technology's cryptographic underpinnings could be endangered by Shor's algorithm can break widely used encryption methods. To address this issue, quantum-resistant cryptography is being developed to secure blockchain systems in a post-quantum world.
- Improved Consensus Mechanisms: Quantum computing could contribute to the development of more efficient consensus mechanisms for blockchain networks. By solving complex problems at speeds unattainable by classical computers, quantum machines could enable faster consensus and validation processes. This could result in quicker confirmation of transactions and enhanced network scalability.
- Quantum-Safe Blockchains: Blockchain projects are exploring the integration of quantum-safe cryptography to ensure the long-term security of their networks. Quantum-resistant cryptographic techniques are being adopted to protect transactions and data from potential quantum attacks.
- Quantum Machine Learning (QML): Quantum computing could accelerate machine learning tasks on the blockchain, leading to smarter and more efficient AI models. Quantum machine learning algorithms may enable faster model training, improved predictive analytics, and enhanced data analysis on blockchain-based AI systems.
- Quantum-Secured Smart Contracts: Quantum-safe smart contracts could provide an extra layer of security for blockchain applications. These contracts would be resistant to quantum attacks, ensuring that the terms and execution of smart contracts remain secure even in a quantum-powered environment.
- Quantum Data Analysis: Quantum computing's ability to process large datasets efficiently can be used in blockchain-based AI systems for data analysis. This can lead to quicker and more accurate information, improving AI-driven decision-making processes.

- Quantum Key Distribution: The techniques can enhance the security of data and transactions on blockchain networks. QKD allows for the creation of ultra-secure encryption keys, making it highly challenging for any potential eavesdropper, including quantum computers, to compromise data security.
- Research and Development: Blockchain and AI researchers are actively improving the efficiency and capabilities of blockchain systems. This research contributes to the ongoing evolution of blockchain technology.

Note that we need to recognize that practical and widespread quantum computing for blockchain applications is still a developing field. As quantum technology advances, its relevance to AI-based blockchain systems will continue to grow. The integration of quantum computing in the blockchain space holds the promise of enhancing security, performance, and the overall functionality of blockchain networks, benefiting various industries and applications. However, it also raises important issues regarding the potential impact of quantum technology on the future of blockchain systems.

15.1.7 ORGANIZATION OF THE WORK

This work is summarized in eight sections.

15.2 EFFECTS OF QUANTUM COMPUTING ON BLOCKCHAIN

The possible effects of quantum computing include blockchain technology in several significant ways, both positively and negatively. Here's an overview of how quantum computing might influence blockchain:

- Quantum-Safe Cryptography: To counter the threat posed by quantum computing, blockchain developers and cryptographic experts are actively researching and implementing quantum-resistant or quantum-safe cryptographic methods.
- Improved Consensus Mechanisms: Quantum computing could potentially be used to enhance the efficiency of consensus mechanisms in blockchain networks. By solving complex mathematical problems more quickly, quantum computers might expedite the transaction validation process, potentially leading to faster block confirmations and increased scalability.
- Quantum-Secured Blockchains: Blockchain projects are exploring the integration of quantum-safe cryptography to ensure the long-term security of their networks. This involves transitioning from traditional cryptographic algorithms to quantum-resistant alternatives to protect against potential quantum attacks.
- Quantum Machine Learning: Algorithms for quantum machine learning might speed up model training, optimize predictive analytics, and improve data processing, benefiting AI-based blockchain applications.
- Quantum Key Distribution: Blockchain networks can employ quantum key distribution techniques to enhance data security. QKD enables the creation of ultra-secure encryption keys, making it highly challenging for quantum computers to breach data privacy or the integrity of blockchain transactions.
- Research and Development: Blockchain and quantum computing researchers are actively finds implications of quantum technology within the blockchain space. This research contributes to the ongoing development and adaptation of blockchain technology in response to the advancing field of quantum computing.

In summary, quantum computing has the potential to both challenge and advance blockchain technology. While it poses a threat to existing cryptographic methods, it also drives the development and adoption of quantum-resistant cryptographic techniques [6–9]. Blockchain projects are exploring ways to harness the capabilities of quantum computing to enhance consensus mechanisms, secure blockchain networks, and accelerate AI and machine learning applications. As quantum technology matures, its impact on blockchain will continue to evolve, and blockchain developers will need to adapt.

15.3 QUANTUM-ENABLED AI-BASED BLOCKCHAIN APPLICATIONS

Quantum-enabled AI-based blockchain applications refer to blockchain systems that harness the potential of quantum computing to enhance the functionality and security of artificial intelligence-driven blockchain networks [3, 10]. These applications use the unique capabilities of quantum computing to address the challenges and opportunities in the blockchain space. Here is some potential quantum-enabled AI-based blockchain applications:

- Quantum-Secured Blockchain: Quantum computing poses a threat to traditional cryptographic methods used in blockchain. Quantum-enabled blockchain applications can implement quantum-resistant encryption techniques to safeguard data, transactions, and the blockchain ledger from quantum attacks.
- Quantum-Safe Smart Contracts: Smart contracts are fundamental to blockchain applications. Quantum-safe smart contracts use quantum-resistant cryptography to ensure that the execution and terms of these contracts remain secure even in a quantum-powered environment.
- Quantum-Enhanced Consensus Mechanisms: By solving complex problems faster, quantum computers can accelerate transaction validation and increase the scalability of blockchain networks.
- Quantum Machine Learning: Quantum computing can be employed to enhance machine learning and data analysis on the blockchain. Quantum machine learning algorithms can speed up model training, improve predictive analytics, and enhance data processing for AI-based blockchain applications.
- Quantum Key Distribution: Blockchain applications can implement quantum key distribution techniques for ultra-secure encryption key generation. This adds an extra layer of security to protect data and transactions on the blockchain.
- Quantum-Enhanced Privacy and Security: Quantum-enabled blockchain applications can enhance privacy features, providing more robust solutions for identity protection and data confidentiality, which are important for various blockchain use cases.
- Quantum-Safe Tokenization: Quantum-safe tokenization methods can be used to represent assets and values on the blockchain. These tokens would be resistant to quantum attacks, ensuring the security of digital assets in a quantum-powered environment.
- Quantum-Enhanced Data Analytics: Quantum computing can accelerate data analysis and decision-making processes in AI-based blockchain applications. This can lead to faster and more accurate information for various use cases, including supply chain optimization and financial forecasting.
- Research and Development: Quantum-enabled AI-based blockchain applications also encompass research and development efforts to discuss innovative solutions that use the unique features of quantum computing to enhance the security and performance of blockchain networks.

15.4 AI-DRIVEN APPLICATIONS IN QUANTUM-POWERED BLOCKCHAIN

AI-driven applications in quantum-powered blockchain networks represent a confluence of quantum computing with artificial intelligence [5, 11 and 12] to create highly sophisticated and secure blockchain systems. Here are some potential applications and use cases in this emerging field:

- Quantum-Secured Transactions: Automation and optimization are possible with AI for secure quantum transactions. The security of transactions can be improved using quantum computing, while AI algorithms can help detect and prevent fraud or suspicious activities in real-time.
- Quantum-Enhanced Consensus Mechanisms: AI-driven consensus mechanisms can use quantum computing for faster and more efficient agreement on the state of the blockchain. This can lead to quicker block confirmations and enhanced network scalability.
- Quantum-Safe Smart Contracts: Quantum-powered smart contracts can be further enhanced by AI. AI algorithms can optimize the execution of smart contracts and improve their performance in complex, multifaceted transactions.
- Quantum Machine Learning: Machine learning can be expedited by quantum computing. tasks on the blockchain. AI-driven quantum machine learning models can provide better predictions, data analysis, and optimization for blockchain-based applications like fraud detection, supply chain management, and recommendation systems.
- Quantum Data Analysis and Information: Quantum-powered blockchain systems can provide rapid and accurate data analysis using AI algorithms. This can enable businesses and organizations to gain meaningful information, make data-driven decisions, and optimize processes efficiently.
- Quantum-Enhanced Privacy and Security: AI can be employed to enhance privacy and security features in quantum-powered blockchains. AI-driven security measures can continuously adapt to emerging threats and vulnerabilities, ensuring the integrity and confidentiality of blockchain data.
- Quantum-Safe Tokens and Digital Assets: Quantum-powered blockchain applications can tokenize assets and values in a quantum-secure manner. AI-driven tokenization methods can facilitate the exchange and management of digital assets while ensuring their security.
- Quantum-Key Management: AI can assist in managing quantum keys for encryption and decryption in quantum-powered blockchains. AI algorithms can optimize the generation, distribution, and storage of quantum keys, ensuring robust security.
- Quantum-Enhanced Supply Chain Management: Quantum computing can optimize supply chain operations on the blockchain. AI-driven applications can provide real-time visibility, predictive analytics, and automated decision-making to enhance supply chain efficiency and reduce costs.
- Quantum-Powered AI-Driven Autonomous Agents: AI-driven autonomous agents on the blockchain can be powered by quantum computing to make highly secure, efficient, and autonomous decisions, such as managing IoT devices, logistics, and resource allocation.
- Quantum-Enhanced Identity Management: Blockchain systems can use quantum-powered AI for secure identity management. This ensures that digital identities are protected against quantum attacks and that access control is robust and efficient.

15.5 OPEN ISSUES AND CHALLENGES IN QUANTUM-POWERED AI-BASED BLOCKCHAIN

The convergence of quantum computing, AI, and blockchain technology provides exciting opportunities, but it also presents several open issues and challenges [4, 13–15] that must be addressed for the development and implementation of quantum-powered AI-based blockchain. Here are some of the key challenges and open issues, as mentioned in Table 15.1.

Hence, addressing these open issues and challenges will be essential for harnessing the potential of quantum-powered AI-based blockchains. As quantum technology continues to advance, a collaborative effort among researchers, developers, policymakers, and industry leaders will play a important role in shaping the future of this technology.

TABLE 15.1

Key Challenges and Open Issues in Quantum-Powered AI-Based Blockchain

Type	Challenges	Solutions
Quantum-Resistant Cryptography	The primary concern is the possible danger that quantum computing poses to existing cryptographic methods used in blockchain. Quantum computers could break encryption algorithms currently in use.	Developing and adopting quantum-resistant cryptography is important to ensure the long-term security of blockchain networks.
Quantum Hardware Development	Scaling and stability issues prevent practical quantum computers with a large enough qubit count and error correction from being developed beyond the experimental stage.	Continued research and development in quantum hardware to achieve practical and reliable quantum machines.
Integration Complexity	Integrating quantum computing capabilities with AI and blockchain can be complex and require specialized expertise.	Developing user-friendly tools and interfaces to simplify the integration process and promote adoption.
Quantum Software Development	Creating programs and algorithms that use quantum computing can be challenging, as it requires a different mindset and skill set compared to classical computing.	Investment in quantum software development and training for developers to bridge the knowledge gap.
Regulatory and Ethical issues	New regulations and ethical issues will be necessary to address quantum-powered blockchain technologies, especially in fields like finance, healthcare, and identity management.	Collaboration between policymakers, technologists, and ethicists to establish guidelines and standards for quantum-powered blockchains.
Limited Practical Quantum Computing	As of now, practical quantum computing capabilities are limited, and it may take time before quantum computers can be effectively used for blockchain and AI applications	While practical quantum computing is under development, focusing on quantum-safe solutions and conducting research and pilot projects is advisable.
Scalability	Scaling quantum-powered AI-based blockchains to handle a large volume of transactions and data efficiently is a complex problem.	Research into scalable consensus mechanisms and data storage solutions designed for quantum-powered blockchains.
Data Privacy and Security	Quantum computing can break existing encryption methods, impacting data privacy. Additionally, ensuring secure quantum key distribution is challenging.	Development of quantum-secure encryption methods and key distribution techniques to protect data and communications.
Quantum Computing Resource Management	Efficient allocation and management of quantum computing resources for AI-based blockchain applications can be complex.	Development of resource management solutions and strategies to optimize quantum computing for blockchain and AI tasks.

15.6   USE CASES/APPLICATIONS IN THE REAL WORLD

15.6.1   QUANTUM-POWERED AI-BLOCKCHAIN–BASED SUPPLY CHAIN MANAGEMENT

Quantum-powered AI-blockchain–based supply chain management represents a cutting-edge approach to enhancing the efficiency, security, and transparency of supply chain operations. This innovative integration of quantum computing, artificial intelligence, and blockchain technology provides numerous benefits and capabilities for managing supply chains [16–18]. Here's an overview of how this integration can transform supply chain management:

- Enhanced Security: Quantum-powered blockchain provides robust encryption and security to protect sensitive supply chain data. Quantum-resistant cryptographic techniques safeguard against potential quantum attacks.
- Real-Time Visibility: AI-driven analytics and quantum-powered blockchain enable real-time tracking of goods, inventory, and shipments, providing stakeholders with accurate, up-to-the-minute visibility into the supply chain.
- Improved Traceability: Blockchain's immutable ledger records every transaction, ensuring complete traceability from raw materials to end products. AI can analyze this data to trace the origin and lifecycle of products.
- Predictive Analytics: AI-powered predictive analytics on quantum-powered blockchains can forecast demand, identify bottlenecks, and optimize inventory management, leading to cost savings and reduced waste.
- Autonomous Decision-Making: Quantum-powered AI-driven agents on the blockchain can autonomously make supply chain decisions, such as routing shipments, managing inventory, and coordinating logistics in response to real-time data.
- Quantum-Secured IoT Integration: Internet of Things devices in the supply chain can use quantum-secured communication to prevent data breaches and ensure the integrity of sensor data.
- Efficient Contract Management: Smart contracts on the blockchain, enhanced by quantum technology, can automate and optimize contract execution, such as payments, delivery confirmations, and quality control.
- Supply Chain Finance: Quantum-enhanced blockchain can facilitate more efficient and secure supply chain financing solutions, including automated invoicing and instant settlements.
- Counterfeit Prevention: Quantum-powered AI can analyze blockchain data to detect counterfeit products, ensuring the authenticity and quality of goods in the supply chain.
- Supplier Verification: AI can verify the credentials and performance of suppliers, while the blockchain provides a transparent and immutable record of supplier history.
- Quantum-Safe Identity Management: Quantum-resistant identity management solutions on the blockchain ensure secure access control, authentication, and authorization within the supply chain ecosystem.
- Energy-Efficient Logistics: Quantum computing can optimize transportation routes, reducing energy consumption and emissions in logistics operations.
- Compliance and Regulatory Reporting: AI can assist in automating compliance checks, and blockchain's immutable record can simplify regulatory reporting and audits.
- Real-Time Quality Control: Quantum-powered AI can continuously monitor quality metrics and detect deviations, triggering real-time adjustments in the manufacturing process.
- Enhanced Resilience: The combination of quantum computing, AI, and blockchain can enhance supply chain resilience by identifying and mitigating risks and vulnerabilities in real-time.

Hence, by integrating quantum-powered AI and blockchain into supply chain management, businesses can streamline operations, reduce costs, improve transparency, and enhance security. This approach not only optimizes traditional supply chain processes but also provides the way for future innovations and sustainability in the supply chain industry.

15.6.2   Quantum-Powered AI-Blockchain–Based Secure Transportation System

Quantum-powered AI-blockchain–based secure transportation systems [19–21] represent a cutting-edge approach to optimizing and securing transportation networks, from smart cities to autonomous vehicles. The integration of quantum computing, artificial intelligence, and blockchain technology can bring numerous benefits to transportation systems. Here's an overview of key components, benefits, and use cases:

Key Components:

- Quantum Computing: Quantum computing enables the processing of complex optimization problems and real-time data analysis for transportation management.
- Artificial Intelligence: AI algorithms drive autonomous vehicles, optimize traffic management, and enhance route planning, reducing congestion and improving safety.
- Blockchain Technology: Blockchain ensures secure and transparent recording of transportation data, including vehicle performance, maintenance, and traffic conditions.
- Internet of Things: IoT devices in vehicles and infrastructure provide real-time data on traffic, road conditions, and vehicle performance.
- Quantum-Secured Communication: Quantum-resistant encryption ensures secure communication between vehicles and transportation infrastructure.
- Decentralized Identity (DID): DID systems enable secure identity verification for drivers and passengers, ensuring privacy and trust.

Benefits:

- Safety and Security: Quantum-secured communication and AI-driven safety measures enhance the security of transportation systems, reducing accidents and minimizing vulnerabilities to cyberattacks.
- Traffic Management: AI-driven traffic management optimizes traffic flow, reducing congestion and emissions while improving transportation efficiency.
- Autonomous Vehicles: AI-powered autonomous vehicles improve road safety; reduce traffic accidents; and provide efficient, on-demand transportation options.
- Supply Chain and Logistics: Blockchain and AI enable the optimization of supply chain operations, reducing delays and ensuring the efficient delivery of goods.
- Quantum-Secured Payments: Quantum-resistant cryptographic methods secure transportation payments and transactions, protecting sensitive financial data.
- Real-Time Data Analysis: Quantum computing and AI provide real-time data analysis for route optimization, predictive maintenance, and incident response.
- Sustainability: Transportation systems can reduce emissions and energy consumption through optimized route planning and traffic management.
- User Privacy: DID systems ensure user privacy and control over personal data in transportation systems.

Use Cases:

- Smart Traffic Management: AI optimizes traffic signals, reroutes vehicles to reduce congestion, and improves traffic flow.
- Autonomous Vehicles: AI-powered autonomous vehicles provide efficient, safe, and convenient transportation options.
- Supply Chain and Logistics Optimization: Blockchain, AI, and quantum computing optimize supply chain and logistics operations, reducing delays and costs.

- Secure Identity Verification: DID systems verify driver and passenger identities securely while protecting privacy.
- Quantum-Secured Payments: Quantum-resistant cryptography secures transportation payments and transactions, preventing fraud.
- Quantum-Secured Communication: Quantum-resistant encryption ensures the security of communication between vehicles, infrastructure, and traffic management systems.
- Predictive Maintenance: AI analyzes real-time data to predict and schedule maintenance for vehicles and infrastructure, reducing breakdowns and improving safety.
- Smart Parking and Charging: AI and blockchain enable efficient parking management and electric vehicle charging solutions.

Hence, quantum-powered AI-blockchain–based secure transportation systems have the potential to revolutionize transportation by improving safety, reducing congestion, enhancing sustainability, and optimizing supply chain operations. However, challenges related to scalability, regulation, and infrastructure updates must be navigated for these systems to reach their full potential.

15.6.3 Decentralized AI-Enabled Banking and Finance Systems

Decentralized AI-enabled banking and finance systems represent a cutting-edge approach to reimagining traditional financial services by incorporating artificial intelligence and decentralized technologies like blockchain [3, 22]. These systems aim to provide enhanced security, efficiency, transparency, and accessibility while reducing the need for intermediaries. Here's an overview of the key components and benefits of such systems:

Key Components:

- Blockchain Technology: Decentralized ledgers powered by blockchain ensure transparency and immutability of financial transactions.
- Smart Contracts: Self-executing smart contracts automate financial agreements, such as lending, borrowing, and investment, without the need for intermediaries.
- Cryptocurrencies and Tokens: Digital currencies and tokens enable cross-border transactions, instant settlements, and programmable financial instruments.
- AI and Machine Learning: It analyzes data, detects fraud, personalizes financial services, and optimizes investment strategies.

Benefits:

- Financial Inclusion: Decentralized systems extend financial services to unbanked and underbanked populations, fostering global financial inclusion.
- Transparency: Blockchain ensures transparency, allowing users to trace and verify all financial transactions and smart contract executions.
- Security: Decentralized systems are more resilient to cyberattacks, thanks to blockchain's security features and quantum-resistant cryptography.
- Efficiency: AI automates processes, reducing the need for manual interventions and streamlining operations for faster, more cost-effective services.
- Reduced Intermediaries: Eliminating intermediaries reduces transaction costs and counterparty risks.
- Smart Investment and Asset Management: AI-driven investment platforms provide personalized investment strategies, portfolio management, and risk assessments.
- Cross-Border Transactions: Digital currencies enable instant, low-cost cross-border transactions without the need for traditional financial institutions.
- Enhanced Privacy: Decentralized identity systems ensure user privacy and control over personal data.

Use Cases:

- Decentralized Lending and Borrowing: Users can lend or borrow funds directly through smart contracts, with interest rates determined by supply and demand.
- Decentralized Exchanges: AI-driven decentralized exchanges provide trading, liquidity provision, and automated market-making.
- Stablecoins and Digital Assets: Decentralized systems can facilitate the issuance and management of stablecoins and digital assets.
- Peer-to-Peer Payments: Digital currencies and tokens enable fast, secure, and low-cost peer-to-peer payments.
- Crowdfunding and Crowdsourcing: Decentralized platforms facilitate crowdfunding, crowdsourcing, and decentralized autonomous organizations (DAOs).
- Insurance and Risk Management: Smart contracts can automatically execute insurance policies and assess claims based on predefined conditions.
- Decentralized Asset Management: AI-powered platforms provide asset management and portfolio diversification strategies.
- Decentralized Identity Verification: DID systems verify user identity securely and efficiently.

Hence, while decentralized AI-enabled banking and finance systems provide numerous benefits, they also face challenges related to regulation, scalability, and user adoption. As these systems continue to evolve, it is essential to navigate these challenges while maximizing the potential for innovation and transformation in the financial industry.

15.6.4   QUANTUM-POWERED AI-BLOCKCHAIN–BASED SECURE VOTING SYSTEMS

In this, we represent a technologically advanced approach to ensuring the integrity, transparency, and security of elections and voting processes. This innovative convergence of quantum computing, artificial intelligence, and blockchain technology provides numerous benefits [23–25] for creating trustworthy and tamper-resistant voting systems. Here's an overview of how this technology can transform secure voting systems:

- Immutable and Transparent Voting Records: Blockchain technology provides a tamper-proof and transparent ledger for recording votes. Each vote is stored as a transaction, making it publicly accessible and auditable.
- Quantum-Resistant Cryptography: Quantum computing's potential to break traditional encryption methods necessitates the use of quantum-resistant cryptographic techniques to secure voter identities and ballots.
- Identity Verification: AI can enhance the identity verification process, using facial recognition, biometrics, and other authentication methods to ensure the eligibility and uniqueness of each voter.
- Secure Digital Voting: Quantum-powered blockchain enables secure digital voting, allowing voters to cast their ballots remotely through secure channels. AI can verify the integrity of votes and the authenticity of voters.
- Real-Time Verification: Quantum-powered AI can validate votes in real time, ensuring that each vote is authentic and free from manipulation.
- Decentralized Voting Infrastructure: Blockchain's decentralized nature ensures that voting data is distributed across multiple nodes, reducing the risk of a single point of failure or tampering.
- Privacy-Preserving Voting: Zero-knowledge proofs and quantum-secured encryption techniques can be employed to preserve voter privacy while maintaining the integrity of the voting process.

- Quantum-Secured Authentication: Quantum-safe authentication mechanisms ensure that only eligible voters can participate, protecting the system from unauthorized access.
- Auditable Results: Blockchain records enable auditors, election officials, and the public to verify the election results independently, ensuring transparency and trust.
- Voter Engagement and Accessibility: AI-powered chatbots and virtual assistants can provide information, answer questions, and guide voters through the process, making voting more accessible and inclusive.
- Resilience Against Cyberattacks: The combination of quantum-resistant cryptography and blockchain's security measures makes the system highly resilient to cyberattacks.
- Election Integrity: The immutability of blockchain and the security of quantum-resistant cryptography ensure the integrity of election results and protect against fraudulent activities.
- Post-Election Verification: AI algorithms can perform post-election verification and analysis, identifying irregularities and ensuring that every vote is counted accurately.
- Quantum Key Management: Quantum key distribution can be employed to protect sensitive voting data and ensure the security of communication channels.
- User-Friendly Interfaces: User-friendly interfaces, driven by AI, can make the voting process more accessible and understandable for all participants.

Hence, quantum-powered AI-blockchain–based secure voting systems have the potential to address issues related to election security, privacy, and transparency. By ensuring that every vote is recorded accurately, securely, and transparently, these systems can play an important role in enhancing the trust and integrity of democratic processes. However, the widespread adoption of such systems would require careful consideration of legal, regulatory, and ethical aspects, along with extensive testing and validation to ensure their reliability and security.

15.7 PROSPECTS FOR QUANTUM-ENABLED AI-BASED BLOCKCHAIN RESEARCH AND INNOVATION FOR THE NEXT GENERATION

The intersection of quantum computing, artificial intelligence, and blockchain technology provides a wealth of opportunities for future research, innovation, and development [3, 21, 26]. Here are some key areas of focus for future exploration in the field of quantum-enabled AI-based blockchain for next-generation applications:

- Quantum-Resistant Cryptography: We need ongoing research on this hot topic, which is required to develop and standardize quantum-resistant cryptographic methods. These techniques will be important for securing blockchain networks against quantum attacks.
- Quantum Key Distribution: We need to develop and implement quantum key distribution methods for secure data transfer and communication within blockchain systems.
- Scalability Solutions: We need to do research into scalable blockchain consensus mechanisms that can efficiently handle the processing demands of quantum-enabled applications.
- Quantum-Safe Smart Contracts: We need innovations in quantum-safe smart contract platforms that are both secure and efficient.
- Quantum Machine Learning: We need to explore quantum-enhanced machine learning algorithms and their applications in blockchain systems.
- Quantum-Powered IoT Integration: We need to investigate the integration of quantum computing with the Internet of Things to enable secure and efficient IoT-based blockchain applications.
- Quantum-Enhanced Data Analysis: We need to do research into quantum-accelerated data analytics for improved information and decision-making within blockchain networks.

- Quantum-Secured Identity Management: We need to have innovations in identity verification and access control solutions that are both quantum secure and privacy preserving.
- Cross-Chain Interoperability: We need to do research into cross-chain interoperability solutions that use quantum computing to facilitate communication and data sharing between different blockchain networks.
- Quantum-Powered Supply Chain Management: We need further developments in using quantum computing to optimize supply chain operations, reduce inefficiencies, and enhance transparency.
- Quantum-Safe Tokens and Digital Assets: We need to do research into quantum-resistant tokenization methods for representing assets and values on blockchain networks.
- Quantum-Enabled Secure Voting Systems: We require advancements in quantum-enhanced secure voting systems to ensure the integrity of elections.
- Quantum-Enhanced Financial Services: We need to do research into quantum-powered financial services, including secure asset management and efficient cross-border transactions.
- Quantum-Enabled Transportation Systems: We need innovation in using quantum computing to optimize traffic management, transportation efficiency, and autonomous vehicle technology.
- Quantum-Powered Healthcare Solutions: We need to do research into the application of quantum computing to healthcare records, privacy, and data analysis within blockchain-based healthcare systems.
- Quantum-Secured Energy and Sustainability: We require research on using quantum computing to optimize energy usage, reduce environmental impact, and enhance sustainability within blockchain systems.
- Quantum-Enabled Environmental Monitoring: We need to develop blockchain-based solutions for real-time environmental monitoring and conservation, with quantum-enhanced data analysis.
- Quantum-Secured Digital Identity: We need innovations in quantum-resistant digital identity systems that protect user privacy and security.

Hence, future research and innovation in these areas will help unlock the full potential of quantum-enabled AI-based blockchain technology, providing more secure, efficient, and scalable solutions for the next generation of blockchain applications. Collaboration between experts in quantum computing, AI, and blockchain will be important to drive these advancements.

15.8 CONCLUSION

The convergence of quantum computing, artificial intelligence, and blockchain technology represents a groundbreaking frontier in the world of information technology. Quantum computing's unprecedented processing power, AI's data-driven intelligence, and blockchain's security and transparency together have the potential to redefine the landscape of next-generation AI-based blockchain systems. The journey toward quantum-enabled AI-based blockchains is a path of both promise and complexity. It holds the potential to create unparalleled efficiencies, security, and transparency across a multitude of industries, finance, supply chain management, healthcare, and more.

However, this transformation does not come without its challenges and intricacies, including the development of quantum-resistant cryptography, scalable consensus mechanisms, and regulatory issues. The challenges and limitations of introducing quantum computing into the blockchain are addressed (in this chapter), such as the need for quantum-resistant cryptographic standards and the scalability of quantum technology in a blockchain context. In summary, the combination of the three promises to advance the capabilities of decentralized systems by introducing quantum-resilient security, enhanced consensus mechanisms, and AI-driven automation. While this intersection is still in its nascent stages, it has the potential to reshape the landscape of blockchain and redefine the future of AI within decentralized networks. Hence, the convergence is filled with more opportunities, and the next generation of AI-based blockchain systems is set to revolutionize how we exchange value, protect data, and make informed decisions in an increasingly digital world.

REFERENCES

1. Fei, S-M., Li, M., & Luo, S. (2023). Quantum information and computation. *Entropy*, 25, 463. https://doi.org/10.3390/e25030463.
2. Nair, M. M., & Tyagi, A. K. (2023). Chapter 11—AI, IoT, blockchain, and cloud computing: The necessity of the future. In R. Pandey, S. Goundar, & S. Fatima (Eds.), *Distributed Computing to Blockchain* (pp. 189–206). Academic Press. ISBN: 9780323961462. https://doi.org/10.1016/B978-0-323-96146-2.00001-2.
3. Tyagi, A. K. (2023). Chapter 2—Decentralized everything: Practical use of blockchain technology in future applications. In R. Pandey, S. Goundar, & S. Fatima (Eds.), *Distributed Computing to Blockchain* (pp. 19–38). Academic Press. ISBN: 9780323961462, https://doi.org/10.1016/B978-0-323-96146-2.00010-3.
4. Nair, M. M., &Tyagi, A. K. (2023). Blockchain technology for next-generation society: Current trends and future opportunities for smart era. In *Blockchain Technology for Secure Social Media Computing*. https://doi.org/10.1049/PBSE019E_ch11.
5. Duan, H. (2022). The principles, algorithms and state-of-art applications of quantum computing. *Journal of Physics: Conference Series*, 2386, 012025. https://doi.org/10.1088/1742-6596/2386/1/012025.
6. Fei, S-M., Li, M., & Luo, S. (2023). Quantum information and computation. *Entropy*, 25, 463. https://doi.org/10.3390/e25030463.
7. Arute, F. et al. (2021). Quantum approximate optimization of non-planar graph problems on a planar superconducting processor. *Nature Physics*, 17(3), 340–345. www.nature.com/articles/s41567-020-01105-x
8. Wecker, D. et al. (2020). Progress and prospects for quantum supremacy in computing. *Frontiers in Physics*, 8, 660. www.frontiersin.org/articles/10.3389/fphy.2020.00660/full.
9. Susindhar A. V., Soni, G., & Tyagi, A. K. (2023). A review on recent trends in quantum computation technology. In A. Tyagi (Ed.), *Handbook of Research on Quantum Computing for Smart Environments* (pp. 48–64). IGI Global. https://doi.org/10.4018/978-1-6684-6697-1.ch003.
10. Sasi, P., Soni, G., Tyagi, A. K., Kakulapati, V., Shyam Mohan J. S., & Singh, R. K. (2023). Quantum computing and the qubit: The future of artificial intelligence. In A.Tyagi (Ed.), *Handbook of Research on Quantum Computing for Smart Environments* (pp. 231–244). IGI Global. https://doi.org/10.4018/978-1-6684-6697-1.ch013.
11. Tyagi, A. K. (Ed.). (2023). *Handbook of Research on Quantum Computing for Smart Environments*. IGI Global. https://doi.org/10.4018/978-1-6684-6697-1.
12. Deekshetha, H. R., &Tyagi, A. K. (2023). Chapter 16—Automated and intelligent systems for next-generation-based smart applications. In A. K. Tyagi & A. Abraham (Eds.), *Data Science for Genomics* (pp. 265–276). Academic Press. https://doi.org/10.1016/B978-0-323-98352-5.00019-7.
13. Tyagi, A. K. (2022). *Handbook of Research on Technical, Privacy, and Security Challenges in a Modern World*. IGI Global. https://doi.org/10.4018/978-1-6684-5250-9.
14. Gomathi, L., Mishra, A. K., & Tyagi, A. K. (2023). Blockchain and machine learning empowered internet of things applications: Current issues, challenges and future research opportunities. In *2023 4th International Conference on Smart Electronics and Communication (ICOSEC)*, Trichy, India (pp. 637–647). https://doi.org/10.1109/ICOSEC58147.2023.10276385.
15. Gomathi, L., Mishra, A. K., & Tyagi, A. K. (2023). Industry 5.0 for Healthcare 5.0: Opportunities, challenges and future research possibilities. In *2023 7th International Conference on Trends in Electronics and Informatics (ICOEI)*, Tirunelveli, India (pp. 204–213). https://doi.org/10.1109/ICOEI56765.2023.10125660.
16. Deshmukh, A., Patil, D. S., Pawar, P. D., Kumari, S., & Muthulakshmi, P. (2023). Recent trends for smart environments with AI and IoT-based technologies: A comprehensive review. In A.Tyagi (Ed.), *Handbook of Research on Quantum Computing for Smart Environments* (pp. 435–452). IGI Global. https://doi.org/10.4018/978-1-6684-6697-1.ch023.
17. Goyal, D., & Tyagi, A. (2020). *A Look at Top 35 Problems in the Computer Science Field for the Next Decade*. https://doi.org/10.1201/9781003052098-40.
18. Pramod, A., Naicker, H. S., & Tyagi, A. K. (2022). Emerging innovations in the near future using deep learning techniques. In *Advanced Analytics and Deep Learning Models*. Wiley Scrivener. https://doi.org/10.1002/9781119792437.ch10.

19. Gheorghiu,V.et al. (2021). Quantum computing: An overview of recent progress. *Annual Review of Condensed Matter Physics*, 12, 247–271. www.annualreviews.org/doi/abs/10.1146/annurev-conmatphys-121919-050502.

20. Sharma, A. (2021). *A Textbook on Modern Quantum Mechanics*. https://doi.org/10.1201/9781003154457.

21. Fernandez-Carames, T. M., & Fraga-Lamas,P. (2020).Towards post-quantum blockchain: A review on blockchain cryptography resistant to quantum computing attacks. *IEEE Access*, 8, 21091–21116, January 23.

22. Flarend, A., & Hilborn, B. (2022). *Quantum Gates and Quantum Circuits*. https://doi.org/10.1093/oso/9780192857972.003.0006.

23. Griffiths, D., &Schroeter,D. (2018). *Introduction to Quantum Mechanics*. https://doi.org/10.1017/9781316995433.

24. Tyagi, A., Kukreja, S., Nair, M. M., & Tyagi, A. K. (2022). Machine learning: Past, present and future. *Neuroquantology*, 20(8). https://doi.org/10.14704/nq.2022.20.8.NQ44468

25. Yanofsky, N., & Mannucci, M. (2008). *Quantum Computing for Computer Scientists*. https://doi.org/10.1017/CBO9780511813887.

26. Tyagi, A. K., Dananjayan, S., Agarwal, D., & Thariq Ahmed, H. F. (2023).Blockchain—Internet of Things applications: Opportunities and challenges for Industry 4.0 and Society 5.0. *Sensors*, 23(2), 947. https://doi.org/10.3390/s23020947.

16 Securing Patient Data in Healthcare with Quantum Cryptography in the Quantum Era

P. Manju Bala, S. Usharani, and A. Balachandar

16.1 INTRODUCTION

The landscape of healthcare has undergone a transformative shift with the rapid digitization of medical records and services, significantly enhancing the efficiency and accessibility of healthcare delivery. Electronic health records (EHRs), telemedicine, and various digital health innovations have streamlined operations, facilitated real-time patient monitoring, and improved overall patient care (Perumal & Nadar, 2020). However, this digitization has also introduced substantial vulnerabilities in information security, exposing complex patient data to cyber extortions (Chengoden et al., 2023). As healthcare systems become increasingly reliant on digital technologies, guaranteeing the security of patient information has become a critical priority. In parallel with the digitization of healthcare, advancements in quantum computing (SaberiKamrposhti et al., 2024) have emerged as a double-edged sword. Quantum computing presents serious challenges to existing encryption techniques, even though it has the potential to solve complicated issues beyond the capabilities of conventional computers. Conventional encryption methods, like Rivest-Shamir-Adleman (RSA) and Elliptic curve cryptography (ECC), are based on statistical puzzles that are too complex for conventional computers to solve computationally. Nevertheless, these methods are susceptible to quantum algorithms, such as Shor's algorithm, which can solve discrete logarithms and factor big numbers with efficiency, making traditional encryption obsolete (Hang et al., 2022). In this regard, using the concepts of quantum physics, quantum cryptography presents a ground-breaking method of data security.

The application of quantum cryptography, in particular quantum key distribution (QKD), offers a means of establishing communication channels that are inherently safe against cyberattacks and eavesdropping (Selvarajan & Mouratidis, 2023). As opposed to traditional encryption techniques, QKD takes advantage of the intrinsic qualities of quantum particles to guarantee that any effort to eavesdrop on the conversation would be quickly discovered since it would disrupt the quantum state (Shuaib et al., 2022). This chapter explores how quantum cryptography is being applied and how it affects patient data security in the healthcare industry. It provides a thorough examination of the present status of healthcare data security, the shortcomings of conventional encryption approaches, and the realistic processes necessary in implementing quantum cryptography techniques, with an emphasis on the observable results of integrating these techniques into healthcare systems (Dash et al., 2019). The chapter also outlines the anticipated gains in data availability, secrecy, and integrity and provides a thorough case study demonstrating the practical applications of quantum cryptography in the medical field.

The rapid digitalization of medical records and services has completely changed the healthcare environment, greatly improving accessibility and efficiency of healthcare delivery. The use of electronic health records, telemedicine, and other developments in digital health have resulted in enhanced

DOI: 10.1201/9781003499459-16

patient care, real-time monitoring of patients, and simplified operations (Ralegankar et al., 2022). Sensitive patient data is now vulnerable to cyberattacks due to significant data security flaws brought about by digitalization. Patient data security has emerged as a top problem as healthcare institutions depend more and more on digital technology ("Limitations and future applications of quantum cryptography," 2021). The digitalization of healthcare is occurring concurrently with the development of quantum computing, which presents a double-edged sword. Quantum computing presents serious risks to existing encryption techniques, even though it has the potential to solve complicated issues that are beyond the capabilities of conventional computers (Aggarwal et al., 2023). Conventional encryption methods, like RSA and ECC, are based on mathematical puzzles that are too complex for conventional computers to solve computationally. Nevertheless, these methods are susceptible to quantum algorithms, such as Shor's algorithm, which solve discrete logarithms and factor big numbers with efficiency, making traditional encryption obsolete.

In this regard, using the ideas of quantum physics, quantum cryptography presents a groundbreaking method of data security. Quantum cryptography (Qu & Sun, 2023), in particular quantum key distribution, offers a way to establish communication channels that are fundamentally safe against cyberattacks and eavesdropping. In contrast to traditional encryption techniques, quantum key distribution leverages the intrinsic characteristics of quantum particles to guarantee that any effort to intercept the communication would be instantly detected since it would disrupt the quantum state (Ahn et al., 2022).

This chapter delves into the implementation and impact of quantum cryptography on securing patient data in the healthcare sector. It focuses on the tangible outcomes of integrating quantum cryptographic techniques into healthcare systems, providing a broad analysis of the recent state of healthcare information security, the weaknesses of traditional encryption methods, and the practical steps involved in deploying QKD. Moreover, the chapter highlights the expected improvements in data integrity, confidentiality, and availability, and presents a detailed case study illustrating the real-world benefits of quantum cryptography in healthcare.

TABLE 16.1

Susceptibilities Presented by Digitization and the Role of Quantum Cryptography

Aspect	Current Situation	Future Direction with Quantum Cryptography
Digital Transformation in Healthcare	• Streamlined operations. • Facilitated real-time patient monitoring	• Continued enhancement through advanced digital tools. • Better patient outcomes and operational efficiency.
Data Security Vulnerabilities	• Increased reliance on digital technologies. • Susceptible to breaches and cyber-attacks.	• Robust solutions to secure patient data. • Mitigating risks associated with cyber threats.
Impact of Quantum Computing	• Open to attack by quantum algorithms, such as Shor's algorithm. • Risks to RSA and ECC encryption.	• Quantum-resistant cryptographic methods. • Safeguarding healthcare data from quantum threats.
Role of Quantum Cryptography	• Classical encryption methods becoming obsolete. • Risking integrity of healthcare data.	• QKD provides resilience to eavesdropping and cyber-attacks. • Ensures data integrity and confidentiality.
Implementation of QKD in Healthcare	• Exploring quantum cryptographic techniques. • Enhancing data security.	• Improved data integrity, confidentiality, and availability. • Real-world benefits through case studies.
Improvements with Quantum Cryptography	• Current measures inadequate against quantum threats. • Risks to patient data privacy and security.	• Adoption strengthens data security. • Ensures protection and improved healthcare services.

16.1.1 The Current Landscape of Healthcare Data Security

Sensitive data pertaining to patients' medical histories, diagnoses, treatment plans, and personal identifying information are all included in the category of healthcare data. This data has been digitalized, which has improved patient care and operational effectiveness by making it simpler to keep, access, and exchange. But it has also made fraudsters' top target when it comes to healthcare data. In the healthcare industry, data breaches can have serious repercussions, such as compromised patient safety, identity theft, and financial loss. Traditional encryption methods (Ukwuoma et al., 2022), such as symmetric encryption (AES) and asymmetric encryption (RSA, ECC), have been the cornerstone of data security in healthcare. These techniques rely on computationally challenging mathematical problems, which prevent attackers from decrypting the data without the necessary keys (Jaime et al., 2023). Nonetheless, the fundamental presumptions of these cryptographic techniques are in jeopardy due to the emergence of quantum computing.

By utilizing the ideas of quantum physics, quantum computing is able to process data at a rate that is not possible for traditional computers. The discrete logarithm issue and the integer factorization problem may be solved tenfold quicker by quantum algorithms like Shor's algorithm than by the most well-known conventional techniques (Davids et al., 2022). This competence directly threatens the security of RSA and ECC, as quantum computers could potentially decrypt data encrypted with these methods in a matter of seconds. Given these advancements, the need for quantum-resistant cryptographic techniques in healthcare is urgent. A workable answer is provided by quantum cryptography, and more especially by quantum key distribution, which offers a secure communication technique that is essentially impervious to the processing capacity of quantum computers (Aparna et al., 2021).

16.2 PRINCIPLES OF QUANTUM CRYPTOGRAPHY

Utilizing the concepts of quantum physics, quantum cryptography establishes safe channels of communication (Zhang et al., 2015). Quantum key distribution, which enables two parties to create a shared secret key that can be used for message encryption and decryption, is the most well-known use of quantum cryptography (Gupta et al., 2023). The foundational characteristics of quantum particles, such photons, which display behaviors like superposition and entanglement, provide the foundation for QKD security (Althobaiti & Dohler, 2021)

16.2.1 Quantum Key Distribution

Two parties, known as Alice and Bob, can create a secure communication channel thanks to QKD techniques. Charles Bennett and Gilles Brassard devised the BB84 protocol, which is the most well-known QKD protocol, in 1984 (Denis & Madhubala, 2021). Alice transmits Bob a sequence of photons encoded with a random quantum state as part of the BB84 protocol. Bob uses bases that are selected at random to measure the photons. Following the broadcast, Alice and Bob compare a portion of their findings in public to make sure no one was listening in on them. The photons' quantum states would be disturbed by any attempt at interception by Eve, the eavesdropper, causing observable inconsistencies in the measurements.

16.2.2 Security Properties of QKD

The no-cloning theorem and the quantum measurement principle are essential to QKD security (Jayanthi et al., 2022). According to the no-cloning theorem, any given unknown quantum state cannot be replicated exactly. This implies that an eavesdropper cannot duplicate the quantum states being transmitted without introducing errors. Additionally, quantum measurement disturbs the quantum state being measured, making any eavesdropping attempt detectable by the communicating parties.

TABLE 16.2

Important Requirements for Quantum Cryptography in the Healthcare Industry, along with a Description, Challenges, and Solutions

Requirement	Description	Challenges	Solutions
Secure Quantum Key Distribution	Implementation of QKD protocols and secure quantum communication channels.	High cost and complexity of QKD systems.	Economies of scale, cost-effective implementation strategies, gradual deployment.
Integration with Existing Systems	Compatibility with current IT infrastructure and use of hybrid cryptographic systems.	Compatibility issues with legacy systems and devices.	Development of APIs, middleware, and hybrid systems for gradual integration.
Scalability	Support for extensive healthcare networks and various devices.	Handling large-scale networks and multiple devices.	Scalable infrastructure, modular deployment, robust network design.
Cost-Effectiveness	Economically feasible implementation and manageable ongoing maintenance costs.	High initial setup and operational costs.	Funding opportunities, grants, cost-benefit analysis, leveraging economies of scale.
User Training and Awareness	Training for healthcare professionals and IT staff, awareness programs for stakeholders.	Resistance to change, lack of knowledge.	Comprehensive training programs, continuous education, stakeholder engagement.
Regulatory Compliance	Adherence to data protection regulations like HIPAA and GDPR.	Keeping up with evolving regulations.	Regular audits, compliance checks, staying informed about regulatory changes.
Robustness and Reliability	Error correction, fault tolerance, and consistent performance.	Quantum communication errors, hardware malfunctions.	Quantum error correction techniques, regular maintenance, robust design.
Data Integrity and Authentication	Ensuring data authenticity and preventing tampering.	Ensuring data has not been altered, verifying identities.	Quantum digital signatures, tamper-proof systems, robust authentication mechanisms.
Future-Proofing	Staying updated with advancements in quantum technology and ensuring upgradability.	Rapid technological changes, future threats.	Research and development, adaptable and upgradeable systems, proactive threat anticipation.
Privacy Preservation	Protecting patient data confidentiality and ensuring anonymity or pseudonymity.	Ensuring patient privacy, complying with regulations.	Robust encryption methods, compliance with privacy standards, patient anonymization techniques.
Secure Quantum Key Distribution	Implementation of QKD protocols and secure quantum communication channels.	High cost and complexity of QKD systems.	Economies of scale, cost-effective implementation strategies, gradual deployment.

16.3   REQUIREMENTS OF QUANTUM CRYPTOGRAPHY FOR HEALTHCARE

16.3.1   Secure Quantum Key Distribution

A fundamental component of quantum cryptography is quantum key distribution, which uses the ideas of quantum physics to enable secure communication. It's critical to deploy QKD protocols like BB84 or E91 in the healthcare industry. These algorithms safely create and distribute cryptographic keys using quantum states. The way the keys are created ensures that any effort at eavesdropping will be noticed because of the disruption to the quantum state. Quantum bits (qubits) must be transmitted over secure quantum communication channels, usually fiber optics, to prevent interception. These channels guarantee the preservation of key distribution security across extended distances. In a healthcare setting, secure QKD can protect sensitive patient data during transmission between hospitals, clinics, and remote healthcare services. It is essential to guarantee the integrity and security of treatment plans, medical records, and private patient data. Strong security measures are becoming more important as telemedicine and electronic health records become more and more integrated into healthcare systems. Healthcare organizations may protect their data from any breaches by implementing QKD, which offers a greater degree of security than traditional cryptography techniques.

16.3.2 INTEGRATION WITH EXISTING SYSTEMS

For quantum cryptography to be practical in healthcare, it must integrate seamlessly with existing IT infrastructure. This involves ensuring compatibility with current systems used for managing patient data, medical records, and communication networks. Initially, hybrid cryptographic systems that combine classical and quantum methods can facilitate a smoother transition. These systems allow healthcare providers to gradually adopt quantum cryptography without overhauling their entire infrastructure. Integration also involves adapting quantum cryptographic protocols to work with various healthcare devices, including medical equipment, patient monitoring systems, and mobile health applications. Ensuring that these devices can communicate securely using quantum-encrypted channels is essential for maintaining data integrity and confidentiality. Moreover, integration requires robust software and hardware solutions that can handle quantum cryptographic operations efficiently. This includes developing APIs and middleware that support quantum key distribution and encryption/decryption processes. The goal is to create a cohesive system where quantum cryptography enhances the security of healthcare data without disrupting the existing workflows and processes. Proper integration ensures that the benefits of quantum cryptography can be fully realized, providing enhanced security for sensitive medical information.

16.3.3 SCALABILITY

Scalability is a critical requirement for the successful deployment of quantum cryptography in healthcare. Healthcare systems are vast and complex, encompassing hospitals, clinics, remote healthcare services, and various other entities. Therefore, the quantum cryptographic system must be scalable to support this extensive network. This involves having the capacity to manage a big number of people and devices without sacrificing performance or security. Network scalability ensures that secure quantum communication channels can be established across different locations, enabling safe transmission of sensitive data. Additionally, the system should be compatible with various devices used in healthcare, from sophisticated medical equipment to handheld devices used by healthcare professionals. Ensuring device compatibility is crucial for maintaining secure communication channels and protecting patient data across the entire healthcare network. Furthermore, the system must be capable of scaling up as the healthcare network grows, accommodating new devices, users, and locations. This requires robust and flexible infrastructure that can adapt to changing demands and increasing data volumes. Scalability also involves ensuring that the system can handle peak loads, such as during large-scale health crises or when dealing with extensive patient records. By ensuring scalability, healthcare institutions can provide secure and efficient services, protecting sensitive information and enhancing overall operational efficiency.

16.3.4 COST-EFFECTIVENESS

Implementing quantum cryptography in healthcare must be economically feasible. This involves assessing the initial setup costs, including the acquisition of quantum cryptographic equipment, secure communication channels, and necessary infrastructure upgrades. While quantum cryptography offers superior security, the cost of implementing it should be justifiable within the budget constraints of healthcare institutions. Ongoing maintenance and operational costs should also be manageable, ensuring that the system remains sustainable in the long term. This includes the costs associated with maintaining and updating quantum cryptographic hardware and software, as well as training staff to use and manage the system effectively. By utilizing economies of scale, negotiating advantageous terms with vendors, and maximizing resource use, cost-effectiveness may be attained. Additionally, healthcare institutions can explore funding opportunities and grants specifically aimed at enhancing cybersecurity in healthcare. Demonstrating the potential cost savings from preventing data breaches and protecting sensitive patient information can also help justify the investment. Ultimately, the goal is to implement a quantum cryptographic system that provides robust security without imposing an excessive financial burden on healthcare providers. By ensuring cost-effectiveness, healthcare institutions can adopt advanced security measures while maintaining financial stability and continuing to provide high-quality care.

16.3.5 User Training and Awareness

Successful implementation of quantum cryptography in healthcare requires comprehensive user training and awareness programs. Healthcare professionals, including doctors, nurses, and administrative staff, as well as IT personnel, need to understand the principles of quantum cryptography and how to use the system effectively. This involves training sessions, workshops, and hands-on practice to familiarize users with quantum cryptographic protocols, key distribution processes, and secure communication practices. Training should cover both the technical aspects and the practical applications of quantum cryptography in healthcare settings. Awareness programs are also essential for educating stakeholders about the benefits of quantum cryptography, the enhanced security it provides, and its role in protecting sensitive patient data. These programs should address common misconceptions, highlight the importance of data security, and demonstrate how quantum cryptography can prevent data breaches and unauthorized access. Additionally, continuous education and updates on advancements in quantum cryptography are crucial for keeping users informed about new threats and emerging technologies. By investing in user training and awareness, healthcare institutions can ensure that their staff is well-equipped to utilize quantum cryptography effectively, thereby maximizing its security benefits and ensuring the protection of patient information.

16.3.6 Regulatory Compliance

One of the most important prerequisites for applying quantum cryptography in healthcare is regulatory compliance. Strict data protection laws, such as the General Data Protection Regulation (GDPR) in the European Union and the Health Insurance Portability and Accountability Act (HIPAA) in the United States, must be followed by healthcare providers. These rules require patient data to be protected, guaranteeing its availability, confidentiality, and integrity. Quantum cryptographic systems must be designed and implemented in a manner that complies with these regulatory requirements. This involves incorporating encryption methods that meet or exceed regulatory standards for data security. Additionally, healthcare providers must adopt industry best practices and standards for quantum cryptography, ensuring that their systems are secure and compliant. Conducting routine audits and assessments is crucial to confirming adherence to regulations and detecting any possible weaknesses. Healthcare organizations should also keep up with the latest developments in quantum cryptography standards and regulations to make sure their systems are compliant and up to date. Healthcare providers may safeguard confidential patient information, stay out of trouble with the law, and keep the confidence of stakeholders and patients by making regulatory compliance a top priority. Effective use of quantum cryptography in healthcare necessitates adherence to data privacy laws.

16.3.7 ROBUSTNESS AND RELIABILITY

Robustness and reliability are essential for the effective implementation of quantum cryptography in healthcare. Quantum cryptographic systems must be designed to handle the unique challenges of quantum communication, ensuring that they are resilient to errors and disruptions. The process entails employing quantum error correction methods to identify and rectify any faults that may arise when transmitting quantum bits (qubits). Another essential component is fault tolerance, which guarantees that the system can function normally even in the case of hardware failures or other problems. Reliable quantum cryptographic systems must provide consistent performance, maintaining secure communication channels and protecting sensitive data at all times. This includes ensuring that the system can handle large volumes of data and high traffic loads without compromising security or performance. Additionally, the system should be able to recover quickly from failures, minimizing downtime and ensuring the continuity of healthcare services. Regular maintenance, monitoring, and updates are necessary to ensure the system remains robust and reliable. By prioritizing robustness and reliability, healthcare institutions can ensure that their quantum cryptographic systems provide consistent and secure protection for patient data, enhancing overall security and operational efficiency.

16.3.8 DATA INTEGRITY AND AUTHENTICATION

Quantum cryptography in healthcare requires data integrity and authenticity to be guaranteed. Treatment plans, medical records, and other sensitive data may be authenticated using quantum digital signatures. With the help of these signatures, you can safely confirm the sender's identity and make sure the data wasn't altered in transit. The implementation of tamper-proof systems is necessary in order to preserve the accuracy and dependability of patient data, prevent illegal alterations, and ensure data integrity. This is especially crucial in the medical field, as patient care and treatment results can be directly impacted by the quality of medical data. Only authorized users should be able to access and edit sensitive data thanks to quantum cryptography systems, which must be built to identify and stop any efforts to fake or alter data. Strong authentication procedures are also required to confirm users' identities when they log into the system, limiting unwanted access and safeguarding patient information. Healthcare organizations may uphold the confidence of patients and stakeholders by guaranteeing data integrity and authenticity, therefore offering dependable and secure safeguarding for confidential data.

16.3.9 FUTURE-PROOFING

Future-proofing is essential for the effective implementation of quantum cryptography in healthcare. As quantum computing and cryptographic technologies continue to evolve, healthcare institutions must ensure that their systems remain secure and up-to-date. This involves staying informed about advancements in quantum technology and being prepared to adopt new protocols and techniques as they become available. Ensuring that the quantum cryptographic system is upgradable is crucial for maintaining long-term security and effectiveness. This includes designing systems that can incorporate new quantum cryptographic methods and technologies without requiring significant overhauls. In order to remain abreast of developments in quantum cryptography and to investigate novel strategies and security-enhancing solutions, healthcare providers should also allocate resources to research and development. Future-proofing also involves anticipating potential threats and vulnerabilities, ensuring that the system can adapt to emerging challenges. By prioritizing future-proofing, healthcare institutions can ensure that their quantum cryptographic systems remain effective and secure, providing robust protection for sensitive patient data in the face of evolving technological landscapes.

16.3.10 Privacy Preservation

Privacy preservation is a fundamental requirement for the implementation of quantum cryptography in healthcare. Healthcare professionals manage extremely sensitive information, such as medical records, treatment plans, and personal information; thus, protecting patient data confidentially is crucial. Systems utilizing quantum cryptography must be created to safeguard this data from illegal access and guarantee its confidentiality. This entails putting in place encryption techniques that offer strong security for patient data, keeping any unauthorized parties from viewing or decoding the data. Additionally, methods for maintaining patient anonymity or pseudonymity are crucial for protecting privacy. These methods can be particularly important in research settings, where anonymized data is used for studies and analyses. Ensuring that patient identities are protected while still allowing for valuable research can enhance both privacy and the advancement of medical knowledge. Quantum cryptographic systems should also be designed to comply with privacy regulations and standards, ensuring that they meet the required criteria for data protection. By prioritizing privacy preservation, healthcare institutions can build trust with patients and stakeholders, ensuring that sensitive information are protected and confidentiality is maintained.

16.4 ALGORITHMS FOR QUANTUM CRYPTOGRAPHY

16.4.1 BB84 Protocol

An innovative quantum key distribution technique called BB84 offers a safe way for two parties to create a shared secret key. The BB84 protocol, which was developed in 1984 by Charles Bennett and Gilles Brassard, makes use of quantum physics to guarantee the security of the key distribution procedure. Using a polarized photon source, Alice, the sender in the BB84 protocol, creates a random sequence of quantum bits (qubits). She choose at random whether of the two bases—the diagonal basis ($\{|+\rangle, |-\rangle\}$) or the rectilinear basis ($\{|0\rangle, |1\rangle\}$)—to encode each bit in. Alice then uses a quantum channel to transmit these qubits to Bob, the recipient. Bob choose at random to measure each qubit in the diagonal or rectilinear basis after receiving the qubits. Bob releases the foundation for each measurement he does after measuring each qubit, but not the measurement's outcome. Alice then makes available to the world the foundation upon which she encoded each qubit. After that, Bob and Alice compare a portion of their measurement bases. The measurement result is stored as a portion of the raw key for each qubit for which the same basis was employed. The bits that correspond to qubits measured in various bases are discarded. Finally, in order to rectify mistakes and extract a more compact, secure key from the raw key, Alice and Bob carry out error reconciliation and privacy amplification. Error reconciliation involves comparing their raw keys and identifying and correcting discrepancies. Privacy amplification involves hashing the corrected key to reduce its information content and ensure its security against eavesdropping attacks. The BB84 protocol provides unconditional security, meaning that any eavesdropping attempt can be detected with a high probability. This makes it a fundamental building block for quantum cryptography and a key algorithm for securing patient data in the quantum era.

16.4.2 E91 Protocol

Another significant quantum key distribution technique that uses quantum entanglement to provide a secure key between two parties is the E91 protocol. The E91 protocol, which was put out by Artur Ekert in 1991, offers a distinct method of key distribution that is essentially distinct from the BB84 system. In the E91 protocol, Alice creates pairs of entangled photons using a quantum entangled source. She sends one photon from each entangled pair to Bob, while keeping the other photon for herself. Bob and Alice use measurement bases that they have picked at random to determine the polarization of their photons. Alice and Bob reveal to the world the measurement bases they used for each pair of photons after measuring their own photons. They then save the measurement data for the pairings in which they utilized the same basis after comparing a subset of their measurement bases. The raw key is formed from these measurement data. To fix mistakes and get a shorter, more secure key from the raw key, Alice and Bob use privacy amplification and error reconciliation, much like in the BB84 protocol. Error reconciliation involves comparing their raw keys and correcting any discrepancies. Privacy amplification involves hashing the corrected key to reduce its information content and ensure its security against eavesdropping attacks. Because any effort to listen in on the entangled photons would disrupt their quantum state and reveal the existence of an eavesdropper, the E91 protocol provides a high degree of security. Because of this characteristic, the E91 protocol is a useful approach for protecting patient data in the quantum age, particularly in situations where it is possible to construct and test quantum entanglement with reliability.

16.5 IMPLEMENTING QKD IN HEALTHCARE SYSTEMS

Integrating QKD in healthcare systems involves several practical steps, including the deployment of quantum cryptographic hardware, integration with existing IT infrastructure, and the establishment of secure quantum communication channels. This section outlines the necessary components and processes for successful implementation.

16.5.1 QUANTUM CRYPTOGRAPHIC HARDWARE

The primary hardware components for QKD include photon sources, single-photon detectors, and quantum channels (typically optical fibers). Photon sources generate the quantum states used for key distribution, while single-photon detectors measure the received photons. Quantum channels provide the medium for transmitting quantum states between the communicating parties.

16.5.2 INTEGRATION WITH EXISTING IT INFRASTRUCTURE

Implementing QKD requires compatibility with existing IT systems and encryption protocols. This involves integrating QKD devices with classical cryptographic systems to enable seamless key management and data encryption. Hybrid encryption schemes, which combine quantum key distribution with classical encryption methods, can facilitate this integration by using quantum-generated keys for classical encryption algorithms.

16.5.3 ESTABLISHING SECURE QUANTUM COMMUNICATION CHANNELS

Setting up secure quantum communication channels involves configuring the QKD hardware and ensuring the integrity of the quantum channels. Optical fibers must be carefully maintained to minimize losses and errors during transmission. Additionally, secure classical communication channels are necessary for key reconciliation and error correction processes.

16.6 EXPECTED OUTCOMES OF IMPLEMENTING QUANTUM CRYPTOGRAPHY IN HEALTHCARE

It is anticipated that the application of quantum cryptography in the healthcare industry would have a number of important effects, the main one being an improvement in patient data security. The benefits in data availability, secrecy, and integrity are quantified in this part, which also shows how quantum cryptography reduces the danger of data breaches and unapproved access.

16.6.1 Enhanced Data Security

The improved security of patient data is the main advantage of quantum cryptography. Because encryption keys are produced and disseminated securely thanks to QKD, it is hard for attackers to intercept or decode data. By doing this, the likelihood of data breaches and illegal access is greatly decreased, shielding private patient data from online risks.

16.6.2 Improved Data Integrity and Confidentiality

Data integrity and secrecy are improved by quantum cryptography, which makes sure that any effort to intercept the transmission will be quickly discovered. This promotes better confidence between patients and healthcare providers by enabling healthcare organizations to safeguard the privacy and accuracy of patient data.

16.6.3 Increased Availability of Secure Communication

By deploying QKD, healthcare organizations can establish highly secure communication channels for transmitting sensitive data. This ensures the availability of secure communication pathways, enabling healthcare professionals to share patient information confidently and efficiently without compromising security.

16.7 MATERIALS AND METHODS

Quantum cryptographic hardware consists of

- **Photon Sources:** Devices capable of generating single photons or entangled photon pairs, essential for QKD protocols.
- **Single-Photon Detectors:** High-efficiency detectors that can accurately measure individual photons, crucial for decoding quantum states.
- **Optical Fibers:** High-quality optical fibers for transmitting quantum states over distances, minimizing loss and maintaining signal integrity.
- **Quantum Random Number Generators (QRNGs):** Devices to generate truly random numbers required for key generation and encryption processes.

16.7.1 Classical Cryptographic Infrastructure

Figure 16.1 shows the classical cryptographic infrastructure. It consists of the following

- Encryption Software: Classical encryption tools compatible with quantum-generated keys, such as AES for data encryption.
- Key Management Systems (KMSs): Systems for storing, managing, and distributing encryption keys securely.
- Network Infrastructure: Existing IT infrastructure, including servers, routers, and secure communication channels for integrating quantum cryptographic systems.

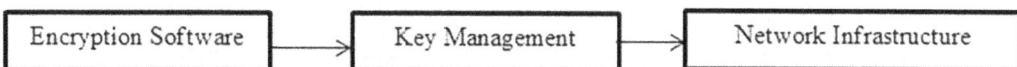

FIGURE 16.1 Cryptographic infrastructure.

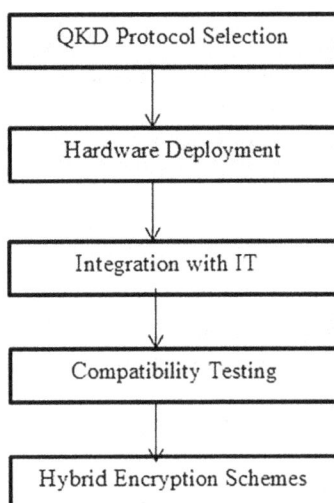

FIGURE 16.2   Steps to implement QKD systems.

16.8   DESIGN AND IMPLEMENTATION OF QKD SYSTEMS

To implement QKD systems, the following steps (Figure 16.2) need to be followed

- **QKD Protocol Selection:** Choose appropriate QKD protocols (e.g., BB84, E91) based on the specific requirements and constraints of the healthcare system.
- **Hardware Deployment:** Install and configure quantum cryptographic hardware, including photon sources, detectors, and optical fibers, within the healthcare network.
- **Integration with IT Infrastructure:** Ensure seamless integration of QKD systems with existing IT infrastructure, including encryption software and key management systems. This involves:
- **Compatibility Testing:** Test the compatibility of quantum cryptographic hardware with existing IT systems.
- **Hybrid Encryption Schemes:** Implement hybrid encryption schemes that combine quantum key distribution with classical encryption methods to enhance security.

16.9   PRACTICAL STEPS FOR IMPLEMENTATION

Initial Planning

- Form a project team consisting of healthcare IT professionals, quantum cryptography experts, and regulatory compliance officers.
- Define the scope and objectives of the QKD implementation project, focusing on securing patient data and enhancing overall data security.

Infrastructure Assessment

- Conduct a thorough assessment of the existing healthcare IT infrastructure to identify areas that require upgrades or modifications for QKD integration.

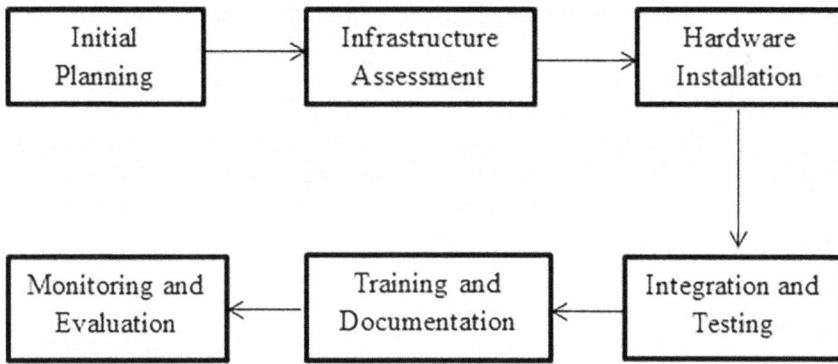

FIGURE 16.3 Practical steps for implementation.

Hardware Installation

- Deploy quantum cryptographic hardware, including photon sources, detectors, and optical fibers, ensuring proper installation and configuration.

Integration and Testing

- Integrate QKD systems with existing IT infrastructure, ensuring compatibility with classical encryption tools and key management systems.
- Conduct extensive testing to verify the functionality and security of the integrated system, including key distribution, error correction, and privacy amplification processes.

Training and Documentation

- Provide training for healthcare IT professionals on the operation and maintenance of QKD systems.
- Document the implementation process, including installation procedures, configuration settings, and troubleshooting guidelines.

Monitoring and Evaluation

- Continuously monitor the performance and security of the QKD system, conducting regular evaluations to ensure sustained protection of patient data.
- Gather and analyze feedback from users to identify areas for improvement and ensure the system meets the needs of healthcare professionals.

16.10 APPLICATIONS OF QUANTUM IN HEALTHCARE

16.10.1 DRUG DISCOVERY AND DEVELOPMENT

Drug research and discovery can benefit greatly from the revolutionary possibilities of quantum computing. Because molecular interactions are so complicated, traditional drug development procedures are generally expensive and time consuming. Drug development takes a lot less time and money because quantum computers can mimic these interactions far more quickly and accurately than conventional computers. By accurately modeling molecular structures and interactions, quantum algorithms can facilitate the development of new drugs and personalized medicine tailored to individual patients' genetic makeup. This capability is particularly crucial for diseases with complex molecular mechanisms, such as cancer and neurological disorders, where traditional approaches have struggled to find effective treatments. Quantum chemistry simulations can provide detailed insights into how drugs interact with target molecules, helping researchers design more potent and specific drugs with fewer side effects. All things considered, quantum computing holds the potential to completely transform the drug discovery process by speeding up the creation of novel treatments and enhancing patient outcomes.

16.10.2   Medical Imaging

Quantum computing can revolutionize medical imaging by enhancing image reconstruction and segmentation techniques. In traditional medical imaging, such as MRI and CT scans, image reconstruction can be time-consuming and prone to artifacts. Quantum algorithms can significantly improve the speed and accuracy of image reconstruction, leading to higher-quality images with reduced radiation exposure for patients. Quantum computing can also improve image segmentation methods, which are essential for locating and examining certain abnormalities or structures in medical imaging. For instance, precise tumor separation from surrounding tissues is crucial for treatment planning in the diagnosis of cancer. Early and more accurate diagnosis can result from more accurate tumor identification and localization thanks to quantum-enhanced picture segmentation. All things considered, quantum computing holds the potential to completely transform medical imaging by enhancing image speed, accuracy, and quality, which would eventually improve patient outcomes.

16.10.3   Genomics and Personalized Medicine

Quantum computing holds immense promise for genomics and personalized medicine. Genomic data is incredibly complex, with billions of base pairs that need to be analyzed to understand an individual's genetic makeup. Rapid genome sequencing and analysis are made possible by the enormous quantity of data that quantum computers can process far more effectively than conventional computers. The capacity to customize therapies based on a patient's genetic profile is essential for personalized medicine. By analyzing genetic data, quantum algorithms can forecast a person's reaction to various medications, enabling medical professionals to choose the most beneficial course of action with the fewest possible negative effects. Quantum computing can also speed up genomics research, improving our knowledge of illnesses and enabling the creation of novel tailored treatments. All things considered, quantum computing holds the potential to completely transform personalized medicine and genomics by facilitating quicker and more precise analysis of genetic data, which will improve patient outcomes.

16.11   CONCLUSION

To sum up, the application of quantum cryptography in the healthcare industry has great promise for improving data security and shielding patient data from online dangers. While the swift digitalization of healthcare has brought about a revolution in medical services, it has also brought to light data security issues that are difficult to resolve using conventional encryption techniques. The necessity for quantum-safe encryption is growing as quantum computing develops. A solution is provided by quantum cryptography, which uses the ideas of quantum physics to establish communication channels that are intrinsically secure. A crucial component of quantum cryptography is quantum key distribution, which creates encryption keys that are nearly impervious to eavesdropping by taking use of quantum entanglement and superposition. The quantum state would be disturbed by any effort to intercept these keys, making it traceable and guaranteeing the communication's security.

Implementing QKD in healthcare systems involves deploying quantum cryptographic hardware, integrating it with existing IT infrastructure, and establishing secure quantum communication channels. While there are challenges such as ensuring compatibility and adjusting encryption protocols, the benefits far outweigh the complexities. Enhanced data security is the primary benefit of implementing quantum cryptography in healthcare. Patient data becomes highly resistant to both current and future cyber threats, ensuring its integrity, confidentiality, and availability. Quantum cryptography offers a strong and long-lasting solution for protecting medical data by reducing the dangers of data breaches and illegal access.

REFERENCES

Aggarwal, L., Sachdeva, S., & Goswami, P. (2023). Quantum healthcare computing using precision based granular approach. *Applied Soft Computing*, *144*, 110458. https://doi.org/10.1016/j.asoc.2023.110458

Ahn, J., Kwon, H., Ahn, B., Park, K., Kim, T., Lee, M., Kim, J., & Chung, J. (2022). Toward quantum secured distributed energy resources: Adoption of Post-Quantum Cryptography (PQC) and Quantum Key Distribution (QKD). *Energies*, *15*(3), 714. https://doi.org/10.3390/en15030714

Althobaiti, O. S., & Dohler, M. (2021). Quantum-Resistant cryptography for the internet of things based on Location-Based lattices. *IEEE Access*, *9*, 133185–133203. https://doi.org/10.1109/access.2021.3115087

Aparna, H., Bhumijaa, B., Santhiyadevi, R., Vaishanavi, K., Sathanarayanan, M., Rengarajan, A., Praveenkumar, P., & El-Latif, A. a. A. (2021). Double layered Fridrich structure to conserve medical data privacy using quantum cryptosystem. *Journal of Information Security and Applications*, *63*, 102972. https://doi.org/10.1016/j.jisa.2021.102972

Chengoden, R., Victor, N., Huynh-The, T., Yenduri, G., Jhaveri, R. H., Alazab, M., Bhattacharya, S., Hegde, P., Maddikunta, P. K. R., & Gadekallu, T. R. (2023). Metaverse for Healthcare: A survey on potential applications, challenges and future directions. *IEEE Access*, *11*, 12765–12795. https://doi.org/10.1109/access.2023.3241628

Dash, S., Shakyawar, S. K., Sharma, M., & Kaushik, S. (2019). Big data in healthcare: Management, analysis and future prospects. *Journal of Big Data*, *6*(1). https://doi.org/10.1186/s40537-019-0217-0

Davids, J., Lidströmer, N., & Ashrafian, H. (2022). Artificial intelligence in medicine using quantum computing in the future of healthcare. In *Springer eBooks* (pp. 423–446). https://doi.org/10.1007/978-3-030-64573-1_338

Denis, R., & Madhubala, P. (2021). Hybrid data encryption model integrating multi-objective adaptive genetic algorithm for secure medical data communication over cloud-based healthcare systems. *Multimedia Tools and Applications*, *80*(14), 21165–21202. https://doi.org/10.1007/s11042-021-10723-4

Gupta, S., Modgil, S., Bhatt, P. C., Jabbour, C. J. C., & Kamble, S. (2023). Quantum computing led innovation for achieving a more sustainable Covid-19 healthcare industry. *Technovation*, *120*, 102544. https://doi.org/10.1016/j.technovation.2022.102544

Hang, L., Chen, C., Zhang, L., & Yang, J. (2022). Blockchain for applications of clinical trials: Taxonomy, challenges, and future directions. *IET Communications*, *16*(20), 2371–2393. https://doi.org/10.1049/cmu2.12488

Jaime, F. J., Muñoz, A., Rodríguez-Gómez, F., & Jerez-Calero, A. (2023). Strengthening privacy and data security in biomedical microelectromechanical systems by IoT communication security and protection in smart healthcare. *Sensors*, *23*(21), 8944. https://doi.org/10.3390/s23218944

Jayanthi, P., Rai, B. K., & Muralikrishna, I. (2022). The potential of quantum computing in healthcare. In *Advances in systems analysis, software engineering, and high performance computing book series* (pp. 81–101). https://doi.org/10.4018/978-1-7998-9183-3.ch006

Limitations and future applications of quantum cryptography. (2021). In *Advances in information security, privacy, and ethics book series*. https://doi.org/10.4018/978-1-7998-6677-0

Perumal, A. M., & Nadar, E. R. S. (2020). RETRACTED ARTICLE: Architectural framework and simulation of quantum key optimization techniques in healthcare networks for data security. *Journal of Ambient Intelligence & Humanized Computing/Journal of Ambient Intelligence and Humanized Computing*, *12*(7), 7173–7180. https://doi.org/10.1007/s12652-020-02393-1

Qu, Z., & Sun, H. (2023). A secure information transmission protocol for healthcare Cyber based on quantum image expansion and Grover search algorithm. *IEEE Transactions on Network Science and Engineering*, *10*(5), 2551–2563. https://doi.org/10.1109/tnse.2022.3187861

Ralegankar, V. K., Bagul, J., Thakkar, B., Gupta, R., Tanwar, S., Sharma, G., & Davidson, I. E. (2022). Quantum Cryptography-as-a-Service for Secure UAV Communication: Applications, challenges, and case study. *IEEE Access*, *10*, 1475–1492. https://doi.org/10.1109/access.2021.3138753

SaberiKamrposhti, M., Ng, K., Chua, F., Abdullah, J., Yadollahi, M., Moradi, M., & Ahmadpour, S. (2024). Post-Quantum Healthcare: A roadmap for cybersecurity resilience in medical data. *Heliyon*, e31406. https://doi.org/10.1016/j.heliyon.2024.e31406

Selvarajan, S., & Mouratidis, H. (2023). Author Correction: A quantum trust and consultative transaction-based blockchain cybersecurity model for healthcare systems. *Scientific Reports*, *13*(1). https://doi.org/10.1038/s41598-023-36573-8

Shuaib, M., Hassan, N. H., Usman, S., Alam, S., Sam, S. M., & Samy, G. a. N. (2022). Effect of quantum computing on blockchain-based electronic health record systems. *2022 4th International Conference on Smart Sensors and Application*. https://doi.org/10.1109/icssa54161.2022.9870964

Ukwuoma, H. C., Arome, G., Thompson, A., & Alese, B. K. (2022). Post-quantum cryptography-driven security framework for cloud computing. *Open Computer Science*, *12*(1), 142–153. https://doi.org/10.1515/comp-2022-0235

Zhang, Y., Wang, S., & Ji, G. (2015). A comprehensive survey on particle swarm optimization algorithm and its applications. *Mathematical Problems in Engineering*, *2015*, 1–38. https://doi.org/10.1155/2015/931256

17 An Analysis of Security Threats in Quantum Computing Information Processing

Kanthavel R., Anju A., Adline Freeda R.,
S. Krithikaa Venket, Dhaya R., Frank Vijay,
and Joseph Fisher

17.1 INTRODUCTION

Although quantum computing has great promise for revolutionizing information processing, it presents new risks and difficulties. As technology advances, it becomes increasingly important to understand these dangers to prepare and secure systems against potential future weaknesses. Utilizing the concepts of superposition and entanglement found in quantum mechanics, quantum computing can execute calculations that are impossible for classical computers. This presents new security risks even if it has enormous potential for industries like optimization, drug development, and cryptography. We can roughly divide these risks into three categories: those that impact current cryptography systems, those that introduce new types of attacks, and those that present unique challenges unique to quantum computing (Gani and Greer, 2023).

The development of quantum computing presents significant risks to today's security and information processing infrastructure. These risks include weaknesses in cryptographic systems, the appearance of attacks special to quantum computing, difficulties with data security and privacy, and problems intrinsic to quantum information processing. To reduce these risks and safeguard data processing in the quantum era, proactive steps such as the implementation of post-quantum cryptography methods, improved network security, and ongoing research are critical [Hossain Faruk et al., 2022]. This chapter also covers the security of quantum software and algorithms, along with the inherent challenges of quantum error correction. Strong error correction techniques are required due to the vulnerability of quantum systems to mistakes and decoherence, and it is crucial to secure quantum programs against both conventional and quantum threats.

17.2 QUANTUM CRYPTANALYSIS

The study of using quantum computing to weaken or strengthen cryptographic systems is known as quantum cryptanalysis. To maintain security, traditional cryptographic techniques focus on the computational challenge of specific mathematical problems, like discrete logarithms and integer factorization. The development of quantum computing, however, presents both enormous opportunities and challenges for the cryptography community [Chen et al., 2024]. The potent powers of quantum computing have led to a fundamental change in the science of cryptography known as quantum cryptanalysis. Although it presents serious risks to already in-use cryptography systems, it also encourages the development of novel quantum-resistant methods and protocols. The area of cryptography must change as quantum technology progresses to guarantee information security and privacy.

DOI: 10.1201/9781003499459-17

TABLE 17.1
QKD's Main Drawbacks

Integrating with Current Networks	– requires implementing new hardware
	– expensive
	– complicated
Price	– requiring specialized hardware like single-photon sources and detectors
	– unaffordable
Scalability	– Challenging to administer
	– maintain the complicated quantum network
	– infrastructure needed for each pair of users,
	– Utilize specialized quantum channels.

Quantum Key Distribution (QKD) Challenges: Quantum key distribution is a technique that securely transfers cryptographic keys between parties by utilizing the principles of quantum physics. Based on the ideas of quantum physics, QKD provides theoretically indestructible security, but several real-world issues have to be resolved. Some of QKD's main drawbacks are listed in Table 17.1.

- **Integrating with Current Networks:** Implementing QKD in current traditional networks necessitates major infrastructure modifications. This requires implementing new hardware, which can be expensive and complicated, such as trusted nodes and quantum repeaters.
- **Price:** When compared to classical cryptography systems, the expense of implementing and maintaining QKD systems, requiring specialized hardware like single-photon sources and detectors, can be unaffordable [4].
- **Scalability:** Reaching a big user base using QKD is difficult. It can be challenging to administer and maintain the complicated quantum network infrastructure needed for each pair of users, or they can utilize specialized quantum channels.

17.3 LIMITATIONS IN THEORETICAL AND FUNDAMENTAL ASPECTS

No-Cloning Theorem: The capacity to magnify quantum signals without erasing the data is also restricted by the no-cloning theorem, which asserts that it is impossible to produce an exact duplicate of any given unknown quantum state while maintaining security.

Quantum Replicators: The development of quantum repeaters—which are required to increase the range of QKD—remains in the experimental phase. Although they are necessary to get over the distance restriction, effective and useful quantum repeaters are still a ways off.

Concept of Quantum Memory: Securing dependable and effective quantum memory is essential for sophisticated QKD procedures and quantum repeaters, although it continues to be a noteworthy technological obstacle. The development of current quantum memory technology is still ongoing. Future cybersecurity will face substantial hurdles from quantum malware and attacks. Even if a lot of these concerns are still theoretical, proactive steps toward safeguarding digital systems are necessary due to the rapid growth of quantum technologies. Effective cybersecurity in the quantum age will depend on implementing post-quantum cryptography approaches, improving quantum security of networks, and remaining alert about new quantum threats [Deshpande, 2022]. Figure 17.1 shows the limitations of using quantum computing.

17.4 QUANTUM MALWARE AND QUANTUM ATTACKS

The concepts and potential of quantum computing are being abused by sophisticated and new forms of malware and exploits known as quantum attacks. Even though these ideas are still mostly theoretical, they represent a new area of cybersecurity difficulties.

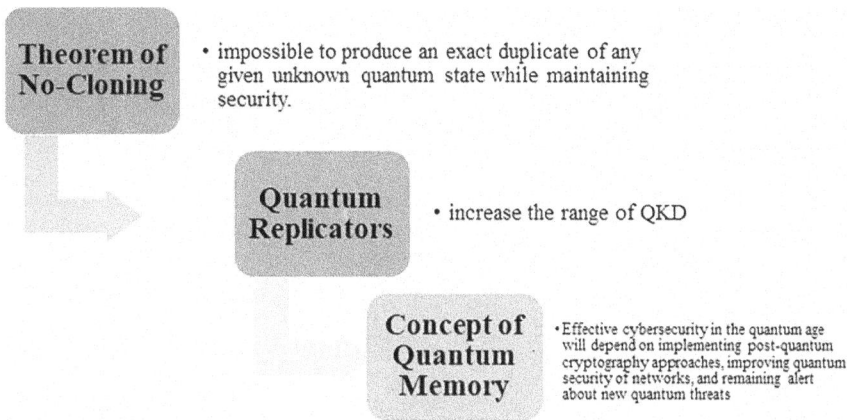

FIGURE 17.1 Limitations of using quantum computing.

- **Quantum Malware:** Malicious software that uses the special capabilities of quantum technology or quantum theories to carry out tasks that are impractical for traditional computer techniques is referred to as quantum malware.
- **Enhanced Attacks Using Cryptography:** Shor's algorithm: RSA and ECC are two popular cryptography systems that could be compromised by quantum malware using Shor's algorithm to factorize big numbers and solve discrete logarithms. Sensitive data could be decrypted far more quickly thanks to this than using traditional techniques.
- **Grover's Algorithm**: The method can search unsorted databases with a quadratic speedup. It could be used by quantum malware to more successfully conduct brute-force assaults against symmetric cryptographic keys, hence lowering the security of such system.
- **Advanced Interception of Data:** Quantum covert channels: Stealthy data exfiltration may be made possible by quantum malware's ability to use quantum superposition and entropy to build hidden communication paths that are difficult to identify with traditional security measures.
- **Attack Optimization:** In order to uncover weaknesses or attack paths in intricate structures more rapidly and efficiently than conventional malware, quantum malware may utilize quantum algorithms to maximize attack techniques.
- **Malware with a quantum resistance:** As cyber-security protocols advance to integrate quantum-resistant algorithms, malware may likewise adjust by utilizing strategies to evade identification and elimination, guaranteeing its continued existence within quantum-secured settings.
- **Quantum Attacks**: Quantum attacks take advantage of the properties of quantum technology to breach data integrity, network protocols, and cryptography systems. Quantum attack types include cryptographic breaks.
- **Public-Key Cryptography:** The basis of modern internet security, public-key cryptosystems like RSA, ECC, and Diffie-Hellman (DH) can be effectively broken by quantum computers employing Shor's algorithm.
- **Symmetric-Key Cryptography:** The key length needed for a particular security level (for example, AES-256 would provide 128-bit protection against a quantum attack) can be practically halved by using Grover's technique to execute brute-force searches on symmetric-key algorithms.
- **Quantum listening in:** QKD Vulnerabilities: Although quantum key distribution systems theoretically offer unbreakable security, there may be issues with real-world applications. For example, side-channel attacks that take advantage of flaws in the device can jeopardize QKD security [Grumbling and Horowitz, 2019]. Attackers that intercept the quantum states during QKD commit intercept-resend attacks, measure them and transmit fresh configurations to the recipient, which can jeopardize the keys that were traded.

17.5 HACKS USING QUANTUM REPLAY

Attackers using quantum technology have the ability to intercept and retransmit quantum data, interfering with quantum methods of communication and perhaps changing the results of quantum transactions.

- **Attacks on Quantum Machine Learning:** Adversarial attacks: By identifying more potent perturbations that avoid detection, quantum algorithms might improve malicious attacks on machine learning models. Data poisoning: The performance of algorithms for machine learning can be harmed by quantum computing's optimal insertion of harmful data pieces into training datasets.
- **Defenses and Mitigations:** Several tactics are being developed to counter the hazards created by quantum malware and quantum attacks:
- **Quantum-Post Cryptography:** Creating and implementing new cryptographic algorithms, such as hash-based, multivariate polynomial-based, lattice-based, and code-based encryption, that can withstand quantum attacks. Standardization efforts: To enable a seamless transition, groups such as National Institute of Standards and Technology (NIST) are striving to standardize post-quantum cryptography methods [Nat Rev Phys 4, 1 (2022)].
- **Security of Quantum Networks:** Better QKD protocols: Creating reliable quantum communication protocols and strengthening QKD systems' security to solve implementation flaws. Error correction and quantum repeaters: employing error-correction methods and quantum repeaters to safeguard long-distance quantum communications.
- **Systems for Hybrid Cryptography:** Classical-quantum combinations: Using hybrid systems that combine quantum and classical cryptography methods to offer a multi-layered resistance against quantum and classical attacks.
- **Constant Observation and Modification:** Proactive security methods include creating countermeasures for new quantum threats and routinely updating security policies to stay up to date with developments in quantum computing. Research and development: Allocating resources towards continuous investigations to foresee and alleviate plausible quantum susceptibilities. The potential of quantum computing has led to a notable advancement in cybersecurity threats in the form of quantum viruses and attacks. Even if these risks are mainly theoretical at the moment, proactive steps to guarantee the integrity of digital systems are required due to the rapid advancement of quantum technology [Murali et al., 2019]. To prepare for the quantum future, it is imperative to implement post-quantum cryptography approaches, strengthen the integrity of quantum connections, and remain watchful for potential quantum threats.

17.6 DATA HARVESTING FOR FUTURE DECRYPTION

A technique known as "data harvesting for future decryption" entails gathering and storing encrypted data with the goal of decrypting it later on, perhaps with the help of quantum computers or other more potent computing resources. This strategy presents a serious long-term risk to data security, especially for sensitive material that must be kept secret for an extended period of time [Orús et al., 2019].

Long-Term Threats to Security:

- **Sensitive Information:** Information that has long-term value or is sensitive (such as financial records, government secrets, or individual medical records) is especially vulnerable.
- **Data Longevity:** A lot of data kinds need to be kept safe for many years because of their extended shelf lives. Within that time range, innovations in quantum computing might make existing secure encryption techniques susceptible.

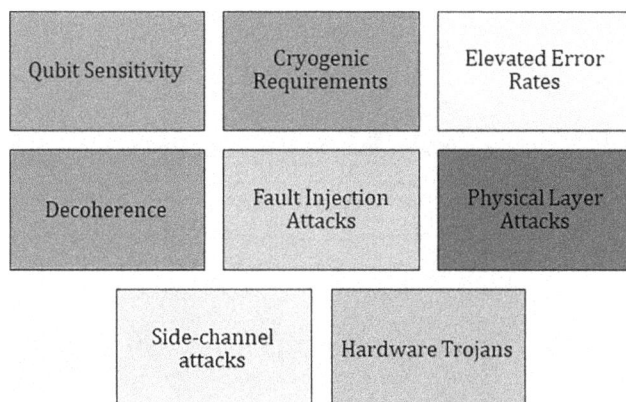

FIGURE 17.2   Main obstacles.

In the age of quantum computing, data collection for potential decryption poses a serious risk. Even now protected sensitive data could become exposed in the potential as quantum technology develops. It is essential to switch to post-quantum cryptography techniques, put strong data management procedures in place, update infrastructure, and inform stakeholders about the changing threat landscape in order to reduce this risk. Sensitive data privacy and security can be preserved throughout time with the help of proactive steps taken today. The particular requirements and characteristics of quantum computing systems pose a unique set of issues for quantum hardware security. A few of the main obstacles are shown in Figure 17.2.

Qubit Sensitivity: The basic building blocks of quantum information, qubits are very susceptible to external influences including mechanical vibrations, electromagnetic fields, and temperature changes. This makes them susceptible to both physical interference and background noise [Hadi et al., 2024].

Cryogenic Requirements: Operating at cryogenic temperatures is necessary for many quantum computing platforms, such as those that rely on superconducting qubits. It is very difficult to ensure and maintain these low temperatures, and any disruption could result in system failure or security breaches [Arute et al., 2019].

Elevated Error Rates: Because qubit operations and interactions with the environment are so delicate, quantum systems are more likely to experience increased error rates. Attackers may use these mistakes to introduce flaws or alter the results of quantum computing.

Decoherence: Interactions with the outside world can readily break quantum coherence, which is the foundation of quantum processing. Attackers may be able to cause decoherence in order to interfere with processes, which results in the loss of quantum information [Ravi et al., 2022].

Fault Injection Attacks: To tamper with calculations or retrieve private data, attackers might purposefully inject faults into quantum systems. A defense against this kind of attack is especially difficult because of the high mistake rates in quantum systems.

Physical Layer Attacks: An attacker can change or harm a system, take information out of it, or interfere with its functions if they have direct physical access to quantum hardware. It is therefore imperative to safeguard the physical infrastructure of quantum computers.

Side-Channel Attacks: Unintentional signals that quantum systems may produce, including electromagnetic radiation or acoustic vibrations, can be received and examined by adversaries to obtain information without authorization.

Hardware Trojans: Malevolent alterations made to quantum hardware during production or upkeep may result in obscure weaknesses that are hard to find but that attackers may take advantage of.

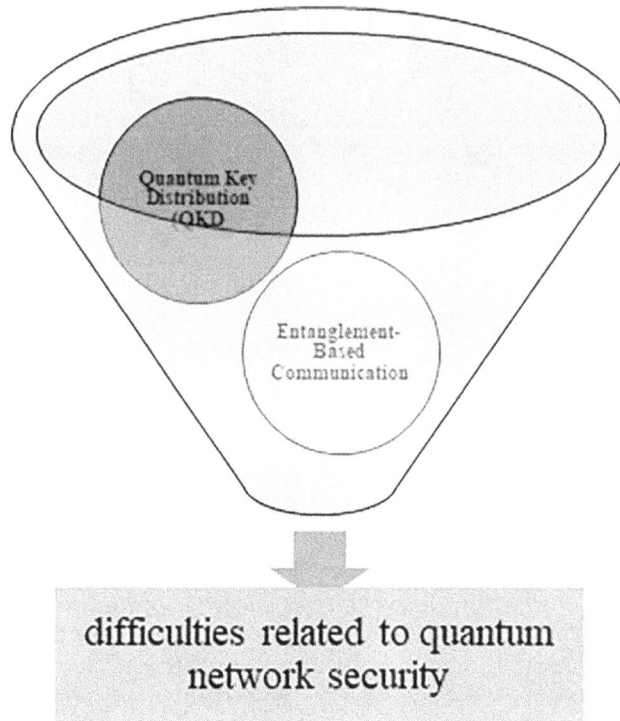

FIGURE 17.3   Difficulties related to quantum network security.

Quantum Network Security: The main goals of quantum network security are data integrity and communication protection. The following are some important considerations and difficulties related to quantum network security, shown in Figure 17.3:

- **Quantum Key Distribution:** QKD encrypts and decrypts communications using quantum mechanics. It is a secure communication technique. Its theoretically secure key exchange is made possible by the entanglement and quantum superposition concepts [Kalinin and Krundyshev, 2023].
- **Entanglement-Based Communication:** Since measurement breaks the entanglement, using entangled particles for communication makes sure that any effort at eavesdropping is discovered. Building long-distance quantum networks requires the employment of quantum repeaters, which increase the range of quantum communication by amplifying signals without changing their quantum state. Creating cryptographic methods that are resistant to attacks from both classical and quantum computers is known as post-quantum cryptography [Montanaro, 2016].

17.7   CHALLENGES

Infrastructure Development: The creation and upkeep of a quantum network necessitate substantial infrastructural advances, such as the currently-underdeveloped quantum repeaters and quantum memory.

Key Distribution and Management: Although QKD offers safe key exchange, it is still a difficult task to manage and distribute these keys across the network.

Integrating Quantum Networks with Classical Infrastructure: There are considerable technological and security obstacles in integrating quantum networks with the current classical infrastructure.

TABLE 17.2
Challenges

Infrastructure Development	– The currently-underdeveloped quantum repeaters and quantum memory.
Key Distribution and Management	– difficult task to manage and distribute
Integrating Quantum Networks with Classical Infrastructure	– Security obstacles in integrating quantum networks with the current classical infrastructure.
Attacks on Quantum Channels	– compromise the security of quantum communications using quantum channels
Error rates and Decoherence	– the high susceptibility of quantum systems to errors and decoherence
Resource Intensity:	– specialised gear, which can be costly and difficult to install.
Standardisation and Protocols	– due to the absence of standardised protocols
	– best practices for quantum network security

Attacks on Quantum Channels: Photon number splitting attacks and channel loss manipulation are two examples of attacks that potentially compromise the security of quantum communications using quantum channels [Cerezo et al., 2022].

Error Rates and Decoherence: The integrity and dependability of quantum communications can be impacted by the high susceptibility of quantum systems to errors and decoherence.

Resource Intensity: In order to generate and detect quantum states, quantum networks need a significant amount of physical and computational resources, including specialized gear, which can be costly and difficult to install.

Standardization and Protocols: It is challenging to guarantee uniform and safe implementation across various systems and organizations due to the absence of standardized protocols and best practices for quantum network security [Han et al., 2024].

17.8 FUTURE DIRECTIONS

Research and development in quantum repeaters will play a critical role in expanding the dependability and range of quantum networks. The resilience of quantum communications will be increased by creating quantum error correction techniques that are more effective. The implementation of quantum network security can be made consistent and secure by establishing best practices and standardized protocols. The creation of hybrid quantum-classical systems can take advantage of the advantages of both technologies, offering a more workable and safe option as we move towards fully quantum networks. By removing financial obstacles and supporting research and development, economic incentives can aid in the broader adoption of quantum network technology.

17.9 CONCLUSION

The rapid development of quantum computing technology presents the promise of unprecedented computational power, but it also introduces a new set of security risks that require management to safeguard the confidentiality and integrity of information processing. This investigation has revealed significant security concerns associated with quantum computing, including the great sensitivity of qubits to external disturbances, the strict cryogenic requirements, and the susceptibility to physical layer and side-channel assaults. Robust error correction techniques are crucial because quantum calculations are highly vulnerable to decoherence and quantum error rates. Hardware Trojans, fault injection attacks, and the potential for malicious alterations during production further complicate the security environment. Furthermore, there are still difficulties in integrating quantum and classical networks, standardizing protocols, and overcoming the financial and technological obstacles to putting safe quantum systems into practice. Notwithstanding these obstacles, entanglement-based communication and quantum key distribution present potential paths towards safe information sharing. Developments in quantum repeaters, enhanced error correction methods, and the creation of uniform security protocols will determine the direction of quantum network security in the future. Furthermore, financial incentives and cross-disciplinary cooperation will be essential to removing the present adoption hurdles and guaranteeing the safe implementation of quantum technology. In summary, whereas quantum computing poses significant security risks, it also offers special chances to improve information processing security. Realizing the full promise of quantum computing in a secure and dependable manner will require addressing these issues via ongoing study, technical innovation, and interdisciplinary collaboration.

REFERENCES

"40 years of quantum computing," *Nature Review Physics* 4, 1 (2022), doi: 10.1038/s42254-021-00410-6

F. Arute et al., "Quantum supremacy using a programmable superconducting processor," *Nature* 574, 505–510 (2019), doi: 10.1038/s41586-019-1666-5

M. Cerezo et al., "Challenges and opportunities in quantum machine learning," *Nature Computational Science* 2, 567–576 (2022), doi: 10.1038/s43588-022-00311-3

F. Chen et al., "NISQ quantum computing: A security-centric tutorial and survey [feature]," *IEEE Circuits and Systems Magazine*, vol. 24, no. 1, pp. 14–32, Firstquarter 2024, doi: 10.1109/MCAS.2024.3349665

S. Deshpande, C. Xu, T. Trochatos, Y. Ding and J. Szefer, "Towards an antivirus for quantum computers," *2022 IEEE International Symposium on Hardware Oriented Security and Trust (HOST)*, McLean, VA, USA, 2022, pp. 37–40, doi: 10.1109/HOST54066.2022.9840181.

P. Gani and R. Greer, "Securing quantum computers: Safeguarding against eavesdropping and side-channel attacks," *2023 IEEE MIT Undergraduate Research Technology Conference (URTC)*, Cambridge, MA, USA, 2023, pp. 1–5, doi: 10.1109/URTC60662.2023.10534941.

E. Grumbling and M. Horowitz, *Quantum Computing: Progress and Prospects*, National Academies of Sciences, Engineering, and Medicine, 2019.

H. J. Hadi, Y. Cao, M. A. Alshara, N. Ahmad, M. S. Riaz and J. Li, "Quantum computing challenges and impact on cyber security," S. Goel and P. R. Nunes de Souza (eds) *Digital Forensics and Cyber Crime. ICDF2C 2023*. Lecture Notes of the Institute for Computer Sciences, Social Informatics and Telecommunications Engineering, vol. 571, 2024, Springer, Cham, doi: 10.1007/978-3-031-56583-0_22

H. Han et al., "Quantum communication based cyber security analysis using artificial intelligence with IoMT," *Optical and Quantum Electronics* 56, 565 (2024), doi: 10.1007/s11082-023-06185-7

M. J. Hossain Faruk, S. Tahora, M. Tasnim, H. Shahriar and N. Sakib, "A review of quantum cybersecurity: Threats, risks and opportunities," *2022 1st International Conference on AI in Cybersecurity (ICAIC)*, Victoria, TX, USA, 2022, pp. 1–8, doi: 10.1109/ICAIC53980.2022.9896970.

M. Kalinin and V. Krundyshev, "Security intrusion detection using quantum machine learning techniques," *Journal of Computer Virology and Hacking Techniques* 19, 125–136 (2023), doi: 10.1007/s11416-022-00435-0

A. Montanaro, "Quantum algorithms: An overview," *npj Quantum Information* 2, 15023 (2016), doi: 10.1038/npjqi.2015.23

P. Murali, N. M. Linke, M. Martonosi, A. J. Abhari, N. H. Nguyen and C. H. Alderete, "Full-stack, real-system quantum computer studies: Architectural comparisons and design insights," *Proceedings of the 46th International Symposium on Computer Architecture (ISCA'19). Association for Computing Machinery*, New York, NY, USA, 2019, pp. 527–540, doi: 10.1145/3307650.3322273

R. Orús, S. Mugel and E. Lizaso, "Quantum computing for finance: Overview and prospects," *Reviews in Physics* 4 (2019).

P. Ravi, A. Chattopadhyay and S. Bhasin, "Security and quantum computing: An overview," *2022 IEEE 23rd Latin American Test Symposium (LATS)*, Montevideo, Uruguay, 2022, pp. 1–6, doi: 10.1109/LATS57337.2022

18 Fortifying Cyber Defenses with IDPS Implementation and Management Best Practices

M. Baritha Begum, R. Thillaikarasi, M. Sandhiya,
R.C. Jeni Gracia, Suresh Balakrishnan T.,
Rengaraj Alias Muralidharan R., Suresh Sankaranarayanan,
and Lakshmi Kanthan Narayanan

18.1 INTRODUCTION

Intrusion detection and prevention systems (IDPSs) are vital parts of an organization's cybersecurity infrastructure. These systems are made to watch network and system activities for harmful actions or rule breaches and react properly. This chapter explores the architecture, functionality, types, and deployment strategies of IDPSs, along with best practices for implementation and maintenance. The concept of intrusion detection dates back to the early days of computing when the primary focus was on securing individual mainframes from unauthorized access. As networking technology advanced, the need for more sophisticated intrusion detection mechanisms became evident. Early intrusion detection systems (IDSs) were primarily signature based, relying on predefined patterns of known threats to detect malicious activities. These systems were effective in identifying known attacks but struggled with new or evolving threats. The advent of the internet and the rapid growth of interconnected networks in the 1990s and 2000s brought about a paradigm shift in cyber threats. Attackers began leveraging more complex techniques, such as polymorphic malware zero-day exploits and advanced persistent threats (APTs), which were capable of bypassing traditional IDSs. This necessitated the development of more advanced systems that could not only detect intrusions but also prevent them in real time. Intrusion prevention systems (IPSs) emerged as an evolution of IDSs, incorporating the ability to actively block or mitigate detected threats. The integration of detection and prevention capabilities led to the development of IDPSs, which combine the functionalities of IDSs and IPSs to provide a more comprehensive security solution. Modern IDPSs employ a variety of detection techniques, including signature-based, anomaly-based, and hybrid methods, to identify and respond to threats more effectively.

The distributed cyber-physical intrusion detection system relies on stacking learning to fortify wide-area protection systems. By amalgamating various detection mechanisms across distributed nodes, it aims to enhance the security of cyber-physical systems [1]. Leveraging a multi-head self-attention gated graph convolutional network, this system focuses on identifying multiple attacks within mobile ad hoc networks (MANETs). Through the fusion of graph convolutional networks and attention mechanisms, it endeavors to heighten intrusion detection accuracy within dynamic and decentralized MANET environments [2]. Aiming at ensuring both security and privacy, this intrusion detection system is tailored for wireless sensor networks. Employing federated learning with Secured Convolutional Neural Network (SCNN)-Bi-LSTM, it boosts reliability while safeguarding sensitive data gathered by sensor nodes [3]. The SCNN is serving as a stalwart defense system, a poll on counter adversarial machine learning attacks in intrusion detection systems is made by deploying advanced defense mechanisms, it reinforces the resilience of intrusion detection systems, thereby ensuring the integrity and dependability of detected intrusions [4].

Tailored to address the intricacies of IoT environments, this intrusion detection system is purpose-built for IoT devices and data. It adeptly navigates resource constraints and diverse communication protocols to detect and mitigate intrusions effectively within IoT networks [5]. Designed to identify and counter poisoning attacks, this personalized federated learning-based intrusion detection system enhances detection accuracy while mitigating the impact of adversarial data manipulation [6]. Tailored to fortify cloud security, this intrusion detection approach harnesses transformer neural networks. By leveraging transformer-based techniques, it enhances the efficiency and effectiveness of intrusion detection, particularly addressing scalability and complexity challenges in cloud environments [7]. Exploring the nuances between feature selection and extraction techniques. The study made by Long et al. optimizes intrusion detection systems within IoT environments. Through comparative analysis, it sheds light on methods to enhance performance and efficiency [8]. IDS-INT employs transformer-based transfer learning to tackle imbalanced network traffic. By harnessing transfer learning, it enhances the detection accuracy of rare and unseen intrusions within imbalanced network environments [9]. This research delves into feature extraction techniques tailored for machine learning-based intrusion detection in IoT networks. By extracting pertinent features from IoT network traffic, the proposed method enhances the efficacy and efficiency of intrusion detection systems within IoT ecosystems [10].

DTL-IDS presents an optimized intrusion detection framework amalgamating deep transfer learning and genetic algorithms. This framework augments adaptability and robustness by leveraging transfer learning while optimizing the detection process using genetic algorithms [11]. Through a comparative examination of machine learning-based intrusion detection systems, this study offers valuable insights into their strengths and weaknesses. Such insights aid in the judicious selection and optimization of intrusion detection systems [12]. Offering a comprehensive overview, this systematic literature review delineates trends, challenges, and advancements in host-based intrusion detection systems (HIDSs). Its findings furnish valuable insights for researchers and practitioners in the field [13]. Tailored for the unique challenges of the Internet of Vehicles (IoV) environment, this intrusion detection system leverages IoV-specific communication patterns and attack scenarios. It enhances the security and resilience of connected vehicle networks against cyber threats [14].

The importance of intrusion detection and prevention systems in the cybersecurity landscape cannot be overstated [15, 16]. Cyber-attacks pose significant risks to organizations, including financial losses, reputational damage, regulatory penalties, and operational disruptions. An effective IDPS offers several critical benefits to mitigate these risks. First, it provides real-time threat detection and prevention by continuously monitoring network traffic and system activities, enabling timely identification and mitigation of malicious actions. This real-time capability is essential for minimizing the impact of attacks and reducing potential damage. Second, an IDPS ensures comprehensive security coverage by integrating both network-based and host-based monitoring, offering a holistic view of the security landscape. This comprehensive approach enables organizations to identify and address both external and internal threats, safeguarding their digital assets effectively. Moreover, modern IDPS solutions feature automated response mechanisms that can automatically respond to detected threats, such as blocking malicious IP addresses or isolating compromised systems. These automated responses reduce response times and limit the potential damage caused by cyber-attacks. Additionally, IDPSs generate enhanced visibility and accountability by providing detailed logs and alerts that offer valuable insights into security incidents. This enhanced visibility facilitates forensic analysis, compliance reporting, and accountability, ensuring organizations can effectively respond to security breaches. Last, IDPSs demonstrate adaptability to emerging threats by integrating advanced detection techniques like machine learning and behavioral analysis. This adaptability enables IDPSs to stay ahead of evolving threats, ensuring organizations are better prepared to handle new and sophisticated attack vectors. Overall, the multifaceted capabilities of

IDPSs play a crucial role in enhancing cybersecurity resilience and protecting organizations from the ever-evolving threat landscape.

18.2 ARCHITECTURE AND FUNCTIONALITY OF IDPSS

The architecture of an intrusion detection and prevention system comprises several key components that collaborate to detect and prevent intrusions effectively. Sensors serve as the frontline observers, whether hardware appliances or software applications, tasked with monitoring network traffic or system activities. They gather data from diverse sources such as network packets, log files, and system processes, providing a wealth of information for analysis as shown in Figure 18.1. Analyzers then come into play, processing and scrutinizing the data collected by sensors. Employing various detection techniques, analyzers discern potential intrusions and trigger alerts or preemptive actions to thwart threats. Management servers serve as the centralized nerve center, overseeing the coordination of sensors and analyzers. They offer a user interface for administrators to configure and monitor the IDPS, facilitating event correlation and report generation.

Databases play a pivotal role by storing data pertaining to detected events, alerts, and logs. This repository of historical data is invaluable for uncovering patterns and trends in security incidents, aiding in forensic analysis and strategic planning. Finally, response systems act swiftly upon detection of intrusions, executing predefined actions to mitigate threats. These responses can range from blocking network traffic and notifying administrators to executing automated scripts for immediate threat containment. Together, these components form a robust architecture that fortifies networks against malicious activities and safeguards organizational assets.

Intrusion detection and prevention systems are critical components in modern cybersecurity frameworks. Their primary function is to monitor, detect, and respond to malicious activities or policy violations within a network or on individual host devices. Understanding the architecture and functionality of IDPSs is essential for implementing effective security measures and protecting digital assets from threats.

The structure of an intrusion detection and prevention system can generally be classified into two primary categories: host-based IDPSs (HIDPSs) and network-based IDPSs (NIDPSs). Each category possesses a unique design crafted to suit its particular surveillance and detection needs. An HIDPS is implemented on individual hosts or endpoints, including servers, workstations, and mobile devices. The architecture typically includes components like an agent, log manager, analysis engine, and response system. The agent is a software component responsible for monitoring system activities such as file access, system calls, and application behavior. The log manager collects and stores logs generated by the agent, which are crucial for analyzing and correlating events to detect intrusions. The analysis engine then processes the collected data to identify suspicious activities using signature-based, anomaly-based, or hybrid detection methods. Finally, the response system executes predefined actions when an intrusion is detected, such as alerting administrators, blocking malicious processes, or isolating the affected host. An HIDPS is particularly effective for detecting insider threats and attacks that originate from within the network.

On the other hand, an NIDPS monitors network traffic to detect malicious activities. Its architecture includes sensors, a traffic collector, an analysis engine, a management server, and a response system. Sensors are deployed at strategic points within the network, such as at the perimeter or critical internal segments, to capture and inspect network packets. The traffic collector aggregates

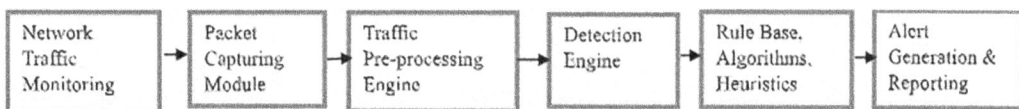

```
Network          Packet          Traffic          Detection     Rule Base,      Alert
Traffic    -->   Capturing  -->  Pre-processing -> Engine    --> Algorithms, -> Generation &
Monitoring       Module          Engine                         Heuristics      Reporting
```

FIGURE 18.1 Intrusion Detection and Prevention System Architecture.

traffic data from various sensors and prepares it for analysis. The analysis engine processes this data to identify suspicious patterns or behaviors, utilizing signature-based, anomaly-based, or hybrid detection techniques. The management server is a centralized component that manages sensors, collects data, and provides a user interface for administrators to configure and monitor the IDPS. Similar to an HIDPS, the response system in an NIDPS takes appropriate actions upon detecting an intrusion, such as sending alerts, dropping malicious packets, or reconfiguring firewall rules. NIDPSs are effective in protecting against external threats and monitoring network-wide traffic.

Intrusion detection and prevention systems utilize diverse detection techniques to pinpoint potential threats, categorized into three primary types: signature-based, anomaly-based, and hybrid detection. Signature-based detection involves matching monitored activities with a repository of established attack signatures, proving adept at recognizing familiar threats but unable to spot novel or unidentified attacks. Anomaly-based detection establishes a norm of typical behavior and flags any deviations from it, offering the potential to uncover unknown threats but susceptible to generating false alarms. Hybrid detection merges the capabilities of signature-based and anomaly-based methods, capitalizing on their respective advantages while mitigating their drawbacks.

The functionality of an IDPS encompasses several key processes, including monitoring, detection, analysis, response, and reporting. The primary function of an IDPS is to continuously monitor network traffic or host activities, capturing data in real time to ensure that no potential threat goes unnoticed. Detection is the core functionality of an IDPS, involving the identification of suspicious activities or policy violations using the aforementioned detection methods. Once a potential threat is detected, the analysis engine processes the data to confirm whether it is a genuine threat. This involves correlating multiple events, analyzing patterns, and eliminating false positives, with advanced IDPSs potentially using machine learning algorithms to enhance accuracy. Upon confirming an intrusion, the IDPS initiates a response to mitigate the threat, which can be passive, such as generating alerts for administrators, or active, such as blocking malicious traffic, terminating suspicious processes, or reconfiguring security policies. The response mechanism is critical for preventing further damage and containing the threat. Finally, the IDPS generates detailed reports on detected intrusions, responses taken, and overall system performance, providing valuable insights for security teams to understand the nature of threats, assess the effectiveness of their security measures, and make informed decisions for future improvements.

Implementing IDPSs offers several benefits for an organization's security posture. Enhanced threat detection is achieved through real-time monitoring and detection of malicious activities, enabling quick identification of threats. Improved response time is facilitated by automated response mechanisms that allow for immediate action upon detecting a threat, minimizing potential damage. Comprehensive visibility is provided by monitoring both network traffic and host activities, offering a holistic view of the security status of an organization's IT infrastructure. Additionally, an IDPS helps ensure regulatory compliance by meeting many regulatory frameworks' requirements for robust security measures to protect sensitive data. Proactive security is also promoted, as IDPSs help organizations adopt a proactive approach to security by identifying and mitigating threats before they can cause significant harm.

While an IDPS offers significant benefits, it also poses several challenges. Anomaly-based detection, for instance, may trigger false positives, resulting in unnecessary alerts and potential disruptions to legitimate activities. Continuous monitoring and analysis, particularly in high-traffic networks or resource-limited environments, can impact system performance. Regular updates to signatures and anomaly detection models are necessary to keep the IDPS effective against evolving threats. Furthermore, configuring and managing an IDPS can be intricate, demanding specialized knowledge and expertise.

IDPSs, encompassing both host-based and network-based systems, are pivotal in safeguarding digital assets by monitoring, detecting, and responding to malicious activities. Leveraging diverse detection methods and robust functionality, an IDPS enhances threat detection, response time, and overall security visibility. Nonetheless, organizations must address the associated challenges to fully harness its benefits. With proper implementation and management, IDPSs can substantially bolster an organization's cybersecurity defenses.

18.3 TYPES OF IDPSS

IDPS can be categorized based on their monitoring scope and detection methods. In Figure 18.2, a block diagram showcases various types of intrusion detection and prevention systems, distinguishing between host-based IDPSs and network-based IDPSs. Each classification employs distinct detection techniques, including signature detection, anomaly detection, and hybrid detection for NIDPS. This visual depiction underscores the synergy among various IDPS components in protecting computing systems and network traffic against potential threats.

18.3.1 Network-Based IDPSs

Network-based intrusion detection and prevention systems are designed to focus on scrutinizing network traffic for any signs of dubious behavior. Their main role is to examine both inbound and outbound data packets in order to pinpoint potential security risks or breaches of policy. NIDPSs are strategically deployed at key points within the network architecture, commonly positioned between the internal network and the perimeter firewall. This strategic placement allows them to intercept and inspect all traffic entering or exiting the network, making them highly effective in detecting and blocking attacks that occur over the network. Examples of such attacks include denial-of-service (DoS) attacks, which flood the network with excessive traffic to disrupt service availability, and network scanning, where adversaries probe for vulnerabilities or open ports. Notable examples of NIDPS solutions include Snort and Suricata, which leverage signature-based and anomaly-based detection techniques to safeguard networks against various cyber threats.

18.3.2 Host-Based IDPSs

Host-based intrusion detection and prevention systems focus on monitoring activities on individual hosts, such as computers or servers. Unlike network-based systems that analyze network traffic, HIDPSs are installed directly on the host machines they protect. This deployment approach enables them to monitor and analyze various aspects of host activity, including file system changes, process execution, and user authentication. By inspecting host-level events and behaviors, HIDPSs can detect insider threats and malicious activities that may not be visible to network-based systems. For example, they can identify unauthorized file modifications, privilege escalations, or suspicious system calls indicative of malware activity. This level of visibility into host behavior enhances the overall security posture by providing early detection and response capabilities at the endpoint level.

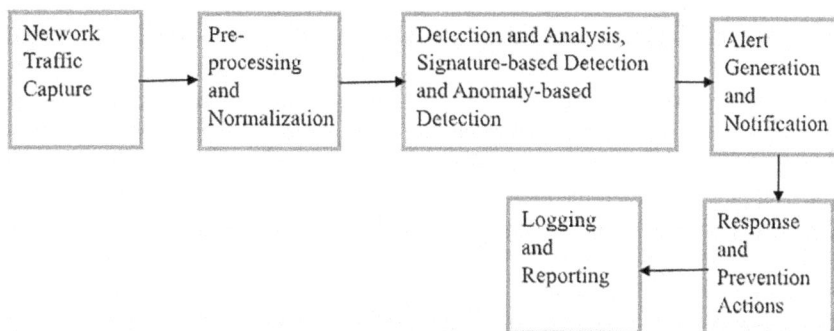

FIGURE 18.2 Types of intrusion detection and prevention systems.

Examples of HIDPS solutions include OSSEC and Tripwire, which offer comprehensive host-based monitoring and protection against a wide range of threats.

18.3.3   HYBRID IDPSs

Hybrid intrusion detection and prevention systems amalgamate the functionalities of both network-based IDPSs and host-based IDPSs to offer comprehensive monitoring capabilities. These systems integrate network-based sensors, which analyze traffic flowing through the network, with host-based sensors, which monitor activities on individual hosts. By combining both types of sensors and analyzers, hybrid IDPSs provide a holistic view of the security landscape, detecting threats at both the network and host levels. This integrated approach enhances detection accuracy and allows for a more nuanced understanding of security incidents, enabling organizations to respond effectively to complex threats. Hybrid IDPSs are deployed by integrating network-based sensors at critical network points and deploying host-based sensors on individual hosts across the network infrastructure. Notable advantages of hybrid IDPSs include their ability to provide a broader and more detailed view of the security landscape, enabling organizations to identify and mitigate threats more effectively. Examples of hybrid IDPSs solutions include IBM QRadar and McAfee ePolicy Orchestrator, which offer advanced capabilities for threat detection, response, and management across hybrid environments.

18.4   DETECTION TECHNIQUES

An intrusion detection and prevention system monitors network traffic to detect and respond to potential threats by employing various detection techniques. These techniques serve as the first line of defense against cyber threats, encompassing methods to identify and thwart malicious activities within networks and individual devices. Understanding these detection techniques is essential for robust cybersecurity.

Signature-based detection, also referred to as rule-based detection, relies on predefined signatures or patterns of known attacks to spot malicious activities. These signatures are typically derived from analyzing past incidents, malware samples, or known vulnerabilities. When observing network traffic or host activities, the IDPS compares behavior against its signature database. If a match is found, indicating a known threat, the IDPS initiates an alert or predefined action to mitigate the risk. However, signature-based detection has limitations, such as its inability to identify new or previously unseen attacks.

In contrast, anomaly-based detection focuses on identifying deviations from normal behavior or expected activity patterns. Instead of predefined signatures, it establishes a baseline of typical behavior for the network or host. Any deviations from this baseline are flagged as potentially suspicious and investigated further. Anomaly detection algorithms utilize statistical analysis, machine learning, or artificial intelligence techniques to identify anomalies. Despite its capability to detect novel threats, anomaly-based detection may produce false positives, alerting on benign activities.

Heuristic-based detection utilizes rules or algorithms to identify suspicious behavior that may indicate a threat. Unlike signature-based detection, which relies on exact matches, heuristic-based detection identifies behaviors with characteristics commonly associated with malicious activities. This method is effective for identifying previously unseen threats or variants of known attacks but may generate false positives if the heuristics are overly sensitive.

Behavioral-based detection monitors and analyzes user, application, and system behavior to detect anomalies or signs of compromise. By establishing a baseline of normal behavior, it identifies deviations indicative of malicious activities, such as unauthorized access attempts or data exfiltration. Behavioral analysis techniques include profiling user activities, tracking system interactions, or monitoring application behavior. While effective against insider threats and sophisticated attacks, it requires comprehensive monitoring and analysis capabilities.

Reputation-based detection uses threat intelligence and reputation data to identify and block known malicious entities, such as IP addresses or domains. It maintains a database of known malicious entities and assesses the reputation or trustworthiness of encountered entities during network or host activities. While effective against known threats, it may be less effective against zero-day attacks or threats with no prior reputation data. Protocol-based detection examines network traffic for anomalies or violations of standard protocols and communication patterns. This technique focuses on identifying deviations from expected protocol behavior, such as unauthorized protocol usage, protocol violations, or unusual protocol sequences. Protocol-based detection is particularly effective for detecting protocol-level attacks, such as protocol fuzzing, packet fragmentation, or protocol abuse. By analyzing network protocols at a granular level, this technique can identify sophisticated attacks that evade traditional signature-based detection methods.

Detection techniques are crucial components of intrusion detection and prevention systems, facilitating the identification and thwarting of malicious activities across networks or individual host devices. Signature-based detection relies on predefined signatures of known attacks, while anomaly-based detection centers on detecting deviations from normal behavior. Supplementary to these are heuristic-based, behavioral-based, reputation-based, and protocol-based detection approaches, which contribute additional layers of defense against a wide range of cyber threats. Understanding the strengths and limitations of each detection technique is imperative for devising effective security measures and mitigating the risks associated with evolving cyber threats. Upon detecting an intrusion, the system issues alerts and notifies administrators, as depicted in Figure 18.3.

Response actions, which can be automated or manual, aim to mitigate the threat by blocking sources or reconfiguring network settings. Comprehensive logs and reports are maintained for auditing and analysis, ensuring ongoing security improvements. IDPSs employ various detection techniques to identify potential security incidents, as shown in Table 18.1.

18.4.1 SIGNATURE-BASED DETECTION

Signature-based detection utilizes pre-established patterns or signatures of recognized threats to detect intrusions. This method depends on a repository of signatures, which are distinct sequences of bytes or patterns representing known malicious behavior. Advantages of this method include its high effectiveness against known threats, as it can quickly and accurately identify malicious activities that match its database of signatures. This makes it a reliable tool for detecting and mitigating threats that have been previously encountered and documented. However, limitations arise because signature-based detection cannot identify new or unknown attacks. Since it depends on predefined signatures, it is ineffective against zero-day exploits or novel attack methods that have not yet been cataloged. This limitation highlights the need for complementary detection techniques to provide a more comprehensive security solution.

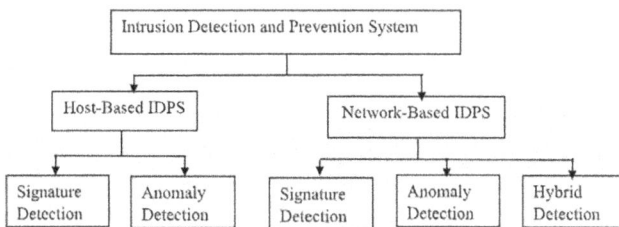

FIGURE 18.3 Block diagram of detection techniques.

TABLE 18.1

Detection Analysis in Character and Features for Different IDPS Detection Techniques

Detection Technique	Advantages	Limitations	Key Features
Signature-Based Detection	—High effectiveness against known threats. Quick and accurate identification of malicious activities.	—Ineffective against unknown or zero-day attacks —Requires regular updates to the signature database.	—Relies on a database of known threat patterns —Predefined sequences of bytes or patterns —High accuracy for known threats.
Anomaly-Based Detection	—Capable of detecting unknown or zero-day attacks —Establishes a baseline of normal behavior.	—Potential for false positives if normal behavior changes —Requires continual updates and fine-tuning.	—Establishes normal behavior baseline —Detects deviations from normal patterns —Suitable for dynamic threat environments.
Hybrid Detection	—Combines strengths of signature-based and anomaly-based methods —Improved detection accuracy.	—More complex to implement and manage —Higher resource requirements.	—Integrates signature-based and anomaly-based techniques —Balances detection accuracy and adaptability —Reduces false positives and negatives.

18.4.2 ANOMALY-BASED DETECTION

Anomaly-based detection establishes a foundation of typical behavior and identifies discrepancies from this foundation. This approach entails observing routine activities and network traffic to construct a blueprint of what is deemed standard for a specific system or environment. Advantages of anomaly-based detection include its ability to identify unknown or zero-day attacks. Since it flags any activity that deviates from the established baseline, it can detect previously unseen threats that do not match known signatures. However, limitations include the potential for false positives if normal behavior changes over time. As network usage patterns evolve, the baseline may need to be continually updated to accurately reflect current normal behavior. Without regular updates and fine-tuning, the system might incorrectly identify legitimate changes as threats, leading to unnecessary alerts and potential alert fatigue among security personnel.

18.4.3 HYBRID DETECTION

Hybrid detection employs both signature-based and anomaly-based methodologies, synergizing their strengths to bolster detection capabilities. It harnesses the predefined patterns or signatures of identified threats from signature-based detection, along with the capacity to pinpoint abnormalities in typical behavior from anomaly-based detection. By integrating these two techniques, hybrid detection achieves a more comprehensive and robust detection capability, capable of identifying both known and unknown threats effectively. One of the advantages of hybrid detection is its ability to balance the strengths of both signature-based and anomaly-based methods. Signature-based detection excels at identifying known threats with high accuracy, while anomaly-based detection can detect previously unseen or zero-day attacks. By combining these techniques, hybrid detection improves overall detection accuracy and reduces the likelihood of false positives and false negatives. However, hybrid detection also comes with its limitations. Implementing and managing hybrid detection systems can be more complex compared to single-method approaches. Integrating signature-based and anomaly-based detection requires careful configuration and tuning to ensure optimal performance. Additionally, managing the increased volume of alerts generated by hybrid detection systems can pose challenges for security teams, requiring additional resources and expertise for effective monitoring and response. Overall, while hybrid detection offers significant advantages in terms of improved detection accuracy, organizations must be prepared to invest the necessary resources and expertise in implementing and managing these more complex detection systems.

18.5   DEPLOYMENT STRATEGIES

Setting up an intrusion detection and prevention system demands meticulous preparation, taking into account the unique requirements and network structure of the organization. Strategies for deployment stand as pivotal elements in IT infrastructure planning, essential for optimizing efficiency, scalability, and security. Organizations must carefully consider various deployment options to align with their business objectives, technological requirements, and budget constraints. In this section, we explore the diverse landscape of deployment strategies, including on-premises, cloud-based, and hybrid approaches, highlighting their benefits, challenges, and implications for modern businesses.

Deploying on-premises means setting up IT infrastructure within the company's physical location, providing complete authority to customize hardware, software, and security measures. This traditional approach provides organizations with a sense of security and compliance, as sensitive data remains within their direct control. Additionally, on-premises deployment is often favored by industries with stringent regulatory requirements, such as finance, healthcare, and government sectors. However, on-premises deployment requires significant upfront investment in infrastructure, maintenance, and skilled personnel. It also lacks the scalability and flexibility of cloud-based solutions, making it less suitable for rapidly growing or fluctuating workloads.

Cloud-based deployment revolutionizes IT infrastructure management by outsourcing computing resources to third-party service providers, offering agility, scalability, and cost-efficiency. Organizations can rapidly provision and scale resources on-demand, paying only for the services they use, without the burden of upfront capital expenditure. Cloud-based solutions also provide geographic redundancy, ensuring high availability and disaster recovery capabilities. Moreover, cloud providers offer a wide range of security features and compliance certifications, enhancing data protection and regulatory compliance. However, cloud-based deployment raises concerns regarding data privacy, vendor lock-in, and potential downtime due to reliance on external service providers. Organizations must carefully evaluate these risks and implement robust governance and security measures to mitigate potential threats.

Hybrid cloud deployment combines the benefits of on-premises and cloud-based solutions, offering a flexible and scalable infrastructure while maintaining control over sensitive data and critical workloads. This deployment model allows organizations to leverage both private and public cloud resources, seamlessly integrating on-premises infrastructure with cloud services. Hybrid cloud deployment is ideal for organizations with dynamic workloads, regulatory compliance requirements, or legacy systems that cannot be migrated to the cloud. By adopting a hybrid cloud strategy, organizations can optimize resource utilization, enhance agility, and mitigate risks associated with cloud adoption. However, managing a hybrid cloud environment requires specialized expertise in networking, security, and governance to ensure seamless integration, data consistency, and compliance across hybrid environments.

Deploying in the public cloud grants organizations access to pooled computing resources and services from third-party providers, fostering swift innovation, global outreach, and cost-effectiveness. Services like IaaS, PaaS, and SaaS empower organizations to deploy applications, databases, and development tools without initial hardware or software investments. Public cloud vendors furnish diverse security features, compliance certifications, and industry-specific solutions to cater to varied organizational needs. Nonetheless, concerns arise regarding data privacy, security, and regulatory adherence as organizations cede control to external providers. Evaluating the pros and cons of public cloud adoption is crucial, necessitating robust security measures, encryption, and access controls to safeguard sensitive data and ensure regulatory compliance. Private cloud deployment entails hosting IT resources within a dedicated environment, offering heightened security, customization, and oversight over infrastructure and data.

Private clouds can be deployed on-premises or hosted by third-party providers, offering organizations flexibility in managing their infrastructure while ensuring data sovereignty and compliance with regulatory requirements. Private cloud solutions provide organizations with the ability to customize infrastructure, security policies, and performance parameters to meet their specific needs and preferences. Additionally, private cloud deployments offer predictable performance, low latency, and high availability, making them ideal for mission-critical workloads, sensitive data, and compliance-driven industries. However, private cloud deployment requires significant upfront investment in infrastructure, expertise, and maintenance, limiting its scalability and agility compared to public cloud solutions. Organizations must carefully assess their requirements, budget constraints, and security concerns when considering private cloud deployment options.

Deployment strategies play a pivotal role in shaping organizations' IT infrastructure, enabling them to maximize efficiency, scalability, and security. On-premises deployment offers control and compliance, but at the cost of scalability and agility. Cloud-based deployment provides agility, scalability, and cost-efficiency, but raises concerns regarding data privacy and vendor lock-in. Hybrid cloud deployment balances control and flexibility, allowing organizations to optimize resource utilization and mitigate risks. Public cloud deployment offers global reach and innovation but requires careful consideration of data privacy and security implications. Private cloud deployment provides security and customization but requires significant upfront investment and expertise. By carefully evaluating the benefits, challenges, and implications of each deployment strategy, organizations can choose the most suitable approach to meet their business objectives and technological requirements in the ever-evolving digital landscape. Cloud-based strategies are further divided into private cloud, hybrid cloud, public cloud, and multi-cloud options. This visualization helps in understanding the different ways organizations can deploy their IT infrastructure to meet specific needs and preferences.

18.5.1 NETWORK PLACEMENT

Strategic placement of IDPS sensors at critical points within the network, such as the perimeter, internal segments, and demilitarized zones (DMZs), ensures comprehensive coverage and effective monitoring. Perimeter deployment involves placing an IDPS at the network boundary to monitor incoming and outgoing traffic, acting as the first line of defense against external threats. This deployment helps in identifying and mitigating threats before they penetrate deeper into the network. Internal deployment entails placing an IDPS within the internal network, which is crucial for detecting lateral movement and insider threats that may bypass perimeter defenses. This helps in identifying malicious activities within the network that could lead to data breaches or internal sabotage. Last, distributed deployment involves using multiple sensors and analyzers at different network segments to achieve comprehensive coverage. By deploying sensors in various locations, such as data centers, departmental networks, and cloud environments, organizations can ensure thorough monitoring and rapid detection of threats across the entire network. This layered approach to deployment enhances the overall security posture, providing robust protection against a wide range of cyber threats.

18.5.2 SCALABILITY AND PERFORMANCE

Ensuring the IDPS can scale with the network size and increased traffic volumes is crucial for maintaining robust and reliable security as an organization grows. Scalability is a key factor, as the IDPS must be capable of handling larger and more complex network environments without degradation in performance. This involves deploying additional sensors, upgrading hardware, or optimizing software configurations to accommodate increased data flow and more devices. Simultaneously, Performance must be carefully balanced with detection capabilities to avoid bottlenecks that could hinder network operations. An effective IDPS should be designed to process high volumes of traffic efficiently while maintaining accurate and timely threat detection. This balance ensures that the security system does not become a choke point, allowing for seamless operation and uninterrupted business activities. By focusing on both scalability and performance, organizations can ensure their IDPS remains effective and responsive, even as their network demands grow.

18.5.3 INTEGRATION WITH EXISTING INFRASTRUCTURE

To ensure optimal performance, an intrusion detection and prevention system should effortlessly merge with present security solutions, including firewalls, security information and event management (SIEM) systems, and endpoint protection platforms. Compatibility is essential to create a unified and cohesive security strategy, allowing for the efficient sharing of threat intelligence and coordinated defense mechanisms. By ensuring the IDPS works harmoniously with these tools, organizations can achieve a holistic security posture that leverages the strengths of each component. Furthermore, Automation plays a crucial role in enhancing the IDPS's efficiency. By implementing automated responses to detected threats, the system can significantly reduce the time to mitigation, swiftly neutralizing potential risks before they escalate into more severe incidents. This automation not only improves response times but also frees up valuable resources, allowing security teams to focus on more complex tasks that require human intervention. Overall, seamless integration and automation are key to maximizing the effectiveness and efficiency of an IDPS within an organization's broader cybersecurity framework.

18.6 BEST PRACTICES FOR IMPLEMENTATION

Effective implementation of an IDPS involves several best practices to maximize its effectiveness and minimize false positives: Effective implementation and maintenance of intrusion detection and prevention systems require adherence to several best practices to maximize security efficacy and minimize operational disruptions. Regular updates are crucial, involving the constant refreshment of signatures and anomaly detection models to defend against emerging threats. This ensures that the IDPS is equipped to recognize and counteract the latest malicious activities. Tuning and calibration of detection thresholds and rules are equally important; by adjusting these parameters regularly, the system can adapt to the evolving network environment, significantly reducing the incidence of false positives and improving detection accuracy. Continuous monitoring is vital for maintaining robust security, necessitating 24/7 surveillance and immediate incident response capabilities to swiftly address any detected threats. Training and awareness programs are essential for personnel, educating staff on responding to IDPS alerts and keeping them informed about the latest threat trends. This knowledge empowers them to act swiftly and appropriately during potential security incidents. Finally, periodic audits are necessary to verify the IDPS's operational integrity. Regular assessments ensure the system functions correctly, adheres to security objectives, and adapts to changing security landscapes, thereby maintaining a strong and resilient cybersecurity posture.

Table 18.2 provides a performance analysis of IDPSs across various dimensions such as detection accuracy, resource consumption, ease of management, and adaptability.

TABLE 18.2
Performance Analysis of IDPSs

Performance Criteria	Signature-Based Detection	Anomaly-Based Detection	Hybrid Detection
Detection Accuracy	High for known threats; low for unknown threats	Moderate; can detect unknown threats but prone to false positives	High; combines accuracy of both methods
Detection Speed	Fast, as it matches against known signatures	Moderate, as it involves baseline comparison	Moderate to fast, depending on the balance of methods used
False Positives	Low for known threats	High, as normal behavior changes can be flagged as anomalies	Moderate; balances false positives from both methods
False Negatives	High for unknown threats	Moderate, depends on the accuracy of the baseline	Low; reduced due to combined approach
Resource Consumption	Low to moderate; depends on the size of the signature database	High; requires significant processing power for baseline analysis	High; requires resources for both signature matching and anomaly detection
Ease of Management	Easy; requires regular signature updates	Complex; requires continuous baseline tuning and monitoring	Complex; needs management of both detection techniques
Adaptability	Low; needs frequent updates to handle new threats	High; can adapt to new and evolving threats	High; leverages adaptability of anomaly detection
Scalability	High; efficient for large datasets of known signatures	Moderate; can become resource-intensive as the environment grows	Moderate; complexity increases with scale
Maintenance Effort	Moderate; regular updates required	High; continuous tuning and adjustments needed	High; requires maintenance of both systems
Cost	Low to moderate; cost mainly for updates	High; significant investment in computational resources	High; involves costs from both methods

In today's digital world, it's crucial to have strong cybersecurity measures because threats are always evolving and becoming more sophisticated. Following best practices is essential to make sure these measures are effective and protect digital assets from potential threats. This article outlines key best practices for cybersecurity, including risk assessment, policy development, access control, employee training, and incident response.

Before implementing any cybersecurity measures, it's essential to conduct a thorough risk assessment. This means identifying and evaluating potential risks and vulnerabilities in the organization's IT systems, applications, and processes. Understanding these risks helps security teams prioritize their efforts, focusing first on the most critical threats. Regular risk assessments are necessary to keep up with evolving threats and changes in the business environment. Clear and concise cybersecurity policies are also fundamental for a strong security framework. These policies should outline guidelines, procedures, and best practices for managing and protecting digital assets like data, systems, and networks. Key areas to cover include data protection, access control, acceptable technology use, incident response, and compliance. Policies should be regularly reviewed and updated to reflect changes in technology, regulations, and threats.

It's crucial to establish efficient access control measures to stop unauthorized entry to sensitive data and resources. This means assigning user roles and privileges with the least amount of access required for their tasks. Strong authentication methods like multi-factor authentication (MFA) should be used, and access rights for past employees or contractors should be reviewed and revoked regularly. Implementing robust identity and access management (IAM) solutions can simplify access control procedures and bolster security.

Employees are frequently seen as the most vulnerable aspect of cybersecurity since their mistakes and oversights can open organizations up to security vulnerabilities. It's crucial to implement thorough cybersecurity training and awareness initiatives for employees to foster a security-oriented culture within the organization. This training should encompass identifying phishing attempts, protecting sensitive data, employing strong passwords, and reporting security breaches. Consistent training sessions and simulated phishing drills can strengthen security awareness and maintain employees' readiness against evolving threats.

Even with top-notch preventive measures, security incidents may still happen. It's vital to have a clear incident response plan ready to handle breaches efficiently. This plan should specify roles, escalation procedures, communication methods, and steps for containing and resolving incidents. Regular testing and drills of this plan are crucial to ensure everyone is prepared. After any incident, reviews should be conducted to learn from the experience and enhance future responses.

Implementing best practices for cybersecurity is essential for organizations. It helps protect digital assets and reduce risks from evolving threats. Organizations can start by conducting thorough risk assessments. They should also develop clear cybersecurity policies and implement effective access control measures. Providing ongoing employee training is crucial. Establishing strong incident response plans is also important. These steps help strengthen security and defend against cyber threats. Cybersecurity is a continuous process. It requires vigilance, adaptability, and a commitment to staying ahead of new threats. By adopting best practices and constantly improving security measures, organizations can better safeguard their data, systems, and reputation in today's digital age.

18.7 CONCLUSION

Intrusion detection and prevention systems are essential for modern cyber security, providing critical capabilities to detect and prevent unauthorized access and malicious activities. By understanding their architecture, types, detection techniques, and best practices for deployment, organizations can effectively implement IDPSs to safeguard their digital assets. As cyber threats keep changing, the strategies and technologies to fight them must also change. This makes IDPSs an important and active part of a strong security plan.

REFERENCES

[1] T. N. Hoang and D. Kim, "Supervised contrastive ResNet and transfer learning for the in-vehicle intrusion detection system," *Expert Systems with Applications*, vol. 238, 2024, doi: 10.1016/j.eswa.2023.122181.

[2] Q. Lu, Q. Gao, J. Li, X. X. Xie, W. Guo, and J. Wang, "Distributed cyber-physical intrusion detection using stacking learning for wide-area protection system," *Computer Communications*, vol. 215, 2024, doi: 10.1016/j.comcom.2023.12.008.

[3] R. Reka, R. Karthick, R. Saravana Ram, and G. Singh, "Multi head self-attention gated graph convolutional network based multi-attack intrusion detection in MANET," *Computers & Security*, vol. 136, 2024, doi: 10.1016/j.cose.2023.103526.

[4] Y. Li, J. Zhang, Y. Yan, Y. Lei, and C. Yin, "Enhancing network intrusion detection through the application of the Dung Beetle Optimized Fusion Model," *IEEE Access*, vol. 12, 2024, doi: 10.1109/ACCESS.2024.3353488.

[5] S. M. S. Bukhari *et al.*, "Secure and privacy-preserving intrusion detection in wireless sensor networks: Federated learning with SCNN-Bi-LSTM for enhanced reliability," *Ad Hoc Networks*, vol. 155, 2024, doi: 10.1016/j.adhoc.2024.103407.

[6] A. Paya, S. Arroni, V. García-Díaz, and A. Gómez, "Apollon: A robust defense system against Adversarial Machine Learning attacks in Intrusion Detection Systems," *Computer & Security*, vol. 136, 2024, doi: 10.1016/j.cose.2023.103546.

[7] A. Kaushik and H. Al-Raweshidy, "A novel intrusion detection system for internet of things devices and data," *Wireless Networks*, vol. 30, no. 1, 2024, doi: 10.1007/s11276-023-03435-0.

[8] Z. Long, H. Yan, G. Shen, X. Zhang, H. He, and L. Cheng, "A transformer-based network intrusion detection approach for cloud security," *Journal of Cloud Computing*, vol. 13, no. 1, 2024, doi: 10.1186/s13677-023-00574-9.

[9] T. T. Thein, Y. Shiraishi, and M. Morii, "Personalized federated learning-based intrusion detection system: Poisoning attack and defense," *Future Generation Computer Systems*, vol. 153, 2024, doi: 10.1016/j.future.2023.10.005.

[10] J. Li, M. S. Othman, H. Chen, and L. M. Yusuf, "Optimizing IoT intrusion detection system: Feature selection versus feature extraction in machine learning," *Journal of Big Data*, vol. 11, no. 1, 2024, doi: 10.1186/s40537-024-00892-y.

[11] M. S. Korium, M. Saber, A. Beattie, A. Narayanan, S. Sahoo, and P. H. J. Nardelli, "Intrusion detection system for cyberattacks in the Internet of Vehicles environment," *Ad Hoc Networks*, vol. 153, 2024, doi: 10.1016/j.adhoc.2023.103330.

[12] H. Satilmis, S. Akleylek, and Z. Y. Tok, "A systematic literature review on host-based intrusion detection systems," *IEEE Access*, vol. 12, 2024, doi: 10.1109/ACCESS.2024.3367004.

[13] A. Singh, J. Prakash, G. Kumar, P. K. Jain, and L. S. Ambati, "Intrusion detection system: A comparative study of machine learning-based IDS," *Journal of Database Management*, vol. 35, no. 1, 2024, doi: 10.4018/JDM.338276.

[14] M. Sarhan, S. Layeghy, N. Moustafa, M. Gallagher, and M. Portmann, "Feature extraction for machine learning-based intrusion detection in IoT networks," *Digital Communications and Networks*, vol. 10, no. 1, 2024, doi: 10.1016/j.dcan.2022.08.012.

[15] S. Latif, W. Boulila, A. Koubaa, Z. Zou, and J. Ahmad, "DTL-IDS: An optimized intrusion detection framework using deep transfer learning and genetic algorithm," *Journal of Network and Computer Applications*, vol. 221, 2024, doi: 10.1016/j.jnca.2023.103784.

[16] F. Ullah, S. Ullah, G. Srivastava, and J. C. W. Lin, "IDS-INT: Intrusion detection system using transformer-based transfer learning for imbalanced network traffic," *Digital Communications and Networks*, vol. 10, no. 1, 2024, doi: 10.1016/j.dcan.2023.03.008.

19 Data Encryption in 6G Networks

A Zero-Knowledge Proof Model

P. Selvaraj, A. Hyils Sharon Magdalene,
Suresh Sankaranarayanan, Rengaraj Alias Muralidharan R.,
Priyanga Subbiah, Saranniya S., and
Lakshmi Kanthan Narayanan

19.1 INTRODUCTION

19.1.1 THE EVOLUTION OF 6G

Sixth-generation (6G) networks are projected to offer ultra-low latency, possibly reaching below 0.1 milliseconds (ms). This near-instantaneous response time opens the door to applications requiring instantaneous communication, such as remote surgery, autonomous vehicles, and augmented reality experiences. By minimizing latency to imperceptible levels, 6G networks aim to blur the line between physical and virtual environments, ushering in a new era of seamless connectivity.

Another key focus of 6G development is the enhancement of spectral efficiency and network coverage. By optimizing spectrum utilization and deploying advanced antenna technologies, 6G networks seek to deliver enhanced coverage, even in remote and challenging environments. This ubiquitous connectivity is essential for enabling ubiquitous connectivity, supporting applications from smart cities and autonomous systems to rural connectivity initiatives. A comparison of communication technology is shown in Table 19.1.

The security challenges in 6G networks are multifaceted and require comprehensive solutions to address effectively. These challenges include the need for secure data encryption, safe key exchange mechanisms, protection against cyber threats and attacks, and the preservation of user privacy in an increasingly connected and data-driven environment. Addressing these security issues is essential to realizing the full potential of 6G networks and ensuring their successful deployment and adoption on a global scale.

19.1.2 NEED FOR SECURITY

Security in networks is paramount due to several reasons:

1. **Data Protection:** Networks, including 6G, carry a large amount of sensitive data ranging from sensitive information to critical business data. Ensuring the security of this data is crucial to prevent unauthorized access, data breaches, identity theft, and financial fraud.
2. **Privacy Concerns:** With the proliferation of connected devices and the IoT, 6G networks will handle massive amounts of personal and sensitive data. Protecting the privacy of users and their data is essential to maintain trust and compliance with regulations such as GDPR.
3. **Cyber Attacks:** As network technologies advance, so do cyber threats. 6G networks are likely to face sophisticated cyber attacks, including ransomware, malware, and DDoS

TABLE 19.1
Comparison between 1G, 2G, 3G, 4G, and 5G

Technology	1G	2G	3G	4G	5G
Deployment in Nigeria	1980s	2001	2010	Right now	2022
Data Rate	2 Kbps	64 Kbps	Up to 2 Mbps	100 Mbps moving 1 Gbps stationary	Higher than 1 Gbps
Technology	Analog	Digital	CDMA 2000, UMTS, EDGE	Wi-Max, Wi-Fi, LTE	World Wide Web
Core Network	PSTN	PSTN	Packet N/W	Internet	Internet
Multiplexing	FDMA	TDMA/CDMA	W-CDMA (wideband code division multiple access)	CDMA	CDMA
Switching	Circuit	Circuit, packet	Packet	All packet	All packet
Primary Services	Analog phone cells	Digital phone calls and messaging	Phone calls, messaging, data	All-IP service (including voice messages)	High speed, high capacity and large broadcast of data in Gbps
Contrast	Mobility	Secure, mass adoption	Better internet experience	Faster broadband internet	Better coverage, no dropped calls

attacks. Robust security measures are needed to mitigate these threats and ensure the continuous operation of critical services.

4. **Trustworthiness of Communication:** Trustworthiness is essential in 6G networks, which aim to provide reliable and low latency communication. Security measures are needed to guarantee the integrity, authenticity, and confidentiality of communication to support mission-critical applications such as remote surgery and autonomous driving.

19.1.3 Data Privacy and Security Issues in 6G

Ensuring data privacy and security is of utmost importance in the 6G wireless communication networks. With the growth of devices, the enormous amount of data generated, and the diverse communication scenarios, multiple significant aspects contribute to the challenges involved in maintaining data privacy and security in 6G.

1. **Increased attack surface:** With the growth of connected devices and the IoT expansion, 6G networks will support more devices than previous generations. This expanded attack surface provides more opportunities for malicious actors to exploit vulnerabilities.
2. **Complexity:** 6G networks are expected to be highly complex, incorporating technologies such as AI, edge computing, and advanced network architectures like network slicing. This complexity can introduce new vulnerabilities and make detecting and mitigating security threats harder.
3. **Privacy concerns:** As the development of 6G networks progresses, it is expected that faster and more extensive data transmission will be possible. However, this advancement also brings concerns about privacy. The large volume of data generated and transmitted by these networks might be at risk of interception and misuse, which could lead to issues related to data privacy and compliance with regulations such as GDPR.

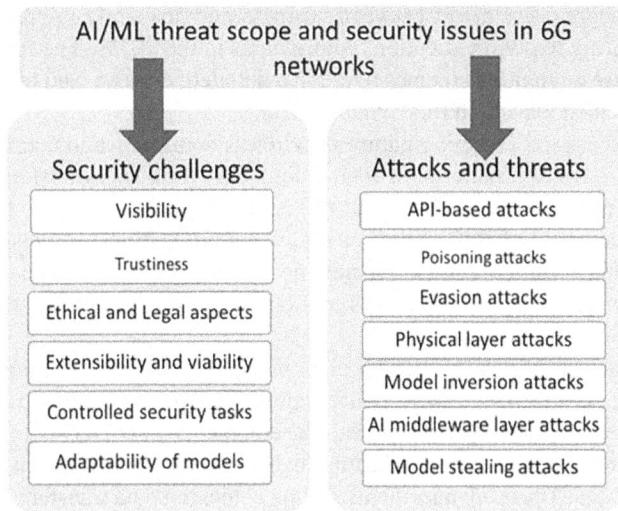

FIGURE 19.1   Security challenges and attacks in 6G networks and examples of these attacks. [1]

4. **AI-driven attacks:** 6G networks will leverage AI and machine learning for various purposes, including network optimization, security analytics, and automation. However, these same technologies are exploited by attackers to launch sophisticated cyber attacks, such as AI-driven malware and social engineering attacks.

5. **Physical layer vulnerabilities:** 6G networks introduces new technologies at the physical layer, such as terahertz communication and free-space optical communication. These technologies could introduce new vulnerabilities, such as eavesdropping or jamming attacks, which has weaknesses in the transmission medium itself.

6. **Zero-day exploits and vulnerabilities:** Despite extensive testing and security measures, zero-day exploits and vulnerabilities are inevitable in any complex system. 6G networks will be no exception, and discovering and exploiting previously unknown vulnerabilities could pose security risks.

19.2   LITERATURE REVIEW

19.2.1   Trends in Data Encryption for 6G Communication Systems

Kaur et al. [2] have examined the new field of sixth-generation wireless technology, which has garnered significant attention since 2019, when research on 6G began. The development of 6G is expected to begin by 2030, and it requires an examination of its possible uses and impact on society, following the timeline of previous wireless generations. 6G has the potential to revolutionize intelligent cities and enhance the quality of life by enabling proactive monitoring, analysis, and planning. The study aims to provide readers with an initial understanding of 6G research and emphasizes the significance of fully autonomous systems in ensuring quality of service and network performance. The work explores the potential uses of 6G technology and examines the challenges that may arise in the future. The authors seek to enhance understanding and foresight regarding the groundbreaking capabilities of 6G while highlighting the significance of addressing the challenges associated with its effective deployment.

Alsharif et al. [3] explore the emerging domain of sixth-generation wireless communication technologies. Their research is motivated by the finalization of fifth-generation (5G) technology standardization efforts and the commencement of global deployment. The work highlights the imperative of continuous innovation to sustain a competitive advantage in wireless networks.

This highlights the cooperative effort between business and academia to create the fundamental structure for 6G, catering to communication requirements in the 2030s. The study aims to comprehensively analyze these contentious themes to attain a detailed, concise, and precise understanding, helping future research endeavors in this dynamic field.

Lipps et al. [4] discuss the changing nature of wireless communication, acknowledging its significant influence on lives and patterns of interaction. They link this transformation to technical breakthroughs such as artificial intelligence (AI) and increasing demands for bandwidth. The study examines the potential of B5G and 6G mobile communications as a response to the limitations of fifth-generation cellular networks in meeting future communication needs beyond 2030. It provides insights into the complex challenges and opportunities influencing the future of mobile communications.

Tonkikh et al. [5] discuss the changing field of mobile communication technologies, emphasizing the critical role of 5G in improving everyday life, safety, and business productivity while also looking ahead to the future transition to 6G networks. The emergence of 6G technology brings the potential for groundbreaking advancements, including high-resolution visualization, wearable displays, and telepresence services. These advancements rely on achieving data transfer rates of up to 1 Tbit/s per user by efficiently using the spectrum in the THz domain, incorporating intelligent technologies, artificial intelligence, and remote presence presents complex technological and statistical obstacles in achieving 6G networks, making it a crucial field for investigation.

W. Jiang et al. [6] recognize the growing ubiquity of fifth-generation mobile communication systems and the imperative to shift focus towards the subsequent generation, 6G. The surge in 5G subscribers and the projected escalation in mobile traffic until 2030 underscores the necessity for exploring the potential of 6G.

Aslam et al. [1] emphasize the significance of 6G cognitive radio (CR) networks in addressing future technology requirements. The study emphasizes new technologies that enable creative applications and specific performance measures, such as worldwide coverage, cost-effectiveness, improved use of radio frequencies, energy efficiency, and safety. The article emphasizes the necessity of achieving worldwide coverage through the utilization of satellite communication systems and the effective allocation of spectrum across several frequency bands. This approach aims to enhance the density of connections and the data transmission speed. Intelligent apps utilizing big data and AI technology will effectively handle various communication circumstances and bandwidth requirements. The article emphasizes the significance of improving network security in decentralized, intelligent, and distributed 6G CR networks. This text explores the future environment of 6G CR network communication and discusses the issues expected to arise throughout its deployment and development.

Abdel Hakeem et al. [7] explore the issues of sixth-generation wireless networks, expected by 2030. Their article discusses emerging technologies like AI and Machine Learning (ML) that will shape 6G networks, highlighting the need for reevaluating security measures. The work introduces a comprehensive security architecture for 6G, addressing challenges at the physical and within AI/ML layers.

Shi et al. [8] investigate the changing environment of innovative applications made possible by fifth-generation mobile communication technology and predict the difficulties and possibilities that will arise with the next sixth-generation technology. Intelligent apps utilizing 5G technology improve everyday life and urban administration. In order to achieve a harmonious equilibrium, the work suggests the implementation of searchable encryption. This specialized encryption framework enables data retrieval based on keywords while guaranteeing the protection of privacy and the accessibility of large amounts of data.

Goldreich et al. [9] investigate the essential inquiry of whether the combination of zero-knowledge protocols maintains their characteristics, uncovering constraints in both sequential and parallel combinations. The work highlights the difficulties in cryptographic protocol design by showing that even powerful versions of zero-knowledge, such as black-box simulation, do not preserve their features when executed in parallel.

Goldreich et al. [10] studied the properties of ZKPs. Zero-knowledge can be classified into auxiliary input and black-box simulation. Auxiliary-input zero-knowledge has been proposed as a more appropriate choice for cryptography applications than the original notion. It has also been shown that protocols that solely include auxiliary subprotocols with input zero knowledge have the same property. The limitations of some types of ZKP systems are also demonstrated, demonstrating that only languages in BPP have ZKPs in specific categories.

Gustavsson et al. [11] examine the challenges faced in modern digital communication networks, particularly in advancing beyond the capabilities of 5G technology. The article discusses the introduction of 5G technology, specifically focusing on the new radio (NR) and its implications. This work provides an overview of the challenges faced while implementing transceivers, mainly when operating at higher carrier frequencies. The text also explores the rise of novel applications such as massive IoT and the increasing need for simultaneous wireless information and power transfer.

Ben-Sasson et al. [12] acknowledge the importance of balancing personal privacy and institutional integrity when dealing with sensitive material, especially in medical and forensic data fields. Privacy safeguards are crucial for preserving human dignity. However, there is a mounting apprehension regarding the possibility of institutions exploiting secrecy, which can result in deceit and the erosion of public confidence. This effectively solves the problem of scalability.

Panait et al. [13] explore the critical need for privacy-preserving identity management solutions in blockchain technology, specifically in public blockchains where the disclosure of sensitive identification data is to be minimized. They emphasize the capability of ZKPs, particularly zero-knowledge succinct non-interactive arguments of knowledge (zk-SNARKs) and zk-STARKs, as effective methods for accomplishing this objective. The research enhance the creation of privacy-preserving solid mechanisms in blockchain systems by utilizing modern cryptographic techniques. These mechanisms are essential for protecting sensitive personal information in identity management operations.

19.2.2 CURRENT ENCRYPTION TECHNIQUES IN 5G NETWORKS

In 5G networks, several security algorithms are employed to protect communication channels; authenticate users and devices; and ensure the confidentiality, integrity, and availability of data. Some of the key security algorithms used in 5G include:

1. **AKA:** It is a fundamental security mechanism used in 5G networks for authenticating users and establishing secure communication channels between mobile devices and the network. It involves mutual authentication between the UE and the network, followed by the derivation of session keys for secure data transmission.
2. **ECDH:** ECDH is a key exchange algorithm utilized in 5G networks to establish shared secret keys between communicating entities. It enables secure key agreement without directly transmitting sensitive information over the network, thus protecting against attacks like eavesdropping and man-in-the-middle.
3. **AES Encryption:** AES is a symmetric encryption algorithm widely used in 5G networks to encrypt data transmitted over the air interface and core network. AES ensures confidentiality by converting plaintext data into ciphertext using a secret encryption key, making it unreadable to unauthorized parties.
4. **Hash Functions (e.g., SHA-256):** Hash functions are cryptographic algorithms used in 5G networks to generate fixed-size hash values from variable-size input data. They are employed for integrity verification, digital signatures, and message authentication codes (MACs). Secure Hash Algorithm 256 (SHA-256) is commonly used in 5G for its strong collision resistance and cryptographic security properties.

Security algorithms play a crucial role in safeguarding 5G networks against various security threats, including eavesdropping, interception, spoofing, tampering, and denial-of-service attacks. By employing robust encryption, authentication, and key management techniques, 5G networks aim to provide a secure and trustworthy environment for users and applications.

19.2.3 Constraints in Current Systems for Future 6G Networks

While the security algorithms used in 5G networks provide a foundation for protecting data and communication channels, their application in 6G networks may face several limitations and challenges due to the unique characteristics and requirements of next-generation wireless systems. Some of the limitations to using these algorithms in 6G networks include:

1. **Increased Complexity:** 6G networks are expected to introduce more complex architectures, heterogeneous communication technologies, and diverse network paradigms compared to 5G. Implementing existing security algorithms in such complex environments may require extensive modifications and enhancements to ensure compatibility and effectiveness.
2. **Higher Data Rates and Throughput:** Compared to 5G, 6G networks enable much greater data rates and throughput, allowing for extremely rapid communication and enormous data interchange. The growing volume of data transmission may be too much for current security methods to handle, which could cause bottlenecks and performance deterioration.
3. **Low Latency Requirements:** In order to support real-time applications like augmented reality, remote surgery, and autonomous vehicles, 6G networks must have ultra-low latency. Time-sensitive applications may not respond as quickly if traditional security techniques involve latency overheads during key exchange, encryption, and decryption processes.
4. **Resource Constraints:** Many devices in 6G networks, such as IoT sensors and wearable devices, are expected to have limited computational resources, memory, and battery life. Putting computationally demanding security methods into practice on devices with limited resources could result in inefficiencies, higher energy usage, and shorter device lifespans.
5. **Adversarial Advances:** As 6G networks evolve, adversaries may develop more sophisticated and targeted attacks to exploit vulnerabilities in existing security algorithms. It is crucial to anticipate and address emerging security threats such as quantum computing-based attacks, side-channel attacks, and advanced evasion techniques.
6. **Privacy Concerns:** With the proliferation of connected devices and the collection of vast amounts of user data in 6G networks, ensuring privacy protection becomes increasingly challenging. Existing security algorithms may need enhancements to address privacy concerns related to data anonymization, user identity protection, and consent management.

To overcome these constraints, creative security solutions that are adapted to the particular needs and difficulties of 6G networks must be created. This could entail creating effective key management plans, lightweight encryption algorithms, and privacy-preserving methods that can function well in fast-paced, dynamic, and resource-constrained contexts.

19.3 SYSTEM ARCHITECTURE AND DESIGN

19.3.1 AES, RSA, and ZKP Algorithm Design

Figure 19.2 shows the proposed algorithm. It integrates three encryption techniques: AES, RSA, and ZKP, to address the previously mentioned issues.

AES: AES is a symmetric encryption technique that secures transmission and storage of data. This technique functions on data blocks of a predetermined size and is compatible with key sizes

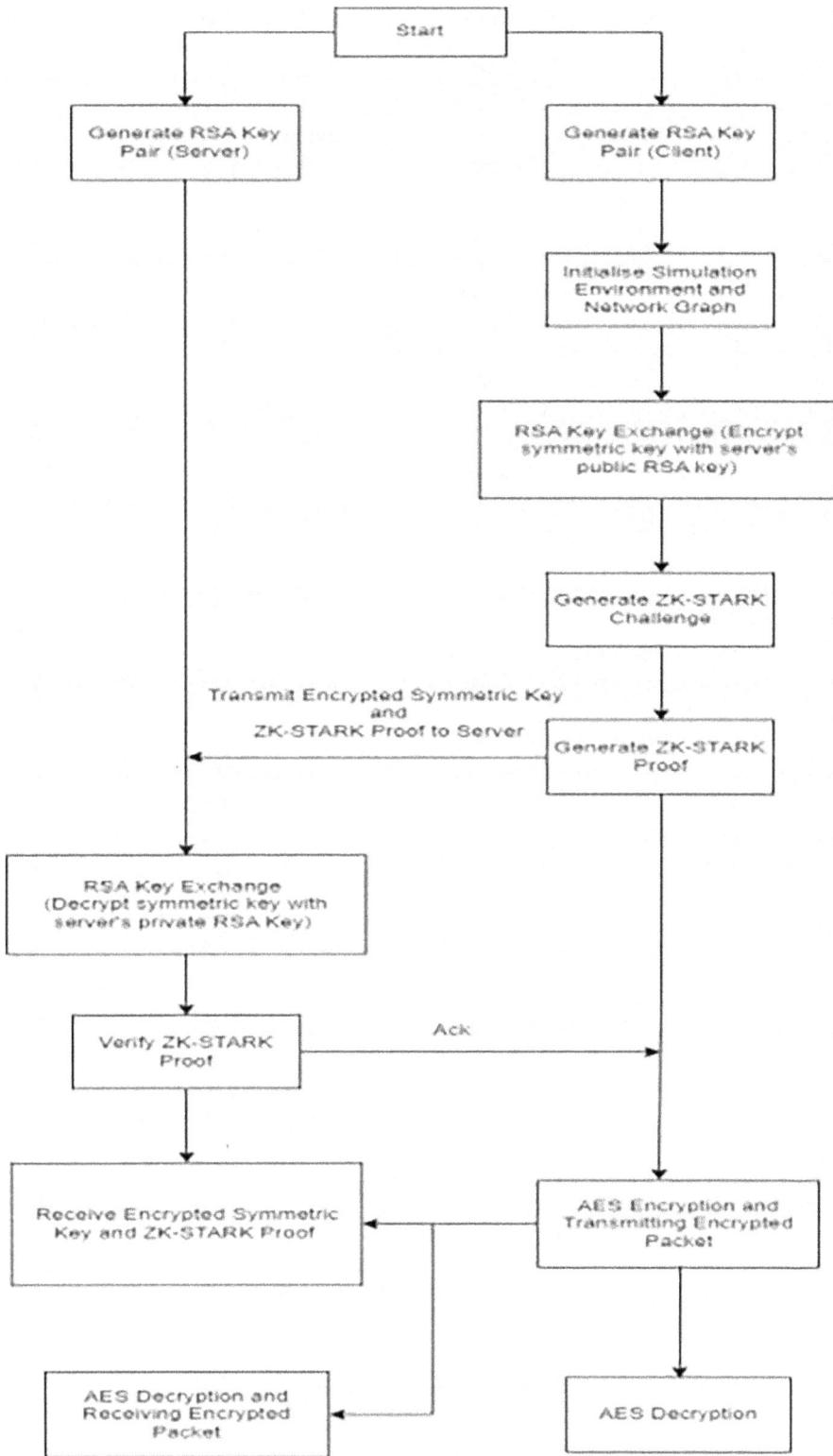

FIGURE 19.2   AES, RSA, and ZKP algorithm architecture.

of 128, 192, or 256 bits. A feature of AES is its use of a symmetric key. AES provides a range of operation modes, including ECB, CBC, and GCM. Each mode is designed for certain applications and offers different levels of security and efficiency. AES is renowned for its efficacy, rapidity, and robust security when employed with suitable key lengths and modes of operation.

RSA: RSA is a widespread asymmetric encryption algorithm that is commonly employed for safe key exchange, digital signatures, and encrypting small data sets. It is dependent on the mathematical characteristics of significant prime numbers and their factorization. The dual key set has a mathematical relationship, but it is practically impossible to calculate one key based on the other. The RSA encryption algorithm offers a range of key sizes, usually between 1024 and 4096 bits. Larger key sizes offer stronger security but result in slower performance. RSA is extensively used in diverse security protocols, such as SSL/TLS for securing web communication, PGP for encrypting emails, and SSH for ensuring secure remote access. Furthermore, it is frequently used in the process of issuing and authenticating digital certificates.

ZKP: A ZKP system enables a prover to convince a verifier of the veracity of a statement without revealing any additional knowledge. Even if the verifier possesses auxiliary information, the system ensures that knowledge gained during the interaction can be obtained independently. This property is crucial for maintaining security in cryptographic protocols and allows for the composition of multiple protocols while preserving security properties.

1. The prover receives authenticated private data, such as a bank statement.
2. The verifier solicits the prover to provide a minimal set of essential personal information. It receives both the response and the proof.
3. The prover calculates an answer to the verifier's query and creates a proof of accurate calculation.
4. The verifier uses the ZKP verification process to validate the correctness of the data. If the algorithm yields a favorable outcome, the verifier places confidence in the response as if it were provided by a trustworthy third party, without possessing any knowledge of the underlying information.

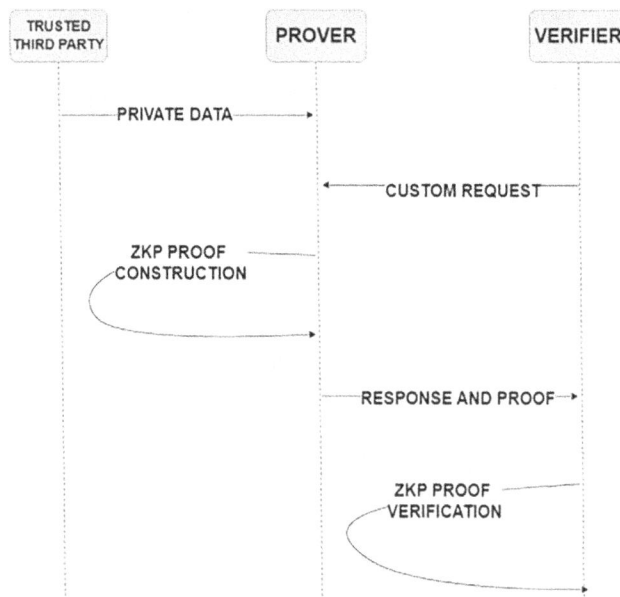

FIGURE 19.3 A basic ZKP architecture.

One notable advancement in ZKPs is the development of zk-STARKs. This type of ZKP offers several advantages over traditional ZKPs, particularly in terms of scalability, transparency, and efficiency. Unlike some other ZKP schemes, zk-STARKs do not rely on trusted setup assumptions, meaning they can be implemented without the need for any trusted parties or parameters. This feature ensures transparency and eliminates potential vulnerabilities associated with trusted setups, making zk-STARKs highly desirable for applications where trust and security are critical.

zk-STARKs have an advantage of scalability. Traditional ZKPs often need help with performance bottlenecks, especially when dealing with large datasets. However, zk-STARKs are designed to scale efficiently, allowing for fast verification even with massive amounts of data. This scalability makes zk-STARKs well-suited for use in high-speed networks like 6G, where large volumes of data need to be processed rapidly.

Scalability: One of the primary challenges in securing 6G networks lies in accommodating the exponential growth of data traffic while ensuring efficient encryption processes. Traditional encryption methods often need help to keep pace with the rapid data transmission rates inherent in 6G networks. In contrast, zk-STARKs offer inherent scalability, enabling fast verification even with large datasets. By leveraging zk-STARKs, we can mitigate the scalability limitations of traditional encryption methods, thereby facilitating seamless data encryption in 6G networks.

National 6G vs 5G performance is shown in Table 19.2.

Transparency: Maintaining transparency in data encryption processes is paramount, particularly in environments where privacy concerns are paramount. Traditional encryption methods often require revealing certain information during verification, raising privacy implications. zk-STARKs, however, enable verification without disclosing any underlying data, ensuring high transparency while preserving privacy. Through zk-STARKs, we can enhance the transparency of data encryption processes within 6G networks, fostering trust and confidence among users.

Effectiveness: Besides scalability and transparency, zk-STARKs offer unparalleled effectiveness in securing data transmission across 6G networks. Combining zk-STARKs with RSA and AES algorithms creates a robust encryption framework capable of withstanding sophisticated cyber threats. Through empirical analysis and simulations, the effectiveness of zk-STARKs is demonstrated in thwarting various security attacks while maintaining optimal performance in 6G network environments.

TABLE 19.2
National 6G Vs 5G Performance

Key Performance Indicator (KPI)	5G	6G
Peak data rate	20 Gbps	1 Tbps
Experience data rate	100 Mbps	1 Gbps
Peak spectral efficiency	30 b/s/Hz	60 b/s/Hz
Experience spectral efficiency	0.3 b/s/Hz	3 b/s/Hz
Maximum bandwidth	1 GHz	100 GHz
Area traffic capacity	10 Mb/s/m^2	1 Gb/s/m^2
Connection density	1 million devices/km^2	10 million devices/km^2
Energy efficiency	–	1 Tb/J
Latency	1 ms	100 μs
Reliability	10^{-5}	10^{-9}
Jitter	–	1 μs
Mobility	500 km/h	1000 km/h

19.3.2 PROPOSED ALGORITHM FRAMEWORK

The algorithm employs a multi-layered approach to secure data transmission in a network environment, designed particularly for 6G networks where stringent security measures are essential. It begins with generating RSA key pairs to facilitate secure communication between sender and receiver.

These keys encrypt and decrypt data packets, ensuring confidentiality and integrity during transmission. ZKP is used to improve the security of the vital exchange process by offering a reliable method of confirming the accuracy of important exchanges without disclosing private data. The algorithm simulates multiple communication sessions, assessing the effectiveness of ZKP in thwarting potential threats and ensuring the security of communication channels. Through visualization of attacker success rates over numerous sessions, the algorithm provides valuable insights into the efficacy of ZKP in fortifying the communication infrastructure of 6G networks against malicious adversaries.

1. **RSA Encryption and Decryption:** The purpose of RSA key pairs is to enable secure communication. Data packets are encrypted using the recipient's public key and decrypted using the recipient's private key during the procedure.
2. **AES Encryption and Decryption:** AES keys are generated for symmetric encryption of data packets. Data packets are encrypted and decrypted using AES in various modes (ECB, CBC, GCM).
3. **Zero-Knowledge Proofs:** ZKP is used to verify the integrity of the critical exchange process, enhancing security against potential threats.
4. **Simulation of Network Transmission:** Simulated network transmission of encrypted data packets between sender and receiver. Visualization of the network graph to illustrate the transmission and decryption processes.
5. **Multiple Session Simulation:** This involves simulating multiple communication sessions to evaluate the effectiveness of ZKP in securing the communication channel.

19.4 PROPOSED METHODOLOGY USING ZKP

The aim of the research is to verify if zero-knowledge proofs are effective in securing the data transfer via networks. In order to ensure the integrity and authenticity of transmitted data, the research work focuses on building a server-client architecture with data packets encrypted using the integrated ZKPs and the AES and RSA algorithms. The study demonstrates the robustness of our communication protocol against potential security threats and weaknesses by applying ZKPs and cryptography approaches.

19.4.1 EXPERIMENTAL SETUP

1. **Hardware Configuration**
   The experimental setup comprises standard desktop machines equipped with Intel Core processors and sufficient RAM to support cryptographic operations efficiently. The server and client machines are connected via a local area network (LAN) to simulate real-world communication scenarios.
2. **Software Environment**
   The Python programming language is used for developing the server-client code base, leveraging cryptography libraries such as PyCrypto and PyCryptodome for implementing encryption.

19.4.2 ENCRYPTION TECHNIQUES

3. AES Encryption
AES encryption is employed to secure the data packets transmitted between the server and the client. The process involves key generation, data encryption using a symmetric key, and subsequent decryption at the receiver's end.

4. RSA Encryption
RSA encryption is used for secure key exchange between the server and the client. The public and private key pairs are generated for encryption and decryption purposes, facilitating the secure transmission of symmetric keys.

5. Zero-Knowledge Proofs
ZKPs are applied in the communication protocol to offer substantial evidence of knowledge without disclosing private data. For effective ZKP verification, zk-SNARKs are used.

19.4.3 EXPERIMENTAL PROCEDURE

6. Data Packet Preparation:
Before transmission, the data packets are prepared by the server for sending to the client. These packets contain sensitive data/ information that needs to be securely transmitted.

7. AES Encryption:
- Key Generation: The server generates a random symmetric encryption key specifically for each data packet. The key is used for encrypting and decrypting the contents of the packet.
- Encryption: The server uses the AES encryption technique to encrypt the data packet by the generated key. AES uses symmetric encryption and uses the same key for both encryption and decryption. Then works with data blocks of size 128 bits.
- AES Mode of Operation: The server selects a mode of operation for AES encryption, such as CBC or GCM, to provide data integrity and confidentiality.

8. RSA Encryption:
- Key Exchange: Using RSA encryption, the server and client exchange keys before encrypting the data packet. The following actions are necessary:
  - The client can encrypt data or create a shared secret key by securely receiving the server's public key.
  - A public key and matching private key are created by the server to form a public-private key pair.
  - Using the public key of the server, the client encrypts a randomly generated symmetric encryption key (for AES encryption) and transmits it back to the server.
- Symmetric Key Encryption: The server uses its private key to decrypt the encrypted symmetric key after receiving it from the client. This guarantees that the symmetric key, which will later be used for AES encryption and decryption, may only be decrypted by the server.

9. Zero-Knowledge Proofs:
- Proof Generation: Before transmitting the encrypted data packet, the server generates a zero-knowledge proof to verify the integrity of the encrypted data without revealing any sensitive information.
- ZKP Incorporation: The ZKP is incorporated into the encrypted data packet, ensuring that the proof of integrity accompanies the encrypted payload during transmission.

10. Data Packet Transmission:
The data packet is fully encrypted using AES and RSA, and accompanied by a ZKP, the server transmits the packet over the network to the client. The network communication may occur over a secure channel (e.g., TLS/SSL) to prevent interception by unauthorized parties.

11. Client-Side Decryption:
- After the client receives the encrypted data packet, it proceeds with the decryption process as follows:
  - The client uses its private key, which was previously shared via RSA with the server, to decrypt the symmetric encryption key.
  - The client uses the AES decryption method to decrypt the contents of the data packet using the decrypted symmetric key.
  - With the help of the included ZKP, the client may confirm that the decrypted data is accurate and hasn't been altered in transit.

19.5   CODING AND TESTING

19.5.1   Proposed Algorithm Code Analysis

Libraries Used:

- SimPy, NetworkX, Matplotlib: These libraries are used for simulation, network visualization, and plotting, respectively.
- Crypto: From this module, functions related to encryption and decryption are imported. This includes AES and RSA encryption algorithms.

Functions Defined:

- generate_rsakey_pair():
  - Generates an RSA key pair for client-side operations.
- rsa_encrypt(plaintext, public_key):
  - Encrypts plaintext using RSA encryption with the provided public key.
- rsa_decrypt(ciphertext, private_key):
  - Decrypts ciphertext using RSA decryption with the provided private key.
- generate_aes_key(key_size=128):
  - Generates an AES key of the specified size aes_encrypt(message, key, mode):
  - Encrypts a message using AES encryption with the specified mode (ECB, CBC, or GCM).
- aes_decrypt(ciphertext, key, mode, iv=None, tag=None):
  - Decrypts ciphertext using AES decryption with the specified mode (ECB, CBC, or GCM).
- generate_zkp_challenge(), generate_zkp(secret, challenge), verify_zkp (secret, challenge, proof):
  - Functions related to zero-knowledge proofs used for secure key exchange.
- network_simulation(env, sender, receiver, encrypted_packet, graph):
  - Simulates the transmission of encrypted packets through a network.
- simulate_transmission(env,graph,use_zkp=True,exit_messages=None,attacker_success=Non e):
  - Simulates the transmission of encrypted data packets.
  - It involves key generation, key exchange using RSA encryption, ZKP, data packet encryption using AES, and packet transmission simulation.
- simulate_multiple_sessions(env, graph, num_sessions):
  - Simulates multiple sessions of data transmission.
  - Measures attacker success rates with and without ZKP.
  - Plots attacker success rates for each session.

Simulation:

- Key Generation and Exchange:
  - RSA key pairs are generated for client-side encryption and decryption.
  - AES keys are generated for symmetric encryption. Then, the symmetric key is encrypted with the server's RSA public key for secure key exchange.
- Data Encryption and Transmission:
  - Data packets are encrypted using AES encryption with specified modes.
  - Encrypted packets are transmitted through a simulated network.
- Zero-Knowledge Proof:
  - ZKP is used to ensure the security of the key exchange process.
  - Challenges and proofs are generated and verified to prevent potential threats.
- Attacker Simulation:
  - The code simulates an attacker attempting to intercept and decrypt the transmitted data.
  - Attacker success rates are measured and compared for sessions with and without ZKP.

Visualization and Analysis:

- Network Visualization:
  - Network graphs are visualized to represent data transmission between client and server.
- Attacker Success Rate Plot:
  - The code plots attacker success rates for sessions with and without ZKP.
  - This analysis helps evaluate the effectiveness of ZKP in securing data transmission.

Conclusion:

- The provided client-side code complements the server-side encryption model by simulating the client's role in secure data transmission.
- It demonstrates key generation, encryption, transmission, and security measures such as ZKP.
- Through simulation and analysis, it evaluates the effectiveness of ZKP in preventing potential security threats during key exchange and data transmission.

19.5.2 System Monitoring Code Analysis

The system monitoring code is written in Python and collects and plots system metrics such as CPU utilization, memory utilization, and network throughput. The code is as follows:

Libraries Used:

- psutil: This library provides functions for retrieving system information such as CPU, memory, disk usage, and network statistics.
- simpy: Used for discrete-event simulation.
- matplotlib.pyplot: Matplotlib is a plotting library for Python, and pyplot is its module providing a MATLAB-like interface for plotting.

Function Defined:

- monitor_system(env, interval=1):
  - This function monitors system metrics like CPU utilization, memory utilization, and network throughput at regular intervals. System metrics are plotted using Matplotlib.
  - It continuously collects data while the simulation is running using psutil.
  - The function runs indefinitely within a SimPy environment, generating metrics plots at each time step.
  - It yields the environment for a timeout at regular intervals specified by interval.

System Monitoring:

- CPU and Memory Utilization:
  - CPU and memory utilization are recorded at each time step and plotted.
  - psutil.cpu_percent(): Returns the current CPU utilization as a percentage.
  - psutil.virtual_memory().percent: Returns the current memory utilization as a percentage.
- Network Throughput:
  - Network throughput is simulated with random values for demonstration purposes.
  - Random throughput values are generated and recorded at each time step and plotted.

Plotting:

- Matplotlib Subplots:
  - Two subplots are created to visualize CPU and memory utilization, and network throughput separately.
  - The first subplot displays CPU and memory utilization over time.
  - The second subplot displays network throughput over time.

Simulation:

- SimPy Environment:
  - The monitor_system is run within a SimPy environment. Its function is processed within this environment.
  - The simulation runs until a specified time limit (until = 10 seconds in this case), after it is stopped.

Summary:

- The provided monitoring system collects and plots system metrics such as CPU utilization, memory utilization, and network throughput. It uses psutil for retrieving system information and Matplotlib for visualization.
- The system is simulated using SimPy to run the monitoring process at regular intervals. This monitoring system is used for observing system behavior and performance analysis over time.

19.6   RESULTS AND DISCUSSION

The programs are designed in VS Code using Python. The test platform is 11 Gen Intel Core i5–11300H 3.10GHz, four cores, and Windows 11. This simulation analyzes the security implications of employing zero-knowledge proofs in data transmission over network channels. Figure 19.4 presents the results obtained from 100 simulation sessions, each assessing the effectiveness of ZKP against potential attackers. The comparison of success rate and session is represented in terms of mean square error.

The x-axis indicates the individual simulation sessions, while the y-axis indicates the attacker's success rate. Two lines are plotted on the graph: one depicting the success rate of attackers when ZKP is utilized in data encryption (labeled "With ZKP"), and the other showing the success rate without employing ZKP (labeled "Without ZKP").The comparison between these two lines reveals the impact of ZKP on thwarting malicious attempts to intercept and decrypt transmitted data. A lower success rate for attackers in sessions utilizing ZKP demonstrates the enhanced security provided by this cryptographic protocol.

The code is also tested to measure its efficiency under general day-to-day network and hardware conditions by monitoring system metrics such as CPU utilization, memory consumption, and network throughput during simulations, as shown in Figures 19.5 and 19.6.

The figures show that the algorithm runs smoothly and easily at a high network throughput when run on a home network while maintaining low system utilization. Next, the effectiveness of

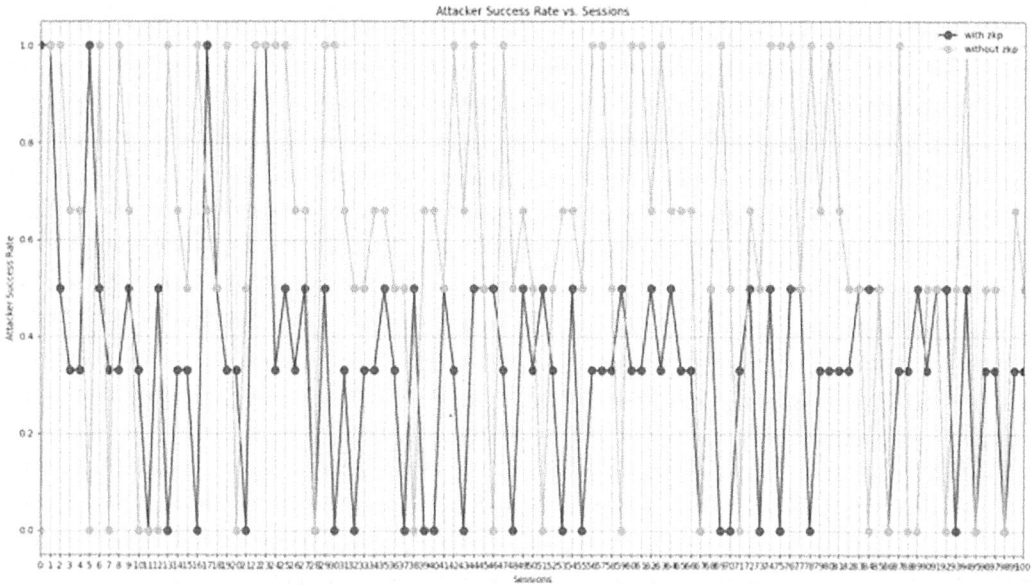

FIGURE 19.4 Attacker success rate vs sessions graph.

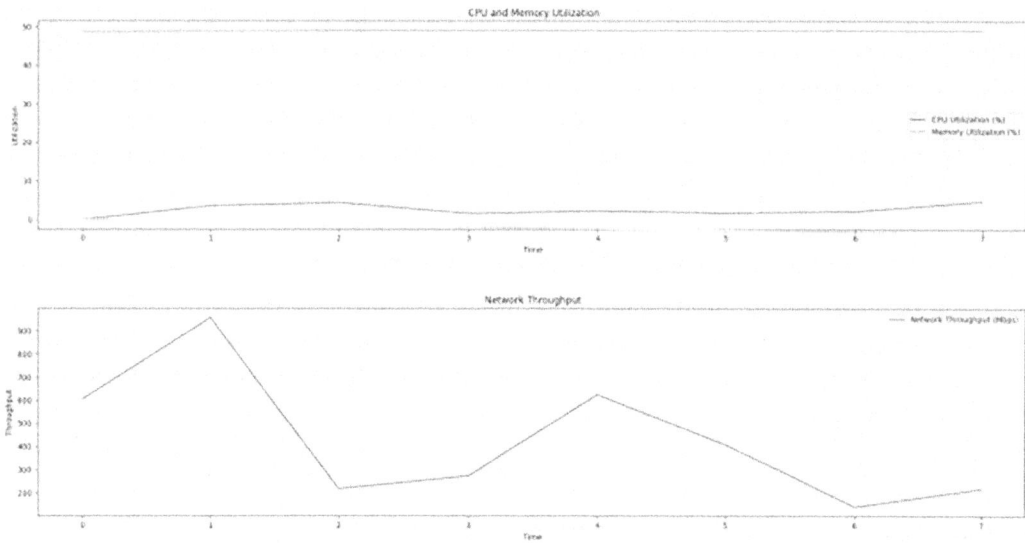

FIGURE 19.5 CPU, memory utilization, and network throughput (idle state).

zero-knowledge proofs as a cryptographic paradigm for protecting data encryption in 6G devices was investigated. The efficiency of ZKP in reducing possible risks to data confidentiality and integrity was assessed using thorough simulations and analysis. The integration of ZKP alongside RSA and AES encryption techniques enhances the security posture of communication channels in 6G networks. By leveraging ZKP for secure key exchange, this work showcased good mitigation in the success rates of attackers attempting to intercept and decrypt transmitted data. The simulation demonstrates the role of ZKP as a robust security measure, particularly in emerging technologies like 6G networks where secure data transmission is paramount. ZKP offers a viable

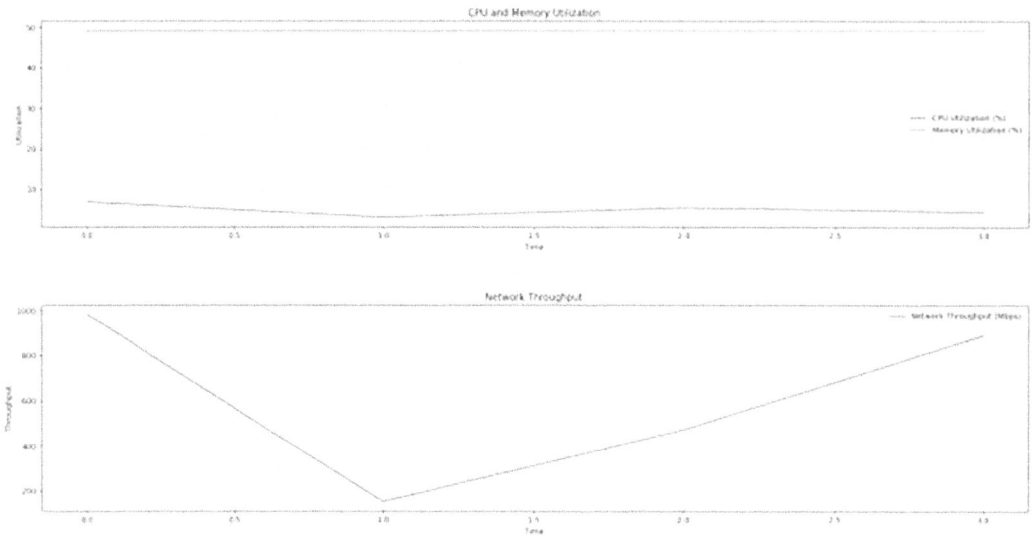

FIGURE 19.6 CPU, memory utilization, and network throughput (busy state).

solution for addressing evolving security challenges and ensuring the privacy and integrity of sensitive information exchanged between devices in next-generation network infrastructures.

The advancements in communication technologies will enhance further research and development efforts which focus on optimizing ZKP protocols that will be integrated into the 6G devices and systems. By focusing on security measures such as ZKP, the path towards establishing a trusted and resilient framework for data encryption in 6G environments is paved, laying the foundation for future secure and trustworthy communication networks.

19.7 CONCLUSION AND FUTURE ENHANCEMENT

This work demonstrates the effectiveness of combining RSA and AES encryption techniques with zero-knowledge proof protocols in securing communication systems. By simulating multiple transmission sessions and measuring attacker success rates, ZKP enhances the security of data transmission over networks.

The improvement involves optimizing the efficiency and speed of encryption and decryption algorithms to better accommodate the high data transfer rates expected in 6G networks.

REFERENCES

[1]. Aslam, Muhammad Muzamil, et al. "Sixth generation (6G) cognitive radio network (CRN) application, requirements, security issues, and key challenges." *Wireless Communications and Mobile Computing 2021* (2021): 1–18.

[2]. Kaur, Jasneet, and M. Arif Khan. "Sixth generation (6G) wireless technology: An overview, vision, challenges and use cases." *2022 IEEE Region 10 Symposium (TENSYMP)*. IEEE (2022).

[3]. Alsharif, Mohammed H., et al. "Sixth generation (6G) wireless networks: Vision, research activities, challenges and potential solutions." *Symmetry* 12.4 (2020): 676.

[4]. Lipps, Christoph, et al. "Towards the sixth generation (6G) wireless systems: Thoughts on physical layer security." *Mobile Communication-Technologies and Applications; 25th ITG-Symposium*. VDE (2021).

[5]. Tonkikh, E. V., K. D. Burobina, and A. A. Shurakhov. "Possible applications of sixth generation communication networks." *2020 Systems of Signals Generating and Processing in the Field of on Board Communications*. IEEE (2020).

[6]. Jiang, W., B. Han, M. A. Habibi, and H. D. Schotten. "The road towards 6G: A comprehensive survey." *IEEE Open Journal of the Communications Society* 2 (2021): 334–366. DOI:10.1109/OJCOMS.2021.3057679.

[7]. Abdel Hakeem, Shimaa A., Hanan H. Hussein, and HyungWon Kim. "Security requirements and challenges of 6G technologies and applications." *Sensors* 22.5 (2022): 1969.

[8]. Shi, Junbin, et al. "Toward data security in 6G networks: A public-key searchable encryption approach." *IEEE Network* 36.4 (2022): 166–173.

[9]. Goldreich, Oded, and Hugo Krawczyk. "On the composition of zero-knowledge proof systems." *SIAM Journal on Computing* 25.1 (1996): 169–192.

[10]. Goldreich, Oded, and Yair Oren. "Definitions and properties of zero-knowledge proof systems." *Journal of Cryptology* 7.1 (1994): 1–32.

[11]. Gustavsson, Ulf, et al. "Implementation challenges and opportunities in beyond-5G and 6G communication." *IEEE Journal of Microwaves* 1.1 (2021): 86–100.

[12]. Ben-Sasson, E., I. Bentov, Y. Horesh, and M. Riabzev. "Scalable, transparent, and post-quantum secure computational integrity." *IACR Cryptology ePrint Archive* 46 (2018).

[13]. Panait, Andreea-Elena, and Ruxandra F. Olimid. "On using zk-SNARKs and zk-STARKs in blockchain-based identity management." *Innovative Security Solutions for Information Technology and Communications: 13th International Conference, SecITC 2020*, Bucharest, Romania, November 19–20, 2020, Revised Selected Papers 13. Springer International Publishing (2021).

Index

For Product Safety Concerns and Information please contact our EU
representative GPSR@taylorandfrancis.com
Taylor & Francis Verlag GmbH, Kaufingerstraße 24, 80331 München, Germany